Middle School 2-2
학교시험 완벽대비

KB100547

2학기 전과정
적중 100 plus

영어 기출문제집

중2

동아 | 이병민

Best Collection

구성과 특징

교과서의 주요 학습 내용을 중심으로 학습 영역별 특성에 맞춰 단계별로 다양한 학습 기회를 제공하여
단원별 학습능력 평가는 물론 중간 및 기말고사 시험 등에 완벽하게 대비할 수 있도록 내용을 구성

Words & Expressions

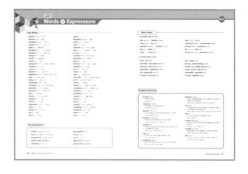

Step1 Key Words 단원별 핵심 단어 설명 및 풀이
Key Expression 단원별 핵심 숙어 및 관용어 설명
Word Power 반대 또는 비슷한 뜻 단어 배우기
English Dictionary 영어로 배우는 영어 단어

Step2 실력평가 단원별 수시평가 대비 주관식, 객관식 문제풀이

Step3 서술형 대비 학업성취도 및 수행능력평가 대비 서술형 문제풀이

Conversation

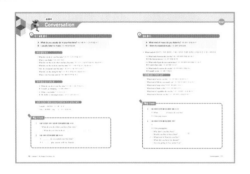

Step1 핵심 의사소통 소통에 필요한 주요 표현 방법 요약
핵심 Check 기본적인 표현 방법 및 활용능력 확인

Step2 대화문 익히기 교과서 대화문 심층 분석 및 확인

Step3 교과서 확인학습 빈칸 채우기를 통한 문장 완성 능력 확인

Step4 기본평가 시험대비 기초 학습 능력 평가

Step5 실력평가 단원별 수시평가 대비 주관식, 객관식 문제풀이

Step6 서술형 대비 학업성취도 및 수행능력평가 대비 서술형 문제풀이

Grammar

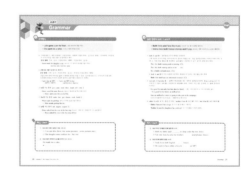

Step1 주요 문법 단원별 주요 문법 사항과 예문을 알기 쉽게 설명
핵심 Check 기본 문법사항에 대한 이해 여부 확인

Step2 기본평가 시험대비 기초 학습 능력 평가

Step3 실력평가 단원별 수시평가 대비 주관식, 객관식 문제풀이

Step4 서술형 대비 학업성취도 및 수행능력평가 대비 서술형 문제풀이

Reading

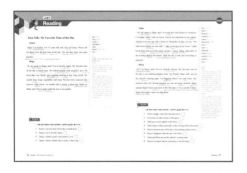

Step1 구문 분석 단원별로 제시된 문장에 대한 구문별 분석과 내용 설명
확인문제 문장에 대한 기본적인 이해와 인지능력 확인

Step2 확인학습A 빈칸 채우기를 통한 문장 완성 능력 확인

Step3 확인학습B 제시된 우리말을 영어로 완성하여 작문 능력 키우기

Step4 실력평가 단원별 수시평가 대비 주관식, 객관식 문제풀이

Step5 서술형 대비 학업성취도 및 수행능력평가 대비 서술형 문제풀이
교과서 구석구석 교과서에 나오는 기타 문장까지 완벽 학습

Composition

|영역별 핵심문제|

단어 및 어휘, 대화문, 문법, 독해 등 각 영역별 기출문제의 출제 유형을 분석하여 실전에 대비하고 연습할 수 있도록 문제를 배열

|단원별 예상문제|

기출문제를 분석한 후 새로운 시험 출제 경향을 더하여 새롭게 출제될 수 있는 문제를 포함하여 시험에 완벽하게 대비할 수 있도록 준비

|서술형 실전 및 창의사고력 문제|

학교 시험에서 점차 늘어나는 서술형 시험에 집중 대비하고 고득점을 취득하는데 만전을 기하기 위한 학습 코너

|단원별 모의고사|

영역별, 단계별 학습을 모두 마친 후 실전 연습을 위한 모의고사

교과서 파헤치기

- **단어Test1~3** 영어 단어 우리말 쓰기, 우리말을 영어 단어로 쓰기, 영영풀이에 해당하는 단어와 우리말 쓰기
- **대화문Test1~2** 대화문 빈칸 완성 및 전체 대화문 쓰기
- **본문Test1~5** 빈칸 완성, 우리말 쓰기, 문장 배열연습, 영어 작문하기 복습 등 단계별 반복 학습을 통해 교과서 지문에 대한 완벽한 습득
- **구석구석지문Test1~2** 지문 빈칸 완성 및 전문 영어로 쓰기

이책의 차례

Contents

Lesson ⑤	Come One, Come All	05~56
Lesson ⑥	In Outer Space	57~108
Lesson ⑦	Can I Trust It?	109~160
Lesson ⑧	Be like Sherlock!	161~212
Special Lesson	Frindle	213~228

| ⟨Insight on the textbook⟩ 교과서 파헤치기 | 01~90 |

| ⟨책 속의 책⟩ 정답 및 해설 | 01~58 |

Lesson 5

Come One, Come All

 의사소통 기능

- 길 묻고 답하기
  A: How can I get to the post office?
  B: Go straight to 1st Street and make a right.
- 소요 시간 말하기
  A: How long will it take to make the sandwiches?
  B: Maybe it will take about an hour.

언어 형식

- 가주어 It
  It is a lot of fun **to throw** colorful powder at everyone.
- 지각동사
  You can **hear** musicians **playing** beautiful live music.

Words & Expressions

Key Words

- **adult** [ədʌ́lt] 명 성인, 어른
- **advertise** [ǽdvərtàiz] 동 광고하다
- **almost** [ɔ́:lmoust] 부 거의
- **amazing** [əméiziŋ] 형 놀라운
- **appear** [əpíər] 동 나타나다
- **arrow** [ǽrou] 명 화살
- **artwork** [á:rtwərk] 명 예술 작품
- **bakery** [béikəri] 명 빵집, 제과점
- **block** [blɑk] 명 블록, 구획
- **boat** [bout] 명 배, 선박
- **celebrate** [séləbrèit] 동 축하하다, 기념하다
- **chase** [tʃeis] 동 뒤쫓다
- **colorful** [kʌ́lərfəl] 형 형형색색의
- **competition** [kàmpətíʃən] 명 대회, 시합, 경쟁
- **completely** [kəmplí:tli] 부 완전히
- **cross** [krɔ:s] 동 가로지르다, 가로질러 건너다
- **dark** [dɑ:rk] 형 어두운
- **decorate** [dékərèit] 동 장식하다
- **during** [djúəriŋ] 전 ~ 동안
- **far** [fɑ:r] 형 먼 부 멀리
- **festival** [féstəvəl] 명 축제

- **firework** [fáiərwə:rk] 명 폭죽, 불꽃놀이
- **follow** [fálou] 동 따르다
- **gather** [gǽðər] 동 모이다, 모으다
- **hold** [hould] 동 개최하다
- **hometown** [hóumtaun] 명 고향
- **huge** [hju:dʒ] 형 거대한
- **last** [læst] 동 지속하다
- **live** [laiv] 형 라이브의, 실황인
- **musician** [mju:zíʃən] 명 음악가
- **near** [niər] 형 가까운, 가까이에 있는
- **neighborhood** [néibərhùd] 명 근처, 이웃, 인근
- **outdoor** [áutdɔ:r] 형 야외의
- **parade** [pəréid] 명 페레이드, 행진
- **pile** [pail] 명 더미
- **post** [poust] 동 게시하다
- **powder** [páudər] 명 가루
- **sail** [seil] 명 돛
- **shape** [ʃeip] 명 형태 동 ~ 모양으로 만들다
- **sled** [sled] 명 썰매
- **solve** [salv] 동 해결하다
- **take** [teik] 동 (시간이) 걸리다, (탈 것을) 타다
- **throw** [θrou] 동 던지다

Key Expressions

- **because of** ~ 때문에
- **between A and B** A와 B 사이에
- **come out** 나오다
- **each other** 서로
- **from beginning to end** 처음부터 끝까지
- **get off** 내리다
- **go on** 지속되다, 계속되다

- **go straight** 앞으로 곧장 가다
- **in front of** ~ 앞에
- **make a left[right]** 왼쪽[오른쪽]으로 돌다
- **more and more** 더욱 더
- **next to** ~ ~ 옆에
- **on one's right** ~의 오른편에
- **out of hand** 손을 쓸 수 없는

Word Power

※ 서로 반대되는 뜻을 가진 단어

- □ **far** 먼 ↔ **near** 가까운
- □ **dark** 어두운 ↔ **bright** 밝은
- □ **outdoor** 야외의 ↔ **indoor** 실내의
- □ **complete** 완전한 ↔ **incomplete** 불완전한
- □ **huge** 거대한 ↔ **tiny** 작은
- □ **get on** (탈 것을) 타다 ↔ **get off** 내리다

- □ **appear** 나타나다 ↔ **disappear** 사라지다
- □ **adult** 어른, 성인 ↔ **child** 아이, 어린이
- □ **live** 살아 있는 ↔ **dead** 죽은
- □ **follow** 뒤따르다 ↔ **precede** 선행하다, 앞서다
- □ **compete** 경쟁하다 ↔ **cooperate** 협력하다, 협동하다
- □ **throw** 던지다 ↔ **receive** 받다

English Dictionary

- □ **adult** 어른
  → a fully grown person
  완전히 자란 사람

- □ **advertise** 광고하다
  → to tell the public about goods to make people buy them
  사람들이 물건을 사게 만들도록 물건에 대해 대중에게 이야기하다

- □ **artwork** 예술 작품
  → objects produced by artists
  예술가들에 의해 만들어진 물체

- □ **celebrate** 축하하다
  → to do something special for an important event, holiday, etc.
  중요한 행사나 휴일 등을 위해 특별한 무언가를 하다

- □ **chase** 뒤쫓다
  → to follow and try to catch
  따라가서 잡으려고 노력하다

- □ **competition** 대회, 경쟁
  → an event or contest in which people compete
  사람들이 경쟁하는 행사 또는 대회

- □ **completely** 완전히
  → totally, fully
  완전히

- □ **decorate** 장식하다
  → to make something look more beautiful by putting things on it
  위에 물건들을 올려놓음으로써 더 아름답게 보이도록 만들다

- □ **festival** 축제
  → a day or period of celebration
  축하하는 날이나 기간

- □ **gather** 모이다
  → to come together to form a group
  모임을 형성하기 위해 함께 모이다

- □ **hold** 개최하다
  → to have a meeting, competition, conversation, etc.
  만남, 경쟁, 대화 등을 갖다

- □ **hometown** 고향
  → the city or town where you were born or grew up
  당신이 태어나거나 자란 도시나 마을

- □ **last** 지속하다
  → to continue in time
  시간에 있어서 계속되다

- □ **lift** 들어올리다
  → to move something or someone to a higher position
  어떤 것이나 어떤 사람을 높은 위치로 옮기다

- □ **live** 라이브의, 실황인
  → given or made when people are watching, not pre-recorded
  미리 녹화되지 않고 사람들이 보고 시청하고 있을 때 주어지거나 만들어진

- □ **pile** 더미
  → a mass of something that has been placed somewhere
  어딘가에 놓여진 무언가의 덩어리

- □ **shape** ~ 모양으로 만들다
  → to make something into a particular shape
  무언가를 특정한 모양으로 만들다

- □ **sled** 썰매
  → a small vehicle used for sliding over snow
  눈 위에서 미끄러지기 위해 사용된 작은 탈 것

서답형

01 다음 짝지어진 단어의 관계가 같도록 빈칸에 알맞은 말을 쓰시오.

> heavy: light = _____ : near

서답형

02 다음 영영풀이가 가리키는 말을 쓰시오.

> the city or town where you were born or grew up

➡ _____

03 다음 중 밑줄 친 부분의 뜻풀이가 바르지 <u>않은</u> 것은?

① That yacht with white <u>sails</u> is my dad's. 항해하다
② He raked the leaves into <u>piles</u>. 더미
③ I heard the band playing <u>live</u> music. 라이브의, 실황의
④ This movie <u>lasts</u> two hours. 지속하다
⑤ The technique is <u>completely</u> new. 완전히

서답형

04 다음 문장의 빈칸에 들어갈 말을 〈보기〉에서 골라 쓰시오.

> ┤ 보기 ├
>
> parade / neighborhood / pile / advertise / regularly

(1) Is there a bakery in this _____?
(2) The band is marching in a _____.
(3) We made a plan to _____ our new product.
(4) He is looking at a _____ of newspapers.
(5) She attended church _____.

중요

05 다음 주어진 문장의 밑줄 친 live와 같은 의미로 쓰인 것은?

> Musicians played beautiful <u>live</u> music.

① This program is <u>live</u> from Time Square.
② We used to <u>live</u> in Jeju-do.
③ Mike needs to find somewhere to <u>live</u>.
④ This moment will <u>live</u> in our memory for a long time.
⑤ Bears can <u>live</u> for several days without food.

06 다음 문장에 공통으로 들어갈 말을 고르시오.

> • You should _____ the sea to get to the island.
> • My brother is waiting to _____ the street.
> • I put a _____ on the map to show where the hotel is.

① follow
② chase
③ parade
④ shape
⑤ cross

서답형

07 다음 우리말에 맞게 빈칸에 알맞은 말을 쓰시오.

(1) 그들은 개 썰매로 이동하곤 했다.
➡ They used to travel by dog _____.
(2) 사진 속의 형형색색의 꽃들을 보세요.
➡ Look at the _____ flowers in the picture.
(3) 시간이 화살처럼 지나갔다.
➡ Time flew like an _____.

01 다음 짝지어진 단어의 관계가 같도록 빈칸에 알맞은 말을 쓰시오.

> complete : incomplete = appear : _____

02 다음 문장의 빈칸에 들어갈 말을 〈보기〉에서 골라 쓰시오.

> ┤ 보기 ├
> almost / live / artwork / fireworks

(1) I'm looking forward to the _____ music performance.
(2) They celebrate the festival with _____.
(3) It's been _____ 5 years since I moved to Korea.
(4) His _____ is going to be displayed in a gallery.

03 다음 우리말에 맞게 주어진 빈칸을 완성하시오.

(1) 나는 이 책을 처음부터 끝까지 읽을 거야.
➡ I'll read this book from beginning _____ _____.
(2) 경쟁이 더욱 더 심해졌다.
➡ The competition became _____ _____ severe.
(3) 언제 그 책이 나왔습니까?
➡ When did the book _____ _____?
(4) 일이 아주 엉망이 되었다.
➡ Things really got _____ _____ _____.

04 다음 우리말을 주어진 단어를 이용하여 영작하시오.

(1) 음악 축제가 언제 열리나요? (will, held)
➡ _____
(2) 나는 크리스마스 트리 장식하는 것을 즐겼다. (enjoyed)
➡ _____
(3) 사람들이 그 가수를 보기 위해 함께 모였다. (gathered)
➡ _____

05 다음 우리말과 일치하도록 주어진 어구를 배열하여 완성하시오.

(1) 사람들이 이틀 동안 여기저기서 축제를 기념한다.
(two / everywhere / days / people / the festival / celebrate / for)
➡ _____
_____
(2) 내가 가장 좋아하는 가수를 직접 본 것은 정말 놀라웠다.
(singer / in / amazing / it / to / see / favorite / person / my / was)
➡ _____
_____
(3) 사람들은 미술가들이 그들의 작품을 만드는 것을 처음부터 끝까지 지켜본다.
(watch / the / shaping / artists / from / end / works / beginning / to / their / people)
➡ _____
_____

Conversation

1 길 묻고 답하기

A How can I get to the post office? 우체국에 어떻게 가나요?

B Go straight to 1st Street and make a right. 1가로 곧장 간 후 오른쪽으로 도세요.

■ 'How can I get to + 장소 명사?'는 '~에 어떻게 갈 수 있나요?'라는 뜻으로 길을 묻는 표현이다. 'How can I go to ~?'로 물을 수도 있다. 대답으로 길을 안내할 때는 보통 'Go straight.'처럼 명령문의 형태로 대답한다.

길 묻고 답하기

- Where can I find the police station? 경찰서가 어디에 있나요?
- Do you know where the library is? 도서관이 어디에 있는지 아세요?
- Is there a bakery around here? 이곳 주위에 빵집이 있나요?
- Walk straight ahead. 앞쪽으로 곧장 걸어가세요.
- You can't miss it. 쉽게 찾을 수 있을 거야.
- It's just around the corner. 그것은 바로 모퉁이를 돌면 있어.
- It's across from the museum. 그것은 박물관 건너편에 있어.

핵심 Check

1. 다음 우리말과 일치하도록 빈칸에 알맞은 말을 쓰시오.

(1) **A:** _____ _____ _____ _____ _____ the museum?

   (박물관에 어떻게 가나요?)

   B: Come out from the school and go straight one block.

   (학교에서 나와서 한 구역 곧장 가세요.)

(2) **A:** Where can I find the theater? (극장이 어디에 있나요?)

   B: _____ _____ _____ and _____ _____ two blocks.

   (길을 건너서 두 구역을 곧장 가세요.)

(3) **A:** _____ _____ _____ _____ around here? (이곳 주위에 병원이 있나요?)

   B: Yes, it's _____ _____ the corner. (네. 그것은 바로 모퉁이를 돌면 있어요.)

❷ 소요 시간 말하기

A How long will it take to make the sandwiches? 샌드위치를 만드는 데 시간이 얼마나 걸릴까?

B Maybe it will take about an hour. 아마도 약 한 시간 정도 걸릴 거야.

■ 'How long will it take to ~?'는 '~하는 데 시간이 얼마가 걸릴까?'라는 뜻으로, 소요 시간을 묻는 표현이다. 대답으로 '(시간이) ~ 걸리다'의 뜻을 나타내는 동사 take를 사용하여 소요 시간을 말한다. 대답할 때는 소요 시간을 구체적으로 말하는 것이 보통이다.

• How long will it take to finish your work? 일을 마치는 데 얼마나 걸리겠어요?

• How long will it take to go to London? 런던까지 가는 데는 얼마나 걸립니까?

• It will take more than an hour. 한 시간 이상 걸릴 것이다.

• It will take about ten minutes on foot. 걸어서 10분 정도 걸립니다.

핵심 Check

2. 다음 우리말과 일치하도록 빈칸에 알맞은 말을 쓰시오.

(1) **A:** How long will it take to clean the classroom? (교실을 청소하는 데 얼마나 걸릴까?)

　　B: It'll ＿＿＿＿ ＿＿＿＿ ＿＿＿＿ ＿＿＿＿ ＿＿＿＿. (약 30분 정도 걸릴 거야.)

(2) **A:** ＿＿＿＿ ＿＿＿＿ ＿＿＿＿ ＿＿＿＿ ＿＿＿＿ ＿＿＿＿ get to the theater?

　　(영화관까지 가는 데 시간이 얼마가 걸릴까?)

　　B: It'll take about 15 minutes ＿＿＿＿ ＿＿＿＿. (버스로 약 15분 정도 걸릴 거야.)

(3) **A:** ＿＿＿＿ ＿＿＿＿ ＿＿＿＿ ＿＿＿＿ ＿＿＿＿ ＿＿＿＿ ＿＿＿＿

　　＿＿＿＿? (교실을 장식하는 데 얼마나 걸릴까?)

　　B: It'll ＿＿＿＿ ＿＿＿＿ ＿＿＿＿ ＿＿＿＿. (약 두 시간 정도 걸릴 거야.)

Conversation 교과서 대화문 익히기

Listen and Speak 1-B

(*A phone rings.*)
Minsu: Hi, Emma. What's up?
Emma: Hey, Minsu. Are you free this Saturday?
Minsu: Yes. Why do you ask?
Emma: Well, ❶how about having lunch together?
Minsu: Sure.
Emma: Let's try the new Chinese restaurant, Ming's. ❷It's near the school.
Minsu: Okay. ❸How can I get there from the school?
Emma: ❹Come out from the school and go straight to Green Street. ❺Make a left, and the restaurant will be on your left.
Minsu: All right. Let's meet at 12 o'clock.
Emma: Wonderful. See you then.

(전화벨이 울린다.)
Minsu: 안녕, Emma. 잘 지내니?
Emma: 안녕, 민수야. 이번 토요일에 한가하니?
Minsu: 응. 왜 묻는 거니?
Emma: 그럼, 함께 점심 먹는 게 어떠니?
Minsu: 좋아.
Emma: Ming's라는 새로 생긴 중국 음식점에 가 보자. 학교 근처에 있어.
Minsu: 좋아. 학교에서 거기까지 어떻게 가니?
Emma: 학교에서 나와서 Green Street까지 곧장 가. 왼쪽으로 돌면 음식점이 네 왼쪽에 있을 거야.
Minsu: 알겠어. 12시에 만나자.
Emma: 좋아. 그때 보자.

❶ 'How about ~?'은 '~하는 게 어때?'라고 제안하는 표현으로 'Why don't we ~?' 또는 'What about ~?'으로 바꾸어 쓸 수 있다.
❷ be near ~: ~와 가깝다
❸ How can I get ~?은 '~에 어떻게 가니?'라고 길을 묻는 표현이다.
❹ 동사원형으로 시작하는 명령문이다.
❺ make a left: 왼쪽으로 돌다(= turn left)

Check(√) True or False

(1) Minsu and Emma will have lunch together.　　　　　　　　T ☐ F ☐

(2) The Chinese restaurant is far from the school.　　　　　　T ☐ F ☐

Real Life Talk

Man: Excuse me. How can I get to Suwon Hwaseong from here?
Mina: It's easy. Do you see the bus stop over there?
Man: Yes, I do.
Mina: Take the No. 11 bus and ❶get off at the sixth stop.
Man: ❷How long will it take to get there?
Mina: It will take ❸about 20 minutes.
Man: Thank you very much.
Mina: No problem. ❹Are you going there for the festival?
Man: Yes. I heard it's a lot of fun.
Mina: I hope you have a great time.

Man: 실례합니다. 여기에서 수원 화성까지 어떻게 가나요?
Mina: 쉬워요. 저쪽에 버스 정류장 보이세요?
Man: 네, 보여요.
Mina: 11번 버스를 타서 여섯 번째 정류장에서 내리세요.
Man: 그곳까지 가는 데 시간이 얼마나 걸릴까요?
Mina: 대략 20분 정도 걸릴 거에요.
Man: 정말 고마워요.
Mina: 별말씀을요. 그곳에 축제 때문에 가시는 건가요?
Man: 네. 그 축제가 무척 재미있다고 들었어요.
Mina: 즐거운 시간 보내길 바라요.

❶ get off: 내리다 ↔ get on: 타다
❷ How long will it take to get there?: '그곳에 가는 데 얼마나 걸리나요?'라는 의미로 소요 시간을 묻는 표현이다.
❸ about: 대략
❹ 수원 화성에 가는 목적을 묻고 있다.

Check(√) True or False

(3) It'll take about 20 minutes for the man to go to Suwon Hwaseong by bus.　　　T ☐ F ☐

(4) Mina wants to visit the festival in Suwon Hwaseong.　　　　T ☐ F ☐

Listen and Speak 1-A

Sora: Excuse me. ❶How can I get to the library?

Tom: Oh, the library? ❷Cross the street and go straight two blocks. Then ❸make a left.

Sora: Thank you very much.

❶ 도서관에 가는 법을 묻는 표현이다.
❷ cross: 건너다
❸ make a left: 왼쪽으로 돌다(= turn left)

Listen and Speak 1-C

A: Excuse me. How can I get to the post office?

B: Go straight to 1st Street and make a right. It will be ❶on your right.

A: Is it ❷far from here?

B: No, it's not.

A: Thank you very much.

❶ on one's right: ~의 오른편에
❷ far: 먼; 멀리

Listen and Speak 2-A

Amy: Jinho, hurry up. We're going to be late for the movie.

Jinho: Okay. ❶How long will it take to get to the theater?

Amy: It will take about 15 minutes ❷by bus.

Jinho: All right. I'm ❸almost ready.

❶ 극장에 가는 소요 시간을 묻고 있다.
❷ by bus: 버스로
❸ almost: 거의

Listen and Speak 2-B

Andy: I'm so excited about the school festival this Friday.

Mike: ❶Me, too. What can we do to advertise ❷ it, Andy?

Andy: How about making posters?

Mike: Great idea. We can post ❸them in our neighborhood.

Andy: Right. ❹How long will it take to make them?

Mike: Well, it will take about three hours.

Andy: Okay, I hope many people come to the festival.

❶ '나도 그래.'라는 의미로 'So am I.'와 바꾸어 쓸 수 있다.
❷ it은 the school festival을 가리킨다.
❸ them은 posters를 가리킨다.
❹ 포스터를 제작하는 데 걸리는 소요 시간을 묻고 있다.

Listen and Speak 2-C

Rachel: Chris, what will you do for the class party?

Chris: I'll make sandwiches.

Rachel: Great idea. How long will it take to make ❶them?

Chris: Maybe it'll take ❷about an hour.

❶ them은 sandwiches를 가리킨다.
❷ about: 약, 대략

• 다음 우리말과 일치하도록 빈칸에 알맞은 말을 쓰시오.

Listen and Speak 1-A

Sora: Excuse me. _____ _____ _____ _____ _____ _____?

Tom: Oh, the library? _____ the street and _____ _____ two blocks. Then _____ a left.

Sora: Thank you very much.

해석

Sora: 실례합니다. 도서관까지 어떻게 가나요?

Tom: 아, 도서관이요? 길을 건너서 두 구역을 곧장 가세요. 그런 다음 왼쪽으로 도세요.

Sora: 정말 고마워요.

Listen and Speak 1-B

(*A phone rings.*)

Minsu: Hi, Emma. _____ _____?

Emma: Hey, Minsu. Are you _____ this Saturday?

Minsu: Yes. _____ do you _____?

Emma: Well, how about _____ lunch together?

Minsu: Sure.

Emma: _____ try the new Chinese restaurant, Ming's. It's _____ the school.

Minsu: Okay. _____ _____ _____ _____ _____ _____?

Emma: _____ _____ from the school and _____ _____ to Green Street. _____ _____ _____, and the restaurant will be _____ _____ _____.

Minsu: All right. _____ _____ at 12 o'clock.

Emma: Wonderful. _____ you _____.

(전화벨이 울린다.)

Minsu: 안녕, Emma. 잘 지내니?

Emma: 안녕, 민수야. 이번 토요일에 한가하니?

Minsu: 응. 왜 묻는 거니?

Emma: 음, 함께 점심 먹는 게 어떠니?

Minsu: 좋아.

Emma: Ming's라는 새로 생긴 중국 음식점에 가 보자. 학교 근처에 있어.

Minsu: 좋아. 학교에서 거기까지 어떻게 가니?

Emma: 학교에서 나와서 Green Street까지 곧장 가. 왼쪽으로 돌면 음식점이 네 왼쪽에 있을 거야.

Minsu: 알겠어. 12시에 만나자.

Emma: 좋아. 그때 보자.

Listen and Speak 1-C

A: Excuse me. _____ _____ I _____ _____ the post office?

B: _____ _____ to 1st Street and _____ a right. It will _____ _____ _____ _____.

A: Is it _____ _____ here?

B: No, it's _____.

A: Thank you very much.

A: 실례합니다. 우체국에 어떻게 갈 수 있나요?

B: 1st Street까지 곧장 가서 오른쪽으로 도세요. 그것은 오른쪽에 있을 거예요.

A: 여기서 먼가요?

B: 아니요, 멀지 않아요.

A: 정말 고마워요.

Listen and Speak 2-A

Amy: Jinho, hurry up. We're going to _____ _____ _____ the movie.

Jinho: Okay. _____ _____ _____ _____ _____ _____ _____ _____ _____ _____?

Amy: It will _____ _____ 15 minutes _____ _____.

Jinho: All right. I'm _____ ready.

Listen and Speak 2-B

Andy: I'm so _____ about the school festival this Friday.

Mike: _____, _____. What can we do to _____ it, Andy?

Andy: How _____ _____ posters?

Mike: Great idea. We can _____ _____ in our _____.

Andy: Right. _____ _____ _____ _____ _____ make them?

Mike: Well, it will _____ _____ three hours.

Andy: Okay, I hope many people _____ _____ the festival.

Real Life Talk

Man: Excuse me. How can I _____ _____ Suwon Hwaseong from here?

Mina: It's easy. Do you see the bus stop _____ _____?

Man: Yes, I do.

Mina: _____ the No. 11 bus and _____ _____ at the sixth stop.

Man: _____ _____ _____ _____ _____ _____ _____?

Mina: It will _____ _____ 20 minutes.

Man: Thank you very much.

Mina: No problem. Are you going there for _____ _____?

Man: Yes. I heard _____ _____ _____ _____ _____.

Mina: I hope you _____ _____ _____ _____.

해석

Amy: 진호야, 서둘러. 우리 영화 시간에 늦겠어.
Jinho: 응. 영화관까지 가는 데 시간이 얼마나 걸릴까?
Amy: 버스로 대략 15분 정도 걸릴 거야.
Jinho: 알겠어. 나 거의 준비됐어.

Andy: 나는 이번 금요일 학교 축제가 정말 기대돼.
Mike: 나도. 축제를 광고하기 위해 무엇을 할 수 있을까, Andy?
Andy: 포스터를 만들면 어떨까?
Mike: 좋은 생각이야. 이 근방에 포스터를 붙일 수 있겠다.
Andy: 맞아. 포스터를 만드는 데 시간이 얼마나 걸릴까?
Mike: 음, 대략 세 시간 정도 걸릴 거야.
Andy: 좋아, 많은 사람들이 축제에 왔으면 좋겠다.

Man: 실례합니다. 여기에서 수원 화성까지 어떻게 가나요?
Mina: 쉬워요. 저쪽에 버스 정류장 보이세요?
Man: 네, 보여요.
Mina: 11번 버스를 타서 여섯 번째 정류장에서 내리세요.
Man: 그곳까지 가는 데 시간이 얼마나 걸릴까요?
Mina: 대략 20분 정도 걸릴 거예요.
Man: 정말 고마워요.
Mina: 별말씀을요. 그곳에 축제 때문에 가시는 건가요?
Man: 네. 그 축제가 무척 재미있다고 들었어요.
Mina: 즐거운 시간 보내길 바라요.

01 다음 대화의 빈칸에 들어갈 말을 〈보기〉에 주어진 단어를 배열하여 완성하시오.

A: How long will it take to get to the pharmacy?

B: _____

┤ 보기 ├

by / car / about / take / it / 5 minutes / will

➡ _____

02 다음 대화가 자연스럽게 이어지도록 순서대로 배열하시오.

(A) Thank you very much.

(B) Excuse me. How can I get to the post office?

(C) Is it far from here?

(D) No, it's not.

(E) Go straight to 1st Street and make a right. It will be on your right.

➡ _____

[03~04] 다음 대화를 읽고 물음에 답하시오.

A: Excuse me. How can I get ⓐto the police station?

B: Go straight to Green Street. ⓑCross the street. Then make a right. The police station is between the flower shop ⓒor the bakery.

A: How ⓓlong will it take to get there?

B: It will take ⓔabout 5 minutes.

A: Thank you very much.

03 위 대화의 밑줄 친 ⓐ~ⓔ 중 어법상 바르지 않은 것을 찾아 바르게 고치시오.

➡ _____

04 위 대화의 내용과 일치하지 않는 것은?

① A는 경찰서를 찾고 있다.

② 경찰서는 꽃가게와 빵집 사이에 위치해 있다.

③ 경찰서까지 5분 정도 걸릴 것이다.

④ 경찰서에 가기 위해 Green Street까지 직진해서 길을 건넌 후 오른쪽으로 돌아야 한다.

⑤ B는 A에게 버스를 타고 경찰서 가는 법을 설명하고 있다.

[01~02] 다음 대화를 읽고 물음에 답하시오.

Amy: Jinho, hurry up. We're going to be late for the movie.

Jinho: Okay. _____(A)_____?

Amy: It will take about 15 minutes ___(B)___ bus.

Jinho: All right. I'm almost ready.

01 위 대화의 빈칸 (A)에 들어갈 말을 〈보기〉의 단어를 배열하여 완성하시오.

┌─ 보기 ├─
take / get / it / the / to / to / theater / how / will / long
└─

➡ _____

02 위 대화의 빈칸 (B)에 들어갈 말로 적절한 것은?

① by   ② at   ③ from
④ on   ⑤ for

[03~04] 다음 대화를 읽고 물음에 답하시오.

Minsu: Hi, Emma. What's up?

Emma: Hey, Minsu. Are you free this Saturday?

Minsu: Yes. Why do you ask?

Emma: Well, (A)how about having lunch together?

Minsu: Sure.

Emma: Let's try the new Chinese restaurant, Ming's. It's near the school.

Minsu: Okay. How can I get there from the school?

Emma: Come out from the school and go straight to Green Street. Make a left, and the restaurant will be on your left.

Minsu: All right. Let's meet at 12 o'clock.

Emma: Wonderful. See you then.

03 위 대화의 밑줄 친 (A)와 의미가 같도록 why를 사용하여 다시 쓰시오.

➡ _____

04 위 대화를 읽고 대답할 수 없는 것은?

① What are Emma and Minsu going to do this Saturday?
② What restaurant are Emma and Minsu going to try?
③ How can Minsu get to Ming's?
④ What time are Emma and Minsu going to meet?
⑤ How long does it take for Emma to go to Ming's?

[05~07] 다음 대화를 읽고 물음에 답하시오.

Andy: I'm so excited about the school festival this Friday.

Mike: Me, too. What can we do to advertise ⓐit, Andy?

Andy: How about making posters?

Mike: Great idea. We can post them in our neighborhood.

Andy: Right. How long will it take to make ⓑ them?

Mike: Well, it will take about three hours.

Andy: Okay, I hope many people come to the festival.

서답형

05 위 대화에서 다음 영영풀이가 나타내는 말을 찾아 쓰시오.

> to tell the public about goods to make people buy them

➡ _____

서답형

06 위 대화의 밑줄 친 ⓐ와 ⓑ가 각각 가리키는 것을 쓰시오.

➡ ⓐ _____ ⓑ _____

07 위 대화의 내용과 일치하지 <u>않는</u> 것은?

① Andy and Mike are excited about the school festival.
② The school festival is going to be held this Friday.
③ Andy and Mike are going to make posters to advertise the school festival.
④ It will take about three hours to make the posters.
⑤ Andy and Mike are going to post the posters with their neighbors.

서답형

[08~10] 다음 대화를 읽고 물음에 답하시오.

Man: Excuse me. How can I get to Suwon Hwaseong from here?
Mina: It's easy. Do you see the bus stop over there?
Man: Yes, I do.
Mina: Take the No. 11 bus and get off at the sixth stop.
Man: How long will it take to get there?
Mina: It will take about 20 minutes.
Man: Thank you very much.

Mina: No problem. Are you going there for the festival?
Man: Yes. I heard it's a lot of fun.
Mina: I hope you have a great time.

08 How will the man go to Suwon Hwaseong?

➡ _____

09 Why does the man want to join the festival?

➡ _____

10 Which bus should the man take to go to Suwon Hwaseong?

➡ _____

서답형

11 다음 대화에 알맞은 말을 〈보기〉에서 골라 쓰시오.

> ┤ 보기 ├
> a right / front / get / one block /
> go straight

A: Excuse me. How can I _____(A)_____ to the market?
B: _____(B)_____ to Green Street. Make _____(C)_____. Go straight _____(D)_____ and cross the street. The market will be in _____(E)_____ of you.
A: Thank you very much.

➡ (A) _____
(B) _____
(C) _____
(D) _____
(E) _____

[01~02] 다음 대화를 읽고 물음에 답하시오.

Sora: Excuse me. _____(A)_____?

Tom: Oh, the library? Cross the street and go straight two blocks. Then ____(B)____.

Sora: Thank you very much.

01 다음 대화의 빈칸 (A)에 들어갈 말을 〈보기〉에 주어진 단어를 배열하여 완성하시오.

┌─ 보기 ┐

get / how / I / to / library / can / the

➡ _____

02 다음 표지판의 내용과 일치하도록 빈칸 (B)를 완성하시오.

➡ _____

[03~05] 다음 대화를 읽고 물음에 답하시오.

Andy: I'm so ⓐexciting about the school festival this Friday.

Mike: Me, too. What can we do ⓑto advertise it, Andy?

Andy: How about ⓒmaking posters?

Mike: Great idea. We can post them in our neighborhood.

Andy: Right. How long will it take to make them?

Mike: Well, it will take ⓓabout three hours.

Andy: Okay, I hope many people ⓔcome to the festival.

03 위 대화의 ⓐ~ⓔ 중 어법상 바르지 않은 것을 찾아 바르게 고치시오.

➡ _____

04 What are Andy and Mike going to advertise?

➡ _____

05 What are Andy and Mike going to make?

➡ _____

06 다음 그림의 내용과 일치하도록 빈칸 (A)와 (B)를 완성하시오.

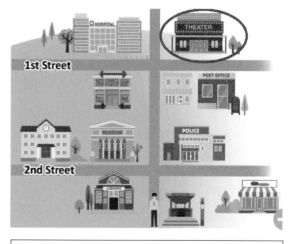

Aram: Excuse me. How can I get to the theater?

Brian: _____(A)_____. It will be on your ____(B)____.

Aram: Thank you so much.

➡ (A) _____
   (B) _____

교과서 Grammar

1 가주어 It

- **It** is a pleasure **to talk** with you. 너와 대화하는 것은 즐거워.
- **It** was difficult **to stop** my bad habit. 나의 나쁜 습관을 멈추는 것은 어려웠다.

■ to부정사구가 문장의 주어로 쓰여 주어가 길어진 경우, 주어부를 문장의 맨 뒤로 보내고 이 자리에 It을 쓰는 것이 가주어 It이다.

- **To exercise** regularly is very important.
  = **It** is very important **to exercise** regularly. 규칙적으로 운동하는 것은 매우 중요하다.

■ 가주어 It은 따로 해석하지 않으며 to부정사구를 주어로 해석해야 한다. to부정사구의 부정은 'not+to V'로 나타낸다.

- **It** is fun **to learn** a foreign language. 외국어를 배우는 것은 재미있다.
- **It** was hard **to say** sorry to you. 너에게 미안하다고 말하는 것은 힘들었어.
- **It** is good **to know** how to say hello. 인사하는 방법을 아는 것은 좋다.
- **It** is important **not to use** your phone while walking. 걷는 동안 휴대 전화기를 사용하지 않는 것이 중요하다.

핵심 Check

1. 다음 우리말과 일치하도록 빈칸에 알맞은 말을 쓰시오.

(1) 아침 일찍 운동하는 것은 좋다.

➡ _____ is good _____ _____ early in the morning.

(2) 부주의하게 운전하는 것은 위험하다.

➡ _____ is dangerous _____ _____ carelessly.

(3) 너의 친구에게 거짓말하는 것은 옳지 않아.

➡ It is wrong _____ _____ to your friend.

② 지각동사

> • I **heard** her **crying**. 나는 그녀가 우는 소리를 들었어.
>
> • They **saw** the boy **playing** the piano. 그들은 그 소년이 피아노를 연주하는 것을 보았다.

■ 지각동사란 신체 감각과 관련된 동사로 보고, 듣고, 느끼는 동사인 see, watch, hear, feel 등이 이에 해당한다. 5형식 동사에 해당하여 목적어와 목적격보어를 취한다.

　• June **heard** the dog **barking** at someone. June은 그 개가 누군가를 향해 짖는 소리를 들었다.

■ '지각동사+목적어+V(ing)'로 쓰이는 경우, 목적어와 목적격보어는 능동 관계가 된다. 동작이 진행 중인 것을 강조하고 싶을 때에는 보통 현재분사를 쓴다. '지각동사+목적어+p.p.'로 쓰이는 경우 목적어와 목적격보어의 관계는 수동이다.

　• We **watched** our children **singing** songs. 우리는 우리 아이들이 노래 부르는 것을 지켜보았다.

　• Did you **see** the glass **broken**? 너는 그 유리잔이 깨어진 것을 봤니?

■ 사역동사의 쓰임과 혼동하지 않도록 한다. 사역동사 make, have, let 역시 5형식 동사로 목적어와 목적격보어를 취하지만, 사역동사의 목적격보어는 원형부정사이며 '목적어가 ~하게 시키다'라는 의미이다.

　• Mom **makes** me **eat** carrots. 엄마는 내가 당근을 먹게 하신다.

　• The teacher **had** us **do** some homework. 그 선생님은 우리가 약간의 숙제를 하도록 시키셨다.

핵심 Check

2. 다음 우리말과 일치하도록 빈칸에 알맞은 말을 쓰시오.

　(1) 그 사냥꾼은 누군가가 그를 따라오는 것을 느꼈다.

　　➡ The hunter ＿＿＿＿ someone ＿＿＿＿ him.

　(2) 우리는 그가 집으로 들어가는 것을 보았다.

　　➡ We ＿＿＿＿ him ＿＿＿＿ the house.

　(3) 아빠는 내가 내 방 청소를 하도록 시키셨다.

　　➡ Dad ＿＿＿＿ me ＿＿＿＿ my room.

01 다음 문장에서 어법상 <u>어색한</u> 부분을 바르게 고쳐 쓰시오.

(1) It is natural for you get angry.

_____ ➡ _____

(2) It was impossible to changing the plan.

_____ ➡ _____

(3) Didn't you hear him said he was busy?

_____ ➡ _____

(4) We watched Jane to dance on the stage.

_____ ➡ _____

02 주어진 단어를 어법에 맞게 빈칸에 쓰시오.

(1) Perry saw her friend _____ off the stairs. (fall)

(2) It is really exciting _____ on a picnic. (go)

(3) I saw the boy _____ the window. (break)

(4) It was fun _____ with your sisters. (play)

03 주어진 단어를 바르게 배열하여 다음 우리말을 영어로 쓰시오. 필요하다면 단어를 추가하거나 변형하시오.

(2) wake up: 일어나다
(3) island: 섬

(1) 나는 그 아기가 우는 소리를 들었어. (cry / the baby / heard / I)

➡ _____

(2) 너가 일찍 일어나는 것은 좋은 생각이야. (early / it / a good idea / for / you / wake up / is)

➡ _____

(3) Emma는 그들이 섬 주변에서 수영하는 것을 보았다. (the island / Emma / them / swim / saw / around)

➡ _____

(4) 사람들은 미술가들이 그들의 작품을 만드는 것을 처음부터 끝까지 지켜본다. (from beginning to end / the artists / people / their / create / watch / works)

➡ _____

01 다음 중 밑줄 친 부분의 쓰임이 다른 하나는?

① It is nice to clean your room by yourself.
② It is not that difficult to speak Korean well.
③ It is under the sofa in the living room.
④ It was hard to tell the truth to her.
⑤ It was easy to find the way to get there.

02 중요
다음 빈칸에 들어갈 말로 가장 적절한 것은?

> James saw his friends _____ football on the playground.

① to play   ② play   ③ played
④ plays   ⑤ to playing

03 다음 우리말을 영어로 바르게 옮긴 것은?

> 이 책을 읽는 것은 어려웠다.

① It is difficult to read this book.
② I was difficult to read this book.
③ It was difficult read this book.
④ It was difficult to read this book.
⑤ It is difficult to reading this book.

서답형
04 주어진 단어를 이용하여 다음 우리말을 영어로 쓰시오.

> 거짓말을 하는 것은 잘못된 일이다.
> (it / wrong)

➡ _____

05 중요
다음 중 어법상 바르지 않은 것은?

① It is good to do your job on your own.
② David saw his brother wearing his cap.
③ It is important to help others.
④ Wendy saw the bus leaving right in front of her eyes.
⑤ Mom made me to wash my clothes every day.

06 다음 빈칸에 들어갈 말이 바르게 짝지어진 것은?

> • I heard the couple _____ last night.
> • Did you feel the house _____?

① to fight – to shake
② fight – shaken
③ fighting – shake
④ fight – to shake
⑤ fighting – shaken

07 다음 중 어법상 바르지 않은 것은?

> I like ①to listen ②to ③the birds ④ to sing when I ⑤get up early in the morning.

①   ②   ③   ④   ⑤

서답형
08 주어진 단어를 바르게 배열하여 다음 우리말을 영어로 쓰시오. 필요하다면 단어를 추가하시오.

> 헬멧을 쓰지 않고 오토바이를 타는 것은 위험해. (dangerous / a helmet / without / a motorcycle / is / it / ride)

➡ _____
_____

09 다음 우리말을 영어로 바르게 옮긴 것을 고르시오.

> 최선을 다하는 것은 중요해.

① It was important to do best.
② It is important to doing your best.
③ It is important do your best.
④ It is important to do your best.
⑤ It is important for doing your best.

10 다음 중 어법상 바르지 <u>않은</u> 것은?

① I saw the man got into the car alone.
② Julia heard Bill talking with someone.
③ It is fun to live in a dormitory.
④ It was careless of you to fall asleep while you were driving.
⑤ It is not easy to learn how to swim.

11 다음 중 쓰임이 <u>다른</u> 하나는?

① It is wrong <u>to say</u> like that to your friend.
② I am so happy <u>to hear</u> the news from you.
③ <u>To see</u> is to believe.
④ It is easy <u>to solve</u> the problem.
⑤ Is it difficult <u>to write</u> a poem?

서답형

12 다음 대화의 빈칸에 알맞은 말을 세 단어로 쓰시오.

> A: Did anybody go out?
> B: I don't think so. I didn't see _____ .

➡ _____

13 다음 빈칸에 들어갈 말로 가장 적절한 것은?

> I didn't hear you _____ in. You must have been very quiet.

① will come   ② come
③ came   ④ to come
⑤ to coming

14 다음 중 (A)~(C)에서 어법상 옳은 것끼리 바르게 짝지은 것은?

> • I saw my friend (A)[running / to run] down the street.
> • It was thoughtful of you (B)[to give / give] her a present.
> • Jason heard somebody (C)[say / to say] something to her.

① to run – give – to say
② to run – to give – to say
③ running – to give – say
④ running – give – say
⑤ running – to give – to say

15 다음 중 주어진 문장의 It과 쓰임이 같은 것은?

> <u>It</u> is kind of you to help your mom.

① <u>It</u> is time to go to bed now.
② <u>It</u> was too dark outside.
③ <u>It</u> was made of 100 blocks of stone.
④ <u>It</u> makes me nervous.
⑤ <u>It</u> is not easy to plant a tree.

서답형

16 주어진 단어를 활용하여 다음 우리말을 영어로 쓰시오.

> 말을 타는 것은 매우 재미있어. (it / lot / of / fun)

➡ _____

17 다음 상황을 읽고 빈칸에 들어갈 말로 가장 적절한 것을 고르시오.

> Brad was walking along the street. I saw that when I drove past in my car.
> → I _____ .

① saw Brad driving past
② heard Brad drive my car
③ saw Brad in my car
④ saw Brad walking along the street
⑤ heard Brad walking with someone

18 다음 중 빈칸에 들어갈 수 없는 말은?

> We _____ the boys playing the guitars.

① watched   ② listened to   ③ saw
④ heard   ⑤ made

19 다음 빈칸에 알맞은 말은?

> A: Did I close the window when I went out?
> B: Yes, you did. I _____ .

① saw you go out
② heard you go out
③ saw you closing the window
④ heard you closed the window
⑤ heard you going out through the window

서답형

20 다음 대화의 밑줄 친 우리말을 영어로 옮기시오.

> A: What was Jane doing then?
> B: 나는 그녀가 누군가에게 전화하고 있는 것을 보았어.

➡ _____

21 빈칸에 알맞은 말이 바르게 짝지어진 것을 모두 고르시오.

> It is fun _____ someone _____ comedy.

① seeing – doing   ② see – doing
③ seeing – to do   ④ to see – do
⑤ see – do

22 다음 중 밑줄 친 부분이 어법상 틀린 것은?

① It is really fun to play tennis with you.
② I want to play computer games.
③ It is exciting to play basketball.
④ Tom was tired of playing alone.
⑤ It is dangerous to playing with a knife.

서답형

23 다음 두 문장을 하나의 문장으로 쓰시오.

> • The boy fell off the tree yesterday.
> • I saw that.

➡ _____

서답형

24 다음 대화를 읽고 빈칸에 알맞은 말을 쓰시오.

> Kelly: What is Jimmy doing over there?
> Amelia: He is using his phone.

➡ Amelia sees Jimmy _____ .

서답형

25 주어진 단어를 활용하여 다음 우리말을 7 단어로 이루어진 한 문장으로 쓰시오.

> 여기에 머무는 것은 안전하지 않아.
> (safe / stay)

➡ _____

01 다음 대화의 빈칸에 알맞은 말을 쓰시오.

> A: How do you know I rode a bike yesterday?
> B: I know because I saw _____.

➡ _____

 02 가주어 It을 이용하여 다음 우리말을 영어로 쓰시오.

> 계단에서 뛰는 것은 나쁘다.

➡ _____

03 다음 두 문장을 하나의 문장으로 쓰시오.

> • The accident happened.
> • Did you see that?

➡ _____

04 다음 빈칸에 알맞은 말을 쓰시오.

> To hear you say that was true.
> = _____ to hear you say that.

➡ _____

 05 주어진 단어를 바르게 배열하여 다음 우리말을 영어로 쓰시오. 한 단어는 두 번 쓰시오.

> 학생들이 학교에서 휴대전화를 이용하도록 허락하는 것은 좋은 생각이 아니다.
> (in school / a good idea / students / allow / cell phones / to / it / not / is / use)

➡ _____
_____

 06 주어진 단어를 이용하여 다음 대화의 빈칸에 알맞은 말을 쓰시오.

> A: Did Susan cross the street?
> B: Yes, she did. I _____.(see)

➡ _____

07 주어진 단어를 이용하여 다음 우리말을 9 단어로 이루어진 한 문장으로 쓰시오.

> 네가 예의 바르게 인사하지 않는 것은 무례하다.
> (it / bow / politely / of)

➡ _____

08 주어진 문장을 지시에 맞게 영어로 쓰시오.

> 물을 절약하는 것은 중요합니다.

(1) to부정사 주어를 써서 작문할 것
  ➡ _____

(2) 가주어를 써서 작문할 것
  ➡ _____

09 다음 빈칸에 알맞은 말을 쓰시오.

> A: Who opened the window?
> B: I saw a man _____ but I don't know who he was.

➡ _____

10 다음 우리말을 영어로 쓰시오.

> 화살을 쏘는 것은 어렵다.

➡ _____

11 다음 대화의 빈칸에 알맞은 말을 7 단어로 쓰시오.

> A: I heard that you carried out a campaign to reduce food waste in school cafeteria. Did it work?
>
> B: It was a little hard _____, but the campaign turned out to be successful.

➡ _____

12 다음 상황을 읽고 빈칸에 알맞은 말을 쓰시오.

> There are many people in the park. Musicians play beautiful live music. Children play catch. Couples sing a song.

➡ In the park, you can hear _____

_____. Also, you can see children _____ and couples

_____.

13 밑줄 친 말의 반의어를 이용하여 빈칸에 알맞은 말을 쓰시오.

> A: Brian, isn't it difficult to look up a word in a dictionary?
>
> B: No. _____

➡ _____

14 다음 우리말을 영어로 쓰시오.

> 나는 누군가가 피아노를 연주하는 소리를 들었다.

➡ _____

15 주어진 문장과 같은 의미의 문장을 쓰시오.

> To be honest and fair is important.

➡ _____

16 다음 중 어법상 어색한 것을 골라 바르게 고치고, 그렇게 고친 이유를 서술하시오.

> Brady saw Clara to do something and wondered what she was doing.

➡ 잘못된 곳: _____ ➡ _____
고친 이유: _____

_____

17 주어진 단어를 활용하여 다음 우리말을 영어로 쓰시오.

> 의사가 되는 것은 쉽지 않아. (It)

➡ _____

18 다음 우리말에 맞게 빈칸에 알맞은 말을 쓰시오.

> 그들이 그 탁자를 옮기는 것을 지켜보는 것은 아주 재미있었다.
> It was a lot of fun _____.

➡ _____

19 다음 우리말을 영어로 쓰시오.

> 나는 어제 누군가가 나를 따라오는 것을 느꼈다.

➡ _____

Let's Party!

Holi, the Festival of Colors

Amala from Delhi, India
출신을 나타내는 전치사 from

Holi is the most popular festival in my country. It is usually in March.
가장 인기 있는(최상급)   = Holi   연도 앞에
During the festival, we say goodbye to cold winter and hello to warm
전치사(~ 동안)   ~에게 작별 인사를 하다
spring. We celebrate the festival everywhere for two days. On the first
전치사(~ 동안)+구체적인 기간   특정 날짜 앞에
day, people gather around a big fire at night and sing and dance. The
등위접속사: sing과 dance를 대등하게 연결
main event begins the next day. Children and adults chase each other
그 다음 날   서로(chase의 목적어)
with *gulal*. What is *gulal*? It is blue, yellow, green and pink powder.

It's a lot of fun to run around and throw colorful powder at everyone.
가주어 It   진주어 to부정사   throw A at B: B를 향해 A를 던지다
We also join street parades!

White Nights Festival

Victor from St. Petersburg, Russia

Have you heard of the *White Nights*? Every summer, this amazing
~에 대해 들어봤니?(경험을 묻는 현재완료)   every+단수명사: 모든 ~, 매 ~   the White
thing happens in my hometown. The night sky does not get completely
Nights를 지칭   get+형용사: (어떤 상태가) 되다
dark.

usually 주로
celebrate 축하하다, 기념하다
gather 모이다. 모으다
adult 어른
chase 뒤쫓다
throw 던지다
parade 퍼레이드, 행진
happen 발생하다
completely 완전히

- 다음 문장이 본문의 내용과 일치하면 T, 일치하지 않으면 F를 쓰시오.

1   Holi is held in India. ⬚

2   People in India celebrate Holi for two weeks. ⬚

3   There is a big fire at night on the second day of Holi. ⬚

4   We can see white nights in Victor's hometown every summer. ⬚

During that time, we hold the White Nights Festival. It usually starts
= the White Nights   = the White Nights Festival
in May and lasts for about a month. During the festival, there is a
                              약
ballet or an opera almost every night. The most popular event is the
                        거의   가장 인기 있는
Scarlet Sails celebration. A boat with red sails slowly appears on the
                              전치사(~가 부착된, ~가 달린)   자동사(수동태 안 됨)
river. Soon, fireworks begin and a water show follows. You can also
                                                (시간, 순서상으로) 뒤를 잇다
hear musicians playing beautiful live music.
지각동사+목적어+현재분사

Kiruna Snow Festival

Ebba from Kiruna, Sweden

Winter is my favorite season because of the Kiruna Snow Festival.
                              ~ 때문에
The festival starts in the last week of January and goes on for five or
                        마지막 주   진행되다
six days. The largest event is the snow design competition. The artists
          가장 큰(최상급)
shape huge piles of snow into animals, buildings, and other beautiful
shape A into B: A를 B의 형태로 만들다
artworks. People watch the artists shaping their works from beginning
              지각동사+목적어+현재분사   처음부터 끝까지(= from start to finish)
to end. My favorite activity is the dog sled ride. It is amazing to fly
              타기, 타는 것(명사)   가주어 It   진주어 to부정사
through a world of snow on a dog sled.

last 지속하다

celebration 축하, 기념, 축하 행사

appear 나타나다

follow 따라가다, 따라오다

fireworks 불꽃놀이

live 라이브의, 실황인

musician 음악가

favorite 가장 좋아하는

competition 대회, 시합, 경쟁

other 다른

from A to B A부터 B까지

sled 썰매

 확인문제

• 다음 문장이 본문의 내용과 일치하면 T, 일치하지 않으면 F를 쓰시오.

1   The White Nights Festival continues for about a month. ☐

2   A boat with no sails appears on the river during the Scarlet Sails celebration. ☐

3   The Kiruna Snow Festival is held in Kiruna. ☐

4   The Kiruna Snow Festival starts in the first week of January. ☐

5   At the Kiruna Snow Festival, artists shape huge piles of snow into animals,

    buildings, and other artworks. ☐

● 우리말을 참고하여 빈칸에 알맞은 말을 쓰시오.

1 Holi, the _____ of Colors

2 Amala _____ Delhi, India

3 Holi is _____ _____ _____ festival in my country.

4 It _____ _____ in March.

5 During the festival, we _____ _____ to cold winter and _____ to warm spring.

6 We _____ the festival everywhere _____ two days.

7 _____ the first day, people _____ _____ a big fire _____ _____ and sing and dance.

8 The main event _____ _____ _____ _____.

9 Children and adults _____ _____ _____ with *gulal*.

10 _____ is *gulal*? It is blue, yellow, green and pink _____.

11 It's a lot of fun _____ _____ _____ and _____ colorful powder _____ everyone.

12 We also _____ _____ _____!

13 _____ _____ Festival

14 Victor _____ St. Petersburg, Russia

15 _____ you _____ _____ the *White Nights*?

16 Every summer, this _____ thing _____ in my hometown.

1 홀리, 색의 축제

2 인도, 델리의 Amala

3 '홀리'는 우리나라에서 가장 인기 있는 축제예요.

4 그것은 보통 3월에 있어요.

5 축제 기간 동안에, 우리는 추운 겨울에게 작별 인사를 하고 따뜻한 봄을 맞는 인사를 해요.

6 우리는 이틀 동안 어디서든 축제를 기념해요.

7 첫째 날, 사람들은 밤에 큰 모닥불 주변에 모여 노래하고 춤을 춰요.

8 주요 행사는 다음 날에 시작돼요.

9 어린이들과 어른들이 'gulal'을 지니고 서로를 쫓아다녀요.

10 'gulal'이 무엇이냐고요? 그것은 파랑, 노랑, 초록, 분홍의 가루예요.

11 주변을 뛰어다니며 형형색색의 가루를 모든 사람들에게 던지는 것은 정말 재미있어요.

12 우리는 거리 행진에도 참가해요!

13 백야 축제

14 러시아, 상트페테르부르크의 Victor

15 '백야'에 대해 들어 봤나요?

16 매년 여름, 이 놀라운 일이 나의 고향에서 벌어져요.

17 The night sky _____ _____ _____ _____ dark.

18 _____ that time, we _____ the White Nights Festival.

19 It usually _____ _____ May and _____ for _____ a month.

20 During the festival, _____ _____ a ballet or an opera _____ _____.

21 The most _____ event is the Scarlet Sails _____.

22 A boat with red sails slowly _____ _____ _____ _____.

23 Soon, fireworks _____ and a water show _____.

24 You can also _____ musicians _____ beautiful live music.

25 Kiruna _____ _____

26 Ebba _____ Kiruna, Sweden

27 Winter is _____ _____ _____ _____ _____ the Kiruna Snow Festival.

28 The festival _____ _____ _____ _____ _____ of January and _____ _____ for five or six days.

29 _____ _____ _____ is the snow design competition.

30 The artists _____ huge piles of snow _____ animals, buildings, and _____ beautiful artworks.

31 People _____ the artists _____ their works _____ beginning _____ end.

32 My _____ _____ is the dog sled ride.

33 It is amazing _____ _____ _____ a world of snow _____ a dog sled.

---

18 그 시기 동안, 우리는 백야 축제를 열어요.

19 축제는 보통 5월에 시작되고 약 한 달 동안 지속돼요.

20 축제 기간 동안 거의 매일 밤 발레나 오페라 공연이 있어요.

21 가장 인기 있는 행사는 '붉은 돛 축하 행사'예요.

22 빨간 돛을 단 배가 강 위에 서서히 나타나요.

23 곧 불꽃놀이가 시작되고 물 쇼가 이어져요.

24 또한 여러분은 음악가들이 아름다운 라이브 음악을 연주하는 것을 들을 수 있어요.

25 키루나 눈 축제

26 스웨덴, 키루나의 Ebba

27 겨울은 키루나 눈 축제 때문에 내가 가장 좋아하는 계절이에요.

28 축제는 1월 마지막 주에 시작해서 5일이나 6일 동안 계속돼요.

29 가장 큰 행사는 '눈 디자인 대회'예요.

30 미술가들이 거대한 눈 덩어리를 동물, 건물, 다른 아름다운 작품의 모양으로 만들어요.

31 사람들은 미술가들이 그들의 작품을 만드는 것을 처음부터 끝까지 지켜봐요.

32 내가 가장 좋아하는 활동은 개썰매 타기예요.

33 개썰매를 타고 눈 세상을 날아가는 것은 정말 놀라워요.

● 우리말을 참고하여 본문을 영작하시오.

1 홀리, 색의 축제

➡ _____

2 인도, 델리의 Amala

➡ _____

3 '홀리'는 우리나라에서 가장 인기 있는 축제예요.

➡ _____

4 그것은 보통 3월에 있어요.

➡ _____

5 축제 기간 동안에, 우리는 추운 겨울에게 작별 인사를 하고 따뜻한 봄을 맞는 인사를 해요.

➡ _____

6 우리는 이틀 동안 어디서든 축제를 기념해요.

➡ _____

7 첫째 날, 사람들은 밤에 큰 모닥불 주변에 모여 노래하고 춤을 춰요.

➡ _____

8 주요 행사는 다음 날에 시작돼요.

➡ _____

9 어린이들과 어른들이 'gulal'을 지니고 서로를 쫓아다녀요.

➡ _____

10 'gulal'이 무엇이냐고요? 그것은 파랑, 노랑, 초록, 분홍의 가루예요.

➡ _____

11 주변을 뛰어다니며 형형색색의 가루를 모든 사람들에게 던지는 것은 정말 재미있어요.

➡ _____

12 우리는 거리 행진에도 참가해요!

➡ _____

13 백야 축제

➡ _____

14 러시아, 상트페테르부르크의 Victor

➡ _____

15 '백야'에 대해 들어 봤나요?

➡ _____

16 매년 여름, 이 놀라운 일이 나의 고향에서 벌어져요.

➡ _____

17 밤하늘이 완전히 어두워지지 않아요.

➡ _____

18 그 시기 동안, 우리는 백야 축제를 열어요.

➡ _____

19 축제는 보통 5월에 시작되고 약 한 달 동안 지속돼요.

➡ _____

20 축제 기간 동안 거의 매일 밤 발레나 오페라 공연이 있어요.

➡ _____

21 가장 인기 있는 행사는 '붉은 돛 축하 행사'예요.

➡ _____

22 빨간 돛을 단 배가 강 위에 서서히 나타나요.

➡ _____

23 곧 불꽃놀이가 시작되고 물 쇼가 이어져요.

➡ _____

24 또한 여러분은 음악가들이 아름다운 라이브 음악을 연주하는 것을 들을 수 있어요.

➡ _____

25 키루나 눈 축제

➡ _____

26 스웨덴, 키루나의 Ebba

➡ _____

27 겨울은 키루나 눈 축제 때문에 내가 가장 좋아하는 계절이에요.

➡ _____

28 축제는 1월 마지막 주에 시작해서 5일이나 6일 동안 계속돼요.

➡ _____

29 가장 큰 행사는 '눈 디자인 대회'예요.

➡ _____

30 미술가들이 거대한 눈 덩어리를 동물, 건물, 다른 아름다운 작품의 모양으로 만들어요.

➡ _____

31 사람들은 미술가들이 그들의 작품을 만드는 것을 처음부터 끝까지 지켜봐요.

➡ _____

32 내가 가장 좋아하는 활동은 개썰매 타기예요.

➡ _____

33 개썰매를 타고 눈 세상을 날아가는 것은 정말 놀라워요.

➡ _____

[01~06] 다음 글을 읽고 물음에 답하시오.

Holi, the Festival of Colors

Amala from Delhi, India

Holi is the most popular festival in my country. It is usually in March. During the festival, we say goodbye to cold winter and hello to warm spring. We celebrate the festival everywhere for two days. On the first day, people gather around a big fire ____ⓐ____ night and sing and dance. The main event begins the next day. Children and adults chase each other with *gulal*. What is *gulal*? It is blue, yellow, green and pink powder. It's a lot of fun ____ⓑ____ around and throw colorful powder ____ⓒ____ everyone. We also join street parades!

01 빈칸 ⓐ와 ⓒ에 공통으로 들어갈 말로 가장 적절한 것은?

① by   ② on   ③ to
④ at   ⑤ in

02 빈칸 ⓑ에 동사 run을 어법에 맞게 쓰시오.

➡ _____

03 다음 중 위 글의 내용과 일치하지 않는 것은?

① Holi is usually in March.
② The festival lasts for two days.
③ There is the main event on the first day.
④ *Gulal* is colorful powder.
⑤ There are street parades at the festival.

04 According to the passage, what is the most popular festival in India?

➡ _____

05 다음 빈칸에 들어갈 말을 위 글에서 찾아 쓰시오.

> If people _____ somewhere, they come together in a group.

➡ _____

06 다음 중 홀리 축제 기간에 볼 수 없는 것은?

① people gathering around a big fire
② people singing and dancing at night
③ street parades
④ adults and children chasing each other with *gulal*
⑤ children throwing colorful balls

[07~10] 다음 글을 읽고 물음에 답하시오.

White Nights Festival

Victor from St. Petersburg, Russia

(A)Have you heard of the *White Nights*? Every summer, (B)this amazing thing happens in my hometown. The night sky does not get completely dark. During that time, we (C)hold the White Nights Festival. It usually starts in May and lasts for about a month. During the festival, there is a ballet or an opera almost every night. The most popular event is the Scarlet Sails celebration. A boat with red sails slowly appears on the river. Soon, fireworks begin and a water show follows. You can also hear musicians playing beautiful live music.

07 밑줄 친 (A)와 현재완료의 용법이 같은 것은?

① We have known each other for ten years.
② Nora has been to Vietnam three times.
③ The employer has just arrived at the airport.
④ David has lost his car key.
⑤ Karen has played the guitar since she was twelve years old.

서답형

08 밑줄 친 (B)가 의미하는 것을 위 글에서 찾아 쓰시오.

➡ _____

09 다음 중 밑줄 친 (C)와 같은 의미로 쓰인 것은?

① Janet held her head because of headache.
② The chair is strong enough to hold your weight.
③ Tom held his girl friend's hand tightly.
④ Can you hold a minute, please?
⑤ We hold our class meeting every Monday.

서답형

10 During the festival, what can you see almost every night? Answer the question with a full sentence.

➡ _____

[11~14] 다음 글을 읽고 물음에 답하시오.

Kiruna Snow Festival

Ebba from Kiruna, Sweden

Winter is my favorite season (A)[because / because of] the Kiruna Snow Festival. The festival starts in the last week of January and goes on for five or six days. The largest event is the snow design competition. The artists shape huge piles of snow into animals, buildings, and (B)[other / another] beautiful artworks. People watch the artists ⓐ _____ their works from beginning to end. My favorite activity is the dog sled ride. It is (C)[amazing / amazed] to fly through a world of snow on a dog sled.

서답형

11 동사 shape를 어법에 맞게 활용하여 빈칸 ⓐ에 쓰시오.

➡ _____

12 (A)~(C)에서 어법상 옳은 것끼리 바르게 묶은 것은?

① because of – another – amazed
② because of – other – amazing
③ because – other – amazed
④ because – other – amazing
⑤ because – another – amazed

13 다음 중 위 글을 읽고 답할 수 없는 것은?

① When does the festival start?
② What is the largest event of the festival?
③ What do the artists do at the festival?
④ What is Ebba's favorite activity?
⑤ How many artists take part in the snow design competition?

서답형

14 How long does the festival last? Answer in English with a full sentence.

➡ _____

[15~19] 다음 글을 읽고 물음에 답하시오.

Holi, the Festival of Colors

Amala ___(A)___ Delhi, India

Holi is ①the most popular festival in my country. It is usually ___(B)___ March. ___(C)___ the festival, we say goodbye to cold winter and hello to warm spring. We celebrate the festival everywhere ②for two days. ③On the first day, people gather around a big fire at night and sing and dance. The main event begins the next day. Children and adults chase each other with *gulal*. What is *gulal*? It is blue, yellow, green and pink powder. It's ④a lot of fun to run around and throw colorful powder at everyone. We also ⑤join with street parades!

15 빈칸 (A)~(C)에 들어갈 말이 바르게 짝지어진 것은?

① from – at – While
② from – in – During
③ at – on – For
④ in – about – At
⑤ in – by – About

16 다음 중 위 글의 내용과 일치하는 것은?

① Holi is not a famous festival in India.
② Holi is held in summer.
③ People celebrate the festival at a special place.
④ People dance and sing on the first night of the festival.
⑤ Amala doesn't like throwing *gulal* at the festival.

17 밑줄 친 ①~⑤ 중 어법상 옳지 <u>않은</u> 것은?

①   ②   ③   ④   ⑤

서답형
18 위 글의 내용에 맞게 빈칸에 알맞은 말을 쓰시오.

> On the last day of the festival, we can see children and adults _____.

➡ _____

서답형
19 If you want to see only the main event of the festival, when should you go to the festival?

➡ _____

[20~23] 다음 글을 읽고 물음에 답하시오.

White Nights Festival

Victor from St. Petersburg, Russia

Have you heard of the *White Nights*? Every summer, this amazing thing happens in my hometown. The night sky does not get completely dark. During that time, we hold the White Nights Festival. It usually starts in May and lasts for about a month. During the festival, there is a ballet or an opera almost every night. The most popular event is the Scarlet Sails celebration. A boat with red sails slowly appears on the river. Soon, fireworks begin and a water show follows. You can also hear musicians ___(A)___ beautiful live music.

서답형
20 play를 어법에 맞게 빈칸 (A)에 쓰시오.

➡ _____

서답형
21 위 글의 내용에 맞게 빈칸에 알맞은 말을 쓰시오.

> The White Nights Festival is held in Victor's hometown _____ _____.

22 다음 중 위 글을 읽고 답할 수 없는 것은?

① Where is Victor from?

② What is Victor mainly talking about?

③ When is the White Nights Festival held?

④ How long does the festival last?

⑤ Where does the boat come from?

23 다음 중 백야 축제에 관한 내용으로 바르지 않은 것은?

① It is held in St. Petersburg in Russia.

② Scarlet Sails celebration is more popular than any other event.

③ There is a boat with red sails.

④ The boat moves really fast on the river.

⑤ After the boat appears, fireworks begin.

[24~28] 다음 글을 읽고 물음에 답하시오.

Kiruna Snow Festival

Ebba from Kiruna, Sweden

Winter is my favorite season because of the Kiruna Snow Festival. The festival starts in ①the last week of January and ②goes on for five or six days. ③The largest event is the snow design competition. The artists shape huge piles of snow into animals, buildings, and other beautiful artworks. People watch the artists shaping their works ④from beginning to end. My favorite activity is the dog sled ride. (A)It is amazing to fly through ⑤a world of snow on a dog sled.

24 다음 중 ①~⑤의 뜻풀이로 바르지 않은 것은?

① 1월 마지막 주   ② 나아가다

③ 가장 큰 행사   ④ 처음부터 끝까지

⑤ 눈 세상

25 Which is NOT true about Ebba?

① She is from Sweden.

② Her favorite season is winter.

③ She likes the dog sled ride.

④ She thinks flying through a world of snow on a dog sled is amazing.

⑤ She can shape huge piles of snow into animals.

26 위 글의 내용에 맞게 빈칸에 알맞은 말을 세 단어로 쓰시오.

> At the Kiruna Snow Festival, you can see the artists _____ from beginning to end.

➡ _____

27 다음 중 위 글의 내용을 잘못 이해한 사람은?

① Kelly: The Kiruna Snow Festival lasts five or six days.

② Susan: I will be able to see many artists in the snow design competition.

③ Jason: Many artists make their works in front of people.

④ Brian: The artists have to make only animals and buildings with snow.

⑤ David: I will ride the dog sled at the festival.

28 다음 중 밑줄 친 (A)와 쓰임이 같은 것을 모두 고르시오.

① It made Jenny upset.

② It is hot and humid outside.

③ It is surprising to meet you here.

④ It was found under the sofa.

⑤ It was difficult for me to study hard.

[01~05] 다음 글을 읽고 물음에 답하시오.

Holi, the Festival of Colors

Amala from Delhi, India

Holi is the most popular festival in my country. It is usually in March. During the festival, we say goodbye to cold winter and hello to warm spring. We celebrate the festival everywhere for two days. On the first day, people gather around a big fire at night and sing and dance. The main event begins the next day. Children and adults chase each other with *gulal*. What is *gulal*? It is blue, yellow, green and pink powder. (A) To run around and throw colorful powder at everyone is a lot of fun. We also join street parades!

01 How long do Indians celebrate the festival? Answer the question with seven words.

➡ _____

02 글의 내용에 맞게 대화의 빈칸에 알맞은 말을 쓰시오.

A: I heard about a festival, Holi.
B: What is it?
A: It is the festival of colors. On the first day of the festival, we can see people _____ a big fire at night and _____.

➡ _____ , _____

03 주어진 단어를 주어로 하여 밑줄 친 문장 (A)를 다시 쓰시오.

➡ It _____
_____

04 글의 내용에 맞게 빈칸에 알맞은 말을 세 단어로 쓰시오.

A: I want to see the festival, Holi.
B: Oh, then you have to go to _____. It is usually held then.

➡ _____

05 What is *gulal*? Answer in English with a full sentence.

➡ _____

[06~11] 다음 글을 읽고 물음에 답하시오.

White Nights Festival

Victor from St. Petersburg, Russia

Have you heard of the *White Nights*? Every summer, this amazing thing happens in (A) my hometown. The night sky does not get completely dark. During that time, we hold the White Nights Festival. (B)It starts in May and lasts for about a month. During the festival, there is a ballet or an opera almost every night. The most popular event is the Scarlet Sails celebration. A boat with red sails slowly appears on the river. Soon, fireworks begin and a water show follows. You can also hear musicians playing beautiful live music.

06 밑줄 친 (A)를 구체적으로 쓰시오.

➡ _____

07 단어 usually를 넣어 밑줄 친 문장 (B)를 다시 쓰시오.

➡ _____

중요

08 위 글에서 백야를 설명하는 문장을 찾아 쓰시오.

➡ _____

09 According to the passage, what kinds of events are at the White Nights Festival?

➡ _____

_____

고난이도

10 다음은 백야 축제를 다녀온 학생이 쓴 일기의 일부이다. 빈칸에 알맞은 말을 다섯 단어로 쓰시오.

> ... I saw a boat _____. It had red sails. Shortly, fireworks began. ...

➡ _____

[11~15] 다음 글을 읽고 물음에 답하시오.

Kiruna Snow Festival

Ebba from Kiruna, Sweden

Winter is my favorite season because of the Kiruna Snow Festival. The festival starts in the last week of January and goes on for five or six days. The largest event is the snow design competition. The artists shape huge piles of snow into animals, buildings, and other beautiful artworks. People watch the artists shaping their works from beginning to end. My favorite activity is the dog sled ride. It is amazing ___(A)___ through a world of snow on a dog sled.

11 동사 fly를 어법에 맞게 빈칸 (A)에 쓰시오.

➡ _____

12 Write the reason why winter is Ebba's favorite season.

➡ _____

_____

고난이도

13 다음 대화의 빈칸에 알맞은 말을 쓰시오.

> A: I heard that you will visit _____ to see the Kiruna Snow Festival.
> B: Yes. I'm so excited.
> A: Then you should see _____.
> It is the largest event at the festival.

➡ _____, _____

14 According to the passage, how long does the Kiruna Snow Festival last? Answer in English with a full sentence.

➡ _____

중요

15 다음은 축제를 방문한 두 사람의 대화이다. 우리말에 맞게 주어진 어구를 바르게 배열하시오.

> A: What are you watching?
> B: 나는 저 미술가가 하나의 거대한 눈 덩어리를 코끼리 모양으로 바꾸는 것을 보고 있어.
> (a huge pile of / an elephant / I / shaping / watching / snow / am / into / the artist)

➡ _____

_____

Listen and Speak 2-C

A: Chris, what will you do for the class party?

B: I'll make sandwiches.

A: Great idea. How long will it take to make them?
= sandwiches

B: Maybe it'll take about an hour.
= Perhaps   대략, ~ 정도

구문해설 • take: (시간이) 걸리다

해석

A: Chris, 학급 파티를 위해 무엇을 할 거니?

B: 나는 샌드위치를 만들 거야.

A: 좋은 생각이야. 그것들을 만드는 데 얼마가 걸릴까?

B: 아마도 약 한 시간 정도 걸릴 거야.

Think and Write

I Love Gangneung

I live in Gangneung. There are beautiful beaches in my neighborhood. It's a
~이 있다 (뒤에 있는 명사에 수의 일치)   나의 이웃에   가주어 It

lot of fun to swim at the beach. There is a famous hanok in Gangneung. It is
진주어(to부정사)

called Ojukheon. Yulgok was born there. The most famous food in Gangneung
수동태   in Ojukheon

is potato tteok. It is soft and sweet. Come and enjoy Gangneung!
= Potato tteok

구문해설 • beach: 해변 • neighborhood: 이웃 • be born: 태어나다

강릉이 정말 좋아요

저는 강릉에 살아요. 나의 이웃에는 아름다운 해변들이 있어요. 해변에서 수영하는 것은 정말 재미있어요. 강릉에는 유명한 한옥이 있어요. 그것은 오죽헌이라고 불려요. 율곡이 거기에서 태어났어요. 강릉에서 가장 유명한 음식은 감자떡이에요. 그것은 부드럽고 달콤해요. 와서 강릉을 즐기세요!

Project Culture

I want to introduce Boryeong Mud Festival. It is held in Daecheon Beach
to부정사를 목적어로 취하는 동사   수동태

in July. There are many interesting events in the festival. First, you can
월, 연도 앞에 쓰는 전치사   흥미를 유발할 때 쓰는 현재분사형 형용사

see people do Ssireum in mud. Also it is fun to do colorful mud body painting
지각동사+목적어+동사원형   가주어   진주어

on your body. Lastly, there is an outdoor concert. You can hear musicians play
지각동사+목적어+동사원형

beautiful musics.

구문해설 • introduce: 소개하다 • mud: 진흙 • festival: 축제 • interesting: 흥미로운
• event: 행사

나는 보령 진흙 축제를 소개하고 싶어요. 그것은 7월에 대천 해수욕장에서 열립니다. 그 축제에는 많은 흥미로운 행사가 있습니다. 우선, 당신은 사람들이 진흙 속에서 씨름하는 것을 볼 수 있어요. 또한 당신의 몸에 형형색색의 진흙을 바르는 것은 재미있어요. 마지막으로, 실외 콘서트가 있습니다. 당신은 음악가들이 아름다운 음악을 연주하는 것을 들을 수 있습니다.

01 다음 짝지어진 단어의 관계가 같도록 빈칸에 알맞은 말을 쓰시오.

_____ : bright = give : receive

02 다음 영영풀이가 가리키는 것을 고르시오.

to follow and try to catch

① chase   ② advertise
③ decorate   ④ hold
⑤ gather

03 다음 중 밑줄 친 부분의 뜻풀이가 바르지 않은 것은?

① Time goes by and you will become an adult soon. 어른
② The painting is my son's latest artwork. 예술 작품
③ We made a poster to advertise our school festival. 광고하다
④ The police officers chased the thief. 체포했다
⑤ There is a competition between players. 경쟁

04 다음 우리말에 맞게 빈칸에 알맞은 말을 쓰시오.

(1) 한 블록 곧장 간 후 왼쪽으로 도세요.
➡ _____ _____ one block and _____ a left.

(2) 우리는 서로 너무 다르다.
➡ We are too different from _____ _____.

(3) 어느 버스 정류장에서 내려야 하나요?
➡ Which bus stop should I _____ _____ at?

05 다음 주어진 문장의 밑줄 친 sail과 같은 의미로 쓰인 것은?

A boat with a red sail appeared on the river.

① After retirement, I want to sail around the world.
② The navigator extended the sail on the boat.
③ The sailors couldn't sail against the wind.
④ The ferry will sail to the Atlantic.
⑤ We are ready to sail to New York.

06 다음 주어진 우리말을 영작하시오.

(1) 당신의 고향은 어디입니까?
➡ _____

(2) 그것은 박물관 건너편에 있어요.
➡ _____

(3) 내 친구들이 내 생일을 축하해 주기 위해 모였다.
➡ _____

[07~08] 다음 대화를 읽고 물음에 답하시오.

Minsu: Hi, Emma. What's up?
Emma: Hey, Minsu. Are you free this Saturday?
Minsu: Yes. Why do you ask?
Emma: Well, how about having lunch together?
Minsu: Sure.
Emma: Let's try the new Chinese restaurant, Ming's. It's near the school.
Minsu: Okay. _____ (A)

Emma: Come out from the school and go straight to Green Street. Make a left, and the restaurant will be on your left.

Minsu: All right. Let's meet at 12 o'clock.

Emma: Wonderful. See you then.

07 위 대화의 빈칸 (A)에 들어갈 말을 <보기>에 주어진 단어를 배열하여 완성하시오.

┌─ 보기 ─┐
the / how / school / from / I / get / there / can

➡ _____

08 위 대화의 내용과 일치하지 <u>않는</u> 것은?

① Emma and Minsu are going to have lunch together this Saturday.
② Emma and Minsu are going to visit Ming's, the new Chinese restaurant.
③ Ming's is located near the school.
④ Minsu should make a left in the front of the school and go straight to Green Street to get to Ming's.
⑤ Emma and Minsu are going to meet at 12 o'clock this Saturday.

[09~10] 다음 대화를 읽고 물음에 답하시오.

Andy: I'm so excited about the school festival this Friday.

Mike: Me, too. What can we do to advertise it, Andy?

Andy: How about making posters?

Mike: Great idea. We can post them in our neighborhood.

Andy: Right. How long will it take to make them?

Mike: Well, it will take about three hours.

Andy: Okay, _____(A)

09 위 대화의 빈칸 (A)에 들어갈 말을 주어진 단어를 배열하여 완성하시오.

┌─ 보기 ─┐
hope / many / the / to / festival / come / I / people

➡ _____

10 위 대화를 읽고 대답할 수 <u>없는</u> 것은?

① What are Andy and Mike looking forward to?
② What do Andy and Mike want to advertise?
③ What do Andy and Mike decide to make?
④ How long will it take to make the poster?
⑤ Where will Andy and Mike make the posters?

[11~13] 다음 대화를 읽고 물음에 답하시오.

Man: Excuse me. How can I (A)[take / get] to Suwon Hwaseong from here?

Mina: It's easy. Do you see the bus stop over there?

Man: Yes, I do.

Mina: Take the No. 11 bus and get (B)[on / off] at the sixth stop.

Man: How (C)[long / far] will it take to get there?

Mina: It will take about 20 minutes.

Man: Thank you very much.

Mina: _____ⓐ_____ Are you going there for the festival?

Man: Yes. I heard it's a lot of fun.

Mina: I hope you have a great time.

11 위 대화의 빈칸 ⓐ에 들어갈 말로 적절하지 <u>않은</u> 것은?

① No problem.　　② You're welcome.
③ Don't mention it.　　④ It's my pleasure.
⑤ Of course not.

12 위 대화의 (A)~(C)에 알맞은 것으로 짝지어진 것은?

	(A)	(B)	(C)
①	take	on	long
②	take	off	far
③	get	off	far
④	get	off	long
⑤	get	on	long

13 위 대화를 읽고 대답할 수 없는 것은?

① What does the man want?
② How can the man get to Suwon Hwaseong?
③ How long will it take to get to Suwon Hwaseong?
④ Why does the man want to visit Suwon Hwaseong?
⑤ Has Mina ever visited the festival of Suwon Hwaseong?

Grammar

14 다음 빈칸에 들어갈 수 없는 것은?

It is good to _____ you laugh.

① see ② hear ③ watch
④ make ⑤ encourage

15 다음 중 밑줄 친 부분의 쓰임이 다른 하나는?

① It is five miles from here to the beach.
② Is it possible to get there in time?
③ Was it cloudy this afternoon?
④ It is five past three.
⑤ It is not dark in this cave.

16 다음 우리말을 영어로 바르게 옮긴 것은?

나는 누군가가 문을 열고 나가는 소리를 들었어.

① I heard someone opened the door and went out.
② I heard someone opened the door and go out.
③ I heard someone open the door and went out.
④ I heard someone open the door and go out.
⑤ I heard someone opening the door and went out.

17 다음 대화의 빈칸에 알맞은 말을 쓰시오.

A: Did you see Tom shouting at someone?
B: Yes, I did. It was surprising _____ _____ _____ _____ _____ because he is known to us as a kind and quiet man.

18 다음 중 어법상 바르지 않은 것은?

① I felt someone pulling my hair.
② It was my fault to believe such a thing.
③ Did you see the boys kicked the ball?
④ To make you laugh is my job.
⑤ The situation made me tell a lot of lies.

19 다음 중 주어진 문장의 밑줄 친 부분과 쓰임이 같은 것은?

It is necessary for you to buy a concert ticket now.

① My brother wanted you to call him.
② Karen went out to eat lunch alone.
③ Do you have a chair to sit on?
④ I didn't plan to do it.
⑤ It is good to hear from you.

영역별 핵심문제 **43**

20 다음 문장에서 어법상 바르지 <u>않은</u> 것을 찾아 바르게 고치시오.

> It is very boring to hearing someone talking constantly.

_____ ➡ _____

21 주어진 단어를 활용하여 다음 우리말을 영어로 쓰시오.

> 영어를 배우는 것은 흥미롭다. (it / excite)

➡ _____

22 다음 중 어법상 <u>틀린</u> 문장의 개수는?

> ⓐ It is impossible to understand her.
> ⓑ Is it possible for me to visit your office?
> ⓒ We listened to the old man told his story from beginning to end.
> ⓓ Yesterday, I saw Kate to wait for a bus alone.
> ⓔ It was not easy to find your house.

① 1개 ② 2개 ③ 3개 ④ 4개 ⑤ 5개

23 빈칸에 들어갈 말이 바르게 짝지어진 것은?

> • It is dangerous _____ the mountain alone.
> • Did you see the man _____ the mountain alone?

① climb – climb
② to climb – climbed
③ to climb – climbing
④ to climb – to climb
⑤ to climbing – climbing

24 다음 우리말을 영어로 쓰시오.

> 나는 누군가가 내 어깨를 만지는 것을 느꼈다.

➡ _____

Reading

[25~28] 다음 글을 읽고 물음에 답하시오.

> **Holi, the Festival of Colors**
> Amala from Delhi, India
> Holi is the most popular festival in my country. ① It is usually in March. During the festival, we say goodbye to cold winter and hello to warm spring. ② We _____ⓐ_____ the festival everywhere for two days. On the first day, people gather around a big fire at night and sing and dance. ③ The main event begins the next day. ④ What is *gulal*? It is blue, yellow, green and pink powder. It's a lot of fun ⓑto run around and throw colorful powder at everyone. ⑤ We also join street parades!

25 다음과 같이 풀이되는 단어를 빈칸 ⓐ에 쓰시오.

> to do something special for an important event, holiday, etc.

➡ _____

26 ①~⑤ 중 주어진 문장이 들어가기에 가장 적절한 곳은?

> Children and adults chase each other with *gulal*.

① ② ③ ④ ⑤

27 위 글의 밑줄 친 ⓑ와 쓰임이 같은 것은?

① Tim went to Rome to see his girlfriend.
② Sarah was sad to hear the news.
③ To see her crying was painful for me.
④ I need something warm to wear.
⑤ The problem was very difficult to solve.

28 다음 중 위 글을 읽고 답할 수 없는 것은?

① What is Holi?
② What do people in India do during the festival?
③ How long does the festival last?
④ When does the main event begin?
⑤ How much *gulal* do people have at the festival?

[29~33] 다음 글을 읽고 물음에 답하시오.

Kiruna Snow Festival
Ebba from Kiruna, Sweden
 Winter is my favorite season because of the Kiruna Snow Festival. The festival starts in the last week of January and (A)goes on for five or six days. The largest event is the snow design competition. The artists shape huge piles of snow into animals, buildings, and other beautiful artworks. People watch the artists shaping their works from beginning to end. My favorite activity is the dog sled ride. It is amazing to fly through a world of snow on a dog sled.

29 다음 중 밑줄 친 (A) 대신에 쓰일 수 있는 것은?

① quits   ② goes by
③ continues   ④ increases
⑤ expects

30 위 글의 내용에 맞게 다음 물음에 완전한 문장의 영어로 답하시오.

Q: What can we see at the snow design competition?

➡ _____

_____

31 다음 대화에서 위 글의 내용과 일치하지 않는 것은?

A: ①As we are here in Sweden, I want to visit Kiruna.
B: ②Oh, there is the snow festival in Kiruna, right?
A: ③Yes. I heard it starts in the last week of January, so we can see the festival.
B: That's nice. ④I'm so excited to see the largest event, the dog sled ride.
A: Me, too. ⑤I will also see how huge piles of snow are turned into various artworks.

①   ②   ③   ④   ⑤

32 위 글의 표현을 이용하여 다음 우리말을 영어로 쓰시오. 주어진 단어를 사용하시오.

미술가들이 그들의 작품을 만드는 것을 처음부터 끝까지 지켜보는 것은 흥미롭다.
(it / interesting)

➡ _____

_____

33 다음과 같이 풀이되는 단어를 위 글에서 찾아 쓰시오.

a small vehicle used for sliding over snow

➡ _____

[01~02] 다음 그림을 보고 물음에 답하시오.

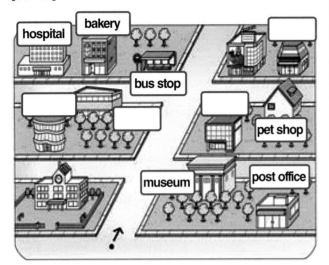

hospital
bakery
bus stop
pet shop
museum
post office

출제율90%

01 다음 대화를 읽고 bank의 위치를 그림에 표시하시오.

> A: Excuse me. Is there a bank around here?
> B: Yes, there is. It's not far from here.
> A: How can I get there?
> B: Go straight two blocks and make a right. It's across from the pet shop. You can't miss it.
> A: Thank you so much.

출제율95%

02 위 그림의 내용과 일치하도록 대화의 빈칸을 완성하시오.

> A: Excuse me. How can I get to the bakery?
> B: _____
> A: Is it far from here?
> B: No, it's not.
> A: Thank you.

➡ _____

_____

출제율100%

03 다음 짝지어진 대화가 어색한 것을 고르시오.

① A: How can I get to the post office?
   B: Go straight to 1st Street and make a right.

② A: How long will it take to make the sandwiches?
   B: Maybe it will take about an hour.

③ A: Do you know where the subway station is?
   B: Sure. Walk straight ahead.

④ A: Is there a pet shop around here?
   B: It's just around the corner.

⑤ A: Where can I find a museum?
   B: It will take about 15 minutes by taxi.

[04~05] 다음 대화를 읽고 물음에 답하시오.

> Man: Excuse me. How can I get to Suwon Hwaseong from here?
> Mina: It's easy. Do you see the bus stop over there?
> Man: Yes, I do.
> Mina: Take the No. 11 bus and get off at the sixth stop.
> Man: (A)그곳까지 가는 데 시간이 얼마나 걸릴까요?
> Mina: It will take about 20 minutes.
> Man: Thank you very much.
> Mina: No problem. Are you going there for the festival?
> Man: Yes. I heard it's a lot of fun.
> Mina: I hope you have a great time.

출제율85%

04 위 대화의 밑줄 친 (A)의 우리말을 주어진 단어를 써서 영어로 옮기시오.

(long, it, get)

➡ _____

출제율 90%

05 위 대화의 내용과 일치하지 <u>않는</u> 것은?

① The man wants to go to Suwon Hwaseong on foot.

② Mina tells the man how to get to Suwon Hwaseong.

③ The man should take the No. 11 bus and get off at the sixth stop to get to Suwon Hwaseong.

④ It will take about 20 minutes for the man to get to Suwon Hwaseong by bus.

⑤ The festival is being held in Suwon Hwaseong.

출제율 95%

06 다음 대화의 내용과 일치하도록 빈칸을 완성하시오.

> Andy: I'm so excited about the school festival this Friday.
>
> Mike: Me, too. What can we do to advertise it, Andy?
>
> Andy: How about making posters?
>
> Mike: Great idea. We can post them in our neighborhood.
>
> Andy: Right. How long will it take to make them?
>
> Mike: Well, it will take about three hours.
>
> Andy: Okay, I hope many people come to the festival.

> Andy and Mike are excited about the school festival this Friday. To advertise it, they decide to _____(A)_____ and post them in _____(B)_____. It will take _____(C)_____ to make them. They want many people to come and enjoy _____(D)_____.

➡ (A) _____

(B) _____

(C) _____

(D) _____

[07~08] 다음 대화를 읽고 물음에 답하시오.

> Minsu: Hi, Emma. What's up?
>
> Emma: Hey, Minsu. Are you free this Saturday?
>
> Minsu: Yes. Why do you ask?
>
> Emma: Well, how about having lunch together?
>
> Minsu: (A) Sure.
>
> Emma: (B) Let's try the new Chinese restaurant, Ming's. It's near the school.
>
> Minsu: (C) Okay. How can I @<u>get</u> there from the school?
>
> Emma: (D) Make a left, and the restaurant will be on your left.
>
> Minsu: (E) All right. Let's meet at 12 o'clock.
>
> Emma: Wonderful. See you then.

출제율 95%

07 위 대화의 (A)~(E) 중에서 다음 문장이 들어가기에 적절한 곳은?

> Come out from the school and go straight to Green Street.

① (A) ② (B) ③ (C) ④ (D) ⑤ (E)

출제율 90%

08 위 대화의 밑줄 친 @<u>get</u>과 같은 의미로 쓰인 것은?

① <u>Get</u> me something to drink, please.

② We're going to be late. Let's <u>get</u> a taxi.

③ I didn't <u>get</u> your letter yesterday.

④ Jane will <u>get</u> the prize at the dancing contest.

⑤ You can <u>get</u> to the city hall by bus.

[09~10] 다음 대화를 읽고 물음에 답하시오.

A: Excuse me. How can I get to the post office?
B: Go straight to 1st Street and make a right. It will be on your right.
A: (A)여기서 먼가요?
B: No, it's not.
A: Thank you very much.

09 ✎출제율 90%
위 대화에 나타난 우체국의 위치를 우리말로 설명하시오.

➡ _____

10 ✎출제율 95%
위 대화의 우리말 (A)를 영작하시오.

➡ _____

11 ✎출제율 100%
다음 빈칸에 들어갈 말이 바르게 짝지어진 것은?

• It is interesting _____ a book.
• David saw me _____ a book in the library.

① reading – to read ② read – reading
③ to read – reading ④ read – to read
⑤ read – read

12 ✎출제율 95%
다음 중 밑줄 친 부분의 쓰임이 <u>다른</u> 하나는?

① <u>It</u> was a bad idea to call you late at night.
② <u>It</u> was my mistake to give you my phone number.
③ <u>It</u> was the hat that I bought for him.
④ <u>It</u> is useful to discuss the issue.
⑤ <u>It</u> is strange for him to say so.

13 ✎출제율 95%
주어진 단어를 활용하여 다음 우리말을 영어로 쓰시오.

나는 Kevin이 프랑스어를 말하는 것을 들었다. (hear / French)

➡ _____

14 ✎출제율 90%
다음 우리말을 영어로 바르게 옮긴 것은?

목표를 정하고 최선을 다하는 것은 중요하다.

① It is important to set a goal and does your best.
② It is important to set a goal and do your best.
③ It is important setting a goal and to do your best.
④ It is important setting a goal and do your best.
⑤ It is important to set a goal and your best.

15 ✎출제율 95%
다음 중 어법상 바르지 <u>않은</u> 것은?

① Jason heard two girls talking to each other loudly.
② It is not easy to take care of a pet.
③ Did you feel the house shaking?
④ I think it is important to listen to other people's opinion carefully.
⑤ Ms. Kim watched her students to solve the problems.

16 ✎출제율 85%
주어진 단어를 활용하여 다음 우리말을 영어로 쓰시오.

그녀가 바이올린을 연주하는 것을 듣는 것은 좋은 기회야. (it / a good chance)

➡ _____

17 ✎출제율 95%
다음 우리말을 영어로 쓰시오.

한 소년이 호수에서 수영하고 있는 것이 보이니?

➡ _____

[18~20] 다음 글을 읽고 물음에 답하시오.

White Nights Festival
Victor from St. Petersburg, Russia
Have you heard ___ⓐ___ the *White Nights*?
[A] During that time, we hold the White Nights Festival. It usually starts in May and lasts for about a month.
[B] A boat with red sails slowly appears on the river. Soon, fireworks begin and a water show follows. You can also hear musicians playing beautiful live music.
[C] Every summer, this amazing thing happens in my hometown. The night sky does not get completely dark.
[D] During the festival, there is a ballet or an opera almost every night. The most popular event is the Scarlet Sails celebration.

18 다음 중 빈칸 ⓐ에 들어갈 말과 같은 말이 들어가는 것은? 출제율 95%

① Emily gets tired _____ eating the same food.
② Jason came up _____ a brilliant idea.
③ My hobby is looking _____ plants in the garden.
④ I really look up _____ King Sejong.
⑤ They had to put _____ their event because of the bad weather.

19 자연스러운 글이 되도록 [A]~[D]를 바르게 나열한 것은? 출제율 90%

① [B] – [D] – [C] – [A]
② [B] – [C] – [A] – [D]
③ [C] – [B] – [D] – [A]
④ [C] – [A] – [D] – [B]
⑤ [D] – [B] – [A] – [C]

20 다음 중 위 글을 읽고 답할 수 없는 것은? 출제율 100%

① Where is St. Petersburg?
② What do people in Russia do during the White Nights?
③ What color of sails does the boat have?
④ What can people see after the firework?
⑤ How many musicians are there at the festival?

[21~22] 다음 글을 읽고 물음에 답하시오.

Holi, the Festival of Colors
Amala from Delhi, India
Holi is the most popular festival in my country. ① It is usually in March. During the festival, we say goodbye to cold winter and hello to warm spring. ② On the first day, people gather around a big fire at night and sing and dance. ③ The main event begins the next day. ④ Children and adults chase each other with *gulal*. ⑤ What is *gulal*? It is blue, yellow, green and pink powder. It's a lot of fun to run around and throw (A)colorful powder at everyone. We also join street parades!

21 ①~⑤ 중 주어진 문장이 들어가기에 가장 적절한 곳은? 출제율 90%

We celebrate the festival everywhere for two days.

①   ②   ③   ④   ⑤

22 밑줄 친 (A)가 가리키는 것을 위 글에서 찾아 쓰시오. 출제율 95%

➡ _____

[01~03] 다음 대화를 읽고 물음에 답하시오.

> Minsu: Hi, Emma. What's up?
> Emma: Hey, Minsu. Are you free this Saturday?
> Minsu: Yes. Why do you ask?
> Emma: Well, how about having lunch together?
> Minsu: Sure.
> Emma: Let's try the new Chinese restaurant, Ming's. It's near the school.
> Minsu: Okay. How can I get there from the school?
> Emma: Come out from the school and go straight to Green Street. Make a left, and the restaurant will be on your left.
> Minsu: All right. Let's meet at 12 o'clock.
> Emma: Wonderful. See you then.

01 What are Emma and Minsu going to do this Saturday?

➡ _____

_____

02 What time are Emma and Minsu going to meet?

➡ _____

03 Minsu가 Ming's를 어떻게 찾아가야 하는지 우리말로 간략히 설명하시오.

➡ _____

_____

04 다음 빈칸에 call을 어법에 맞게 쓰시오.

> • I heard someone _____ my name.
> • I heard my name _____.

05 주어진 단어를 활용하여 다음 우리말을 영어로 쓰시오.

> 나의 영어 실력을 향상시키는 것은 필수적이다.
> (it / essential / skill / improve)

➡ _____

06 다음 대화의 빈칸에 알맞은 말을 다섯 단어로 쓰시오.

> A: Do you think that having a balanced diet is important?
> B: Sure. It is really important _____.

➡ _____

07 다음 두 문장을 하나의 문장으로 쓰시오.

> • The cat jumped up onto the chair.
> • Did you see that?

➡ _____

08 주어진 단어를 바르게 배열하여 다음 우리말을 영어로 쓰시오.

> 나는 그 소년이 수영장에서 수영하고 있는 것을 보았다.
> (in / the boy / I / the pool / saw / swimming)

➡ _____

[09~11] 다음 글을 읽고 물음에 답하시오.

Holi, the Festival of Colors
Amala from Delhi, India
Holi is the most popular festival in my country. It is usually in March. During the festival, we say goodbye to cold winter and hello to warm spring. We celebrate the festival everywhere for two days. On the first day, people gather around a big fire at night and sing and dance. The main event begins the next day. Children and adults chase each other with *gulal*. What is *gulal*? It is blue, yellow, green and pink powder. (A)주변을 뛰어다니며 형형색색의 가루를 모든 사람들에게 던지는 것은 정말 재미있어요. We also join street parades!

09 주어진 단어를 활용하여 밑줄 친 우리말 (A)를 영어로 쓰시오.

(a lot of / run around / colorful)

➡ _____

_____

10 위 글의 내용에 맞게 빈칸에 알맞은 말을 세 단어로 쓰시오.

A: Did you _____ _____ _____
at the Holi festival?
B: Yeah. People march in public to celebrate the festival. It was amazing.

11 When do people in India celebrate Holi? Answer in English with a full sentence.

➡ _____

[12~14] 다음 글을 읽고 물음에 답하시오.

I live in Gangneung. There are beautiful beaches in my neighborhood. It's a lot of fun to swim at the beach. Many people swim there. There is a famous hanok in Gangneung. It is called Ojukheon. Yulgok was born there. The most famous food in Gangneung is potato tteok. It is soft and sweet. Come and enjoy Gangneung!

12 다음 질문에 4 단어로 이루어진 한 문장으로 답하시오.

Q: Where is Ojukheon?

➡ _____

13 According to the passage, what can we see at the beach in Gangneung? Answer in English with a full sentence.

➡ _____

14 위 글의 내용에 맞게 빈칸에 알맞은 말을 쓰시오.

A: How is potato tteok?
B: _____

➡ _____

01 다음 지도에서 나타내는 Ming's의 위치와 일치하도록 빈칸에 알맞은 말을 넣어 가는 길을 설명하시오.

> Emma: Let's try the new Chinese restaurant, Ming's. It's near the school.
>
> Minsu: Okay. How can I get there from the school?
>
> Emma: _____
>
> Minsu: All right. Let's meet at 12 o'clock.
>
> Emma: Wonderful. See you then.

➡ _____

02 주어진 단어와 지각동사를 이용하여 축제에서 볼 수 있는 다양한 사람들을 묘사해 보시오.

> children   merchants   people

(1) _____

(2) _____

(3) _____

03 주어진 단어와 가주어 It과 진주어 to부정사를 활용하여 학교생활에서 유의해야 할 점에 대해 〈보기〉와 같이 써 보시오.

> important, necessary, essential, dangerous

┌─ 보기 ─────────────────────────────────────┐
It is important not to fall asleep during the class.
└──┘

(1) _____

(2) _____

(3) _____

(4) _____

단원별 모의고사

01 다음 영영풀이가 가리키는 것을 고르시오.

> a small vehicle used for sliding over snow

① firework   ② sled
③ boat   ④ sail
⑤ shape

02 다음 주어진 문장의 밑줄 친 hold와 같은 의미로 쓰인 것은?

> We hold the White Nights Festival.

① Did Emily hold a large box?
② It is hard to hold a business meeting because of all this noise.
③ The girl was holding her mother's hand.
④ I'll hold the door for you.
⑤ Would you hold my place, please?

03 다음 대화의 빈칸에 들어갈 말로 어색한 것은?

> Sora: Excuse me. _____
> Tom: Oh, the library? Cross the street and go straight two blocks. Then make a left.
> Sora: Thank you very much.

① How can I get to the library?
② Where can I find the library?
③ Do you know where the library is?
④ Is there the library around here?
⑤ How long will it take to get to the library?

04 다음 우리말에 맞게 빈칸에 알맞은 말을 쓰시오.

(1) 그녀는 창문에 돌을 던졌다.
  ➡ She _____ stones at the window.
(2) Kate는 토론 대회에 참가했다.
  ➡ Kate took part in the debate _____.
(3) 마을이 거대한 시장으로 변하였다.
  ➡ The village was changed into the _____ market.

05 다음 문장의 빈칸에 들어갈 말을 〈보기〉에서 골라 쓰시오.

> ┤ 보기 ├
> go on / in front of / more and more / because of

(1) The festival will _____ for 5 days.
(2) _____ people are using the tablet PC.
(3) The boys couldn't go on a picnic _____ the bad weather.
(4) I felt so nervous _____ a large group of people.

06 다음 대화의 밑줄 친 우리말을 영작하시오.

> Amy: Jinho, hurry up. We're going to be late for the movie.
> Jinho: Okay. How long will it take to get to the theater?
> Amy: 버스로 약 15분 걸릴 거야.
> Jinho: All right. I'm almost ready.

➡ _____

[07~08] 다음 대화를 읽고 물음에 답하시오.

Man: Excuse me. How can I get to Suwon Hwaseong from here?
Mina: ⓐ It's easy. Do you see the bus stop over there?
Man: Yes, I do.
Mina: Take the No. 11 bus and get ___ⓑ___ at the sixth stop.
Man: How long will it take to get there?
Mina: It will take about 20 minutes.
Man: Thank you very much.
Mina: No problem. Are you going there for the festival?
Man: Yes. I heard it's a lot of fun.
Mina: I hope you have a great time.

07 위 글의 밑줄 친 ⓐ가 가리키는 것을 우리말로 쓰시오.

➡ _____

08 위 글의 빈칸 ⓑ에 알맞은 말을 쓰시오.

➡ _____

09 다음 대화의 내용과 일치하지 <u>않는</u> 것은?

Rachel: Chris, what will you do for the class party?
Chris: I'll make sandwiches.
Rachel: Great idea. How long will it take to make them?
Chris: Maybe it'll take about an hour.
Rachel: Then, I'll decorate the classroom.
Chris: Sounds great.

① Rachel과 Chris는 학급 파티를 준비하고 있다.
② Chris는 학급 파티를 위해 샌드위치를 만들 것이다.
③ Chris는 샌드위치를 만드는 데 약 한 시간이 걸릴 것이다.
④ Rachel은 교실을 장식할 것이다.
⑤ Rachel은 교실을 장식하는 데 약 한 시간이 걸릴 것이다.

10 다음 주어진 우리말과 일치하도록 주어진 단어를 모두 배열하여 완성하시오.

(1) 너의 집에서 학교까지 가는 데 얼마나 걸리니?
(from / get / school / to / to / it / take / how / long / house / your / does)
➡ _____

(2) 은행까지 어떻게 가나요?
(the / to / I / get / can / bank / how)
➡ _____

(3) 길을 건너서 한 구역 곧장 가세요.
(street / and / the / cross / one / go / straight / block)
➡ _____

(4) 지하철로 대략 10분 정도 걸릴 거야.
(will / by / it / about / take / subway / 10 minutes)
➡ _____

11 다음 대화가 자연스럽게 이어지도록 순서대로 배열하시오.

(A) Maybe it'll take about an hour.
(B) I'll decorate the classroom.
(C) What will you do for the class party?
(D) Great idea. How long will it take to do it?

➡ _____

[12~13] 다음 대화를 읽고 물음에 답하시오.

A: How long does it take to get to school from your house?
B: It usually takes (a)about 10 minutes.
A: How do you go to school?
B: _____ (A)

12 위 대화의 빈칸 (A)에 들어갈 말로 적절한 것은?

① I walk to school.
② Go straight two blocks and you can find it on your right.
③ It will take about thirty minutes.
④ I'll decorate the classroom.
⑤ I'm almost ready.

13 위 대화의 밑줄 친 (a)와 같은 의미로 쓰인 것은?

① What is this book about?
② It is a story about wild animals.
③ My father is always worried about me.
④ We walked about five miles in the desert.
⑤ I can't understand why she's so angry about him.

14 다음 중 어법상 바르지 않은 것은?

① It is so great to be here with you.
② It is annoying to hear her to sing the same song.
③ Polly heard someone pounding on the door.
④ Christine saw her friend bounce a ball alone.
⑤ It is strange for him to be late today.

15 주어진 단어를 이용하여 다음 우리말을 영어로 쓰시오.

그녀는 비가 지붕 위로 떨어지는 소리를 들었다. (fall on)

➡ _____

16 다음 중 빈칸에 들어갈 말이 바르게 짝지어진 것은?

- Hamilton heard Simon _____ the blackboard.
- It was really irritating to hear someone _____ the blackboard.

① to scratch – to scratch
② scratching – to scratch
③ scratch – scratch
④ scratch – to scratch
⑤ scratch – scratched

17 다음 중 빈칸에 들어갈 수 있는 말을 모두 고르시오.

Jane _____ Thomas kick the wall.

① saw ② made
③ wanted ④ heard
⑤ would like

18 주어진 단어를 활용하여 다음 우리말을 영어로 쓰시오.

James는 무언가가 그의 팔을 무는 것을 느꼈다. (bite)

➡ _____

[19~20] 다음 글을 읽고 물음에 답하시오.

White Nights Festival
Victor from St. Petersburg, Russia
Have you heard of the *White Nights*? Every summer, this amazing thing happens in my hometown. The night sky does not get completely dark. (A)[While / During] that time, we hold the White Nights Festival. It usually starts in May and lasts for about a month. During the festival, there is a ballet or an opera almost every night. The most popular event is the Scarlet Sails celebration. A boat with red sails slowly (B)[appears / is appeared] on the river. Soon, fireworks begin and a water show follows. You can also hear musicians (C)[playing / to play] beautiful live music.

19 (A)~(C)에서 어법상 옳은 것끼리 바르게 짝지은 것은?

① While – appears – playing
② While – appears – to play
③ While – is appeared – to play
④ During – appears – playing
⑤ During – is appeared – playing

20 다음 중 위 글의 내용과 일치하지 <u>않는</u> 것은?

① You can experience the White Nights in Russia.
② It is hard to see something at night during the White Nights.
③ The White Nights Festival continues for about a month.
④ Musicians play live music at the festival.
⑤ You can see a ballet or an opera during the festival.

[21~23] 다음 글을 읽고 물음에 답하시오.

Kiruna Snow Festival
Ebba from Kiruna, Sweden
Winter is my favorite season (A)<u>because of</u> the Kiruna Snow Festival. The festival starts in the last week of January and goes on for five or six days. The largest event is the snow design competition. The artists shape huge piles of snow into animals, buildings, and other beautiful artworks. People watch the artists shaping their works from beginning to end. My favorite activity is the dog sled ride. (B)<u>개 썰매를 타고 눈 세상을 날아가는 것은 놀라워요.</u>

21 다음 중 밑줄 친 (A)를 대신하여 쓰일 수 있는 것은?

① because   ② due to   ③ since
④ as   ⑤ for

22 다음 중 위 글의 내용과 일치하는 것은?

① Ebba is not fond of the Kiruna Snow Festival.
② The festival lasts over a week.
③ The artists compete in the event by making something into a particular shape with snow.
④ There is only one mass of snow at the festival.
⑤ It is hard for people to watch the artists shape their works.

23 주어진 단어를 활용하여 밑줄 친 우리말 (B)를 영어로 쓰시오.

(it / through / on a dog sled)

➡ _____

_____

Lesson 6

In Outer Space

의사소통 기능

- 알고 있는지 묻기

  A: Do you know who he is?

  B: Yes, I do. He is Albert Schweitzer.

- 용도 말하기

  A: What is it for?

  B: It's for making ink.

언어 형식

- 동등 비교

  A year on Mars is about twice **as long as** a year on Earth.

- 접속사 although

  Although there are many movies about Mars, no one has been there yet.

Words & Expressions

Key Words

□ **adapt** [ədǽpt] 동 적응하다

□ **although** [ɔːlðóu] 접 (비록) ~이긴 하지만

□ **apply** [əplái] 동 지원하다

□ **average** [ǽvəridʒ] 명 평균

□ **blind** [blaind] 형 시각 장애가 있는, 눈이 먼

□ **brave** [breiv] 형 용감한

□ **communicate** [kəmjú:nəkèit] 동 의사소통하다

□ **curious** [kjúəriəs] 형 호기심이 많은, 궁금한

□ **deaf** [def] 형 청각 장애가 있는, 귀가 먹은

□ **decorate** [dékərèit] 동 장식하다

□ **difference** [dífərəns] 명 차이

□ **electricity** [ilektrísəti] 명 전기

□ **environment** [inváiərənmənt] 명 환경, 주위의 상황

□ **exhibition** [èksəbíʃən] 명 전시회

□ **farther** [fá:rðər] 형 더 먼 (far의 비교급) 부 더 멀리

□ **following** [fálouiŋ] 형 다음에 나오는

□ **friendly** [fréndli] 형 친절한, 상냥한

□ **half** [hæf] 명 절반

□ **include** [inklú:d] 동 포함하다

□ **invention** [invénʃən] 명 발명

□ **inventor** [invéntər] 명 발명가

□ **lastly** [lǽstli] 부 마지막으로

□ **lead** [li:d] 동 이끌다, 안내하다, 생활을 하다, 지내다

□ **length** [leŋkθ] 명 기간, 길이

□ **Mars** [ma:rz] 명 화성

□ **mission** [míʃən] 명 임무

□ **necessary** [nésəsèri] 형 필요한, 없어서는 안 될

□ **organization** [ɔ̀rgənizéiʃən] 명 조직, 단체

□ **outgoing** [áutgouiŋ] 형 활발한

□ **peel** [pi:l] 동 껍질을 벗기다

□ **planet** [plǽnit] 명 행성

□ **produce** [prədjú:s] 동 생산하다

□ **promise** [prámis] 동 약속하다

□ **reason** [rí:zn] 명 이유

□ **sense of humor** 유머 감각

□ **several** [sévərəl] 형 몇몇의

□ **similar** [símələr] 형 비슷한

□ **slice** [slais] 동 (얇게) 썰다, 자르다

□ **solar system** 태양계

□ **space** [speis] 명 우주, 공간

□ **spread** [spred] 동 바르다, 펼치다

□ **stick** [stik] 명 나뭇가지, 막대

Key Expressions

□ **be curious about** ~에 대해 궁금해 하다

□ **be good at** ~을 잘하다

□ **be made of** ~로 만들어지다, ~로 구성되다

□ **cheer up** 기운을 내다, ~을 격려하다

□ **from now on** 지금부터

□ **get along with** ~와 잘 지내다

□ **have a great time** 즐거운 시간을 보내다

□ **in addition** 게다가

□ **look for** ~을 찾다

□ **make an invention** 발명하다

□ **miss out** 놓치다

□ **on average** 평균적으로

Word Power

※ 서로 반대되는 뜻을 가진 단어

☐ **wide** 넓은 → **narrow** 좁은

☐ **include** 포함하다 → **exclude** 제외하다

☐ **necessary** 필요한 → **unnecessary** 불필요한

☐ **produce** 생산하다 → **consume** 소비하다

※ 행성을 나타내는 단어

☐ **Mercury** 수성　　☐ **Venus** 금성　　☐ **Earth** 지구　　☐ **Mars** 화성

☐ **Jupiter** 목성　　☐ **Saturn** 토성　　☐ **Uranus** 천왕성　　☐ **Neptune** 해왕성

☐ **Pluto** 명왕성

※ 사람의 성격을 묘사하는 형용사

☐ **creative** 창의적인　　☐ **curious** 호기심이 많은　　☐ **friendly** 친절한　　☐ **brave** 용감한

☐ **strong** 강한　　☐ **outgoing** 활발한　　☐ **shy** 수줍음이 많은　　☐ **generous** 관대한

English Dictionary

☐ **adapt** 적응하다
→ to change your behavior in order to live in a new situation successfully
새로운 환경에서 성공적으로 살아가기 위해 당신의 행동을 바꾸다

☐ **apply** 지원하다
→ to ask formally for something such as a job, admission to a school, etc.
직장, 학교의 입학 허가 등과 같은 무언가를 공식적으로 요청하다

☐ **blind** 시각 장애가 있는, 눈이 먼
→ not able to see
볼 수 없는

☐ **deaf** 청각 장애가 있는, 귀가 먹은
→ not able to hear anything
어떤 것도 들을 수 없는

☐ **difference** 차이
→ the way in which two things are not like each other
두 가지 것들이 서로 같지 않은 방식

☐ **environment** 환경
→ the conditions that surround someone or something
누군가 또는 무언가를 둘러싸고 있는 주위의 상황

☐ **half** 절반
→ one of two equal parts into which something can be divided
무언가가 나누어질 수 있는 두 개의 똑같은 부분 중 하나

☐ **length** 기간
→ the amount of time that something lasts
무언가가 지속되는 시간의 양

☐ **mission** 임무
→ a task or job that someone is given to do
누군가에게 하도록 주어진 업무나 일

☐ **organization** 조직, 단체
→ a group such as a club or business that is formed for a particular purpose
특정한 목적을 위해 형성된 모임이나 사업과 같은 모임

☐ **peel** 껍질을 벗기다
→ to remove the skin from a fruit, vegetable, etc.
과일, 야채 등으로부터 껍질을 제거하다

☐ **similar** 비슷한
→ like somebody or something but not exactly the same
누군가 또는 무언가와 비슷하지만 완전히 같지는 않은

☐ **slice** (얇게) 썰다, 자르다
→ to cut something into thin pieces
무언가를 얇은 조각으로 자르다

☐ **stick** 나뭇가지, 막대
→ a thin piece of wood that has been broken from a tree
나무로부터 부러진 얇은 나무 조각

서답형

01 다음 짝지어진 단어의 관계가 같도록 빈칸에 알맞은 말을 쓰시오.

> increase : decrease = _____ : exclude

02 다음 주어진 단어 중 나머지 넷과 성격이 다른 것은?

① Mercury   ② Venus
③ Saturn   ④ Jupiter
⑤ Galaxy

중요

03 다음 영영풀이가 가리키는 것을 고르시오.

> a group such as a club or business that is formed for a particular purpose

① organization   ② mission
③ length   ④ average
⑤ invention

서답형

04 다음 괄호 안에서 알맞은 단어를 고르시오.

(1) Her (miss / mission) in life was to work for poor people.
(2) (Although / But) he was hungry, he could not eat.
(3) Could you (peel / feel) an orange for me?
(4) I need to (look after / look for) the book to do my homework.
(5) There are (several / severe) similar stores at the mall.

중요

05 다음 중 밑줄 친 부분의 뜻풀이가 바르지 <u>않은</u> 것은?

① <u>Although</u> he is short, he is very strong. 비록 ~일지라도
② I have to <u>adapt</u> quickly to the new system. 적응하다
③ Her grandfather is <u>blind</u>. 눈이 먼
④ Alice grew up in a good <u>environment</u>. 환경
⑤ He is a member of a large international <u>organization</u>. 유기체

서답형

06 다음 주어진 우리말과 일치하도록 빈칸에 알맞은 말을 쓰시오.

(1) 그는 일주일에 한 번씩 귀가 먼 아이들을 돕는다.
➡ He helps _____ children once a week.
(2) 10과 6의 평균값은 8이다.
➡ The _____ of 10 and 6 is 8.
(3) 나는 몇몇 다른 회사에 지원했다.
➡ I _____ to several different companies.

07 다음 밑줄 친 space의 의미가 나머지 넷과 <u>다른</u> 것은?

① In <u>space</u>, there is no gravity.
② The Earth looks beautiful from <u>space</u>.
③ Do you know who the first woman in <u>space</u> was?
④ I want to study <u>space</u> engineering in university.
⑤ There is not enough <u>space</u> between the two houses.

01 다음 주어진 우리말과 일치하도록 빈칸에 알맞은 말을 써 넣으시오.

(1) 그는 배드민턴을 잘 친다.

➡ He ＿＿＿＿＿＿＿ playing badminton.

(2) 많은 팬들이 그의 새 앨범에 대해 궁금해 하고 있다.

➡ Many fans ＿＿＿＿＿＿＿ his new album.

(3) 평균적으로 캥거루는 6년에서 8년 동안 산다.

➡ ＿＿＿＿＿＿＿, kangaroos live for 6 to 8 years.

02 다음 문장의 빈칸에 들어갈 말을 〈보기〉에서 골라 쓰시오.

┌─ 보기 ─┐
curious / blind / exhibition / similar / difference
└─────┘

(1) She is ＿＿＿＿ in one eye.

(2) He is such a ＿＿＿＿ boy, always asking questions.

(3) There's no ＿＿＿＿ between the two bags.

(4) The brothers look very ＿＿＿＿.

(5) There are several famous paintings at the ＿＿＿＿.

03 다음 우리말에 맞게 주어진 단어를 사용하여 영작하시오.

(1) 우리는 매우 비슷한 관심사를 갖고 있다. (interests)

➡ ＿＿＿＿＿＿＿＿＿＿＿＿＿＿

(2) 물은 생명을 위해 필요하다. (life)

➡ ＿＿＿＿＿＿＿＿＿＿＿＿＿＿

(3) 여행 기간은 5일입니다. (trip)

➡ ＿＿＿＿＿＿＿＿＿＿＿＿＿＿

04 다음 영영풀이가 가리키는 말을 한 단어로 쓰시오.

┌─────────────────────┐
│ not able to see │
└─────────────────────┘

➡ ＿＿＿＿＿＿＿＿＿＿＿

05 다음 주어진 우리말과 일치하도록 주어진 어구를 배열하여 완성하시오.

(1) 나는 자원봉사 프로그램에 지원할 것이다.
(apply / the / program / volunteer / I'll / for)

➡ ＿＿＿＿＿＿＿＿＿＿＿＿＿＿

(2) 나는 평균적으로 한 달에 3권의 책을 읽는다.
(read / month / average / three books / I / a / on)

➡ ＿＿＿＿＿＿＿＿＿＿＿＿＿＿

(3) 이 공은 저 공의 절반 크기이다.
(ball / that / of / one / the size / this / half / is)

➡ ＿＿＿＿＿＿＿＿＿＿＿＿＿＿

06 대화의 내용과 일치하도록 다음 글의 빈칸을 완성하시오.

┌─────────────────────────────┐
│ Sumi: Do you know what this is? │
│ Kevin: No, I don't. What is it? │
│ Sumi: It's a Soccket. │
│ Kevin: A Soccket? What is it for? │
│ Sumi: It produces electricity when you │
│ 　　　play with it. │
│ Kevin: Wow, that's great! │
└─────────────────────────────┘
⬇
┌─────────────────────────────┐
│ I think Sumi's Soccket is the best │
│ invention. When we play with it, it │
│ produces ＿＿＿＿. It is very useful when │
│ we don't have any ＿＿＿＿. │
└─────────────────────────────┘

➡ ＿＿＿＿＿＿＿＿＿＿＿

Conversation

① 알고 있는지 묻기

> **A** Do you know who he is? 그가 누구인지 아니?
>
> **B** Yes, I do. He is Albert Schweitzer. 응, 알아. 그는 Albert Schweitzer야.

■ 어떤 것에 관해 알고 있는지 물을 때는 'Do you know ~?'를 이용해 표현한다. 특정 인물에 관해 알고 있는지 물을 때는 'Do you know who ~ is?'로 표현하고, 사물에 관해 알고 있는지 물을 때는 'Do you know what ~ is?'로 표현한다.

알고 있는지 묻기

- Do you know who Jane Goodall is? Jane Goodall이 누구인지 알고 있니?
- Do you know about her? 그녀에 관해 알고 있니?
- Guess who she is. 그녀가 누군지 맞혀 봐.
- Can you guess what this is? 이게 무엇인지 추측할 수 있겠니?

핵심 Check

1. 다음 우리말과 일치하도록 빈칸에 알맞은 말을 쓰시오.

(1) **A:** He was an artist. He painted *the Mona Lisa*. Do you know _____ _____

_____? (그는 미술가야. 그는 모나리자를 그렸어. 그가 누구인지 아니?)

   B: Yes, I do. He is Leonardo Da Vinci. (응, 알아. 그는 Leonardo Da Vinci야.)

(2) **A:** It looks like a man. It is made of snow. _____ _____ _____

_____ _____? (그것은 사람처럼 보여. 눈으로 만들어졌어. 무엇인지 알겠니?)

   B: No, I don't. What is it? (아니, 모르겠어. 뭐니?)

   A: It's a snowman. (눈사람이야.)

(3) **A:** It's for a rainy day. It has different colors. _____ what it is.

   (그것은 비 오는 날을 위한 것이야. 그것은 여러 가지 색들을 갖고 있어. 무엇인지 맞혀 봐.)

   B: It's an umbrella. (우산이야.)

② 용도 말하기

A What is it for? 그것은 용도가 무엇이니?

B It's for making ink. 잉크를 만들기 위한 것이야.

■ 'What is it for?' 또는 'What are they for?'는 '용도가 무엇이니?'라는 뜻으로 특정 물건의 사용 목적이나 용도를 묻는 표현이다. 이에 대한 대답은 'It is[They are] for ~.'를 사용하여 물건의 사용 목적이나 용도를 말할 수 있다.

용도 말하기

- What is it for? 그것은 용도가 무엇이니?
- What are they used for? 그것들은 무엇을 위해 사용되니?

핵심 Check

2. 다음 우리말과 일치하도록 빈칸에 알맞은 말을 쓰시오.

(1) **A:** I've never seen it before. _____ _____ _____ _____?

(나는 전에 그것을 본 적이 없어. 그것은 용도가 무엇이니?)

B: It's for decorating your hair. (네 머리 장식을 위한 것이야.)

(2) **A:** Jane, _____ _____ this. It's a *Jige*. (Jane, 이것 좀 봐. 이것은 지게야.)

B: I have never seen it before. What is it _____?

(그것을 전에 본 적이 없어요. 용도가 무엇이에요?)

(3) **A:** _____ _____ _____ _____ _____? (그것들은 무엇을 위해 사용되나요?)

B: They are used for carrying many different things.

(그것들은 많은 다른 물건들을 옮기는 데 사용된다.)

Listen and Speak 1-B

Ms. Lee: Hello, class! Jisu is today's ❶speaker for show and tell. Jisu?

Jisu: Hi, class! Do you know ❷who this man is? His name is Alexander Graham Bell. Bell was an ❸inventor. He ❹was interested in sound. What did he invent? Yes, the telephone! His mother and wife were ❺deaf. So he also made some inventions for deaf people and opened a school for ❻them.

Ms. Lee: 안녕하세요, 여러분! 지수가 오늘의 물건 가져와서 발표하기의 발표자예요. 지수야?

Jisu: 안녕, 얘들아! 이 사람이 누구인지 아니? 그의 이름은 Alexander Graham Bell이야. Bell은 발명가였어. 그는 소리에 관심이 있었어. 그가 무엇을 발명했지? 맞아, 전화기야! 그의 어머니와 아내는 청각 장애가 있었어. 그래서 그는 청각 장애인들을 위한 몇몇 발명품도 만들었고 그들을 위한 학교를 열었어.

❶ speaker: 발표자 show and tell 물건 가져와서 발표하기
❷ 간접의문문의 어순으로 '의문사+주어+동사'의 순서로 이어진다.
❸ inventor: 발명가
❹ be interested in: ~에 관심이 있다 = have an interest in
❺ deaf: 청각 장애가 있는
❻ them은 deaf people을 가리킨다.

Check(√) True or False

(1) Alexander Graham Bell invented the telephone. T☐ F☐

(2) Alexander Graham Bell was not able to hear. T☐ F☐

Real Life Talk – Step 1

Judy: How was your weekend, Hojin?

Hojin: I ❶had a great time. I went to a science ❷exhibition with my brother.

Judy: Did you? I heard there were so many interesting things.

Hojin: Yes. Look at this. I bought it there. Do you know what it is?

Judy: Well, I'm not sure. What is it?

Hojin: It's a VR headset.

Judy: A VR headset? ❸What is it for?

Hojin: If you wear ❹it, you can experience another world.

Judy: Sounds cool. May I try it?

Hojin: Sure. Here you go.

Judy: 주말은 어땠니, 호진아?

Hojin: 즐거운 시간을 보냈어. 남동생과 과학 전시회에 갔었어.

Judy: 그랬니? 흥미로운 것들이 굉장히 많다고 들었어.

Hojin: 응. 이것 좀 봐. 거기에서 샀어. 이게 무엇인지 아니?

Judy: 음, 잘 모르겠어. 뭐니?

Hojin: VR 헤드셋이야.

Judy: VR 헤드셋? 용도가 뭐니?

Hojin: 그것을 쓰면 다른 세상을 경험할 수 있어.

Judy: 멋지다. 내가 써 봐도 될까?

Hojin: 물론이지. 여기 있어.

❶ have a great time: 즐거운 시간을 보내다
❷ exhibition: 전시회
❸ 용도를 묻는 표현이다.
❹ it은 a VR headset을 가리킨다.

Check(√) True or False

(3) Hojin went to a science exhibition and bought the VR headset. T☐ F☐

(4) The VR headset is for experiencing another world. T☐ F☐

Listen and Speak 1-A

> **Brian:** Do you know what this is?
>
> **Amy:** Um, it ❶looks like a ❷glue stick.
>
> **Brian:** No, it's a butter stick.
>
> **Amy:** Oh, is there butter in it?
>
> **Brian:** Yes, you can ❸spread butter on the bread with ❹it.

❶ look like+명사(구): ～처럼 보이다
❷ glue: 풀
❸ spread: 바르다
❹ it은 a butter stick을 가리킨다.

 Listen and Speak 2-A

> **Jane:** ❶This looks interesting. ❷What is it for?
>
> **Mike:** It's for ❸slicing eggs.
>
> **Jane:** Really? May I try it?
>
> **Mike:** Sure, here is an egg.

❶ look+형용사: ～처럼 보이다
❷ 용도를 묻는 표현으로 'What is it used for?'로 바꾸어 쓸 수 있다.
❸ slice: 썰다

❶ look at: ～을 보다
❷ them은 slippers를 가리킨다.
❸ just: 단지, 오직
❹ put on: ～을 입다, 신다
❺ from now on: 지금부터
❻ worry about: ～에 대해 걱정하다

 Listen and Speak 2-C

> **A:** Jane, look at this. It's a meok.
>
> **B:** I have never seen ❶it before. What is ❶it for?
>
> **A:** ❶It's for making ink.
>
> **B:** Oh, really? ❷That's interesting.

❶ it은 모두 meok(먹)을 가리킨다.
❷ That sounds interesting.으로 바꾸어 쓸 수 있다.

 Real Life Talk – Step 2

> **A:** Do you know what this is?
>
> **B:** No, I don't. What is it?
>
> **A:** It's a Clean Straw.
>
> **B:** A Clean Straw? What is it for?
>
> **A:** It cleans water ❶while you drink.
>
> **B:** Wow, that's great!

❶ while은 '～하는 동안에'를 뜻하며 'while+주어+동사'가 이어지는 반면 during은 명사(구)가 이어진다.

Listen and Speak 2-B

> **Tom:** Mom, ❶look at these slippers. I made ❷them in science class.
>
> **Mom:** Why did you make slippers in science class?
>
> **Tom:** They are not ❸just for wearing.
>
> **Mom:** Then, what are they for?
>
> **Tom:** You can ❹put them on and clean the floor.
>
> **Mom:** Oh, so you will clean your room ❺from now on?
>
> **Tom:** Sure. Don't ❻worry about my room, Mom.

● 다음 우리말과 일치하도록 빈칸에 알맞은 말을 쓰시오.

Listen & Speak 1-A

Brian: Do you know _____ this is?

Amy: Um, it _____ _____ a glue stick.

Brian: No, it's a _____ _____.

Amy: Oh, _____ _____ butter in it?

Brian: Yes, you can _____ butter on the bread with it.

Brian: 너는 이것이 무엇인지 아니?
Amy: 음, 막대 모양 풀 같아 보여.
Brian: 아니, 막대 모양 버터야.
Amy: 오, 그 안에 버터가 있니?
Brian: 응, 그걸로 빵 위에 버터를 바를 수 있어.

Listen & Speak 1-B

Ms. Lee: Hello, class! Jisu is today's speaker for show and tell. Jisu?

Jisu: Hi, class! Do you know _____ _____ _____ _____?
His name is Alexander Graham Bell. Bell was an _____. He _____ _____ _____ sound. _____ did he _____?
Yes, the telephone! His mother and wife were _____. So he also made some _____ for deaf people and opened a school for them.

Ms. Lee: 안녕하세요, 여러분! 지수가 오늘의 물건 가져와서 발표하기의 발표자예요. 지수야?
Jisu: 안녕, 얘들아! 이 사람이 누구인지 아니? 그의 이름은 Alexander Graham Bell이야. Bell은 발명가였어. 그는 소리에 관심이 있었어. 그가 무엇을 발명했지? 맞아, 전화기야! 그의 어머니와 아내는 청각 장애가 있었어. 그래서 그는 청각 장애인들을 위한 몇몇 발명품도 만들었고 그들을 위한 학교를 열었어.

Listen & Speak 2-A

Jane: This looks _____. What is it for?

Mike: It's for _____ _____.

Jane: Really? May I _____ it?

Mike: Sure, _____ _____ an egg.

Jane: 이거 흥미롭게 생겼네. 용도가 뭐야?
Mike: 달걀을 얇게 썰기 위한 거야.
Jane: 정말? 내가 해 봐도 돼?
Mike: 물론이지, 여기 달걀이 있어.

Listen & Speak 2-B

Tom: Mom, _____ _____ these slippers. I made them in science class.

Mom: _____ did you _____ slippers in science class?

Tom: They are _____ _____ for wearing.

Mom: Then, _____ are they _____?

Tom: You can _____ _____ _____ and clean the floor.

Mom: Oh, so you will clean your room _____ _____ _____?

Tom: Sure. Don't _____ _____ my room, Mom.

해석

Tom: 엄마, 이 슬리퍼를 보세요. 과학 시간에 만들었어요.
Mom: 왜 과학 시간에 슬리퍼를 만들었니?
Tom: 단지 신기 위한 게 아니에요.
Mom: 그럼 용도가 무엇이니?
Tom: 슬리퍼를 신고 바닥을 청소할 수 있어요.
Mom: 오, 그럼 앞으로는 네가 네 방을 청소하겠구나?
Tom: 물론이에요. 제 방은 걱정 마세요, 엄마.

Listen & Speak 2-C

A: Jane, _____ _____ this. It's a meok.

B: I _____ _____ _____ it before. _____ is it _____?

A: It's _____ _____ _____.

B: Oh, really? That's _____.

A: Jane, 이것 좀 봐. 먹이야.
B: 나는 그것을 전에 본 적이 없어. 용도가 무엇이니?
A: 잉크를 만들기 위한 거야.
B: 오, 정말? 그거 흥미롭다.

Real Life Talk – Step 1

Judy: _____ _____ your weekend, Hojin?

Hojin: I had a _____ _____. I went to a _____ _____ with my brother.

Judy: Did you? I heard _____ _____ so many interesting things.

Hojin: Yes. Look at this. I bought it there. Do you know _____ _____ _____?

Judy: Well, I'm _____ _____. What is it?

Hojin: It's a VR headset.

Judy: A VR headset? _____ _____ _____ _____?

Hojin: If you _____ it, you can experience _____ _____.

Judy: Sounds cool. May I _____ it?

Hojin: Sure. Here you go.

Judy: 주말은 어땠니, 호진아?
Hojin: 즐거운 시간을 보냈어. 남동생과 과학 전시회에 갔었어.
Judy: 그랬니? 흥미로운 것들이 굉장히 많다고 들었어.
Hojin: 응. 이것 좀 봐. 거기에서 샀어. 이게 무엇인지 아니?
Judy: 음, 잘 모르겠어. 뭐니?
Hojin: VR 헤드셋이야.
Judy: VR 헤드셋? 용도가 뭐니?
Hojin: 그것을 쓰면 다른 세상을 경험할 수 있어.
Judy: 멋지다. 내가 써 봐도 될까?
Hojin: 물론이지. 여기 있어.

[01~02] 다음 대화를 읽고 물음에 답하시오.

> Jane: This looks interesting. (A)What is it for?
> Mike: It's for slicing eggs.
> Jane: Really? May I try it?
> Mike: Sure, here is an egg.

01 위 대화의 밑줄 친 (A)의 의도로 적절한 것은?

① 용도 묻기   ② 직업 묻기
③ 사용 방법 묻기   ④ 취미 묻기
⑤ 선호도 묻기

02 What is Jane going to do with an egg?

➡ _____

[03~04] 다음 대화를 읽고 물음에 답하시오.

> Sue: Do you know what this is?
> Jack: No, I don't. What is it?
> Sue: It's a Clean Straw.
> Jack: A Clean Straw? What is it for?
> Sue: _____
> Jack: Wow, that's great!

03 위 대화의 주제로 적절한 것은?

① a new invention
② how to make a Clean Straw
③ how to use a Clean Straw
④ Sue's creativity
⑤ how to use Jack's invention

04 위 대화의 빈칸에 들어갈 말을 주어진 단어를 모두 배열하여 완성하시오.

┌─ 보기 ┌
│ water / you / it / cleans / drink / while │

➡ _____

01 다음 짝지어진 대화가 <u>어색한</u> 것은?

① A: This looks interesting. What is it?
　B: It's for slicing eggs.

② A: What are they for?
　B: They are for cleaning the floor.

③ A: What is it used for?
　B: You can use it for decorating your hair.

④ A: I've never seen this machine.
　B: This is for peeling apples.

⑤ A: What are they for?
　B: They are bineyos.

서답형

02 다음 대화가 자연스럽게 이어지도록 순서대로 배열하시오.

(A) It's for slicing eggs.
(B) Sure, here is an egg.
(C) Really? May I try it?
(D) This looks interesting. What is it for?

➡ _____

[03~04] 다음 대화를 읽고 물음에 답하시오.

Judy: How was your weekend, Hojin?
Hojin: I had a great time. I went to a science exhibition with my brother.
Judy: Did you? I heard there (A)[was / were] so many interesting things.
Hojin: Yes. Look at this. I bought it there. Do you know what it is?
Judy: Well, I'm not sure. What is it?
Hojin: It's a VR headset.
Judy: A VR headset? What is it for?
Hojin: If you wear it, you can experience (B)[another / other] world.
Judy: (C)[Sound / Sounds] cool. May I try it?
Hojin: Sure. Here you go.

중요

03 위 대화의 밑줄 친 (A)~(C)에 들어갈 말이 바르게 짝지어진 것은?

	(A)	(B)	(C)
①	was	another	Sound
②	was	other	Sounds
③	were	another	Sounds
④	were	other	Sound
⑤	were	another	Sound

서답형

04 위 대화의 내용과 일치하도록 다음 빈칸을 완성하시오.

Hojin visited a science exhibition with his brother last weekend. Hojin was so excited because there were _____(A)_____ to experience. He bought a VR headset, which made him _____(B)_____.

➡ (A) _____
　(B) _____

[05~06] 다음 대화를 읽고 물음에 답하시오.

Tom: Mom, (A)look at these slippers. I made them in science class.
Mom: (B)Why did you make slippers in science class?
Tom: (C)They are not just for wearing.
Mom: Then, what are they for?
Tom: (D)You can put on them and clean the floor.
Mom: (E)Oh, so you will clean your room from now on?
Tom: Sure. Don't worry about my room, Mom.

05 위 대화의 (A)~(E) 중 어법상 <u>어색한</u> 문장을 찾아 바르게 고쳐 쓰시오.

➡ _____

 위 대화의 내용과 일치하지 <u>않는</u> 것은?

① Tom은 과학 시간에 슬리퍼를 만들었다.
② Tom은 슬리퍼를 단지 신기 위한 것이 아니라 청소할 수 있는 용도로 만들었다.
③ Tom은 앞으로 그의 방은 직접 청소할 것이다.
④ Tom은 엄마에게 그의 방은 걱정 말라고 말했다.
⑤ Tom은 엄마가 신을 수 있는 편안한 슬리퍼를 만들었다.

[07~08] 다음 대화를 읽고 물음에 답하시오.

Ms. Lee: Hello, class! Jisu is today's speaker for show and tell. Jisu?

Jisu: Hi, class! Do you know who this man is? His name is Alexander Graham Bell. Bell was an __(A)__ . He was interested in sound. What did he invent? Yes, the telephone! His mother and wife were deaf. So he also made some __(B)__ for deaf people and opened a school for them.

07 위 대화의 빈칸 (A)와 (B)에 invent를 알맞은 형태로 써 넣으시오.

➡ (A) _____ (B) _____

08 위 대화를 읽고 대답할 수 <u>없는</u> 질문은?

① Who was the speaker for show and tell?
② What did Alexander Graham Bell invent?
③ What was Alexander Graham Bell interested in?
④ What did Alexander Graham Bell do for deaf people?
⑤ What was the problem with Alexander Graham Bell's telephone?

[09~10] 다음 대화를 읽고 물음에 답하시오.

Brian: _____(A)_____

Amy: Um, it looks like a glue stick.

Brian: No, it's a butter stick.

Amy: Oh, is there butter in it?

Brian: Yes, you can spread butter on the bread with it.

09 위 대화의 빈칸 (A)에 들어갈 말을 다음 〈보기〉에 주어진 단어를 모두 배열하여 완성하시오.

┌─ 보기 ─┐
know / do / what / is / this / you
└─────┘

➡ _____

10 For what can the butter stick be used?

➡ _____

11 다음 주어진 문장 다음에 대화가 자연스럽게 이어지도록 순서대로 배열하시오.

┌─────────────────────────┐
Do you know what this is?
└─────────────────────────┘

(A) A Clean Straw? What is it for?
(B) It's a Clean Straw.
(C) It cleans water while you drink.
(D) Wow, that's great!
(E) No, I don't. What is it?

➡ _____

[01~02] 다음 대화를 읽고 물음에 답하시오.

> Jane: This looks interesting. (A)용도가 뭐예요? (for)
>
> Mike: It's for slicing eggs.
>
> Jane: Really? May I try it?
>
> Mike: Sure, here is an egg.

01 위 대화의 밑줄 친 (A)의 우리말을 주어진 단어를 사용하여 4 단어로 영작하시오.

➡ _____

02 위 대화에서 설명하는 물건의 용도를 우리말로 간략히 설명하시오.

➡ _____

[03~05] 다음 대화를 읽고 물음에 답하시오.

> Irene: Jane, look at this. It's a meok.
>
> Jane: (A)나는 그것을 전에 본 적이 없어. (before, never) What is it for?
>
> Irene: It's for making ink.
>
> Jane: Oh, really? That's interesting.

03 위 대화의 밑줄 친 (A)의 우리말을 주어진 단어를 사용하여 6단어로 영작하시오.

➡ _____

04 What are Irene and Jane talking about?

➡ _____

05 What is a meok used for?

➡ _____

06 다음 대화의 내용과 일치하도록 주어진 표의 빈칸을 완성하시오.

> Sue: Do you know what this is?
>
> Jack: No, I don't. What is it?
>
> Sue: It's a Clean Straw.
>
> Jack: A Clean Straw? What is it for?
>
> Sue: It cleans water while you drink.
>
> Jack: Wow, that's great!

Sue's Invention		
Name	(A)	
Use	It _____ (B) _____ while you drink.	

➡ (A) _____ (B) _____

07 다음 대화의 내용과 일치하도록 표를 완성하시오.

> Ms. Lee: Hello, class! Jisu is today's speaker for show and tell. Jisu?
>
> Jisu: Hi, class! Do you know who this man is? His name is Alexander Graham Bell. Bell was an inventor. He was interested in sound. What did he invent? Yes, the telephone! His mother and wife were deaf. So he also made some inventions for deaf people and opened a school for them.

<Who is Alexander Graham Bell?>

Occupation	(A)
Interest	(B)
Achievement	(C)
Problems	(D)
Contribution	(E)

➡ (A) _____

(B) _____

(C) _____

(D) _____

(E) _____

교과서 Grammar

① 동등 비교

> • Jane is **as tall as** Mike. Jane은 Mike만큼 키가 크다.
> • My allowance is two times **as much as** my brother. 내 용돈은 내 남동생보다 두 배나 많다.

■ 'as+형용사/부사+as'는 두 대상을 비교하며 서로 동등할 때 쓰는 표현이다. '~만큼 …한'이라는 의미로 쓰인다. 서로가 같지 않음을 나타내는 동등비교의 부정형은 'not+as[so]+형용사/부사+as'의 형태로 쓰인다.

- Your flower is **as beautiful as** mine. 너의 꽃은 내 꽃만큼 아름다워.
- Karen's pumpkin pie is **not as[so] delicious as** her mother's.
  Karen의 호박파이는 그녀의 어머니 파이만큼 맛있지 않다.
- The river is **not as[so] clean as** it used to be. 그 강은 예전만큼 깨끗하지 않다.

■ 동등 비교를 이용하여 배수 표현이 가능하다. '배수사(twice, three times 등)+as+형용사/부사+as'의 형태이며 '~의 몇 배 만큼 …한'이라는 의미로 쓰인다.

- This ball is twice **as big as** that ball. 이 공은 저 공보다 두 배나 크다.
- The demand is three times **as great as** the supply. 수요가 공급의 세 배이다.

■ 비교급은 일반적으로 형용사나 부사의 어미에 -er을 붙여서 만든다. 불규칙 변화하는 비교급 good-better, well-better, many-more, little-less 등이 있으며 의미에 따라 비교급 형태가 달라지는 것들에 유의한다.

- The man looks **older than** his age. 그 남자는 자신의 나이보다 더 나이 들어 보인다.
- He is **less clever than** his elder sister. 그는 누나보다 덜 영리하다.

핵심 Check

1. 다음 우리말과 일치하도록 빈칸에 알맞은 말을 쓰시오.

(1) 개는 토끼만큼 빨리 달린다.
➡ Dogs run _____ _____ _____ rabbits.

(2) 이것은 저것보다 두 배나 좋다.
➡ This is _____ _____ _____ _____ that.

(3) 나는 너만큼 용감하지 못해.
➡ I am _____ _____ _____ _____ you.

② 접속사 although

- **Although** I was tired, I did my homework. 나는 피곤했지만, 숙제를 했다.
- **Although** I like to swim in the river, I hate summer.
  내가 강에서 수영하는 것을 좋아한다 해도, 나는 여름이 싫어.

■ '비록 ~이지만[~일지라도]'라는 의미로 쓰이는 although는 양보의 부사절을 이끄는 접속사이다. 이에 해당하는 접속사로는 though, even though, even if 등이 있다.

- **Though** he is old, he is quite strong. 그가 나이가 많다 할지라도, 꽤 힘이 세다.
- **Even though** she didn't invite me, I went to her party.
  그녀가 날 초대하지 않았지만, 나는 그녀의 파티에 갔다.
- **Even if** the cookies look great, they don't taste good. 그 쿠키들이 보기에는 좋지만, 맛이 있지는 않다.

■ 부사절을 이끄는 접속사는 주절의 앞뒤에 모두 위치할 수 있으며, 주절 앞에 올 경우 콤마를 쓴다.

- **Although** he wasn't hungry, he had dinner with her. 배가 고프지 않았지만, 그는 그녀와 함께 저녁을 먹었다.
- The waiters at the restaurant were polite **although** the service was slow.
  서비스가 느리긴 했지만, 그 식당의 웨이터들은 친절했다.
- **Although** I like the house, it's too far from my school. 나는 그 집을 좋아하지만, 학교에서 너무 멀다.

■ Despite(= In spite of)와 혼동하지 않도록 주의하자. Despite는 '~일지라도'라는 의미를 갖지만, 전치사로 명사구를 이끈다.

- **Despite** being late for the meeting, I had all the work done.

  = **Although** I was late for the meeting, I had all the work done.
  비록 회의에 늦었다 할지라도, 나는 모든 일을 처리하였다.

핵심 Check

2. 다음 우리말과 일치하도록 빈칸에 알맞은 말을 쓰시오.

(1) 물을 많이 마셨지만, 나는 목이 말랐다.
➡ _____ I drank a lot of water, I was thirsty.

(2) 졸렸지만 Julia는 공부했다.
➡ Julia studied _____ she was _____.

(3) 곤경에 처했다 해도, 너는 평정을 유지해야 한다.
➡ _____ _____ you are in trouble, you have to remain cool.

Grammar 시험대비 기본평가

01 다음 문장에서 어법상 <u>어색한</u> 부분을 바르게 고쳐 쓰시오.

(1) Because she was scared, she bravely went out.

_____ ➡ _____

(2) Kick the ball as hardly as you can.

_____ ➡ _____

(3) His speech is not as bored as it sounds.

➡ _____

02 다음 우리말에 맞게 주어진 말을 이용해 빈칸에 알맞은 말을 쓰시오.

(1) 진짜 과학은 공상 과학 소설만큼 재미있을 수 있다. (interesting)

= Real science can be _____ science fiction.

(2) 그는 대단히 침착했어요. (cool)

= He was _____ a cucumber.

(3) 내가 Sally만큼 예쁘지 않다고 생각하니? (pretty)

= Do you think I am _____ Sally?

(4) 그녀가 무례하다 할지라도, 그들은 그녀를 고용했다. (even)

= _____ she was rude, they hired her.

> (2) (as) cool as a cucumber: (곤란한 상황에서) 대단히 침착한

03 주어진 어구를 바르게 배열하여 다음 우리말을 영어로 쓰시오.

(1) 그녀는 부자였지만 계속해서 돈을 저축했다. (money / although / saving / she / rich / she / kept / was)

➡ _____

(2) 수영하는 법을 배우는 것은 보이는 것만큼 어렵지 않아요. (looks / as / it / as / learning / difficult / how / swim / is / to / not)

➡ _____

(3) 그들만큼 우리도 슬퍼요. (they / are / are / we / sad / as / as)

➡ _____

(4) 그녀는 예전만큼 매력적이지 않아. (used to / she / she / is / attractive / not / as / be / as)

➡ _____

> (1) keep Ving: 계속해서 V하다
> (2) how to V: V하는 방법
> (4) attractive: 매력적인

01 다음 중 빈칸에 들어갈 말로 알맞지 <u>않은</u> 것은?

> Julia is as _____ as Kelly.

① friendly   ② tall   ③ lovely
④ beautifully   ⑤ kind

02 다음 우리말을 영어로 바르게 옮긴 것은?

> 그것은 기차만큼 빠르게 달릴 수 없어요.

① It runs faster than a train.
② It runs as fast as a train.
③ A train doesn't run faster than it.
④ A train runs as fast as it.
⑤ It can't run as fast as a train.

03 다음 중 어법상 바르지 <u>않은</u> 것은?

> ①Even though ②what I said yesterday, I
> ③still love you ④as much as I ⑤can.

①   ②   ③   ④   ⑤

04 다음 중 빈칸에 들어갈 말이 <u>다른</u> 하나는?

① _____ the news made him so sad, he started to cry.
② _____ it rained, we didn't go out.
③ _____ I was very tired, I couldn't sleep.
④ _____ Maria works out regularly, she is healthy.
⑤ _____ he was hungry, he wanted to eat something.

05 다음 문장을 지시대로 다시 쓰시오.

> David is 178cm tall. Richard is 182cm tall.

(1) tall, as ~ as를 사용할 것.
➡ _____

(2) short, as ~ as를 사용할 것.
➡ _____

06 다음 빈칸에 들어갈 말이 바르게 짝지어진 것은?

> • Sarah passed the exam _____ she didn't do her best.
> • Clark passed the exam _____ he studied hard.

① despite – because of
② although – when
③ in spite of – because
④ though – because
⑤ because – although

07 다음 중 어법상 바르지 <u>않은</u> 것은?

① Your hair is twice as long as mine.
② Despite the bad weather, we were happy.
③ Call me as soon as you know something.
④ June is not as smart as Einstein.
⑤ Although he slept well last night, he is refreshed.

08 동등비교를 이용하여 주어진 문장과 같은 의미의 문장을 쓰시오.

> James is richer than Barry.

➡ _____

서답형

09 as ~ as를 이용하여 다음 문장과 같은 의미의 문장을 쓰시오.

> Brad is younger than he looks.

➡ _____

10 다음 대화의 밑줄 친 부분과 같은 의미의 문장은?

> A: How much did it cost? Seventy dollars?
> B: Not as much as that.

① I bought it for seventy dollars.
② It cost more than seventy dollars.
③ It didn't cost at all.
④ It cost seventy dollars.
⑤ It cost less than seventy dollars.

11 다음 중 주어진 문장의 빈칸에 들어갈 말과 같은 말이 들어가는 것은? (2개)

> _____ Kelly has a beautiful voice, she doesn't like to sing.

① _____ you called me, I was doing something.
② _____ I like June, I don't like the way she behaves.
③ _____ you are late again, you will be punished.
④ _____ they were poor, they were happy together.
⑤ _____ she is diligent, Emily works hard.

12 다음 중 어법상 바르지 않은 것은?

① Despite the pain, he kept walking.
② The first rope is three times as thick as the second rope.
③ His jacket is not as fancy as me.
④ I don't skip my meal although I am busy all the time.
⑤ You can have it as much as you want.

13 다음 중 어법상 옳은 것끼리 바르게 짝지은 것은?

> • [Although / In spite of] what he heard, he couldn't accept it.
> • I came in as [quiet / quietly] as possible.
> • Sally's house is [bigger / as big as] than Toms' house.

① Although – quiet – bigger
② In spite of – quietly – bigger
③ Although – quitely – bigger
④ In spite of – quiet – as big as
⑤ Although – quitely – as big as

서답형

14 주어진 단어를 활용하여 다음 우리말을 영어로 쓰시오.

> 비록 그가 막 자신의 방을 청소했다 할지라도, 방은 여전히 더럽다.
> (just / still / though)

➡ _____

15 다음 우리말을 영어로 쓰시오.

> 너의 가방은 내 가방보다 두 배나 커.

➡ _____

16 주어진 문장과 같은 의미의 문장은?

> James still feels quite tired, but he felt a lot more tired yesterday.

① James feels more tired than he did yesterday.
② James feels as tired as he did yesterday.
③ James didn't feel as tired as he did the other day.
④ James doesn't feel as tired as he did yesterday.
⑤ James didn't feel more tired than he did yesterday.

17 다음 중 어법상 옳은 문장의 개수는?

> ⓐ Kevin is not as more creative as Jim.
> ⓑ Despite his success, Brad had trouble finding a publisher for his works.
> ⓒ Julian spends as more money as she wants.
> ⓓ Karl didn't hurry even though he was late for the meeting.
> ⓔ My time is as precious as your time.

① 1개   ② 2개   ③ 3개   ④ 4개   ⑤ 5개

18 다음 빈칸에 들어갈 말로 적절한 것을 <u>모두</u> 고르시오.

> _____ all my effort, my voice kept shaking.

① Though   ② Even if
③ Despite   ④ Because of
⑤ In spite of

19 다음 중 빈칸에 들어갈 수 <u>없는</u> 것은?

> Tom didn't give up _____ he kept failing.

① even though   ② although
③ though   ④ even if
⑤ unless

20 다음 빈칸에 들어갈 말로 적절한 것은?

> • Despite applying for tens of jobs, Mark is still out of job.
> = _____, Mark is still out of job.

① Because he applied for tens of jobs
② Even though he applied for tens of jobs
③ When he applied for tens of jobs
④ Although applied for tens of jobs
⑤ In spite applying for tens of jobs

21 다음 문장에서 어법상 <u>틀린</u> 것을 고쳐 문장을 다시 쓰시오.

> It is not as cheaper as I expected.

➡ _____

22 다음 우리말을 영어로 바르게 옮긴 것을 <u>모두</u> 고르시오.

> 그 영화는 내가 생각했던 것보다 짧았어.

① The movie was not as long as I thought.
② The movie was longer than I thought.
③ The movie was not as short as I thought.
④ The movie was shorter than I thought.
⑤ The movie was much longer than I thought.

Grammar **77**

01 동등 비교 표현을 이용하여 다음 문장과 같은 의미의 문장을 쓰시오.

> You spent more money than me.

➡ _____

02 주어진 형용사를 내용과 어법에 맞게 빈칸에 쓰시오.

> long   comfortable   fast   heavy

(1) I'm sorry I'm late, but I got here _____ I could.

(2) I'm going to sleep on the floor although it is _____ the bed.

(3) You can stay here _____ you like.

(4) Your box weighs 5 kilograms. My box weighs 10 kilograms. My box is _____ yours.

03 양보의 접속사를 이용하여 주어진 문장과 같은 의미의 문장을 쓰시오.

> In spite of being sick, Joe continues working.

➡ _____

04 다음 우리말을 영어로 쓰시오.

> BTS는 Justin Bieber만큼 유명하다.

➡ _____

05 주어진 단어를 이용하여 다음 우리말을 영어로 쓰시오. 콤마를 사용하지 마시오.

> 비록 네가 Bradley만큼 똑똑하다 할지라도, 너는 그만큼 현명하지는 못하다.
> (smart / wise)

➡ _____

_____

06 다음 두 문장을 하나의 문장으로 연결하시오.

> • It rained a lot.
> • The traffic was bad.
> • We have an important job.

> • We arrived on time.
> • We are not well paid.
> • We enjoyed our holiday.

➡ _____
➡ _____
➡ _____

07 지시에 맞게 다음 우리말을 영어로 쓰시오.

> 거북이는 토끼만큼 빠르지 않다.

(1) 동등 비교를 이용하여 문장을 쓰시오.
➡ _____

(2) slow를 이용하여 문장을 쓰시오.
➡ _____

08 주어진 단어를 이용하여 다음 문장과 같은 의미의 문장을 쓰시오.

> The new school was nearer than Tom expected.
> (not, as)

➡ _____

09 주어진 어휘를 어법에 맞게 빈칸에 쓰시오.

> despite   although   in spite of   though

(1) _____ our effort, we failed to win the first prize.

(2) Dana accepted the job _____ the salary was rather low.

(3) Dad can't quit smoking _____ the doctor's repeated warning.

(4) _____ he lied about everything, we decided to forgive him.

10 다음 문장을 동등 비교 문장을 이용하여 하나의 문장으로 쓰시오.

> Daivd has lived here for quite a long time. But I've lived here longer than he.

➡ _____

11 알맞은 접속사를 이용하여 주어진 문장과 같은 의미의 문장을 쓰시오.

> Despite being poor, Helen never lost her sense of humor.

➡ _____
_____

12 주어진 어구를 이용하여 다음 우리말을 영어로 쓰시오.

> 비록 이야기가 유치하긴 했지만, 나는 그 영화를 즐겼다. 그러나 그것은 내가 예상했던 것만큼 유치하지는 않았다.
> (although / silly / enjoy the film)

➡ _____
_____

13 주어진 어구를 바르게 배열하여 다음 우리말을 영어로 쓰시오.

> 그가 책을 출판했지만, 누구도 그 사실을 몰랐다.
> (the fact / though / knew / he / no one / a book / published)

➡ _____

14 다음 문장과 같은 의미의 문장을 완성하시오.

> The yellow car is not as expensive as the red car.

➡ The red car _____.
➡ The yellow car _____.

15 적절한 접속사를 이용하여 다음 우리말을 영어로 쓰시오.

> 어제 나는 배가 고팠지만, 아무것도 먹지 않았다.

➡ _____
_____

Reading

Fly Me to Mars

Live on MARS!
(어떤 장소에) 살다(자동사)
Do you want to live on another planet?
또 다른(another+단수명사)
The Korea Space Organization (KSO) is looking for people to go to
to부정사의 형용사적 용법(people 수식)
MARS! Our mission is to build a city on Mars.
to부정사의 명사적 용법(~하는 것)
We are looking for someone…

who is healthy.
주격 관계대명사(선행사: someone)
who is creative and curious.

who can get along with others.
= other people
who can adapt to a new environment quickly.
~에 적응하다
To apply, send us a short video. The video must include the answers
to부정사의 부사적 용법 중 목적(~하기 위해서)
to the following questions:

1. Why do you want to go to Mars?

2. Do you have a good sense of humor?

3. Why are you the perfect person for this mission?

This is a chance of a lifetime, so don't miss out!
부정명령문(~하지 마라)

Mars, the Second Earth?

Although there are many books and movies about Mars, no one has
many books에 수의 일치   누구도 ~하지 않다
been there yet. These days, scientists are looking at Mars as a new
아직   요즈음   (자격, 기능) ~로(서)
home. In fact, NASA and some companies are trying to send people
사실
there right now.

 확인문제

● 다음 문장이 본문의 내용과 일치하면 T, 일치하지 않으면 F를 쓰시오.

1 To apply, you need to be healthy and creative. ☐

2 Getting along with others is not an important matter. ☐

3 Many people have been to Mars. ☐

4 NASA wants to send people to Mars. ☐

organization 조직, 단체
mission 임무
get along with ~와 잘 지내다
adapt 적응하다
environment 환경, 주위의 상황
apply 지원하다
include 포함하다
following 다음에 나오는
chance 기회
lifetime 일생
miss out 놓치다
although (비록) ~이긴 하지만

The big question is, "Can people live on Mars?" Many scientists believe so for several reasons. First, they think that there is water on Mars. This is great because water is necessary for all life. Second, Mars has hard land to build houses and buildings on. Third, the length of day and night on Mars is similar to that on Earth. In addition, Mars also has four seasons. So, people can lead similar lives. Lastly, Mars is not very far. It is the second closest planet to Earth.

그렇게(부사) / 명사절 접속사(+완전한 문장) / 이유를 나타내는 접속사 / to부정사의 형용사적 용법(hard land 수식) / = the length of day and night / 게다가 / 마지막으로 / = Mars / the+서수(second)+최상급: 두 번째로 가까운 행성

Mars, however, has some differences from Earth. First, Mars is about half the size of Earth. It is the second smallest planet in the solar system. Second, a year on Mars is about twice as long as a year on Earth. Third, Mars is much colder than Earth. On average, it is about –60°C on Mars. This is because Mars is farther away from the Sun than Earth.

접속부사 / 대략(전치사) / ~의 절반의 크기 / 배수사+as+형용사 원급+as: ~배 만큼 …한 / 훨씬(비교급 강조부사) / 평균적으로 / 비인칭 주어(날짜, 날씨, 거리, 요일, 명암, 온도 등을 나타낼 때 씀) / 더 멀리(far의 비교급)

Although no one can answer the big question right now, it is exciting to imagine this new world. Who knows? You could be the first Korean on Mars!

= Can people live on Mars? / 가주어 / 진주어 / 조동사 can보다 상대적으로 약한 가능성을 나타냄

several 몇몇의
necessary 필요한, 없어서는 안 될
length 길이, 기간
similar 비슷한
in addition 게다가
lead 생활을 하다, 지내다
half 절반
solar system 태양계
twice 두 배
on average 평균적으로
exciting 신이 나는

확인문제

● 다음 문장이 본문의 내용과 일치하면 T, 일치하지 않으면 F를 쓰시오.

1 Many scientists think that it is possible for people to live on Mars. ☐

2 It is hard to say that there is water on Mars. ☐

3 Mars has fewer seasons as Earth has. ☐

4 Earth is about two times bigger than Mars. ☐

5 Being farther away from the Sun makes Mars colder than Earth. ☐

● 우리말을 참고하여 빈칸에 알맞은 말을 쓰시오.

1 Live _____ MARS!

2 Do you want _____ _____ _____ another planet?

3 The Korea Space Organization (KSO) is _____ _____ _____ _____ _____ to MARS!

4 Our mission is _____ _____ a city _____ Mars.

5 We are looking for someone…

_____ is _____ .

_____ is _____ and _____ .

_____ can _____ _____ _____ others.

_____ can _____ _____ a new environment quickly.

6 _____ _____ , send us a short video.

7 The video _____ _____ the answers _____ the following questions:

8 1. Why do you _____ _____ _____ to Mars?

2. Do you have _____ _____ _____ _____ humor?

3. Why are you the perfect person _____ _____ _____ ?

9 This is _____ _____ _____ a lifetime, so don't _____ out!

10 Mars, _____ _____ _____ ?

11 _____ there are _____ _____ and _____ about Mars, no one has been there _____ .

12 These days, scientists are _____ _____ Mars _____ a new home.

13 _____ _____ , NASA and some companies _____ _____ _____ _____ people there right now.

1 화성에서 살아요!

2 다른 행성에서 살고 싶은가요?

3 한국 우주 기구(KSO)는 화성에 갈 사람들을 찾고 있습니다!

4 우리의 임무는 화성에 도시를 세우는 것입니다.

5 우리는 다음과 같은 사람을 찾고 있습니다.
건강한 사람.
창의적이고 호기심이 많은 사람.
다른 사람들과 잘 지낼 수 있는 사람.
새로운 환경에 빨리 적응할 수 있는 사람.

6 지원하려면 우리에게 짧은 동영상을 보내세요.

7 동영상은 다음의 질문에 관한 답을 포함해야 합니다.

8 1. 당신은 왜 화성에 가고 싶은가요?

2. 당신은 유머 감각이 있나요?

3. 왜 당신이 이 임무에 적합한 사람인가요?

9 이것은 일생에 단 한 번뿐인 기회이므로 놓치지 마세요!

10 화성, 제 2의 지구?

11 화성에 관한 많은 책과 영화가 있긴 하지만, 아직 화성에 가 본 사람은 아무도 없다.

12 요즘, 과학자들은 화성을 새로운 거주지로 보고 있다.

13 사실, NASA와 몇몇 회사들은 그곳에 사람들을 보내기 위해 바로 지금도 노력하고 있다.

14 The big question is, "_____ _____ _____ _____ Mars?"

15 Many scientists _____ _____ for several reasons.

16 First, they think _____ there is _____ on Mars.

17 This is great _____ water is _____ _____ all life.

18 Second, Mars has _____ _____ _____ _____ houses and buildings _____.

19 Third, the length of day and night on Mars _____ _____ _____ that on Earth.

20 _____ _____, Mars also _____ _____ _____ _____.

21 So, people can _____ _____ _____.

22 Lastly, Mars is not _____ _____.

23 It is _____ _____ _____ planet to Earth.

24 Mars, _____, has _____ _____ _____ Earth.

25 First, Mars is _____ _____ the size of Earth.

26 It is _____ _____ _____ planet in the _____ system.

27 Second, a year on Mars is _____ _____ _____ _____ a year on Earth.

28 Third, Mars is _____ _____ than Earth.

29 _____ _____, it is about −60℃ on Mars.

30 This is _____ Mars is _____ _____ from the Sun than Earth.

31 _____ no one can _____ the big question right now, it is _____ _____ _____ this new world.

32 Who knows? You could be _____ _____ _____ _____ Mars!

14 중요한 질문은 "화성에서 사람 들어 살 수 있는가?"이다.

15 많은 과학자들은 몇몇 이유로 그렇게 믿고 있다.

16 첫째, 그들은 화성에 물이 있다 고 생각한다.

17 물은 모든 생명체에 필수적이기 때문에 이것은 중요하다.

18 둘째, 화성은 집과 건물을 지을 수 있는 단단한 땅을 가지고 있 다.

19 셋째, 화성의 낮과 밤의 길이는 지구의 낮과 밤의 길이와 비슷 하다.

20 게다가, 화성은 사계절도 있다.

21 그래서 사람들이 비슷한 생활을 할 수 있다.

22 마지막으로, 화성은 그렇게 멀 지 않다.

23 화성은 지구에서 두 번째로 가 까운 행성이다.

24 그러나 화성은 지구와 다른 점 이 몇 개 있다.

25 첫째, 화성은 지구의 약 절반 크 기이다.

26 화성은 태양계에서 두 번째로 작은 행성이다.

27 둘째, 화성에서의 일 년은 지구 에서의 일 년보다 약 두 배 길다.

28 셋째, 화성은 지구보다 훨씬 더 춥다.

29 평균적으로, 화성의 기온은 약 섭씨 영하 60도이다.

30 이것은 화성이 지구보다 태양에 서 더 멀리 떨어져 있기 때문이 다.

31 비록 누구도 그 중요한 질문에 지금 당장 답할 수는 없지만, 이 새로운 세상을 상상하는 것은 신이 난다.

32 누가 알겠는가? 당신이 화성에 발을 디디는 첫 번째 한국인이 될 수도 있다!

● 우리말을 참고하여 본문을 영작하시오.

1 화성에서 살아요!

➡ _____

2 다른 행성에서 살고 싶은가요?

➡ _____

3 한국 우주 기구(KSO)는 화성에 갈 사람들을 찾고 있습니다!

➡ _____

4 우리의 임무는 화성에 도시를 세우는 것입니다.

➡ _____

5 우리는 다음과 같은 사람을 찾고 있습니다.
건강한 사람. 창의적이고 호기심이 많은 사람. 다른 사람들과 잘 지낼 수 있는 사람.
새로운 환경에 빨리 적응할 수 있는 사람.

➡ _____

_____

6 지원하려면 우리에게 짧은 동영상을 보내세요.

➡ _____

7 동영상은 다음의 질문에 관한 답을 포함해야 합니다.

➡ _____

8 1. 당신은 왜 화성에 가고 싶은가요?

2. 당신은 유머 감각이 있나요?

3. 왜 당신이 이 임무에 적합한 사람인가요?

➡ 1. _____

2. _____

3. _____

9 이것은 일생에 단 한 번뿐인 기회이므로 놓치지 마세요!

➡ _____

10 화성, 제 2의 지구?

➡ _____

11 화성에 관한 많은 책과 영화가 있긴 하지만, 아직 화성에 가 본 사람은 아무도 없다.

➡ _____

12 요즘, 과학자들은 화성을 새로운 거주지로 보고 있다.

➡ _____

13 사실, NASA와 몇몇 회사들은 그곳에 사람들을 보내기 위해 바로 지금도 노력하고 있다.

➡ _____

14 중요한 질문은 "화성에서 사람들이 살 수 있는가?"이다.
➡ _____

15 많은 과학자들은 몇몇 이유로 그렇게 믿고 있다.
➡ _____

16 첫째, 그들은 화성에 물이 있다고 생각한다.
➡ _____

17 물은 모든 생명체에 필수적이기 때문에 이것은 중요하다.
➡ _____

18 둘째, 화성은 집과 건물을 지을 수 있는 단단한 땅을 가지고 있다.
➡ _____

19 셋째, 화성의 낮과 밤의 길이는 지구의 낮과 밤의 길이와 비슷하다.
➡ _____

20 게다가, 화성은 사계절도 있다.
➡ _____

21 그래서 사람들이 비슷한 생활을 할 수 있다.
➡ _____

22 마지막으로, 화성은 그렇게 멀지 않다.
➡ _____

23 화성은 지구에서 두 번째로 가까운 행성이다.
➡ _____

24 그러나 화성은 지구와 다른 점이 몇 개 있다.
➡ _____

25 첫째, 화성은 지구의 약 절반 크기이다.
➡ _____

26 화성은 태양계에서 두 번째로 작은 행성이다.
➡ _____

27 둘째, 화성에서의 일 년은 지구에서의 일 년보다 약 두 배 길다.
➡ _____

28 셋째, 화성은 지구보다 훨씬 더 춥다.
➡ _____

29 평균적으로, 화성의 기온은 약 섭씨 영하 60도이다.
➡ _____

30 이것은 화성이 지구보다 태양에서 더 멀리 떨어져 있기 때문이다.
➡ _____

31 비록 누구도 그 중요한 질문에 지금 당장 답할 수는 없지만, 이 새로운 세상을 상상하는 것은 신이 난다.
➡ _____

32 누가 알겠는가? 당신이 화성에 발을 디디는 첫 번째 한국인이 될 수도 있다!
➡ _____

[01~03] 다음 글을 읽고 물음에 답하시오.

Live on MARS!

Do you want to live ___(A)___ another planet?

The Korea Space Organization (KSO) is looking ___(B)___ people to go to MARS! Our mission is to build a city ___(C)___ Mars.

We are looking for someone...

who is healthy.

who is creative and curious.

who can get along with others.

who can adapt to a new environment quickly.

01 빈칸 (A)와 (C)에 공통으로 들어갈 말은?

① at   ② by   ③ of

④ to   ⑤ on

02 다음 중 빈칸 (B)에 들어갈 말과 같은 말이 들어가는 것은?

① What brought _____ the change?

② James came back to care _____ the baby.

③ Can you please turn _____ the light?

④ I will pick you _____ at three.

⑤ Put _____ your coat. It's still cold.

03 다음 중 KSO에서 찾고 있는 사람과 가장 거리가 먼 사람은?

① Minsu is perfectly healthy.

② Jimmy is interested in many things.

③ Kelly makes friends easily wherever she goes.

④ Sheldon has hard time adjusting to a new environment.

⑤ Penny is inventive and exercises regularly.

[04~05] 다음 글을 읽고 물음에 답하시오.

To apply, send us a short video. The video must include the answers to the following questions:

1. Why do you want to go to Mars?

2. Do you have a good sense of humor?

3. Why are you the perfect person for this mission?

This is a chance of a lifetime, so (A)don't miss out!

04 다음 중 위 글을 읽고 답할 수 없는 질문은?

① What do we need to send to apply?

② How many questions do we need to answer?

③ What must be included in the video?

④ Where should we send the video?

⑤ How many videos should we send?

05 빈칸에 알맞은 말을 써서 글쓴이가 밑줄 친 (A)와 같이 말한 이유를 서술하시오.

➡ It's because _____.

[06~09] 다음 글을 읽고 물음에 답하시오.

Mars, the Second Earth?

Although there are many books and movies about Mars, no one has been there yet. ① These days, scientists are looking at Mars as a new home. ② In fact, NASA and some companies are trying to send people there right now. ③ Many scientists believe so for ___(A)___ reasons. ④ First, they think that there is water on Mars. ⑤ This is great because water is necessary for all life.

06 다음 중 빈칸 (A)에 들어갈 말로 적절하지 <u>않은</u> 것은?

① several ② a few
③ a number of ④ some
⑤ a great deal of

07 ①~⑤ 중 주어진 문장이 들어가기에 가장 적절한 곳은?

> The big question is, "Can people live on Mars?"

① ② ③ ④ ⑤

08 다음 중 위 글의 내용과 일치하지 <u>않는</u> 것은?

① There is no one who has been to Mars.
② We can easily find books and movies about Mars.
③ All living things need water to live.
④ Scientists believe that there is water on Mars.
⑤ NASA thinks that it is impossible to send people to Mars.

서답형

09 According to the passage, what is essential for all life? Answer the question in English with a full sentence.

➡ _____

[10~15] 다음 글을 읽고 물음에 답하시오.

Second, Mars has hard land to build houses and buildings ___(A)___. Third, the length of day and night on Mars is similar to (B)<u>that</u> on Earth. In addition, Mars also has four seasons. So, people can lead similar lives. Lastly, Mars is not very far. It is the second closest planet to Earth. Mars, however, has some differences from Earth.

10 다음 중 빈칸 (A)에 들어갈 말로 가장 적절한 것은?

① at ② on ③ by
④ in ⑤ to

서답형

11 밑줄 친 (B)가 가리키는 것을 위 글에서 찾아 쓰시오.

➡ _____

12 다음 중 위 글에 이어질 내용으로 가장 적절한 것은?

① the similarity between Earth and Mars
② how to build houses on Mars
③ merits of living on Mars
④ differences between Mars and Earth
⑤ difficulties of living on another planet

13 According to the passage, which is NOT true about Mars?

① It has hard land.
② It has four seasons.
③ It is not very far from Earth.
④ The length of day and night on Mars is similar to that on Earth.
⑤ It is the closest planet to Earth.

서답형

14 Write the reason why it is possible that people can lead similar lives on Mars. Use the phrase "It's because."

➡ _____

_____

서답형

15 How close is Mars to Earth? Answer the question in English.

➡ _____

[16~20] 다음 글을 읽고 물음에 답하시오.

Mars, however, has some differences (A)[from / to] Earth. First, Mars is about half the size of Earth. It is the second smallest planet (B)[on / in] the solar system. Second, a year on Mars is about twice as long as a year on Earth. Third, Mars is much colder than Earth. On average, it is about −60℃ on Mars. ⓐ This is because Mars is farther away from the Sun than Earth.

(C)[Because / Although] no one can answer the big question right now, ⓑit is exciting to imagine ⓒthis new world. Who knows? You could be the first Korean on Mars!

16 (A)~(C)에서 어법상 옳은 것끼리 바르게 짝지은 것은?

① from – on – Because
② to – in – Although
③ from – on – Although
④ to – on – Because
⑤ from – in – Although

서답형

17 밑줄 친 ⓐ가 의미하는 것을 우리말로 쓰시오.

➡ _____

18 다음 중 밑줄 친 ⓑ와 쓰임이 같은 것은?

① It is getting hotter and hotter.
② It is five kilometers from here to the station.
③ It looks like rain.
④ It is difficult to get there on time.
⑤ It will be soon Thanksgiving.

서답형

19 밑줄 친 ⓒ가 가리키는 것을 위 글에서 찾아 쓰시오.

➡ _____

20 다음 중 위 글을 읽고 답할 수 없는 질문은?

① How many differences are there between Earth and Mars?
② How big is Mars?
③ How cold is Mars?
④ What is the average temperature of Earth?
⑤ Which is farther away from the Sun, Earth or Mars?

[21~23] 다음 글을 읽고 물음에 답하시오.

Do you want to live on another planet? The Korea Space Organization (KSO) is looking for people to go to MARS! Our mission is __(A)__ a city on Mars.

We are looking for someone...

who is healthy.

who is creative and curious.

who can get along with others.

who can adapt to a new environment quickly.

To apply, send us a short video. The video must include the answers to the following questions:

1. Why do you want to go to Mars?
2. Do you have a good sense of humor?
3. Why are you the perfect person for this mission?

This is a chance of a lifetime, so don't miss out!

서답형

21 동사 build를 어법에 맞게 빈칸 (A)에 쓰시오.

서답형 ➡ _____

22 다음과 같이 풀이되는 단어를 위 글에서 찾아 쓰시오.

a large, round object in space that moves around a star

➡ _____

23 다음 중 위 글의 내용과 일치하지 <u>않는</u> 것은?

① KSO is looking for someone creative.
② KSO needs people who can get used to a new environment quickly.
③ Making a short video is necessary for you to apply.
④ You should answer some questions at the interview.
⑤ KSO needs someone who has curiosity.

[24~30] 다음 글을 읽고 물음에 답하시오.

Although there are many books and movies about Mars, no one has been there yet. These days, scientists are looking at Mars ①<u>as</u> a new home. In fact, NASA and some companies are trying ②<u>to send</u> people there right now.

The big question is, "Can people live on Mars?" Many scientists believe so ③<u>for</u> several reasons. First, they think (A)<u>that</u> there is water on Mars. This is great ④<u>because</u> water is necessary for all life. Second, Mars has hard land to build houses and buildings on. Third, the length of day and night on Mars is similar to ⑤<u>those</u> on Earth. (B) , Mars also has four seasons.

24 다음 중 밑줄 친 (A)와 쓰임이 <u>다른</u> 하나는?

① The idea <u>that</u> Tom can swim that far is hard to accept.
② Danny suggests <u>that</u> we do exercise regularly.
③ He is the man <u>that</u> I have met at a party before.
④ It is not true <u>that</u> Kelly cheated on the exam.
⑤ Jason told me <u>that</u> he was not going to attend the class meeting.

25 다음 중 빈칸 (B)에 들어갈 말로 가장 적절한 것은?

① Therefore ② Besides
③ However ④ On the other hand
⑤ For example

서답형
26 What are NASA and some companies trying to do? Answer in English. Use the word 'to.'

➡ _____

_____

27 다음 중 위 글의 제목으로 가장 적절한 것은?

① Build a New House
② Mars, the Second Earth?
③ Where Do You Want to Live?
④ What Scientists Think about Earth
⑤ Mars, a New Resource for Water

서답형
28 위 글의 내용에 맞게 빈칸에 알맞은 말을 쓰시오.

There are several reasons why scientists believe that _____.

➡ _____

29 ①~⑤ 중 어법상 <u>어색한</u> 것은?

① ② ③ ④ ⑤

30 다음 중 위 글에서 반의어를 찾을 수 <u>없는</u> 것은?

① old ② die ③ vital
④ soft ⑤ different

[01~05] 다음 글을 읽고 물음에 답하시오.

Live on MARS!

Do you want to live on another planet?

The Korea Space Organization (KSO) is looking for people to go to MARS! Our mission is to build a city on Mars.

We are looking for someone...

who is healthy.

who is creative and curious.

who can get along with others.

who can adapt to a new environment quickly.

To apply, send us a short video. The video must include the answers to the following questions:

1. Why do you want to go to Mars?

2. Do you have a good sense of humor?

3. Why are you the perfect person for (A) this mission?

This is (B)일생에 단 한번뿐인 기회, so don't miss out!

01 밑줄 친 (A)가 의미하는 것을 우리말로 쓰시오.

➡ _____

02 밑줄 친 우리말 (B)를 영어로 쓰시오.

➡ _____

03 다음은 화성으로 가려는 사람의 지원서이다. 빈칸에 알맞은 말을 위 글에서 찾아 쓰시오.

> I am as _____ as an athlete. Also, I
> _____, so I always
> make people laugh.

➡ _____

04 위 글의 내용에 맞게 빈칸에 알맞은 말을 쓰시오.

> You should send _____ _____
> _____ _____ _____ in order to
> apply.

05 According to the passage, what must the video contain? Answer in English with a full sentence. Use the word 'some.'

➡ _____

[06~10] 다음 글을 읽고 물음에 답하시오.

Although there are many books and movies about Mars, no one has been there yet. These days, scientists are looking at Mars as a new home. In fact, NASA and some companies are trying to send people there right now.

The big question is, "Can people live on Mars?" Many scientists believe so for several reasons. First, they think that there is water on Mars. (A)This is great because water is necessary for all life. Second, Mars has hard land to build houses and buildings on. Third, the length of day and night on Mars is similar to that on Earth. In addition, Mars also has four seasons. So, people can lead similar lives. Lastly, Mars is not very far. It is the second closest planet to Earth.

06 밑줄 친 (A)가 가리키는 것을 위 글에서 찾아 쓰시오.

➡ _____

07 빈칸에 알맞은 말을 위 글에서 찾아 세 단어로 쓰시오.

> Life on Mars will _____ life on Earth.

08 위 글의 내용에 맞게 빈칸에 알맞은 말을 아홉 단어로 쓰시오.

> No one has been to Mars yet _____
>
> _____ .

➡ _____

09 위 글의 내용에 맞게 빈칸에 알맞은 말을 여섯 단어로 쓰시오.

> It is possible to _____
> because it has hard land.

➡ _____

10 How many seasons does Mars have? Answer in English with a full sentence.

➡ _____

[11~14] 다음 글을 읽고 물음에 답하시오.

Mars, however, has _____(A)_____ from Earth. First, Mars is about half the size of Earth. It is the second smallest planet in the solar system. Second, a year on Mars is about twice as long as _____(B)_____. Third, Mars is much colder than Earth. On average, it is about −60℃ on Mars. This is because Mars is farther away from the Sun than Earth.

Although no one can answer the big question right now, it is exciting to imagine this new world. Who knows? You could be the first Korean on Mars!

11 빈칸 (A)에 알맞은 말을 두 단어로 쓰시오.

➡ _____

12 빈칸 (B)에 알맞은 말을 어법에 맞게 쓰시오.

➡ _____

13 Why is Mars much colder than Earth? Answer in English with a full sentence.

➡ _____

14 위 글의 내용에 맞게 빈칸에 알맞은 말을 쓰시오.

> Mars is _____ to the Sun as Earth.

[15~17] 다음 글을 읽고 물음에 답하시오.

My name is Suji Lee from Korea. I'm 15 years old. I want to go to Mars because I've been curious about space. I'm friendly and I enjoy _____(A)_____. I'm good at taking photos. I'm the perfect person for this mission because I can adapt to a new environment quickly. Although I'm young, I can communicate well with others. (B)저에게 화성에서 살 기회를 주세요!

15 make friends를 어법에 맞게 빈칸 (A)에 쓰시오.

➡ _____

16 밑줄 친 우리말 (B)를 영어로 쓰시오.

➡ _____

17 Write the reason why she is the perfect person for the mission she wants to participate in.

➡ _____

구석구석

Real Life Talk - Step 2

A: Do you know what this is?
    간접의문문(의문사+주어+동사: 어순 주의)

B: No, I don't. What is it?

A: It's a Clean Straw.

B: A Clean Straw? What is it for?
        용도를 묻는 표현

A: It cleans water while you drink.
        (~ 동안에)+주어+동사. *cf.* during (~ 동안에)+명사(구)

B: Wow, that's great!

A: 너는 이것이 무엇인지 아
   니?

B: 아니. 그건 뭐니?

A: Clean Straw야.

B: Clean Straw? 용도가
   뭐니?

A: 네가 물을 마시는 동안 물
   을 깨끗이 해주는 거야.

B: 와, 멋지다!

Think and Write

My name is Suji Lee from Korea. I'm 15 years old. I want to go to Mars
                                                      to부정사를 목적어로 취하는 동사

because I've been curious about space. I'm friendly and I enjoy making
          현재완료(계속 용법)   동명사를 목적어로 취하는 동사

friends. I'm good at taking photos. I'm the perfect person for this mission
                     동명사: 전치사 at의 목적어

because I can adapt to a new environment quickly. Although I'm young, I can
              ~에 적응하다   양보의 부사절을 이끄는 접속사

communicate well with others. Give me the chance to live on Mars!
                        other people   to부정사의 형용사적 용법

구문해설 • **from:** ~ 출신인   • **Mars:** 화성   • **curious:** 호기심 있는   • **be good at:** ~을 잘하다
       • **perfect:** 완벽한   • **mission:** 임무   • **communicate:** 의사소통하다   • **chance:** 기회

제 이름은 수지이고 한국 출
신입니다. 저는 15살입니다.
저는 쭉 우주에 호기심을 가
져왔기 때문에 화성에 가고
싶습니다. 저는 상냥하고 친
구들을 사귀는 것을 좋아합니
다. 저는 사진을 잘 찍습니
다. 저는 새로운 환경에 빨리 적
응할 수 있기 때문에 이 임무
에 적합한 사람입니다. 비록
저는 어리지만, 다른 사람들
과 의사소통을 잘할 수 있습
니다. 저에게 화성에서 살 기
회를 주세요!

Project

Neptune

It has 14 moons. It's a very cold planet. It's named after the god of the sea. It's
Neptune   수동태   바다의 신

the farthest planet from the Sun in the solar system.
far의 최상급: 가장 먼

구문해설 • **Neptune:** 해왕성   • **moon:** 위성, 달   • **be named after:** ~의 이름을 따다
       • **the solar system:** 태양계

해왕성

그것은 14개의 위성을 가지고
있다. 그곳은 아주 추운 행성
이다. 그것은 바다의 신의 이
름을 딴 것이다. 그것은 태양
계에서 태양과 가장 멀리 떨
어져 있다.

영역별 핵심문제

01 다음 주어진 단어 중 나머지 넷과 성격이 <u>다른</u> 것은?

① friendly   ② brave

③ curious   ④ outgoing

⑤ pretty

02 다음 영영풀이가 가리키는 것을 고르시오.

> to remove the skin from a fruit, vegetable, etc.

① peel   ② slice

③ cut   ④ boil

⑤ reduce

03 다음 빈칸에 들어갈 알맞은 말은?

> _____ we ran to the bus stop, we missed the bus.

① As   ② If   ③ Since

④ Because   ⑤ Although

04 다음 중 밑줄 친 부분의 뜻풀이가 바르지 <u>않은</u> 것은?

① I will <u>peel</u> an apple for my little sister. 껍질을 벗기다

② <u>Several</u> people came to the meeting. 몇몇의

③ <u>Mars</u> is a planet in the solar system. 목성

④ We collected dry <u>sticks</u> for the campfire. 나뭇가지

⑤ She has an important <u>mission</u>. 임무

05 다음 우리말에 맞게 빈칸에 알맞은 말을 쓰시오.

(1) 나는 그녀에 대한 나의 생각을 말할 만큼 충분히 용감하지 않았다.

➡ I wasn't _____ enough to tell her what I thought of her.

(2) 우리는 오로지 이메일로 의사소통한다.

➡ We _____ only by email.

(3) 그는 빵 위에 버터를 발랐다.

➡ He _____ butter on bread.

06 다음 주어진 문장의 밑줄 친 lead[led]와 같은 의미로 쓰인 것은?

> I want to <u>lead</u> a happy life.

① This road will <u>lead</u> you to the library.

② I tried to <u>lead</u> the discussion.

③ If I could be born again, I would like to <u>lead</u> a luxury life.

④ Eating too much sugar can <u>lead</u> to health problems.

⑤ My teacher <u>led</u> us out into the grounds.

07 다음 문장에 공통으로 들어갈 말을 고르시오.

> • I visited the factory that _____s parts for the airplanes.
> • They will _____ a TV series about Korean history.
> • Creativity is needed to _____ artworks.

① promise   ② produce

③ spread   ④ build

⑤ apply

Conversation

[08~10] 다음 대화를 읽고 물음에 답하시오.

Ms. Lee: Hello, class! (A)Jisu is today's speaker for show and tell. Jisu?

Jisu: Hi, class! (B)Do you know who is this man? His name is Alexander Graham Bell. Bell was an inventor. (C)He was interested in sound. What did he invent? Yes, the telephone! (D)His mother and wife were deaf. (E)So he also made some inventions for deaf people and opened a school for them.

08 위 대화에서 다음 주어진 영영풀이가 가리키는 말을 찾아 쓰시오.

not able to hear anything

➡ _____

09 위 대화의 (A)~(E) 중 어법상 어색한 문장을 고른 후 바르게 고쳐 쓰시오.

➡ _____

10 위 대화의 내용과 일치하지 <u>않는</u> 것은?

① 지수는 Alexander Graham Bell에 대해 발표하였다.

② Alexander Graham Bell은 소리에 관심이 있었다.

③ Alexander Graham Bell은 청각 장애인을 위해 전화기를 발명하였다.

④ Alexander Graham Bell의 어머니와 아내는 청각 장애가 있었다.

⑤ Alexander Graham Bell은 청각 장애인들을 위한 학교를 열었다.

[11~12] 다음 대화를 읽고 물음에 답하시오.

Brian: (A)Do you know what this is?

Amy: Um, (B)it looks a glue stick.

Brian: No, it's a butter stick.

Amy: Oh, is there butter in it?

Brian: Yes, you can spread butter on the bread with it.

11 위 대화의 밑줄 친 (A)와 바꾸어 쓸 수 있는 것은?

① Have you ever heard about this?

② Guess what this is.

③ Do you want to know about this?

④ How can I get to know this?

⑤ Can you explain this?

12 위 대화의 밑줄 친 (B)를 어법에 맞게 고쳐 쓰시오.

➡ _____

[13~14] 다음 대화를 읽고 물음에 답하시오.

Judy: How was your weekend, Hojin?

Hojin: (A) I went to a science exhibition with my brother.

Judy: (B) Did you? I heard there were so many interesting things.

Hojin: (C) Yes. Look at this. I bought it there. Do you know what it is?

Judy: (D) Well, I'm not sure. What is it?

Hojin: (E) It's a VR headset.

Judy: A VR headset? What is it for?

Hojin: If you wear it, you can experience another world.

Judy: Sounds cool. May I try it?

Hojin: Sure. Here you go.

13 위 대화의 (A)~(E) 중 다음 주어진 문장이 들어가기에 적절한 곳은?

> I had a great time.

① (A) ② (B) ③ (C) ④ (D) ⑤ (E)

14 위 대화의 내용과 일치하지 <u>않는</u> 것은?

① Hojin은 주말에 남동생과 과학 전시회에 갔었다.
② Judy는 과학 전시회에는 흥미로운 것들이 굉장히 많다고 들었다.
③ Hojin은 VR 헤드셋을 과학 전시회에서 구매하였다.
④ VR 헤드셋을 쓰면 다른 세상을 경험할 수 있다.
⑤ Judy는 Hojin에게 VR 헤드셋의 용도를 설명하였다.

Grammar

15 주어진 단어를 활용하여 다음 우리말을 영어로 쓰시오.

> 비록 흐렸지만, 나는 선글라스를 썼다.
> (it / put on)

➡ _____

_____

16 다음 빈칸에 들어갈 말이 바르게 짝지어진 것은?

> • Christine couldn't get to sleep _____ there was a lot of noise.
> • Tom managed to get to sleep _____ the noise.

① when – although
② because – despite
③ as – even though
④ because of – even if
⑤ since – when

17 다음 우리말을 영어로 바르게 옮긴 것을 <u>모두</u> 고르시오.

> 그 시험은 내가 생각했던 것만큼 어렵지 않았어.

① The exam was not as difficult as I thought.
② The exam was as easy as I thought.
③ The exam was not as easy as I thought.
④ The exam was more difficult than I thought.
⑤ The exam was easier than I thought.

18 다음 중 밑줄 친 부분의 쓰임이 <u>잘못된</u> 것은?

① Kevin feels okay <u>although</u> he has a cold.
② Tony is in good shape <u>because</u> he gets a lot of exercise.
③ <u>Even though</u> he was busy, he answered all of my questions.
④ Angela doesn't speak French <u>because</u> she lived in Paris for years.
⑤ <u>Though</u> Jason is not rich, he always donates some money to the poor.

19 다음 중 주어진 문장과 같은 의미의 문장은?

> Susan used to have longer hair.

① Susan's hair is as long as it used to be.
② Susan's hair is not as short as it used to be.
③ Susan't hair is as short as it used to be.
④ Susan has longer hair than she used to have.
⑤ Susan's hair is not as long as it used to be.

20 다음 중 문맥상 어색한 문장은?

① Even though I told the truth, nobody believed me.
② Victoria is not as smart as you think.
③ I drive my car a lot because gas is so expensive.
④ Jackson has twice as many candies as I have.
⑤ We must be as kind to her as we can.

21 다음 빈칸에 들어갈 말로 가장 적절한 것은?

• I eat less meat than you do.
= I _____ you do.

① eat as much meat as
② don't eat meat like
③ eat as little meat as
④ don't eat as much meat as
⑤ eat as much meat like

22 다음 빈칸에 들어갈 말과 같은 말이 들어가는 것은?

Larry didn't understand the joke _____ he laughed anyway.

① Tom wasn't tired _____ he took enough rest.
② I didn't wake up _____ the phone rang many times.
③ Stop talking _____ someone wants to talk to you.
④ He has been busy _____ he came here.
⑤ Give him this note _____ you see him.

23 두 문장의 의미가 통하도록 빈칸에 알맞은 말을 쓰시오.

• You watch TV more than me.
= I don't _____ you.

➡ _____

24 지시에 맞게 다음 우리말을 영어로 쓰시오.

테니스는 축구만큼 인기 있지 않지만, 나는 축구보다 테니스를 더 좋아한다.
(동등 비교, 비교급을 한 번씩 사용할 것)

➡ _____
_____

Reading

[25~29] 다음 글을 읽고 물음에 답하시오.

Mars, the Second Earth?

____(A)____ there are many books and movies about Mars, no one (a)has been there yet. These days, scientists are looking at Mars as a new home. In fact, NASA and some companies are trying to send people there right now.

The big question is, "Can people live on Mars?" Many scientists believe so for several reasons. First, (b)they think that there is water on Mars. This is great because water is necessary for all life. Second, Mars has hard land to build houses and buildings on. Third, the length of day and night on Mars is similar to that on Earth. In addition, Mars also has four seasons. ____(B)____, people can lead similar lives. Lastly, Mars is not very far. It is the second closest planet to Earth.

25 빈칸 (A)에 들어갈 말로 적절한 것을 <u>모두</u> 고르시오.

① Even though ② Because
③ Although ④ Since
⑤ As

26 다음 중 (B)에 들어갈 말로 적절한 것은?

① However ② Therefore
③ For example ④ In addition
⑤ On the contrary

27 다음 중 밑줄 친 (a)와 쓰임이 같은 것은?

① Have you ever <u>visited</u> the museum?
② They <u>have just arrived</u> at the airport.
③ David <u>has gone</u> to the theater.
④ We <u>have known</u> each other for a year.
⑤ She <u>hasn't finished</u> her homework yet.

28 다음 중 위 글을 읽고 답할 수 <u>없는</u> 것은?

① Who considers Mars as a new home?
② Why do scientists believe people can live on Mars?
③ What is viewed as a new home by scientists?
④ How long does it take to get to Mars?
⑤ What makes it possible to build houses and buildings on Mars?

29 밑줄 친 (b)가 가리키는 것을 위 글에서 찾아 쓰시오.

➡ _____

[30~33] 다음 글을 읽고 물음에 답하시오.

Mars, however, has some differences from Earth. First, ⓐMars is about half the size of Earth. It is the second smallest planet in the solar system. Second, a year on Mars is about twice as long as a year on Earth. Third, Mars is (A)[much / very] colder than Earth. On average, it is about –60℃ on Mars. (B)[This is because / This is why] Mars is farther away from the Sun than Earth.

Although no one can answer the big question right now, it is (C)[exciting / excited] ⓑto imagine this new world. Who knows? You could be the first Korean on Mars!

30 위 글의 밑줄 친 ⓐ를 참고하여 다음 대화에 알맞은 말을 네 단어로 쓰시오.

A: Do you know that Earth is _____ Mars?
B: Really? I didn't know Mars is that small.

➡ _____

31 (A)~(C)에서 어법상 옳은 것끼리 바르게 묶은 것은?

① much – This is because – exciting
② much – This is why – excited
③ much – This is because – excited
④ very – This is why – exciting
⑤ very – This is because – exciting

32 다음 중 밑줄 친 ⓑ와 쓰임이 <u>다른</u> 하나는?

① <u>To sing</u> a song is my hobby.
② Is it possible <u>to change</u> her mind?
③ Is there anything <u>to ask</u>?
④ It is always fun <u>to talk</u> with her.
⑤ <u>To be</u> angry with them is not helpful.

33 위 글의 내용에 맞게 빈칸에 알맞은 말을 쓰시오.

Mercury is the smallest planet in the solar system. So, Mars is _____ _____ _____ _____ Mercury.

출제율 90%

01 다음 대화의 (A)~(C)에 들어갈 말로 적절한 것은?

> Irene: Jane, (A)[look / to look] at this. It's a meok.
>
> Jane: I (B)[was / have] never seen it before. What is it for?
>
> Irene: It's for making ink.
>
> Jane: Oh, really? That's (C)[interesting / interested].

	(A)	(B)	(C)
①	look	was	interesting
②	look	have	interesting
③	look	have	interested
④	to look	have	interested
⑤	to look	was	interested

출제율 95%

02 다음 대화가 자연스럽게 이어지도록 순서대로 배열하시오.

> (A) Yes, you can spread butter on the bread with it.
> (B) Um, it looks like a glue stick.
> (C) Do you know what this is?
> (D) Oh, is there butter in it?
> (E) No, it's a butter stick.

➡ _____

[03~05] 다음 대화를 읽고 물음에 답하시오.

Tom: Mom, look ⓐat these slippers. I made them in science class.

Mom: Why did you make slippers in science class?

Tom: They are not just for wearing.

Mom: Then, what are they ⓑfor?

Tom: You can put them ⓒoff and clean the floor.

Mom: Oh, so you will clean your room from now ⓓon?

Tom: Sure. Don't worry ⓔabout my room, Mom.

출제율 85%

03 위 대화의 밑줄 친 ⓐ~ⓔ 중 문맥상 어색한 것을 찾아 바르게 고치시오.

➡ _____

출제율 90%

04 What are the slippers Tom made for?

➡ _____
_____

출제율 100%

05 위 대화를 읽고 대답할 수 없는 것은?

① What did Tom do in science class?
② What are the slippers Tom made for?
③ What did Tom promise his mom to do?
④ What can Tom do by wearing slippers?
⑤ What did Tom use to make the slippers in science class?

[06~08] 다음 대화를 읽고 물음에 답하시오.

Ms. Lee: Hello, class! Jisu is today's speaker for show and tell. Jisu?

Jisu: Hi, class! Do you know who this man is? His name is Alexander Graham Bell. Bell was an ___(A)___. He was interested in sound. What did he invent? Yes, the telephone! His mother and wife were deaf. So he also made some inventions for deaf people and opened a school for them.

[10~11] 다음 대화를 읽고 물음에 답하시오.

06 위 대화의 빈칸 (A)에 다음 주어진 영영풀이가 가리키는 말을 쓰시오.

> a person who has invented something or whose job is inventing things

➡ _____

07 What did Alexander Graham Bell have an interest in?

➡ _____

08 What did Alexander Graham Bell do for deaf people?

➡ _____
_____

09 다음 짝지어진 대화가 어색한 것은?

① A: Do you know who she is?
　 B: Um, it looks like a glue stick.
② A: Do you know what it is?
　 B: No, I don't. What is it?
③ A: Do you know who he is?
　 B: Yes, I do. He is Albert Schweitzer.
④ A: Guess what it is.
　 B: I don't have any idea. Would you give me some hints?
⑤ A: Do you know about this man?
　 B: Sure. I have seen him before.

[10~11] 다음 대화를 읽고 물음에 답하시오.

A: Do you know what this is?
B: No, I don't. What is ⓐit?
A: It's a Soccket.
B: A Soccket? What is ⓑit for?
A: ⓒIt produces electricity when you play with ⓓit.
B: Wow, ⓔIt sounds great!

10 위 대화에서 소개된 Soccket의 용도를 우리말로 간략히 설명하시오.

➡ _____

11 위 대화의 밑줄 친 ⓐ~ⓔ 중 나머지 넷과 가리키는 대상이 다른 것은?

① ⓐ　　② ⓑ　　③ ⓒ　　④ ⓓ　　⑤ ⓔ

12 다음 중 빈칸에 들어갈 말로 가장 적절한 것은?

> I didn't get hurt _____ I fell down the stairs.

① because　　② unless
③ though　　④ as soon as
⑤ but

13 다음 중 어법상 바르지 않은 것은?

① I don't know as many people as you.
② Even though I mailed the letter a week ago, it has not arrived yet.
③ The building is not as high as I expected.
④ I didn't return his call although he called me several times.
⑤ Your backpack is three times as big as me.

14 두 문장의 의미가 통하도록 빈칸에 알맞은 말을 여섯 단어로 쓰시오.

> • We played better than them.
> = They _____ .

➡ _____

15 다음 우리말을 영어로 바르게 옮긴 것을 <u>모두</u> 고르시오. *출제율 90%*

> 사과는 배만큼 크지 않다.

① An apple is as big as a pear.
② A pear is not as big as an apple.
③ An apple is not bigger than a pear.
④ A pear is as small as an apple.
⑤ An apple is not as big as a pear.

16 다음 중 서로 의미가 같지 <u>않은</u> 것은? *출제율 95%*

① Despite the rain, we went to the zoo last week.
　= We went to the zoo although it rained last week.
② The river is two times longer than the Han River.
　= The river is two times as long as the Han River.
③ Although my grandmother is ninety years old, she is still young at heart.
　= My grandmother is still young at heart even though she is ninety years old.
④ The festival was more exciting than we thought.
　= The festival was as exciting as we thought.
⑤ Today is not as cold as yesterday.
　= Yesterday was colder than today.

17 주어진 어구를 활용하여 다음 우리말을 영어로 쓰시오. *출제율 95%*

> 그 빵은 어제만큼 촉촉하지 않더라도, 여전히 맛있다.
> (though / moist / it was / still)

➡ _____

_____

18 다음 빈칸에 알맞은 말을 쓰시오. *출제율 90%*

> Halla Mountain is 1950 meters high. Fuji Mountain is 3776 meters high. Fuji Mountain is almost _____ _____ as _____ as Halla Mountain.

[19~22] 다음 글을 읽고 물음에 답하시오.

> ___(A)___ there are many books and movies about Mars, no one has been there ①ago. These days, scientists are looking at Mars as a new home. In fact, NASA and some companies ② are trying to send people there right now. The big question is, "Can people live on Mars?" Many scientists believe so for several reasons. First, they think that ③there is water on Mars. This is great ④because water is necessary for all life. Second, Mars has hard land to build houses and buildings on. Third, the length of day and night on Mars ⑤is similar to that on Earth. In addition, Mars also has four seasons. So, people can lead similar lives.

19 다음 중 빈칸 (A)에 들어갈 말과 같은 말이 들어가는 것은? *출제율 95%*

① _____ you ask me a question, I will answer it.
② Stop bothering me _____ I am trying to study.
③ _____ I am broke, I don't need your help.
④ You will miss the bus _____ you wake up early.
⑤ It has been five years _____ you met me.

20 ①~⑤ 중 어법상 바르지 <u>않은</u> 것은? *출제율 100%*

①　　　　②　　　　③　　　　④　　　　⑤

21 다음 중 위 글의 내용과 일치하는 것은?

① It is hard to find books and movies about Mars.
② Many people have already been to Mars.
③ People keep contacting NASA to go to Mars.
④ It is difficult to build houses on Mars.
⑤ Many scientists think that people can live on Mars.

22 What is the fourth reason that scientists believe people can live on Mars? Answer in English with four words.

➡ _____

[23~26] 다음 글을 읽고 물음에 답하시오.

In addition, Mars also has four ①seasons. So, people can lead similar lives.

[A] It is the second smallest planet in ②the solar system. Second, a year on Mars is about twice as long as a year on Earth. Third, Mars is much colder than Earth.

[B] Lastly, Mars is not very far. It is the second closest planet to Earth. Mars, however, has some ③differences from Earth. First, Mars is about ④half the size of Earth.

[C] On ⑤average, it is about –60℃ on Mars. This is because Mars is farther away from the Sun than Earth.

Although no one can answer the big question right now, it is exciting to imagine this new world. Who knows? You could be the first Korean on Mars!

23 자연스러운 글이 되도록 [A]~[C]를 바르게 나열하시오.

➡ _____

24 밑줄 친 ①~⑤의 뜻풀이가 잘못된 것은?

① the main periods into which a year can be divided
② the sun and the planets that move around it
③ the way in which two things are not like each other
④ to cut something into pieces
⑤ the sum of the values in a set divided by their number

25 다음 우리말을 영어로 쓰시오.

화성은 내가 생각했던 것만큼 멀지 않다.

➡ _____

26 다음 중 위 글을 읽고 답할 수 없는 것은?

① Where can people lead similar lives?
② What is the smallest planet in the solar system?
③ How long is a year on Mars?
④ Why is Mars much colder than Earth?
⑤ How big is Earth compared with Mars?

[01~03] 다음 대화를 읽고 물음에 답하시오.

Judy: How was your weekend, Hojin?

Hojin: I had a great time. I went to a science exhibition with my brother.

Judy: Did you? I heard there were so many interesting things.

Hojin: Yes. Look at this. I bought it there. Do you know what it is?

Judy: Well, I'm not sure. What is it?

Hojin: It's a VR headset.

Judy: A VR headset? What is it for?

Hojin: If you wear it, you can experience another world.

Judy: Sounds cool. May I try it?

Hojin: Sure. Here you go.

01 With whom did Hojin go to the science exhibition?

➡ _____

02 What did Hojin buy at the science exhibition?

➡ _____

03 What is the VR headset for?

➡ _____

[04~05] 다음 대화를 읽고 물음에 답하시오.

Tom: Mom, look at these slippers. I made them in science class.

Mom: Why did you make slippers in science class?

Tom: They are not just for wearing.

Mom: Then, what are they for?

Tom: You can put them on and clean the floor.

Mom: Oh, so you will clean your room from now on?

Tom: Sure. Don't worry about my room, Mom.

04 In what class did Tom make slippers?

➡ _____

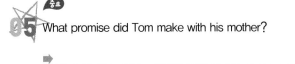

05 What promise did Tom make with his mother?

➡ _____

06 적절한 접속사를 사용하여 다음 대화의 빈칸에 알맞은 말을 쓰시오.

> A: You turned on the air conditioner. Is the room still hot?
>
> B: Yes. _____

➡ _____
_____

07 적절한 접속사를 이용하여 다음 두 문장을 하나의 문장으로 연결하시오.

> • Hannah invited Tom to her party. But he didn't come without saying a word.

➡ _____
_____

08 주어진 문장과 같은 의미의 문장을 동등 비교 표현을 이용하여 쓰시오.

> • Sally got up earlier than James.

➡ James _____ .

➡ Sally _____ .

09 다음 글을 읽고 지시에 맞게 빈칸에 알맞은 말을 쓰시오.

> Jason works very hard. He works 10 hours a day. Amelia works hard, but not that hard. She works 7 hours a day. Tom doesn't work very hard. He works only 5 hours a day.

(1) 동등 비교 표현을 이용하여

➡ Amelia _____ Jason.

(2) 비교급을 이용하여

➡ But she _____ Tom.

10 주어진 문장과 의미가 통하도록 빈칸에 알맞은 말을 8 단어로 쓰시오.

> • Health and happiness are more important than money.
> = Money _____.

➡ _____

[11~12] 다음 글을 읽고 물음에 답하시오.

> Mars, the Second Earth?
>
> Although ①there are many books and movies about Mars, no one has been there yet. These days, scientists are looking at Mars as a new home. ②In fact, NASA and some companies are trying to send people there right now.
>
> The big question is, "Can people live on Mars?" ③Many scientists believe so for several reasons. First, they think that there is water on Mars. This is great because water is necessary for all life. Second, ④Mars has hard land to build houses and buildings. Third, the length of day and night on Mars is similar to that on Earth. ⑤In addition, Mars also has four seasons.

11 ①~⑤ 중 어법상 틀린 문장을 찾아 바르게 고쳐 쓰시오.

_____

➡ _____

12 According to the passage, who thinks that there is water on Mars? Answer in English with a full sentence.

➡ _____

[13~14] 다음 글을 읽고 물음에 답하시오.

> Mars, however, has some differences from Earth. First, (A)화성은 지구의 약 절반 크기이다. It is the second smallest planet in the solar system. Second, a year on Mars is about two times longer than a year on Earth. Third, Mars is much colder than Earth. On average, it is about −60℃ on Mars. This is because Mars is farther away from the Sun than Earth.

13 밑줄 친 우리말 (A)를 주어진 말을 써서 영어로 쓰시오. (about, size)

➡ _____

14 위 글의 내용에 맞게 다음 글의 빈칸을 채우시오.

> I read about Mars today. Mars is not exactly the same as Earth. One of the most surprising differences is that a year on Mars is about _____ _____ _____ _____ a year on Earth.

01 다음 대화를 읽고 대화의 내용과 일치하도록 빈칸을 완성하시오.

> Tom: Mom, look at these slippers. I made them in science class.
>
> Mom: Why did you make slippers in science class?
>
> Tom: They are not just for wearing.
>
> Mom: Then, what are they for?
>
> Tom: You can put them on and clean the floor.
>
> Mom: Oh, so you will clean your room from now on?
>
> Tom: Sure. Don't worry about my room, Mom.

> Mon. Sep. 5th, 2019
>
> Today, I made special (A)_____ in science class. I came up with the idea to wipe the floor without any cloth. So, my slippers were designed not only for wearing but also for (B)_____. I promised my mother to (C)_____ myself.

02 다음 세 사람에 관한 이야기를 읽고 빈칸에 알맞은 말을 쓰시오. 괄호 안의 단어를 이용할 것.

> Jennifer: I am 25. I usually get up at 8. I don't have a car. I work at home.
>
> Michael: I am 27. I get up at 7:15. My car is gray. It takes 15 minutes to go to work.
>
> Christine: I am 27. I usually get up at 8. My car is black. It takes 45 minutes to go to work.

(1) Jennifer _____ Michael and Christine. (as)

(2) Jennifer and Christine _____ Michael. (as)

(3) Christine spends _____ Michael to go to work.

03 양보의 부사절 접속사를 활용하여 다음 문장을 하나의 문장으로 쓰시오.

> (1) The length of day and night on Mars is similar to that on Earth. A year on Mars is about twice as long as a year on Earth.
>
> (2) Mars has four seasons like Earth. Mars is much colder than Earth.
>
> (3) Mars has hard land to build houses and buildings on. It is really expensive to build them on Mars.

(1) _____

(2) _____

(3) _____

단원별 모의고사

01 다음 문장에 공통으로 들어갈 말을 고르시오.

> • Would you tell me the _____ for your absence?
> • Without any _____, Tom left for England.
> • We tried to _____ out the answers to the questions.

① promise   ② reason
③ difference   ④ way
⑤ find

02 다음 문장의 빈칸에 들어갈 말을 〈보기〉에서 골라 쓰시오. 필요하면 어형 변화를 할 것.

> ┤ 보기 ├
> inventor / deaf / planet / organization / slice

(1) Wash and _____ the tomatoes.
(2) Thomas Edison was a great _____.
(3) Tony is a leader of an international _____.
(4) He's _____ in his right ear. So you should speak up.
(5) Mercury is the smallest of all the _____.

03 다음 우리말에 맞게 빈칸에 알맞은 말을 쓰시오.

(1) Alice와 잘 지내는 것은 불가능하다.
➡ It's impossible to _____ Alice.

(2) 그는 훌륭한 유머 감각이 있다.
➡ He has a good _____.

(3) 그는 영어를 매우 잘한다. 게다가, 그는 또한 스페인어와 독일어도 한다.
➡ He speaks English very well. _____, he speaks Spanish and German, too.

04 다음 대화가 자연스럽게 이어지도록 순서대로 배열하시오.

> (A) Why did you make slippers in science class?
> (B) Then, what are they for?
> (C) They are not just for wearing.
> (D) You can put them on and clean the floor.
> (E) Mom, look at these slippers. I made them in science class.

➡ _____

05 다음 영어 뜻풀이에 해당하는 말은?

> the sun and the planets that move around it

① earth   ② sky
③ galaxy   ④ universe
⑤ solar system

[06~07] 다음 대화를 읽고 물음에 답하시오.

> Judy: How was your weekend, Hojin?
> Hojin: I had a great time. I went to a science exhibition with my brother.
> Judy: Did you? I heard there were so many interesting things.
> Hojin: Yes. Look at this. I bought it there. Do you know what it is?
> Judy: Well, I'm not sure. What is it?
> Hojin: It's a VR headset.
> Judy: A VR headset? _____(A)_____
> Hojin: (B)그것을 쓰면 다른 세상을 경험할 수 있어.
> Judy: Sounds cool. May I try it?
> Hojin: Sure. Here you go.

06 위 대화의 빈칸 (A)에 들어갈 수 있는 말을 <u>모두</u> 고르시오.

① What should I do?
② What is it for?
③ What can I do for you?
④ What is it used for?
⑤ What do you do?

07 위 대화의 밑줄 친 우리말 (B)를 <보기>에 주어진 단어를 모두 배열하여 완성하시오.

┌─ 보기 ┼─
it / world / can / experience / you / another / if / wear / you
└──────

➡ _____

08 다음 대화의 빈칸에 들어갈 말로 적절한 것은?

A: I've never seen it. What is it for?
B: _____

① It looks like a stick.
② It is made of wood.
③ It is for decorating your hair.
④ How about wearing it?
⑤ I don't know how to use it.

[09~11] 다음 대화를 읽고 물음에 답하시오.

Ms. Lee: Hello, class! Jisu is today's speaker for show and tell. Jisu?

Jisu: Hi, class! Do you know (A)[who / which] this man is? ⓐ His name is Alexander Graham Bell. ⓑ Bell was an inventor. ⓒ He was (B)[interesting / interested] in sound. ⓓ Yes, the telephone! His mother and wife were deaf. ⓔ So he also made some inventions for deaf people and (C)[opened / opening] a school for them.

09 위 대화의 (A)~(C)에 들어갈 말로 바르게 짝지어진 것은?

	(A)	(B)	(C)
①	who	interesting	opened
②	who	interested	opening
③	who	interested	opened
④	which	interested	opening
⑤	which	interesting	opened

10 위 대화의 ⓐ~ⓔ 중 주어진 문장이 들어가기에 적절한 곳은?

What did he invent?

① ⓐ   ② ⓑ   ③ ⓒ   ④ ⓓ   ⑤ ⓔ

11 위 대화의 내용과 일치하지 <u>않는</u> 것은?

① Alexander Graham Bell invented the telephone.
② Alexander Graham Bell had an interest in sound.
③ Bell's mother and wife were not able to hear.
④ Alexander Graham Bell opened the school for his family.
⑤ Jisu introduced Alexander Graham Bell to her class.

12 다음 주어진 우리말과 일치하도록 주어진 단어를 모두 배열하여 완성하시오.

(1) Jimin은 반 친구들과 잘 지내는 것 같지 않다. (classmates / get / to / along / with / his / seem / doesn't / Jimin)

➡ _____

(2) 태양계에서 가장 큰 행성은 무엇인가? (the / solar / what / planet / system / is / biggest / the / in)

➡ _____

13 다음 중 어법상 옳은 문장의 개수는?

ⓐ Although I felt sorry for her, I didn't apologize to her.

ⓑ Tom is richer than me. I am not as rich as Tom.

ⓒ Miranda went for a walk despite it was cold outside.

ⓓ I drink two times as much water as you are.

ⓔ The garden looks as tidy than it used to.

① 1개 ② 2개 ③ 3개 ④ 4개 ⑤ 5개

14 동등 비교 표현을 이용하여 다음 빈칸에 알맞은 말을 쓰시오.

Dad and I went for a run. Dad ran ten kilometers. I stopped after seven kilometers. I _____ Dad.

➡ _____

15 다음 우리말을 영어로 바르게 옮기지 <u>않은</u> 것은?

① 그녀의 병은 생각보다 심각하지 않았다.
   → Her illness was not as serious as we thought.

② 비록 네가 몸이 약하더라도, 항상 남을 도와라.
   → Always help others although you are weak.

③ 배가 부르진 않지만, 더 먹고 싶지 않아.
   → Though I am not full, I don't want to eat more.

④ 형편없는 성적에도 불구하고, 엄마는 나를 벌주지 않으셨다.
   → Despite the poor grade, Mom didn't punish me.

⑤ 그의 배낭은 나의 배낭보다 세 배 만큼 무겁다.
   → His backpack is three times as heavier as my backpack.

16 주어진 단어를 활용하여 다음 우리말을 영어로 쓰시오.

이 쿠키가 그 케이크만큼 맛있지 않더라도, 나는 이 쿠키를 먹을 거야.

(as ~ as / have)

➡ _____
_____

17 다음 빈칸에 알맞은 말을 쓰시오.

Bella couldn't finish her homework _____ there wasn't enough time. But Helen did everything she had to do _____ there wasn't enough time.

[18~21] 다음 글을 읽고 물음에 답하시오.

Do you want to live on another planet?
The Korea Space Organization (KSO) is looking ⓐ[at / for] people to go to MARS! Our mission is to build a city on Mars.
We are looking for someone...
who is healthy.
who is creative and curious.
who can get along with others.
who can ⓑ[adopt / adapt] to a new environment quickly.
Send us a short video (A)to apply. The video must ⓒ[include / exclude] the answers to the following questions:
1. Why do you want to go to Mars?
2. (B)당신은 훌륭한 유머 감각이 있나요?
3. Why are you the perfect person for this mission?

18 ⓐ~ⓒ에서 글의 흐름상 옳은 것끼리 바르게 짝지은 것은?

① for – adapt – exclude
② for – adapt – include
③ at – adopt – exclude
④ at – adopt – include
⑤ at – adapt – include

19 다음 중 밑줄 친 (A)와 쓰임이 같은 것은?

① I have many friends to play with.
② It is surprising for you to say so.
③ Anna went to the market to buy milk.
④ To jog in the morning makes me happy.
⑤ We decided to make a cake for Mom's birthday.

20 적절한 대명사를 이용하여 다음 물음에 완전한 문장의 영어로 답하시오.

> Q: What is the mission of KSO?

➡ _____

21 밑줄 친 우리말 (B)를 영어로 쓰시오.

➡ _____

[22~25] 다음 글을 읽고 물음에 답하시오.

The big question is, "Can people live on Mars?" Many scientists believe so for ① several reasons. First, they think that there is water on Mars. ②This is great because water is necessary for all life. Second, Mars has hard ③land to build houses and buildings on. Third, the length of day and night on Mars ④ is similar to that on Earth. In addition, Mars also has four seasons. So, people can lead similar lives. Lastly, Mars is not very far. It is the second closest planet to Earth.

_____(A)_____, Mars has some differences from Earth. First, Mars is about half the size of Earth. It is the second smallest planet in the solar system. Second, a year on Mars is about twice as long as a year on Earth. Third, Mars is much colder than Earth. On average, it is about –60℃ on Mars. This is because Mars is ⑤nearer to the Sun than Earth.

22 다음 중 빈칸 (A)에 들어갈 말로 가장 적절한 것은?

① For example   ② However
③ Therefore   ④ Thus
⑤ Moreover

23 다음 중 위 글의 내용과 일치하는 것은?

① Scientists don't think that it is possible for people to live on Mars.
② Mars doesn't have proper land to build houses on.
③ Mars is close to Earth and has four seasons.
④ Mars is the second smallest planet in the universe.
⑤ Mars is not as cold as Earth.

24 ①~⑤ 중 글의 흐름상 어색한 것을 골라 바르게 고치시오.

_____ ➡ _____

25 위 글의 표현을 이용하여 다음 우리말을 영어로 쓰시오.

> 화성은 지구와 다른 점이 몇 개 있지만, 과학자들은 사람들이 화성에서 살 수 있다고 믿는다.

➡ _____
_____

Lesson 7

Can I Trust It?

🎙 의사소통 기능

- 추천 요청하기

  A: Can you recommend a musical for me?

  B: How about *The Lion King*?

- 만족 여부 묻고 답하기

  A: How do you like your bicycle?

  B: I'm really happy with it.

🎙 언어 형식

- so ~ that

  The movie is **so** boring **that** I want to cry.

- 목적격 관계대명사

  In the ad, "Best Picture" is the award **which** the movie won.

Words & Expressions

교과서

Key Words

- adventure [ədvéntʃər] 명 모험
- advertisement [ədvərtáizmənt] 명 광고
- author [ɔ́:θər] 명 작가
- award [əwɔ́:rd] 명 상
- backpack [bǽkpæk] 명 배낭
- belief [bilí:f] 명 신념, 생각
- boring [bɔ́:riŋ] 형 지루한
- connection [kənékʃən] 명 관련성, 연관성
- desert [dézərt] 명 사막
- difference [dífərəns] 명 차이점
- else [els] 부 또 다른
- especially [ispéʃəli] 부 특히
- explain [ikspléin] 동 설명하다
- express [iksprés] 동 나타내다, 표현하다
- fantasy [fǽntəsi] 명 공상
- friendship [fréndʃip] 명 우정
- genre [ʒɑ́:nrə] 명 장르
- lie [lai] 동 거짓말하다
- lift [lift] 동 들어 올리다
- meal [mi:l] 명 식사
- mix [miks] 동 섞다

- navy [néivi] 명 남색
- novel [návəl] 명 소설
- opinion [əpínjən] 명 의견
- perfect [pə́:rfikt] 형 완벽한
- pocket [pákit] 명 주머니
- prove [pru:v] 동 증명하다
- purple [pə́:rpl] 명 보라색, 자색
- recommend [rèkəménd] 동 추천하다
- side [said] 명 옆면, 측면
- simple [símpl] 형 간단한, 단순한
- solve [sɑlv] 동 해결하다, 풀다
- strongly [strɔ́:ŋli] 부 강력하게
- touching [tʌ́tʃiŋ] 형 감동적인
- traditional [trədíʃənl] 형 전통적인
- trip [trip] 명 여행
- trust [trʌst] 동 믿다, 신뢰하다
- truth [tru:θ] 명 진실, 사실
- unlike [ənláik] 전 ~와 달리
- wisely [wáizli] 부 현명하게
- worth [wə:rθ] 형 가치가 있는
- yet [jet] 부 아직

Key Expressions

- based on ~을 바탕으로
- check out ~을 확인하다
- for example 예를 들면
- from now on 지금부터
- full of ~로 가득한
- hold on 기다려, 멈춰

- look for ~을 찾다
- main character 주인공
- make a choice 선택하다
- number one (인기 순위) 1위
- right now 지금
- worth it 그만한 가치가 있는

Word Power

※ 서로 반대되는 뜻을 가진 어휘

- □ **simple** 간단한, 단순한 ↔ **complex** 복잡한
- □ **true** 사실의, 진실의 ↔ **false** 거짓의
- □ **boring** 지루한 ↔ **exciting** 신나는
- □ **perfect** 완벽한 ↔ **imperfect** 불완전한
- □ **ancient** 고대의 ↔ **modern** 현대의

- □ **worth** 가치가 있는 ↔ **worthless** 가치가 없는
- □ **wise** 지혜로운 ↔ **foolish** 미련한, 어리석은
- □ **fact** 사실 ↔ **opinion** 의견
- □ **like** ~처럼, ~같이 ↔ **unlike** ~와 달리
- □ **similarity** 유사점 ↔ **difference** 차이점

※ 색을 나타내는 단어

- □ **navy** 남색
- □ **orange** 주황색
- □ **burgundy** 진홍색

- □ **purple** 보라색
- □ **ivory** 상아색
- □ **violet** 보라색

- □ **gray** 회색
- □ **silver** 은색

- □ **brown** 갈색
- □ **khaki** 카키색

English Dictionary

- □ **advertisement** 광고
  → a notice, picture or short film telling people about something
  사람들에게 무언가에 대해 이야기하는 게시, 그림 또는 짧은 영화

- □ **award** 상
  → a prize such as money, etc. for something that somebody has done
  누군가가 한 무언가에 대한 돈 등과 같은 상

- □ **connection** 관련성
  → the way in which two things are related to each other
  두 개가 서로 관련되어 있는 방식

- □ **explain** 설명하다
  → to tell somebody about something in a way that is easy to understand
  이해하기 쉬운 방식으로 무언가에 대해 누군가에게 이야기하다

- □ **express** 나타내다, 표현하다
  → to show what you think or feel
  당신이 생각하거나 느끼는 것을 보여주다

- □ **lie** 거짓말하다
  → to say or write something that is not true
  사실이 아닌 무언가를 말하거나 쓰다

- □ **lift** 들어 올리다
  → to move something to a higher position
  무언가를 더 높은 위치로 옮기다

- □ **meal** 식사
  → the foods eaten or prepared at one time
  한 번에 먹거나 준비되는 음식

- □ **mix** 섞다
  → to add something to something else
  무언가를 다른 무언가에 더하다

- □ **opinion** 의견
  → ideas or feelings about something
  무언가에 대한 생각 또는 느낌

- □ **pocket** 주머니
  → a small bag that is attached to something
  무언가에 붙어 있는 작은 자루

- □ **prove** 증명하다
  → to use facts, evidence, etc. to show that something is true
  무언가가 진실이라는 것을 보여 주기 위해 사실, 증거 등을 사용하다

- □ **trust** 신뢰하다, 믿다
  → to believe that something is true
  무언가가 사실이라고 믿다

- □ **truth** 진실, 사실
  → the real facts about something
  무언가에 대한 실제의 사실

01 다음 짝지어진 단어의 관계가 같도록 빈칸에 알맞은 말을 쓰시오.

> tall : short = _____ : complex

02 다음 영영풀이가 가리키는 것을 고르시오.

> a prize such as money, etc. for something that somebody has done

① penalty   ② award
③ fare   ④ fee
⑤ price

03 다음 중 밑줄 친 부분의 뜻풀이가 바르지 <u>않은</u> 것은?

① I saw an <u>advertisement</u> for a ski camp in Toronto. 광고
② There is a <u>connection</u> between pollution and the death of plants. 관련성
③ The steak was <u>especially</u> good. 특히
④ Give me a chance. I'll <u>prove</u> it to you. 제공하다
⑤ My favorite color is <u>purple</u>. 보라색

서답형
04 다음 우리말에 맞게 빈칸에 알맞은 말을 써 넣으시오.

(1) 말로는 내 기분을 표현할 수 없다.
  ➡ Words cannot _____ my feelings.
(2) 같은 광고가 3개의 잡지에 등장했다.
  ➡ The same _____ appeared in three magazines.
(3) 그는 승리할 것이라는 자신의 능력에 강한 신념을 갖고 있다.
  ➡ He has a strong _____ in his ability to win.

05 다음 주어진 문장의 밑줄 친 touching과 같은 의미로 쓰인 것은?

> The movie was so <u>touching</u> that I cried a lot.

① My daughter is <u>touching</u> a pet.
② Who is the boy <u>touching</u> an ant?
③ What a <u>touching</u> love story!
④ Avoid <u>touching</u> your eyes and nose with dirty hands.
⑤ <u>Touching</u> the keyboard, she told me about the plan.

06 다음 문장에 공통으로 들어갈 말을 고르시오.

> • My father served three years in the _____.
> • I dressed my son in the new _____ suit.
> • It's not bad, but I prefer the _____ skirt.

① navy   ② pink   ③ yellow
④ purple   ⑤ brown

서답형
07 다음 문장의 빈칸에 들어갈 말을 〈보기〉에서 골라 쓰시오.

> ┤ 보기 ├
> beliefs, purple, genre, friendship

(1) Do you know the girl wearing the _____ jacket?
(2) You must respect other people's _____.
(3) Which _____ do you like most?
(4) A strong _____ grew between the two people.

Words & Expressions **서술형 시험대비**

01 다음 짝지어진 단어의 관계가 같도록 빈칸에 알맞은 말을 쓰시오.

> similar : different = similarity : _____

02 다음 우리말에 맞게 빈칸에 알맞은 말을 쓰시오.

(1) 나는 네게 거짓말하지 않았다. 모든 것은 진실이야.

➡ I didn't _____ to you. Everything is true.

(2) 주머니에 구멍이 났다.

➡ I have a hole in my _____.

(3) 그 만화 영화는 소설을 바탕으로 한다.

➡ The animation is _____ on a novel.

03 다음 문장의 빈칸에 들어갈 말을 〈보기〉에서 골라 쓰시오.

> ┌── 보기 ──┐
> fantasy, traditional, connection, author, desert, award

(1) I'm interested in _____ Korean culture.

(2) The land of Australia is primarily _____.

(3) This novel was written by a famous _____.

(4) There is a _____ between health and eating habits.

(5) Emma was really happy when she won the _____.

(6) I like to read _____ novels.

04 다음 우리말을 주어진 단어를 이용하여 영작하시오.

(1) 지금부터 축구 경기를 시작하겠습니다. (from, start, let's, playing)

➡ _____

(2) 나가기 전에, 전등을 다시 확인해 주세요. (light, you, check)

➡ _____

(3) 누가 이 영화의 주인공입니까? (main, this)

➡ _____

05 다음 우리말과 일치하도록 주어진 어구를 모두 배열하여 영작하시오.

(1) 게임 규칙을 설명해 줄 수 있나요?
(explain / the game / can / of / the rules / you)

➡ _____

(2) 당신이 빨간색과 파란색을 섞으면 보라색을 얻을 수 있어요.
(purple / get / you / blue / red / with / mix / you / can / if)

➡ _____

(3) 그가 유리창을 깨지 않았다는 것을 증명할 수 있어요.
(that / I / the window / didn't / can / break / prove / he)

➡ _____

(4) 신문에 난 그 광고 봤니?
(you / see / did / the advertisement / the newspaper / on)

➡ _____

Conversation

① 추천 요청하기 및 추천하기

A Can you recommend a musical for me? 제게 뮤지컬을 추천해 줄 수 있나요?

B How about *The Lion King*? *The Lion King*은 어때?

■ 'Can you recommend ∼?'는 '∼을 추천해 줄 수 있나요?'라는 뜻으로 상대방에게 무엇인가를 추천해 달라고 부탁하는 표현이다. 대답으로 "How about ∼?", "Why don't you ∼?", "I recommend ∼", "Try ∼", "I think ∼." 등의 표현을 사용해 추천해 줄 수 있다.

추천 요청하기

• What would you recommend? 무엇을 추천하나요?

• What do you think would be the best? 무엇이 가장 좋다고 생각하나요?

• Can you suggest a good movie? 좋은 영화를 추천해 줄 수 있나요?

추천하기

• How about *Frozen*? The music is so beautiful. *Frozen*은 어때? 음악이 매우 아름다워.

• Why don't you read *Frindle*? The story is really touching.
*Frindle*을 읽어 보는 게 어때? 이야기가 정말 감동적이야.

• I recommend *Beauty and the Beast*. 나는 미녀와 야수를 추천해요.

• Try Antonio's. It's a good restaurant. Antonio's에 가 봐. 좋은 식당이야.

• I think this backpack is much better than that one. 제 생각에 이 배낭이 저것보다 훨씬 나을 거 같아요.

핵심 Check

1. 다음 주어진 우리말과 일치하도록 빈칸을 완성하시오.

(1) **A:** Can you _____ a movie for me? (영화를 추천해 줄 수 있나요?)

  B: _____ _____ *Spider Man*? It's interesting. (*Spiderman* 어때? 재밌어.)

(2) **A:** _____ _____ _____ a good novel for me? (제게 좋은 소설을 제안해 주시겠어요?)

  B: _____ don't you read *Harry Potter*? (*Harry Potter*를 읽어 보는 게 어때요?)

(3) **A:** _____ _____ _____ _____ _____ _____ the best musical?
(최고의 뮤지컬이 무엇인 거 같아요?)

  B: I think *The Phantom of the Opera* is the best. (저는 오페라의 유령이 최고인 것 같아요.)

2 만족 여부 묻고 답하기

> **A** How do you like your bicycle? 네 자전거는 마음에 드니?
> **B** I'm really happy with it. 정말 마음에 들어.

- 'How do you like ~?'는 '~이 마음에 드니?'라는 뜻으로 특정 물건이나 장소 등에 대해 만족하는지를 묻는 표현이다. 이에 대한 대답으로 만족을 표현할 때는 'I'm happy with ~.'로, 불만족을 표현할 때는 'I'm not happy with ~.'로, 표현할 수 있다.

만족 여부 묻기

- How do you like your new sneakers? 새 운동화가 마음에 드니?
- What do you like about the movie? 그 영화의 무엇이 마음에 드니?

만족 여부 답하기

- I'm satisfied with my job. 내 일에 만족해.
- I'm disappointed with the decision. 나는 그 결정에 실망했어.
- I'm pleased with the food. 음식이 마음에 들어.
- It's perfect. 완벽해.
- It's fantastic. 매우 좋아.

핵심 Check

2. 다음 주어진 우리말과 일치하도록 빈칸을 완성하시오.

(1) **A:** _____ _____ _____ _____ your new pants? (새 바지가 마음에 드니?)
B: I'm really happy with them. (정말 마음에 들어.)

(2) **A:** How do you like your jacket? (재킷이 마음에 드니?)
B: _____ _____ _____ _____ _____. (만족스럽지 않아.)

(3) **A:** _____ _____ _____ _____ about the bicycle?
(그 자전거의 무엇이 마음에 드니?)
B: It's light and fast. (가볍고 빨라요.)

Listen and Speak 1 - B

W: ❶May I help you?

B: Yes. I'm ❷looking for a ❸backpack. Can you recommend ❹one?

W: ❺How about this red one? Red is the most popular color ❻these days.

B: My old backpack was red, so I want a different color.

W: How about this navy one? It has side pockets.

B: Oh, that looks good. I'll take ❼it.

W: 도와드릴까요?

B: 네. 배낭을 찾고 있어요. 하나 추천해 주시겠어요?

W: 이 빨간 배낭은 어떤가요? 빨간색은 요즘 가장 인기 있는 색이에요.

B: 제 옛 배낭이 빨간색이어서 다른 색을 원해요.

W: 이 남색 배낭은 어떤가요? 양옆에 주머니가 있어요.

B: 오, 좋아 보여요. 그걸로 살게요.

❶ 'May I help you?'는 '도와드릴까요?'라고 도움을 제안하는 표현으로 'How can I help you?' 또는 'Do you need any help?' 등으로 바꾸어 표현할 수 있다.

❷ look for: ~을 찾다　　❸ backpack: 배낭　　❹ one = a backpack

❺ 'How about ~?'은 '~하는 게 어때?'라고 추천하는 표현으로 'What about ~?'으로 바꾸어 쓸 수 있다.

❻ these days: 요즘 cf. those days: 그 당시에

❼ it은 the navy backpack with side pockets를 가리킨다.

Check(√) True or False

(1) The boy already had a red backpack.　　　　T ☐ F ☐

(2) The boy bought the backpack with side pockets.　　　　T ☐ F ☐

Listen and Speak 2 - B

Jack: Hi, Suji. ❶How did you like your trip to Gyeongju?

Suji: I was very happy with it.

Jack: Where did you visit?

Suji: I visited Cheomseongdae. It was great.

Jack: Where else did you go?

Suji: Bulguksa. It was a wonderful place.

Jack: Sounds like the perfect trip.

Suji: Yeah, but ❷walking up to Seokguram was difficult.

Jack: But I'm sure it was ❸worth it.

Jack: 안녕, 수지야. 경주 여행은 어땠니?

Suij: 매우 즐거웠어.

Jack: 어디를 방문했니?

Suij: 첨성대를 방문했어. 좋았어.

Jack: 또 어디를 방문했니?

Suij: 불국사. 멋진 곳이었어.

Jack: 완벽한 여행이었던 것 같네.

Suij: 응, 하지만 석굴암까지 걸어 올라가는 것은 힘들었어.

Jack: 하지만 그것이 그만한 가치가 있었을 것이라고 확신해.

❶ 경주 여행이 마음에 들었는지 묻는 표현이다.

❷ 동명사가 주어이므로 동사는 단수 형태로 쓰였다.

❸ worth it: 그만한 가치가 있는

Check(√) True or False

(3) Suji was happy with her trip to Gyeongju.　　　　T ☐ F ☐

(4) It was not hard for Suji to walk up to Seokguram.　　　　T ☐ F ☐

Listen and Speak 1-A

Brian: Can you ❶recommend a good movie?

Emily: Try *Star Wars*. I really liked ❷it.

Brian: Oh, I haven't seen ❷it yet.

Emily: ❷It's the ❸number one movie ❹right now.

❶ recommend: 추천하다
❷ it은 *Star Wars*를 가리킨다.
❸ number one: 1위의
❹ right now: 지금

Listen and Speak 1-C

A: Jiho, can you recommend a musical for me?

B: ❶How about *The Lion King*? The dancing is fantastic.

A: Okay. ❷Sounds good.

B: ❸I'm sure you'll like ❹it.

❶ How about ~?: ~는 어때?(=What about ~?)
❷ Sounds good.에는 앞 문장을 받는 주어 That이 생략되었다.
❸ I'm sure ~.: 나는 ~라고 확신해.
❹ it은 *The Lion King*을 가리킨다.

Listen and Speak 2-A

Sue: Tom, you got a new smartphone.

Tom: Yes, I did. I'm really happy with ❶it.

Sue: ❷What do you like most about ❶it?

Tom: I love the camera. It ❸takes great pictures.

❶ it은 a new smartphone을 가리킨다.
❷ 무엇이 마음에 드는지 묻는 표현이다.
❸ take a picture: 사진을 찍다

Real Life Talk – Step 1

Brian: Mina, can you recommend a good pizza restaurant?

Mina: ❶Why don't you try Antonio's? ❷It's my favorite.

Brian: What do you like about ❷it?

Mina: The food is delicious. I recommend the bulgogi pizza.

Brian: How are the prices?

Mina: I think the prices are good, too.

Brian: Sounds like a good restaurant. How do you like the service?

Mina: It's ❸a little slow on the weekends.

Brian: Okay. I'll ❹check it out. Thanks.

Mina: No problem. Enjoy your meal!

❶ How about trying Antonio's?로 바꾸어 쓸 수 있다.
❷ It은 Antonio's를 가리킨다.
❸ a little: 조금
❹ check out: ~을 확인하다

Real Life Talk – Step 2

Amy: Yujin, can you recommend a book for me?

Yujin: How about *The Little Prince*?

Amy: What do you like about ❶the book?

Yujin: I like the ❷main character. ❸He is very special.

Amy: Sounds good. I'll read it.

❶ the book은 *The Little Prince*를 가리킨다.
❷ main character: 주인공
❸ He = the main character

● 다음 우리말과 일치하도록 빈칸에 알맞은 말을 쓰시오.

Listen & Speak 1-A

Brian: Can you _____ a good movie?

Emily: Try *Star Wars*. I really liked it.

Brian: Oh, I haven't seen it _____.

Emily: It's the _____ _____ movie right now.

해석

Brian: 좋은 영화를 추천해 줄래?
Emily: 'Star Wars'를 봐. 정말 좋았어.
Brian: 오, 나는 아직 그 영화를 본 적이 없어.
Emily: 지금 1위 영화야.

Listen & Speak 1-B

W: May I _____ you?

B: Yes. I'm looking for a _____. Can you _____ _____?

W: _____ _____ this red one? Red is the most popular color _____ _____.

B: My old backpack was red, so I want a _____ color.

W: How about this _____ one? It has side _____.

B: Oh, that looks good. I'll _____ it.

W: 도와드릴까요?
B: 네. 배낭을 찾고 있어요. 하나 추천해 주시겠어요?
W: 이 빨간 배낭은 어떤가요? 빨간색은 요즘 가장 인기 있는 색이에요.
B: 제 옛 배낭이 빨간색이어서 다른 색을 원해요.
W: 이 남색 배낭은 어떤가요? 양옆에 주머니가 있어요.
B: 오, 좋아 보여요. 그걸로 살게요.

Listen & Speak 2-A

Sue: Tom, you _____ a new smartphone.

Tom: Yes, I did. I'm really happy with it.

Sue: What do you _____ _____ _____ _____?

Tom: I love the camera. It _____ great pictures.

Sue: Tom, 새 스마트폰을 샀구나.
Tom: 응, 그래. 나는 정말 만족스러워.
Sue: 무엇이 가장 마음에 드니?
Tom: 카메라가 정말 좋아. 멋진 사진을 찍어.

Listen & Talk 2-B

Jack: Hi, Suji. How did you _____ your _____ to Gyeongju?

Suji: I was very _____ with it.

Jack: Where did you visit?

Suji: I visited Cheomseongdae. It was great.

Jack: _____ _____ did you go?

Suji: Bulguksa. It was a _____ _____.

Jack: Sounds like the _____ _____.

Suji: Yeah, but _____ _____ to Seokguram was difficult.

Jack: But I'm sure it was _____ _____.

Real Life Talk – Step 1

Brian: Mina, _____ _____ _____ a good pizza restaurant?

Mina: _____ _____ you try Antonio's? It's my favorite.

Brian: What do you like _____ it?

Mina: The food is _____. I _____ the bulgogi pizza.

Brian: How are _____ _____ ?

Mina: I _____ the prices are good, _____.

Brian: _____ _____ a good restaurant. _____ do you like _____ _____ ?

Mina: It's a little _____ on the weekends.

Brian: Okay. I'll _____ _____ _____. Thanks.

Mina: No _____. _____ your meal!

Real Life Talk – Step 2

Amy: Yujin, can you _____ _____ _____ _____ _____ _____ ?

Yujin: How _____ *The Little Prince*?

Amy: _____ do you _____ about the book?

Yujin: I like the _____ _____. He is very _____.

Amy: _____ good. I'll read it.

[01~02] 다음 대화를 읽고 물음에 답하시오.

Brian: _____?
Emily: Try *Star Wars*. I really liked it.
Brian: Oh, I haven't seen it yet.
Emily: It's the number one movie right now.

01 위 대화의 빈칸에 들어갈 말을 〈보기〉에 주어진 단어를 모두 배열하여 영작하시오.

┤ 보기 ├
you / recommend / a / movie / can / good

➡ _____

02 위 대화의 내용과 일치하지 <u>않는</u> 것은?

① Brian은 Emily에게 좋은 영화를 추천해 줄 것을 요청하였다.
② Emily는 *Star Wars*를 볼 것을 추천하였다.
③ Emily는 *Star Wars*가 정말 좋았다.
④ Brain은 아직 *Star Wars*를 보지 않았다.
⑤ Brian은 지금 1위 영화를 보았다.

[03~04] 다음 대화를 읽고 물음에 답하시오.

Sue: Tom, you got a new smartphone.
Tom: Yes, I did. I'm really happy with (B)it.
Sue: (A)무엇이 가장 마음에 드니?
Tom: I love the camera. (C)It takes great pictures.

03 위 대화의 밑줄 친 (A)의 우리말을 주어진 단어를 모두 배열하여 영작하시오.

┤ 보기 ├
you / it / about / what / most / do / like

➡ _____

04 위 대화의 밑줄 친 (B)와 (C)의 it이 가리키는 것을 각각 찾아 쓰시오.

➡ (B) _____ (C) _____

[01~03] 다음 대화를 읽고 불음에 답하시오.

Jack: Hi, Suji. ①How did you like your trip to Gyeongju?

Suji: I was very happy ②with it.

Jack: Where did you visit?

Suji: I visited Cheomseongdae. It was great.

Jack: Where else did you go?

Suji: Bulguksa. It was a wonderful place.

Jack: ③Sounds like the perfect trip.

Suji: Yeah, ___(A)___ walking up to Seokguram ④were difficult.

Jack: ___(A)___ I'm sure it was ⑤worth it.

서답형

01 위 대화의 ①~⑤ 중 어법상 어색한 것을 찾아 바르게 고치시오.

➡ _____

02 위 대화의 빈칸 (A)에 들어갈 말로 적절한 것은?

① and / And ② but / But
③ so / So ④ for / For
⑤ because / Because

중요

03 위 대화의 내용과 일치하지 <u>않는</u> 것은?

① Suji was satisfied with her trip to Gyeongju.

② Suji visited both Cheomseongdae and Bulguksa.

③ It was difficult for Suji to walk up to Seokguram.

④ Jack didn't think that it was worth while walking up to Cheomseongdae.

⑤ Suji thought that Bulguksa was a great place.

[04~05] 다음 대화를 읽고 물음에 답하시오.

Amy: Yujin, (A)내게 책을 추천해 줄래?(can)

Yujin: How about *The Little Prince*?

Amy: What do you like about the book?

Yujin: I like the main character. He is very special.

Amy: Sounds good. I'll read it.

서답형

04 위 대화의 밑줄 친 (A)의 우리말을 주어진 단어를 사용하여 영작하시오.

➡ _____

서답형

05 What does Yujin like about *The Little Prince*? Answer in English.

➡ _____

[06~08] 다음 대화를 읽고 물음에 답하시오.

Brian: Mina, can you recommend a good pizza restaurant?

Mina: (A) It's my favorite.

Brian: (B) What do you like about ⓐit?

Mina: (C) The food is delicious. I recommend the bulgogi pizza.

Brian: (D) How are the prices?

Mina: (E) I think the prices are good, too.

Brian: Sounds like a good restaurant. How do you like the service?

Mina: ⓑIt's a little slow on the weekends.

Brian: Okay. I'll check it out. Thanks.

Mina: No problem. Enjoy your meal!

06 위 대화의 (A)~(E) 중 주어진 문장이 들어가기에 적절한 곳은?

> Why don't you try Antonio's?

① (A)　② (B)　③ (C)　④ (D)　⑤ (E)

서답형

07 위 대화에서 밑줄 친 ⓐ와 ⓑ가 각각 가리키는 것을 찾아 쓰시오.

➡ ⓐ _____　ⓑ _____

08 위 대화의 내용과 일치하지 <u>않는</u> 것은?

① 미나는 괜찮은 피자 식당으로 Antonio's를 추천하였다.
② Antonio's는 미나가 가장 좋아하는 곳이다.
③ 미나는 Antonio's의 불고기 피자를 추천하였다.
④ 미나는 Antonio's의 가격이 괜찮다고 생각한다.
⑤ Antonio's의 서비스는 주중에는 좀 느리다.

[09~10] 다음 대화를 읽고 물음에 답하시오.

W: May I help you?
B: (A) Yes. I'm looking for a backpack. Can you recommend one?
W: (B) Red is the most popular color these days.
B: (C) My old backpack was red, so I want a different color.
W: (D) How about this navy one? It has side pockets.
B: (E) Oh, that looks good. I'll take it.

09 위 대화의 (A)~(E) 중 주어진 문장이 들어가기에 적절한 곳은?

> How about this red one?

① (A)　② (B)　③ (C)　④ (D)　⑤ (E)

중요

10 위 대화를 읽고 대답할 수 <u>없는</u> 질문은?

① What was the boy looking for?
② What did the woman recommend at first?
③ Why didn't the boy want the red backpack?
④ What did the boy decide to buy?
⑤ How many pockets did the boy's old backpack have?

[11~12] 다음 대화를 읽고 물음에 답하시오.

Sue: Tom, you got a new smartphone.
Tom: Yes, I did. _____(A)_____
Sue: What do you like most about it?
Tom: I love the camera. It takes great pictures.

11 위 대화의 빈칸 (A)에 들어갈 말로 <u>어색한</u> 것은?

① I'm really happy with it.
② I'm satisfied with it.
③ I'm disappointed with it.
④ I'm pleased with it.
⑤ It's fantastic.

중요

12 위 대화를 읽고 대답할 수 <u>없는</u> 질문은?

① What did Tom get?
② Does Tom like his new smartphone?
③ What does Tom like most about his smartphone?
④ Why does Tom love the camera in his smartphone?
⑤ When did Tom take great pictures?

[01~03] 다음 대화를 읽고 물음에 답하시오.

Brian: Can you recommend a good movie?

Emily: Try *Star Wars*. I really liked it.

Brian: Oh, (A)나는 아직 그것을 본 적이 없어. (yet)

Emily: It's the number one movie right now.

01 위 대화의 밑줄 친 (A)의 우리말을 주어진 단어를 사용하여 영작하시오.

➡ _____

02 What movie did Emily recommend to Brian?

➡ _____

03 What is the number one movie now?

➡ _____

[04~06] 다음 대화를 읽고 물음에 답하시오.

W: May I help you?

B: Yes. I'm looking for a backpack. Can you recommend one?

W: How about this red one? Red is the most popular color these days.

B: My old backpack was red, so I want a different color.

W: How about this navy one? It has side pockets.

B: Oh, that looks good. I'll take it.

04 What is the most popular color nowadays?

➡ _____

05 What is the feature of the navy backpack?

➡ _____

06 Why didn't the boy want to take the red backpack?

➡ _____

[07~08] 다음 대화를 읽고 물음에 답하시오.

Jack: Hi, Suji. ___(A)___ did you like your trip to Gyeongju?

Suji: I was very happy with it.

Jack: ___(B)___ did you visit?

Suji: I visited Cheomseongdae. It was great.

Jack: ___(C)___ else did you go?

Suji: Bulguksa. It was a wonderful place.

Jack: Sounds like the perfect trip.

Suji: Yeah, but walking up to Seokguram was difficult.

Jack: But I'm sure it was worth it.

07 위 대화의 빈칸 (A), (B), (C)에 들어갈 알맞은 의문사를 쓰시오.

➡ (A) _____ (B) _____ (C) _____

08 위 대화의 내용과 일치하도록 Suji의 일기를 완성하시오.

Sun, Nov 3rd, 2019

I took a trip to ___(A)___ . It was a really nice and beautiful city. I visited ___(B)___ as well as Cheomseongdae. They are wonderful places. When I walked up to ___(C)___ , I was tired but it was worth while to do it. I was so happy with the perfect trip to Gyeongju.

➡ (A) _____ (B) _____ (C) _____

Grammar

1 so ~ that

> • The hot chocolate was **so** hot **that** Jeremy couldn't drink it.
> 그 핫 초콜릿은 너무 뜨거워서 Jeremy는 그것을 마실 수 없었다.
>
> • I am **so** hungry **that** I could eat a horse.
> 나는 배가 너무 고파서 말 한 마리를 다 먹을 수 있을 정도야.

- 'so+형용사/부사+that ~'은 '너무 …해서 ~하다'는 의미로 원인과 결과를 나타낼 때 사용한다.

  - This book is **so** interesting **that** I can't put it down. 이 책은 너무 재미있어서 내려놓을 수가 없어.

  - The sun is **so** hot **that** I have to drink lots of water. 태양이 너무 뜨거워서 나는 많은 물을 마셔야만 한다.

  - The fox was **so** playful **that** he wanted to make play with the crane.
    그 여우는 장난기가 너무 많아서 학을 골탕 먹이고 싶었다.

- 'so ~ that 주어 can't …'는 '너무 ~해서 …할 수 없다'는 의미로 'too ~ to V'로 표현할 수 있고, 'so ~ that 주어 can'은 '너무 ~해서 …할 수 있다'는 의미로 '~ enough to V'로 표현할 수 있다.

  - I am **so** tired **that** I can't play with you.

    = I am **too** tired **to** play with you. 나는 너무 피곤해서 너와 함께 놀 수 없어.

  - Julia was **so** tall **that** she played basketball very well.

    = Julia was tall **enough to** play basketball very well. Julia는 충분히 키가 커서 농구를 아주 잘했다.

핵심 Check

1. 다음 우리말과 같도록 빈칸에 알맞은 말을 쓰시오.

   (1) 불빛이 너무 밝아서 나는 눈을 뜰 수 없어.

   ➡ The light is _____ _____ _____ I can't open my eyes.

   (2) 그것은 너무 작아서 사람들은 그것을 보기 위해 현미경이 필요해요.

   ➡ It is _____ _____ _____ people need a microscope to see it.

   (3) James는 너무 게을러서 모두가 그를 싫어한다.

   ➡ James is _____ _____ _____ everyone hates him.

② 목적격 관계대명사

> • Mr. Han **whom** everyone respects teaches English.
> 모두가 존경하는 한 선생님은 영어를 가르친다.
>
> • The jacket **which** Sam got from his mother looks fancy.
> Sam이 엄마에게서 받은 재킷은 멋져 보인다.

■ 관계대명사는 두 개의 문장을 하나로 이어주는 접속사 역할을 하면서 동시에 (대)명사 역할을 한다. 전치사의 목적어 혹은 동사의 목적어였던 (대)명사를 목적격 관계대명사로 만들어 문장을 하나로 이어준다.

- There were many children at the zoo **which** Tom and Jane visited. 〈동사의 목적어〉
  Tom과 Jane이 방문했던 동물원에는 아이들이 많았다.

- Those boys **who[whom]** the woman is looking after look very cute. 〈전치사의 목적어〉
  그 여자가 돌보고 있는 저 소년들은 매우 귀여워 보인다.

■ 목적격 관계대명사 who(m), which는 that으로 대체할 수 있으며, 생략 가능하다. 관계대명사가 전치사의 목적어로 사용된 경우 전치사는 동사 뒤에 그대로 두거나, 전치사를 관계대명사 앞으로 보낼 수 있다. 단, 관계대명사 that은 전치사의 목적어로 쓰일 수 없음에 유의하자.

- The hotel (**which/that**) you stay in is famous for its breakfast.
  = The hotel **in which** you stay is famous for its breakfast.
  = The hotel in that you stay is famous for its breakfast. (×) 네가 머물고 있는 그 호텔은 아침식사로 유명하다.

- The missing girl (**who(m)/that**) people were looking for was found at the train station.
  = The missing girl for **whom** people were looking was found at the train station.
  = The missing girl for that people were looking was found at the train station. (×)
  사람들이 찾던 그 실종 소녀가 기차역에서 발견되었다.

- Tell me about the cats (**which/that**) you take care of on the streets.
  네가 길에서 돌보는 고양이들에 관해서 말해 줘.

핵심 Check

2. 다음 우리말과 같도록 빈칸에 알맞은 말을 쓰시오.

(1) 나는 Elizabeth가 만든 드레스를 입고 싶다.
➡ I want to wear the dress _____ _____ _____.

(2) Chris는 그가 어제 잃어버린 지갑을 찾고 있다.
➡ Chris is looking for the wallet _____ _____ _____ yesterday.

(3) 나는 Molly가 정말 좋아했던 책을 가지고 있다.
➡ I have the book _____ _____ _____.

(4) 그녀는 꿈에서 본 남자를 찾고 있어.
➡ She is looking for a man _____ _____ _____ in her dream.

Grammar 시험대비 기본평가

01 다음 문장에서 어법상 <u>어색한</u> 부분을 바르게 고쳐 쓰시오.

(1) The areas who you mentioned have some problems.

_____ ➡ _____

(2) Tell me about the patients which you cared for in the hospital.

_____ ➡ _____

(3) This necklace is very expensive that you will be shocked.

_____ ➡ _____

(4) Suji was so tired to do her homework.

_____ ➡ _____

02 다음 우리말과 같은 의미가 되도록 빈칸에 알맞은 말을 쓰시오.

(1) Tom이 많이 좋아하는 그 소녀는 내 친구이다.

= The girl _____ _____ _____ so much is my friend.

(2) 그 문제는 너무 쉬워서 모두가 그것을 풀 수 있다.

= The problem is _____ _____ _____ everyone can solve it.

(3) 그는 매우 부유해서 그가 원하는 어떤 것도 할 수 있다.

= He is _____ _____ _____ he can do anything _____ he wants.

(4) 내가 앉아 있는 이 의자는 편안하다.

= This chair _____ _____ _____ _____ is comfortable.

03 주어진 어구를 바르게 배열하여 다음 우리말을 영어로 쓰시오. 필요하다면 어형을 바꾸고 단어를 추가하시오.

> (4) commute: 통근 (거리)

(1) 그녀는 좋아하지 않는 음식에 손도 대지 않았다. (she / she / didn't / didn't / like / touch / the food / that)

➡ _____

(2) 그 여자가 돌보고 있는 저 아기들은 매우 귀여워 보인다. (very cute / those babies / look after / look / whom / is / the woman)

➡ _____

(3) 구두가 너무 꼭 끼어서 내 발이 아파. (tight / hurt / the shoes / my feet / are / that)

➡ _____

(4) 그녀의 출퇴근 거리가 너무 멀어서 그녀는 차를 샀다. (a car / her commute / bought / so / she / far / was)

➡ _____

01 다음 우리말을 영어로 바르게 옮긴 것은?

> 그녀는 너무 피곤해서 일찍 잤어.

① She is very tired to go to bed early.
② She was too tired to go to bed early.
③ She was so tired that she couldn't go to sleep.
④ She was so tired that she went to bed early.
⑤ She went to bed so early that she was tired.

02 다음 중 어법상 바르지 <u>않은</u> 것은?

> The woman ①whom I ②met yesterday ③was ④very friendly ⑤that I wanted to be friends with her.

　　①　　　②　　　③　　　④　　　⑤

03 다음 주어진 문장의 빈칸에 들어갈 말로 적절한 것을 <u>모두</u> 고르시오.

> The sofa _____ they bought last week looks expensive.

① whose　　② which　　③ who
④ that　　　⑤ what

04 목적격 관계대명사를 이용하여 다음 두 문장을 하나의 문장으로 쓰시오.

> • The book was written by my mother.
> • You borrowed the book from the library.

➡ _____

_____

05 주어진 문장과 같은 의미의 문장은?

> Tom was too scared to go out at night.

① Tom was scared enough to go out at night.
② Tom was very scared of going out at night.
③ Tom was so scared that he couldn't go out at night.
④ Tom was so scared that he could go out at night.
⑤ Tom was scared to go out at night.

06 다음 중 어법상 바르지 <u>않은</u> 것은?

① Minji is so smart that she can solve all the problems.
② The bike which Jason rides are fancy.
③ I know the house in which we used to live.
④ Some friends you invited are a little rude.
⑤ I was so upset that I didn't answer her phone.

07 다음 빈칸에 들어갈 말이 바르게 짝지어진 것은?

> James kicked a ball so _____ that his foot hurt. The ball _____ James kicked was not found.

① hardly – whose　② hardly – that
③ hard – who　　　④ hard – whose
⑤ hard – that

서답형

08 주어진 단어를 활용하여 다음 우리말을 영어로 쓰시오.

> 그 컴퓨터는 너무 작아서 내가 가지고 다닐 수 있다. (so / carry around)

➡ _____
_____

09 다음 중 밑줄 친 부분을 생략할 수 <u>없는</u> 것은?

① The boy <u>whom</u> you ran across was one of my students.
② The banana <u>which</u> Jane ate was not hers.
③ Where are the coins <u>that</u> were under the sofa?
④ The car <u>that</u> Jimmy washed looked clean and shiny.
⑤ The children <u>whom</u> you play with are there.

10 다음 중 that의 쓰임이 나머지 넷과 <u>다른</u> 하나는?

① It is certain <u>that</u> Brady is alive.
② <u>That</u> he worried about you is true.
③ I lost the hat <u>that</u> you had bought for me.
④ I told her <u>that</u> he was playing the piano.
⑤ Do you think <u>that</u> there will be lots of homework?

서답형

11 주어진 상황을 읽고 하나의 문장으로 표현하시오.

> There was an important examination. Julia studied hard to pass the exam. At last, she passed it.

➡ _____
_____

서답형

12 주어진 단어를 이용하여 알맞은 대답을 쓰시오.

> **A**: Why were you late?
> **B**: (that / traffic / heavy / here / be / on time)

➡ _____
_____

13 다음 빈칸에 공통으로 들어갈 말로 가장 적절한 것은?

> • The movie was so boring _____ most people fell asleep.
> • The plants _____ you cared for look very similar.

① who   ② which   ③ that
④ what   ⑤ whose

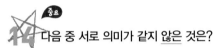

14 다음 중 서로 의미가 같지 <u>않은</u> 것은?

① Amelia was too talkative to listen to others.
= Amelia was so talkative that she couldn't listen to others.
② I lent you some money. What will you do with it?
= What will you do with the money that I lent you?
③ The boys are too noisy to be in the library.
= The boys are so noisy that they can't be in the library.
④ Jacky wrote a popular song. People loved the song.
= Jacky wrote a popular song which people loved.
⑤ Where is the dog? It follows you all the time.
= Where is the dog you follow all the time?

15 같은 의미가 되도록 빈칸에 알맞은 말을 쓰시오.

> • The concert made me excited.
> • We watched the concert last week.
> = The concert _____ made me excited.

➡ _____

16 다음 빈칸에 들어갈 말로 가장 적절한 것은?

> • My teeth were so painful that I went to the dentist.
> = I went to the dentist _____ my teeth were so painful.

① although　　② because
③ when　　④ as soon as
⑤ unless

17 다음 우리말을 영어로 바르게 옮긴 것은?

> 그 노래가 나를 너무 슬프게 해서 나는 라디오를 껐다.

① The song was sad that I turned off the radio.
② The song made me so sad that I turned off the radio.
③ The song was too sad to turn off the radio.
④ I was so sad that I turned off the radio.
⑤ The song made me sadly so that I turned off the radio.

서답형
18 같은 의미의 문장이 되도록 빈칸에 알맞은 말을 쓰시오.

> • The song was beautiful.
> • They sang the song together.
> = The song _____.

➡ _____

19 주어진 문장과 같은 의미의 문장은?

> I was so busy that I couldn't have lunch.

① I was busy although I couldn't have lunch.
② I was busy enough to have lunch.
③ I was busy because I couldn't have lunch.
④ I was busy having lunch.
⑤ I was too busy to have lunch.

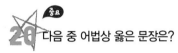

20 다음 중 어법상 옳은 문장은?

① The necklace you wear look beautiful.
② The dress was so beautiful that I can't take my eyes off it.
③ The students whose you teach are noisy.
④ The apple you brought is tasty.
⑤ The man was so diligently that everyone liked him.

서답형
21 괄호 안의 말을 써서 주어진 문장과 같은 의미의 문장을 쓰시오.

> I can't talk in front of many people because I am too shy. (so ~ that)

➡ _____

서답형
22 다음 우리말을 영어로 쓸 때 빈칸에 알맞은 말을 쓰시오.

> 내가 흥미 있는 과목은 영어입니다.
> (subject / interested)

(1) The subject _____ _____ _____ in is English.
(2) The subject in _____ _____ _____ _____ is English.

01 주어진 단어를 바르게 배열하여 다음 우리말을 영어로 쓰시오.

> 네가 나에게 소개해 준 그 소녀는 매우 인기 있어.
> (very / is / me / popular / the girl / introduced / you / to / whom)

➡ _____

02 다음 대화를 읽고 빈칸에 알맞은 말을 쓰시오.

> A: Why didn't Sandra carry the box?
> B: It was too heavy.

➡ The box _____

_____ .

03 다음 두 문장을 하나의 문장으로 쓸 때 빈칸에 알맞은 말을 쓰시오.

> Ross wrote a poem. The poem was so amazing that I was moved to tears.

➡ The poem _____

_____ .

04 다음 빈칸에 알맞은 말을 쓰시오.

(1) The cats _____ you take care of look happy.

(2) The guests _____ are in the hall want something cold to drink.

(3) Some people _____ we can see over there are interested in our artworks.

05 주어진 문장과 같은 의미의 문장을 지시에 맞게 쓰시오. 주어 Penny로 문장을 시작할 것.

> Penny was too sick to eat anything.

(1) because를 써서

➡ _____

(2) so ~ that을 써서

➡ _____

06 자연스러운 문장이 되도록 두 문장을 연결하시오.

> • The car is not his.
> • Kevin picked some roses.
> • I know the person.

> • Catherine planted roses.
> • You took a trip with him.
> • Tom is driving a car.

(1) The car _____ .
(2) Kevin _____ .
(3) I _____ .

07 다음 대화를 읽고 빈칸에 알맞은 말을 쓰시오.

> A: Do you need to buy a coat, Avian?
> B: I don't need to buy another coat because I already have a coat which is really warm.

➡ Avian's coat is _____

_____ .

08 〈보기〉와 같이 두 문장을 하나의 문장으로 쓰시오.

> ── 보기 ──
> I was very grateful to her. I made a pie for her.
> → I was so grateful to her that I made a pie for her.

(1) Sally speaks English very well. You would think it is her native language.

➡ _____

_____

(2) The music was very loud. You could hear it from miles away.

➡ _____

_____

(3) Gabriel is very beautiful. Any man would love to be with her.

➡ _____

_____

09 원인과 결과를 나타내는 구문을 이용하여 다음 문장과 같은 의미의 문장을 쓰시오.

> The soup burned my tongue because it was too hot.

➡ _____

10 주어진 단어를 활용하여 다음 우리말을 영어로 쓰시오.

> Jody는 Ms. Galler가 찾고 있는 학생이다.
> (look for)

➡ _____

_____

11 다음 우리말을 영어로 쓰시오.

(1) 네가 어제 본 소년은 나의 남동생이야.

➡ _____

_____

(2) 그녀가 입고 있는 드레스는 유명한 사람에 의해 디자인된 거야.

➡ _____

_____

12 주어진 단어를 바르게 배열하여 다음 우리말을 영어로 쓰시오.

> 내가 가장 자주 전화하는 사람들은 나의 엄마와 내 여동생들이다.
> (my sisters / I / my mother / are / and / often / call / the people / most / whom)

➡ _____

_____

13 다음 대화를 읽고 빈칸에 알맞은 말을 쓰시오.

> A: Lisa must be really happy.
> B: Why do you say so, Jason?
> A: I can see her dancing in the room.

➡ According to Jason, Lisa is _____ she is dancing in the room.

14 주어진 문장을 'so'를 이용하여 하나의 문장으로 표현하시오.

> The party was very enjoyable. Therefore, no one wanted to leave.

➡ _____

_____

15 주어진 단어를 활용하여 다음 우리말을 영어로 쓰시오.

> 그녀는 너무 일찍 일어나서 피곤했어요.
> (so / early)

➡ _____

Making Good Choices

Emma: What are you doing, Kyle?

Kyle: Oh, Emma. I'm watching the movie, *Y-Men 7* on my computer.
<u>the movie</u> = *Y-Men 7* 동격   ~로(수단)

Emma: How is it?

Kyle: Don't ask. It's so boring that I want to cry.
원인과 결과(너무 ~해서 …하다)

Emma: I'm sorry to hear that.
감정의 원인

Kyle: I'm so mad. The movie advertisement said it was "The Most

Exciting Movie of the Year."
of+명사(비교의 범위를 나타냄)

Emma: Well, you can't believe everything that you read.
목적격 관계대명사

Kyle: They lied on the advertisement. I'm going to ask for my money

back.

Emma: Hold on, Kyle! They didn't really lie because they used
(부정문에서) 꼭, 사실   이유를 나타내는 접속사

opinions, not facts.
A. not B: B가 아니라 A

Kyle: Huh? I'm not following you.
I can't understand you. = I don't get it.

Emma: Opinions express people's feelings like, "The desert is
전치사(~와 같은)

beautiful." You can't say that it's true or not. But, facts can
say의 목적어를 이끄는 명사절 접속사

be proven. For example, "The Atacama Desert is in Chile," is a
조동사가 있는 수동태

fact. You can check that on the map.
= The Atacama Desert is in Chile.

Kyle: Okay…. But what's the connection with movies?

---

boring 지루한
advertisement 광고
believe 믿다
lie 거짓말하다
ask for A back A를 돌려달라고 청하다
opinion 의견
express 나타내다, 표현하다
for example 예를 들어
check ~을 확인하다
connection 관련성

확인문제

● 다음 문장이 본문의 내용과 일치하면 T, 일치하지 <u>않으면</u> F를 쓰시오.

1 Kyle feels like crying because of the movie. ☐

2 Emma tells Kyle to believe what he reads. ☐

3 It is hard to say that they told a lie on the advertisement. ☐

Emma: Let me explain. What's your favorite movie?
let+목적어+동사원형: 목적어가 ~하게 하다

Kyle: It's *Forrest Gump*.

Emma: Okay. Let's look for its advertisement. What does it say?
it = Forrest Gump   = its advertisement

Kyle: It says, "Winner of 6 Academy Awards including Best Picture."
~라고 되어[쓰여] 있다   수상작   전치사(~을 포함하여)

Emma: See? It uses facts unlike the *Y-Men 7* advertisement. Do you
전치사(~와는 달리)

see the difference?
알다, 이해하다

Kyle: Not exactly. The *Y-Men 7* ad says "Most Exciting Movie" and the
정확히는 아니다

Forrest Gump ad says "Best Picture." Aren't they both opinions?
= 'Most Exciting Movie'와 'Best Picture'

Emma: That's a great question, Kyle. When people use words like
전치사(~와 같은)

"best" or "most," they are usually expressing opinions. But in the

Forrest Gump ad, "Best Picture" is the award which the movie
목적격 관계대명사(선행사: award)

won. We can check that on the Internet. That's a fact.
"Best Picture" is the award which the movie won

Kyle: Aha! From now on I'm only going to trust ads with facts.
지금부터   ~을 가진, ~이 있는

Emma: It's not that simple. Most ads mix facts with opinions. So you
지시부사(그렇게, 그 정도로)

have to make a smart choice based on both of them.
facts and opinions

Kyle: Got it! Emma, do you want to watch the rest of *Y-Men 7* with me?
알았어!

Emma: Thanks, but no thanks. Enjoy the rest of the movie!
상대방이 권해 줘서 고맙지만 거절하고 싶을 때 쓸 수 있는 표현

explain 설명하다	
favorite 가장 좋아하는	
difference 차이	
both 둘 다	
trust 믿다	
simple 간단한	
mix A with B A와 B를 섞다	
make a choice 선택하다	
based on ~을 바탕으로	
rest 나머지	

📎 **확인문제**

● 다음 문장이 본문의 내용과 일치하면 T, 일치하지 않으면 F를 쓰시오.

1 Emma's favorite movie is *Forrest Gump*. ☐

2 *Forrest Gump* won seven Academy Awards. ☐

3 People use words like 'best' or 'most' when telling opinions. ☐

4 Kyle wants Emma to watch the movie with him. ☐

● 우리말을 참고하여 빈칸에 알맞은 말을 쓰시오.

1 Emma: What _____ you _____, Kyle?

2 Kyle: Oh, Emma. I'm _____ the movie, *Y-Men 7* _____ my computer.

3 Emma: _____ is it?

4 Kyle: Don't ask. It's _____ _____ _____ I want to cry.

5 Emma: I'm sorry _____ _____ _____ .

6 Kyle: I'm so mad. The movie _____ said _____ was "_____ _____ _____ _____ of the Year."

7 Emma: Well, you can't believe _____ _____ _____ _____ .

8 Kyle: They lied on the advertisement. I'm going to _____ _____ _____ _____ _____ .

9 Emma: _____ _____ , Kyle! They didn't really _____ _____ they used opinions, not facts.

10 Kyle: Huh? I'm _____ _____ _____ .

11 Emma: Opinions _____ _____ _____ like, "The desert is beautiful."

12 You can't say _____ it's true or not. But, facts _____ _____ _____ .

13 _____ _____ , "The Atacama Desert is in Chile," is a fact. You can _____ _____ _____ _____ _____ _____ .

14 Kyle: Okay…. But what's _____ _____ _____ movies?

15 Emma: _____ _____ _____ . What's your favorite movie?

1 Emma: Kyle, 뭐 하고 있니?

2 Kyle: Emma. 나는 컴퓨터로 영화 "Y-Men 7"을 보고 있어.

3 Emma: 어때?

4 Kyle: 묻지 마. 너무 지루해서 울고 싶어.

5 Emma: 유감이야.

6 Klye: 난 정말 화가 나. 영화 광고에는 이것이 "올해의 가장 흥미진진한 영화"라고 쓰여 있었어.

7 Emma: 음, 넌 네가 읽는 것을 모두 믿을 수는 없어.

8 Kyle: 그들은 광고에 거짓말을 한 거야. 돈을 환불해 달라고 해야겠어.

9 Emma: 기다려, Kyle! 그들은 사실이 아닌 의견을 사용했기 때문에 꼭 거짓말을 한 것은 아니야.

10 Kyle: 뭐라고? 네 말을 이해하지 못하겠어.

11 Emma: 의견은 "사막은 아름다워."와 같이 사람들의 감정을 표현하는 것이야.

12 그것이 사실인지 아닌지 말할 수는 없어. 하지만 사실은 증명할 수 있어.

13 예를 들면, "아타카마 사막은 칠레에 있다."는 사실이야. 넌 그것을 지도에서 확인할 수 있어.

14 Kyle: 알겠어… 하지만 그게 영화와 무슨 관련이 있니?

15 Emma: 설명해 줄게. 네가 가장 좋아하는 영화가 뭐니?

16 Kyle: _____ *Forrest Gump*.

17 Emma: Okay. Let's _____ _____ _____ _____. What does it say?

18 Kyle: _____ _____, "Winner of 6 Academy Awards including Best Picture."

19 Emma: See? It _____ _____ _____ the *Y-Men 7* advertisement.

20 Do you see _____ _____?

21 Kyle: Not _____. The *Y-Men 7* ad _____ "Most Exciting Movie" and the *Forrest Gump* ad _____ "Best Picture."

22 _____ they _____ _____?

23 Emma: That's a great question, Kyle. When people use _____ _____ "best" or "most," they are _____ _____ _____.

24 But in the *Forrest Gump* ad, "Best Picture" is the award _____ _____ _____ _____.

25 We can check _____ _____ _____ _____. That's a fact.

26 Kyle: Aha! _____ _____ _____ I'm only going to _____ ads _____ facts.

27 Emma: It's not _____. Most ads _____ facts _____ opinions.

28 So you have to _____ _____ _____ _____ based on _____ of them.

29 Kyle: Got it! Emma, do you want _____ _____ the rest of *Y-Men 7* with me?

30 Emma: Thanks, but no thanks. Enjoy _____ the movie!

---

16 Kyle: "Forest Gump"야.

17 Emma: 좋아. 그 영화의 광고를 찾아보자. 뭐라고 쓰여 있니?

18 Kyle: "Best Picture를 포함하여 아카데미 6개 부문 수상작"이라 고 쓰여 있어.

19 Emma: 알겠니? "Y-Men 7" 광 고와는 달리 사실을 사용하고 있어.

20 차이를 알겠니?

21 Kyle: 잘 모르겠어. "Y-Men 7" 광고는 "Most Exciting Movie" 라고 쓰여 있고 "Forest Gump" 광고는 "Best Picture"라고 쓰여 있잖아.

22 둘 다 의견 아니니?

23 Emma: 좋은 질문이야, Kyle. 사 람들이 'best'나 'most'와 같은 말을 사용할 때, 그들은 대개 의 견을 표현하는 거야.

24 하지만 "Forest Gump" 광고에 서 "Best Picture"는 영화가 받 은 상이야.

25 우리는 인터넷에서 그것을 확인 할 수 있어. 그건 사실이야.

26 Kyle: 아하! 지금부터 사실로 이 루어진 광고만 믿겠어.

27 Emma: 그렇게 간단하지는 않 아. 대부분의 광고는 사실과 의 견이 섞여 있어.

28 그러니 그 둘을 바탕으로 현명 한 선택을 해야 해.

29 Kyle: 알겠어! Emma, "Y-Men 7"의 남은 부분을 나와 함께 볼 래?

30 Emma: 고맙지만 사양할게. 영 화의 남은 부분 잘 봐!

● 우리말을 참고하여 본문을 영작하시오.

1 ▶ Emma: Kyle, 뭐 하고 있니?

➡ _____

2 ▶ Kyle: Emma. 나는 컴퓨터로 영화 "Y-Men 7"을 보고 있어.

➡ _____

3 ▶ Emma: 어때?

➡ _____

4 ▶ Kyle: 묻지 마. 너무 지루해서 울고 싶어.

➡ _____

5 ▶ Emma: 유감이야.

➡ _____

6 ▶ Klye: 난 정말 화가 나. 영화 광고에는 이것이 "올해의 가장 흥미진진한 영화"라고 쓰여 있었어.

➡ _____

7 ▶ Emma: 음, 넌 네가 읽는 것을 모두 믿을 수는 없어.

➡ _____

8 ▶ Kyle: 그들은 광고에 거짓말을 한 거야. 돈을 환불해 달라고 해야겠어.

➡ _____

9 ▶ Emma: 기다려, Kyle! 그들은 사실이 아닌 의견을 사용했기 때문에 꼭 거짓말을 한 것은 아니야.

➡ _____

10 ▶ Kyle: 뭐라고? 네 말을 이해하지 못하겠어.

➡ _____

11 ▶ Emma: 의견은 "사막은 아름다워."와 같이 사람들의 감정을 표현하는 것이야.

➡ _____

12 ▶ 그것이 사실인지 아닌지 말할 수는 없어. 하지만 사실은 증명할 수 있어.

➡ _____

13 ▶ 예를 들면, "아타카마 사막은 칠레에 있다."는 사실이야. 넌 그것을 지도에서 확인할 수 있어.

➡ _____

14 ▶ Kyle: 알겠어…. 하지만 그게 영화와 무슨 관련이 있니?

➡ _____

15 ▶ Emma: 설명해 줄게. 네가 가장 좋아하는 영화가 뭐니?

➡ _____

16 Kyle: "Forest Gump"야.

➡ _____

17 Emma: 좋아. 그 영화의 광고를 찾아보자. 뭐라고 쓰여 있니?

➡ _____

18 Kyle: "Best Picture를 포함하여 아카데미 6개 부문 수상작"이라고 쓰여 있어.

➡ _____

19 Emma: 알겠니? "Y-Men 7" 광고와는 달리 사실을 사용하고 있어.

➡ _____

20 차이를 알겠니?

➡ _____

21 Kyle: 잘 모르겠어. "Y-Men 7" 광고는 "Most Exciting Movie"라고 쓰여 있고 "Forest Gump" 광고는 "Best Picture"라고 쓰여 있잖아.

➡ _____

22 둘 다 의견 아니니?

➡ _____

23 Emma: 좋은 질문이야, Kyle. 사람들이 'best'나 'most'와 같은 말을 사용할 때, 그들은 대개 의견을 표현하는 거야.

➡ _____

24 하지만 "Forest Gump" 광고에서 "Best Picture"는 영화가 받은 상이야.

➡ _____

25 우리는 인터넷에서 그것을 확인할 수 있어. 그건 사실이야.

➡ _____

26 Kyle: 아하! 지금부터 사실로 이루어진 광고만 믿겠어.

➡ _____

27 Emma: 그렇게 간단하지는 않아. 대부분의 광고는 사실과 의견이 섞여 있어.

➡ _____

28 그러니 그 둘을 바탕으로 현명한 선택을 해야 해.

➡ _____

29 Kyle: 알겠어! Emma, "Y-Men 7"의 남은 부분을 나와 함께 볼래?

➡ _____

30 Emma: 고맙지만 사양할게. 영화의 남은 부분 잘 봐!

➡ _____

[01~05] 다음 글을 읽고 물음에 답하시오.

Emma: What are you doing, Kyle?

Kyle: Oh, Emma. I'm watching the movie, *Y-Men 7* on my computer.

Emma: How is it?

Kyle: Don't ask. It's so boring that I want to cry.

Emma: I'm sorry to hear that.

Kyle: I'm so mad. The movie advertisement said it was "The Most Exciting Movie of the Year."

Emma: Well, you can't believe everything ___(A)___ you read.

Kyle: They lied on the advertisement. I'm going to ask for my money back.

Emma: (B)Hold on, Kyle! They didn't really lie because they used opinions, not facts.

01 빈칸 (A)에 들어갈 말로 적절한 것을 모두 고르시오.

① which   ② that   ③ what
④ whose   ⑤ who

02 다음 중 위 글의 내용과 일치하지 않는 것은?

① Kyle is watching *Y-Men 7*.
② Emma is wondering what Kyle is doing.
③ Kyle is satisfied with the movie.
④ Kyle wants to get his money back.
⑤ Kyle thinks that he was fooled by the movie advertisement.

서답형

03 다음과 같이 풀이되는 단어를 위 글에서 찾아 쓰시오.

> ideas or feelings about something.

➡ _____

서답형

04 Write the reason why Kyle wants to cry. Answer in English with the phrase 'It's because.'

➡ _____

05 다음 중 밑줄 친 (B)를 대신하여 쓰일 수 있는 것은?

① Go ahead   ② Wait
③ Let me see   ④ Watch out
⑤ Way to go

[06~09] 다음 글을 읽고 물음에 답하시오.

Kyle: Huh? I'm not following you.

Emma: Opinions express people's feelings like, "The desert is beautiful." You can't say that it's true or not. But, facts can be proven. ___(A)___, "The Atacama Desert is in Chile," is a fact. You can check (B)that on the map.

Kyle: Okay.... But what's the connection with movies?

Emma: Let me explain. What's your favorite movie?

Kyle: It's *Forrest Gump*.

Emma: Okay. Let's look for its advertisement. What does it say?

Kyle: It says, "Winner of 6 Academy Awards including Best Picture."

Emma: See? It uses facts unlike the *Y-Men 7* advertisement. Do you see the difference?

06 다음 중 빈칸 (A)에 들어갈 말로 가장 적절한 것은?

① However   ② Therefore
③ Also   ④ For example
⑤ Nevertheless

서답형

07 밑줄 친 (B)가 가리키는 것을 15자 이내의 우리말로 쓰시오.

➡ _____

08 다음 중 위 글을 읽고 답할 수 <u>없는</u> 질문은?

① What is opinion?

② Where is the Atacama Desert?

③ What is Emma's favorite movie?

④ How many academy awards did *Forrest Gump* win?

⑤ What does *Forrest Gump* advertisement say?

09 According to the passage, which one is a fact?

① Jimmy is the kindest person I have ever met.

② I think the river is dangerous to swim in.

③ It seems that the butterfly is saying hello to me.

④ Mrs. Simpson looked upset today.

⑤ Barack Obama is the 44th president of the United States of America.

[10~15] 다음 글을 읽고 물음에 답하시오.

> **Kyle:** Not exactly. The *Y-Men 7* ad says "Most Exciting Movie" and the *Forrest Gump* ad says "Best Picture." Aren't they both ①opinion?
>
> **Emma:** That's a great question, Kyle. When people use words like "best" or "most," they are usually expressing opinions. But ②in the *Forrest Gump* ad, "Best Picture" is the award ③which the movie won. We can check that ④on the Internet. That's ___(A)___ .
>
> **Kyle:** Aha! (B)지금부터 I'm only going to trust ⑤ads with facts.

Emma: It's not that simple. Most ads mix facts with opinions. So you have to make a smart choice based on (C)both of them.

서답형

10 빈칸 (A)에 알맞은 말을 위 글에서 찾아 어법에 맞게 쓰시오.

➡ _____

11 밑줄 친 우리말 (B)를 영어로 바르게 옮긴 것은?

① For a long time   ② For the time being

③ From now on   ④ From time to time

⑤ Now and then

서답형

12 밑줄 친 (C)가 가리키는 것을 영어로 쓰시오.

➡ _____

13 ①~⑤ 중 어법상 바르지 <u>않은</u> 것은?

①   ②   ③   ④   ⑤

서답형

14 What do people usually use when they express their opinions? Answer in English with a full sentence.

➡ _____

_____

15 다음 중 위 글의 내용과 일치하지 <u>않는</u> 것은?

① There is a phrase "Most Exciting Movie" in the ad of *Y-Men 7*.

② *Forrest Gump* won the Best Picture award.

③ The ad of *Forrest Gump* used a fact.

④ There are many ads using only facts.

⑤ Kyle finally understands the difference between opinions and facts.

[16~20] 다음 글을 읽고 물음에 답하시오.

Emma: What are you doing, Kyle?

Kyle: Oh, Emma. I'm watching the movie, *Y-Men 7* on my computer.

Emma: (A)[What / How] is it?

Kyle: Don't ask. It's so (B)[boring / bored] that I want to cry.

Emma: I'm sorry ⓐto hear that.

Kyle: I'm so mad. The movie advertisement said it was "The Most Exciting Movie of the Year."

Emma: Well, you can't believe everything that you read.

Kyle: They lied on the advertisement. I'm going (C)[asking / to ask] for my money back.

Emma: Hold on, Kyle! They didn't really lie _____ⓑ_____ they used opinions, not facts.

16 다음 중 밑줄 친 ⓐ와 쓰임이 같은 것은?

① David wants me to go with him to the theater.

② It is fun to spend time with you.

③ There are some cookies to give her friends.

④ There is a chance to win the race.

⑤ I am so happy to have such a nice teacher.

17 다음 중 빈칸 ⓑ에 들어갈 말로 가장 적절한 것은?

① so   ② while   ③ and

④ because   ⑤ though

서답형

18 What is Kyle doing? Answer in English with a full sentence.

➡ _____

19 (A)~(C)에서 어법상 옳은 것을 바르게 짝지은 것은?

① What – boring – asking

② What – boring – to ask

③ What – bored – to ask

④ How – boring – to ask

⑤ How – bored – asking

서답형

20 According to the passage, what did the movie advertisement say about the movie?

➡ _____

_____

[21~25] 다음 글을 읽고 물음에 답하시오.

Kyle: Huh? I'm not following you.

Emma: Opinions express people's feelings like, "The desert is beautiful." ① You can't say that it's true or not. ② But, facts can (A)[prove / be proven]. ③ For example, "The Atacama Desert is in Chile," is a fact. ④

Kyle: Okay.... But what's the connection with movies? ⑤

Emma: Let me (B)[explain / to explain]. What's your favorite movie?

Kyle: It's *Forrest Gump*.

Emma: Okay. Let's look for its advertisement. What does it say?

Kyle: It says, "Winner of 6 Academy Awards (C)[including / included] Best Picture."

Emma: See? It uses facts unlike the *Y-Men 7* advertisement. Do you see the difference?

21 ①~⑤ 중 주어진 문장이 들어가기에 가장 적절한 곳은?

You can check that on the map.

① ② ③ ④ ⑤

22 (A)~(C)에서 어법상 옳은 것을 바르게 짝지은 것은?

① be proven – explain – included
② be proven – explain – including
③ prove – to explain – included
④ prove – explain – including
⑤ prove – to explain – including

서답형

23 위 글의 내용을 참고하여 다음 빈칸에 알맞은 말을 쓰시오.

> According to the passage, "She is the most beautiful baby I've ever seen," is _____. On the other hand, "Mountain Everest is the highest mountain in the world." is _____.

24 According to the passage, who says an opinion?

① Jane: King Sejong invented Hanguel.
② Tim: Canada is rich in natural resources.
③ Brad: The longest river in the world is the Nile in Egypt.
④ Zoe: Going to the beach alone is not safe.
⑤ Kelly: Tom's house is located near the river.

25 다음 중 위 글의 내용과 일치하지 <u>않는</u> 것은?

① People's feelings are expressed in opinions.
② Emma wants to know what Kyle's favorite movie is.
③ Emma is explaining the difference between opinions and facts.
④ The *Forrest Gump* ad uses facts.
⑤ *Forrest Gump* won seven Academy Awards.

[26~29] 다음 글을 읽고 물음에 답하시오.

Emma: Do you see the difference?
(A) That's a great question. When people use words like "best" or "most," they are usually expressing opinions. But in the *Forrest Gump* ad, "Best Picture" is the award which the movie won. We can check (a)that on the Internet. That's a fact.
(B) It's not that simple. Most ads mix facts __ⓐ__ opinions. So you have to make a smart choice based on both of them.
(C) Aha! From now on I'm only going to trust ads __ⓑ__ facts.
(D) Not exactly. The *Y-Men 7* ad says "Most Exciting Movie" and the *Forrest Gump* ad says "Best Picture." Aren't they both opinions?

서답형

26 자연스러운 대화가 되도록 (A)~(D)를 바르게 나열하시오.

➡ _____

27 다음 중 빈칸 ⓐ와 ⓑ에 공통으로 들어갈 말은?

① in   ② by   ③ with   ④ to   ⑤ at

서답형

28 밑줄 친 (a)가 가리키는 것을 우리말로 쓰시오.

➡ _____

서답형

29 위 글의 내용에 맞게 빈칸에 알맞은 말을 쓰시오.

> We can find both _____ in most ads.

➡ _____

[01~05] 다음 글을 읽고 물음에 답하시오.

Emma: What are you doing, Kyle?

Kyle: Oh, Emma. I'm watching the movie, *Y-Men 7* on my computer.

Emma: How is it?

Kyle: Don't ask. (A)너무 지루해서 울고 싶어.

Emma: I'm sorry to hear that.

Kyle: I'm so mad. The movie advertisement said it was "The Most Exciting Movie of the Year."

Emma: Well, you can't believe everything that you read.

Kyle: They lied on the advertisement.
          (a)

Emma: Hold on, Kyle! (B)They didn't really lie because they used opinions, not facts.

01 주어진 단어를 바르게 배열하여 빈칸 (a)에 들어갈 말을 쓰시오.

(back / am / to / I / ask / money / for / my / going)

➡ _____

02 밑줄 친 우리말 (A)를 영어로 쓰시오.

➡ _____

03 주어진 단어를 이용하여 밑줄 친 (B)와 같은 의미의 문장을 쓰시오.

(not A but B / so)

➡ _____
_____

04 What is the title of the movie that Kyle is watching?

➡ _____

05 글의 내용에 맞게 빈칸에 알맞은 말을 쓰시오.

Unlike the movie advertisement, Kyle did not feel _____ while he was watching the movie.

[06~10] 다음 글을 읽고 물음에 답하시오.

Kyle: Huh? I'm not following you.

Emma: Opinions express people's feelings like, "The desert is beautiful." You can't say that it's true or not. But, facts can ___(A)___. For example, "(B)The Atacama Desert is in Chile," is a fact. You can check that on the map.

Kyle: Okay.... But what's the connection with movies?

Emma: Let me explain. What's your favorite movie?

Kyle: It's *Forrest Gump*.

Emma: Okay. Let's look for its advertisement. What does it say?

Kyle: It says, "Winner of 6 Academy Awards including Best Picture."

Emma: See? (C)It uses facts unlike the *Y-Men 7* advertisement. Do you see the difference?

06 ⭐중요 주어진 단어를 빈칸 (A)에 어법에 맞게 쓰시오.

prove

➡ _____

07 How can you know the underlined sentence (B) is a fact? Find the answer in the above passage.

➡ _____

08 다음 문장은 밑줄 친 문장 (C)를 읽고 알 수 있는 것이다. 빈칸에 알맞은 말을 쓰시오.

➡ The *Y-Men 7* ad _____.

09 고난이도 위 글의 표현을 이용하여 다음 우리말을 영어로 쓰시오.

6개의 아카데미상을 수상한 그 영화를 보았니?

➡ _____

10 ⭐중요 According to the passage, what is Kyle's favorite movie? Answer in English with a full sentence.

➡ _____

[11~14] 다음 글을 읽고 물음에 답하시오.

Kyle: Not exactly. The *Y-Men 7* ad says "Most Exciting Movie" and the *Forrest Gump* ad says "Best Picture." _____ (A)

Emma: That's a great question, Kyle. When people use words like "best" or "most," they are usually expressing opinions. But in the *Forrest Gump* ad, (B)"Best Picture" is the award which the movie won. We can check that on the Internet. That's a fact.

Kyle: Aha! From now on I'm only going to trust ads with facts.

Emma: It's not that simple. Most ads mix facts with opinions. So you have to make a smart choice based on both of them.

11 ⭐중요 주어진 단어를 바르게 나열하여 빈칸 (A)에 알맞은 말을 쓰시오.

(opinions / they / aren't / both)?

➡ _____

12 밑줄 친 문장 (B)를 두 문장으로 나누어 쓰시오.

➡ _____

13 고난이도 주어진 어구를 바르게 배열하여 다음 우리말을 영어로 쓰시오.

'best'나 'most'와 같은 말을 사용하는 사람들은 대개 의견을 표현하는 중이다. (opinions / people / use / are / expressing / usually / 'best' or 'most' / who / like / words)

➡ _____

_____

14 위 글의 내용에 맞게 빈칸에 알맞은 말을 쓰시오.

When we make a decision, we should _____ our choice on _____ _____ _____.

Listen and Speak 2-C

A: How do you like your bicycle?

'〜이 마음에 드니?' (만족하는지를 묻는 표현)

B: I'm not happy with it.

= the bicycle을 가리킨다.

A: Why not?

= Why are you not satisfied with it?

B: It's too heavy.

A: 자전거가 마음에 드니?

B: 마음에 들지 않아.

A: 왜?

B: 너무 무거워.

Think and Write

Harry Potter is a fantasy novel. It was written by J. K. Rowling. Harry Potter

인칭대명사(Harry Potter 지칭)

is the main character of the book. When Harry goes to magic school, his

주인공

adventures begin. I especially like the friendship of Harry and his friends. The

book was so interesting that I couldn't put it down. I strongly recommend it to

흥미를 유발할 때 현재분사 so+형용사/부사+that ...: 너무 〜해서 …하다

everyone.

구문해설 • a fantasy novel: 공상 소설   • adventure: 모험   • especially: 특히
• friendship: 우정   • put A down: 〜를 내려놓다   • recommend: 추천하다

"해리포터"는 공상 소설이다. 이 책은 J. K. Rowling에 의해 쓰였다. Harry Potter 는 이 책의 주인공이다. Harry가 마법 학교에 가면서 그의 모험은 시작된다. 나는 특히 Harry와 그의 친구들의 우정을 좋아한다. 이 책은 너무 재미있어서 나는 책을 놓을 수가 없었다. 나는 모두에게 이 책을 강력히 추천한다.

Project

Korean folk village

Facts: It is located in Yongin. There are Korean traditional houses. Visitors

〜에 위치해 있다   〜이 있다 (뒤에 나오는 명사에 수의 일치)

can watch nongak and juljtagi.

Opinions: It's a fun place in Yongin. Korean traditional houses are beautiful.

Nongak and juljtagi will be exciting.

감정을 유발할 때 현재분사

구문해설 • folk village: 민속촌   • traditional: 전통적인   • exciting: 신나는

한국 민속촌

사실: 그것은 용인에 있습니다. 한국 전통 가옥이 있습니다. 방문객들은 농악과 줄타기를 볼 수 있습니다.

의견: 그곳은 용인에 있는 재미있는 장소입니다. 한국 전통 가옥들은 아름답습니다. 농악과 줄타기는 신이 날 것입니다.

Words & Expressions

01 다음 짝지어진 단어의 관계가 같도록 빈칸에 알맞은 말을 쓰시오.

increase : decrease = empty : _____

02 다음 영영풀이가 가리키는 것을 고르시오.

to say or write something that is not true

① explain ② tell

③ present ④ lie

⑤ express

03 다음 중 밑줄 친 부분의 뜻풀이가 바르지 않은 것은?

① I like this pocket on the back of the suitcase. 주머니

② I can trust her word. 신뢰하다

③ She answered wisely. 현명하게

④ This book is worth reading. 세계

⑤ The bag comes in navy and green. 남색

04 다음 주어진 우리말과 일치하도록 주어진 단어를 모두 배열하여 영작하시오.

(1) 선물이 마음에 드니?

(you / how / like / the / present / do)

➡ _____

(2) 그의 주장을 증명할 증거가 없다.

(no / his / evidence / is / to / claim / there / prove)

➡ _____

05 주어진 단어를 이용해서 다음 우리말에 맞게 빈칸에 알맞은 말을 쓰시오.

(1) 가격을 비교해 보고 선택하는 게 어때?

➡ Why don't you _____ after comparing the prices? (make)

(2) 나는 네가 다시 한 번 서류를 확인해야 할 것 같아.

➡ I think you should _____ the documents again. (out)

(3) 야외 시장은 사람들로 가득 차 있었다.

➡ The outdoor market was _____ people. (of)

06 다음 주어진 문장의 밑줄 친 lie와 같은 의미로 쓰인 것은?

Why did you lie to me? I'm so disappointed with you.

① I want to go home and lie on the bed.

② Lie down here and take a rest.

③ I'm innocent because I didn't lie for a second.

④ My children usually lie on the right side when they sleep.

⑤ You can't lie on the floor.

07 다음 문장에 공통으로 들어갈 말을 고르시오.

• This gallery is _____ a visit.
• This movie is _____ watching.
• This souvenir is _____ $100.

① worth ② cost

③ price ④ value

⑤ expense

Conversation

[08~09] 다음 대화를 읽고 물음에 답하시오.

> Brian: (A)Can you recommend a good movie?
> Emily: _____(B)_____ I really liked it.
> Brian: Oh, I haven't seen it yet.
> Emily: It's the number one movie right now.

08 위 대화의 밑줄 친 (A)와 바꾸어 쓸 수 있는 것은?

① What do you think about a good movie?
② Would you recommend a good movie?
③ What is a good movie?
④ Do you want to see a good movie?
⑤ What should I do to find a good movie?

09 위 대화의 빈칸 (B)에 들어갈 말로 어색한 것은?

① Try *Star Wars*.
② How about watching *Star Wars*?
③ Why did you watch *Star Wars*?
④ What about watching *Star Wars*?
⑤ I recommend *Star Wars*.

[10~12] 다음 대화를 읽고 물음에 답하시오.

> W: May I help you?
> B: Yes. I'm looking for a backpack. Can you recommend one?
> W: How about this red one? Red is the most popular color (A)these days.
> B: My old backpack was red, so I want a different color.
> W: How about this navy one? It has side pockets.
> B: Oh, that looks good. I'll take it.

10 위 대화의 여자와 소년의 관계로 적절한 것은?

① doctor – patient
② clerk – customer
③ guide – tourist
④ teacher – student
⑤ writer – reader

11 위 대화의 밑줄 친 (A)와 바꾸어 쓸 수 있는 것은?

① those days
② nowadays
③ in the past
④ the day before
⑤ in the future

12 위 대화의 내용과 일치하지 <u>않는</u> 것은?

① 소년은 배낭을 찾고 있다.
② 요즘 빨간색이 가장 인기 있는 색이다.
③ 소년의 옛 배낭이 빨간색이었다.
④ 남색 배낭은 양옆에 주머니가 있다.
⑤ 소년은 주머니가 있는 빨간색 가방을 샀다.

[13~15] 다음 대화를 읽고 물음에 답하시오.

> Jack: Hi, Suji. (A)경주 여행은 어땠니?
> (Gyeongju, trip, how, like)
> Suji: I was very happy with it.
> Jack: Where did you visit?
> Suji: I visited Cheomseongdae. It was great.
> Jack: Where else did you go?
> Suji: Bulguksa. It was a wonderful place.
> Jack: Sounds like the perfect trip.
> Suji: Yeah, but walking up to Seokguram was difficult.
> Jack: But I'm sure it was worth it.

13 위 대화의 밑줄 친 (A)의 우리말을 주어진 단어를 사용하여 영작하시오.

➡ _____

14 위 대화에서 다음 주어진 영영풀이가 나타내는 말을 찾아 쓰시오.

> important, good or enjoyable enough for something

➡ _____

15 위 대화를 읽고 대답할 수 <u>없는</u> 질문은?

① Where did Suji travel?
② How did Suji like her trip to Gyeongju?
③ What did Suji think of Bulguksa?
④ What does Jack think about walking up to Seokguram?
⑤ How long did it take for Suji to walk up to Seokguram?

16 다음 짝지어진 대화가 <u>어색한</u> 것을 고르시오.

① A: Can you recommend a musical for me?
   B: How about *The Lion King*?
② A: How do you like your bicycle?
   B: I'm really happy with it.
③ A: Would you recommend a good movie?
   B: Why don't you try *Star Wars*?
④ A: How do you like your jacket?
   B: I'm not satisfied with it.
⑤ A: What do you like about your backpack?
   B: I like it so much.

Grammar

17 다음 중 주어진 문장의 밑줄 친 부분과 쓰임이 같은 것은?

> The health-care worker <u>that</u> I spoke to was helpful.

① Hudson said <u>that</u> he refused the job offer.
② It is true <u>that</u> I don't like your attitude.
③ Patrick woke up so late <u>that</u> he couldn't attend the meeting again.
④ The fact <u>that</u> you lied to the police officer doesn't change.
⑤ This is the same kind of watch <u>that</u> I lost.

18 주어진 문장과 같은 의미의 문장은?

> We postponed our trip because the weather was bad.

① The weather was bad enough that we postponed our trip.
② The weather was so bad that we postponed our trip.
③ Although the weather was bad, we postponed our trip.
④ Because we postponed our trip, the weather was bad.
⑤ The weather was too bad to postpone our trip.

19 다음 빈칸에 들어갈 말로 적절한 것을 <u>모두</u> 고르시오.

> The children _____ Mr. Smith adopted are from three different countries.

① who   ② that   ③ whose
④ which   ⑤ whom

20 주어진 문장과 같은 의미의 문장을 쓰시오.

> We went swimming because it was so hot yesterday. (so ~ that을 이용)

➡ _____

21 다음 중 빈칸에 들어갈 말로 적절한 것은?

> • She was so embarrassed that she wanted to run away and hide.
> = She wanted to run away and hide _____ she was embarrassed.

① although   ② because   ③ so
④ unless   ⑤ therefore

22 다음 중 의미가 나머지 넷과 <u>다른</u> 하나는?

① Maya is so afraid of flying that she can't travel by plane.

② Maya can't travel by plane because she is afraid of flying.

③ Maya is afraid of flying, so she can't travel by plane.

④ Maya is too afraid of flying to travel by plane.

⑤ Although Maya is afraid of flying, she travels by plane.

23 주어진 단어를 이용하여 다음 우리말을 영어로 쓰시오.

> 그 남자가 훔친 약은 그의 아들을 위한 것이었다.
> (drug)

➡ _____

24 다음 중 밑줄 친 부분이 생략 가능하지 <u>않은</u> 것은?

① The painting <u>which</u> you drew looks amazing.

② The car <u>that</u> Brian borrowed from his brother was dirty.

③ A girl <u>who</u> was called Puddle fell in love with my brother.

④ I ordered an expensive meal at the restaurant <u>which</u> Clark runs.

⑤ Joy saw a man looking into the car <u>which</u> Tom bought.

25 다음 두 문장을 하나의 문장으로 쓰시오.

> We eat the carrots. My grandfather grew them on the farm.

➡ _____

_____

26 'so ~ that'을 이용하여 다음 두 문장을 한 문장으로 쓰시오.

> There are many leaves on a single tree. It is impossible to count them.

➡ _____

_____

27 주어진 단어를 이용하여 다음 우리말을 영어로 쓰시오.

> 네가 지난주에 방문한 박물관에 관해 말해 줘.
> (tell / visit)

➡ _____

_____

Reading

[28~30] 다음 글을 읽고 물음에 답하시오.

Emma: What are you doing, Kyle?

Kyle: Oh, Emma. I'm watching the movie, *Y-Men 7* on my computer.

Emma: How is it?

Kyle: Don't ask. (A)It's so boring that I want to cry.

Emma: I'm sorry to hear that.

Kyle: I'm so mad. The movie advertisement said it was "The Most Exciting Movie of the Year."

Emma: Well, you can't believe everything that you read.

Kyle: They lied on the advertisement. I'm going to ask for my money back.

Emma: Hold on, Kyle! They didn't really lie because they used opinions, not facts.

28 주어진 단어를 이용하여 다음 우리말을 영어로 쓰시오.

> Kyle이 선택한 영화는 광고에서 의견을 사용하였다. (chose / in the advertisement)

➡ _____

_____

29 다음 중 밑줄 친 (A)와 쓰임이 같은 것을 <u>모두</u> 고르시오.

① <u>It</u> is exciting to meet them this weekend.

② <u>It</u> is ten miles to Boston.

③ <u>It</u> will make our cake creamy.

④ <u>It</u> was windy and dark yesterday.

⑤ <u>It</u> means that they will quit as soon as possible.

30 다음 중 위 글을 읽고 답할 수 <u>없는</u> 질문은?

① What is Kyle doing?

② Why does Kyle want to cry?

③ How does Kyle feel about the movie?

④ Why does Kyle think they lied on the advertisement?

⑤ What does Emma think about Kyle?

[31~33] 다음 글을 읽고 물음에 답하시오.

Kyle: Not exactly. The *Y-Men 7* ad says "Most Exciting Movie" and the *Forrest Gump* ad says "Best Picture." Aren't they both opinions?

Emma: That's a great question, Kyle. When people use words like "best" or "most," they are usually expressing opinions. But in the *Forrest Gump* ad, "Best Picture" is the award ____(A)____ the movie won. We can check that on the Internet. That's a fact.

Kyle: Aha! From now on I'm only going to trust ads with facts.

Emma: (B)It's not that simple. Most ads mix facts with opinions. So you have to make a smart choice based on both of them.

31 다음 중 빈칸 (A)에 들어갈 말과 <u>다른</u> 하나는?

① I don't know _____ she is.

② The boys _____ you are looking at are my friends.

③ There are some flowers _____ Tom picked.

④ Many students _____ I teach are diligent.

⑤ A girl and a cat _____ are sitting together look happy.

32 다음은 좋은 영화를 고르기 위해 어떤 광고를 신뢰해야 하는지에 대한 조언이다. 올바른 조언을 한 사람은?

① Ben: Don't trust ads because they are full of lies.

② Amelia: Find ads which are full of facts.

③ Clark: Watch only movies that use opinions in their ads.

④ Molly: Choose a movie which only uses words like 'best' or 'most' in the ad.

⑤ Kevin: Check both facts and opinions and choose wisely.

33 Write the reason why Emma says like the underlined (B). Use the phrase "It's because."

➡ _____

01 다음 영영풀이가 가리키는 것을 고르시오. *출제율 90%*

> to add something to something else

① divide　　　② prove
③ lift　　　　④ advertise
⑤ mix

02 다음 우리말에 맞게 빈칸에 알맞은 말을 쓰시오. *출제율 95%*

(1) 시간을 현명하게 써야 한다.
　➡ You should spend your time _____.
(2) 좋은 식당을 추천해 줄래요?
　➡ Can you _____ a good restaurant?
(3) 나는 강력하게 그의 의견에 동의한다.
　➡ I _____ agree with his idea.

03 다음 문장의 빈칸에 들어갈 말을 〈보기〉에서 골라 쓰시오. *출제율 100%*

> ┤ 보기 ├
> hold on / right now / look for / number one / worth it

(1) Paris was the _____ destination for tourists.
(2) Would you help me _____ the information about Korean history?
(3) I'm working at the oil company _____.
(4) _____ for a moment. I'll bring my phone.
(5) I'm sure it'll _____.

04 다음 주어진 문장에 이어지는 대화가 자연스럽게 이어지도록 순서대로 배열하시오. *출제율 90%*

> May I help you?

(A) How about this red one? Red is the most popular color these days.
(B) Oh, that looks good. I'll take it.
(C) My old backpack was red, so I want a different color.
(D) How about this navy one? It has side pockets.
(E) Yes. I'm looking for a backpack. Can you recommend one?

➡ _____

05 다음 대화의 빈칸에 들어갈 말로 어색한 것은? *출제율 95%*

> A: How do you like your bicycle?
> B: I'm not satisfied with it.
> A: _____
> B: It's too heavy.

① What's wrong?
② Why not?
③ What's the problem?
④ What's the matter?
⑤ What do you like about it?

[06~08] 다음 대화를 읽고 물음에 답하시오.

Jack: Hi, Suji. (A)[What / How] did you like your trip to Gyeongju?
Suji: 여행은 매우 즐거웠어. (happy, it)
Jack: Where did you visit?
Suji: I visited Cheomseongdae. It was great.
Jack: Where else did you go?
Suji: Bulguksa. It was a wonderful place.
Jack: (B)[Sound / Sounds] like the perfect trip.
Suji: Yeah, but (C)[walk / walking] up to Seokguram was difficult.
Jack: But I'm sure it was worth it.

06 위 대화의 밑줄 친 우리말을 주어진 단어를 사용하여 영어로 쓰시오.

➡ _____

07 위 대화의 (A)~(C)에 들어갈 말로 적절한 것으로 짝지어진 것은?

	(A)	(B)	(C)
①	What	Sound	walk
②	What	Sounds	walking
③	How	Sounds	walk
④	How	Sounds	walking
⑤	How	Sound	walk

08 Check the places which Suji liked during the trip.

Cheomseongdae · Gyeongju National Museum · Seokguram · Bulguksa

➡ _____

09 다음 대화의 빈칸에 들어갈 말로 어색한 것은?

> **Bomi:** Jiho, can you recommend a musical for me?
>
> **Jiho:** How about *The Lion King*? _____
>
> **Bomi:** Okay. Sounds good.
>
> **Jiho:** I'm sure you'll like it.

① The story is exciting.

② The dancing is fantastic.

③ The music is so beautiful.

④ It is so popular these days.

⑤ I was so bored that I couldn't focus on it.

10 다음 대화의 내용과 일치하지 <u>않는</u> 것은?

> **Brian:** Mina, can you recommend a good pizza restaurant?
>
> **Mina:** Why don't you try Antonio's? It's my favorite.
>
> **Brian:** What do you like about it?
>
> **Mina:** The food is delicious. I recommend the bulgogi pizza.
>
> **Brian:** How are the prices?
>
> **Mina:** I think the prices are good, too.
>
> **Brian:** Sounds like a good restaurant. How do you like the service?
>
> **Mina:** It's a little slow on the weekends.
>
> **Brian:** Okay. I'll check it out. Thanks.
>
> **Mina:** No problem. Enjoy your meal!

① Brian is looking for a good pizza restaurant.

② Mina has eaten bulgogi pizza at Antonio's.

③ Mina thinks that the prices of Antonio's are resonable.

④ The service of Antonio's is a little slow on Saturdays and Sundays.

⑤ Brian is going to Antonio's to check whether the price is good or not.

11 다음 중 밑줄 친 부분의 쓰임이 <u>다른</u> 하나는?

① The girl <u>who</u> you invited didn't come.

② The man <u>who</u> gave me this ticket looks scary.

③ Can you tell me <u>who</u> they are?

④ The reporter <u>who</u> they hate wrote an article.

⑤ Tom is the boy <u>who</u> read lots of books.

12 다음 우리말을 영어로 바르게 옮긴 것은?
출제율 90%

> Jamie는 일을 너무 열심히 해서 병이 들었다.

① Jamie worked hardly to make himself sick.
② Jamie worked so that hard to become sick.
③ Jamie worked too hard to make himself sick.
④ Jamie worked so hard that he became sick.
⑤ Jamie worked so hardly that he became sick.

13 주어진 단어를 바르게 배열하여 다음 우리말을 영어로 쓰시오.
출제율 95%

> 네가 나에게서 빌려간 펜을 돌려줄래?
> (from / borrowed / the pen / me / can / you / back / give / you / me / that)

➡ _____

14 다음 중 빈칸에 들어갈 말로 가장 적절한 것은?
출제율 100%

> That is the chair _____ your brother used to sit.

① which
② on which
③ who
④ on that
⑤ that

15 다음 중 문장을 잘못 바꿔 쓴 것은?
출제율 90%

① Thomas is the man. You have to meet him.
= Thomas is the man you have to meet.
② This is the copy machine. Polly bought it.
= This is the copy machine that Polly bought.
③ Sally is too tired to do it.
= Sally is so tired that she can't do it.
④ Joe is looking at the candle. Maya made it.
= Joe is looking at the candle which Maya made.
⑤ Chris didn't know the man that his sister talked to.
= Chris didn't know the man to that his sister talked.

16 주어진 단어를 활용하여 다음 우리말을 영어로 쓰시오.
출제율 95%

> 그 역기는 너무 가벼워서 내가 들어 올릴 수 있었어. (barbell / lift)

➡ _____

[17~21] 다음 글을 읽고 물음에 답하시오.

Kyle: Huh? (A)I'm not following you.
Emma: Opinions express people's feelings like, "The desert is beautiful." You can't say (B)that it's true or not. But, facts can be proven. For example, "The Atacama Desert is in Chile," is a fact. You can check that on the map.
Kyle: Okay.... But what's the connection with movies?
Emma: Let me explain. What's your favorite movie?
Kyle: It's *Forrest Gump*.

Emma: Okay. Let's look for its advertisement. What does it say?

Kyle: It says, "Winner of 6 Academy Awards including Best Picture."

Emma: See? It uses facts unlike the *Y-Men 7* advertisement. Do you see the difference?

Kyle: Not exactly. The *Y-Men 7* ad says "Most Exciting Movie" and the *Forrest Gump* ad says "Best Picture." Aren't they both opinions?

17 출제율 95%

다음 중 밑줄 친 (A) 대신에 쓸 수 있는 것은?

① I can't go after you.
② I can't understand you.
③ You are following me.
④ I need to follow up something.
⑤ It is hard to catch up with you.

18 출제율 100%

다음 중 밑줄 친 (B)와 쓰임이 다른 것은?

① He thinks that his friends are nice.
② Do you know the fact that the movie is bad?
③ It is true that she bought two tickets.
④ He is the boy that you want to see.
⑤ They said that I had to deal with the problem.

19 출제율 90%

글의 내용에 맞게 빈칸에 알맞은 말을 쓰시오.

Unlike _____, _____ cannot be proven.

20 출제율 85%

What are they mainly talking about? Answer in English with a full sentence.

➡ _____

_____

21 출제율 95%

다음 중 의견에 해당하는 것은?

① Bulguksa is located in Gyeongju.
② The Han River is not as long as the Nile River.
③ Watching movies is interesting.
④ Bill Gates founded Microsoft.
⑤ Mother Teresa was born in 1910.

[22~24] 다음 글을 읽고 물음에 답하시오.

Charlotte's Web is a children's novel. It was written by E. B. White. A little pig named Wilbur is the main character of the book. When Wilbur is in danger, his friend Charlotte helps him out. I especially like the friendship of Wilbur and Charlotte. _____(A)_____ I strongly recommend it to everyone.

22 출제율 90%

주어진 어구를 바르게 배열하여 빈칸 (A)에 들어갈 말을 쓰시오.

(touching / many times / the book / that / I / so / read / was / it)

➡ _____

23 출제율 95%

다음 중 위 글을 읽고 답할 수 <u>없는</u> 질문은?

① When did Charlotte help Wilbur?
② Who wrote the novel?
③ What is the name of the main character?
④ Who is Wilbur's friend?
⑤ How many friends does Wilbur have?

24 출제율 90%

다음 두 문장을 하나의 문장으로 쓰시오.

Charlotte's Web is a children's novel. E. B. White wrote the book.

➡ _____

[01~03] 다음 대화를 읽고 물음에 답하시오.

Brian: Mina, can you recommend a good pizza restaurant?

Mina: Why don't you try Antonio's? It's my favorite.

Brian: What do you like about it?

Mina: The food is delicious. I recommend the bulgogi pizza.

Brian: How are the prices?

Mina: I think the prices are good, too.

Brian: Sounds like a good restaurant. How do you like the service?

Mina: It's a little slow on the weekends.

Brian: Okay. I'll check it out. Thanks.

Mina: No problem. Enjoy your meal!

01 What is Mina's favorite restaurant?

➡ _____

02 중요 Which food does Mina recommend?

➡ _____

03 What does Mina think about the service?

➡ _____

04 중요 다음 대화가 자연스럽게 이어지도록 순서대로 배열하시오.

(A) What do you like most about it?
(B) Yes, I did. I'm really happy with it.
(C) Tom, you got a new smartphone.
(D) I love the camera. It takes great pictures.

➡ _____

05 다음 두 문장을 하나의 문장으로 쓰시오.

I can't find the cup. My husband likes to use it.

➡ _____

06 지시에 맞게 주어진 문장과 같은 의미의 문장을 쓰시오. 각각 The wind를 주어로 시작할 것.

The wind was strong, so it blew my hat off my head.

(1) because를 이용하여

➡ _____
_____

(2) so ~ that을 이용하여

➡ _____
_____

07 중요 두 문장이 같은 의미가 되도록 빈칸에 알맞은 말을 쓰시오.

• Peter fell in love with a woman. She left him a few weeks ago.
= The woman _____ a few weeks ago.

➡ _____
_____

08 다음 우리말에 맞게 빈칸에 알맞은 말을 쓰시오.

The cookies _____ was _____ I ate all of them.
네가 구운 쿠키가 너무 맛있어서 내가 모두 먹어 버렸어.

09 주어진 단어를 활용하여 다음 우리말을 영어로 쓰시오.

> 그 보석은 너무 귀해서 값을 매길 수가 없다.
> (jewel / precious / that / priceless)

➡ _____

[10~13] 다음 글을 읽고 물음에 답하시오.

Kyle: Huh? I'm not following you.

Emma: Opinions express people's feelings like, "The desert is beautiful." You can't say that it's true or not. But, facts can be proven. For example, "The Atacama Desert is in Chile," is a fact. You can check that on the map.

Kyle: Okay.... But what's the connection with movies?

Emma: Let me explain. What's your favorite movie?

Kyle: It's *Forrest Gump*.

Emma: Okay. Let's look for its advertisement. What does it say?

Kyle: It says, "Winner of 6 Academy Awards including Best Picture."

Emma: See? It uses facts unlike the *Y-Men 7* advertisement. Do you see the difference?

10 What does the advertisement say about *Forrest Gump*?

➡ _____
_____

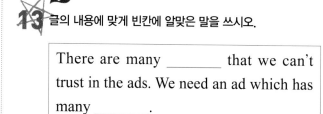

11 What is Emma using to explain the difference between facts and opinions? Answer in English.

➡ _____

12 According to the passage, what is the difference between facts and opinions? Answer in Korean.

➡ _____

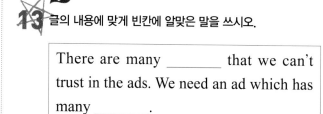

13 글의 내용에 맞게 빈칸에 알맞은 말을 쓰시오.

> There are many _____ that we can't trust in the ads. We need an ad which has many _____.

[14~15] 다음 글을 읽고 물음에 답하시오.

Harry Potter is a fantasy novel. It was written by J. K. Rowling. Harry Potter is the main character of the book. When Harry goes to magic school, his adventures begin. I especially like the friendship of Harry and his friends. (A)그 책은 아주 재미있어서 나는 책을 놓을 수가 없었다. I strongly recommend it to everyone.

14 밑줄 친 우리말 (A)를 영어로 쓰시오.

➡ _____
_____

15 What is the genre of the book, *Harry Potter*?

➡ _____

01 다음 대화의 내용과 일치하도록 Mina의 소개문을 완성하시오.

> Brian: Mina, can you recommend a good pizza restaurant?
> Mina: Why don't you try Antonio's? It's my favorite.
> Brian: What do you like about it?
> Mina: The food is delicious. I recommend the bulgogi pizza.
> Brian: How are the prices?
> Mina: I think the prices are good, too.
> Brian: Sounds like a good restaurant. How do you like the service?
> Mina: It's a little slow on the weekends.
> Brian: Okay. I'll check it out. Thanks.
> Mina: No problem. Enjoy your meal!

> I'll introduce my favorite restaurant, Antonio's. It is a good pizza restaurant. I recommend (A)_____, which is so delicious. The (B)_____ are reasonable. If you visit there on the weekends, the service can be (C)_____. How about trying Antonio's?

02 'so ~ that' 구문을 이용하여 다음 두 문장을 하나의 문장으로 써 보시오.

> Tom was busy. He couldn't answer the phone.
> The waves were high. We couldn't swim in the sea.

(1) _____

(2) _____

03 한국 민속촌에 관한 다음 글을 읽고 Facts와 Opinions를 구별하시오.

> I want to introduce Korean folk village. It is located in Yongin. It's a fun place in Yongin. There are Korean traditional houses. They are beautiful. Visitors can watch nongak and jultagi. Nongak and jultagi are very exciting to see.

Facts	Opinions

단원별 모의고사

[01~03] 다음 대화를 읽고 물음에 답하시오.

Jack: Hi, Suji. How did you like your trip to Gyeongju?
Suji: I was very happy with it.
Jack: Where did you visit?
Suji: I visited Cheomseongdae. It was great.
Jack: Where else did you go?
Suji: Bulguksa. It was a wonderful place.
Jack: _____ (A) _____
Suji: Yeah, but walking up to Seokguram was difficult.
Jack: But I'm sure it was worth it.

01 위 대화의 빈칸 (A)에 들어갈 말로 어색한 것은?

① That sounds great.
② Sounds like the perfect trip.
③ You seem to enjoy it a lot.
④ You seem to like it so much.
⑤ I'm sorry to hear that.

02 위 대화에서 알 수 있는 Suji의 심경으로 적절한 것은?

① disappointed ② satisfied
③ nervous ④ gloomy
⑤ upset

03 How was it to walk up to Seokguram for Suji?

➡ _____

[04~06] 다음 대화를 읽고 물음에 답하시오.

W: May I help you?
B: Yes. I'm looking for a backpack. Can you ___(A)___ one?
W: How about this red one? Red is the most popular color these days.
B: My old backpack was red, so I want a different color.
W: _____(B)_____ It has side pockets.
B: Oh, that looks good. I'll take it.

04 위 대화의 빈칸 (A)에 들어갈 수 있는 단어를 고르시오.

① watch ② guess
③ recommend ④ advise
⑤ introduce

05 위 대화의 빈칸 (B)에 들어갈 말로 어색한 것은?

① How about this navy one?
② I recommend this navy one.
③ What about this navy one?
④ Why don't you choose this navy one?
⑤ How was this navy one?

06 위 대화의 내용과 일치하도록 소년의 일기의 빈칸을 완성하시오.

Mon, Nov 4th, 2019
I was excited because I bought the new backpack. I used to wear the (A)_____ color backpack, so I wanted to buy (B)_____. The clerk recommended (C)_____, which had (D)_____. I liked it a lot and bought it. I'm looking forward to wearing the new backpack tomorrow.

[07~09] 다음 대화를 읽고 물음에 답하시오.

> Sue: Tom, you got a new smartphone.
> Tom: Yes, I did. I'm really happy with it.
> Sue: What do you like most about it?
> Tom: I love the camera. It takes great pictures.

07 What are Tom and Sue talking about?

➡ _____

08 How does Tom like his new smartphone?

➡ _____

09 What does Tom like most about his smartphone?

➡ _____

[10~11] 다음 대화를 읽고 물음에 답하시오.

> Brian: Mina, can you recommend a good pizza restaurant?
> Mina: Why don't you try Antonio's? It's my ⓐ favorite.
> Brian: What do you like about it?
> Mina: The food is delicious. I recommend the bulgogi pizza.
> Brian: How are the prices?
> Mina: I think the prices are good, too.
> Brian: ⓑSounds like a good restaurant. How do you like the service?
> Mina: It's ⓒa little slow on the weekends.
> Brian: Okay. I'll ⓓcheck out it. Thanks.
> Mina: No problem. ⓔEnjoy your meal!

10 위 대화의 밑줄 친 ⓐ~ⓔ 중 어법상 어색한 것을 찾아 바르게 고치시오.

➡ _____

11 위 대화를 읽고 대답할 수 없는 질문은?

① What is Mina's favorite restaurant?
② What food did Mina recommend Brian to try at Antonio's?
③ How was the price of Antonio's?
④ When was the service of Antonio's slow?
⑤ How much was the bulgogi pizza at Antonio's?

12 다음 우리말에 맞게 주어진 단어를 사용하여 영작하시오.

(1) 버터를 설탕과 함께 섞으세요. (mix)

➡ _____

(2) Jack이 의자를 들어 올렸다. (lifted)

➡ _____

(3) 너는 진실을 말하고 있니? (telling)

➡ _____

13 다음 중 의미가 <u>다른</u> 하나는?

① It was so fine that we went out.
② We went out because of the fine weather.
③ It was fine, so we went out.
④ It was too fine for us to go out.
⑤ As it was fine, we went out.

14 다음 중 쓰임이 <u>다른</u> 하나는?

① The doll that Rose carries around all the time is made by her mother.
② I know the fact that she doesn't trust anyone.
③ The vase that the boy broke was not expensive.
④ The paper that Danny tore into pieces was an important document.
⑤ Who is the woman that Lisa is talking to?

15 주어진 단어를 활용하여 다음 우리말을 영어로 쓰시오.

> 그의 연설은 너무 유명해서 모두가 그것에 관해 알았다. (speech / that)

➡ _____

_____

16 다음 중 어법상 바르지 <u>않은</u> 것은?

① Are these the keys you lost the other day?

② Is there anything that I can do for you?

③ The dog is so smart that everyone loves him.

④ What is the name of the movie that you are going to see?

⑤ The women whom I work with in the office is friendly.

17 주어진 문장과 같은 의미의 문장을 아홉 단어로 이루어진 한 문장으로 쓰시오.

> My mouth is frozen because it is so cold.

➡ _____

[18~23] 다음 글을 읽고 물음에 답하시오.

Emma: What are you doing, Kyle?
Kyle: ① _____
Emma: ② _____
Kyle: ③ _____
Emma: ④ _____
Kyle: I'm so mad. The movie advertisement said that it was "The Most Exciting Movie of the Year."
Emma: Well, you can't believe everything that you read.
Kyle: They lied on the advertisement. I'm going to ask for my money back.

Emma: Hold ___ⓐ___, Kyle! They didn't really ⓑlie because they used opinions, not facts.
Kyle: Huh? (A)I'm not following you.
Emma: Opinions express people's feelings like, "The desert is beautiful." You can't say (B)that it's true or not. But, facts can be ⓒproven. For example, "The Atacama Desert is in Chile," is a fact. You can check that on the map.
Kyle: Okay.... But what's (C)the connection with movies?
Emma: Let me explain. What's ⓓyour favorite movie?
Kyle: It's *Forrest Gump*.
Emma: Okay. Let's ⓔlook for its advertisement. What does (D)it say?
Kyle: It says, "Winner of 6 Academy Awards (E)including Best Picture."
Emma: See? It uses facts ⓕlike the *Y-Men 7* advertisement. Do you see the difference?

18 자연스러운 대화가 되도록 ①~④에 들어갈 말을 바르게 나열한 것은?

> ⓐ How is it?
> ⓑ I'm sorry to hear that.
> ⓒ Oh, Emma. I'm watching the movie, *Y-Men 7* on my computer.
> ⓓ Don't ask. It's so boring that I want to cry.

① ⓑ – ⓐ – ⓓ – ⓒ　　② ⓑ – ⓓ – ⓒ – ⓐ
③ ⓒ – ⓐ – ⓓ – ⓑ　　④ ⓒ – ⓑ – ⓐ – ⓓ
⑤ ⓓ – ⓑ – ⓐ – ⓒ

19 빈칸 ⓐ에 들어갈 말로 가장 적절한 것은?

① in　　② at　　③ by　　④ on　　⑤ out

20 다음 중 위 글의 내용과 일치하는 것은?

① It is hard to prove facts.

② Ads always tell lies about their products.

③ We had better believe everything that we read.

④ It is not allowed to use opinions in ads.

⑤ People who advertise products use not only facts but also opinions.

21 다음 중 (A)~(E)에 관한 설명으로 바르지 않은 것은?

① (A): 'I can't understand you.'로 바꾸어 쓸 수 있다.

② (B): 접속사로 동사 say의 목적어가 되는 명사절을 이끌고 있다.

③ (C): the way in which two things are related to each other로 풀이되는 말이다.

④ (D): "Forest Gump"를 가리키는 대명사이다.

⑤ (E): '~을 포함하여'라는 의미의 전치사이다.

22 밑줄 친 ⓑ~ⓕ 중 내용상 어색한 것을 골라 바르게 고치시오.

➡ _____

23 글의 내용에 맞게 빈칸에 알맞은 말을 쓰시오.

> According to the passage, if something can be proven, it is a _____. However, if it is hard to say something is true or not, you can say it is _____ _____.

[24~25] 다음 글을 읽고 물음에 답하시오.

> *Charlotte's Web* is a children's novel. It was written by E. B. White. A little pig named Wilbur is the main character of the book. When Wilbur is in danger, his friend Charlotte helps him out. I especially like the friendship of Wilbur and Charlotte. The book was so touching that I read it many times. I strongly recommend it to everyone.

24 Which is NOT true about the passage?

① The writer of the book is E. B. White.

② Wilbur is the name of the main character.

③ Wilbur and Charlotte are friends.

④ Charlotte ignores Wilbur when he is in danger.

⑤ The writer read the book many times.

25 위 글의 표현을 이용하여 다음 우리말을 영어로 쓰시오.

> 내가 읽은 책은 너무 감동적이어서 나는 그것을 너에게 추천하고 싶어.

➡ The book _____

    I want to _____.

Lesson 8

Be like Sherlock!

 의사소통 기능

- 도움 요청하기

  A: Can you help me mop the floor?

  B: No problem.

- 추측하기

  A: I guess you're playing the piano.

  B: You're right.

 언어 형식

- something+형용사

  Is there **something wrong**?

- 간접의문문

  Could you tell me **when this happened**?

Key Words

- **afraid** [əfréid] 형 걱정하는, 두려워하는
- **anymore** [ènimɔ́ːr] 부 이제는, 지금은, 더 이상
- **anyway** [éniwèi] 부 어차피
- **broken** [bróukən] 형 깨진, 부서진
- **bronze** [brɑnz] 명 청동
- **call** [kɔːl] 동 전화를 걸다, 부르다
- **carry** [kǽri] 동 나르다, 옮기다
- **clue** [kluː] 명 단서, 실마리
- **crime** [kraim] 명 범죄
- **dangerous** [déindʒərəs] 형 위험한
- **detective** [ditéktiv] 명 탐정
- **else** [els] 부 또 다른
- **favor** [féivər] 명 호의, 친절, 부탁
- **feather** [féðər] 명 깃털
- **flash** [flæʃ] 명 섬광, 번쩍임
- **footprint** [fútprìnt] 명 발자국
- **handprint** [hǽndprint] 명 손자국
- **horror** [hɔ́ːrər] 명 공포
- **inside** [ìnsáid] 전 ~ 안에
- **leave** [liːv] 동 ~을 두고 가다
- **lightning** [láitniŋ] 명 번개
- **lose** [luːz] 동 잃어버리다

- **mop** [mɑp] 동 대걸레로 닦다
- **playground** [pléigràund] 명 운동장
- **poem** [póuəm] 명 시
- **post** [poust] 동 게시하다, 공고하다
- **principal** [prínsəpəl] 명 교장
- **real** [ríːəl] 형 진짜의, 실제의
- **refrigerator** [rifrídʒərèitər] 명 냉장고
- **rush** [rʌʃ] 동 (급히) 움직이다, 서두르다
- **silver** [sílvər] 명 은
- **steal** [stiːl] 동 훔치다
- **strange** [streindʒ] 형 이상한
- **stranger** [stréindʒər] 명 낯선 사람, 모르는 사람
- **suddenly** [sʌ́dnli] 부 갑자기
- **talent** [tǽlənt] 명 재능
- **talent show** 장기 자랑 대회
- **text** [tekst] 동 문자 메시지를 보내다 명 문자
- **thief** [θiːf] 명 도둑
- **thirsty** [θɔ́ːrsti] 형 목마른
- **thunder** [θʌ́ndər] 명 천둥
- **treasure** [tréʒər] 명 보물
- **water** [wɔ́ːtər] 동 물을 주다
- **wonder** [wʌ́ndər] 동 궁금해 하다

Key Expressions

- **a few** 몇몇의, 조금의
- **ask ~ a favor** ~에게 부탁을 하다
- **at the moment** 그 순간에, 그때에
- **bring ~ back** ~을 돌려주다
- **do ~ a favor** ~의 부탁을 들어주다
- **get into trouble** 곤경에 빠지다
- **look for** ~을 찾다
- **make one's round** 순찰을 돌다

- **not ~ anymore** 더 이상 ~ 않다
- **on the way home** 집에 가는[오는] 길에
- **right now** 지금, 곧, 당장
- **run across** ~을 가로질러[건너서] 뛰다
- **rush over** 달려가다
- **take care of** ~을 돌보다
- **wash the dishes** 설거지하다
- **win first place** 일등을 하다

Word Power

※ 서로 반대되는 뜻을 가진 어휘

- □ **inside** ~ 안에 ↔ **outside** ~ 밖에
- □ **low** 낮은 ↔ **high** 높은
- □ **safe** 안전한 ↔ **dangerous** 위험한
- □ **completely** 완전히 ↔ **partially** 부분적으로

- □ **ask** 묻다 ↔ **answer** 대답하다
- □ **leave** 떠나다 ↔ **arrive** 도착하다
- □ **find** 찾다 ↔ **lose** 잃어버리다
- □ **catch** 잡다 ↔ **run away** 도망가다

※ 수사 관련 어휘

- □ **crime** 범죄
- □ **clue** 단서
- □ **investigation** 조사, 수사

- □ **detective** 탐정
- □ **suspect** 용의자
- □ **judge** 판사

- □ **witness** 증인
- □ **victim** 피해자

English Dictionary

- □ **anyway** 어쨌든
  → in any case
  어떤 경우에든
- □ **bronze** 청동
  → a yellowish-brown metal containing copper and tin
  구리와 주석을 포함한 황갈색의 금속
- □ **clue** 단서, 실마리
  → something that helps a person find something
  누군가가 무언가를 찾도록 도와주는 어떤 것
- □ **crime** 범죄
  → activities that involve breaking the law
  법을 어기는 것을 포함하는 행동들
- □ **detective** 탐정
  → a person whose job is to find information about something or someone
  무언가 또는 누군가에 관한 정보를 찾는 것이 직업인 사람
- □ **else** 또 다른
  → in addition to something already mentioned
  이미 언급된 무언가에 더하여
- □ **flash** 섬광, 번쩍임
  → a bright light that shines for a short time
  짧은 시간 동안 빛나는 밝은 빛
- □ **footprint** 발자국
  → a mark left by a foot or shoe
  발 또는 신발에 의해 남겨진 자국

- □ **horror** 공포
  → a strong feeling of shock and fear
  충격과 두려움의 강한 느낌
- □ **lightning** 번개
  → a powerful flash of light in the sky and usually followed by thunder
  보통 천둥이 뒤따라오는 하늘의 강력한 빛의 번쩍임
- □ **mop** 대걸레로 닦다
  → to clean the floor with a mop
  대걸레로 바닥을 닦다
- □ **principal** 교장
  → the person in charge of a school
  학교를 담당하고 있는 사람
- □ **rush** (급히) 행동하다
  → to move or do something very quickly
  매우 빠르게 무언가를 하거나 움직이다
- □ **steal** 훔치다
  → to take something that does not belong to you in a wrong way
  잘못된 방식으로 당신에게 속하지 않은 무언가를 취하다
- □ **talent** 재능
  → a natural and special ability to do something well
  무언가를 잘하는 타고난, 특별한 능력
- □ **thief** 도둑
  → someone who steals things from another person
  다른 사람으로부터 무언가를 훔치는 사람

서답형

01 다음 짝지어진 단어의 관계가 같도록 빈칸에 알맞은 말을 쓰시오.

> top : bottom = _____ : outside

02 다음 영영풀이가 가리키는 것을 고르시오.

> a natural and special ability to do something well

① feather ② talent
③ footprint ④ text
⑤ treasure

 중요

03 다음 중 밑줄 친 부분의 뜻풀이가 바르지 않은 것은?

① This small school has just three teachers and one principal. 교장
② Lightning struck a big tree. 가벼운
③ There is something strange in the sky. 이상한
④ Suddenly the power went out. 갑자기
⑤ The thief stole the computer equipment. 도둑

04 다음 주어진 문장의 밑줄 친 post와 같은 의미로 쓰인 것은?

> What did you post on the bulletin board?

① There was a lot of post this morning.
② I want to post the advertisement on the websites.
③ Has the post come yet?
④ I was waiting for the next post with my friends.
⑤ I sent some presents to my cousins by post.

중요

05 다음 문장에 공통으로 들어갈 말을 고르시오.

> • Emma is really good at paraphrasing the _____.
> • I needed Brian's help, so I sent a _____ to ask him a favor.
> • He memorized the whole _____ of the speech.
> • I'll _____ you before I drop by your office.
>
> *paraphrase: 바꿔 쓰다

① book ② text
③ call ④ article
⑤ poem

서답형

06 다음 우리말에 맞게 빈칸에 알맞은 말을 쓰시오.

(1) 나는 오늘 식물에 물을 주지 않았다.
   ➡ I didn't _____ the plant today.
(2) 도둑이 내 지갑을 가져갔다.
   ➡ A _____ took my purse.
(3) 나는 음악적 재능이 없다.
   ➡ I have no musical _____.
(4) 나는 토요일에 내 사촌들을 돌볼 것이다.
   ➡ I'll _____ my cousins on Saturday.
(5) 나는 집에 오는 길에 Jane을 만났다.
   ➡ I met Jane _____.
(6) 그는 밤에 순찰을 돌고 있었다.
   ➡ He was making _____ at night.

01 다음 짝지어진 단어의 관계가 같도록 빈칸에 알맞은 말을 쓰시오.

> leave : arrive = find : _____

02 다음 문장의 빈칸에 들어갈 말을 〈보기〉에서 골라 쓰시오.

> ┌─ 보기 ─┐
> afraid / refrigerator / carry / poem / clue
> / thunder

(1) What did you put in the _____?
(2) I can't sleep because of the _____.
(3) We need a _____ to catch the thief.
(4) I'm _____ of singing in front of the audience.
(5) In English class, we studied rhyme on the _____.
(6) Can you help me _____ these heavy boxes?

03 다음 우리말에 맞게 빈칸에 알맞은 말을 쓰시오.

(1) 이상한 소음이 그녀를 깨웠다.
➡ A _____ noise woke her up.
(2) 그는 갑자기 그가 해야 할 일을 깨달았다.
➡ He _____ realized what he had to do.
(3) 선생님은 학생들의 시험 성적을 게시판에 게시하지 않을 것이다.
➡ The teacher won't _____ the students' exam grades on the board.

04 다음 우리말과 일치하도록 주어진 어구를 모두 배열하여 영작하시오.

(1) 그의 인생은 더 이상 행복하지 않았다.
(happy / his / anymore / not / was / life)
➡ _____

(2) 우리는 곤경에 처할 때, 이겨내기 위해 노력해야 한다. (종속절로 시작할 것.)
(we / a trouble / we / to / overcome / into / try / should / when / get)
➡ _____
_____

(3) 그는 장기 자랑 대회에서 1등을 하였다.
(show / first / the talent / in / he / won / place)
➡ _____

05 다음 주어진 단어를 사용하여 우리말을 영작하시오.

(1) 범죄율이 증가하고 있다. (rate, rise)
➡ _____
(2) 그는 춤추는 재능을 보였다. (talent, for)
➡ _____
(3) 그녀의 개는 천둥을 두려워한다. (afraid)
➡ _____
(4) 바닥을 닦아 줄 수 있나요? (could, mop)
➡ _____
(5) 그녀는 그 문제를 해결하기 위해 탐정을 고용했다. (hire)
➡ _____
(6) 그녀의 가방이 깃털만큼 가볍다. (as)
➡ _____

Conversation

교과서

① 도움 요청하기

A Can you help me mop the floor? 바닥 닦는 것 좀 도와줄래?
B No problem. 좋아.

■ "Can you ~?"는 상대방에게 도움을 요청할 때 사용할 수 있는 표현이다. "Can you help me mop the floor?"와 같이 도움이 필요한 사항을 구체적으로 말하며 도움을 요청할 수 있다. 도움 요청을 승낙할 경우에는 "Sure.", "Of course.", "No problem." 등으로 답하고, 거절할 경우에는 "Sorry, I can't." 또는 "I'm afraid I can't."로 답하고 도울 수 없는 이유를 덧붙여 말할 수 있다.

도움 요청하기

- Can I ask you a favor? 부탁 좀 드려도 될까요?
- Can you do me a favor? 부탁 좀 들어 주실래요?
- Can you give me a hand? 좀 도와주시겠어요?
- Can you help me out, please? 좀 도와주실 수 있으세요?
- I have a favor to ask. 부탁하고 싶은 것이 있어.
- I need your help. 나 네 도움이 필요해.
- Please help me (to) ~. 나 좀 도와주세요.
- Would you mind helping me (to) ~? 나를 좀 도와주시겠어요?

도움 요청을 수락하거나 거절하는 표현

- 수락: Sure. / No problem. / Of course.
- 거절: I'm afraid not. / I don't think I can do that.

핵심 Check

1. 다음 주어진 우리말과 일치하도록 빈칸을 완성하시오.

(1) **A**: Can you do me a _____? (부탁 좀 들어줄래?)

B: Sure. What is it? (물론이지. 무엇인데?)

A: _____ _____ _____ carry these books?

(이 책들을 나르는 것을 도와줄래?)

(2) **A**: I have a _____ to ask. (부탁하고 싶은 게 있어.)

B: _____ _____ _____? (무엇인데?)

A: Can you help me _____ this notice on the bulletin board?

(게시판에 이 공지를 붙이는 것을 도와줄래?)

B: I'm _____ I can't. (미안하지만 못할 것 같아.)

② 추측하기

> **A** I guess you're playing the piano. 나는 네가 피아노를 치고 있는 거 같아.
>
> **B** You're right. 맞아.

■ "I guess ~."는 어떤 것을 추측하여 말할 때 사용하는 표현으로, "I guess" 뒤에 자신이 추측하는 내용을 말한다.

추측하기

- I think the dog took your sock. 나는 그 개가 네 양말을 가져갔다고 생각해.
- Maybe it will snow tonight. 아마도 오늘밤 눈이 올 것 같다.
- I suppose prices will go up. 추측컨대 물가가 오를 것 같다.
- It's difficult to say, but I think the Korean team will win the game.
  말하긴 어렵지만 내 생각에는 한국 팀이 경기를 이길 것 같아.

핵심 Check

2. 다음 주어진 우리말과 일치하도록 빈칸을 완성하시오.

(1) **A:** _____ what I'm doing. (내가 무엇을 하고 있는지 추측해 봐.)

   B: _____ _____ you're fishing. (네가 낚시하고 있는 것 같아.)

   A: You're right. (맞아.)

(2) **A:** I guess you're going up a ladder. (네가 사다리를 올라가는 것 같아.)

   B: You're _____. Guess again. (틀렸어. 다시 추측해 봐.)

(3) **A:** _____ it will grow even bigger. (아마도 이게 더 크게 자랄 것 같아.)

   B: I think so, too. (나도 그렇게 생각해.)

Listen and Speak 1-B

Narae: Tony, can you do me a favor?

Tony: Sure. What is it, Narae?

Narae: Can you ❶take care of my dog this weekend? My family is going to visit my grandmother in Busan.

Tony: Oh, ❷I'm sorry but I can't. My mom doesn't like dogs.

Narae: Oh, what should I do?

Tony: ❸Why don't you ask Sumin? Her family loves dogs.

Narae: Okay. I'll call ❹her right now.

Narae: Tony야, 부탁 하나 해도 될까?

Tony: 물론이지. 뭔데, 나래야?

Narae: 이번 주말에 내 개를 돌봐 줄 수 있니? 우리 가족은 부산에 계신 할머니를 방문할 예정이야.

Tony: 오, 미안하지만 안 돼. 엄마가 개를 좋아하지 않으셔.

Narae: 오, 어떻게 해야 하지?

Tony: 수민이에게 물어보는 게 어때? 그녀의 가족은 개를 정말 좋아해.

Narae: 알겠어. 지금 당장 그녀에게 전화해야겠다.

❶ take care of: ~을 돌보다
❷ 부탁을 거절하는 표현이다.
❸ Why don't you ~? = How about ~? = What about ~?: ~하는 게 어때?
❹ her는 Sumin을 가리킨다.

Check(√) True or False

(1) Narae is going to visit Busan this weekend.   T ☐ F ☐

(2) Tony is going to help Narae this weekend.   T ☐ F ☐

Listen and Speak 2-B

G: Good morning, classmates! Nine months ❶have passed so fast, and we are almost ❷at the end of this school year. We all had a wonderful year. I guess ❸only a few of us will be in the same class next year. Don't be a stranger. Say hello when we see ❹each other, okay? Thank you.

G: 좋은 아침이야, 학급 친구들아! 9개월은 아주 빨리 지나갔고, 우리는 이번 학년의 거의 막바지에 있어. 우리 모두는 멋진 한 해를 보냈어. 우리 중 극소수가 내년에 같은 반이 될 거라고 생각해. 모르는 사람처럼 지내지 말자. 서로 만나면 인사말을 건네자. 알겠지? 고마워.

❶ 과거부터 지금까지 이어지는 것을 나타내기 위해 현재완료 시제가 사용되었다.
❷ at the end of: ~의 끝에
❸ only a few: 극소수의, few: 거의 없는
❹ each other: 서로

Check(√) True or False

(3) The girl asks her classmates not to be strangers next year.   T ☐ F ☐

(4) The girl felt bored in this school year.   T ☐ F ☐

Listen and Speak 1-A

Emily: Jinsu, can I ask you a favor?

Jinsu: Sure. What is it?

Emily: Can you help me ❶wash the dishes?

Jinsu: ❷No problem.

❶ wash the dishes: 설거지하다
❷ 도움 요청을 수락하는 표현으로 Sure. 또는 Of course.로 바꾸어 쓸 수 있다.

Listen and Speak 1-C

A: ❶Can you do me a favor?

B: Sure. What is it?

A: Can you help me ❷mop the floor?

B: No problem. / ❸Sorry, I can't.

❶ 상대방에게 도움을 요청할 때 사용하는 표현으로 Can I ask you a favor?와 바꿔 쓸 수 있다.
❷ mop: 대걸레로 닦다
❸ 도움 요청에 거절하는 표현으로 I'm afraid I can't.로 바꿔 쓸 수 있다.

Listen and Speak 2-A

Brian: Did you see my baseball glove?

Jane: Yes, I saw ❶it under the table.

Brian: Really? It's not ❷there anymore.

Jane: Then I guess Spot took ❶it.

Brian: Oh, there ❸he is. You bad dog, Spot!

❶ it은 Brian's baseball glove를 가리킨다.
❷ there는 under the table을 가리킨다.
❸ he는 Spot을 가리킨다.

Listen and Speak 2-C

A: ❶Guess what I'm doing.

B: ❷I guess you're playing the piano.

A: You're wrong. Guess again.

B: I guess you're ❸working on the computer.

A: That's right.

❶ 자신의 동작에 대해 상대방의 추측을 유도하는 표현이다.
❷ I guess (that)+주어+동사 ~.는 어떤 것을 추측하여 말할 때 사용하는 표현이다.
❸ work on the computer: 컴퓨터로 일하다

Real Life Talk – Step 1

Brian: Mom, I can't find my smartphone. Can you help me find ❶it?

Mom: Are you sure you lost ❶it ❷inside the house?

Brian: Yes. I just ❸texted my friend a few minutes ago.

Mom: Where were you ❹at the time?

Brian: In the kitchen. I was making a sandwich.

Mom: Then I guess you left ❶it somewhere in the kitchen.

Brian: I already checked the kitchen, Mom.

Mom: Well, let's check ❺it again. Oh, here it is. Inside the refrigerator.

Brian: Thanks, Mom. You are the greatest!

Mom: You're welcome, honey.

❶ it은 Brian's smartphone을 가리킨다.
❷ inside: ~ 안에 ↔ outside: ~ 밖에
❸ text: 문자 메시지를 보내다
❹ at the time: 그때
❺ it은 the kitchen을 가리킨다.

Real Life Talk – Step 2

A: Can you help me find my baseball glove?

B: Okay. Where did you see it last?

A: On the bench.

B: ❶I guess a dog took your baseball glove. I can see its ❷footprints on the bench.

❶ 추측을 나타내는 표현이다.
❷ footprint: 발자국

● 다음 우리말과 일치하도록 빈칸에 알맞은 말을 쓰시오.

Listen and Speak 1-A

Emily: Jinsu, can I ask you a _____?

Jinsu: Sure. What is it?

Emily: Can you help me _____ _____ _____?

Jinsu: No problem.

Emily: 진수야, 부탁 하나 해도 될까?
Jinsu: 물론이지. 뭔데?
Emily: 설거지하는 것 좀 도와줄래?
Jinsu: 좋아.

Listen and Speak 1-B

Narae: Tony, can you do me a favor?

Tony: Sure. What is it, Narae?

Narae: Can you _____ _____ _____ my dog this weekend? My family is going to visit my grandmother in Busan.

Tony: Oh, _____ _____ _____ _____ _____. My mom doesn't like dogs.

Narae: Oh, _____ _____ _____ _____?

Tony: _____ _____ _____ ask Sumin? Her family loves dogs.

Narae: Okay. I'll call her _____ _____.

Narae: Tony야, 부탁 하나 해도 될까?
Tony: 물론이지. 뭔데, 나래야?
Narae: 이번 주말에 내 개를 돌봐 줄 수 있니? 우리 가족은 부산에 계신 할머니를 방문할 예정이야.
Tony: 오, 미안하지만 안 돼. 엄마께서 개를 좋아하지 않으셔.
Narae: 오, 어떻게 해야 하지?
Tony: 수민이에게 물어보는 게 어때? 그녀의 가족은 개를 정말 좋아해.
Narae: 알겠어. 지금 당장 그녀에게 전화해야겠다.

Listen and Speak 1-C

A: Can you _____ _____ _____ _____?

B: Sure. What is it?

A: Can you _____ _____ _____ the floor?

B: No _____. / Sorry, I _____.

A: 부탁 하나 해도 될까?
B: 물론이지. 뭔데?
A: 바닥 닦는 것을 도와줄래?
B: 좋아. / 미안하지만 못해.

Listen and Speak 2-A

Brian: Did you see my baseball glove?

Jane: Yes, I saw it _____ _____ _____.

Brian: Really? It's not there _____.

Jane: Then I _____ Spot took it.

Brian: Oh, there _____ _____. You bad dog, Spot!

Brian: 내 야구 글러브 보았니?
Jane: 그래, 탁자 아래에서 봤어.
Brian: 정말? 더 이상 그곳에 없어.
Jane: 그럼 Spot이 가져간 것 같구나.
Brian: 오, 저기 있네. 이런 나쁜 개, Spot!

Listen and Speak 2-B

G: Good morning, classmates! Nine months _____ _____ so fast, and we are almost _____ _____ _____ _____ this school year. We all had a _____ _____ . I guess only _____ _____ of us will be in the same class next year. Don't be a _____ . Say hello when we see _____ _____ , okay? Thank you.

Listen and Speak 2-C

A: Guess _____ _____ _____ .

B: _____ _____ you're playing the piano.

A: You're _____ . Guess again.

B: I guess you're _____ _____ the computer.

A: That's _____ .

Real Life Talk - Step 1

Brian: Mom, I can't find my smartphone. _____ _____ _____ _____ find it?

Mom: Are you sure you lost it _____ the house?

Brian: Yes. I just _____ my friend a few minutes ago.

Mom: _____ _____ you at the time?

Brian: In the kitchen. I _____ _____ a sandwich.

Mom: Then I guess you left it _____ in the kitchen.

Brian: I already _____ the kitchen, Mom.

Mom: Well, _____ _____ _____ _____ . Oh, here _____ _____ . Inside the _____ .

Brian: Thanks, Mom. You are the greatest!

Mom: You're _____ , honey.

Real Life Talk - Step 2

A: Can you _____ _____ _____ my baseball glove?

B: Okay. Where _____ you _____ it _____ ?

A: On the bench.

B: I _____ a dog _____ your baseball glove. I can _____ _____ _____ on the bench.

해석

G: 좋은 아침이야, 학급 친구들아! 9개 월은 아주 빨리 지나갔고, 우리는 이 번 학년의 거의 막바지에 있어. 우리 모두는 멋진 한 해를 보냈어. 우리 중 극소수가 내년에 같은 반이 될 거 라고 생각해. 모르는 사람처럼 지내 지 말자. 서로 만나면 인사말을 건네 자. 알겠지? 고마워.

A: 내가 무엇을 하고 있는지 맞혀 봐.
B: 너는 피아노를 치고 있는 것 같아.
A: 틀렸어. 다시 맞혀 봐.
B: 너는 컴퓨터로 일하고 있는 것 같아.
A: 맞아.

Brian: 엄마, 제 스마트폰을 찾을 수가 없어요. 제가 그것을 찾는 걸 도 와주시겠어요?
Mom: 집 안에서 잃어버린 것이 확실하 니?
Brian: 네. 불과 몇 분 전에 친구에게 문자 메시지를 보냈어요.
Mom: 너는 그때 어디에 있었니?
Brian: 부엌요. 샌드위치를 만들고 있 었어요.
Mom: 그럼 네가 부엌 어딘가에 놓은 것 같구나.
Brian: 이미 부엌은 확인했어요, 엄마.
Mom: 음, 다시 확인해 보자. 오, 여기 있구나. 냉장고 안에 있어.
Brian: 고마워요, 엄마. 엄마는 최고예 요!
Mom: 천만에, 애야.

A: 내 야구 글러브를 찾는 것을 도와줄 래?
B: 응. 그것을 어디에서 마지막으로 봤 니?
A: 벤치 위에서.
B: 개가 네 야구 글러브를 가져간 것 같 아. 벤치 위에 발자국을 볼 수 있어.

[01~02] 다음 대화를 읽고 물음에 답하시오.

Emily: Jinsu, (A)부탁 하나 해도 될까?
Jinsu: Sure. What is it?
Emily: Can you help me wash the dishes?
Jinsu: _____ (B)

01 위 대화의 밑줄 친 (A)의 우리말을 주어진 단어를 모두 배열하여 영작하시오.

┌─ 보기 ─┐
ask / I / favor / a / you / can

➡ _____

02 위 대화의 빈칸 (B)에 들어갈 말로 나머지 넷과 의도가 <u>다른</u> 것은?

① Of course.
② No problem.
③ I'll give you a hand.
④ Sure.
⑤ I'm afraid I can't.

[03~04] 다음 대화를 읽고 물음에 답하시오.

Brian: Did you see my baseball glove?
Jane: Yes, I saw it under the table.
Brian: Really? (A)It's not there anymore.
Jane: (B)Then I guess Spot took it.
Brian: Oh, there he is. You bad dog, Spot!

03 위 대화의 밑줄 친 (A)가 가리키는 것을 영어로 쓰시오.

➡ _____

04 위 대화의 밑줄 친 (B)의 의도로 적절한 것은?

① 확신 표현하기　　　② 제안하기
③ 추측하기　　　　　④ 계획 말하기
⑤ 도움 요청하기

[01~03] 다음 대화를 읽고 물음에 답하시오.

> Narae: Tony, can you do me a favor?
> Tony: Sure. What is it, Narae?
> Narae: Can you take care of my dog this weekend? My family is going to visit my grandmother in Busan.
> Tony: Oh, (A)I'm sorry but I can't. My mom doesn't like dogs.
> Narae: Oh, what should I do?
> Tony: (B)Why don't you ask Sumin? Her family loves dogs.
> Narae: Okay. I'll call her right now.

01 위 대화의 밑줄 친 (A)와 바꾸어 쓸 수 있는 것은?

① I'm afraid I can't.　② All right.
③ No problem.　④ Of course.
⑤ Sounds good.

02 위 대화의 밑줄 친 (B)와 바꾸어 쓸 수 없는 것은? (2개)

① How about asking Sumin?
② I think you can ask Sumin.
③ I can ask Sumin.
④ What about asking Sumin?
⑤ How did you ask Sumin?

03 위 대화의 내용과 일치하지 않는 것은?

① Narae는 주말에 가족들과 함께 부산에 갈 것이다.
② Narae는 Tony에게 그녀의 개를 돌봐 줄 것을 요청하였다.
③ Tony의 엄마는 개를 좋아하지 않는다.
④ Sumin의 가족은 개를 아주 좋아한다.
⑤ Narae는 Tony에게 개를 맡긴 후 부산에 갈 것이다.

서답형
04 다음 대화가 자연스럽게 이어지도록 순서대로 배열하시오.

> (A) Really? It's not there anymore.
> (B) Oh, there he is. You bad dog, Spot!
> (C) Yes, I saw it under the table.
> (D) Then I guess Spot took it.
> (E) Did you see my baseball glove?

➡ _____

[05~06] 다음 대화를 읽고 물음에 답하시오.

> Amy: Can you help me find my baseball glove?
> Jack: Okay. Where did you see it last?
> Amy: On the bench.
> Jack: (A)개가 네 야구 글러브를 가져간 것 같구나.(guess, took) I can see its footprints on the bench.

서답형
05 위 대화의 밑줄 친 (A)의 우리말을 주어진 단어를 이용하여 영작하시오.

➡ _____

06 위 대화의 내용과 일치하지 않는 것은?

① Amy needs help to find her baseball glove.
② Amy saw her baseball glove on the bench last.
③ Jack thinks that a dog took Amy's baseball glove.
④ Jack saw a dog running away with a baseball glove.
⑤ Jack finds a dog's footprints on the bench.

[07~09] 다음 대화를 읽고 물음에 답하시오.

Brian: Mom, I can't find my smartphone. Can you help me ⓐfinding it?

Mom: Are you sure you lost it inside the house?

Brian: Yes. I just ⓑtexted my friend a few minutes ago.

Mom: Where were you at the time?

Brian: In the kitchen. I ⓒwas making a sandwich.

Mom: Then I guess you left it ⓓsomewhere in the kitchen.

Brian: I already checked the kitchen, Mom.

Mom: Well, let's check ⓔit again. Oh, here it is. Inside the refrigerator.

Brian: Thanks, Mom. You are the greatest!

Mom: You're welcome, honey.

서답형

07 위 대화의 밑줄 친 ⓐ~ⓔ 중 어법상 어색한 것을 찾아 바르게 고치시오.

➡ _____

08 위 대화를 읽고 대답할 수 없는 질문은?

① What is Brian looking for?
② What does Brian ask his mom to do?
③ What was Brian doing in the kitchen?
④ Why did Brian text to his friend?
⑤ Where did his mom find the smartphone?

중요

09 위 대화에서 나타난 Brian의 심경 변화로 적절한 것은?

① happy → worried
② lonely → irritated
③ confused → pleased
④ satisfied → dissatisfied
⑤ nervous → upset

[10~12] 다음 글을 읽고 물음에 답하시오.

Sujin: Good morning, classmates! Nine months have (A)[passed / passing] so fast, and we are almost at the end of this school year. We all had a wonderful year. I guess only (B)[a little / a few] of us will be in the same class next year. Don't be a stranger. Say hello when we see (C)[each other / other], okay? Thank you.

서답형

10 위 글에서 주어진 영영풀이가 가리키는 말을 찾아 쓰시오.

> people who are in the same class as you at school or college

➡ _____

중요

11 위 글의 (A)~(C)에 들어갈 말로 바르게 짝지어진 것은?

	(A)	(B)	(C)
①	passed	a little	each other
②	passed	a few	each other
③	passed	a few	other
④	passing	a few	other
⑤	passing	a little	other

12 위 글의 내용과 일치하지 않는 것은?

① 9개월이 아주 빨리 지나갔다.
② 수진과 학급 친구들은 이번 학년의 거의 막바지에 있다.
③ 수진은 학급 친구들에게 모르는 사람처럼 지내지 말 것을 당부하였다.
④ 수진은 학급 친구들에게 학급이 달라져도 서로 만나면 인사말을 할 것을 요청하였다.
⑤ 수진과 학급 친구들은 대부분 내년에 같은 반이 될 것이다.

[01~02] 다음 글을 읽고 물음에 답하시오.

Sujin: Good morning, classmates! Nine months have passed so fast, and we are almost at the end of this school year. We all had a wonderful year. (A)우리 중 극소수만이 내년에 같은 반이 될 거라고 생각해. Don't be a stranger. Say hello when we see each other, okay? Thank you.

01 위 글에서 주어진 영영풀이에 해당하는 말을 찾아 쓰시오.

> a person that you do not know

➡ _____

02 위 글의 밑줄 친 (A)의 우리말을 〈보기〉에 주어진 어구를 모두 배열하여 영작하시오.

┌─── 보기 ───┐
in / next / guess / I / a few of / us / be / will / the same / year / only / class
└──────────┘

➡ _____

_____

[03~05] 다음 대화를 읽고 물음에 답하시오.

Brian: Mom, I can't find my smartphone. (A)제가 그것을 찾는 것을 도와주시겠어요? (help, can)
Mom: Are you sure you lost it inside the house?
Brian: Yes. I just texted my friend a few minutes ago.
Mom: Where were you at the time?
Brian: In the kitchen. I was making a sandwich.
Mom: Then I guess you left it somewhere in the kitchen.

Brian: I already checked the kitchen, Mom.
Mom: Well, let's check it again. Oh, here it is. Inside the refrigerator.
Brian: Thanks, Mom. You are the greatest!
Mom: You're welcome, honey.

03 위 대화의 밑줄 친 (A)의 우리말을 주어진 단어를 사용하여 영작하시오.

➡ _____

04 Where did Brian use his smartphone last?

➡ _____

05 Where was Brian's smartphone?

➡ _____

[06~07] 다음 대화를 읽고 물음에 답하시오.

Amy: Can you help me find my baseball glove?
Jack: Okay. Where did you see it last?
Amy: On the bench.
Jack: I guess a dog took your baseball glove. I can see its ___(A)___ s on the bench.

06 위 대화의 빈칸 (A)에 다음 주어진 영영풀이가 나타내는 말을 쓰시오.

> a mark left by a foot or shoe

➡ _____

07 Why does Jack think a dog took Amy's baseball glove?

➡ _____

Grammar

1 something+형용사

> • She has **something cute**. 그녀는 귀여운 무언가를 가지고 있다.
> • I know **someone dependable**. 나는 의지할 만한 누군가를 알아요.

■ '-body, -thing, -one'으로 끝나는 부정대명사는 형용사가 뒤에서 수식한다. 이러한 대명사에는 somebody, something, someone, anybody, anything, anyone, nobody, nothing, no one 등이 있다.

  • I need **something exciting**. 나는 신나는 무언가가 필요해.

  • Do you have **anything long**? 길쭉한 무언가를 가지고 있니?

  • Catherine did **something terrible**. Catherine은 무언가 끔찍한 일을 저질렀다.

  • Didn't you bring **anything small**? 어떤 작은 것을 가지고 오지 않았니?

■ 위의 대명사를 to부정사와 형용사가 동시에 수식할 때 어순은 '대명사+형용사+to부정사'이다.

  • Is there **someone brave** to tell the truth? 그 사실을 말할 용감한 누군가가 있나요?

  • They want **something valuable** to have. 그들은 가지기에 귀중한 어떤 것을 원해요.

  • He knew **nothing important** to tell. 그는 말하기에 중요한 것을 아무것도 몰랐다.

핵심 Check

1. 다음 우리말과 일치하도록 빈칸에 알맞은 말을 쓰시오.

  (1) 그는 어떤 시끄러운 소리를 들었다.
    ➡ He heard _____ _____.

  (2) 그의 차에 무슨 문제가 있어.
    ➡ There is _____ _____ with his car.

  (3) 음식에 이상한 것이 있다.
    ➡ There is _____ _____ in the food.

② 간접의문문

- I don't know **what she is doing**. 나는 그녀가 무엇을 하고 있는지 몰라요.
- Tell me **why he came late**. 그가 왜 늦게 왔는지 말해 줘.

■ 간접의문문은 명사절을 이끌며 주어, 목적어, 보어 역할을 한다. 의문사가 있는 간접의문문은 '의문사+주어+동사' 어순으로 쓰인다. 직접의문문인 '의문사+동사+주어 ~?'의 어순과 혼동하지 않도록 유의한다.

- Where is she going? 〈직접의문문〉

  Can you tell me **where she is going**? 〈간접의문문〉 그녀가 어디에 가고 있는지 말해 줄 수 있니?

- Ted didn't know how she broke in his house. Ted는 어떻게 그녀가 그의 집에 침입했는지 몰랐다.
- Do you remember **when she went out**? 그녀가 언제 나갔는지 기억하니?

■ 다음과 같이 의문사가 주어 역할을 하는 경우가 있다. 이때에는 '의문사+동사'의 어순이 된다.

- June doesn't know **who built the house**. June은 누가 그 집을 지었는지 모른다.

■ 의문사가 없는 경우 간접의문문의 어순은 'if/whether+주어+동사'로 쓴다.

- Can you tell me? + Do you know her?

  → Can you tell me **if[whether] you know her**? 네가 그녀를 아는지 말해 줄래?

- I wonder **whether they came to the party in time**. 나는 그들이 제때에 그 파티에 왔는지 궁금해.
- Branda tried to guess **if they needed her help**.
  Branda는 그들이 그녀의 도움을 필요로 하는지 추측하려고 애썼다.

핵심 Check

2. 다음 우리말과 일치하도록 빈칸에 알맞은 말을 쓰시오.

(1) 나는 그 영화가 언제 시작하는지 몰라.

➡ I don't know _____ _____ _____ _____.

(2) 그가 무엇을 먹었는지 말해 줘.

➡ Tell me _____ _____ _____.

(3) 그 시계가 얼마인지 아니?

➡ Do you know _____ _____ _____ _____ _____?

Grammar 시험대비 기본평가

01 다음 문장에서 어법상 <u>어색한</u> 부분을 바르게 고쳐 쓰시오.

(1) Is there nice anyone like you?

_____ ➡ _____

(2) Can you tell me where can I find the church?

_____ ➡ _____

(3) Tell me something to see pretty in your class.

_____ ➡ _____

(4) May I ask that you are a student?

_____ ➡ _____

02 다음 빈칸에 괄호 안의 단어를 바르게 배열하시오.

(1) Do you know _____? (is / she / who)

(2) I don't understand _____. (angry / her / what / made)

(3) Is there _____? (on / comfortable / to / sit / something)

(4) Can you tell me _____? (is / old / how / she)

(5) Is _____? (cold / there / something)

03 주어진 단어를 바르게 배열하여 다음 우리말을 영어로 쓰시오.

(1) sweet: 달콤한

(1) 달콤한 무언가를 먹고 싶어. (sweet / I / eat / to / want / something)

➡ _____

(2) 이것보다 더 큰 무언가를 가지고 있니? (this / have / you / than / anything / do / bigger)

➡ _____

(3) Jason은 엄마가 그를 어떻게 찾았는지 모른다. (him / know / his mom / doesn't / found / Jason / how)

➡ _____

(4) 우리는 그들이 언제 올지 몰라요. (come / we / when / they / will / don't / know)

➡ _____

01 다음 우리말을 영어로 옮길 때 다섯 번째로 오는 단어는?

> 나는 다채롭고 아름다운 무언가를 보고 싶어.

① to   ② colorful   ③ and
④ see   ⑤ something

02 다음 중 빈칸에 들어갈 말로 가장 적절한 것은?

> Can you tell me _____?

① when are you going there
② who called you last night
③ where do they want to meet
④ how will you keep the promise
⑤ what does she choose to eat

03 다음 빈칸에 들어갈 말이 바르게 짝지어진 것은?

> • Is there _____?
> • I wonder _____.

① something excited – what are they
② something excite – whether they do
③ something do – what do they do
④ anything exciting – what they are
⑤ anything doing – if they do

서답형

04 주어진 단어를 바르게 배열하여 다음 우리말을 영어로 쓰시오.

> 그녀에게는 함께 대화할 친절한 사람이 없어.
> (with / anyone / have / she / kind / talk /
> doesn't / to)

➡ _____

05 다음 빈칸에 들어갈 말로 적절하지 않은 것은?

> Daisy knows someone _____.

① friendly   ② lovely   ③ lonely
④ lively   ⑤ politely

06 다음 중 문장의 전환이 바르지 않은 것은?

① 그가 언제 숙제를 했는지 궁금해.
  → I wonder when he did his homework.
② 나는 귀중한 무언가를 원해요.
  → I want something precious.
③ 그가 그것을 좋아하는지 물어봐도 될까?
  → May I ask him whether he likes it?
④ 누가 그녀를 봤는지 아니?
  → Do you know who she saw?
⑤ 저기에 작은 무언가가 있어.
  → There is something small there.

07 다음 중 빈칸에 들어갈 말로 적절한 것을 모두 고르시오.

> David wanted to know _____ Julia
> went home.

① if   ② who   ③ which
④ whether   ⑤ what

서답형

08 다음 빈칸에 알맞은 말을 쓰시오.

> 우리가 언제 만날지 기억나지 않아.
> I can't remember _____ _____
> _____ _____ _____ _____.

09 다음 중 어법상 바르지 않은 것은?

① They don't know if Molly will take part in the race.
② Jimmy has something big.
③ I remember how they made the cake.
④ Do you know why he stopped his car?
⑤ I have something to talk about fun.

10 다음 중 대화의 빈칸에 들어갈 말로 가장 적절한 것은?

> A: Can you tell me _____?
> B: Go straight one block and turn left.

① when I go out to have dinner
② how can I get to the bakery
③ why you want to go there
④ how I can get to the police office
⑤ how long one block is

11 다음 중 우리말을 영어로 바르게 옮긴 것은?

> 누가 그 공을 찼는지 나는 알고 싶어.

① I want to know who the ball kicked.
② I want to know who did you kick the ball.
③ I want to know who kicked the ball.
④ I want to know whom you kicked the ball.
⑤ I want to know how you kicked the ball.

서답형
12 주어진 단어를 활용하여 다음 우리말을 영어로 쓰시오.

> 처리해야 할 중요한 무언가가 있어.
> (there / deal with)

➡ _____

13 다음 중 빈칸에 들어갈 말이 바르게 짝지어진 것은?

> • I'm looking for something _____.
> • Remember what _____.

① fresh to eat – is he saying to you
② fresh to eat – he said to you
③ fresh to eat – does he say to you
④ eat fresh to – he said to you
⑤ eat to fresh – did he say to you

14 다음 두 문장을 하나의 문장으로 바르게 옮기지 않은 것은?

① Tell me. Why did you leave me?
  → Tell me why you left me.
② I wonder. What made you so happy?
  → I wonder what made you so happy.
③ Can I ask you? Are you mad at me?
  → Can I ask you if you are mad at me?
④ I don't know. Who helped you?
  → I don't know who you helped.
⑤ Do you remember? What's his name?
  → Do you remember what his name is?

15 다음 빈칸에 들어갈 수 없는 것은?

> I want someone _____ right now.

① reliable   ② fun   ③ cute
④ to talk to   ⑤ care

서답형
16 주어진 단어를 바르게 배열하여 다음 우리말을 영어로 쓰시오.

> 나는 그가 지금 누구와 이야기하고 있는지 궁금해. (wonder / with / I / talking / is / he / who / now)

➡ _____

17 다음 중 주어진 문장의 밑줄 친 부분과 쓰임이 같은 것은?

> You didn't tell me <u>who</u> gave this file for the meeting.

① The boy <u>who</u> plays the piano looks handsome.
② There are many people <u>who</u> want to participate in the marathon.
③ Let me guess <u>who</u> will help us to prepare the meal.
④ Can you tell me about the woman <u>who</u> is swimming in our pool?
⑤ We ran with the employees <u>who</u> donated their blood.

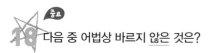

18 다음 중 어법상 바르지 않은 것은?

> A: ①<u>Is there</u> ②<u>something</u> wrong?
> B: Yes, there ③<u>is</u>. Someone ④<u>stole</u> my money. I think I know ⑤<u>who is he</u>.

①   ②   ③   ④   ⑤

서답형

19 주어진 단어를 활용하여 다음 우리말을 영어로 쓰시오.

> 언제 이게 발생했는지 말해 주겠니?
> (could / happen)

➡ _____

서답형

20 다음 두 문장을 하나의 문장으로 쓰시오.

> • Do you know?
> • Who brought this T-shirt?

➡ _____

21 다음 빈칸에 들어갈 말로 가장 적절한 것은?

> Tell me. Is he going to sing the song?
> = Tell me _____ he is going to sing the song.

① that   ② why   ③ if
④ how   ⑤ when

22 다음 중 우리말을 영어로 바르게 옮기지 않은 것은?

① 새로운 것은 없습니다.
   → There is nothing new.
② 누가 그 꽃을 꺾었는지 아니?
   → Do you know who picked the flower?
③ 우리는 무거운 것은 필요 없어요.
   → We don't need heavy anything.
④ 왜 울고 있는지 물어봐도 될까?
   → Can I ask you why you are crying?
⑤ 누가 문을 두드렸는지는 중요하지 않아.
   → Who knocked the door doesn't matter.

23 여덟 개의 단어를 이용하여 다음 우리말을 영어로 쓸 때 다섯 번째와 여섯 번째 오는 단어를 바르게 짝지은 것은?

> 그는 다른 사람들을 위해 뭔가 좋은 일을 하려고 애쓴다.

① to – do
② do – something
③ something – good
④ good – for
⑤ for – others

서답형

24 다음 대화의 빈칸에 알맞은 말을 쓰시오.

> A: We have a medical experiment, so we need _____ _____ _____ _____.
> B: Oh, I know someone like that. Mr. Han is very strong and healthy.

01 주어진 단어를 활용하여 다음 우리말을 영어로 쓰시오.

> 나는 믿을 만한 누군가가 필요해. (reliable)

➡ _____

02 다음 두 문장을 하나의 문장으로 쓰시오.

(1) Do you know? How does she bake these cookies?
➡ _____

(2) I'll ask Jason. Where does he live?
➡ _____

(3) Do you remember? What is Brad's last name?
➡ _____

(4) I wonder. Will they go abroad to study English?
➡ _____
_____

(5) Can you tell me? Is she going to run or walk?
➡ _____
_____

(6) I don't understand. What did they want to do?
➡ _____

(7) I want to know. Who made the decision last night?
➡ _____

03 다음 우리말을 영어로 쓰시오.

> 그가 몇 살인지 알려 줘. (let / know)

➡ _____

04 다음 대화의 빈칸에 알맞은 말을 쓰시오.

> A: I can't remember _____ home.
> B: You came home at 10 p.m.

➡ _____

05 주어진 단어를 활용하여 다음 우리말을 영어로 쓰시오.

> A: 나는 어제 파티에서 흥미로운 어떤 사람을 만났어. (someone / at a party)
> B: 그가 누구였는지 내게 말해 줘. (tell)

➡ A: _____
  B: _____

06 주어진 어구를 바르게 배열하여 다음 우리말을 영어로 쓰시오.

> Mike는 존경받을 만한 용감한 누군가를 만나길 원했다.
> (to be admired / wanted / Mike / brave / meet / to / someone)

➡ _____
_____

07 주어진 단어를 활용하여 다음 대화를 완성하시오.

> A: I'd like to know _____.(what / about)
> B: The story is about a princess and seven dwarfs.

➡ _____

08 빈칸에 알맞은 단어를 넣어 다음 대화를 완성하시오.

> A: Look! I found _____ _____.
> B: It looks really strange. Do you know what _____ _____ ?
> A: I have no idea.

09 다음 빈칸에 공통으로 들어갈 알맞은 말을 쓰시오.

> • I will drive the car _____ you lend me yours.
> • Did they tell you _____ they had lunch together?

10 주어진 단어를 활용하여 다음 우리말을 8단어로 이루어진 한 문장의 영어로 쓰시오.

> 나는 이 트리를 장식할 다채로운 무언가가 필요해.
> (colorful / decorate / something)

➡ _____

11 다음 대화를 영어로 쓰시오. 한 칸에 하나의 단어만 쓰시오.

> A: 나는 그가 무엇을 원하는지 모르겠어.
> (_____ _____ _____ _____
> _____ _____.)
> B: 그는 다른 무언가를 원해. (_____
> _____ _____ _____.)

12 주어진 단어를 활용하여 다음 우리말을 영어로 쓰시오.

> 이 단어가 무엇을 의미하는지 아니?
> (mean)

➡ _____

13 대화의 빈칸에 알맞은 말을 세 단어로 쓰시오.

> A: It's so hot. I want _____ _____ _____. Do you have any?
> B: Oh, yes. I have a bottle of water.

14 다음 문장에서 어법상 바르지 <u>않은</u> 것을 바르게 고쳐 쓰시오.

> I don't remember where did I put my purse yesterday.

➡ _____
_____

15 다음 그림에 맞게 대화 내용을 완성하시오. 주어진 단어를 활용하시오.

> A: I wonder _____ _____ _____ watching.
> B: They are watching _____ _____ in the theater.

> (surprising / what / something)

Reading

The Missing Gold!

Mr. Reese, the principal, ran across the wet playground.
_{콤마로 연결된 동격 관계}

"Shirley! Shirley! I need your help!"

Shirley was an eighth grade student at Bakersville Middle School.
_{eight의 서수}
She was also the best detective in the whole town.

"Is there something wrong?" asked Shirley.
_{-thing으로 끝나는 부정대명사는 형용사가 뒤에서 수식}

"Someone has stolen the gold medal for the talent show!"
_{결과 용법의 현재완료}

Mr. Reese took Shirley to the scene of the crime. There was a case
_{take A to B: A를 B로 데려가다}
with a broken window. The silver and bronze medals were still there.
_{~이 있는}   _{= in the case}
But the gold medal was missing. There was a poem in its place.
_{없어진, 실종된(형용사)}

> Tomorrow is the talent show.
>
> Where did the gold medal go?
>
> Look high and low.
> _{구석구석 살펴라}
> You can't catch me. You're too slow.

Shirley asked, "Could you tell me when this happened?"
_{간접의문문: 의문사+주어+동사}

"A little after nine last night. I was making my rounds when I heard a
_{9시 조금 지나서}   _{make one's rounds: 순찰을 돌다, 순찰하다}
scream. I rushed over and found Jocelyn and the case like this."
                       _{이와 같은 (모습의)}

"I wonder who else was here last night."
_{간접의문문: 의문사+주어+동사(동사 wonder의 목적어로 쓰임)}

"Sylvia and Harry. They were also practicing for the talent show. I'll
call them to my office."
_{call A to B A를 B로 부르다}

 확인문제

● 다음 문장이 본문의 내용과 일치하면 T, 일치하지 않으면 F를 쓰시오.

1 The ground was wet when Mr. Reese ran across it. ☐

2 Shirley went to the scene of the crime alone. ☐

3 The thief stole the medal without breaking anything. ☐

4 Mr. Reese knew who was at the school last night. ☐

---

principal 교장
run across ~을 가로질러 뛰다
detective 탐정
steal 훔치다
talent show 장기 자랑 대회
scene 현장
crime 범죄
broken 깨진, 부서진
silver 은
bronze 동
thief 도둑
else 또 다른

Jocelyn was a ninth grade student with short curly red hair.

"I was practicing my song and I became thirsty. I stepped outside the classroom to get some water. It was completely dark. Suddenly, there was a loud sound of thunder. I think the thief broke the window at that moment. Lightning followed right after and it became bright for a second or two. Then I saw someone running away from the case."

"Did you see the thief's face?"

"No, I only saw the thief's back. But the thief had short hair."

Next was an eighth grade student, Sylvia. She was tall with long black hair. She said, "I was reading my poem aloud in the classroom. I heard a scream and went outside. There was a girl next to the case. With the flash from the lightning, it was like a horror movie. I got scared so I ran straight home."

"Did you hear the window break?"

"No, the thunder was too loud. Well, I didn't do it. I was going to win first place anyway."

Harry, a seventh grader, had short blonde hair. He said, "Hey, you got the wrong guy. I was practicing my dance moves. I went home a little before nine. I didn't take one step outside the classroom until then."

"Did you hear anything strange?"

"How could I? My music was really loud."

"Did you see anyone on the way home?"

"No, I heard someone singing really badly, but I didn't see anyone."

Shirley said, "I don't need to hear anymore." Then she turned to the thief.

"Why don't you bring the medal back before you get into some real trouble?"

curly	곱슬머리의
completely	완전히
suddenly	갑자기
thunder	천둥
thief	도둑
at that moment	그 순간에, 그 때에
lightning	번개
flash	섬광, 번쩍임
horror	공포
win first place	일등을 하다, 우승하다
anyway	어쨌든, 어차피
strange	이상한
on the way home	집에 가는[오는] 길에
not ~ anymore	더 이상 ~ 않다
get into trouble	곤경에 빠지다
real	진짜의, 실제의

 확인문제

● 다음 문장이 본문의 내용과 일치하면 T, 일치하지 않으면 F를 쓰시오.

1 Jocelyn knew nothing about the thief. ☐

2 Harry heard someone sing poorly on the way home. ☐

3 Shirley found out who had stolen the medal. ☐

● 우리말을 참고하여 빈칸에 알맞은 말을 쓰시오.

1 Mr. Reese, the principal, _____ _____ the wet playground.

2 "Shirley! Shirley! I _____ your _____!"

3 Shirley was an _____ _____ student at Bakersville Middle School.

4 She was also _____ _____ _____ in the whole town.

5 "Is there _____ _____?" asked Shirley.

6 "Someone _____ _____ the gold medal _____ the talent show!"

7 Mr. Reese _____ Shirley _____ the _____ of the crime.

8 There _____ a case with a _____ window.

9 The silver and bronze medals _____ _____ _____.

10 But the gold medal was _____. There was _____ _____ in _____ _____.

11 Tomorrow is the talent show. _____ _____ the gold medal _____?

12 Look _____ _____ _____. You can't catch me. You're _____ slow.

13 Shirley asked, "Could you tell me _____ _____ _____?"

14 "A little _____ nine last night. I was _____ _____ _____ when I heard a scream. I _____ _____ and found Jocelyn and the case like this."

15 "I wonder _____ _____ _____ _____ last night."

16 "Sylvia and Harry. They were also _____ for the talent show. I'll _____ to my office."

17 Jocelyn was a _____ student with short _____ red hair.

1 Reese 교장은 젖은 운동장을 달려왔다.

2 "Shirley! Shirley! 네 도움이 필요하구나!"

3 Shirley는 Bakersville 중학교의 8학년 학생이었다.

4 그녀는 또한 그 마을 최고의 탐정이었다.

5 "무슨 일이 있나요?" Shirley가 물었다.

6 "누군가 장기 자랑 대회 금메달을 훔쳐갔어!"

7 Reese 교장은 Shirley를 범죄 현장으로 데려갔다.

8 유리창이 깨진 진열장이 있었다.

9 은메달과 동메달은 그곳에 그대로 있었다.

10 하지만 금메달은 사라졌다. 그 자리에는 시가 있었다.

11 내일은 장기 자랑 대회다. 금메달은 어디로 갔을까?

12 구석구석 찾아라. 당신은 나를 잡을 수 없어. 당신은 너무 느려.

13 Shirley는 "언제 이 사건이 일어났는지 말씀해 주시겠어요?"라고 물었다.

14 "어젯밤 9시가 조금 넘은 후에. 내가 순찰을 돌고 있었을 때 비명 소리가 들렸어. 나는 달려가서 Jocelyn과 이 상태인 진열장을 발견했지."

15 "어젯밤에 또 다른 누가 여기 있었는지 궁금해요."

16 "Sylvia와 Harry가 있었어. 그 두 사람 또한 장기 자랑을 위해 연습 중이었어. 내가 그들을 내 사무실로 부르마."

17 Jocelyn은 빨간색 짧은 곱슬머리를 가진 9학년 학생이었다.

18 "I was _____ my song and I became _____. I _____ the classroom _____ _____ some water. _____ was _____ dark. _____, there was a loud sound of _____. I think the thief _____ the window at that moment. _____ _____ right after and it became bright for a second or two. Then I saw someone _____ _____ from the case."

19 "Did you see the thief's _____?"

20 "No, I only saw the thief's _____. But the thief had _____ hair."

21 Next was an _____ _____ student, Sylvia. She was tall _____ _____ _____ _____ hair.

22 She said, "I was _____ my poem _____ in the classroom. I heard a scream and went outside. There was a girl _____ _____ the case. With the _____ from the lightning, it was _____ _____ _____ _____. I got _____ so I ran straight home."

23 "Did you _____ the window _____?"

24 "No, the thunder was _____ _____. Well, I didn't do it. I _____ _____ _____ _____ first place anyway."

25 Harry, a seventh grader, had _____ _____ hair.

26 He said, "Hey, you got the _____ guy. I was practicing my dance _____. I went home _____ _____ _____ nine. I didn't _____ one step _____ the classroom _____ then."

27 "Did you hear _____ _____?"

28 "_____ _____ I? My music was really loud."

29 "Did you see anyone _____ _____ _____ _____ _____?"

30 "No, I heard someone _____ really badly, but I didn't see anyone."

31 Shirley said, "I don't need _____ _____ _____." Then she _____ _____ the thief.

32 "Why don't you _____ _____ _____ before you get into some real trouble?"

18 "저는 제 노래를 연습하고 있었는데 목이 말랐어요. 저는 물을 가지러 교실 밖으로 나갔어요. 완전히 어두웠어요. 갑자기, 커다란 천둥소리가 났어요. 저는 도둑이 그 순간에 유리창을 깼다고 생각해요. 번개가 바로 뒤따랐고 1~2초 정도 밝아졌어요. 그때 저는 누군가가 진열장에서 도망치는 걸 봤어요."

19 "도둑의 얼굴을 봤나요?"

20 "아니요, 도둑의 뒷모습만 봤어요. 하지만 그 도둑은 짧은 머리였어요."

21 다음은 8학년 학생인 Sylvia였다. 그녀는 긴 검은색 머리에 키가 컸다.

22 그녀는 말했다. "저는 교실에서 큰 소리로 제 시를 낭송하고 있었어요. 비명 소리를 듣고 밖으로 나갔어요. 진열장 옆에 한 소녀가 있었어요. 번개의 번쩍임과 어우러져 그것은 공포 영화 같았어요. 저는 겁이 나서 곧장 집으로 달려갔어요."

23 "창이 깨지는 소리를 들었나요?"

24 "아니요, 천둥소리가 너무 컸어요. 음, 제가 그런 게 아니에요. 저는 어쨌든 1등을 할 거였으니까요."

25 7학년인 Harry는 짧은 금발을 가지고 있었다.

26 그는 말했다. "이봐요, 사람을 잘못 짚었어요. 저는 제 춤 동작을 연습하고 있었어요. 저는 9시 조금 전에 집에 갔어요. 저는 그때까지 교실 밖으로 한 발자국도 나가지 않았어요."

27 "이상한 소리라도 들었나요?"

28 "제가 어떻게 듣겠어요? 제 음악 소리가 정말 컸어요."

29 "집에 가는 길에 누군가를 보았나요?"

30 "아니요, 누군가가 노래를 정말 끔찍하게 부르는 소리는 들었지만 누구도 보진 못했어요."

31 Shirley는 "더 이상 들을 필요는 없겠네요."라고 말했다. 그리고 나서 그녀는 도둑을 향했다.

32 "정말 곤경에 빠지기 전에 금메달을 돌려주는 게 어때요?"

● 우리말을 참고하여 본문을 영작하시오.

1 Reese 교장은 젖은 운동장을 달려왔다.

➡ _____

2 "Shirley! Shirley! 네 도움이 필요하구나!"

➡ _____

3 Shirley는 Bakersville 중학교의 8학년 학생이었다.

➡ _____

4 그녀는 또한 그 마을 최고의 탐정이었다.

➡ _____

5 "무슨 일이 있나요?" Shirley가 물었다.

➡ _____

6 "누군가 장기 자랑 대회 금메달을 훔쳐갔어!"

➡ _____

7 Reese 교장은 Shirley를 범죄 현장으로 데려갔다.

➡ _____

8 유리창이 깨진 진열장이 있었다.

➡ _____

9 은메달과 동메달은 그곳에 그대로 있었다.

➡ _____

10 하지만 금메달은 사라졌다. 그 자리에는 시가 있었다.

➡ _____

11 내일은 장기 자랑 대회다. 금메달은 어디로 갔을까?

➡ _____

12 구석구석 찾아라. 당신은 나를 잡을 수 없어. 당신은 너무 느려.

➡ _____

13 Shirley는 "언제 이 사건이 일어났는지 말씀해 주시겠어요?"라고 물었다.

➡ _____

14 "어젯밤 9시가 조금 넘은 후에. 내가 순찰을 돌고 있었을 때 비명 소리가 들렸어. 나는 달려가서 Jocelyn과 이 상태인 진열장을 발견했지."

➡ _____

➡ _____

15 "어젯밤에 또 다른 누가 여기 있었는지 궁금해요."

➡ _____

16 "Sylvia와 Harry가 있었어. 그 두 사람 또한 장기 자랑을 위해 연습 중이었어. 내가 그들을 내 사무실로 부르마."

➡ _____

17 Jocelyn은 빨간색 짧은 곱슬머리를 가진 9학년 학생이었다.

➡ _____

18 "저는 제 노래를 연습하고 있었는데 목이 말랐어요. 저는 물을 가지러 교실 밖으로 나갔어요. 완전히 어두웠어요. 갑자기, 커다란 천둥소리기 났어요. 저는 도둑이 그 순간에 유리창을 깼다고 생각해요. 번개가 바로 뒤따랐고 1~2초 정도 밝아졌어요. 그때 저는 누군가가 진열장에서 도망치는 걸 봤어요."

➡ _____

_____

_____

19 "도둑의 얼굴을 봤나요?"

➡ _____

20 "아니요, 도둑의 뒷모습만 봤어요. 하지만 그 도둑은 짧은 머리였어요."

➡ _____

21 다음은 8학년 학생인 Sylvia였다. 그녀는 긴 검은색 머리에 키가 컸다.

➡ _____

22 그녀는 말했다. "저는 교실에서 큰 소리로 제 시를 낭송하고 있었어요. 비명 소리를 듣고 밖으로 나갔어요. 진열장 옆에 한 소녀가 있었어요. 번개의 번쩍임과 어우러져 그것은 공포 영화 같았어요. 저는 겁이 나서 곧장 집으로 달려갔어요."

➡ _____

_____

_____

23 "창이 깨지는 소리를 들었나요?"

➡ _____

24 "아니요, 천둥소리가 너무 컸어요. 음, 제가 그런 게 아니에요. 저는 어쨌든 1등을 할 거였으니까요."

➡ _____

25 7학년인 Harry는 짧은 금발을 가지고 있었다.

➡ _____

26 그는 말했다. "이봐요, 사람을 잘못 짚었어요. 저는 제 춤 동작을 연습하고 있었어요. 저는 9시 조금 전에 집에 갔어요. 저는 그때까지 교실 밖으로 한 발자국도 나가지 않았어요."

➡ _____

27 "이상한 소리라도 들었나요?"

➡ _____

28 "제가 어떻게 듣겠어요? 제 음악 소리가 정말 컸어요."

➡ _____

29 "집에 가는 길에 누군가를 보았나요?"

➡ _____

30 "아니요, 누군가가 노래를 정말 끔찍하게 부르는 소리는 들었지만 누구도 보진 못했어요."

➡ _____

31 Shirley는 "더 이상 들을 필요는 없겠네요."라고 말했다. 그러고 나서 그녀는 도둑을 향했다.

➡ _____

32 "정말 곤경에 빠지기 전에 금메달을 돌려주는 게 어때요?"

➡ _____

[01~04] 다음 글을 읽고 물음에 답하시오.

Mr. Reese, the principal, ①ran across the wet playground.

"Shirley! Shirley! I need your help!"

Shirley was an eighth grade student at Bakersville Middle School. She was also the best detective in the whole town.

"Is there something wrong?" asked Shirley.

"Someone has stolen the gold medal for the talent show!"

Mr. Reese ②took Shirley to ③the scene of the crime. There was ④a case with a broken window. The silver and bronze medals were still (A)there. But the gold medal was missing. There was a poem in its place.

Tomorrow is the talent show.
Where did the gold medal go?
⑤Look high and low.
You can't catch me. You're too slow.

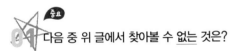 다음 중 위 글에서 찾아볼 수 <u>없는</u> 것은?

① a man who ran across the playground
② a case with a gold medal
③ a poem written by someone
④ a case with a silver and bronze medals
⑤ a man and a girl going to the scene of the crime

서답형

02 밑줄 친 (A)가 의미하는 것을 영어로 쓰시오.

➡ _____

03 ①~⑤ 중 단어의 의미풀이가 바르지 <u>않은</u> 것은?

① 가로질러 뛰었다　② 데려갔다
③ 범죄의 현장　　　④ 사건
⑤ 구석구석 찾아라

서답형

04 다음 물음에 세 단어로 이루어진 한 문장의 영어로 답하시오.

Q: What happened to the gold medal for the talent show?

➡ _____

[05~08] 다음 글을 읽고 물음에 답하시오.

Shirley asked, "Could you tell me when this happened?"

"A little after nine last night. I was making my rounds when I heard a scream. I rushed over and found Jocelyn and the case like this."

"I wonder who else was here last night."

"Sylvia and Harry. They were also practicing for the talent show. I'll call ⓐthem to my office."

Jocelyn was a ninth grade student with short curly red hair.

"I was practicing my song and I became thirsty. I stepped outside the classroom to get some water. ⓑIt was completely dark. Suddenly, there was a loud sound of thunder. I think the thief broke the window at that moment. Lightning followed right after and it became bright for a second or two. Then I saw someone running away from the case."

"Did you see the thief's face?"

"No, I only saw the thief's back. But the thief had short hair."

서답형

05 밑줄 친 ⓐ가 가리키는 것을 영어로 쓰시오.

➡ _____

Which one is NOT true about Jocelyn?

① She had short curly hair.

② She became thirsty while practicing.

③ She drank water in the classroom.

④ She heard a sound of thunder.

⑤ She practiced songs for the talent show.

07 다음 중 밑줄 친 ⓑ와 쓰임이 같은 것은?

① It was my mistake to bring you here.

② It was cloudy and windy.

③ It climbs a tree by itself.

④ It is true that she stole my money.

⑤ It belongs to my brother.

서답형

08 According to the passage, what did Jocelyn know about the thief? Answer in English with a full sentence.

➡ _____

[09~13] 다음 글을 읽고 물음에 답하시오.

Next was an eighth grade student, Sylvia. She was tall with long black hair. She said, "I was ①reading my poem aloud in the classroom. I heard a scream and went outside. There was a girl next to the case. With ②the flash from the lightning, it was like a horror movie. I got ③scared so I ran straight home."

"Did you hear the window break?"

"No, the thunder was too loud. Well, I didn't do it. I was going to win first place anyway."

Harry, a seventh grader, had short blonde hair. He said, "Hey, you got the ④wrong guy. I was practicing my dance moves. I went home a little before nine. I didn't take one step outside the classroom until then."

"Did you hear anything strange?"

"How could I? My music was really ⑤quiet."

"Did you see anyone on the way home?"

"No, I heard someone singing really badly, but I didn't see anyone."

Shirley said, "I don't need to hear anymore." Then she turned to the ___(A)___.

"Why don't you bring the medal back before you get into some real trouble?"

서답형

09 다음과 같이 풀이되는 단어를 빈칸 (A)에 쓰시오.

> a person who steals something from another person

➡ _____

서답형

10 ①~⑤ 중 글의 흐름상 어색한 것은?

①   ②   ③   ④   ⑤

서답형

11 위 글의 내용에 맞게 빈칸에 알맞은 말을 쓰시오.

> Shirley: I wonder _____.
>
> Harry: No, I just heard someone singing badly.

➡ _____

서답형

12 Write the reason why Sylvia didn't hear the window break.

➡ It was because _____.

다음 중 위 글을 읽고 답할 수 없는 질문은?

① Where was Sylvia reading her poem?

② Why did Sylvia go outside?

③ Why did Sylvia see a horror movie?

④ What was Harry doing?

⑤ When did Harry go home?

[14~17] 다음 글을 읽고 물음에 답하시오.

Mr. Reese, the principal, ran across the wet playground.

"Shirley! Shirley! I need your help!"

Shirley was an eighth grade student at Bakersville Middle School. She was also the best detective in the whole town.

"Is there something wrong?" asked Shirley.

"Someone has stolen the gold medal for the talent show!"

Mr. Reese took Shirley to the scene of the crime. There was a case with a broken window. The silver and bronze medals were still there. But the gold medal was missing. There was a poem in its place.

> Tomorrow is the talent show.
> Where did the gold medal go?
> Look high and low.
> You can't catch me. You're too slow.

Shirley asked, "Could you tell me _____(A)_____?"

"A little after nine last night. I was making my rounds when I heard a scream. I rushed over and found Jocelyn and the case like this."

"I wonder who else was here last night."

"Sylvia and Harry. They were also practicing for the talent show. I'll call them to my office."

서답형

14 단어 this를 이용하여 빈칸 (A)에 들어갈 알맞은 말을 3단어로 쓰시오.

➡ _____

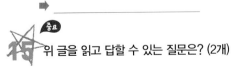

15 위 글을 읽고 답할 수 있는 질문은? (2개)

① When did Mr. Reese find Shirley?

② Where does Shirley live?

③ How many cases did Shirley solve?

④ When did the medal disappear?

⑤ When is the talent show?

16 Choose what we can know from the poem. (2개)

① The gold medal was placed somewhere high.

② The talent show was going to be held the next day.

③ The person who wrote it wondered who took the medal.

④ The thief wrote the poem.

⑤ The person who wrote it wanted someone to catch him or her.

서답형

17 위 글의 내용에 맞게 빈칸에 알맞은 말을 쓰시오.

> The thief took only _____.

[18~22] 다음 글을 읽고 물음에 답하시오.

Jocelyn was a ninth grade student with short curly red hair.

"I was practicing my song and I became thirsty. ① I stepped outside the classroom to get some water. ② It was completely dark. ③ Suddenly, there was a loud sound of thunder. ④ I think the thief broke the window at that moment. Lightning followed right after and it became bright for a second or two. ⑤"

"Did you see the thief's face?" asked Shirley.

"No, I only saw the thief's back. But the thief had short hair."

Next was an eighth grade student, Sylvia. She was tall with long black hair. She said, "I was reading my poem aloud in the classroom. I heard a scream and went outside. There was a girl next to the case. With the flash from the lightning, it was like a horror movie. I got scared so I ran straight home."

"Did you hear the window break?" asked Shirley.

"No, the thunder was too loud. Well, I didn't do it. I was going to win first place anyway."

18 ①~⑤ 중 주어진 문장이 들어가기에 가장 적절한 곳은?

> Then I saw someone running away from the case.

①　　　②　　　③　　　④　　　⑤

19 Sylvia가 교실 밖을 나와 느낀 감정으로 가장 적절한 것은?

① interested　　② happy　　③ sad
④ frightened　　⑤ bored

20 Which one is NOT true about the passage?

① Shirley wondered if Jocelyn saw the thief's face.
② Sylvia was an eighth grade student.
③ Sylvia was reading a poem when there was thunder.
④ Sylvia saw a girl beside the case.
⑤ The sound of the thunder was very loud.

21 According to the passage, why did Jocelyn step outside the classroom? Answer in English with a full sentence.

➡ _____

22 다음 물음에 완전한 문장의 영어로 답하시오.

> Q: What did Sylvia look like?

➡ _____

[23~25] 다음 글을 읽고 물음에 답하시오.

Harry, a seventh grader, had short blonde hair. He said, "Hey, you got the wrong guy. I was practicing my dance moves. I went home a little before nine. I didn't take one step outside the classroom until then."

"Did you hear (A)[strange anything / anything strange]?"

"ⓐHow could I? My music was really loud."

"Did you see anyone on the way home?"

"No, I heard someone (B)[singing / to sing] really badly, but I didn't see anyone."

Shirley said, "I don't need to hear anymore." Then she turned to the thief.

"Why don't you (C)[bring / bringing] the medal back before you get into some real trouble?"

23 (A)~(C)에서 어법상 옳은 것을 바르게 짝지은 것은?

① anything strange – to sing – to bring
② anything strange – singing – bring
③ strange anything – singing – to bring
④ strange anything – singing – bring
⑤ strange anything – to sing – to bring

24 밑줄 친 ⓐ의 의미로 가장 적절한 것은?

① It was my fault.
② I heard someone talk.
③ It was impossible.
④ I could hear something.
⑤ I couldn't practice well.

25 What was Harry doing in the classroom? Answer in English with a full sentence.

➡ _____

[01~04] 다음 글을 읽고 물음에 답하시오.

Mr. Reese, the principal, ran across the wet playground.

"Shirley! Shirley! I need your help!"

Shirley was an eighth grade student at Bakersville Middle School. She was also the best detective in the whole town.

"_____(A)_____" asked Shirley.

"Someone has stolen the gold medal for the talent show!"

Mr. Reese took Shirley to the scene of the crime. There was a case with a broken window. The silver and bronze medals were still there. But the gold medal was missing. There was a poem in its place.

Tomorrow is the talent show.
Where did the gold medal go?
Look high and low.
You can't catch me. You're too slow.

01 주어진 단어를 바르게 배열하여 빈칸 (A)에 알맞은 말을 쓰시오.

(wrong / there / something / is)?

➡ _____

02 위 글의 등장인물에 대한 정보를 완성하시오.

• Mr. Reese: the _____ of Bakersville Middle School.
• Shirley: an _____ grade student / the _____ _____ in the town

03 Where were silver and bronze medals for the talent show? Answer in English with six words.

➡ _____

04 다음은 Shirley의 일기 중 일부이다. 빈칸에 알맞은 말을 쓰시오.

When I was walking, I heard someone _____ my name. It was _____.
He said somebody _____ _____ _____ _____ for the talent show. I went to the scene of the crime with him. I saw the window of the case _____. There was a _____ instead of _____ _____ _____.

[05~07] 다음 글을 읽고 물음에 답하시오.

Shirley asked, "Could you tell me when this happened?"

"A little after nine last night. I was making my rounds when I heard a scream. I rushed over and found Jocelyn and the case like this."

"I wonder who else was here last night."

"Sylvia and Harry. They were also practicing for the talent show. I'll call them to my office."

Jocelyn was a ninth grade student with short curly red hair.

"I was practicing my song and I became thirsty. I stepped outside the classroom to get some water. It was completely dark. Suddenly, there was a loud sound of thunder. I think the thief broke the window (A)at that moment. Lightning followed right after and it became bright for a second or two. Then I saw someone running away from the case."

"Did you see the thief's face?"

"No, I only saw the thief's back. But the thief had short hair."

05 밑줄 친 (A)가 의미하는 것을 10자 이내의 우리말로 쓰시오.

➡ _____

06 위 글의 내용에 맞게 빈칸에 알맞은 말을 쓰시오.

> **Shirley:** I'd like to ask _____ _____
> _____ _____ when you
> heard a scream.
> **Mr. Reese:** I was making my rounds when
> I heard a scream.

07 ⭐중요
Who was in the school at the time of the accident? Answer in English with a full sentence.

➡ _____
_____

[08~13] 다음 글을 읽고 물음에 답하시오.

Next was an eighth grade student, Sylvia. She was tall with long black hair. She said, "I was reading my poem aloud in the classroom. I heard a scream and went outside. There was a girl next to the case. With the flash from the lightning, it was like a horror movie. I got scared so I ran straight home."

"Did you hear the window break?"

"No, the thunder was too loud. Well, I didn't do it. I was going to win first place anyway."

Harry, a seventh grader, had short blonde hair. He said, "Hey, you got the wrong guy. I was practicing my dance moves. I went home a little before nine. I didn't take one step outside the classroom until then."

"Did you hear anything strange?"

"How could I? My music was really loud."

"Did you see anyone on the way home?"

"No, I heard someone singing really badly, but I didn't see anyone."

Shirley said, "I don't need to hear anymore." Then she turned to the thief.

"Why don't you bring the medal back before you get into some real trouble?"

08 ⭐중요
Write the reason why Harry couldn't hear anything strange. Use the phrase 'It was because.'

➡ _____

09 What did Sylvia see when she went outside? Answer in English with a full sentence.

➡ _____

10 According to the passage, why did Sylvia run straight home?

➡ _____

11 ⭐중요
According to what Sylvia said, what made the crime scene look like a horror movie? Answer in English with six words.

➡ _____

12 다음 중 글의 내용과 일치하지 <u>않는</u> 것 <u>두 개</u>를 찾아 바르게 고치시오.

> Sylvia was tall. She was reading her poem for the talent show. She heard a scream and went home. She heard someone breaking the window.

➡ _____, _____

13 주어진 단어를 활용하여 Shirley가 한 말을 영어로 쓰시오.

> 나는 누가 금메달을 훔쳤는지 알아냈어.
> (find out)

➡ _____

해석

Think and Write

When Rapunzel was a baby, a witch put her in a tall tower. Rapunzel grew up in the tower. She had long hair. The witch used it to climb up the tower. The witch always said, "The world outside is very dangerous." One day, a prince heard Rapunzel singing beautifully. He said, "Come down. The world outside is wonderful." Rapunzel said, "I don't know who is telling the truth." Rapunzel was confused. Finally, she made up her mind. She cut her hair and came down from the tower. When she faced the world for the first time, she couldn't believe her eyes. "What a beautiful world!"

(to부정사의 부사적 용법 중 목적(~하기 위해서))
(지각동사+목적어+Ving)
(간접의문문(의문대명사+동사))
(처음으로)
('S+V'가 생략된 감탄문)

구문해설
- put someone in ~: …을 ~에 가두다 · grow up: 자라다 · climb up: ~을 오르다
- wonderful: 아름다운 · confused: 혼란스러운 · make up one's mind: 결심하다
- face: ~에 직면하다, 마주하다

Rapunzel이 아기였을 때, 한 마녀가 그녀를 높은 탑에 가뒀다. Rapunzel은 그 탑에서 자랐다. 그녀는 긴 머리카락을 가지고 있었다. 마녀는 탑을 올라가기 위해 그 머리카락을 이용했다. 마녀는 항상 "바깥세상은 매우 위험해."라고 말했다. 어느 날, 한 왕자가 Rapunzel이 노래를 아름답게 부르고 있는 것을 들었다. 그는 "내려와요. 바깥세상은 멋져요."라고 말했다. Rapunzel은 "누가 사실을 말하고 있는지 모르겠어."라고 말했다. Rapunzel은 혼란스러워. 마침내, 그녀는 결심했다. 그녀는 머리카락을 자르고 탑에서 내려왔다. 그녀가 처음으로 세상과 마주했을 때, 그녀는 자신의 눈을 믿을 수 없었다. "정말 아름다운 세상이야!"

Project

To the treasure hunters,

Hello. We have hidden our treasure in the classroom. It is something delicious. Do you want to know where it is? Then follow the steps. First, look for a plant near the window. Look under the plant. You'll find a key. Second, pick up the key and walk to the back of the classroom. You'll see the lockers. The treasure is in the third locker from the left. It is locked, so use the key to open it. Got it? Help yourself.

(현재완료)
(부정대명사는 형용사가 뒤에서 수식)
(간접의문문(의문사+주어+동사))
(~ 아래를 보아라)
(왼쪽에서부터) (= The third locker) (부사적 용법(목적))

From Group 5

구문해설
- hide(hid-hidden): 숨기다 · delicious: 맛있는 · step: 단계 · pick up: 주워들다
- locker: 사물함 · treasure: 보물 · Got it?: 알겠니?

보물 사냥꾼들에게,

안녕. 우리는 교실에 우리 보물을 숨겼어. 그것은 맛있는 것이야. 그것이 어디에 있는지 알고 싶어? 그러면 다음 단계를 따라 봐. 우선, 창문 옆에 있는 식물을 찾아. 그 식물 아래를 봐. 너는 열쇠 하나를 찾을 거야. 두 번째, 그 열쇠를 들고 교실 뒤쪽으로 걸어가. 너는 사물함을 볼 거야. 보물은 왼쪽에서 세 번째 사물함 안에 있어. 그것은 잠겼으니 그것을 열기 위해 열쇠를 사용해. 알겠지? 많이 먹으렴.

Check Up

A: Can you do me a favor?
(상대방에게 도움을 요청하는 표현(=Can I ask you a favor?))
B: Sure. What is it?
(도움 요청에 승낙하는 표현(=Of course. = No problem.))
A: Can you help me blow up these balloons?

B: No problem.
(상대방의 요청에 승낙하는 표현)

구문해설
- blow up: (입으로) 불다

A: 부탁 하나 해도 될까?
B: 물론이지. 뭔데?
A: 이 풍선들을 부는 것 좀 도와줄 수 있니?
B: 좋아.

영역별 핵심문제

Words & Expressions

01 다음 짝지어진 단어의 관계가 같도록 빈칸에 알맞은 말을 쓰시오.

> hand : foot = handprint : _____

02 다음 중 밑줄 친 부분의 뜻풀이가 바르지 <u>않은</u> 것은?

① This information is a valuable <u>clue</u>. 단서
② The boy's eyes were wide with <u>horror</u>. 공포
③ He left his <u>footprints</u> on the sand. 발자국
④ The city can be a <u>dangerous</u> place to live in. 위험한
⑤ Can I ask you a <u>favor</u>? 맛, 풍미

03 다음 주어진 문장의 밑줄 친 principal과 <u>다른</u> 의미로 쓰인 것은?

> Mr. Kim, the <u>principal</u>, ran across the wet playground.

① I talked about my career with the <u>principal</u> for an hour.
② Bad weather is one of the <u>principal</u> causes to cancel the event.
③ My grandfather used to work at the elementary school as a <u>principal</u>.
④ The <u>principal</u> usually manages the teachers and the students.
⑤ I met the <u>principal</u> on the way home tonight.

04 다음 문장의 빈칸에 들어갈 말을 〈보기〉에서 골라 쓰시오.

> ┤ 보기 ├
> broken / footprint / thirsty / detective

(1) I felt so _____ after running the playground.
(2) Do you know what a _____ does to find the thief?
(3) He found the _____ which could be a clue.
(4) Don't touch the _____ window with your hand.

05 다음 주어진 문장에 공통으로 들어갈 말을 고르시오.

> • You have to _____ the gate and show your ID card.
> • I believe that my son will _____ the test.
> • Would you _____ me the bread and knife?
> • Time _____(e)s so fast.

① cross
② pass
③ steal
④ water
⑤ lose

06 다음 우리말을 주어진 단어를 이용하여 영작하시오.

(1) 그녀는 내게 은목걸이를 주었다. (necklace) (6 words)
  ➡ _____

(2) 제가 당신 방으로 당신 짐을 옮겨드릴게요. (carry, luggage) (7 words)
  ➡ _____

(3) 이 이야기는 하늘을 나는 마녀에 관한 것이다. (who, witch) (11 words)
  ➡ _____

Conversation

[07~08] 다음 대화를 읽고 물음에 답하시오.

Emily: (A)Can I ask you a favor?
Jinsu: Sure. What is it?
Emily: _____ (B)
Jinsu: No problem.

07 위 대화의 밑줄 친 (A)와 바꾸어 쓸 수 없는 것은?

① Can you do me a favor?
② Can you give me a hand?
③ Can you help me out?
④ Would you mind helping me?
⑤ How can I help you?

08 위 대화의 빈칸 (B)에 들어갈 말을 〈보기〉에 주어진 단어를 모두 배열하여 영작하시오.

┌── 보기 ──┐
you / the / dishes / me / wash / help / can
└────────┘

➡ _____

09 다음 짝지어진 대화가 어색한 것을 고르시오.

① A: Guess what I'm doing.
   B: I guess you're going up a ladder.
② A: Can you guess what I'm doing?
   B: Hmm.... I think you're flying a kite.
③ A: I think you're working on the computer.
   B: You're wrong. Guess again.
④ A: I guess you're fishing.
   B: That's right.
⑤ A: I guess you're playing the piano.
   B: That's too bad.

[10~12] 다음 대화를 읽고 물음에 답하시오.

Narae: Tony, ⓐcan you do me a favor? (hand)
Tony: (A) Sure. What is it, Narae?
Narae: (B) My family is going to visit my grandmother in Busan.
Tony: (C) Oh, I'm sorry but I can't. My mom doesn't like dogs.
Narae: (D) Oh, what should I do?
Tony: (E) Why don't you ask Sumin? Her family loves dogs.
Narae: Okay. I'll call her right now.

10 위 대화의 (A)~(E) 중 주어진 문장이 들어가기에 적절한 곳은?

┌─────────────────────────┐
Can you take care of my dog this weekend?
└─────────────────────────┘

① (A)   ② (B)   ③ (C)   ④ (D)   ⑤ (E)

11 위 대화의 밑줄 친 ⓐ와 의미가 같도록 주어진 단어를 사용하여 다시 쓰시오.

➡ _____

12 위 대화를 읽고 대답할 수 없는 질문은?

① What is Narae going to do this weekend?
② Where does Narae's grandmother live?
③ What is Narae asking Tony to do?
④ Why can't Tony help Narae?
⑤ How does Narae take care of her dog?

[13~14] 다음 글을 읽고 물음에 답하시오.

Sujin: Good morning, classmates! Nine months have passed so fast, and we are almost at the end of this school year. We all had a wonderful year. I guess only a few of us will be in the same class next year. Don't be a stranger. Say hello when we see each other, okay? Thank you.

13 When is Sujin making this speech?

➡ _____

14 What is Sujin asking her classmates to do?

➡ _____

_____

[15~16] 다음 대화를 읽고 물음에 답하시오.

> Brian: Mom, I can't find my smartphone. Can you help me find ⓐit?
>
> Mom: Are you sure you lost ⓑit inside the house?
>
> Brian: Yes. I just texted my friend a few minutes ago.
>
> Mom: Where were you at the time?
>
> Brian: In the kitchen. I was making a sandwich.
>
> Mom: Then I guess you left ⓒit somewhere in the kitchen.
>
> Brian: I already checked the kitchen, Mom.
>
> Mom: Well, let's check ⓓit again. Oh, here ⓔit is. Inside the refrigerator.
>
> Brian: Thanks, Mom. You are the greatest!
>
> Mom: You're welcome, honey.

15 위 대화의 ⓐ~ⓔ 중 가리키는 대상이 나머지 넷과 다른 것은?

① ⓐ　② ⓑ　③ ⓒ　④ ⓓ　⑤ ⓔ

16 위 대화의 내용과 일치하지 않는 것은?

① Brian은 스마트폰을 찾고 있다.
② Brian은 몇 분 전에 친구에게 문자 메시지를 보냈다.
③ 엄마는 Brian이 부엌 어딘가에 핸드폰을 놓은 것 같다고 추측하였다.
④ 엄마는 부엌에서 Brian을 위해 샌드위치를 만들고 있었다.
⑤ 엄마는 냉장고 안에서 Brian의 스마트폰을 찾았다.

Grammar

17 다음 중 빈칸에 들어갈 말로 알맞지 않은 것은?

> I'd like to know _____.

① who you met an hour ago
② who made you this skirt
③ who your purse found
④ who invited you to the party
⑤ who you want to talk to

18 다음 우리말을 영어로 옮길 때 다섯 번째와 여섯 번째로 오는 단어를 바르게 묶은 것은?

> 나는 내 생일 파티에 신나는 무엇인가를 하고 싶다.

① do – something
② something – exciting
③ exciting – for
④ for – my
⑤ my – birthday

19 다음 우리말을 영어로 바르게 옮긴 것은?

> 누가 너를 그 파티에 초대했는지 말해 줄래?

① Can you tell me who you will invite to the party?
② Can you tell me whom you invited to the party?
③ Can you tell me who invite to the party?
④ Can you tell me who invited you to the party?
⑤ Can you tell me who is going to invite you?

20 다음 두 문장을 하나의 문장으로 쓰시오.

> Do you know? What color is her bag?

➡ _____

21 빈칸에 들어갈 말로 가장 적절한 것은?

> I have _____.

① to tell you important something
② something to tell you important
③ to you something important tell
④ you to tell you something important
⑤ something important to tell you

22 다음 중 어법상 옳은 것을 바르게 짝지은 것은?

> • Let's decide what [should we do / we should do].
> • I have something [to do interesting / interesting to do].
> • They will ask [that / if] you live alone.

① should we do – to do interesting – that
② should we do – interesting to do – that
③ should we do – interesting to do – if
④ we should do – interesting to do – if
⑤ we should do – to do interesting – if

23 다음 중 어법상 바르지 <u>않은</u> 것은?

① There is something wrong with this computer.
② I want to have something cute.
③ I don't know what Tim took to the party.
④ Patrick wondered whether they would agree with his idea.
⑤ There is nothing to keep precious.

24 주어진 단어를 활용하여 다음 우리말을 7 단어로 이루어진 한 문장의 영어로 쓰시오.

> 그녀는 자기 엄마를 위해 특별한 것을 샀다.
> (special / for)

➡ _____

25 빈칸에 들어갈 말로 가장 적절한 것은?

> A: Why did she come late?
> B: I don't know _____. But she said she was sorry for being late.

① why she hates me
② why she was sorry
③ why she came late
④ why she comes lately
⑤ why she was coming

26 주어진 단어를 바르게 배열하여 다음 우리말을 영어로 쓰시오.

> 나는 기댈 만한 믿음직한 누군가가 필요해.
> (need, I, depend, trustful, to, someone, on)

➡ _____

Reading

[27~28] 다음 글을 읽고 물음에 답하시오.

Mr. Reese, the principal, ran across the wet playground.
"Shirley! Shirley! I need your help!"
Shirley was an eighth grade student at Bakersville Middle School. She was also the best detective in the whole town.
"Is there something wrong?" asked Shirley.
"Someone has stolen the gold medal for the talent show!"
Mr. Reese took Shirley to (A)the scene of the crime. There was a case with a broken window. The silver and bronze medals were still there. But the gold medal was missing. There was a poem in its place.

Tomorrow is the talent show.
Where did the gold medal go?
Look high and low.
You can't catch me. You're too slow.

Shirley asked, "Could you tell me when this happened?"

"A little after nine last night. I was making my rounds when I heard a scream. I rushed over and found Jocelyn and the case like this."

"I wonder who else was here last night."

"Sylvia and Harry. They were also practicing for the talent show. I'll call them to my office."

27 Which one is NOT true about the underlined (A)?

① There was a case whose window was broken.
② The gold medal was missing.
③ Mr. Reese was the first man that arrived at the crime scene.
④ The thief didn't take the other medals.
⑤ The thief left a poem.

28 위 글의 내용과 일치하지 않는 것은?

① The playground was wet.
② Mr. Reese ran across the playground, calling Shirley's name.
③ Shirley wondered when the accident happened.
④ Mr. Reese wasn't at school when the accident happened.
⑤ Mr. Reese knew who was at school last night.

[29~31] 다음 글을 읽고 물음에 답하시오.

When Rapunzel was a baby, a witch put her in a tall tower. Rapunzel grew up in the tower. She had long hair.

(A) He said, "Come down. The world outside is wonderful. Rapunzel said, "I don't know who is telling the truth." Rapunzel was confused.

(B) The witch used it to climb up the tower. The witch always said, "The world outside is very dangerous." One day, a prince heard Rapunzel singing beautifully.

(C) Finally, she made up her mind. She cut her hair and came down from the tower. When she faced the world for the first time, she couldn't believe her eyes. "What a beautiful world!"

29 자연스러운 글이 되도록 (A)~(C)를 바르게 배열한 것은?

① (A) – (C) – (B)   ② (B) – (A) – (C)
③ (B) – (C) – (A)   ④ (C) – (A) – (B)
⑤ (C) – (B) – (A)

30 What did Rapunzel do before she came down from the tower? Answer in English with four words.

➡ _____

31 다음 중 위 글을 읽고 답할 수 없는 질문은?

① Who put Rapunzel in a tall tower?
② Where did Rapunzel grow up?
③ Why did Rapunzel feel confused?
④ How did the witch climb up the tower?
⑤ What did Rapunzel use to come down from the tower?

출제율 90%

01 다음 영영풀이가 가리키는 것을 고르시오.

> a yellowish-brown metal containing copper and tin

① gold   ② silver   ③ bronze
④ diamond   ⑤ glass

출제율 100%

02 다음 대화가 자연스럽게 이어지도록 순서대로 배열하시오.

> (A) No problem.
> (B) Sure. What is it?
> (C) Jinsu, can I ask you a favor?
> (D) Can you help me wash the dishes?

➡ _____

[03~04] 다음 대화를 읽고 물음에 답하시오.

Brian: Mom, I can't find my smartphone. Can you help me find it?
Mom: (A) Are you sure you lost it inside the house?
Brian: (B) Yes. I just texted my friend a few minutes ago.
Mom: (C) Where were you at the time?
Brian: (D) I was making a sandwich.
Mom: (E) Then I guess you left it somewhere in the kitchen.
Brian: I already checked the kitchen, Mom.
Mom: Well, let's check it again. Oh, here it is. Inside the refrigerator.
Brian: Thanks, Mom. You are the greatest!
Mom: You're welcome, honey.

출제율 90%

03 위 대화의 (A)~(E) 중 주어진 문장이 들어가기에 적절한 곳은?

> In the kitchen.

① (A)   ② (B)   ③ (C)   ④ (D)   ⑤ (E)

출제율 95%

04 위 대화의 내용과 일치하는 것은?

① Brian and his mom were making a sandwich.
② His mom texted Brian a few minutes ago.
③ Brian helped his mom find her smartphone.
④ Brian is sure that he left his smartphone in the kitchen.
⑤ Brian's smartphone was discovered in the refrigerator.

[05~06] 다음 대화를 읽고 물음에 답하시오.

Narae: Tony, can you do me a favor?
Tony: Sure. What is it, Narae?
Narae: (A)이번 주말에 내 개를 돌봐 줄 수 있니? (can, take) My family is going to visit my grandmother in Busan.
Tony: Oh, I'm sorry but I can't. My mom doesn't like dogs.
Narae: _____(B)_____
Tony: Why don't you ask Sumin? Her family loves dogs.
Narae: Okay. I'll call her right now.

출제율 90%

05 위 대화의 밑줄 친 (A)의 우리말을 주어진 단어를 이용하여 영작하시오.

➡ _____

출제율 95%

06 위 대화의 빈칸 (A)에 들어갈 말로 적절한 것을 모두 고르시오.

① I don't know what to do.
② What can I do for you?
③ Oh, what should I do?
④ Can you give me a hand?
⑤ Would you help me out?

[07~08] 다음 글을 읽고 물음에 답하시오.

> **Sujin:** Good morning, classmates! ①Nine months have passed so fast, and we are almost at the end of this school year. ② We all had a wonderful year. ③I guess only a few of us will be in the same class next year. Don't be a stranger. ④You should learn how to turn the stranger into your friends. ⑤Say hello when we see each other, okay? Thank you.

출제율 95%

07 다음 ①~⑤ 중 글의 흐름상 어색한 것을 고르시오.

①   ②   ③   ④   ⑤

출제율 100%

08 위 대화를 읽고 대답할 수 <u>없는</u> 것은?

① Who are the listeners?
② When is Sujin making this speech?
③ How many months have passed after this school year began?
④ What is Sujin asking her classmates to do?
⑤ What should Sujin do whenever she meets strangers?

[09~10] 다음 대화를 읽고 물음에 답하시오.

> **Emily:** Jinsu, can I ask you a favor?
> **Jinsu:** Sure. What is it?
> **Emily:** (A)Can you help me wash the dishes? (give)
> **Jinsu:** No problem.

출제율 90%

09 What does Emily ask Jinsu to do?

➡ _____

출제율 90%

10 위 대화의 밑줄 친 (A)와 같은 의미가 되도록 주어진 단어를 이용하여 바꿔 쓰시오.

➡ _____

출제율 100%

11 다음 빈칸에 들어갈 말로 적절하지 <u>않은</u> 것은?

> _____ who the man is?

① Does she know
② Can you tell me
③ Do they remember
④ Does it happen
⑤ Do you want to know

출제율 95%

12 다음 대화의 빈칸에 알맞은 말로 가장 적절한 것은?

> **A:** I wonder _____.
> **B:** It was James. He found the flag.

① who bought the flag
② how James found the flag
③ who found the flag
④ when James brought the flag
⑤ where James found the flag

출제율 90%

13 다음 우리말을 영어로 바르게 옮긴 것은?

> 당신과 함께 논의할 중요한 것이 있습니다.

① There are some important things to discuss.
② There are important something to discuss with you.
③ There is something important to discuss about you.
④ There is something important to discuss with you.
⑤ There is something discuss with you important.

14 다음 중 어법상 올바른 문장은?

① Tell me who the ball kicked.
② They need old someone.
③ Ask her that she likes to eat pizza with us.
④ Did you know what would he want from you?
⑤ Judy wants something powerful.

15 다음 대화의 빈칸에 알맞은 말을 쓰시오.

> A: It's very cold. I want something _____ _____ _____.
> B: Here, you can wear my coat. It will make you warm.

16 다음 두 문장을 하나의 문장으로 쓰시오.

> • Please ask him.
> • What time can he pick me up?

➡ _____

17 다음 대화의 빈칸에 알맞은 말을 쓰시오.

> A: Do you know _____ ?
> B: Yes. My grandfather built it.

➡ _____

[18~20] 다음 글을 읽고 물음에 답하시오.

When Rapunzel was a baby, a witch put her in a tall tower. Rapunzel grew up in the tower. She had long hair. The witch used it to climb up the tower. The witch always said, "The world outside is very dangerous." One day, a prince heard Rapunzel singing beautifully. He said, "Come down. The world outside is wonderful. Rapunzel said, "I don't know (A)누가 사실을 말하고 있는지." Rapunzel was confused. ___(B)___, she made up her mind. She cut her hair and came down from the tower. When she faced the world for the first time, she couldn't believe her eyes. "What a beautiful world!"

18 밑줄 친 우리말 (A)를 영어로 쓰시오.

➡ _____

19 빈칸 (B)에 들어갈 말로 가장 적절한 것은?

① For example ② Therefore
③ Moreover ④ Finally
⑤ In addition

20 다음 중 위 글의 내용과 일치하지 않는 것은?

① Rapunzel grew up in the tall tower because of the witch.
② The witch had long hair.
③ The prince told Rapunzel that the world outside was wonderful.
④ The prince wanted Rapunzel to come down.
⑤ Rapunzel felt the world outside was beautiful.

[21~25] 다음 글을 읽고 물음에 답하시오.

Jocelyn was a ninth grade student with short curly red hair.

"I was practicing my song and I became thirsty.

(A) I think the thief broke the window at that moment. Lightning followed right after and it became bright for a second or two.

(B) Suddenly, there was a loud sound of thunder.

(C) I stepped outside the classroom to get some water. It was completely dark.

(D) Then I saw someone running away from the case."

"Did you see the thief's face?"

"No, I only saw the thief's back. But the thief had short hair."

Next ①was an eighth grade student, Sylvia. She was tall with long black hair. She said, "I was reading my poem ②aloud in the classroom. I heard a scream and went outside. There was a girl ③next to the case. With the flash from the lightning, it was like a horror movie. I got scared ④so I ran straight home."

"Did you hear the window ⑤to break?"

"No, the thunder was too loud. Well, I didn't do it. I was going to win first place anyway."

21 자연스러운 내용이 되도록 (A)~(D)를 바르게 배열하시오.

➡ _____

22 ①~⑤ 중 어법상 바르지 <u>않은</u> 것은?

① ② ③ ④ ⑤

23 다음 중 위 글의 내용을 바르게 이해한 사람은?

① Jacky: Jocelyn must be really scared to see the thief's face.

② Polly: I think Sylvia is the thief. Because she had short hair.

③ Jason: Jocelyn is the same grade student as Sylvia.

④ Teo: Sylvia is confident enough to think that she is going to win first place.

⑤ Christine: Jocelyn saw the thief when he broke the case. He must be really scared.

24 위 글의 내용에 맞게 빈칸에 알맞은 말을 쓰시오.

The gold medal was stolen. Shirley wanted to find out _____ _____ it, so she talked with some students who were at school when the accident happened. Jocelyn was _____ _____ _____ and Sylvia was _____ _____ _____ in the classroom.

25 다음 중 위 글을 읽고 답할 수 <u>없는</u> 것은?

① What does Jocelyn look like?

② What was Sylvia doing in the classroom?

③ How long did it became bright when lightning stroke?

④ Why did Sylvia go outside?

⑤ What time did Sylvia hear a scream?

[01~03] 다음 대화를 읽고 물음에 답하시오.

Narae: Tony, can you do me a favor?

Tony: Sure. What is it, Narae?

Narae: Can you take care of my dog this weekend? My family is going to visit my grandmother in Busan.

Tony: Oh, I'm sorry but I can't. My mom doesn't like dogs.

Narae: Oh, what should I do?

Tony: Why don't you ask Sumin? Her family loves dogs.

Narae: Okay. I'll call her right now.

01 What does Narae ask Tony to do?

➡ _____

_____

02 Who doesn't like dogs?

➡ _____

03 Why does Tony recommend Narae to ask Sumin?

➡ _____

04 다음 대화의 빈칸에 알맞은 말을 7 단어로 쓰시오.

A: I want to ask _____ .

B: Donna says she was satisfied with your service.

A: That's good to know. Thank you.

➡ _____

05 주어진 단어를 활용하여 다음 우리말을 영어로 쓰시오.

나는 그녀가 어떤 둥근 것을 가지고 있는지 궁금해요. (wonder / something)

➡ _____

06 주어진 단어를 바르게 배열하여 다음 우리말을 영어로 쓰시오.

나는 그것이 영어로 뭐라고 불리는지 기억할 수 없어.

(in / English / what / called / remember / is / it / can't / I)

➡ _____

07 다음 대화의 빈칸에 알맞은 말을 쓰시오.

A: Do you want something?

B: Yes, I want _____ _____

_____ .

A: Then, how about eating ice cream? It is really sweet.

08 다음 두 문장을 하나의 문장으로 쓰시오.

• I really don't understand.

• Why is she crying?

➡ _____

When Rapunzel was a baby, a witch put her in a tall tower. Rapunzel grew up in the tower. She had long hair. The witch used it to climb up the tower. The witch always said, "The world outside is very dangerous." One day, a prince heard Rapunzel singing beautifully. He said, "Come down. The world outside is wonderful. Rapunzel said, "I don't know who is telling the truth." Rapunzel was confused. Finally, she made up her mind. She cut her hair and came down from the tower. When she faced the world for the first time, (A)she couldn't believe her eyes. "What a beautiful world!"

09 What did the witch use in order to climb up the tower? Answer in English with a full sentence.

➡ _____

10 주어진 어구를 바르게 배열하여 밑줄 친 (A)의 이유를 설명하시오.

> (what the witch said / because / unlike / beautiful / outside / the world / was)

➡ _____
_____

[11~15] 다음 글을 읽고 물음에 답하시오.

Mr. Reese, the principal, ran across the wet playground.

"Shirley! Shirley! I need your help!"

Shirley was an eighth grade student at Bakersville Middle School. She was also the best detective in the whole town.

"Is there something wrong?" asked Shirley.

"Someone has stolen the gold medal for the talent show!"

Mr. Reese took Shirley to the scene of the crime. There was a case with a broken window. The silver and bronze medals were still there. But the gold medal was missing. There was a poem in (A)its place.

Shirley asked, "Could you tell me when this happened?"

"A little after nine last night. I was making my rounds when I heard a scream. I rushed over and found Jocelyn and the case like this."

11 When and where did the accident happen? Answer in English with a full sentence.

➡ _____

12 What did Mr. Reese find when he rushed over?

➡ _____

13 Where did Mr. Reese take Shirley?

➡ _____

14 Who is Mr. Reese? Answer in English with a full sentence.

➡ _____

15 밑줄 친 (A)its가 지칭하는 것을 위 글에서 찾아 쓰시오.

➡ _____

01 다음 대화를 읽고 대화의 내용과 일치하도록 Narea의 일기를 완성하시오.

Narae: Tony, can you do me a favor?

Tony: Sure. What is it, Narae?

Narae: Can you take care of my dog this weekend? My family is going to visit my grandmother in Busan.

Tony: Oh, I'm sorry but I can't. My mom doesn't like dogs.

Narae: Oh, what should I do?

Tony: Why don't you ask Sumin? Her family loves dogs.

Narae: Okay. I'll call her right now.

Today, I was worried about my dog, Pony. I will visit my grandmother this weekend, so I had to find someone who can (A)_____ my dog. At first, I asked Tony to look after my dog. Unfortunately, he can't help me because (B)_____.
I didn't know what to do. Then, Tony recommended Sumin because (C)_____.
I made a call to Sumin and asked her a favor. She said she could help me during this weekend. I was happy and really appreciated her.

02 다음 두 사람의 대화를 읽고 빈칸에 알맞은 말을 쓰시오.

David: Who is your favorite actor?

Alison: My favorite actor is Tom Cruz.

David: When was he born?

Alison: He was born in 1962.

David: Is he married?

Alison: Yes, he was.

I talked with David about my favorite actor. David wondered _____, so I answered it was Tom Cruz. Then, he wanted me to tell him _____.
I told him that Tom Cruz was born in 1962. David also would like to know _____, so I answered, "Yes, he was."

단원별 모의고사

01 다음 영영풀이가 가리키는 것을 고르시오.

> someone who steals things from another person

① detective   ② thief
③ lawyer   ④ policeman
⑤ judge

02 다음 문장의 빈칸에 들어갈 말을 〈보기〉에서 골라 알맞은 형태로 쓰시오.

┌─── 보기 ───┐
bring back / at the moment / rush over / run across / win first place
└─────────────┘

(1) I wanted to _____, so I did my best.
(2) I was so nervous that I couldn't say anything _____.
(3) I saw my brother _____ here.
(4) I felt so thirsty after _____ the road.
(5) I need to _____ this book _____ by 12 o'clock.

03 다음 문장에 공통으로 들어갈 말을 고르시오.

> • You should not use the _____ of a camera in the museum.
> • That _____ means danger.
> • A red light on the screen will _____ when you touch it.
> • I saw a _____ of lightning in the dark.

① flash   ② light   ③ call
④ clue   ⑤ favor

04 다음 우리말과 일치하도록 주어진 단어를 모두 배열하여 영작하시오.

(1) 도둑이 어제 금메달을 훔쳤다.
(stole / the / medal / yesterday / gold / a / thief)
➡ _____

(2) 이 풍선들을 부는 것을 도와주시겠어요?
(balloons / me / blow / can / these / you / help / up)
➡ _____

(3) 우리 장기 자랑 사진 좀 보내 줄래?
(talent / you / me / some / of / show / pictures / will / send / our)
➡ _____
_____

[05~07] 다음 대화를 읽고 물음에 답하시오.

> Brian: Did you see my baseball glove?
> Jane: Yes, I saw it under the table.
> Brian: Really? It's not there anymore.
> Jane: Then (A)I guess Spot took it.
> Brian: Oh, there he is. You bad dog, Spot!

05 위 대화의 밑줄 친 (A)와 바꾸어 쓸 수 있는 것을 모두 고르시오.

① I doubt that Spot took it.
② I think Spot took it.
③ I'm certain that Spot took it.
④ Maybe Spot took it.
⑤ I don't know whether Spot took it.

06 What was Brian looking for?
➡ _____

07 Who took Brian's baseball glove?

➡ _____

08 다음 대화가 자연스럽게 이어지도록 순서대로 배열하시오.

> (A) Okay. Where did you see it last?
> (B) On the bench.
> (C) Can you help me find my baseball glove?
> (D) I guess a dog took your baseball glove. I can see its footprints on the bench.

➡ _____

09 다음 짝지어진 대화가 <u>어색한</u> 것을 고르시오.

① A: Can you help me mop the floor?
　 B: Of course.
② A: Can you do me a favor?
　 B: Sure. What is it?
③ A: Can you help me clean the board?
　 B: I'm afraid I can't.
④ A: Would you mind helping me carry these books?
　 B: No problem.
⑤ A: Can you give me a hand?
　 B: You should wash your hands first.

[10~11] 다음 대화를 읽고 물음에 답하시오.

Brian: Mom, I can't find my smartphone. Can you help me find it?
Mom: Are you sure you (A)[lost / losing] it inside the house?
Brian: Yes. I just (B)[texted / texting] my friend a few minutes ago.

Mom: Where were you at the time?
Brian: In the kitchen. I was making a sandwich.
Mom: Then I guess you left it (C)[anywhere / somewhere] in the kitchen.
Brian: I already checked the kitchen, Mom.
Mom: Well, let's check it again. Oh, here it is. Inside the refrigerator.
Brian: Thanks, Mom. You are the greatest!
Mom: You're welcome, honey.

10 위 대화의 괄호 (A)~(C)에 들어갈 말로 알맞은 것끼리 짝지어진 것은?

	(A)	(B)	(C)
①	lost	texted	anywhere
②	lost	texting	somewhere
③	lost	texted	somewhere
④	losing	texting	somewhere
⑤	losing	texted	anywhere

11 위 대화의 내용과 일치하도록 빈칸을 완성하시오.

> Brian felt confused when he couldn't find _____(A)_____ . He asked his mother to help find it. Brian was sure that it must be inside _____(B)_____ because he just texted his friend a few minutes ago. He was making _____(C)_____ in the kitchen, so his mom checked the kitchen again. Finally, his mom found it inside _____(D)_____ .

➡ (A) _____ (B) _____
　 (C) _____ (D) _____

12 다음 중 우리말을 영어로 <u>잘못</u> 옮긴 것은?

① Clair는 공원에서 무엇인가 차가운 것을 마셨다.
→ Clair drank something cold at the park.

② 그가 내일 몇 시에 올지 알려줘.
→ Let me know what time he will come tomorrow.

③ 그 학교가 여기에서 얼마나 먼지 아니?
→ Do you know how the school is far from here?

④ 해야 할 즐거운 것이 있어.
→ There is something pleasant to do.

⑤ 누가 너에게 그 편지를 보냈는지 나는 몰라.
→ I don't know who sent you the letter.

13 빈칸에 알맞은 말로 가장 적절한 것은?

> I want to ask this. Are you married?
> = I want to ask _____.

① when are you married
② that you are married
③ whether you are married
④ who you are married
⑤ if you will marry or not

14 다음 중 어법상 바르지 <u>않은</u> 것은?

① I want to see something touching.
② They need someone reliable to be with.
③ Do you understand what I'm saying?
④ Tell her when does she have to move out.
⑤ Polly had nothing precious.

15 주어진 단어를 활용하여 다음 우리말을 영어로 쓰시오.

> 그가 어디에 있는지 내게 말해 줄 수 있니?
> (can / tell)

➡ _____

16 다음 우리말에 맞게 빈칸에 알맞은 말을 쓰시오.

> 그 과학자는 중요한 무언가를 발견했다.
> The scientist found _____ _____.

[17~20] 다음 글을 읽고 물음에 답하시오.

Mr. Reese, the principal, ran across the wet playground.

"Shirley! Shirley! I need your help!"

Shirley was an eighth grade student at Bakersville Middle School. She was also the best detective in the whole town.

"Is there something wrong?" asked Shirley.

"Someone has stolen the gold medal for the talent show!"

Mr. Reese took Shirley to the scene of the crime. There was a case with a broken window. The silver and bronze medals were still there. But the gold medal was missing. There was a poem in its place.

Shirley asked Mr. Reese, "Could you tell me ⓐ_____ this happened?"

"A little after nine last night. I was making my rounds ⓑ_____ I heard a scream. I rushed over and found Jocelyn and the case like this."

"_____ⓒ_____"

"Sylvia and Harry. They were also practicing for the talent show. I'll call them to my office."

Jocelyn was a ninth grade student with short curly red hair.

"I was practicing my song and I became thirsty. I stepped outside the classroom (A) to get some water. It was completely dark. Suddenly, there was a loud sound of thunder. I think the thief broke the window at that moment. Lightning followed right after and it became bright for a second or two. Then I saw someone running away from the case."

"Did you see the thief's face?"

"No, I only saw the thief's back. But the thief had short hair."

17 빈칸 ⓐ와 ⓑ에 공통으로 들어갈 말로 가장 적절한 것은?

① how   ② when   ③ why
④ who   ⑤ where

18 다음 중 빈칸 ⓒ에 들어갈 말로 가장 적절한 것은?

① I'd like to know how the case was broken.
② I wonder when you saw her.
③ Can you tell me who else was here last night?
④ Tell me who broke the case.
⑤ Do you know who saw the thief?

19 다음 중 밑줄 친 (A)와 쓰임이 같은 것은?

① They wanted to make *bibimbap*.
② You must listen to many songs to make your own song.
③ It is important to keep your friends' secret.
④ Is there something comfortable to wear?
⑤ To exercise regularly is essential.

20 According to what Jocelyn said, what did she see when there was lightning?

➡ _____

[21~23] 다음 글을 읽고 물음에 답하시오.

Next was an eighth grade student, Sylvia. She was tall with long black hair. She said, "I was reading my poem aloud in the classroom. I heard a scream and went outside. There was a girl next to the case. With the flash from the lightning, it was like a horror movie. I got scared so I ran straight home."

"Did you hear the window broken?"

"No, the thunder was too loud. Well, I didn't do it. I was going to win first place anyway."

Harry, a seventh grader, had short blonde hair. He said, "Hey, you got the wrong guy. I was practicing my dance moves. I went home a little before nine. I didn't take one step outside the classroom until then."

"Did you hear anything strange?"

"How could I? My music was really loud."

"Did you see anyone on the way home?"

"No, I heard someone singing really badly, but I didn't see anyone."

21 When did Harry go home? Answer in English with a full sentence.

➡ _____

22 위 글에서 어법상 어색한 것을 하나 찾아 전체 문장을 어법에 맞게 다시 쓰시오.

➡ _____

23 다음 중 위 글을 읽고 답할 수 없는 것은?

① Why did Sylvia go straight home?
② Why did Sylvia get scared?
③ What was Harry going to do for the talent show?
④ What did Harry hear on the way home?
⑤ Who won first place?

Frindle

Words & Expressions

Key Words

- □ **agree** [əgríː] 동 동의하다
- □ **article** [áːrtikl] 명 (신문의) 기사
- □ **bark** [baːrk] 동 (개가) 짖다
- □ **borrow** [bárou] 형 빌리다
- □ **classmate** [klǽsmèit] 명 급우, 반 친구
- □ **cool** [kuːl] 형 멋진
- □ **cover** [kávər] 동 보도하다, 덮다
- □ **cute** [kjuːt] 형 귀여운
- □ **date** [deit] 동 날짜를 적다 명 날짜
- □ **decide** [disáid] 동 결정하다
- □ **dictionary** [díkʃənèri] 명 사전
- □ **entire** [intáiər] 형 전체의, 온
- □ **envelope** [énvəlòup] 명 봉투
- □ **excited** [iksáitid] 형 신이 난
- □ **extra** [ékstrə] 형 여분의, 추가의
- □ **funny** [fʌ́ni] 형 재미있는
- □ **grade** [greid] 명 학년
- □ **graduate** [grǽdʒuèit, -it] 동 졸업하다

- □ **inside** [ìnsáid] 부 안에, 내부에
- □ **local** [lóukəl] 형 지역의, 지방의
- □ **mean** [miːn] 동 의미하다
- □ **meaning** [míːniŋ] 명 의미
- □ **nearby** [nìərbái] 형 인근의, 가까이의
- □ **package** [pǽkidʒ] 명 소포
- □ **perfectly** [pə́ːrfiktli] 부 완벽하게
- □ **pleased** [pliːzd] 형 기쁜, 기뻐하는
- □ **punish** [pʌ́niʃ] 동 처벌하다, 벌주다
- □ **quickly** [kwíkli] 부 재빨리, 빠르게
- □ **receive** [risíːv] 동 받다
- □ **reporter** [ripɔ́ːrtər] 명 기자
- □ **satisfied** [sǽtisfàid] 형 만족하는
- □ **signature** [sígnətʃər] 명 서명
- □ **situation** [sìtʃuéiʃən] 명 상황
- □ **spread** [spred] 동 퍼지다, 확산되다
- □ **vocabulary** [voukǽbjulèri] 명 어휘
- □ **war** [wɔːr] 명 전쟁

Key Expressions

- □ **be excited about** ~에 신이 나다
- □ **be famous for** ~로 유명하다
- □ **be over** ~이 끝나다
- □ **be worried about** ~에 대해 걱정하다
- □ **by the time** 그때까지, ~할 때까지
- □ **find out about** ~에 대해 알게 되다
- □ **have no choice** 선택의 여지가 없다, 대안이 없다

- □ **hold up** 쥐다, 잡다
- □ **look up** (사전 등에서) 찾아보다
- □ **more and more** 더욱 더, 갈수록 더
- □ **on the way home** 집으로 가는 길에
- □ **out of hand** 손을 쓸 수 없는
- □ **take out** ~을 꺼내다
- □ **turn+나이** ~ 살이 되다

Word Power

※ 서로 반대되는 뜻을 가진 어휘

- □ **agree** 동의하다 ↔ **disagree** 반대하다
- □ **cover** 덮다 ↔ **uncover** 덮개를 벗기다
- □ **excited** 신이 난 ↔ **boring** 지루한
- □ **quickly** 재빨리 ↔ **slowly** 천천히
- □ **pleased** 기쁜 ↔ **unpleased** 기뻐하지 않는, 불쾌한
- □ **satisfied** 만족한 ↔ **dissatisfied** 만족스럽지 않은

- □ **borrow** 빌리다 ↔ **lend** 빌려주다
- □ **entire** 전체의 ↔ **partial** 부분적인
- □ **inside** 안에 ↔ **outside** 밖에
- □ **receive** 받다 ↔ **give** 주다
- □ **hate** 미워하다 ↔ **like** 좋아하다
- □ **more and more** 점점 더 ↔ **less and less** 점점 적게[덜]

English Dictionary

- □ **agree** 동의하다
  → to have the same opinion as somebody
  누군가와 같은 의견을 갖다

- □ **borrow** 빌리다
  → to take and use something that belongs to somebody else, and return it to them at a later time
  다른 누군가에게 속한 무언가를 가져다가 사용하고 나중에 그것을 그들에게 돌려주다

- □ **classmate** 급우
  → a person who is or was in the same class as you at school or college
  학교 또는 대학에서 당신과 같은 학급에 있거나 있었던 사람

- □ **dictionary** 사전
  → a book that gives a list of the words of a language in alphabetical order and explains what they mean, or gives a word for them in a foreign language
  알파벳 순서로 한 언어의 단어들의 목록을 제공하고 그들이 의미하는 것을 설명하거나 그것들에 대해 외국어에 있는 단어를 제공하는 책

- □ **entire** 전체의
  → including everything, everyone or every part
  모든 것, 모든 사람 또는 모든 부분을 포함하는

- □ **envelope** 봉투
  → a flat paper container used for sending letters in
  편지를 보내기 위해 사용되는 납작한 종이 용기

- □ **extra** 여분의
  → more than is usual, expected, or than exists already
  보통 기대되는 것 이상의 또는 이미 존재하는 것 이상의

- □ **graduate** 졸업하다
  → to complete a course in education
  교육에서 한 과정을 완료하다

- □ **package** 소포
  → a box, bag, etc. in which things are wrapped or packed
  물건들이 포장되거나 채워 넣어지는 상자, 가방 등

- □ **punish** 처벌하다
  → to make somebody suffer because they have broken the law or done something wrong
  누군가가 법을 어기거나 무언가를 잘못했기 때문에 고통을 주다

- □ **reporter** 기자
  → a person who collects and reports news for newspapers, radio or television
  신문, 라디오 또는 텔레비전에 뉴스를 모아 보도하는 사람

- □ **signature** 서명
  → your name as you usually write it, for example at the end of a letter
  예를 들어 편지 끝에 당신이 보통 쓰는 당신의 이름

- □ **situation** 상황
  → all the circumstances and things that are happening at a particular time and in a particular place
  특정 시간과 특정 장소에서 일어나는 모든 주위의 사정

- □ **vocabulary** 어휘
  → all the words that a person knows or uses
  한 사람이 알거나 사용하는 모든 단어들

Frindle

Nick Allen <u>was excited about</u> starting fifth grade, but he <u>was worried</u>
~에 신났다   ~에 대해 걱정했다
<u>about</u> one thing — <u>Mrs. Granger's English class.</u> Mrs. Granger
                        one thing과 동격
<u>was famous for</u> her difficult vocabulary lessons.
~으로 유명했다

In the first class, Mrs. Granger said, "Everyone should have a good
dictionary. You can <u>look up</u> the meanings of new words in <u>it</u>."
                    ~을 찾다   a good dictionary
"Mrs. Granger? Who decides the meanings of words? I mean, who
<u>decided that</u> 'dog' means <u>an animal that</u> barks?" Nick asked.
    명사절 접속사   주격 관계대명사
"You did, Nick. You, me, and the entire town and country. We all
agreed. That <u>gives the word its meaning</u>."
            give+간접목적어+직접목적어
Nick wasn't satisfied. "When did I agree?" he said to <u>himself</u>.
                                                        재귀대명사(주어와 목적어가 같을 때 목적어로 재귀대명사 사용)
<u>On the way home</u>, he <u>decided to</u> test Mrs. Granger's idea. He <u>took</u>
집으로 가는 길에   to부정사를 목적어로 취하는 동사   ~을 꺼냈다
<u>out</u> a pen and said, "From today, this is a *frindle*."

The next day, he <u>asked five friends to use</u> the word *frindle*. During
                    to부정사를 목적격보어로 취하는 동사
class, Nick said, "Mrs. Granger, I forgot my *frindle* today." His friend,
John, held up a pen and said, "I have an extra *frindle*. Do you want to
borrow my *frindle*?" Mrs. Granger was not pleased. She said, "Your
new word is cute, but it already has a perfectly good name — a pen."

Nick's classmates <u>found this funny</u> and <u>began</u> to use the word more
                    find+목적어+목적격보어   to부정사와 동명사 모두를 목적어로 취할 수 있음
and more. In just three days, it became the cool word at school.

vocabulary: 어휘
dictionary: 사전
bark: 짖다
entire: 전체의, 온
satisfied: 만족하는
extra: 여분의
borrow: 빌리다

● 다음 문장이 본문의 내용과 일치하면 T, 일치하지 <u>않으면</u> F를 쓰시오.

1 Nick decided to test Mrs. Granger's idea. ☐

2 Mrs. Granger didn't like the idea that students called a pen a *frindle*. ☐

Mrs. Granger said to Nick after class, "This is getting out of hand. Can you tell your friends to stop saying *frindle*?"

"I'm sorry, but I can't stop it. It started as my word, but now it's the students' word."

"Very well. Then I have no choice." Mrs. Granger took out an envelope and asked Nick to sign and date the back. She said, "I'll give this letter to you when all this is over."

Nick thought, "She really hates me."

Next week, Mrs. Granger began a war with *frindle*. She said that she would punish any student for using it. But this only made things worse. The students wanted to use the word more and more. *Frindle* quickly spread to nearby middle and high schools. Shortly after, a local newspaper reporter wrote an article on the situation and everyone in town knew about it. A month later, a national television station covered the news and everyone found out about *frindle*. By the time Nick graduated from elementary school, most students in the country used the word.

Time flew by and Nick turned 21. One day, he received a package. Inside it, he found a pen, an envelope and a dictionary. The envelope had his signature from fifth grade. The dictionary had a yellow note. It said, "Check page 541."

---

more and more: 더욱 더
out of hand: 손을 쓸 수 없는
envelope: 봉투
date: 날짜를 적다
punish: 처벌하다
spread: 퍼지다
nearby: 인근의, 가까이의
local: 지역의, 지방의
article: (신문의) 기사
situation: 상황
cover: 보도하다
graduate: 졸업하다
receive: 받다
signature: 서명

확인문제

● 다음 문장이 본문의 내용과 일치하면 T, 일치하지 않으면 F를 쓰시오.

1 Mrs. Granger wanted students to stop saying *frindle*. ☐

2 Nick thought Mrs. Granger hated him. ☐

3 Students gave up using the word *frindle*. ☐

4 When Nick graduated from elementary school, the word *frindle* was used by most students in the country. ☐

5 There was no signature on the envelope. ☐

● 우리말을 참고하여 빈칸에 알맞은 말을 쓰시오.

1 Nick Allen _____ _____ _____ starting fifth grade, but he _____ _____ _____ one thing — Mrs. Granger's English class.

2 Mrs. Granger _____ _____ _____ her difficult vocabulary lessons.

3 In the first class, Mrs. Granger said, "Everyone _____ _____ _____ _____ _____. You _____ _____ _____ the meanings of new words in it."

4 "Mrs. Granger? Who decides _____ _____ of words? I mean, who decided that 'dog' _____ an animal that barks?" Nick asked.

5 "You did, Nick. You, me, and the _____ _____ and country. We all _____. That gives the word _____ _____."

6 Nick wasn't _____. "When _____ _____ _____?" he said to _____.

7 _____ the way home, he _____ to test Mrs. Granger's idea.

8 He _____ _____ a pen and said, "_____ today, this is a *frindle*."

9 The next day, he _____ five friends _____ _____ the word *frindle*.

10 _____ class, Nick said, "Mrs. Granger, I forgot my *frindle* today."

11 His friend, John, _____ _____ a pen and said, "I have an _____ *frindle*. Do you want _____ _____ my *frindle*?"

12 Mrs. Granger was not _____.

13 She said, "Your new word is cute, _____ it _____ _____ a perfectly good name — a pen."

14 Nick's classmates _____ this _____ and began _____ _____ the word more and more.

15 _____ just three days, it _____ the _____ _____ at school.

1 Nick Allen은 5학년이 시작되는 것이 신났지만, 한 가지가 걱정되었다. 그것은 Granger 선생님의 영어 수업이었다.

2 Granger 선생님은 어려운 어휘 수업으로 유명했다.

3 첫 번째 시간에 Granger 선생님은 말했다. "모두 좋은 사전을 가지고 있어야 해요. 여러분은 사전에서 새 단어의 뜻을 찾을 수 있어요."

4 "Granger 선생님? 단어의 뜻은 누가 정하나요? 그러니까, '개'는 짖는 동물을 뜻한다고 누가 정했나요?" Nick이 물었다.

5 "네가 그랬지, Nick. 너와 나, 그리고 온 마을과 나라가 말이야. 우리 모두가 동의했단다. 그게 그 단어에게 의미를 부여하는 거야."

6 Nick은 마음에 들지 않았다. "내가 언제 동의했지?" 그는 혼잣말을 했다.

7 집에 가는 길에 Nick은 Granger 선생님의 생각을 시험하기로 결심했다.

8 그는 펜을 하나 꺼내서 말했다. "오늘부터 이것은 'frindle'이야."

9 그 다음날 Nick은 다섯 명의 친구들에게 단어 'frindle'을 사용해 달라고 부탁했다.

10 수업 중에 Nick이 말했다. "Granger 선생님, 오늘 'frindle'을 빠뜨리고 왔어요."

11 Nick의 친구인 John이 펜을 하나 들고서는 말했다. "나한테 여분의 'frindle'이 있어. 내 'frindle'을 빌리고 싶니?"

12 Granger 선생님은 즐거워하지 않았다.

13 선생님이 말했다. "너희들의 새 단어는 귀엽지만, 그건 이미 'pen'이라는 완벽하게 좋은 이름이 있단다."

14 Nick의 학급 친구들은 이것을 재미있어 했고 더욱 더 그 단어를 사용하기 시작했다.

15 단지 3일 만에 학교에서 그것은 멋진 단어가 되었다.

16 Mrs. Granger _____ _____ Nick after class, "This is _____ _____ _____ _____. Can you tell your friends _____ _____ _____*frindle*?"

17 "I'm sorry, but I can't _____ _____. It started _____ my word, but now it's the students' word."

18 "Very well. Then I have _____ _____."

19 Mrs. Granger _____ _____ an envelope and _____ Nick _____ _____ and _____ the back.

20 She said, "_____ _____ this letter _____ _____ when all this _____ _____."

21 Nick thought, "She really _____ me."

22 Next week, Mrs. Granger _____ a war _____ *frindle*.

23 She said that she would _____ any student _____ _____ it.

24 But this only made _____ _____.

25 The students wanted _____ _____ the word _____ _____ _____.

26 *Frindle* quickly _____ _____ _____ middle and high schools.

27 _____ _____, a local newspaper reporter _____ an article _____ the situation and everyone in town _____ _____ _____.

28 A month later, a national television station _____ the news and everyone _____ _____ _____*frindle*.

29 _____ _____ _____ Nick _____ _____ elementary school, most students in the country _____ the word.

30 Time _____ _____ and Nick turned 21. One day, he _____ a package.

31 _____ _____, he _____ a pen, an envelope and a dictionary.

32 The envelope had his _____ _____ fifth grade.

33 The dictionary had a _____ _____. _____ _____, "Check page 541."

16 Granger 선생님은 수업 후에 Nick에게 말했다. "점점 손을 쓸 수 없게 되어 가는구나. 네 친구들에게 'frindle'을 말하는 것을 멈춰달라고 말해 줄래?"

17 "죄송하지만, 멈추게 할 수가 없어요. 그건 제 단어로 시작됐지만, 이제 그건 학생들의 단어예요."

18 "좋아. 그러면 선택의 여지가 없구나."

19 Granger 선생님은 봉투를 하나 꺼내더니 Nick에게 뒷면에 서명을 하고 날짜를 적게 했다.

20 선생님은 말했다. "이 모든 것이 끝나면 내가 이 편지를 너에게 줄게."

21 Nick은 생각했다. "선생님은 내가 정말 싫은가봐."

22 다음 주에 Granger 선생님은 'frindle'과의 전쟁을 시작했다.

23 선생님은 그 단어를 사용한다면 어떤 학생이든 벌을 줄 것이라고 말했다.

24 하지만 이것은 상황을 더 나쁘게 만들 뿐이었다.

25 학생들은 그 단어를 더욱 더 사용하고 싶어했다.

26 'frindle'은 근처의 중학교와 고등학교로 빠르게 퍼져 나갔다.

27 곧 지역 신문 기자가 그 상황에 관한 기사를 썼고, 마을의 모든 사람들이 그것에 관해 알게 되었다.

28 한 달 후에 한 전국 텔레비전 방송사에 서 그 소식을 다루었고, 모든 사람들이 'frindle'에 관해 알게 되었다.

29 Nick이 초등학교를 졸업할 때쯤에는 이 나라의 대부분의 학생들이 그 단어를 사용했다.

30 시간은 흘러 Nick은 21살이 되었다. 어느 날 Nick은 소포를 하나 받았다.

31 소포 안에는 펜 한 자루, 봉투 한 장, 그리고 사전 한 권이 있었다.

32 봉투에는 5학년 때의 그의 서명이 있었다.

33 사전에는 노란색 쪽지가 있었다. "541쪽을 확인해 봐."라고 적혀 있었다.

● 우리말을 참고하여 본문을 영작하시오.

1 Nick Allen은 5학년이 시작되는 것이 신났지만, 한 가지가 걱정되었다. 그것은 Granger 선생님의 영어 수업이었다.

➡ _____

_____

2 Granger 선생님은 어려운 어휘 수업으로 유명했다.

➡ _____

3 첫 번째 시간에 Granger 선생님은 말했다. "모두 좋은 사전을 가지고 있어야 해요. 여러분은 사전에서 새 단어의 뜻을 찾을 수 있어요."

➡ _____

4 "Granger 선생님? 단어의 뜻은 누가 정하나요? 그러니까, '개'는 짖는 동물을 뜻한다고 누가 정했나요?" Nick이 물었다.

➡ _____

5 "네가 그랬지, Nick. 너와 나, 그리고 온 마을과 나라가 말이야. 우리 모두가 동의했단다. 그게 그 단어에게 의미를 부여하는 거야."

➡ _____

_____

6 Nick은 마음에 들지 않았다. "내가 언제 동의했지?" 그는 혼잣말을 했다.

➡ _____

7 집에 가는 길에 Nick은 Granger 선생님의 생각을 시험하기로 결심했다.

➡ _____

8 그는 펜을 하나 꺼내서 말했다. "오늘부터 이것은 'frindle'이야."

➡ _____

9 그 다음날 Nick은 다섯 명의 친구들에게 단어 'frindle'을 사용해 달라고 부탁했다.

➡ _____

10 수업 중에 Nick이 말했다. "Granger 선생님, 오늘 'frindle'을 빠뜨리고 왔어요."

➡ _____

11 Nick의 친구인 John이 펜을 하나 들고서는 말했다. "나한테 여분의 'frindle'이 있어. 내 'frindle'을 빌리고 싶니?"

➡ _____

12 Granger 선생님은 즐거워하지 않았다.

➡ _____

13 선생님이 말했다. "너희들의 새 단어는 귀엽지만, 그건 이미 'pen'이라는 완벽하게 좋은 이름이 있단다."

➡ _____

14 Nick의 학급 친구들은 이것을 재미있어 했고 더욱 더 그 단어를 사용하기 시작했다.

➡ _____

_____

15 단지 3일 만에 학교에서 그것은 멋진 단어가 되었다.

➡ _____

16 Granger 선생님은 수업 후에 Nick에게 말했다. "점점 손을 쓸 수 없게 되어 가는구나. 네 친구들에게 'frindle'을 말하는 것을 멈춰달라고 말해 줄래?"

➡ _____

_____

17 "죄송하지만, 멈추게 할 수가 없어요. 그건 제 단어로 시작됐지만, 이제 그건 학생들의 단어예요."

➡ _____

18 "좋아. 그러면 선택의 여지가 없구나."

➡ _____

19 Granger 선생님은 봉투를 하나 꺼내더니 Nick에게 뒷면에 서명을 하고 날짜를 적게 했다.

➡ _____

20 선생님은 말했다. "이 모든 것이 끝나면 내가 이 편지를 너에게 줄게."

➡ _____

21 Nick은 생각했다. "선생님은 내가 정말 싫은가봐."

➡ _____

22 다음 주에 Granger 선생님은 'frindle'과의 전쟁을 시작했다.

➡ _____

23 선생님은 그 단어를 사용한다면 어떤 학생이든 벌을 줄 것이라고 말했다.

➡ _____

24 하지만 이것은 상황을 더 나쁘게 만들 뿐이었다.

➡ _____

25 학생들은 그 단어를 더욱 더 사용하고 싶어했다.

➡ _____

26 'frindle'은 근처의 중학교와 고등학교로 빠르게 퍼져 나갔다.

➡ _____

27 곧 지역 신문 기자가 그 상황에 관한 기사를 썼고, 마을의 모든 사람들이 그것에 관해 알게 되었다.

➡ _____

28 한 달 후에 한 전국 텔레비전 방송사에 서 그 소식을 다루었고, 모든 사람들이 'frindle'에 관해 알게 되었다.

➡ _____

29 Nick이 초등학교를 졸업할 때쯤에는 이 나라의 대부분의 학생들이 그 단어를 사용했다.

➡ _____

30 시간은 흘러 Nick은 21살이 되었다. 어느 날 Nick은 소포를 하나 받았다.

➡ _____

31 소포 안에는 펜 한 자루, 봉투 한 장, 그리고 사전 한 권이 있었다.

➡ _____

32 봉투에는 5학년 때의 그의 서명이 있었다.

➡ _____

33 사전에는 노란색 쪽지가 있었다. "541쪽을 확인해 봐."라고 적혀 있었다.

➡ _____

서술형 실전문제

01 다음 짝지어진 단어의 관계가 같도록 빈칸에 알맞은 말을 쓰시오.

> increase : decrease = _____ : disagree

02 다음 문장의 빈칸에 들어갈 말을 〈보기〉에서 골라 쓰시오.

> ┤ 보기 ├
> signature / package / envelope / bark

(1) Why did your dogs _____ last night?

(2) I put my _____ to the document.

(3) Look at the back of the _____, please.

(4) I was so happy when I received my _____ from my sister.

03 다음 우리말을 주어진 단어를 사용하여 영작하시오.

(1) 나는 제주도로 가는 수학여행에 매우 신났었다. (school trip, about)

➡ _____

(2) 나는 수학 시험이 끝난 후 안도감을 느꼈다. (over, test, relaxed)

➡ _____

04 주어진 문장과 같은 의미의 문장을 쓰시오.

(1) David was too tired to meet us last night.

➡ _____

(2) They are tall enough to touch the ceiling.

➡ _____

05 주어진 단어를 이용하여 우리말을 영어로 옮기시오.

(1) 나는 네가 야채를 먹길 원해. (want / vegetables)

➡ _____

(2) 그 의사는 나의 아버지에게 규칙적으로 운동하라고 조언했다. (advise)

➡ _____

06 주어진 단어를 어법에 맞게 빈칸에 쓰시오.

(1) Mr. Park encourages us _____ our best all the time. (do)

(2) I don't want you _____ my books. (borrow)

(3) We found the situation _____. (interest)

[07~12] 다음 글을 읽고 물음에 답하시오.

Nick Allen was excited about starting fifth grade, but he was worried about one thing — Mrs. Granger's English class. Mrs. Granger was famous for her difficult vocabulary lessons. In the first class, Mrs. Granger said, "Everyone should have a good dictionary. You can look up the meanings of new words in it."

"Mrs. Granger? Who decides the meanings of words? I mean, who decided that 'dog' means an animal that barks?" Nick asked.

"You did, Nick. You, me, and the entire town and country. We all agreed. That gives the word its meaning."

Nick wasn't satisfied. "When did I agree?" he said to himself.

On the way home, he decided to test Mrs. Granger's idea. He took out a pen and said, "From today, this is a *frindle*." The next day, he asked five friends to use the word *frindle*. During class, Nick said, "Mrs. Granger, I forgot my *frindle* today." His friend, John, held up a pen and said, "I have an extra *frindle*. Do you want to borrow my *frindle*?" Mrs. Granger was not pleased. She said, "ⓐ Your new word is cute, but it already has a perfectly good name — a pen."

07 What was Nick Allen excited about? Answer in English with a full sentence.

➡ _____

08 What did Mrs. Granger want her students to have? Answer in English with nine words.

➡ _____

09 According to Mrs. Granger, what can students do with a dictionary?

➡ _____

10 밑줄 친 ⓐ가 의미하는 것을 위 글에서 찾아 쓰시오.

➡ _____

11 What did Nick do to test Mrs. Granger's idea? Answer in English with six words.

➡ _____

12 Who was Nick's English teacher?

➡ _____

[13~15] 다음 글을 읽고 물음에 답하시오.

Nick's classmates found this funny and began to use the word more and more. In just three days, it became the cool word at school.

Mrs. Granger said to Nick after class, "This is getting out of hand. Can you tell your friends to stop saying *frindle*?"

"I'm sorry, but I can't stop ⓐit. It started as my word, but now it's the students' word."

"Very well. Then I have no choice." Mrs. Granger took out an envelope and asked Nick to sign and date the back. She said, "I'll give this letter to you when all this is over."

Nick thought, "She really hates me."

(A) She said that she would punish any student for using it.

(B) The students wanted to use the word more and more.

(C) But this only made things worse.

(D) Next week, Mrs. Granger began a war with *frindle*.

Frindle quickly spread to nearby middle and high schools.

13 밑줄 친 ⓐ가 의미하는 것을 우리말로 쓰시오.

➡ _____

14 자연스러운 글이 되도록 (A)~(D)를 바르게 나열하시오.

➡ _____

15 What did Mrs. Granger ask Nick to do after she took out the envelope?

➡ _____

출제율 95%

01 다음 영영풀이가 나타내는 말을 고르시오.

> to make somebody suffer because they have broken the law or done something wrong

① borrow　　② punish
③ bark　　　④ cover
⑤ spread

출제율 100%

02 다음 문장의 빈칸에 들어갈 말을 〈보기〉에서 골라 적절한 형태로 쓰시오.

> ┤ 보기 ├
> take out / out of hand / hold up /
> look up / have no choice

(1) He ＿＿＿＿＿＿＿ a candy from his pocket and gave it to me.
(2) Did you ＿＿＿＿＿＿＿ the meanings of new words in the dictionary?
(3) I ＿＿＿＿＿＿ but to do this work.
(4) The problem is getting ＿＿＿＿＿＿＿.
(5) Would you ＿＿＿＿＿＿＿ this board for a while?

출제율 90%

03 다음 문장의 빈칸에 공통으로 들어갈 말로 적절한 것은?

> • The officer gave the letter and asked me to ＿＿＿＿ at the bottom.
> • Have you checked the ＿＿＿＿ and time of the invitation?
> • Did you fix on a ＿＿＿＿ for your journey?

① date　　　② cover
③ receive　　④ spread
⑤ choice

출제율 90%

04 다음 주어진 문장의 밑줄 친 covered와 같은 의미로 쓰인 것은?

> The TV reporter covered the car accident in the morning.

① She covered her eyes with her hands.
② The CNN will cover all the major competition.
③ Be careful. Snow covered the road.
④ Would you cover the seeds with soil?
⑤ Let's cover the label before taking a picture.

출제율 95%

05 다음 밑줄 친 단어의 뜻이 바르지 않은 것은?

① The entire system was broken down. 전체의
② Do you know who planted the tree nearby the red house? 가까이에, 인근의
③ I was pleased with your present. 불쾌한
④ Parents should punish their children in a proper way. 처벌하다
⑤ What do you want to do after you graduate from high school? 졸업하다

출제율 85%

06 다음 우리말을 주어진 단어를 사용하여 영작하시오.

(1) James는 점점 더 많은 시간을 컴퓨터 게임하는 데 쓴다. (and, more)
➡ ＿＿＿＿＿＿＿＿＿＿＿＿＿＿＿＿＿
＿＿＿＿＿＿＿＿＿＿＿＿＿＿＿＿＿

(2) 나의 영어 선생님은 재미있는 수업으로 유명하다. (funny, for)
➡ ＿＿＿＿＿＿＿＿＿＿＿＿＿＿＿＿＿
＿＿＿＿＿＿＿＿＿＿＿＿＿＿＿＿＿

07 다음 중 어법상 바르지 <u>않은</u> 것은?

① They forced me to help them.

② Carry was pleased with my gift.

③ Colin is not as handsome as Paul.

④ Although he was busy, he visited us.

⑤ The accident caused us being more careful.

08 다음 중 우리말을 영어로 바르게 옮긴 것은?

> 나는 네가 나를 초대하면 좋겠어.

① I like to invite you.

② I would like to invite you.

③ I would like you to invite me.

④ I want you to invite yourself.

⑤ I would like you invite me.

09 다음 문장과 같은 의미의 문장은?

> Jamie was so interested in the book that he couldn't put it down.

① Jamie was interested in the book enough to put it down.

② Jamie was so interested in the book to put it down.

③ Jamie was too interested in the book to put it down.

④ Jamie was very interested in the book so he put it down.

⑤ Jamie was so interested in the book that he could put it down.

10 다음 중 빈칸에 들어갈 수 <u>없는</u> 말은?

> David _____ us to find his wallet.

① forced   ② allowed

③ wanted   ④ encouraged

⑤ made

11 다음 빈칸에 들어갈 말로 가장 적절한 것은?

> I want to know. Did she arrive home safely?
> = I want to know _____ she arrived home safely.

① how   ② whether   ③ why

④ when   ⑤ that

12 다음 우리말에 맞게 빈칸에 알맞은 말을 쓰시오.

> 누가 이 편지를 너에게 줬는지 말해 줄래?
> Can you tell me _____?

➡ _____

13 다음 중 어법상 <u>어색한</u> 것은?

① We hope to find your son soon.

② Did you decide to get more interesting job?

③ She didn't let me to make the cookies.

④ He taught us to think reasonably.

⑤ They advised me to do the right thing.

14 주어진 단어를 활용하여 다음 우리말을 영어로 쓰시오.

> 그 선생님은 나를 초조하게 만들어. (make)

➡ _____

[15~20] 다음 글을 읽고 물음에 답하시오.

Nick Allen was excited about starting fifth grade, but he was worried about one thing — Mrs. Granger's English class. Mrs. Granger was famous for her difficult vocabulary lessons.

In the first class, Mrs. Granger said, "Everyone should have a good dictionary. You can look up the meanings of new words in it."

"Mrs. Granger? Who decides the meanings of words? I mean, who decided that 'dog' means an animal that barks?" Nick asked.

"You (A)did, Nick. You, me, and the entire town and country. We all agreed. (B)That gives the word its meaning."

Nick wasn't satisfied. "When did I agree?" he said to himself.

📝 출제율 90%
15 밑줄 친 (A)가 의미하는 것을 위 글에서 찾아 쓰시오.

➡ _____

📝 출제율 95%
16 다음 중 밑줄 친 (B)가 의미하는 것으로 가장 적절한 것은?

① 반 친구들의 설명
② 선생님의 어휘 수업
③ 사회 구성원의 동의
④ 국가의 엄격한 법
⑤ 가족의 따뜻한 사랑

📝 출제율 85%
17 What was Mrs. Granger famous for? Answer in English with a full sentence.

➡ _____

📝 출제율 100%
18 다음 중 위 글의 내용과 일치하지 <u>않는</u> 것은?

① Nick Allen was a fifth grader.
② Mrs. Granger taught English to students.
③ Mrs. Granger wanted students to have a good dictionary.
④ Mrs. Granger wondered who decided the meanings of words.
⑤ Nick didn't feel satisfied with what Mrs. Granger said.

📝 출제율 90%
19 What was Nick worried about?

➡ _____

📝 출제율 95%
20 다음 중 위 글에서 반의어를 찾을 수 <u>없는</u> 것은?

① disagree ② easy ③ old
④ whole ⑤ unknown

[21~26] 다음 글을 읽고 물음에 답하시오.

On the way home, Nick decided to ⓐtest Mrs. Granger's idea. He took out a pen and said, "From today, this is a ①*frindle*."

[A] Mrs. Granger was not pleased. She said, "②Your new word is cute, but it ⓑalready has ③a perfectly good name — a pen."

[B] His friend, John, held up a pen and said, "I have an extra *frindle*. Do you want to ⓒlend my *frindle*?"

[C] The next day, he asked five friends to use the word *frindle*. During class, Nick said, "Mrs. Granger, I forgot my *frindle* today."

Nick's classmates found (A)this ⓓfunny and began to use ④the word more and more. In just three days, ⑤it became the ⓔcool word at school.

21 자연스러운 글이 되도록 [A]~[C]를 바르게 나열하시오.

➡ _____

22 밑줄 친 (A)this가 의미하는 것을 우리말로 쓰시오.

➡ _____

23 ①~⑤ 중 의미하는 것이 <u>다른</u> 것을 고르시오.

① ② ③ ④ ⑤

24 How did Mrs. Granger feel about the new word? Answer in English with a full sentence.

➡ _____

25 ⓐ~ⓔ 중 글의 흐름상 <u>어색한</u> 것은?

① ⓐ ② ⓑ ③ ⓒ ④ ⓓ ⑤ ⓔ

26 다음 중 위 글을 읽고 답할 수 <u>없는</u> 것은?

① What did Nick decide to do on the way home?

② What did Nick ask his friends to do?

③ When did Nick tell Mrs. Granger that he forgot his *frindle*?

④ How many classmates were there in Nick's class?

⑤ How long did it take for the word *frindle* to become the cool word at school?

[27~32] 다음 글을 읽고 물음에 답하시오.

Mrs. Granger said to Nick after class, "This is ⓐgetting out of hand. Can you tell your friends to stop (A)[saying / to say] *frindle*?"

"I'm sorry, but I can't stop it. It started as my word, but now it's the students' word."

"Very well. Then I have no choice." Mrs. Granger took out an envelope and asked Nick (B)[signing / to sign] and date the back. She said, "I'll give this letter to you when all this is over."

Nick thought, "She really hates me."

Next week, Mrs. Granger began a war with *frindle*. She said that she would punish any student for using it. But this only made things worse. The students wanted (C)[using / to use] the word more and more.

27 다음 중 밑줄 친 ⓐ의 의미로 가장 적절한 것은?

① possible to deal with

② beyond my control

③ easy to solve

④ difficult to ask

⑤ hard to get along with

28 (A)~(C)에서 어법상 옳은 것끼리 바르게 묶은 것은?

① to say – to sign – to use

② to say – signing – using

③ saying – to sign – to use

④ saying – signing – using

⑤ saying – to sign – using

출제율95%

29 다음 중 위 글의 내용과 일치하는 것은?

① Mrs. Granger told students that they should call a pen a *frindle*.
② The word Nick made became the students' word.
③ Mrs. Granger wrote letters to all of the students.
④ Mrs. Granger thought there were many choices.
⑤ What Mrs. Granger said made things better.

출제율85%

30 When will Mrs. Granger give the letter to Nick?

➡ _____

출제율90%

31 What did Mrs. Granger say in order to make her students stop using the word, *frindle*?

➡ _____
_____

출제율95%

32 What happened after Mrs. Granger began a war with *frindle*?

➡ _____

[33~36] 다음 글을 읽고 물음에 답하시오.

Frindle quickly spread to nearby middle and high schools. Shortly after, a local newspaper reporter wrote an article on the situation and everyone in town knew about it. A month later, a national television station @covered the news and everyone found out about *frindle*. By the time Nick graduated from elementary school, most students in the country used the word.

Time flew by and Nick turned 21. One day, he received a package. Inside it, he found a pen, an envelope and a dictionary. The envelope had his signature from fifth grade. The dictionary had a yellow note. It said, "Check page 541."

출제율100%

33 다음 중 위 글을 읽고 대답할 수 <u>없는</u> 것은?

① Who wrote the article on the situation?
② What happened shortly after *frindle* quickly spread to nearby middle and high schools?
③ How old was Nick when he received a package from Mrs. Granger?
④ What was said in the letter?
⑤ How did Nick feel when the word *frindle* became popular?

출제율90%

34 By the time Nick graduated from elementary school, what happened to the word, *frindle*?

➡ _____
_____

출제율95%

35 What did Nick find inside the package?

➡ _____

출제율85%

36 다음 중 밑줄 친 @와 같은 의미로 쓰인 것은?

① Snow <u>covered</u> the ground.
② <u>Cover</u> the chicken loosely with foil.
③ Much of the country is <u>covered</u> by forest.
④ The front <u>cover</u> of the book is pretty.
⑤ The BBC will <u>cover</u> all the major games.

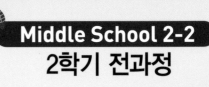

중간 + 기말

plus

영어 기출문제집

영어 중 **2**

동아 | 이병민

Best Collection

내용문의 중등영어발전소 적중100 편집부 TEL 070-7707-0457

INSIGHT
on the textbook

교과서 파헤치기

영어 기출 문제집

적중 100 plus
2학기 전과정

영어 중 2

동아 | 이병민

INSIGHT
on the textbook
교과서 파헤치기

Lesson **5** **Come One, Come All**

Lesson **6** **In Outer Space**

Lesson **7** **Can I Trust It?**

Lesson **8** **Be like Sherlock!**

Lesson **S** **Frindle**

※ 다음 영어를 우리말로 쓰시오.

01 arrow	_____
02 neighborhood	_____
03 appear	_____
04 dark	_____
05 solve	_____
06 decorate	_____
07 far	_____
08 firework	_____
09 follow	_____
10 gather	_____
11 shape	_____
12 amazing	_____
13 huge	_____
14 last	_____
15 advertise	_____
16 competition	_____
17 festival	_____
18 sled	_____
19 almost	_____
20 completely	_____
21 post	_____

22 musician	_____
23 celebrate	_____
24 outdoor	_____
25 chase	_____
26 pile	_____
27 artwork	_____
28 powder	_____
29 adult	_____
30 colorful	_____
31 hold	_____
32 throw	_____
33 hometown	_____
34 bakery	_____
35 each other	_____
36 out of hand	_____
37 from beginning to end	_____
38 between A and B	_____
39 go on	_____
40 because of	_____
41 more and more	_____
42 on one's right	_____
43 in front of	_____

※ 다음 우리말을 영어로 쓰시오.

01	빵집, 제과점		22	장식하다
02	축하하다, 기념하다		23	모이다, 모으다
03	형형색색의		24	광고하다
04	페레이드, 행진		25	해결하다
05	(시간이) 걸리다		26	지속하다
06	~ 동안		27	나타나다
07	돛		28	근처, 이웃, 인근
08	예술 작품		29	대회, 시합, 경쟁
09	뒤쫓다		30	불꽃놀이
10	개최하다		31	거대한
11	고향		32	화살
12	배, 선박		33	완전히
13	가로지르다		34	따르다
14	라이브의, 실황인		35	더욱 더
15	가까운, 가까이에 있는		36	내리다
16	가루		37	서로
17	야외의		38	~ 앞에
18	블록, 구획		39	~ 때문에
19	더미		40	~ 옆에
20	성인, 어른		41	지속되다, 계속되다
21	던지다		42	A와 B 사이에
			43	처음부터 끝까지

※ 다음 영영풀이에 알맞은 단어를 <보기>에서 골라 쓴 후, 우리말 뜻을 쓰시오.

1 _____ : to move something or someone to a higher position: _____

2 _____ : a fully grown person: _____

3 _____ : to follow and try to catch: _____

4 _____ : objects produced by artists: _____

5 _____ : an event or contest in which people compete: _____

6 _____ : a day or period of celebration: _____

7 _____ : a small vehicle used for sliding over snow: _____

8 _____ : to continue in time: _____

9 _____ : the city or town where you were born or grew up: _____

10 _____ : to come together to form a group: _____

11 _____ : to have a meeting, competition, conversation, etc.: _____

12 _____ : a mass of something that has been placed somewhere: _____

13 _____ : to tell the public about goods to make people buy them: _____

14 _____ : to make something into a particular shape: _____

15 _____ : to do something special for an important event, holiday, etc.: _____

16 _____ : to make something look more beautiful by putting things on it: _____

보기			
sled	chase	artwork	lift
decorate	pile	hometown	competition
adult	celebrate	advertise	last
shape	hold	gather	festival

※ 다음 우리말과 일치하도록 빈칸에 알맞은 말을 쓰시오.

Listen and Speak 1-A

Sora: Excuse me. _____ _____ _____ _____ _____ _____ _____?

Tom: Oh, the library? _____ the street and _____ _____ two blocks. Then _____ _____ _____.

Sora: _____ _____ very much.

Listen and Speak 1-B

(*A phone rings.*)

Minsu: Hi, Emma. _____ _____?

Emma: Hey, Minsu. _____ you _____ _____ _____ _____?

Minsu: Yes. _____ _____ you _____?

Emma: Well, how _____ _____ _____ together?

Minsu: Sure.

Emma: _____ _____ the new _____ _____, Ming's. It's _____ the school.

Minsu: Okay. _____ _____ _____ _____ _____ _____ _____ _____ _____ _____?

Emma: _____ _____ from the school and _____ _____ to Green Street. _____ _____ _____, and the restaurant will _____ _____ _____ _____.

Minsu: _____ _____. _____ _____ _____ 12 o'clock.

Emma: Wonderful. _____ _____ _____.

Listen and Speak 1-C

A: _____ _____. How _____ I _____ _____ the post office?

B: _____ _____ to 1st Street and _____ _____ _____. It _____ _____ _____ _____ _____.

A: _____ it _____ _____ here?

B: _____, it's _____.

A: _____ _____ very much.

Sora: 실례합니다. 도서관까지 어떻게 가나요?

Tom: 아, 도서관이요? 길을 건너서 두 구역을 곧장 가세요. 그런 다음 왼쪽으로 도세요.

Sora: 정말 고마워요.

(전화벨이 울린다.)

Minsu: 안녕, Emma. 잘 지내니?

Emma: 안녕, 민수야. 이번 토요일에 한가하니?

Minsu: 응. 왜 묻는 거니?

Emma: 음, 함께 점심 먹는 게 어떠니?

Minsu: 좋아.

Emma: Ming's라는 새로 생긴 중국 음식점에 가 보자. 학교 근처에 있어.

Minsu: 좋아. 학교에서 거기까지 어떻게 가니?

Emma: 학교에서 나와서 Green Street까지 곧장 가. 왼쪽으로 돌면 음식점이 네 왼쪽에 있을 거야.

Minsu: 알겠어. 12시에 만나자.

Emma: 좋아. 그때 보자.

A: 실례합니다. 우체국에 어떻게 갈 수 있나요?

B: 1st Street까지 곧장 가서 오른쪽으로 도세요. 그것은 오른쪽에 있을 거예요.

A: 여기서 먼가요?

B: 아니요, 멀지 않아요.

A: 정말 고마워요.

Listen and Speak 2-A

Amy: Jinho, _____ _____. We're _____ _____ _____ _____ _____ the movie.

Jinho: Okay. _____ _____ _____ _____ _____ _____ _____ _____ _____?

Amy: It will _____ _____ 15 minutes _____ _____.

Jinho: All right. I'm _____ _____.

Amy: 진호야, 서둘러. 우리 영화 시간에 늦겠어.
Jinho: 응. 영화관까지 가는 데 시간이 얼마나 걸릴까?
Amy: 버스로 대략 15분 정도 걸릴 거야.
Jinho: 알겠어. 나 거의 준비됐어.

Listen and Speak 2-B

Andy: I'm so _____ _____ the school festival _____ _____.

Mike: _____, _____. What _____ we _____ _____ _____ _____ it, Andy?

Andy: How _____ _____ posters?

Mike: Great idea. We _____ _____ _____ _____ in our _____.

Andy: Right. _____ _____ _____ _____ _____ _____ _____ make them?

Mike: Well, it will _____ _____ _____ _____.

Andy: Okay, _____ _____ many people _____ _____ _____.

Andy: 나는 이번 금요일 학교 축제가 정말 기대돼.
Mike: 나도. 축제를 광고하기 위해 무엇을 할 수 있을까, Andy?
Andy: 포스터를 만들면 어떨까?
Mike: 좋은 생각이야. 이 근방에 포스터를 붙일 수 있겠다.
Andy: 맞아. 포스터를 만드는 데 시간이 얼마나 걸릴까?
Mike: 음, 대략 세 시간 정도 걸릴 거야.
Andy: 좋아, 많은 사람들이 축제에 왔으면 좋겠다.

Real Life Talk

Man: _____ me. _____ _____ I _____ _____ Suwon Hwaseong from here?

Mina: It's _____. Do you see the bus stop _____ _____?

Man: Yes, _____ _____.

Mina: _____ the No. 11 bus and _____ _____ at the sixth stop.

Man: _____ _____ _____ _____ _____ _____ _____?

Mina: It will _____ _____ _____ _____ _____.

Man: Thank you _____ _____.

Mina: No _____. _____ you _____ there for _____ _____?

Man: Yes. I heard _____ _____ _____ _____.

Mina: _____ _____ you _____ _____ _____.

Man: 실례합니다. 여기에서 수원 화성까지 어떻게 가나요?
Mina: 쉬워요. 저쪽에 버스 정류장 보이세요?
Man: 네, 보여요.
Mina: 11번 버스를 타서 여섯 번째 정류장에서 내리세요.
Man: 그곳까지 가는 데 시간이 얼마나 걸릴까요?
Mina: 대략 20분 정도 걸릴 거예요.
Man: 정말 고마워요.
Mina: 별말씀을요. 그곳에 축제 때문에 가시는 건가요?
Man: 네. 그 축제가 무척 재미있다고 들었어요.
Mina: 즐거운 시간 보내길 바라요.

※ 다음 우리말에 맞도록 대화를 영어로 쓰시오.

Listen and Speak 1-A

Sora: _____

Tom: _____

Sora: _____

Sora: 실례합니다. 도서관까지 어떻게 가나요?
Tom: 아, 도서관이요? 길을 건너서 두 구역을 곧장 가세요. 그런 다음 왼쪽으로 도세요.
Sora: 정말 고마워요.

Listen and Speak 1-B

(*A phone rings.*)

Minsu: _____

Emma: _____

Minsu: _____

Emma: _____

Minsu: _____

Emma: _____

Minsu: _____

Emma: _____

Minsu: _____

Emma: _____

(전화벨이 울린다.)
Minsu: 안녕, Emma. 잘 지내니?
Emma: 안녕, 민수야. 이번 토요일에 한가하니?
Minsu: 응. 왜 묻는 거니?
Emma: 음, 함께 점심 먹는 게 어떠니?
Minsu: 좋아.
Emma: Ming's라는 새로 생긴 중국 음식점에 가 보자. 학교 근처에 있어.
Minsu: 좋아. 학교에서 거기까지 어떻게 가니?
Emma: 학교에서 나와서 Green Street까지 곧장 가. 왼쪽으로 돌면 음식점이 네 왼쪽에 있을 거야.
Minsu: 알겠어. 12시에 만나자.
Emma: 좋아. 그때 보자.

Listen and Speak 1-C

A: _____

B: _____

A: _____

B: _____

A: _____

A: 실례합니다. 우체국에 어떻게 갈 수 있나요?
B: 1st Street까지 곧장 가서 오른쪽으로 도세요. 그것은 오른쪽에 있을 거예요.
A: 여기서 먼가요?
B: 아니요, 멀지 않아요.
A: 정말 고마워요.

Listen and Speak 2-A

Amy: _____

Jinho: _____

Amy: _____

Jinho: _____

Listen and Speak 2-B

Andy: _____

Mike: _____

Andy: _____

Mike: _____

Andy: _____

Mike: _____

Andy: _____

Real Life Talk

Man: _____

Mina: _____

Man: _____

Mina: _____

Man: _____

Mina: _____

Man: _____

Mina: _____

Man: _____

Mina: _____

Amy: 진호야, 서둘러. 우리 영화 시간에 늦겠어.
Jinho: 응. 영화관까지 가는 데 시간이 얼마나 걸릴까?
Amy: 버스로 대략 15분 정도 걸릴 거야.
Jinho: 알겠어. 나 거의 준비됐어.

Andy: 나는 이번 금요일 학교 축제가 정말 기대돼.
Mike: 나도. 축제를 광고하기 위해 무엇을 할 수 있을까, Andy?
Andy: 포스터를 만들면 어떨까?
Mike: 좋은 생각이야. 이 근방에 포스터를 붙일 수 있겠다.
Andy: 맞아. 포스터를 만드는 데 시간이 얼마나 걸릴까?
Mike: 음, 대략 세 시간 정도 걸릴 거야.
Andy: 좋아, 많은 사람들이 축제에 왔으면 좋겠다.

Man: 실례합니다. 여기에서 수원 화성까지 어떻게 가나요?
Mina: 쉬워요. 저쪽에 버스 정류장 보이세요?
Man: 네, 보여요.
Mina: 11번 버스를 타서 여섯 번째 정류장에서 내리세요.
Man: 그곳까지 가는 데 시간이 얼마나 걸릴까요?
Mina: 대략 20분 정도 걸릴 거에요.
Man: 정말 고마워요.
Mina: 별말씀을요. 그곳에 축제 때문에 가시는 건가요?
Man: 네. 그 축제가 무척 재미있다고 들었어요.
Mina: 즐거운 시간 보내길 바라요.

※ 다음 우리말과 일치하도록 빈칸에 알맞은 것을 골라 쓰시오.

1 Holi, the _____ of _____
A. Colors   B. Festival

2 Amala _____ _____, India
A. from   B. Delhi

3 Holi is the _____ _____ festival in _____ country.
A. popular   B. my   C. most

4 It _____ _____ _____ March.
A. usually   B. is   C. in

5 _____ the festival, we _____ goodbye to cold winter and _____ to warm spring.
A. say   B. during   C. hello

6 We _____ the festival _____ _____ two days.
A. everywhere   B. for   C. celebrate

7 _____ the first day, people _____ _____ a big fire _____ night and sing and dance.
A. around   B. at   C. on   D. gather

8 The _____ event _____ the _____ day.
A. next   B. main   C. begins

9 Children and adults _____ _____ _____ with *gulal*.
A. each   B. chase   C. other

10 _____ is *gulal*? It is blue, yellow, _____ and pink _____.
A. powder   B. what   C. green

11 It's a lot of fun to _____ _____ and _____ colorful powder _____ everyone.
A. throw   B. run   C. at   D. around

12 We _____ _____ street _____!
A. join   B. parades   C. also

13 _____ _____ Festival
A. Nights   B. White

14 Victor _____ St. _____, _____
A. Russia   B. Petersburg   C. from

15 _____ you _____ _____ the *White Nights*?
A. heard   B. have   C. of

16 _____ summer, this _____ thing _____ in my hometown.
A. amazing   B. every   C. happens

1 홀리, 색의 축제

2 인도, 델리의 Amala

3 '홀리'는 우리나라에서 가장 인기 있는 축제예요.

4 그것은 보통 3월에 있어요.

5 축제 기간 동안에, 우리는 추운 겨울에게 작별 인사를 하고 따뜻한 봄을 맞는 인사를 해요.

6 우리는 이틀 동안 어디서든 축제를 기념해요.

7 첫째 날, 사람들은 밤에 큰 모닥불 주변에 모여 노래하고 춤을 춰요.

8 주요 행사는 다음 날에 시작돼요.

9 어린이들과 어른들이 'gulal'을 지니고 서로를 쫓아다녀요.

10 'gulal'이 무엇이냐고요? 그것은 파랑, 노랑, 초록, 분홍의 가루예요.

11 주변을 뛰어다니며 형형색색의 가루를 모든 사람들에게 던지는 것은 정말 재미있어요.

12 우리는 거리 행진에도 참가해요!

13 백야 축제

14 러시아, 상트페테르부르크의 Victor

15 '백야'에 대해 들어 봤나요?

16 매년 여름, 이 놀라운 일이 나의 고향에서 벌어져요.

17 The night sky does not _____ _____ _____.
A. completely   B. get   C. dark

18 _____ that time, we _____ the White Nights Festival.
A. hold   B. during

19 It usually starts _____ May and _____ for _____ a month.
A. lasts   B. about   C. in

20 During the festival, _____ is a ballet or an opera _____ _____ night.
A. every   B. there   C. almost

21 The _____ _____ event is the Scarlet Sails _____.
A. celebration   B. popular   C. most

22 A boat _____ red sails slowly _____ the river.
A. appears   B. with   C. on

23 Soon, fireworks _____ and a water show _____.
A. follows   B. begin

24 You can _____ _____ musicians _____ beautiful live music.
A. playing   B. hear   C. also

25 _____ Snow _____
A. Festival   B. Kiruna

26 Ebba _____ _____, Sweden
A. Kiruna   B. from

27 Winter is my _____ season _____ _____ the Kiruna Snow Festival.
A. because   B. favorite   C. of

28 The festival _____ in the _____ week of January and _____ _____ for five or six days.
A. on   B. last   C. goes   D. starts

29 The _____ _____ is the snow design _____.
A. competition   B. event   C. largest

30 The artists _____ huge piles of snow _____ animals, buildings, and _____ beautiful artworks.
A. shape   B. other   C. into

31 People _____ the artists _____ their works beginning _____ end.
A. shaping   B. to   C. from   D. watch

32 My favorite _____ is the dog _____ _____.
A. sled   B. activity   C. ride

33 It is amazing _____ fly _____ a world of snow _____ a dog sled.
A. on   B. through   C. to

17 밤하늘이 완전히 어두워지지 않아요.

18 그 시기 동안, 우리는 백야 축제를 열어요.

19 축제는 보통 5월에 시작되고 약 한 달 동안 지속돼요.

20 축제 기간 동안 거의 매일 밤 발레나 오페라 공연이 있어요.

21 가장 인기 있는 행사는 '붉은 돛 축하 행사'예요.

22 빨간 돛을 단 배가 강 위에 서서히 나타나요.

23 곧 불꽃놀이가 시작되고 물 쇼가 이어져요.

24 또한 여러분은 음악가들이 아름다운 라이브 음악을 연주하는 것을 들을 수 있어요.

25 키루나 눈 축제

26 스웨덴, 키루나의 Ebba

27 겨울은 키루나 눈 축제 때문에 내가 가장 좋아하는 계절이에요.

28 축제는 1월 마지막 주에 시작해서 5일이나 6일 동안 계속돼요.

29 가장 큰 행사는 '눈 디자인 대회'예요.

30 미술가들이 거대한 눈 덩어리를 동물, 건물, 다른 아름다운 작품의 모양으로 만들어요.

31 사람들은 미술가들이 그들의 작품을 만드는 것을 처음부터 끝까지 지켜봐요.

32 내가 가장 좋아하는 활동은 개썰매 타기예요.

33 개썰매를 타고 눈 세상을 날아가는 것은 정말 놀라워요.

Step2

※ 다음 우리말과 일치하도록 빈칸에 알맞은 말을 쓰시오.

1 Holi, the _____ _____ _____

2 Amala _____ _____, _____

3 Holi is _____ _____ _____ _____ in my country.

4 It _____ _____ _____ _____.

5 _____ the festival, we _____ _____ to cold winter and _____ to _____ _____.

6 We _____ the festival everywhere _____ _____ _____.

7 _____ the first day, people _____ _____ a big fire _____ _____ and _____ _____.

8 The _____ event _____ _____ _____ _____.

9 Children and adults _____ _____ _____ _____ _____ *gulal*.

10 _____ is *gulal*? It is blue, yellow, green and pink _____.

11 It's a lot of fun _____ _____ _____ and _____ colorful powder _____ _____.

12 We _____ _____ _____ _____!

13 _____ _____ Festival

14 Victor _____ St. Petersburg, _____

15 _____ _____ _____ _____ the *White Nights*?

16 Every summer, this _____ thing _____ in my hometown.

1 홀리, 색의 축제

2 인도, 델리의 Amala

3 '홀리'는 우리나라에서 가장 인기 있는 축제예요.

4 그것은 보통 3월에 있어요.

5 축제 기간 동안에, 우리는 추운 겨울에게 작별 인사를 하고 따뜻한 봄을 맞는 인사를 해요.

6 우리는 이틀 동안 어디서든 축제를 기념해요.

7 첫째 날, 사람들은 밤에 큰 모닥불 주변에 모여 노래하고 춤을 춰요.

8 주요 행사는 다음 날에 시작돼요.

9 어린이들과 어른들이 'gulal'을 지니고 서로를 쫓아다녀요.

10 'gulal'이 무엇이냐고요? 그것은 파랑, 노랑, 초록, 분홍의 가루예요.

11 주변을 뛰어다니며 형형색색의 가루를 모든 사람들에게 던지는 것은 정말 재미있어요.

12 우리는 거리 행진에도 참가해요!

13 백야 축제

14 러시아, 상트페테르부르크의 Victor

15 '백야'에 대해 들어 봤나요?

16 매년 여름, 이 놀라운 일이 나의 고향에서 벌어져요.

17 The night sky _____ _____ _____ _____ .

18 _____ that time, we _____ the White Nights Festival.

19 It _____ _____ _____ May and _____ _____ _____ a month.

20 _____ the festival, _____ _____ a ballet or an opera _____ _____ _____ .

21 The _____ _____ event is the Scarlet Sails _____ .

22 A boat with red sails slowly _____ _____ _____ _____ _____ .

23 Soon, _____ _____ and a water show _____ .

24 You can _____ _____ musicians _____ beautiful live music.

25 Kiruna _____ _____

26 Ebba _____ _____ , _____

27 Winter is _____ _____ _____ _____ _____ the Kiruna Snow Festival.

28 The festival _____ _____ _____ _____ _____ of January and _____ _____ _____ five or six days.

29 _____ _____ _____ is the snow design _____ .

30 The artists _____ _____ _____ of snow _____ animals, buildings, and _____ beautiful artworks.

31 People _____ the artists _____ their works _____ _____ _____ _____ .

32 My _____ _____ is the _____ _____ _____ .

33 _____ is _____ _____ _____ _____ a world of snow _____ a dog sled.

17 밤하늘이 완전히 어두워지지 않아요.

18 그 시기 동안, 우리는 백야 축제를 열어요.

19 축제는 보통 5월에 시작되고 약한 달 동안 지속돼요.

20 축제 기간 동안 거의 매일 밤 발레나 오페라 공연이 있어요.

21 가장 인기 있는 행사는 '붉은 돛 축하 행사'예요.

22 빨간 돛을 단 배가 강 위에 서서히 나타나요.

23 곧 불꽃놀이가 시작되고 물 쇼가 이어져요.

24 또한 여러분은 음악가들이 아름다운 라이브 음악을 연주하는 것을 들을 수 있어요.

25 키루나 눈 축제

26 스웨덴, 키루나의 Ebba

27 겨울은 키루나 눈 축제 때문에 내가 가장 좋아하는 계절이에요.

28 축제는 1월 마지막 주에 시작해서 5일이나 6일 동안 계속돼요.

29 가장 큰 행사는 '눈 디자인 대회'예요.

30 미술가들이 거대한 눈 덩어리를 동물, 건물, 다른 아름다운 작품의 모양으로 만들어요.

31 사람들은 미술가들이 그들의 작품을 만드는 것을 처음부터 끝까지 지켜봐요.

32 내가 가장 좋아하는 활동은 개썰매 타기예요.

33 개썰매를 타고 눈 세상을 날아가는 것은 정말 놀라워요.

※ 다음 문장을 우리말로 쓰시오.

1 Holi, the Festival of Colors

➡ _____

2 Amala from Delhi, India

➡ _____

3 Holi is the most popular festival in my country.

➡ _____

4 It is usually in March.

➡ _____

5 During the festival, we say goodbye to cold winter and hello to warm spring.

➡ _____

6 We celebrate the festival everywhere for two days.

➡ _____

7 On the first day, people gather around a big fire at night and sing and dance.

➡ _____

8 The main event begins the next day.

➡ _____

9 Children and adults chase each other with *gulal*.

➡ _____

10 What is *gulal*? It is blue, yellow, green and pink powder.

➡ _____

11 It's a lot of fun to run around and throw colorful powder at everyone.

➡ _____

12 We also join street parades!

➡ _____

13 White Nights Festival

➡ _____

14 Victor from St. Petersburg, Russia

➡ _____

15 Have you heard of the *White Nights*?

➡ _____

16 Every summer, this amazing thing happens in my hometown.

➡ _____

17 The night sky does not get completely dark.

➡ _____

18 During that time, we hold the White Nights Festival.

➡ _____

19 It usually starts in May and lasts for about a month.

➡ _____

20 During the festival, there is a ballet or an opera almost every night.

➡ _____

21 The most popular event is the Scarlet Sails celebration.

➡ _____

22 A boat with red sails slowly appears on the river.

➡ _____

23 Soon, fireworks begin and a water show follows.

➡ _____

24 You can also hear musicians playing beautiful live music.

➡ _____

25 Kiruna Snow Festival

➡ _____

26 Ebba from Kiruna, Sweden

➡ _____

27 Winter is my favorite season because of the Kiruna Snow Festival.

➡ _____

28 The festival starts in the last week of January and goes on for five or six days.

➡ _____

29 The largest event is the snow design competition.

➡ _____

30 The artists shape huge piles of snow into animals, buildings, and other beautiful artworks.

➡ _____

31 People watch the artists shaping their works from beginning to end.

➡ _____

32 My favorite activity is the dog sled ride.

➡ _____

33 It is amazing to fly through a world of snow on a dog sled.

➡ _____

※ 다음 괄호 안의 단어들을 우리말에 맞도록 바르게 배열하시오.

1 (the / Colors / Holi, / of / Festival)
➡ _____

2 (from / Amala / India / Delhi,)
➡ _____

3 (is / Holi / most / the / festival / popular / country. / my / in)
➡ _____

4 (is / it / usually / March. / in)
➡ _____

5 (the / during / festival, / say / we / to / goodbye / cold / and / winter / spring. / warm / to / hello)
➡ _____

6 (celebrate / we / festival / the / for / everywhere / days. / two)
➡ _____

7 (the / day, / on / first / people / around / gather / fire / big / a / night / at / and / dance. / and / sing)
➡ _____

8 (main / the / begins / event / day. / next / the)
➡ _____

9 (and / children / chase / adults / other / each / *gulal*. / with)
➡ _____

10 (*gulal*? / is / what // is / it / blue, / green / yellow, / and / powder. / pink)
➡ _____

11 (a / it's / of / lot / fun / run / to / around / and / colorful / throw / everyone. / at / powder)
➡ _____

12 (join / also / we / parades! / street)
➡ _____

13 (Nights / White / Festival)
➡ _____

14 (from / Victor / Russia / St. Petersburg)
➡ _____

15 (you / have / of / heard / *Nights*? / *White* / the)
➡ _____

16 (summer, / every / amazing / this / happens / thing / hometown. / my / in)
➡ _____

1 홀리, 색의 축제

2 인도, 델리의 Amala

3 '홀리'는 우리나라에서 가장 인기 있는 축제예요.

4 그것은 보통 3월에 있어요.

5 축제 기간 동안에, 우리는 추운 겨울에게 작별 인사를 하고 따뜻한 봄을 맞는 인사를 해요.

6 우리는 이틀 동안 어디서든 축제를 기념해요.

7 첫째 날, 사람들은 밤에 큰 모닥불 주변에 모여 노래하고 춤을 춰요.

8 주요 행사는 다음 날에 시작돼요.

9 어린이들과 어른들이 'gulal'을 지니고 서로를 쫓아다녀요.

10 'gulal'이 무엇이냐고요? 그것은 파랑, 노랑, 초록, 분홍의 가루예요.

11 주변을 뛰어다니며 형형색색의 가루를 모든 사람들에게 던지는 것은 정말 재미있어요.

12 우리는 거리 행진에도 참가해요!

13 백야 축제

14 러시아, 상트페테르부르크의 Victor

15 '백야'에 대해 들어 봤나요?

16 매년 여름, 이 놀라운 일이 나의 고향에서 벌어져요.

17 (night / sky / the / not / does / completely / dark. / get)

➡ _____

18 (that / during / time, / hold / we / the / White / Festival. / Nights)

➡ _____

19 (usually / it / in / starts / May / and / for / lasts / about / month. / a)

➡ _____

20 (the / festival, / during / is / there / ballet / a / or / opera / an / night. / every / almost)

➡ _____

21 (most / the / is / event / popular / Scarlet / the / celebration. / Sails)

➡ _____

22 (boat / a / red / with / sails / appears / slowly / river. / the / on)

➡ _____

23 (fireworks / soon, / begin / and / water / a / follows. / show)

➡ _____

24 (can / you / hear / also / playing / musicians / music. / live / beautiful)

➡ _____

25 (Festival / Snow / Kiruna)

➡ _____

26 (from / Sweden / Ebba / Kiruna,)

➡ _____

27 (is / winter / favorite / season / my / of / because / the / Festival. / Snow / Kiruna)

➡ _____

28 (festival / starts / the / in / last / the / week / January / of / and / on / goes / for / days. / six / or / five)

➡ _____

➡ _____

29 (largest / the / event / is / snow / the / competition. / design)

➡ _____

30 (artists / shape / the / piles / huge / snow / of / animals, / into / buildings, / and / artworks. / beautiful / other)

➡ _____

➡ _____

31 (watch / people / artists / the / shaping / works / their / from / end. / to / beginning)

➡ _____

➡ _____

32 (favorite / my / activity / is / dog / the / ride. / sled)

➡ _____

33 (is / it / amazing / fly / to / a / through / world / snow / of / on / sled. / dog / a)

➡ _____

17 밤하늘이 완전히 어두워지지 않아요.

18 그 시기 동안, 우리는 백야 축제를 열어요.

19 축제는 보통 5월에 시작되고 약 한 달 동안 지속돼요.

20 축제 기간 동안 거의 매일 밤 발레나 오페라 공연이 있어요.

21 가장 인기 있는 행사는 '붉은 돛 축하 행사'예요.

22 빨간 돛을 단 배가 강 위에 서서히 나타나요.

23 곧 불꽃놀이가 시작되고 물 쇼가 이어져요.

24 또한 여러분은 음악가들이 아름다운 라이브 음악을 연주하는 것을 들을 수 있어요.

25 키루나 눈 축제

26 스웨덴, 키루나의 Ebba

27 겨울은 키루나 눈 축제 때문에 내가 가장 좋아하는 계절이에요.

28 축제는 1월 마지막 주에 시작해서 5일이나 6일 동안 계속돼요.

29 가장 큰 행사는 '눈 디자인 대회'예요.

30 미술가들이 거대한 눈 덩어리를 동물, 건물, 다른 아름다운 작품의 모양으로 만들어요.

31 사람들은 미술가들이 그들의 작품을 만드는 것을 처음부터 끝까지 지켜봐요.

32 내가 가장 좋아하는 활동은 개썰매 타기예요.

33 개썰매를 타고 눈 세상을 날아가는 것은 정말 놀라워요.

※ 다음 우리말을 영어로 쓰시오.

1 홀리, 색의 축제

➡ _____

2 인도, 델리의 Amala

➡ _____

3 '홀리'는 우리나라에서 가장 인기 있는 축제예요.

➡ _____

4 그것은 보통 3월에 있어요.

➡ _____

5 축제 기간 동안에, 우리는 추운 겨울에게 작별 인사를 하고 따뜻한 봄을 맞는 인사를 해요.

➡ _____

6 우리는 이틀 동안 어디서든 축제를 기념해요.

➡ _____

7 첫째 날, 사람들은 밤에 큰 모닥불 주변에 모여 노래하고 춤을 춰요.

➡ _____

8 주요 행사는 다음 날에 시작돼요.

➡ _____

9 어린이들과 어른들이 'gulal'을 지니고 서로를 쫓아다녀요.

➡ _____

10 'gulal'이 무엇이냐고요? 그것은 파랑, 노랑, 초록, 분홍의 가루예요.

➡ _____

11 주변을 뛰어다니며 형형색색의 가루를 모든 사람들에게 던지는 것은 정말 재미있어요.

➡ _____

12 우리는 거리 행진에도 참가해요!

➡ _____

13 백야 축제

➡ _____

14 러시아, 상트페테르부르크의 Victor

➡ _____

15 '백야'에 대해 들어 봤나요?

➡ _____

16 매년 여름, 이 놀라운 일이 나의 고향에서 벌어져요.

➡ _____

17 밤하늘이 완전히 어두워지지 않아요.
➡ _____

18 그 시기 동안, 우리는 백야 축제를 열어요.
➡ _____

19 축제는 보통 5월에 시작되고 약 한 달 동안 지속돼요.
➡ _____

20 축제 기간 동안 거의 매일 밤 발레나 오페라 공연이 있어요.
➡ _____

21 가장 인기 있는 행사는 '붉은 돛 축하 행사'예요.
➡ _____

22 빨간 돛을 단 배가 강 위에 서서히 나타나요.
➡ _____

23 곧 불꽃놀이가 시작되고 물 쇼가 이어져요.
➡ _____

24 또한 여러분은 음악가들이 아름다운 라이브 음악을 연주하는 것을 들을 수 있어요.
➡ _____

25 키루나 눈 축제
➡ _____

26 스웨덴, 키루나의 Ebba
➡ _____

27 겨울은 키루나 눈 축제 때문에 내가 가장 좋아하는 계절이에요.
➡ _____

28 축제는 1월 마지막 주에 시작해서 5일이나 6일 동안 계속돼요.
➡ _____

29 가장 큰 행사는 '눈 디자인 대회'예요.
➡ _____

30 미술가들이 거대한 눈 덩어리를 동물, 건물, 다른 아름다운 작품의 모양으로 만들어요.
➡ _____

31 사람들은 미술가들이 그들의 작품을 만드는 것을 처음부터 끝까지 지켜봐요.
➡ _____

32 내가 가장 좋아하는 활동은 개썰매 타기예요.
➡ _____

33 개썰매를 타고 눈 세상을 날아가는 것은 정말 놀라워요.
➡ _____

※ 다음 우리말과 일치하도록 빈칸에 알맞은 말을 쓰시오.

Listen and Speak 2 - C

1. A: Chris, what _____ you _____ for the _____ _____?

2. B: I'll _____ _____.

3. A: Great idea. _____ _____ will it _____ _____ make them?

4. B: _____ it'll _____ _____ _____ _____.

1. A: Chris, 학급 파티를 위해 무엇을 할 거니?
2. B: 나는 샌드위치를 만들 거야.
3. A: 좋은 생각이야. 그것들을 만드는 데 얼마가 걸릴까?
4. B: 아마도 약 한 시간 정도 걸릴 거야.

Think and Write

1. I _____ Gangneung

2. I _____ _____ Gangneung.

3. _____ _____ beautiful beaches in my _____.

4. It's _____ _____ fun _____ _____ at the beach.

5. There is a _____ _____ _____ Gangneung.

6. It _____ _____ Ojukheon. Yulgok _____ _____ there.

7. _____ _____ _____ _____ in Gangneung is potato tteok.

8. It is soft and sweet. _____ _____ _____ Gangneung!

1. 강릉이 정말 좋아요
2. 저는 강릉에 살아요.
3. 나의 이웃에는 아름다운 해변들이 있어요.
4. 해변에서 수영하는 것은 정말 재미있어요.
5. 강릉에는 유명한 한옥이 있어요.
6. 그것은 오죽헌이라고 불려요. 율곡이 거기에서 태어났어요.
7. 강릉에서 가장 유명한 음식은 감자떡이에요.
8. 그것은 부드럽고 달콤해요. 와서 강릉을 즐기세요!

Project Culture

1. I want _____ _____ Boryeong Mud Festival.

2. It _____ _____ _____ Daecheon Beach _____ _____.

3. There are _____ _____ _____ in the festival.

4. First, you can _____ _____ _____ Ssireum in mud.

5. Also _____ is fun _____ colorful mud body _____ on your body.

6. _____, there is an _____ _____.

7. You can _____ _____ _____ beautiful musics.

1. 나는 보령 진흙 축제를 소개하고 싶어요.
2. 그것은 7월에 대천 해수욕장에서 열립니다.
3. 축제에는 많은 흥미로운 행사가 있습니다.
4. 우선, 당신은 사람들이 진흙 속에서 씨름하는 것을 볼 수 있어요.
5. 또한 당신의 몸에 형형색색의 진흙을 바르는 것은 재미있어요.
6. 마지막으로, 실외 콘서트가 있습니다.
7. 당신은 음악가들이 아름다운 음악을 연주하는 것을 들을 수 있습니다.

※ 다음 우리말을 영어로 쓰시오.

Listen and Speak 2 - C

1. A: Chris, 학급 파티를 위해 무엇을 할 거니?
➡ _____

2. B: 나는 샌드위치를 만들 거야.
➡ _____

3. A: 좋은 생각이야. 그것들을 만드는 데 얼마가 걸릴까?
➡ _____

4. B: 아마도 약 한 시간 정도 걸릴 거야.
➡ _____

Think and Write

1. 강릉이 정말 좋아요
➡ _____

2. 저는 강릉에 살아요.
➡ _____

3. 나의 이웃에는 아름다운 해변들이 있어요.
➡ _____

4. 해변에서 수영하는 것은 정말 재미있어요.
➡ _____

5. 강릉에는 유명한 한옥이 있어요.
➡ _____

6. 그것은 오죽헌이라고 불려요. 율곡이 거기에서 태어났어요.
➡ _____

7. 강릉에서 가장 유명한 음식은 감자떡이에요.
➡ _____

8. 그것은 부드럽고 달콤해요. 와서 강릉을 즐기세요!
➡ _____

Project Culture

1. 나는 보령 진흙 축제를 소개하고 싶어요.
➡ _____

2. 그것은 7월에 대천 해수욕장에서 열립니다.
➡ _____

3. 그 축제에는 많은 흥미로운 행사가 있습니다.
➡ _____

4. 우선, 당신은 사람들이 진흙 속에서 씨름하는 것을 볼 수 있어요.
➡ _____

5. 또한 당신의 몸에 형형색색의 진흙을 바르는 것은 재미있어요.
➡ _____

6. 마지막으로, 실외 콘서트가 있습니다.
➡ _____

7. 당신은 음악가들이 아름다운 음악을 연주하는 것을 들을 수 있습니다.
➡ _____

※ 다음 영어를 우리말로 쓰시오.

01	inventor		22	following
02	lastly		23	several
03	apply		24	length
04	environment		25	adapt
05	blind		26	necessary
06	promise		27	organization
07	communicate		28	curious
08	similar		29	peel
09	deaf		30	mission
10	average		31	difference
11	decorate		32	slice
12	space		33	electricity
13	outgoing		34	in addition
14	brave		35	miss out
15	exhibition		36	on average
16	although		37	from now on
17	farther		38	be made of
18	friendly		39	get along with
19	include		40	cheer up
20	spread		41	make an invention
21	invention		42	be curious about
			43	be good at

※ 다음 우리말을 영어로 쓰시오.

01	발명		22	나뭇가지, 막대
02	눈이 먼		23	전시회
03	비슷한		24	용감한
04	전기		25	생산하다
05	청각 장애가 있는		26	임무
06	평균		27	(비록) ~이긴 하지만
07	장식하다		28	포함하다
08	약속하다		29	지원하다
09	발명가		30	다음에 나오는
10	마지막으로		31	몇몇의
11	필요한		32	기간, 길이
12	조직, 단체		33	적응하다
13	(얇게) 썰다, 자르다		34	차이
14	환경, 주위의 상황		35	놓치다
15	호기심이 많은, 궁금한		36	지금부터
16	의사소통하다		37	~와 잘 지내다
17	친절한, 상냥한		38	평균적으로
18	이유		39	게다가
19	태양계		40	~로 구성되다
20	껍질을 벗기다		41	~에 대해 궁금해 하다
21	활발한		42	기운을 내다, ~을 격려하다
			43	즐거운 시간을 보내다

※ 다음 영영풀이에 알맞은 단어를 <보기>에서 골라 쓴 후, 우리말 뜻을 쓰시오.

1 _____ : not able to see: _____

2 _____ : the amount of time that something lasts: _____

3 _____ : a task or job that someone is given to do: _____

4 _____ : to cut something into thin pieces: _____

5 _____ : not able to hear anything: _____

6 _____ : to put a layer of something on top of something else: _____

7 _____ : like somebody or something but not exactly the same: _____

8 _____ : to remove the skin from a fruit, vegetable, etc.: _____

9 _____ : the way in which two things are not like each other: _____

10 _____ : the conditions that surround someone or something: _____

11 _____ : one of two equal parts into which something can be divided: _____

12 _____ : a person who has invented something or whose job is inventing things: _____

13 _____ : to change your behavior in order to live in a new situation successfully: _____

14 _____ : a thin piece of wood that has been broken from a tree: _____

15 _____ : to ask formally for something such as a job, admission to a school, etc.: _____

16 _____ : a group such as a club or business that is formed for a particular purpose: _____

보기

mission	difference	slice	environment
peel	blind	length	apply
half	inventor	organization	adapt
stick	similar	deaf	spread

※ 다음 우리말과 일치하도록 빈칸에 알맞은 말을 쓰시오.

Listen & Speak 1-A

Brian: Do you know _____ _____ _____?

Amy: Um, it _____ _____ a glue stick.

Brian: No, it's a _____ _____.

Amy: Oh, _____ _____ _____ _____ _____?

Brian: Yes, you _____ _____ _____ on the bread _____ it.

Brian: 너는 이것이 무엇인지 아니?
Amy: 음, 막대 모양 풀 같아 보여.
Brian: 아니, 막대 모양 버터야.
Amy: 오, 그 안에 버터가 있니?
Brian: 응, 그걸로 빵 위에 버터를 바를 수 있어.

Listen & Speak 1-B

Ms. Lee: Hello, class! Jisu is today's speaker for _____ _____ _____. Jisu?

Jisu: Hi, class! Do you know _____ _____ _____ _____? His name is Alexander Graham Bell. Bell was an _____. He _____ _____ _____ sound. _____ did he _____? Yes, the telephone! His mother and wife were _____. So he also _____ _____ _____ for _____ _____ and _____ a school for them.

Ms. Lee: 안녕하세요, 여러분! 지수가 오늘의 물건 가져와서 발표하기의 발표자예요. 지수야?
Jisu: 안녕, 얘들아! 이 사람이 누구인지 아니? 그의 이름은 Alexander Graham Bell이야. Bell은 발명가였어. 그는 소리에 관심이 있었어. 그가 무엇을 발명했지? 맞아, 전화기야! 그의 어머니와 아내는 청각 장애가 있었어. 그래서 그는 청각 장애인들을 위한 몇몇 발명품도 만들었고 그들을 위한 학교를 열었어.

Listen & Speak 2-A

Jane: This _____ _____. _____ is it _____?

Mike: It's _____ _____ _____.

Jane: Really? May I _____ it?

Mike: Sure, _____ _____ _____ _____ _____.

Jane: 이거 흥미롭게 생겼네. 용도가 뭐야?
Mike: 달걀을 얇게 썰기 위한 거야.
Jane: 정말? 내가 해 봐도 돼?
Mike: 물론이지, 여기 달걀이 있어.

Listen & Speak 2-B

Tom: Mom, _____ _____ these slippers. I made them _____ _____ _____.

Mom: _____ did you _____ slippers in science class?

Tom: They are _____ _____ _____ _____.

Mom: Then, _____ are they _____?

Tom: You can _____ _____ _____ and _____ _____ _____.

Mom: Oh, so you _____ _____ your room _____ _____ _____?

Tom: Sure. _____ _____ _____ my room, Mom.

Tom: 엄마, 이 슬리퍼를 보세요. 과학 시간에 만들었어요.
Mom: 왜 과학 시간에 슬리퍼를 만들었니?
Tom: 단지 신기 위한 게 아니에요.
Mom: 그럼 용도가 무엇이니?
Tom: 슬리퍼를 신고 바닥을 청소할 수 있어요.
Mom: 오, 그럼 앞으로는 네가 네 방을 청소하겠구나?
Tom: 물론이에요. 제 방은 걱정 마세요, 엄마.

Listen & Speak 2-C

A: Jane, _____ _____ this. It's a meok.

B: I _____ _____ _____ it _____. _____ is it _____?

A: It's _____ _____ _____.

B: Oh, really? That's _____.

A: Jane, 이것 좀 봐. 먹이야.
B: 나는 그것을 전에 본 적이 없어. 용도가 무엇이니?
A: 잉크를 만들기 위한 거야.
B: 오, 정말? 그거 흥미롭다.

Real Life Talk – Step 1

Judy: _____ _____ your weekend, Hojin?

Hojin: I _____ _____ _____ _____. I went to a _____ _____ _____ my brother.

Judy: Did you? I _____ _____ _____ so many interesting things.

Hojin: Yes. _____ _____ this. I bought it there. Do you know _____ _____ _____?

Judy: Well, I'm _____ _____. What is it?

Hojin: It's a VR headset.

Judy: A VR headset? _____ _____ _____ _____?

Hojin: If you _____ it, you _____ _____ _____ _____.

Judy: _____ cool. May I _____ it?

Hojin: Sure. _____ you _____.

Judy: 주말은 어땠니, 호진아?
Hojin: 즐거운 시간을 보냈어. 남동생과 과학 전시회에 갔었어.
Judy: 그랬니? 흥미로운 것들이 굉장히 많다고 들었어.
Hojin: 응. 이것 좀 봐. 거기에서 샀어. 이게 무엇인지 아니?
Judy: 음, 잘 모르겠어. 뭐니?
Hojin: VR 헤드셋이야.
Judy: VR 헤드셋? 용도가 뭐니?
Hojin: 그것을 쓰면 다른 세상을 경험할 수 있어.
Judy: 멋지다. 내가 써 봐도 될까?
Hojin: 물론이지. 여기 있어.

※ 다음 우리말에 맞도록 대화를 영어로 쓰시오.

Listen & Speak 1-A

Brian: _____

Amy: _____

Brian: _____

Amy: _____

Brian: _____

해석

Brian: 너는 이것이 무엇인지 아니?
Amy: 음, 막대 모양 풀 같아 보여.
Brian: 아니, 막대 모양 버터야.
Amy: 오, 그 안에 버터가 있니?
Brian: 응, 그걸로 빵 위에 버터를 바를
 수 있어.

Listen & Speak 1-B

Ms. Lee: _____

Jisu: _____

_____

_____

_____

Ms. Lee: 안녕하세요, 여러분! 지수
 가 오늘의 물건 가져와서
 발표하기의 발표자예요. 지
 수야?
Jisu: 안녕, 얘들아! 이 사람이 누
 구인지 아니? 그의 이름은
 Alexander Graham Bell이야.
 Bell은 발명가였어. 그는 소리
 에 관심이 있었어. 그가 무엇을
 발명했지? 맞아, 전화기야! 그
 의 어머니와 아내는 청각 장애
 가 있었어. 그래서 그는 청각
 장애인들을 위한 몇몇 발명품
 도 만들었고 그들을 위한 학교
 를 열었어.

Listen & Speak 2-A

Jane: _____

Mike: _____

Jane: _____

Mike: _____

Jane: 이거 흥미롭게 생겼네. 용도가
 뭐야?
Mike: 달걀을 얇게 썰기 위한 거야.
Jane: 정말? 내가 해 봐도 돼?
Mike: 물론이지, 여기 달걀이 있어.

Listen & Speak 2-B

Tom: _____

Mom: _____

Tom: _____

Mom: _____

Tom: _____

Mom: _____

Tom: _____

Tom: 엄마, 이 슬리퍼를 보세요. 과학 시간에 만들었어요.
Mom: 왜 과학 시간에 슬리퍼를 만들었니?
Tom: 단지 신기 위한 게 아니에요.
Mom: 그럼 용도가 무엇이니?
Tom: 슬리퍼를 신고 바닥을 청소할 수 있어요.
Mom: 오, 그럼 앞으로는 네가 네 방을 청소하겠구나?
Tom: 물론이에요. 제 방은 걱정 마세요, 엄마.

Listen & Speak 2-C

A: _____

B: _____

A: _____

B: _____

A: Jane, 이것 좀 봐. 먹이야.
B: 나는 그것을 전에 본 적이 없어. 용도가 무엇이니?
A: 잉크를 만들기 위한 거야.
B: 오, 정말? 그거 흥미롭다.

Real Life Talk – Step 1

Judy: _____

Hojin: _____

Judy: _____

Hojin: _____

Judy: _____

Hojin: _____

Judy: _____

Hojin: _____

Judy: _____

Hojin: _____

Judy: 주말은 어땠니, 호진아?
Hojin: 즐거운 시간을 보냈어. 남동생과 과학 전시회에 갔었어.
Judy: 그랬니? 흥미로운 것들이 굉장히 많다고 들었어.
Hojin: 응. 이것 좀 봐. 거기에서 샀어. 이게 무엇인지 아니?
Judy: 음, 잘 모르겠어. 뭐니?
Hojin: VR 헤드셋이야.
Judy: VR 헤드셋? 용도가 뭐니?
Hojin: 그것을 쓰면 다른 세상을 경험할 수 있어.
Judy: 멋지다. 내가 써 봐도 될까?
Hojin: 물론이지. 여기 있어.

※ 다음 우리말과 일치하도록 빈칸에 알맞은 것을 골라 쓰시오.

1 _____ _____ MARS!
　　A. on　　　　　　B. Live

2 Do you want to _____ _____ _____ planet?
　　A. another　　　B. on　　　　　C. live

3 The Korea Space Organization (KSO) is _____ _____ people _____ go to MARS!
　　A. for　　　　　B. to　　　　　C. looking

4 Our mission is _____ _____ a city _____ Mars.
　　A. build　　　　B. on　　　　　C. to

5 We are looking for someone…
who is _____.
who is creative and _____.
who can get _____ with others.
who can _____ to a new environment quickly.
　　A. adapt　　　　B. curious　　　C. healthy　　　D. along

6 _____ _____, _____ us a short video.
　　A. apply　　　　B. to　　　　　C. send

7 The video _____ the answers _____ the _____ questions:
　　A. following　　B. include　　　C. to　　　D. must

8 1. _____ do you _____ to _____ to Mars?
　　A. want　　　　B. go　　　　　C. why
2. Do you have a _____ _____ of _____?
　　A. humor　　　　B. sense　　　C. good
3. Why are you the _____ person _____ this _____?
　　A. perfect　　　B. mission　　　C. for

9 This is a _____ of a lifetime, _____ don't _____ _____!
　　A. chance　　　B. out　　　　C. miss　　　D. so

10 Mars, _____ _____ _____?
　　A. Earth　　　　B. Second　　　C. the

11 _____ there are many books and movies about Mars, no _____ has _____ there _____.
　　A. one　　　　　B. yet　　　　C. although　　　D. been

12 _____ days, scientists are _____ _____ Mars _____ a new home.
　　A. as　　　　　B. these　　　　C. at　　　D. looking

13 _____ _____, NASA and some companies are _____ to send people there _____ now.
　　A. right　　　　B. fact　　　　C. trying　　　D. in

1　화성에서 살아요!

2　다른 행성에서 살고 싶은가요?

3　한국 우주 기구(KSO)는 화성에 갈 사람들을 찾고 있습니다!

4　우리의 임무는 화성에 도시를 세우는 것입니다.

5　우리는 다음과 같은 사람을 찾고 있습니다.
건강한 사람.
창의적이고 호기심이 많은 사람.
다른 사람들과 잘 지낼 수 있는 사람.
새로운 환경에 빨리 적응할 수 있는 사람.

6　지원하려면 우리에게 짧은 동영상을 보내세요.

7　동영상은 다음의 질문에 관한 답을 포함해야 합니다.

8　1. 당신은 왜 화성에 가고 싶은가요?
2. 당신은 유머 감각이 있나요?
3. 왜 당신이 이 임무에 적합한 사람인가요?

9　이것은 일생에 단 한 번뿐인 기회이므로 놓치지 마세요!

10　화성. 제 2의 지구?

11　화성에 관한 많은 책과 영화가 있긴 하지만, 아직 화성에 가 본 사람은 아무도 없다.

12　요즘. 과학자들은 화성을 새로운 거주지로 보고 있다.

13　사실, NASA와 몇몇 회사들은 그곳에 사람들을 보내기 위해 바로 지금도 노력하고 있다.

14 The _____ question is, "Can people _____ _____ Mars?"
    A. on   B. live   C. big

15 Many scientists _____ _____ for _____ _____.
    A. reasons   B. believe   C. several   D. so

16 First, they _____ there is _____ on Mars.
    A. that   B. water   C. think

17 This is great _____ water is _____ _____ all life.
    A. for   B. because   C. necessary

18 Second, Mars has _____ _____ to _____ houses and buildings _____.
    A. on   B. land   C. build   D. hard

19 Third, the _____ of day and night on Mars is _____ _____ on Earth.
    A. similar   B. length   C. to   D. that

20 _____ _____, Mars also _____ four _____.
    A. seasons   B. addition   C. has   D. in

21 _____, people can _____ similar _____.
    A. lives   B. so   C. lead

22 _____, Mars is not _____ _____.
    A. far   B. lastly   C. very

23 It is _____ _____ _____ planet to Earth.
    A. second   B. the   C. closest

24 Mars, _____, has some _____ _____ Earth.
    A. differences   B. from   C. however

25 First, Mars is _____ _____ the _____ of Earth.
    A. half   B. size   C. about

26 It is the _____ _____ planet in the _____ _____.
    A. solar   B. second   C. smallest   D. system

27 Second, a _____ on Mars is _____ _____ as long _____ a year on Earth.
    A. twice   B. as   C. about   D. year

28 Third, Mars is _____ _____ _____ Earth.
    A. colder   B. than   C. much

29 _____ _____, it is _____ −60℃ on Mars.
    A. about   B. average   C. on

30 This is _____ Mars is _____ _____ from the Sun _____ Earth.
    A. farther   B. because   C. than   D. away

31 _____ no one can _____ the big question right now, it is _____ to _____ this new world.
    A. answer   B. imagine   C. exciting   D. although

32 Who knows? You could _____ _____ first _____ _____ Mars!
    A. Korean   B. on   C. be   D. the

14 중요한 질문은 "화성에서 사람들이 살 수 있는가?"이다.

15 많은 과학자들은 몇몇 이유로 그렇게 믿고 있다.

16 첫째, 그들은 화성에 물이 있다고 생각한다.

17 물은 모든 생명체에 필수적이기 때문에 이것은 중요하다.

18 둘째, 화성은 집과 건물을 지을 수 있는 단단한 땅을 가지고 있다.

19 셋째, 화성의 낮과 밤의 길이는 지구의 낮과 밤의 길이와 비슷하다.

20 게다가, 화성은 사계절도 있다.

21 그래서 사람들이 비슷한 생활을 할 수 있다.

22 마지막으로, 화성은 그렇게 멀지 않다.

23 화성은 지구에서 두 번째로 가까운 행성이다.

24 그러나 화성은 지구와 다른 점이 몇 개 있다.

25 첫째, 화성은 지구의 약 절반 크기이다.

26 화성은 태양계에서 두 번째로 작은 행성이다.

27 둘째, 화성에서의 일 년은 지구에서의 일 년보다 약 두 배 길다.

28 셋째, 화성은 지구보다 훨씬 더 춥다.

29 평균적으로, 화성의 기온은 약 섭씨 영하 60도이다.

30 이것은 화성이 지구보다 태양에서 더 멀리 떨어져 있기 때문이다.

31 비록 누구도 그 중요한 질문에 지금 당장 답할 수는 없지만, 이 새로운 세상을 상상하는 것은 신이 난다.

32 누가 알겠는가? 당신이 화성에 발을 디디는 첫 번째 한국인이 될 수도 있다!

※ 다음 우리말과 일치하도록 빈칸에 알맞은 말을 쓰시오.

1 _____ _____ MARS!

2 Do you want _____ _____ _____ _____ planet?

3 The _____ _____ _____ (KSO) is _____ _____ _____ _____ _____ to MARS!

4 _____ _____ is _____ _____ a city _____ Mars.

5 We _____ _____ _____ someone…

_____ is _____.

_____ is _____ and _____.

_____ can _____ _____ _____ others.

_____ can _____ a _____ _____ quickly.

6 _____ _____ , _____ _____ a short video.

7 The video _____ _____ the answers _____ the _____ _____:

8 1. Why do you _____ _____ _____ to Mars?

2. Do you have _____ _____ _____ _____ _____?

3. Why are you the _____ _____ _____?

9 This is _____ _____ a lifetime, so _____ _____ out!

10 Mars, _____ _____ _____?

11 _____ there are _____ _____ and _____ about Mars, no one _____ _____ there _____.

12 _____ _____, scientists are _____ _____ Mars _____ a new home.

13 _____ _____, NASA and some companies _____ _____ _____ people there _____ _____.

---

1 화성에서 살아요!

2 다른 행성에서 살고 싶은가요?

3 한국 우주 기구(KSO)는 화성에 갈 사람들을 찾고 있습니다!

4 우리의 임무는 화성에 도시를 세우는 것입니다.

5 우리는 다음과 같은 사람을 찾고 있습니다.
건강한 사람.
창의적이고 호기심이 많은 사람.
다른 사람들과 잘 지낼 수 있는 사람.
새로운 환경에 빨리 적응할 수 있는 사람.

6 지원하려면 우리에게 짧은 동영상을 보내세요.

7 동영상은 다음의 질문에 관한 답을 포함해야 합니다.

8 1. 당신은 왜 화성에 가고 싶은가요?
2. 당신은 유머 감각이 있나요?
3. 왜 당신이 이 임무에 적합한 사람인가요?

9 이것은 일생에 단 한 번뿐인 기회이므로 놓치지 마세요!

10 화성, 제 2의 지구?

11 화성에 관한 많은 책과 영화가 있긴 하지만, 아직 화성에 가 본 사람은 아무도 없다.

12 요즘, 과학자들은 화성을 새로운 거주지로 보고 있다.

13 사실, NASA와 몇몇 회사들은 그곳에 사람들을 보내기 위해 바로 지금도 노력하고 있다.

14 The big question is, "_____ _____ _____ _____ Mars?"

15 Many scientists _____ _____ for _____ _____ .

16 First, they think _____ there is _____ _____ Mars.

17 This is great _____ water is _____ _____ all life.

18 Second, Mars has _____ _____ _____ _____ _____ houses and buildings _____ .

19 Third, the _____ of day and night on Mars _____ _____ _____ _____ on Earth.

20 _____ _____ , Mars also _____ _____ _____ .

21 So, people _____ _____ _____ _____ .

22 Lastly, Mars is _____ _____ _____ .

23 It is _____ _____ _____ _____ to Earth.

24 Mars, _____ , has _____ _____ _____ Earth.

25 First, Mars is _____ _____ the size of Earth.

26 It is _____ _____ _____ planet in the _____ system.

27 Second, a year on Mars is _____ _____ _____ _____ _____ a year on Earth.

28 Third, Mars is _____ _____ _____ Earth.

29 _____ _____ , it is _____ −60℃ on Mars.

30 This is _____ Mars is _____ _____ _____ the Sun than Earth.

31 _____ no one can _____ the big question _____ _____ , it is _____ _____ _____ this new world.

32 Who knows? You could be _____ _____ _____ Mars!

14 중요한 질문은 "화성에서 사람들이 살 수 있는가?"이다.

15 많은 과학자들은 몇몇 이유로 그렇게 믿고 있다.

16 첫째, 그들은 화성에 물이 있다고 생각한다.

17 물은 모든 생명체에 필수적이기 때문에 이것은 중요하다.

18 둘째, 화성은 집과 건물을 지을 수 있는 단단한 땅을 가지고 있다.

19 셋째, 화성의 낮과 밤의 길이는 지구의 낮과 밤의 길이와 비슷하다.

20 게다가, 화성은 사계절도 있다.

21 그래서 사람들이 비슷한 생활을 할 수 있다.

22 마지막으로, 화성은 그렇게 멀지 않다.

23 화성은 지구에서 두 번째로 가까운 행성이다.

24 그러나 화성은 지구와 다른 점이 몇 개 있다.

25 첫째, 화성은 지구의 약 절반 크기이다.

26 화성은 태양계에서 두 번째로 작은 행성이다.

27 둘째, 화성에서의 일 년은 지구에서의 일 년보다 약 두 배 길다.

28 셋째, 화성은 지구보다 훨씬 더 춥다.

29 평균적으로, 화성의 기온은 약 섭씨 영하 60도이다.

30 이것은 화성이 지구보다 태양에서 더 멀리 떨어져 있기 때문이다.

31 비록 누구도 그 중요한 질문에 지금 당장 답할 수는 없지만, 이 새로운 세상을 상상하는 것은 신이 난다.

32 누가 알겠는가? 당신이 화성에 발을 디디는 첫 번째 한국인이 될 수도 있다!

※ 다음 문장을 우리말로 쓰시오.

1 Live on MARS!

➡ _____

2 Do you want to live on another planet?

➡ _____

3 The Korea Space Organization (KSO) is looking for people to go to MARS!

➡ _____

4 Our mission is to build a city on Mars.

➡ _____

5 We are looking for someone... who is healthy. who is creative and curious.

who can get along with others. who can adapt to a new environment quickly.

➡ _____

_____

6 To apply, send us a short video.

➡ _____

7 The video must include the answers to the following questions:

➡ _____

8 1. Why do you want to go to Mars?

2. Do you have a good sense of humor?

3. Why are you the perfect person for this mission?

➡ 1. _____

2. _____

3. _____

9 This is a chance of a lifetime, so don't miss out!

➡ _____

10 Mars, the Second Earth?

➡ _____

11 Although there are many books and movies about Mars, no one has been there yet.

➡ _____

12 These days, scientists are looking at Mars as a new home.

➡ _____

13 In fact, NASA and some companies are trying to send people there right now.

➡ _____

14 The big question is, "Can people live on Mars?"

➡ _____

15 Many scientists believe so for several reasons.

➡ _____

16 First, they think that there is water on Mars.

➡ _____

17 This is great because water is necessary for all life.

➡ _____

18 Second, Mars has hard land to build houses and buildings on.

➡ _____

19 Third, the length of day and night on Mars is similar to that on Earth.

➡ _____

20 In addition, Mars also has four seasons.

➡ _____

21 So, people can lead similar lives.

➡ _____

22 Lastly, Mars is not very far.

➡ _____

23 It is the second closest planet to Earth.

➡ _____

24 Mars, however, has some differences from Earth.

➡ _____

25 First, Mars is about half the size of Earth.

➡ _____

26 It is the second smallest planet in the solar system.

➡ _____

27 Second, a year on Mars is about twice as long as a year on Earth.

➡ _____

28 Third, Mars is much colder than Earth.

➡ _____

29 On average, it is about −60°C on Mars.

➡ _____

30 This is because Mars is farther away from the Sun than Earth.

➡ _____

31 Although no one can answer the big question right now, it is exciting to imagine this new world.

➡ _____

32 Who knows? You could be the first Korean on Mars!

➡ _____

※ 다음 괄호 안의 단어들을 우리말에 맞도록 바르게 배열하시오.

1 (MARS / on / Live)
➡ _____

2 (want / you / do / live / to / planet? / another / on)
➡ _____

3 (Korea / The / Oraganization / Space / (KSO) / looking / is / for / MARS! / to / go / people / to)
➡ _____

4 (mission / our / to / is / a / build / Mars. / on / city)
➡ _____

5 (are / we / for / looking / someone... / is / who / healthy. // who / curious. / and / creative / is // can / who / with / get / others. / along // can / who / to / adapt / a / environment / new / quickly.)
➡ _____
_____

6 (apply, / to / us / send / video. / short / a)
➡ _____

7 (video / the / include / must / answers / the / to / following / the / questions:)
➡ _____

8 1. (do / why / want / you / go / to / Mars? / to)
2. (you / do / have / good / a / sense / humor? / of)
3. (are / why / the / you / person / perfect / mission? / this / for)
➡ 1. _____
2. _____
3. _____

9 (is / this / chance / a / of / lifetime, / a / don't / so / out! / miss)
➡ _____

10 (the / Mars, / Earth? / Second)
➡ _____

11 (there / although / many / are / books / and / about / movies / Mars, / one / no / been / has / yet. / there)
➡ _____
_____

12 (days / these / are / scientists / looking / at / as / Mars / home. / new / a)
➡ _____

13 (fact, / in / NASA / and / companies / some / trying / are / send / to / there / people / now. / right)
➡ _____
_____

1 화성에서 살아요!

2 다른 행성에서 살고 싶은가요?

3 한국 우주 기구(KSO)는 화성에 갈 사람들을 찾고 있습니다!

4 우리의 임무는 화성에 도시를 세우는 것입니다.

5 우리는 다음과 같은 사람을 찾고 있습니다.
건강한 사람.
창의적이고 호기심이 많은 사람.
다른 사람들과 잘 지낼 수 있는 사람.
새로운 환경에 빨리 적응할 수 있는 사람.

6 지원하려면 우리에게 짧은 동영상을 보내세요.

7 동영상은 다음의 질문에 관한 답을 포함해야 합니다.

8 1. 당신은 왜 화성에 가고 싶은가요?
2. 당신은 유머 감각이 있나요?
3. 왜 당신이 이 임무에 적합한 사람인가요?

9 이것은 일생에 단 한 번뿐인 기회이므로 놓치지 마세요!

10 화성, 제 2의 지구?

11 화성에 관한 많은 책과 영화가 있긴 하지만, 아직 화성에 가 본 사람은 아무도 없다.

12 요즘, 과학자들은 화성을 새로운 거주지로 보고 있다.

13 사실, NASA와 몇몇 회사들은 그곳에 사람들을 보내기 위해 바로 지금도 노력하고 있다.

14 (big / the / is, / question / people / "can / live / Mars?" / on)
➡ _____

15 (scientists / many / so / believe / for / reasons. / several)
➡ _____

16 (first, / think / they / there / that / water / is / Mars. / on)
➡ _____

17 (is / this / because / great / is / water / for / necessary / life. / all)
➡ _____

18 (second, / has / Mars / land / hard / build / to / houses / and / on. / buildings)
➡ _____

19 (the / third, / length / day / of / night / and / Mars / on / similar / is / that / to / Earth. / on)
➡ _____

20 (addition, / in / also / Mars / four / seasons. / has)
➡ _____

21 (people / so, / lead / can / lives. / similar)
➡ _____

22 (Mars / lastly, / not / is / far. / very)
➡ _____

23 (is / it / second / the / planet / closest / Earth. / to)
➡ _____

24 (however, / Mars, / some / has / differences / Earth. / from)
➡ _____

25 (Mars / first, / about / is / the / half / Earth. / of / size)
➡ _____

26 (is / it / second / the / planet / smallest / the / in / system. / solar)
➡ _____

27 (a / second, / year / Mars / on / about / is / as / twice / long / as / year / a / Earth. / on)
➡ _____

28 (Mars / third, / is / colder / much / Earth. / than)
➡ _____

29 (average, / on / is / it / about / on / –60°C / Mars.)
➡ _____

30 (is / this / Mars / because / farther / is / from / away / the / Earth. / than / Sun)
➡ _____

31 (no / although / one / answer / can / big / the / right / question / now, / is / it / to / exciting / this / imagine / world. / new)
➡ _____
_____

32 (knows? / who // could / you / the / be / Korean / first / Mars! / on)
➡ _____

14 중요한 질문은 "화성에서 사람들이 살 수 있는가?"이다.

15 많은 과학자들은 몇몇 이유로 그렇게 믿고 있다.

16 첫째, 그들은 화성에 물이 있다고 생각한다.

17 물은 모든 생명체에 필수적이기 때문에 이것은 중요하다.

18 둘째, 화성은 집과 건물을 지을 수 있는 단단한 땅을 가지고 있다.

19 셋째, 화성의 낮과 밤의 길이는 지구의 낮과 밤의 길이와 비슷하다.

20 게다가, 화성은 사계절도 있다.

21 그래서 사람들이 비슷한 생활을 할 수 있다.

22 마지막으로, 화성은 그렇게 멀지 않다.

23 화성은 지구에서 두 번째로 가까운 행성이다.

24 그러나 화성은 지구와 다른 점이 몇 개 있다.

25 첫째, 화성은 지구의 약 절반 크기이다.

26 화성은 태양계에서 두 번째로 작은 행성이다.

27 둘째, 화성에서의 일 년은 지구에서의 일 년보다 약 두 배 길다.

28 셋째, 화성은 지구보다 훨씬 더 춥다.

29 평균적으로, 화성의 기온은 약 섭씨 영하 60도이다.

30 이것은 화성이 지구보다 태양에서 더 멀리 떨어져 있기 때문이다.

31 비록 누구도 그 중요한 질문에 지금 당장 답할 수는 없지만, 이 새로운 세상을 상상하는 것은 신이 난다.

32 누가 알겠는가? 당신이 화성에 발을 디디는 첫 번째 한국인이 될 수도 있다!

※ **다음 우리말을 영어로 쓰시오.**

1 화성에서 살아요!

➡ _____

2 다른 행성에서 살고 싶은가요?

➡ _____

3 한국 우주 기구(KSO)는 화성에 갈 사람들을 찾고 있습니다!

➡ _____

4 우리의 임무는 화성에 도시를 세우는 것입니다.

➡ _____

5 우리는 다음과 같은 사람을 찾고 있습니다.
건강한 사람. 창의적이고 호기심이 많은 사람. 다른 사람들과 잘 지낼 수 있는 사람.
새로운 환경에 빨리 적응할 수 있는 사람.

➡ _____

_____

6 지원하려면 우리에게 짧은 동영상을 보내세요.

➡ _____

7 동영상은 다음의 질문에 관한 답을 포함해야 합니다.

➡ _____

8 1. 당신은 왜 화성에 가고 싶은가요?

2. 당신은 유머 감각이 있나요?

3. 왜 당신이 이 임무에 적합한 사람인가요?

➡ 1. _____

2. _____

3. _____

9 이것은 일생에 단 한 번뿐인 기회이므로 놓치지 마세요!

➡ _____

10 화성, 제 2의 지구?

➡ _____

11 화성에 관한 많은 책과 영화가 있긴 하지만, 아직 화성에 가 본 사람은 아무도 없다.

➡ _____

12 요즘, 과학자들은 화성을 새로운 거주지로 보고 있다.

➡ _____

13 사실, NASA와 몇몇 회사들은 그곳에 사람들을 보내기 위해 바로 지금도 노력하고 있다.

➡ _____

14 중요한 질문은 "화성에서 사람들이 살 수 있는가?"이다.
➡ _____

15 많은 과학자들은 몇몇 이유로 그렇게 믿고 있다.
➡ _____

16 첫째, 그들은 화성에 물이 있다고 생각한다.
➡ _____

17 물은 모든 생명체에 필수적이기 때문에 이것은 중요하다.
➡ _____

18 둘째, 화성은 집과 건물을 지을 수 있는 단단한 땅을 가지고 있다.
➡ _____

19 셋째, 화성의 낮과 밤의 길이는 지구의 낮과 밤의 길이와 비슷하다.
➡ _____

20 게다가, 화성은 사계절도 있다.
➡ _____

21 그래서 사람들이 비슷한 생활을 할 수 있다.
➡ _____

22 마지막으로, 화성은 그렇게 멀지 않다.
➡ _____

23 화성은 지구에서 두 번째로 가까운 행성이다.
➡ _____

24 그러나 화성은 지구와 다른 점이 몇 개 있다.
➡ _____

25 첫째, 화성은 지구의 약 절반 크기이다.
➡ _____

26 화성은 태양계에서 두 번째로 작은 행성이다.
➡ _____

27 둘째, 화성에서의 일 년은 지구에서의 일 년보다 약 두 배 길다.
➡ _____

28 셋째, 화성은 지구보다 훨씬 더 춥다.
➡ _____

29 평균적으로, 화성의 기온은 약 섭씨 영하 60도이다.
➡ _____

30 이것은 화성이 지구보다 태양에서 더 멀리 떨어져 있기 때문이다.
➡ _____

31 비록 누구도 그 중요한 질문에 지금 당장 답할 수는 없지만, 이 새로운 세상을 상상하는 것은 신이 난다.
➡ _____

32 누가 알겠는가? 당신이 화성에 발을 디디는 첫 번째 한국인이 될 수도 있다!
➡ _____

※ 다음 우리말과 일치하도록 빈칸에 알맞은 말을 쓰시오.

Real Life Talk - Step 2

1. A: Do you know _____ _____ _____?

2. B: _____, I _____. _____ is _____?

3. A: It's a _____ _____.

4. B: A Clean Straw? _____ _____ _____ _____?

5. A: It cleans water _____ _____ _____.

6. B: Wow, _____ _____!

1. A: 너는 이것이 무엇인지 아니?
2. B: 아니. 그게 뭐니?
3. A: Clean Straw야.
4. B: Clean Straw? 용도가 뭐니?
5. A: 네가 물을 마시는 동안 물을 깨끗이 해주는 거야.
6. B: 와, 멋지다!

Think and Write

1. My name is Suji Lee _____ _____. I'm 15 _____ _____.

2. I _____ _____ go to Mars _____ I've _____ _____ _____ space.

3. I'm _____ and I _____ _____ _____.

4. I'm _____ _____ _____ photos.

5. I'm the _____ _____ for this mission because I can _____ to a _____ _____ quickly.

6. _____ I'm young, I can _____ _____ _____ _____.

7. Give me _____ _____ _____ _____ on Mars!

1. 제 이름은 수지이고 한국 출신입니다. 저는 15살입니다.
2. 저는 쭉 우주에 호기심을 가져왔기 때문에 화성에 가고 싶습니다.
3. 저는 상냥하고 친구들을 사귀는 것을 좋아합니다.
4. 저는 사진을 잘 찍습니다.
5. 저는 새로운 환경에 빨리 적응할 수 있기 때문에 이 임무에 적합한 사람입니다.
6. 비록 저는 어리지만, 다른 사람들과 의사소통을 잘할 수 있습니다.
7. 저에게 화성에서 살 기회를 주세요!

Project

1. _____

2. It has 14 _____. It's a very _____ _____.

3. It's _____ _____ the _____ _____ _____ _____.

4. It's _____ _____ _____ from the Sun in _____ _____ _____.

1. 해왕성
2 그것은 14개의 위성을 가지고 있다. 그곳은 아주 추운 행성이다.
3 그것은 바다의 신의 이름을 딴 것이다.
4 그것은 태양계에서 태양과 가장 멀리 떨어져 있다.

※ 다음 우리말을 영어로 쓰시오.

Real Life Talk - Step 2

1. A: 너는 이것이 무엇인지 아니?
   ➡ _____

2. B: 아니. 뭐니?
   ➡ _____

3. A: Clean Straw야.
   ➡ _____

4. B: Clean Straw? 용도가 뭐니?
   ➡ _____

5. A: 네가 물을 마시는 동안 물을 깨끗이 해주는 거야.
   ➡ _____

6. B: 와, 멋지다!
   ➡ _____

Think and Write

1. 제 이름은 수지이고 한국 출신입니다. 저는 15살입니다.
   ➡ _____

2. 저는 쭉 우주에 호기심을 가져왔기 때문에 화성에 가고 싶습니다.
   ➡ _____

3. 저는 상냥하고 친구들을 사귀는 것을 좋아합니다.
   ➡ _____

4. 저는 사진을 잘 찍습니다.
   ➡ _____

5. 저는 새로운 환경에 빨리 적응할 수 있기 때문에 이 임무에 적합한 사람입니다.
   ➡ _____

6. 비록 저는 어리지만, 다른 사람들과 의사소통을 잘할 수 있습니다.
   ➡ _____

7. 저에게 화성에서 살 기회를 주세요!
   ➡ _____

Project

1. 해왕성
   ➡ _____

2. 그것은 14개의 위성을 가지고 있다. 그곳은 아주 추운 행성이다.
   ➡ _____

3. 그것은 바다의 신의 이름을 딴 것이다.
   ➡ _____

4. 그것은 태양계에서 태양과 가장 멀리 떨어져 있다.
   ➡ _____

※ 다음 영어를 우리말로 쓰시오.

01	author	
02	backpack	
03	perfect	
04	connection	
05	trip	
06	award	
07	difference	
08	mix	
09	trust	
10	adventure	
11	traditional	
12	explain	
13	simple	
14	friendship	
15	especially	
16	unlike	
17	truth	
18	lie	
19	advertisement	
20	worth	
21	fantasy	

22	belief	
23	strongly	
24	lift	
25	wisely	
26	meal	
27	prove	
28	express	
29	solve	
30	navy	
31	recommend	
32	boring	
33	touching	
34	opinion	
35	for example	
36	full of	
37	based on	
38	from now on	
39	hold on	
40	make a choice	
41	right now	
42	check out	
43	worth it	

단어 Test

※ 다음 우리말을 영어로 쓰시오.

01	믿다, 신뢰하다	_____
02	작가	_____
03	완벽한	_____
04	감동적인	_____
05	나타내다, 표현하다	_____
06	지루한	_____
07	여행	_____
08	남색	_____
09	모험	_____
10	보라색, 자색	_____
11	소설	_____
12	의견	_____
13	광고	_____
14	주머니	_____
15	간단한, 단순한	_____
16	상	_____
17	가치가 있는	_____
18	특히	_____
19	식사	_____
20	우정	_____
21	강력하게	_____

22	들어 올리다	_____
23	해결하다, 풀다	_____
24	증명하다	_____
25	설명하다	_____
26	전통적인	_____
27	차이점	_____
28	섞다	_____
29	공상	_____
30	추천하다	_____
31	신념, 생각	_____
32	~와 달리	_____
33	현명하게	_____
34	진실, 사실	_____
35	~을 확인하다	_____
36	~을 찾다	_____
37	지금부터	_____
38	선택하다	_____
39	예를 들면	_____
40	~로 가득한	_____
41	~을 바탕으로	_____
42	지금	_____
43	기다려, 멈춰	_____

※ 다음 영영풀이에 알맞은 단어를 <보기>에서 골라 쓴 후, 우리말 뜻을 쓰시오.

1 _____ : to believe that something is true: _____

2 _____ : ideas or feelings about something: _____

3 _____ : to add something to something else: _____

4 _____ : to move something to a higher position: _____

5 _____ : the real facts about something: _____

6 _____ : the foods eaten or prepared at one time: _____

7 _____ : to show what you think or feel: _____

8 _____ : to say or write something that is not true: _____

9 _____ : a small bag that is attached to something: _____

10 _____ : to tell someone that something is good or useful: _____

11 _____ : a notice, picture or short film telling people about something:
_____

12 _____ : the way in which two things are related to each other: _____

13 _____ : to tell somebody about something in a way that is easy to understand:
_____

14 _____ : to use facts, evidence, etc. to show that something is true: _____

15 _____ : a prize such as money, etc. for something that somebody has done:
_____

16 _____ : a large area of land that has very little water and very few plants growing
on it: _____

보기			
award	explain	advertisement	lie
mix	opinion	desert	express
prove	connection	pocket	recommend
trust	lift	meal	truth

Step1

※ 다음 우리말과 일치하도록 빈칸에 알맞은 말을 쓰시오.

Listen & Speak 1-A

Brian: Can you _____ _____ _____ _____ ?

Emily: Try *Star Wars*. I _____ _____ it.

Brian: Oh, I _____ _____ it _____ .

Emily: It's the _____ _____ movie _____ _____ .

Brian: 좋은 영화를 추천해 줄래?
Emily: 'Star Wars'를 봐. 정말 좋았어.
Brian: 오, 나는 아직 그 영화를 본 적이 없어.
Emily: 지금 1위 영화야.

Listen & Speak 1-B

W: May I _____ you?

B: Yes. I'm _____ _____ a _____ . Can you _____ _____ ?

W: _____ _____ this red one? Red is _____ _____ _____
_____ _____ _____ .

B: _____ _____ _____ was red, so I want a _____ _____ .

W: _____ _____ this _____ one? It _____ _____ _____ .

B: Oh, that _____ _____ . I'll _____ it.

W: 도와드릴까요?
B: 네. 배낭을 찾고 있어요. 하나 추천해 주시겠어요?
W: 이 빨간 배낭은 어떤가요? 빨간색은 요즘 가장 인기 있는 색이에요.
B: 제 옛 배낭이 빨간색이어서 다른 색을 원해요.
W: 이 남색 배낭은 어떤가요? 양옆에 주머니가 있어요.
B: 오, 좋아 보여요. 그걸로 살게요.

Listen & Speak 2-A

Sue: Tom, you _____ a _____ _____ .

Tom: Yes, I did. I'm _____ _____ _____ it.

Sue: _____ do you _____ _____ _____ ?

Tom: I love the camera. It _____ _____ _____ .

Sue: Tom, 새 스마트폰을 샀구나.
Tom: 응, 그래. 나는 정말 만족스러워.
Sue: 무엇이 가장 마음에 드니?
Tom: 카메라가 정말 좋아. 멋진 사진을 찍어.

Listen & Speak 2-B

Jack: Hi, Suji. _____ _____ you _____ your _____ to Gyeongju?

Suji: I was very _____ _____ it.

Jack: _____ did you _____?

Suji: I _____ Cheomseongdae. It was great.

Jack: _____ _____ _____ you _____?

Suji: Bulguksa. It was a _____ _____.

Jack: _____ _____ the _____ _____.

Suji: Yeah, but _____ _____ to Seokguram _____ _____.

Jack: But _____ _____ it was _____ _____.

Jack: 안녕, 수지야. 경주 여행은 어땠니?
Suij: 매우 즐거웠어.
Jack: 어디를 방문했니?
Suij: 첨성대를 방문했어. 좋았어.
Jack: 또 어디를 방문했니?
Suij: 불국사. 멋진 곳이었어.
Jack: 완벽한 여행이었던 것 같네.
Suij: 응, 하지만 석굴암까지 걸어 올라가는 것은 힘들었어.
Jack: 하지만 그것이 그만한 가치가 있었을 것이라고 확신해.

Real Life Talk – Step 1

Brian: Mina, _____ _____ _____ _____ a good pizza restaurant?

Mina: _____ _____ you try Antonio's? It's _____ _____.

Brian: _____ do you _____ _____ it?

Mina: The food is _____. I _____ the bulgogi pizza.

Brian: _____ are _____ _____?

Mina: I _____ the prices are good, _____.

Brian: _____ _____ a good restaurant. _____ do you _____ _____ _____?

Mina: It's a _____ _____ on the weekends.

Brian: Okay. I'll _____ _____ _____. Thanks.

Mina: No _____. _____ your meal!

Brian: 미나야, 괜찮은 피자 식당을 추천해 줄래?
Mina: Antonio's에 가 보는 게 어때? 내가 가장 좋아하는 곳이야.
Brian: 무엇이 좋은데?
Mina: 음식이 맛있어. 나는 불고기 피자를 추천해.
Brian: 가격은 어때?
Mina: 가격도 괜찮다고 생각해.
Brian: 괜찮은 식당 같네. 서비스는 어때?
Mina: 주말에는 좀 느려.
Brian: 알겠어. 내가 확인해 볼게. 고마워.
Mina: 천만에. 맛있게 먹어!

Real Life Talk – Step 2

Amy: Yujin, can you _____ _____ _____ _____ _____?

Yujin: _____ _____ The Little Prince?

Amy: _____ _____ _____ _____ about the book?

Yujin: I like the _____ _____. He is very _____.

Amy: _____ good. I'll _____ it.

Amy: Yujin아, 내게 책을 추천해 줄래?
Yujin: '어린 왕자' 어때?
Amy: 책의 무엇이 마음에 드니?
Yujin: 나는 주인공이 마음에 들어. 그는 매우 특별해.
Amy: 좋은 책 같네. 내가 읽어 볼게.

※ 다음 우리말에 맞도록 대화를 영어로 쓰시오.

Listen & Speak 1-A

Brian: _____

Emily: _____

Brian: _____

Emily: _____

Brian: 좋은 영화를 추천해 줄래?
Emily: 'Star Wars'를 봐. 정말 좋았어.
Brian: 오, 나는 아직 그 영화를 본 적이
없어.
Emily: 지금 1위 영화야.

Listen & Speak 1-B

W: _____

B: _____

W: _____

B: _____

W: _____

B: _____

W: 도와드릴까요?
B: 네. 배낭을 찾고 있어요. 하나 추천해
주시겠어요?
W: 이 빨간 배낭은 어떤가요? 빨간색은
요즘 가장 인기 있는 색이에요.
B: 제 옛 배낭이 빨간색이어서 다른 색을
원해요.
W: 이 남색 배낭은 어떤가요? 양옆에 주
머니가 있어요.
B: 오, 좋아 보여요. 그걸로 살게요.

Listen & Speak 2-A

Sue: _____

Tom: _____

Sue: _____

Tom: _____

Sue: Tom, 새 스마트폰을 샀구나.
Tom: 응, 그래. 나는 정말 만족스러워.
Sue: 무엇이 가장 마음에 드니?
Tom: 카메라가 정말 좋아. 멋진 사진을
찍어.

Listen & Speak 2-B

Jack: _____

Suji: _____

Jack: _____

Suji: _____

Jack: _____

Suji: _____

Jack: _____

Suji: _____

Jack: _____

Jack: 안녕, 수지야. 경주 여행은 어땠니?

Suij: 매우 즐거웠어.

Jack: 어디를 방문했니?

Suij: 첨성대를 방문했어. 좋았어.

Jack: 또 어디를 방문했니?

Suij: 불국사. 멋진 곳이었어.

Jack: 완벽한 여행이었던 것 같네.

Suij: 응, 하지만 석굴암까지 걸어 올라 가는 것은 힘들었어.

Jack: 하지만 그것이 그만한 가치가 있었을 것이라고 확신해.

Real Life Talk – Step 1

Brian: _____

Mina: _____

Brian: _____

Mina: _____

Brian: _____

Mina: _____

Brian: _____

Mina: _____

Brian: _____

Mina: _____

Brian: 미나야, 괜찮은 피자 식당을 추천해 줄래?

Mina: Antonio's에 가 보는 게 어때? 내가 가장 좋아하는 곳이야.

Brian: 무엇이 좋은데?

Mina: 음식이 맛있어. 나는 불고기 피자를 추천해.

Brian: 가격은 어때?

Mina: 가격도 괜찮다고 생각해.

Brian: 괜찮은 식당 같네. 서비스는 어때?

Mina: 주말에는 좀 느려.

Brian: 알겠어. 내가 확인해 볼게. 고마워.

Mina: 천만에. 맛있게 먹어!

Real Life Talk – Step 2

Amy: _____

Yujin: _____

Amy: _____

Yujin: _____

Amy: _____

Amy: Yujin아, 내게 책을 추천해 줄래?

Yujin: '어린 왕자' 어때?

Amy: 책의 무엇이 마음에 드니?

Yujin: 나는 주인공이 마음에 들어. 그는 매우 특별해.

Amy: 좋은 책 같네. 내가 읽어 볼게.

※ 다음 우리말과 일치하도록 빈칸에 알맞은 것을 골라 쓰시오.

1 Emma: What _____ you _____, Kyle?
    A. doing   B. are

2 Kyle: Oh, Emma. I'm _____ the movie, *Y-Men 7* _____ my _____.
    A. on   B. watching   C. computer

3 Emma: _____ is _____?
    A. it   B. how

4 Kyle: _____ ask. It's _____ _____ _____ I want to cry.
    A. so   B. don't   C. that   D. boring

5 Emma: I'm _____ _____ _____ that.
    A. to   B. sorry   C. hear

6 Kyle: I'm so _____. The movie _____ _____ it was "The Most Exciting Movie of the Year."
    A. advertisement   B. mad   C. said

7 Emma: Well, you can't _____ _____ _____ you _____.
    A. that   B. believe   C. everything   D. read

8 Kyle: They _____ _____ the advertisement. I'm going to ask _____ my money _____.
    A. for   B. on   C. back   D. lied

9 Emma: _____ on, Kyle! They didn't really _____ they used _____, not facts.
    A. hold   B. because   C. lie   D. opinions

10 Kyle: Huh? I'm _____ _____ _____.
    A. you   B. following   C. not

11 Emma: Opinions _____ people's _____ _____, "The desert is beautiful."
    A. like   B. express   C. feelings

12 You can't say _____ it's true or _____. But, _____ can be _____.
    A. not   B. that   C. proven   D. facts

13 _____ _____, "The Atacama Desert is in Chile," is a fact. You can _____ that _____ the map.
    A. on   B. check   C. example   D. for

14 Kyle: Okay…. But what's _____ _____ _____ movies?
    A. with   B. connection   C. the

15 Emma: _____ me _____. What's your _____ movie?
    A. explain   B. favorite   C. let

1 Emma: Kyle, 뭐 하고 있니?

2 Kyle: Emma. 나는 컴퓨터로 영화 "Y-Men 7"을 보고 있어.

3 Emma: 어때?

4 Kyle: 묻지 마. 너무 지루해서 울고 싶어.

5 Emma: 유감이야.

6 Klye: 난 정말 화가 나. 영화 광고에는 이것이 "올해의 가장 흥미진진한 영화"라고 쓰여 있었어.

7 Emma: 음, 넌 네가 읽는 것을 모두 믿을 수는 없어.

8 Kyle: 그들은 광고에 거짓말을 한 거야. 돈을 환불해 달라고 해야겠어.

9 Emma: 기다려, Kyle! 그들은 사실이 아닌 의견을 사용했기 때문에 꼭 거짓말을 한 것은 아니야.

10 Kyle: 뭐라고? 네 말을 이해하지 못하겠어.

11 Emma: 의견은 "사막은 아름다워."와 같이 사람들의 감정을 표현하는 것이야.

12 그것이 사실인지 아닌지 말할 수는 없어. 하지만 사실은 증명할 수 있어.

13 예를 들면, "아타카마 사막은 칠레에 있다."는 사실이야. 넌 그것을 지도에서 확인할 수 있어.

14 Kyle: 알겠어… 하지만 그게 영화와 무슨 관련이 있니?

15 Emma: 설명해 줄게. 네가 가장 좋아하는 영화가 뭐니?

16 Kyle: _____ *Forrest* _____.

A. *Gump*   B. it's

17 Emma: Okay. _____ look for _____ _____. What does it _____?

A. say   B. its   C. let's   D. advertisement

18 Kyle: It _____, "Winner of 6 Academy _____ _____ Best Picture."

A. says   B. including   C. Awards

19 Emma: See? It _____ _____ _____ the *Y-Men 7* advertisement.

A. unlike   B. uses   C. facts

20 _____ you _____ the _____?

A. see   B. difference   C. do

21 Kyle: Not _____. The *Y-Men 7* ad _____ "Most Exciting Movie" and the *Forrest Gump* _____ says "Best Picture."

A. says   B. ad   C. exactly

22 _____ they _____ _____?

A. opinions   B. aren't   C. both

23 Emma: That's a great _____, Kyle. When people use words _____ "best" or "most," they are usually _____ _____.

A. like   B. expressing   C. question   D. opinions

24 But in the *Forrest Gump* _____, "Best Picture" is the _____ which the _____ _____.

A. award   B. movie   C. ad   D. won

25 We can _____ that _____ the Internet. That's a _____.

A. fact   B. on   C. check

26 Kyle: Aha! _____ now _____ I'm only going to _____ ads _____ facts.

A. with   B. from   C. trust   D. on

27 Emma: It's not _____ _____. Most ads _____ facts _____ opinions.

A. with   B. mix   C. simple   D. that

28 So you _____ to _____ a smart _____ based on _____ of them.

A. both   B. choice   C. make   D. have

29 Kyle: _____ it! Emma, do you want to _____ the _____ of *Y-Men 7* _____ me?

A. rest   B. watch   C. with   D. got

30 Emma: Thanks, but _____ _____. Enjoy the _____ of the movie!

A. rest   B. thanks   C. no

16 Kyle: "Forest Gump"야.

17 Emma: 좋아. 그 영화의 광고를 찾아보자. 뭐라고 쓰여 있니?

18 Kyle: "Best Picture를 포함하여 아카데미 6개 부문 수상작"이라고 쓰여 있어.

19 Emma: 알겠니? "Y-Men 7" 광고와는 달리 사실을 사용하고 있어.

20 차이를 알겠니?

21 Kyle: 잘 모르겠어. "Y-Men 7" 광고는 "Most Exciting Movie"라고 쓰여 있고 "Forest Gump" 광고는 "Best Picture"라고 쓰여 있잖아.

22 둘 다 의견 아니니?

23 Emma: 좋은 질문이야, Kyle. 사람들이 'best'나 'most'와 같은 말을 사용할 때, 그들은 대개 의견을 표현하는 거야.

24 하지만 "Forest Gump" 광고에서 "Best Picture"는 영화가 받은 상이야.

25 우리는 인터넷에서 그것을 확인할 수 있어. 그건 사실이야.

26 Kyle: 아하! 지금부터 사실로 이루어진 광고만 믿겠어.

27 Emma: 그렇게 간단하지는 않아. 대부분의 광고는 사실과 의견이 섞여 있어.

28 그러니 그 둘을 바탕으로 현명한 선택을 해야 해.

29 Kyle: 알겠어! Emma, "Y-Men 7"의 남은 부분을 나와 함께 볼래?

30 Emma: 고맙지만 사양할게. 영화의 남은 부분 잘 봐!

※ 다음 우리말과 일치하도록 빈칸에 알맞은 말을 쓰시오.

1 Emma: _____ _____ you _____, Kyle?

2 Kyle: Oh, Emma. I'm _____ _____ _____, *Y-Men 7* _____ my computer.

3 Emma: _____ is _____?

4 Kyle: _____ ask. It's _____ _____ _____ I want _____ _____.

5 Emma: I'm _____ _____ _____ _____ _____.

6 Kyle: I'm so _____. The movie _____ said _____ was "_____ _____ _____ _____ of the Year."

7 Emma: Well, you _____ _____ _____ _____ _____ _____ _____.

8 Kyle: They _____ _____ the advertisement. I'm going to _____ _____ _____ _____ _____.

9 Emma: _____ _____, Kyle! They didn't really _____ _____ they _____ _____, not _____.

10 Kyle: Huh? I'm _____ _____ _____.

11 Emma: Opinions _____ _____ _____ like, "The desert is beautiful."

12 You can't say _____ it's _____ _____ _____. But, facts _____ _____ _____.

13 _____ _____, "The Atacama Desert is in Chile," is a fact. You can _____ _____ _____ _____ _____.

14 Kyle: Okay…. But what's _____ _____ _____ movies?

15 Emma: _____ _____ _____. What's your favorite movie?

---

1 Emma: Kyle, 뭐 하고 있니?

2 Kyle: Emma. 나는 컴퓨터로 영화 "Y-Men 7"을 보고 있어.

3 Emma: 어때?

4 Kyle: 묻지 마. 너무 지루해서 울고 싶어.

5 Emma: 유감이야.

6 Klye: 난 정말 화가 나. 영화 광고에는 이것이 "올해의 가장 흥미진진한 영화"라고 쓰여 있었어.

7 Emma: 음, 넌 네가 읽는 것을 모두 믿을 수는 없어.

8 Kyle: 그들은 광고에 거짓말을 한 거야. 돈을 환불해 달라고 해야겠어.

9 Emma: 기다려, Kyle! 그들은 사실이 아닌 의견을 사용했기 때문에 꼭 거짓말을 한 것은 아니야.

10 Kyle: 뭐라고? 네 말을 이해하지 못하겠어.

11 Emma: 의견은 "사막은 아름다워."와 같이 사람들의 감정을 표현하는 것이야.

12 그것이 사실인지 아닌지 말할 수는 없어. 하지만 사실은 증명할 수 있어.

13 예를 들면, "아타카마 사막은 칠레에 있다."는 사실이야. 넌 그것을 지도에서 확인할 수 있어.

14 Kyle: 알겠어… 하지만 그게 영화와 무슨 관련이 있니?

15 Emma: 설명해 줄게. 네가 가장 좋아하는 영화가 뭐니?

16 Kyle: _____ *Forrest Gump*.

17 Emma: Okay. _____ _____ _____ _____ _____. What does it say?

18 Kyle: _____ _____, "Winner of 6 Academy Awards _____ Best Picture."

19 Emma: See? It _____ _____ _____ the *Y-Men 7* advertisement.

20 Do you see _____ _____?

21 Kyle: Not _____. The *Y-Men 7* ad _____ "Most Exciting Movie" and the *Forrest Gump* ad _____ "Best Picture."

22 _____ they _____ _____?

23 Emma: That's a great question, Kyle. When people use _____ _____ "best" or "most," they are _____ _____ _____.

24 But in the *Forrest Gump* ad, "Best Picture" is the _____ _____ _____ _____ _____.

25 We can _____ _____ _____ _____ _____. That's a fact.

26 Kyle: Aha! _____ _____ _____ I'm only going to _____ ads _____ facts.

27 Emma: It's not _____ _____. Most ads _____ _____ _____ _____.

28 So you have to _____ _____ _____ _____ of them.

29 Kyle: Got it! Emma, do you want _____ _____ _____ of *Y-Men 7* with me?

30 Emma: Thanks, but _____ _____. Enjoy _____ _____ the movie!

---

16 Kyle: "Forest Gump"야.

17 Emma: 좋아. 그 영화의 광고를 찾아보자. 뭐라고 쓰여 있니?

18 Kyle: "Best Picture를 포함하여 아카데미 6개 부문 수상작"이라고 쓰여 있어.

19 Emma: 알겠니? "Y-Men 7" 광고와는 달리 사실을 사용하고 있어.

20 차이를 알겠니?

21 Kyle: 잘 모르겠어. "Y-Men 7" 광고는 "Most Exciting Movie" 라고 쓰여 있고 "Forest Gump" 광고는 "Best Picture"라고 쓰여 있잖아.

22 둘 다 의견 아니니?

23 Emma: 좋은 질문이야, Kyle. 사람들이 'best'나 'most'와 같은 말을 사용할 때, 그들은 대개 의견을 표현하는 거야.

24 하지만 "Forest Gump" 광고에서 "Best Picture"는 영화가 받은 상이야.

25 우리는 인터넷에서 그것을 확인할 수 있어. 그건 사실이야.

26 Kyle: 아하! 지금부터 사실로 이루어진 광고만 믿겠어.

27 Emma: 그렇게 간단하지는 않아. 대부분의 광고는 사실과 의견이 섞여 있어.

28 그러니 그 둘을 바탕으로 현명한 선택을 해야 해.

29 Kyle: 알겠어! Emma, "Y-Men 7"의 남은 부분을 나와 함께 볼래?

30 Emma: 고맙지만 사양할게. 영화의 남은 부분 잘 봐!

※ 다음 문장을 우리말로 쓰시오.

1 Emma: What are you doing, Kyle?

➡ _____

2 Kyle: Oh, Emma. I'm watching the movie, *Y-Men 7* on my computer.

➡ _____

3 Emma: How is it?

➡ _____

4 Kyle: Don't ask. It's so boring that I want to cry.

➡ _____

5 Emma: I'm sorry to hear that.

➡ _____

6 Kyle: I'm so mad. The movie advertisement said it was "The Most Exciting Movie of the Year."

➡ _____

7 Emma: Well, you can't believe everything that you read.

➡ _____

8 Kyle: They lied on the advertisement. I'm going to ask for my money back.

➡ _____

9 Emma: Hold on, Kyle! They didn't really lie because they used opinions, not facts.

➡ _____

10 Kyle: Huh? I'm not following you.

➡ _____

11 Emma: Opinions express people's feelings like, "The desert is beautiful."

➡ _____

12 You can't say that it's true or not. But, facts can be proven.

➡ _____

13 For example, "The Atacama Desert is in Chile," is a fact. You can check that on the map.

➡ _____

14 Kyle: Okay.... But what's the connection with movies?

➡ _____

15 Emma: Let me explain. What's your favorite movie?

➡ _____

16 Kyle: It's *Forrest Gump*.

➡ _____

17 Emma: Okay. Let's look for its advertisement. What does it say?

➡ _____

18 Kyle: It says, "Winner of 6 Academy Awards including Best Picture."

➡ _____

19 Emma: See? It uses facts unlike the *Y-Men 7* advertisement.

➡ _____

20 Do you see the difference?

➡ _____

21 Kyle: Not exactly. The *Y-Men 7* ad says "Most Exciting Movie" and the *Forrest Gump* ad says "Best Picture."

➡ _____

_____

22 Aren't they both opinions?

➡ _____

23 Emma: That's a great question, Kyle. When people use words like "best" or "most," they are usually expressing opinions.

➡ _____

24 But in the *Forrest Gump* ad, "Best Picture" is the award which the movie won.

➡ _____

25 We can check that on the Internet. That's a fact.

➡ _____

26 Kyle: Aha! From now on I'm only going to trust ads with facts.

➡ _____

27 Emma: It's not that simple. Most ads mix facts with opinions.

➡ _____

28 So you have to make a smart choice based on both of them.

➡ _____

29 Kyle: Got it! Emma, do you want to watch the rest of *Y-Men 7* with me?

➡ _____

30 Emma: Thanks, but no thanks. Enjoy the rest of the movie!

➡ _____

※ 다음 괄호 안의 단어들을 우리말에 맞도록 바르게 배열하시오.

1 (Emma: / are / what / doing, / you / Kyle?)
➡ _____

2 (Kyle: / Emma. / oh, // watching / I'm / movie, / the / on / 7 / *Y-Men* / computer. / my)
➡ _____

3 (Emma: / is / it? / how)
➡ _____

4 (Kyle: / ask. / don't // so / it's / that / boring / cry. / to / want / I)
➡ _____

5 (Emma: / sorry / I'm / that. / hear / to)
➡ _____

6 (Klye: / so / mad. / I'm // movie / the / advertisement / it / said / was / Most / "The / Movie / Exciting / of / Year." / the)
➡ _____

7 (Emma: / well, / can't / you / everything / believe / that / read. / you)
➡ _____

8 (Kyle: / lied / they / the / on / advertisement. // going / I'm / ask / to / my / for / back. / money)
➡ _____

9 (Emma: / on, / hold / Kyle! // didn't / they / lie / really / they / because / used / opinions, / facts. / not)
➡ _____

10 (Kyle: / huh? // not / I'm / you. / following)
➡ _____

11 (Emma: / express / opinions / feelings / people's / like, / desert / "the / beautiful." / is)
➡ _____

12 (can't / you / say / it's / that / or / true / not. // but, / can / proven. / be / facts)
➡ _____

13 (example, / for / "The / Desert / Atacama / in / is / Chile," / fact. / a / is // can / you / that / check / map. / the / on)
➡ _____

14 (Kyle: / okay / ..... / what's / but / connection / the / movies? / with)
➡ _____

15 (Emma: / me / let / explain. // your / what's / movie? / favorite)
➡ _____

---

1 Emma: Kyle, 뭐 하고 있니?

2 Kyle: Emma. 나는 컴퓨터로 영화 "Y-Men 7"을 보고 있어.

3 Emma: 어때?

4 Kyle: 묻지 마. 너무 지루해서 울고 싶어.

5 Emma: 유감이야.

6 Klye: 난 정말 화가 나. 영화 광고에는 이것이 "올해의 가장 흥미진진한 영화"라고 쓰여 있었어.

7 Emma: 음, 넌 네가 읽는 것을 모두 믿을 수는 없어.

8 Kyle: 그들은 광고에 거짓말을 한 거야. 돈을 환불해 달라고 해야겠어.

9 Emma: 기다려, Kyle! 그들은 사실이 아닌 의견을 사용했기 때문에 꼭 거짓말을 한 것은 아니야.

10 Kyle: 뭐라고? 네 말을 이해하지 못하겠어.

11 Emma: 의견은 "사막은 아름다워."와 같이 사람들의 감정을 표현하는 것이야.

12 그것이 사실인지 아닌지 말할 수는 없어. 하지만 사실은 증명할 수 있어.

13 예를 들면, "아타카마 사막은 칠레에 있다."는 사실이야. 넌 그것을 지도에서 확인할 수 있어.

14 Kyle: 알겠어… 하지만 그게 영화와 무슨 관련이 있니?

15 Emma: 설명해 줄게. 네가 가장 좋아하는 영화가 뭐니?

16 (Kyle: / *Forrest* / it's / *Gump*.)
➡ _____

17 (Emma: / okay. / look / let's / for / advertisement. / its // say? / what / it / does)
➡ _____

18 (Kyle: / says, / it / "winner / 6 / of / Awards / Academy / Best / Picture." / including)
➡ _____

19 (Emma: / see? // uses / it / unlike / facts / the / advertisement. / 7 / *Y-Men*)
➡ _____

20 (you / do / see / difference? / the)
➡ _____

21 (Kyle: / exactly. / not // *Y-Men 7* / the / says / ad / "Most Exciting Movie" / and / says / the / "Best Picture." / *Forrest Gump* / ad)
➡ _____

22 (they / aren't / opinions? / both)
➡ _____

23 (Emma: / a / questions, / that's / Kyle. // people / when / words / use / "most," / or / "best" / like / are / they / usually / opinions. / expressing)
➡ _____

24 (in / but / *Forrest Gump* / the / ad, / "Best Picture" / the / is / which / award / won. / movie / the)
➡ _____

25 (can / we / that / check / the / on / Internet. // fact. / a / that's)
➡ _____

26 (Kyle: / aha! // now / from / on / only / I'm / to / going / trust / facts. / with / ads)
➡ _____

27 (Emma: / not / it's / simple. / that // ads / most / facts / mix / opinions. / with)
➡ _____

28 (you / so / to / have / make / smart / a / based / choice / both / on / them. / of)
➡ _____

29 (Kyle: / it! / got / Emma, / you / do / want / watch / to / rest / the / *Y-Men 7* / of / me? / with)
➡ _____

30 (Emma: / but / thanks, / thanks. / no // the / enjoy / rest / movie! / of / the)
➡ _____

16 Kyle: "Forest Gump"야.

17 Emma: 좋아. 그 영화의 광고를 찾아보자. 뭐라고 쓰여 있니?

18 Kyle: "Best Picture를 포함하여 아카데미 6개 부문 수상작"이라고 쓰여 있어.

19 Emma: 알겠니? "Y-Men 7" 광고와는 달리 사실을 사용하고 있어.

20 차이를 알겠니?

21 Kyle: 잘 모르겠어. "Y-Men 7" 광고는 "Most Exciting Movie"라고 쓰여 있고 "Forest Gump" 광고는 "Best Picture"라고 쓰여 있잖아.

22 둘 다 의견 아니니?

23 Emma: 좋은 질문이야, Kyle. 사람들이 'best'나 'most'와 같은 말을 사용할 때, 그들은 대개 의견을 표현하는 거야.

24 하지만 "Forest Gump" 광고에서 "Best Picture"는 영화가 받은 상이야.

25 우리는 인터넷에서 그것을 확인할 수 있어. 그건 사실이야.

26 Kyle: 아하! 지금부터 사실로 이루어진 광고만 믿겠어.

27 Emma: 그렇게 간단하지는 않아. 대부분의 광고는 사실과 의견이 섞여 있어.

28 그러니 그 둘을 바탕으로 현명한 선택을 해야 해.

29 Kyle: 알겠어! Emma, "Y-Men 7"의 남은 부분을 나와 함께 볼래?

30 Emma: 고맙지만 사양할게. 영화의 남은 부분 잘 봐!

※ 다음 우리말을 영어로 쓰시오.

1 Emma: Kyle, 뭐 하고 있니?

➡ _____

2 Kyle: Emma. 나는 컴퓨터로 영화 "Y-Men 7"을 보고 있어.

➡ _____

3 Emma: 어때?

➡ _____

4 Kyle: 묻지 마. 너무 지루해서 울고 싶어.

➡ _____

5 Emma: 유감이야.

➡ _____

6 Klye: 난 정말 화가 나. 영화 광고에는 이것이 "올해의 가장 흥미진진한 영화"라고 쓰여 있었어.

➡ _____

7 Emma: 음, 넌 네가 읽는 것을 모두 믿을 수는 없어.

➡ _____

8 Kyle: 그들은 광고에 거짓말을 한 거야. 돈을 환불해 달라고 해야겠어.

➡ _____

9 Emma: 기다려, Kyle! 그들은 사실이 아닌 의견을 사용했기 때문에 꼭 거짓말을 한 것은 아니야.

➡ _____

10 Kyle: 뭐라고? 네 말을 이해하지 못하겠어.

➡ _____

11 Emma: 의견은 "사막은 아름다워."와 같이 사람들의 감정을 표현하는 것이야.

➡ _____

12 그것이 사실인지 아닌지 말할 수는 없어. 하지만 사실은 증명할 수 있어.

➡ _____

13 예를 들면, "아타카마 사막은 칠레에 있다."는 사실이야. 넌 그것을 지도에서 확인할 수 있어.

➡ _____

14 Kyle: 알겠어…. 하지만 그게 영화와 무슨 관련이 있니?

➡ _____

15 Emma: 설명해 줄게. 네가 가장 좋아하는 영화가 뭐니?

➡ _____

16 Kyle: "Forest Gump"야.

➡ _____

17 Emma: 좋아. 그 영화의 광고를 찾아보자. 뭐라고 쓰여 있니?

➡ _____

18 Kyle: "Best Picture를 포함하여 아카데미 6개 부문 수상작"이라고 쓰여 있어.

➡ _____

19 Emma: 알겠니? "Y-Men 7" 광고와는 달리 사실을 사용하고 있어.

➡ _____

20 차이를 알겠니?

➡ _____

21 Kyle: 잘 모르겠어. "Y-Men 7" 광고는 "Most Exciting Movie"라고 쓰여 있고 "Forest Gump" 광고는 "Best Picture"라고 쓰여 있잖아.

➡ _____

22 둘 다 의견 아니니?

➡ _____

23 Emma: 좋은 질문이야, Kyle. 사람들이 'best'나 'most'와 같은 말을 사용할 때, 그들은 대개 의견을 표현하는 거야.

➡ _____

24 하지만 "Forest Gump" 광고에서 "Best Picture"는 영화가 받은 상이야.

➡ _____

25 우리는 인터넷에서 그것을 확인할 수 있어. 그건 사실이야.

➡ _____

26 Kyle: 아하! 지금부터 사실로 이루어진 광고만 믿겠어.

➡ _____

27 Emma: 그렇게 간단하지는 않아. 대부분의 광고는 사실과 의견이 섞여 있어.

➡ _____

28 그러니 그 둘을 바탕으로 현명한 선택을 해야 해.

➡ _____

29 Kyle: 알겠어! Emma, "Y-Men 7"의 남은 부분을 나와 함께 볼래?

➡ _____

30 Emma: 고맙지만 사양할게. 영화의 남은 부분 잘 봐!

➡ _____

※ 다음 우리말과 일치하도록 빈칸에 알맞은 말을 쓰시오.

Listen and Speak 2 - C

1. A: _____ _____ _____ _____ your bicycle?

2. B: I'm _____ _____ _____ it.

3. A: Why _____?

4. B: It's _____ _____.

Think and Write

1. *Harry Potter* is a _____ _____.

2. It _____ _____ _____ J. K. Rowling.

3. Harry Potter is _____ _____ _____ of the book.

4. When Harry goes to _____ _____, his _____ begin.

5. I _____ _____ the _____ of Harry and his friends.

6. The book was _____ _____ _____ I couldn't _____ it _____.

7. I _____ _____ it to everyone.

1. "해리포터"는 공상 소설이다.
2. 이 책은 J. K. Rowling에 의해 쓰였다.
3. Harry Potter는 이 책의 주인공이다.
4. Harry가 마법 학교에 가면서 그의 모험은 시작된다.
5. 나는 특히 Harry와 그의 친구들의 우정을 좋아한다.
6. 이 책은 너무 재미있어서 나는 책을 놓을 수가 없었다.
7. 나는 모두에게 이 책을 강력히 추천한다.

Project

1. Korean _____ _____

2. Facts: It _____ _____ _____ Yongin.

3. There are _____ _____ _____.

4. Visitors _____ _____ nongak and jultagi.

5. Opinions: It's _____ _____ _____ in Yongin.

6. Korean _____ _____ are beautiful.

7. Nongak and jultagi _____ _____ _____.

1. 한국 민속촌
2. 사실: 그것은 용인에 있습니다.
3. 한국 전통 가옥이 있습니다.
4. 방문객들은 농악과 줄타기를 볼 수 있습니다.
5. 의견: 그곳은 용인에 있는 재미있는 장소입니다.
6. 한국 전통 가옥들은 아름답습니다.
7. 농악과 줄타기는 신이 날 겁니다.

※ 다음 우리말을 영어로 쓰시오.

Listen and Speak 2 - C

1. A: 자전거가 마음에 드니?
➡ _____

2. B: 마음에 들지 않아.
➡ _____

3. A: 왜?
➡ _____

4. B: 너무 무거워.
➡ _____

Think and Write

1. "해리포터"는 공상 소설이다.
➡ _____

2. 이 책은 J. K. Rowling에 의해 쓰였다.
➡ _____

3. Harry Potter는 이 책의 주인공이다.
➡ _____

4. Harry가 마법 학교에 가면서 그의 모험은 시작된다.
➡ _____

5. 나는 특히 Harry와 그의 친구들의 우정을 좋아한다.
➡ _____

6. 이 책은 너무 재미있어서 나는 책을 놓을 수가 없었다.
➡ _____

7. 나는 모두에게 이 책을 강력히 추천한다.
➡ _____

Project

1. 한국 민속촌
➡ _____

2. 사실: 그것은 용인에 있습니다.
➡ _____

3. 한국 전통 가옥이 있습니다.
➡ _____

4. 방문객들은 농악과 줄타기를 볼 수 있습니다.
➡ _____

5. 의견: 그곳은 용인에 있는 재미있는 장소입니다.
➡ _____

6. 한국 전통 가옥들은 아름답습니다.
➡ _____

7. 농악과 줄타기는 신이 날 겁니다.
➡ _____

※ 다음 영어를 우리말로 쓰시오.

01	horror	22	stranger
02	post	23	detective
03	broken	24	wonder
04	thirsty	25	favor
05	bronze	26	call
06	feather	27	suddenly
07	rush	28	footprint
08	flash	29	thief
09	poem	30	lightning
10	strange	31	carry
11	thunder	32	mop
12	clue	33	principal
13	afraid	34	talent
14	refrigerator	35	take care of
15	text	36	a few
16	handprint	37	right now
17	inside	38	win first place
18	treasure	39	not ~ anymore
19	crime	40	on the way home
20	dangerous	41	rush over
21	steal	42	get into trouble
		43	at the moment

※ 다음 우리말을 영어로 쓰시오.

01	발자국	
02	은	
03	청동	
04	번개	
05	낯선 사람, 모르는 사람	
06	나르다, 옮기다	
07	냉장고	
08	위험한	
09	갑자기	
10	궁금해 하다	
11	깃털	
12	깨진, 부서진	
13	재능	
14	범죄	
15	(급히) 움직이다, 서두르다	
16	시	
17	섬광, 번쩍임	
18	단서, 실마리	
19	도둑	
20	잃어버리다	
21	손자국	

22	교장	
23	호의, 친절, 부탁	
24	목마른	
25	공포	
26	훔치다	
27	이상한	
28	탐정	
29	～ 안에	
30	물을 주다	
31	대걸레로 닦다	
32	보물	
33	게시하다, 공고하다	
34	천둥	
35	몇몇의, 조금의	
36	집에 가는(오는) 길에	
37	더 이상 ～ 않다	
38	지금, 곧, 당장	
39	～을 돌보다	
40	그 순간에, 그때에	
41	～을 돌려주다	
42	곤경에 빠지다	
43	달려가다	

※ 다음 영영풀이에 알맞은 단어를 <보기>에서 골라 쓴 후, 우리말 뜻을 쓰시오.

1 _____ : in any case: _____

2 _____ : a mark left by a foot or shoe: _____

3 _____ : a strong feeling of shock and fear: _____

4 _____ : the person in charge of a school: _____

5 _____ : activities that involve breaking the law: _____

6 _____ : someone who steals things from another person: _____

7 _____ : in addition to something already mentioned: _____

8 _____ : a bright light that shines for a short time: _____

9 _____ : to clean the floor with a mop: _____

10 _____ : to move or do something very quickly: _____

11 _____ : a natural and special ability to do something well: _____

12 _____ : something that helps a person find something: _____

13 _____ : a yellowish-brown metal containing copper and tin: _____

14 _____ : a person whose job is to find information about something or someone:
   _____

15 _____ : to take something that does not belong to you in a wrong way: _____

16 _____ : a powerful flash of light in the sky and usually followed by thunder:
   _____

보기			
crime	lightning	footprint	principal
bronze	thief	talent	clue
anyway	detective	flash	rush
steal	else	horror	mop

※ 다음 우리말과 일치하도록 빈칸에 알맞은 말을 쓰시오.

Listen and Speak 1-A

Emily: Jinsu, can I _____ you a _____?

Jinsu: _____. What is it?

Emily: Can you help me _____ _____ _____?

Jinsu: No _____.

Emily: 진수야, 부탁 하나 해도 될까?
Jinsu: 물론이지. 뭔데?
Emily: 설거지하는 것 좀 도와줄래?
Jinsu: 좋아.

Listen and Speak 1-B

Narae: Tony, can you _____ _____ a _____?

Tony: Sure. What is it, Narae?

Narae: Can you _____ _____ _____ my dog this weekend? My family is _____ _____ _____ my grandmother in Busan.

Tony: Oh, _____ _____ _____ _____ _____. My mom doesn't like dogs.

Narae: Oh, _____ _____ _____ _____?

Tony: _____ _____ _____ ask Sumin? Her family _____ dogs.

Narae: Okay. I'll _____ her _____ _____.

Narae: Tony야, 부탁 하나 해도 될까?
Tony: 물론이지. 뭔데, 나래야?
Narae: 이번 주말에 내 개를 돌봐 줄 수 있니? 우리 가족은 부산에 계신 할머니를 방문할 예정이야.
Tony: 오, 미안하지만 안 돼. 엄마께서 개를 좋아하지 않으셔.
Narae: 오, 어떻게 해야 하지?
Tony: 수민이에게 물어보는 게 어때? 그녀의 가족은 개를 정말 좋아해.
Narae: 알겠어. 지금 당장 그녀에게 전화해야겠다.

Listen and Speak 1-C

A: Can you _____ _____ _____ _____?

B: Sure. What is it?

A: Can you _____ _____ _____ the floor?

B: No _____. / _____, I _____.

A: 부탁 하나 해도 될까?
B: 물론이지. 뭔데?
A: 바닥 닦는 것을 도와줄래?
B: 좋아. / 미안하지만 못해.

Listen and Speak 2-A

Brian: Did you see my _____ _____?

Jane: Yes, I saw it _____ _____ _____.

Brian: Really? It's _____ there _____.

Jane: Then I _____ Spot _____ it.

Brian: Oh, there _____ _____. You bad dog, Spot!

Brian: 내 야구 글러브 보았니?
Jane: 그래, 탁자 아래에서 봤어.
Brian: 정말? 더 이상 그곳에 없어.
Jane: 그럼 Spot이 가져간 것 같구나.
Brian: 오, 저기 있네. 이런 나쁜 개, Spot!

Listen and Speak 2-B

G: Good morning, classmates! Nine months _____ _____ so fast, and we are almost _____ _____ _____ _____ this school year. We all had a _____ _____. I guess only _____ _____ of us will _____ _____ _____ _____ next year. Don't be a _____. Say hello when we see _____ _____, okay? Thank you.

G: 좋은 아침이야, 학급 친구들아! 9개월은 아주 빨리 지나갔고, 우리는 이번 학년의 거의 막바지에 있어. 우리 모두는 멋진 한 해를 보냈어. 우리 중 극소수가 내년에 같은 반이 될 거라고 생각해. 모르는 사람처럼 지내지 말자. 서로 만나면 인사말을 건네자. 알겠지? 고마워.

Listen and Speak 2-C

A: Guess _____ _____ _____.
B: _____ _____ you're _____ the piano.
A: You're _____. _____ again.
B: I _____ you're _____ _____ the computer.
A: That's _____.

A: 내가 무엇을 하고 있는지 맞혀 봐.
B: 너는 피아노를 치고 있는 것 같아.
A: 틀렸어. 다시 맞혀 봐.
B: 너는 컴퓨터로 일하고 있는 것 같아.
A: 맞아.

Real Life Talk - Step 1

Brian: Mom, I _____ _____ my smartphone. _____ _____ _____ _____ find it?
Mom: _____ _____ _____ you lost it _____ the house?
Brian: Yes. I just _____ my friend _____ _____ _____ ago.
Mom: _____ _____ you _____ _____ _____?
Brian: In the kitchen. I _____ _____ a sandwich.
Mom: Then I guess you left it _____ in the kitchen.
Brian: I _____ _____ the kitchen, Mom.
Mom: Well, _____ _____ _____ _____ _____. Oh, here _____ . Inside the _____.
Brian: Thanks, Mom. You are the _____!
Mom: You're _____, honey.

Brian: 엄마, 제 스마트폰을 찾을 수가 없어요. 제가 그것을 찾는 걸 도와주시겠어요?
Mom: 집 안에서 잃어버린 것이 확실하니?
Brian: 네. 불과 몇 분 전에 친구에게 문자 메시지를 보냈어요.
Mom: 너는 그때 어디에 있었니?
Brian: 부엌에요. 샌드위치를 만들고 있었어요.
Mom: 그럼 네가 부엌 어딘가에 놓은 것 같구나.
Brian: 이미 부엌은 확인했어요, 엄마.
Mom: 음, 다시 확인해 보자. 오, 여기 있구나. 냉장고 안에 있어.
Brian: 고마워요, 엄마. 엄마는 최고예요!
Mom: 천만에, 애야.

Real Life Talk - Step 2

A: Can you _____ _____ _____ my baseball glove?
B: Okay. Where _____ you _____ it _____?
A: _____ the bench.
B: I _____ a dog _____ your baseball glove. I can _____ _____ _____ on the bench.

A: 내 야구 글러브를 찾는 것을 도와줄래?
B: 응. 그것을 어디에서 마지막으로 봤니?
A: 벤치 위에서.
B: 개가 네 야구 글러브를 가져간 것 같아. 벤치 위에 발자국을 볼 수 있어.

※ 다음 우리말에 맞도록 대화를 영어로 쓰시오.

Listen and Speak 1-A

Emily: _____

Jinsu: _____

Emily: _____

Jinsu: _____

Emily: 진수야, 부탁 하나 해도 될까?
Jinsu: 물론이지. 뭔데?
Emily: 설거지하는 것 좀 도와줄래?
Jinsu: 좋아.

Listen and Speak 1-B

Narae: _____

Tony: _____

Narae: _____

_____

Tony: _____

Narae: _____

Tony: _____

Narae: _____

Narae: Tony야, 부탁 하나 해도 될까?
Tony: 물론이지. 뭔데, 나래야?
Narae: 이번 주말에 내 개를 돌봐 줄 수 있니? 우리 가족은 부산에 계신 할머니를 방문할 예정이야.
Tony: 오, 미안하지만 안 돼. 엄마께서 개를 좋아하지 않으셔.
Narae: 오, 어떻게 해야 하지?
Tony: 수민이에게 물어보는 게 어때? 그녀의 가족은 개를 정말 좋아해.
Narae: 알겠어. 지금 당장 그녀에게 전화해야겠다.

Listen and Speak 1-C

A: _____

B: _____

A: _____

B: _____

A: 부탁 하나 해도 될까?
B: 물론이지. 뭔데?
A: 바닥 닦는 것을 도와줄래?
B: 좋아. / 미안하지만 못해.

Listen and Speak 2-A

Brian: _____

Jane: _____

Brian: _____

Jane: _____

Brian: _____

Brian: 내 야구 글러브 보았니?
Jane: 그래, 탁자 아래에서 봤어.
Brian: 정말? 더 이상 그곳에 없어.
Jane: 그럼 Spot이 가져간 것 같구나.
Brian: 오, 저기 있네. 이런 나쁜 개, Spot!

Listen and Speak 2-B

G: _____

_____

_____

_____

G: 좋은 아침이야, 학급 친구들아! 9개월은 아주 빨리 지나갔고, 우리는 이번 학년의 거의 막바지에 있어. 우리 모두는 멋진 한 해를 보냈어. 우리 중 극소수가 내년에 같은 반이 될 거라고 생각해. 모르는 사람처럼 지내지 말자. 서로 만나면 인사말을 건네자. 알겠지? 고마워.

Listen and Speak 2-C

A: _____

B: _____

A: _____

B: _____

A: _____

A: 내가 무엇을 하고 있는지 맞혀 봐.
B: 너는 피아노를 치고 있는 것 같아.
A: 틀렸어. 다시 맞혀 봐.
B: 너는 컴퓨터로 일하고 있는 것 같아.
A: 맞아.

Real Life Talk - Step 1

Brian: _____

Mom: _____

Brian: _____

Mom: _____

Brian: _____

Mom: _____

Brian: _____

Mom: _____

Brian: _____

Mom: _____

Brian: 엄마, 제 스마트폰을 찾을 수가 없어요. 제가 그것을 찾는 걸 도와주시겠어요?
Mom: 집 안에서 잃어버린 것이 확실하니?
Brian: 네. 불과 몇 분 전에 친구에게 문자 메시지를 보냈어요.
Mom: 너는 그때 어디에 있었니?
Brian: 부엌이에요. 샌드위치를 만들고 있었어요.
Mom: 그럼 네가 부엌 어딘가에 놓은 것 같구나.
Brian: 이미 부엌은 확인했어요, 엄마.
Mom: 음, 다시 확인해 보자. 오, 여기 있구나. 냉장고 안에 있어.
Brian: 고마워요, 엄마. 엄마는 최고예요!
Mom: 천만에, 얘야.

Real Life Talk - Step 2

A: _____

B: _____

A: _____

B: _____

A: 내 야구 글러브를 찾는 것을 도와줄래?
B: 응. 그것을 어디에서 마지막으로 봤니?
A: 벤치 위에서.
B: 개가 네 야구 글러브를 가져간 것 같아. 벤치 위에 발자국을 볼 수 있어.

※ 다음 우리말과 일치하도록 빈칸에 알맞은 것을 골라 쓰시오.

1 Mr. Reese, the principal, _____ _____ the _____ playground.
A. across B. ran C. wet

2 "Shirley! Shirley! I _____ your _____!"
A. help B. need

3 Shirley was an _____ _____ _____ at Bakersville Middle School.
A. grade B. eighth C. student

4 She was also the _____ _____ in the _____ town.
A. detective B. whole C. best

5 "Is there _____ _____?" asked Shirley.
A. wrong B. something

6 "Someone _____ _____ the gold medal _____ the talent show!"
A. for B. stolen C. has

7 Mr. Reese _____ Shirley _____ the _____ of the crime.
A. to B. took C. scene

8 There was a _____ _____ a _____ window.
A. broken B. case C. with

9 The silver and _____ medals were _____ _____.
A. there B. bronze C. still

10 But the gold medal was _____. There was a _____ in _____ _____.
A. place B. missing C. poem D. its

11 Tomorrow is the talent show. _____ _____ the gold medal _____?
A. go B. did C. where

12 Look high and _____. You can't _____ me. You're _____ slow.
A. too B. low C. catch

13 Shirley asked, "Could you tell me _____ _____ _____?"
A. this B. when C. happened

14 "A little _____ nine last night. I was making my _____ when I heard a scream. I _____ _____ and found Jocelyn and the case like this."
A. rounds B. after C. over D. rushed

15 "I _____ _____ _____ _____ here last night."
A. else B. wonder C. was D. who

16 "Sylvia and Harry. They were also _____ _____ the talent show. I'll _____ _____ to my office."
A. call B. practicing C. them D. for

17 Jocelyn was a _____ _____ student with short _____ red hair.
A. grade B. curly C. ninth

---

1 Reese 교장은 젖은 운동장을 달려왔다.

2 "Shirley! Shirley! 네 도움이 필요하구나!"

3 Shirley는 Bakersville 중학교의 8학년 학생이었다.

4 그녀는 또한 그 마을 최고의 탐정이었다.

5 "무슨 일이 있나요?" Shirley가 물었다.

6 "누군가 장기 자랑 대회 금메달을 훔쳐갔어!"

7 Reese 교장은 Shirley를 범죄 현장으로 데려갔다.

8 유리창이 깨진 진열장이 있었다.

9 은메달과 동메달은 그곳에 그대로 있었다.

10 하지만 금메달은 사라졌다. 그 자리에는 시가 있었다.

11 내일은 장기 자랑 대회다. 금메달은 어디로 갔을까?

12 구석구석 찾아라. 당신은 나를 잡을 수 없어. 당신은 너무 느려.

13 Shirley는 "언제 이 사건이 일어났는지 말씀해 주시겠어요?"라고 물었다.

14 "어젯밤 9시가 조금 넘은 후에. 내가 순찰을 돌고 있었을 때 비명 소리가 들렸어. 나는 달려가서 Jocelyn과 이 상태인 진열장을 발견했지."

15 "어젯밤에 또 다른 누가 여기 있었는지 궁금해요."

16 "Sylvia와 Harry가 있었어. 그 두 사람 또한 장기 자랑을 위해 연습 중이었어. 내가 그들을 내 사무실로 부르마."

17 Jocelyn은 빨간색 짧은 곱슬머리를 가진 9학년 학생이었다.

18 "I was practicing my song and I became _____. I stepped outside the classroom to get some water. It was _____ dark. Suddenly, there was a loud sound of _____. I think the thief broke the window at that moment. Lightning followed right after and it became bright for a second or two. Then I saw someone running _____ from the case."

    A. thunder   B. away   C. thirsty   D. completely

19 "Did you _____ the _____ _____?"

    A. face   B. see   C. thief's

20 "No, I _____ saw the _____ _____. But the thief had _____ hair."

    A. short   B. back   C. thief's   D. only

21 Next was an _____ _____ student, Sylvia. She was tall _____ _____ black hair.

    A. with   B. grade   C. long   D. eighth

22 She said, "I was reading my poem _____ in the classroom. I heard a scream and went outside. There was a girl next to the case. With the _____ from the lightning, it was _____ a horror movie. I got _____ so I ran straight home."

    A. flash   B. aloud   C. scared   D. like

23 "Did you _____ the window _____?"

    A. break   B. hear

24 "No, the thunder was _____ _____. Well, I didn't do it. I was _____ to _____ first place anyway."

    A. loud   B. win   C. going   D. too

25 Harry, a _____ grader, had _____ _____ hair.

    A. short   B. seventh   C. blonde

26 He said, "Hey, you got the _____ guy. I was practicing my dance _____. I went home a _____ before nine. I didn't take one step _____ the classroom until then."

    A. little   B. outside   C. moves   D. wrong

27 "Did you hear _____ _____?"

    A. strange   B. anything

28 "_____ _____ I? My music was really _____."

    A. could   B. loud   C. how

29 "Did you see anyone _____ the _____ _____?"

    A. way   B. on   C. home

30 "No, I _____ someone _____ really _____, but I didn't see _____."

    A. singing   B. heard   C. anyone   D. badly

31 Shirley said, "I don't _____ to hear _____." Then she _____ _____ the thief.

    A. anymore   B. need   C. to   D. turned

32 "Why don't you _____ the medal _____ before you get _____ some real _____?"

    A. into   B. bring   C. trouble   D. back

---

18 "저는 제 노래를 연습하고 있었는데 목이 말랐어요. 저는 물을 가지러 교실 밖으로 나갔어요. 완전히 어두웠어요. 갑자기, 커다란 천둥소리가 났어요. 저는 도둑이 그 순간에 유리창을 깼다고 생각해요. 번개가 바로 뒤 따랐고 1~2초 정도 밝아졌어요. 그때 저는 누군가가 진열장에서 도망치는 걸 봤어요."

19 "도둑의 얼굴을 봤나요?"

20 "아니요, 도둑의 뒷모습만 봤어요. 하지만 그 도둑은 짧은 머리였어요."

21 다음은 8학년 학생인 Sylvia였다. 그녀는 긴 검은색 머리에 키가 컸다.

22 그녀는 말했다. "저는 교실에서 큰 소리로 제 시를 낭송하고 있었어요. 비명 소리를 듣고 밖으로 나갔어요. 진열장 옆에 한 소녀가 있었어요. 번개의 번쩍임과 어우러져 그것은 공포 영화 같았어요. 저는 겁이 나서 곧장 집으로 달려갔어요."

23 "창이 깨지는 소리를 들었나요?"

24 "아니요, 천둥소리가 너무 컸어요. 음, 제가 그런 게 아니에요. 저는 어쨌든 1등을 할 거였으니까요."

25 7학년인 Harry는 짧은 금발을 가지고 있었다.

26 그는 말했다. "이봐요, 사람을 잘못 짚었어요. 저는 제 춤 동작을 연습하고 있었어요. 저는 9시 조금 전에 집에 갔어요. 저는 그때까지 교실 밖으로 한 발자국도 나가지 않았어요."

27 "이상한 소리라도 들었나요?"

28 "제가 어떻게 듣겠어요? 제 음악 소리가 정말 컸어요."

29 "집에 가는 길에 누군가를 보았나요?"

30 "아니요, 누군가가 노래를 정말 끔찍하게 부르는 소리는 들었지만 누구도 보진 못했어요."

31 Shirley는 "더 이상 들을 필요는 없겠네요."라고 말했다. 그러고 나서 그녀는 도둑을 향했다.

32 "정말 곤경에 빠지기 전에 금메달을 돌려주는 게 어때요?"

※ 다음 우리말과 일치하도록 빈칸에 알맞은 말을 쓰시오.

1 Mr. Reese, the principal, _____ _____ the _____ playground.

2 "Shirley! Shirley! I _____ _____ _____!"

3 Shirley was _____ _____ _____ _____ at Bakersville Middle School.

4 She was also _____ _____ _____ in the _____ town.

5 "Is there _____ _____?" _____ Shirley.

6 "Someone _____ _____ the gold medal _____ the _____ _____!"

7 Mr. Reese _____ Shirley _____ the _____ of the crime.

8 There _____ _____ _____ with a _____ window.

9 The silver and _____ medals _____ _____ _____.

10 But the gold medal was _____. There was _____ _____ in _____ _____.

11 Tomorrow is the talent show. _____ _____ the gold medal _____?

12 Look _____ _____ _____. You can't catch me. You're _____ _____.

13 Shirley asked, "Could you tell me _____ _____ _____?"

14 "A little _____ nine last night. I was _____ _____ _____ when I heard a scream. I _____ _____ and found Jocelyn and the case _____ this."

15 "I wonder _____ _____ _____ _____ last night."

16 "Sylvia and Harry. They were also _____ _____ the talent show. I'll _____ _____ to my office."

17 Jocelyn was a _____ _____ student _____ _____ _____ red hair.

1 Reese 교장은 젖은 운동장을 달려왔다.

2 "Shirley! Shirley! 네 도움이 필요하구나!"

3 Shirley는 Bakersville 중학교의 8학년 학생이었다.

4 그녀는 또한 그 마을 최고의 탐정이었다.

5 "무슨 일이 있나요?" Shirley가 물었다.

6 "누군가 장기 자랑 대회 금메달을 훔쳐갔어!"

7 Reese 교장은 Shirley를 범죄 현장으로 데려갔다.

8 유리창이 깨진 진열장이 있었다.

9 은메달과 동메달은 그곳에 그대로 있었다.

10 하지만 금메달은 사라졌다. 그 자리에는 시가 있었다.

11 내일은 장기 자랑 대회. 금메달은 어디로 갔을까?

12 구석구석 찾아라. 당신은 나를 잡을 수 없어. 당신은 너무 느려.

13 Shirley는 "언제 이 사건이 일어났는지 말씀해 주시겠어요?"라고 물었다.

14 "어젯밤 9시가 조금 넘은 후에. 내가 순찰을 돌고 있었을 때 비명 소리가 들렸어. 나는 달려가서 Jocelyn과 이 상태인 진열장을 발견했지."

15 "어젯밤에 또 다른 누가 여기 있었는지 궁금해요."

16 "Sylvia와 Harry가 있었어. 그 두 사람 또한 장기 자랑을 위해 연습 중이었어. 내가 그들을 내 사무실로 부르마."

17 Jocelyn은 빨간색 짧은 곱슬머리를 가진 9학년 학생이었다.

18 "I was _____ my song and I _____ _____ . I _____ _____ the classroom _____ _____ some water. _____ was _____ dark. _____ , there was a loud sound of _____ . I think the thief _____ the window at that moment. _____ _____ right after and it became bright for _____ _____ or _____ . Then I _____ someone _____ _____ from the case."

19 "Did you see the _____ _____ ?"

20 "No, I _____ _____ the thief's _____ . But the thief had _____ hair."

21 Next was an _____ _____ student, Sylvia. She was tall _____ _____ _____ hair.

22 She said, "I was _____ my poem _____ in the classroom. I heard a scream and _____ _____ . There was a girl _____ _____ the case. With the _____ from the lightning, it was _____ _____ _____ _____ _____ . I got _____ so I _____ _____ home."

23 "Did you _____ the window _____ ?"

24 "No, the thunder was _____ _____ . Well, I didn't do it. I _____ _____ _____ _____ first place anyway."

25 Harry, a _____ grader, had _____ _____ hair.

26 He said, "Hey, you got the _____ guy. I was practicing my dance _____ . I went home _____ _____ _____ nine. I didn't _____ one step _____ the classroom _____ then."

27 "Did you _____ _____ ?"

28 "_____ _____ I? My music was really loud."

29 "Did you see anyone _____ _____ _____ _____ ?"

30 "No, I _____ _____ _____ really badly, but I didn't see anyone."

31 Shirley said, "I don't _____ _____ _____ _____ ." Then she _____ _____ the thief.

32 "Why don't you _____ _____ _____ before you _____ _____ some real _____ ?"

---

18 "저는 제 노래를 연습하고 있었는데 목이 말랐어요. 저는 물을 가지러 교실 밖으로 나갔어요. 완전히 어두웠어요. 갑자기, 커다란 천둥소리가 났어요. 저는 도둑이 그 순간에 유리창을 깼다고 생각해요. 번개가 바로 뒤따랐고 1~2초 정도 밝아졌어요. 그때 저는 누군가가 진열장에서 도망치는 걸 봤어요."

19 "도둑의 얼굴을 봤나요?"

20 "아니요, 도둑의 뒷모습만 봤어요. 하지만 그 도둑은 짧은 머리였어요."

21 다음은 8학년 학생인 Sylvia였다. 그녀는 긴 검은색 머리에 키가 컸다.

22 그녀는 말했다. "저는 교실에서 큰 소리로 제 시를 낭송하고 있었어요. 비명 소리를 듣고 밖으로 나갔어요. 진열장 옆에 한 소녀가 있었어요. 번개의 번쩍임과 어우러져 그것은 공포 영화 같았어요. 저는 겁이 나서 곧장 집으로 달려갔어요."

23 "창이 깨지는 소리를 들었나요?"

24 "아니요, 천둥소리가 너무 컸어요. 음, 제가 그런 게 아니에요. 저는 어쨌든 1등을 할 거였으니까요."

25 7학년인 Harry는 짧은 금발을 가지고 있었다.

26 그는 말했다. "이봐요, 사람을 잘못 짚었어요. 저는 제 춤 동작을 연습하고 있었어요. 저는 9시 조금 전에 집에 갔어요. 저는 그때까지 교실 밖으로 한 발자국도 나가지 않았어요."

27 "이상한 소리라도 들었나요?"

28 "제가 어떻게 듣겠어요? 제 음악 소리가 정말 컸어요."

29 "집에 가는 길에 누군가를 보았나요?"

30 "아니요, 누군가가 노래를 정말 끔찍하게 부르는 소리는 들었지만 누구도 보진 못했어요."

31 Shirley는 "더 이상 들을 필요는 없겠네요."라고 말했다. 그러고 나서 그녀는 도둑을 향했다.

32 "정말 곤경에 빠지기 전에 금메달을 돌려주는 게 어때요?"

※ 다음 문장을 우리말로 쓰시오.

1 Mr. Reese, the principal, ran across the wet playground.
➡ _____

2 "Shirley! Shirley! I need your help!"
➡ _____

3 Shirley was an eighth grade student at Bakersville Middle School.
➡ _____

4 She was also the best detective in the whole town.
➡ _____

5 "Is there something wrong?" asked Shirley.
➡ _____

6 "Someone has stolen the gold medal for the talent show!"
➡ _____

7 Mr. Reese took Shirley to the scene of the crime.
➡ _____

8 There was a case with a broken window.
➡ _____

9 The silver and bronze medals were still there.
➡ _____

10 But the gold medal was missing. There was a poem in its place.
➡ _____

11 Tomorrow is the talent show. Where did the gold medal go?
➡ _____

12 Look high and low. You can't catch me. You're too slow.
➡ _____

13 Shirley asked, "Could you tell me when this happened?"
➡ _____

14 "A little after nine last night. I was making my rounds when I heard a scream. I rushed over and found Jocelyn and the case like this."
➡ _____
_____

15 "I wonder who else was here last night."
➡ _____

16 "Sylvia and Harry. They were also practicing for the talent show. I'll call them to my office."
➡ _____

17 Jocelyn was a ninth grade student with short curly red hair.
➡ _____

18 "I was practicing my song and I became thirsty. I stepped outside the classroom to get some water. It was completely dark. Suddenly, there was a loud sound of thunder. I think the thief broke the window at that moment. Lightning followed right after and it became bright for a second or two. Then I saw someone running away from the case."

➡ _____

_____

_____

19 "Did you see the thief's face?"

➡ _____

20 "No, I only saw the thief's back. But the thief had short hair."

➡ _____

21 Next was an eighth grade student, Sylvia. She was tall with long black hair.

➡ _____

22 She said, "I was reading my poem aloud in the classroom. I heard a scream and went outside. There was a girl next to the case. With the flash from the lightning, it was like a horror movie. I got scared so I ran straight home."

➡ _____

_____

23 "Did you hear the window break?"

➡ _____

24 "No, the thunder was too loud. Well, I didn't do it. I was going to win first place anyway."

➡ _____

25 Harry, a seventh grader, had short blonde hair.

➡ _____

26 He said, "Hey, you got the wrong guy. I was practicing my dance moves. I went home a little before nine. I didn't take one step outside the classroom until then."

➡ _____

_____

27 "Did you hear anything strange?"

➡ _____

28 "How could I? My music was really loud."

➡ _____

29 "Did you see anyone on the way home?"

➡ _____

30 "No, I heard someone singing really badly, but I didn't see anyone."

➡ _____

31 Shirley said, "I don't need to hear anymore." Then she turned to the thief.

➡ _____

32 "Why don't you bring the medal back before you get into some real trouble?"

➡ _____

※ 다음 괄호 안의 단어들을 우리말에 맞도록 바르게 배열하시오.

1 (Reese, / Mr. / principal, / the / across / ran / wet / playground. / the)
➡ _____

2 ("Shirley! / I / Shirley! / help!" / your / need)
➡ _____

3 (was / Shirley / eighth / an / grade / student / Bakersville / at / School. / Middle)
➡ _____

4 (was / she / the / also / best / in / detective / the / town. / whole)
➡ _____

5 (there / "is / wrong?" / something / Shirley. / asked)
➡ _____

6 (has / "someone / the / stolen / medal / gold / for / show!" / talent / the)
➡ _____

7 (Reese / Mr. / took / to / Shirley / the / crime. / of / the / scene)
➡ _____

8 (was / there / case / a / with / window. / broken / a)
➡ _____

9 (silver / the / and / medals / bronze / were / there. / still)
➡ _____

10 (the / but / gold / was / medal / missing. // was / there / poem / a / place. / its / in)
➡ _____

11 (is / tomorrow / the / show. / talent // did / where / gold / go? / medal / the)
➡ _____

12 (high / look / low. / and // you / catch / can't / me. // too / you're / slow.)
➡ _____

13 (asked, / Shirley / "could / tell / you / me / this / happened?" / when)
➡ _____

14 (little / "a / after / last / nine / night. // I / making / was / rounds / my / when / heard / I / scream. / a // I / over / rushed / and / Jocelyn / found / and / case / the / this." / like)
➡ _____
_____

15 (wonder / "I / else / who / was / last / night." / here)
➡ _____

16 (Harry. / and / "Sylvia // were / they / practicing / also / for / talent / the / show. // call / I'll / to / them / . office." / my)
➡ _____

17 (was / Jocelyn / a / grade / ninth / student / with / curly / short / hair. / red)
➡ _____

1 Reese 교장은 젖은 운동장을 달려왔다.

2 "Shirley! Shirley! 네 도움이 필요하구나!"

3 Shirley는 Bakersville 중학교의 8학년 학생이었다.

4 그녀는 또한 그 마을 최고의 탐정이었다.

5 "무슨 일이 있나요?" Shirley가 물었다.

6 "누군가 장기 자랑 대회 금메달을 훔쳐갔어!"

7 Reese 교장은 Shirley를 범죄 현장으로 데려갔다.

8 유리창이 깨진 진열장이 있었다.

9 은메달과 동메달은 그곳에 그대로 있었다.

10 하지만 금메달은 사라졌다. 그 자리에는 시가 있었다.

11 내일은 장기 자랑 대회다. 금메달은 어디로 갔을까?

12 구석구석 찾아라. 당신은 나를 잡을 수 없어. 당신은 너무 느려.

13 Shirley는 "언제 이 사건이 일어났는지 말씀해 주시겠어요?"라고 물었다.

14 "어젯밤 9시가 조금 넘은 후에. 내가 순찰을 돌고 있었을 때 비명 소리가 들렸어. 나는 달려가서 Jocelyn과 이 상태인 진열장을 발견했지."

15 "어젯밤에 또 다른 누가 여기 있었는지 궁금해요."

16 "Sylvia와 Harry가 있었어. 그 두 사람 또한 장기 자랑을 위해 연습 중이었어. 내가 그들을 내 사무실로 부르마."

17 Jocelyn은 빨간색 짧은 곱슬머리를 가진 9학년 학생이었다.

18 ("I / practicing / was / song / and / my / became / thirsty. / I // I / outside / stepped / classroom / the / to / some / get / water. // was / it / dark. / completely // suddenly, / was / there / loud / a / sound / of / thunder. // I / the / think / thief / the / broke / window / of / that / at / moment. // lightning / right / followed / after / and / it / bright / became / a / for / second / two. / or // then / saw / I / running / someone / away / the / case." / from)

➡ _____

_____

_____

_____

19 (you / "did / see / thief's / the / face?")

➡ _____

20 ("no, / only / I / saw / thief's / the / back. // but / thief / the / hair." / short / had)

➡ _____

21 (was / next / eighth / an / student, / grade / Sylvia. // was / she / with / tall / black / long / hair.)

➡ _____

22 (said, / she / "I / reading / was / poem / my / in / aloud / classroom. / the // I / heard / scream / a / and / outside. / went // was / there / girl / a / to / next / case. / the // the / with / from / flash / lightning, / the / was / it / like / horror / movie. / a // I / scared / got / I / so / home." / straight / ran)

➡ _____

_____

_____

23 (you / "did / hear / the / break?" / window)

➡ _____

24 (the / "no, / was / thunder / loud. / too // well, / didn't / I / it. / do // was / I / to / going / win / place / first / anyway.")

➡ _____

_____

25 (a / Harry, / grader, / seventh / had / hair. / blonde / short)

➡ _____

26 (said, / he / "hey, / got / you / wrong / the / guy. // was / practicing / I / dance / moves. / my // went / I / home / little / a / nine. / before // didn't / I / one / take / step / outside / the / then." / until / classroom)

➡ _____

_____

27 (you / "did / anything / hear / strange?")

➡ _____

28 (could / "how / I? // music / my / really / was / loud.")

➡ _____

29 (you / "did / anyone / see / the / on / home?" / way)

➡ _____

30 ("no, / heard / I / singing / someone / really / badly, / I / but / see / didn't /. anyone.")

➡ _____

31 (said, / Shirley / "I / need / don't / hear / to / anymore." // she / then / to / turned / thief. / the)

➡ _____

32 ("why / you / don't / bring / medal / the / before / back / get / you / into / real / trouble?" / some)

➡ _____

18 "저는 제 노래를 연습하고 있었는데 목이 말랐어요. 저는 물을 가지러 교실 밖으로 나갔어요. 완전히 어두웠어요. 갑자기, 커다란 천둥소리가 났어요. 저는 도둑이 그 순간에 유리창을 깼다고 생각해요. 번개가 바로 뒤따랐고 1~2초 정도 밝아졌어요. 그때 저는 누군가가 진열장에서 도망치는 걸 봤어요."

19 "도둑의 얼굴을 봤나요?"

20 "아니요, 도둑의 뒷모습만 봤어요. 하지만 그 도둑은 짧은 머리였어요."

21 다음은 8학년 학생인 Sylvia였다. 그녀는 긴 검은색 머리에 키가 컸다.

22 그녀는 말했다. "저는 교실에서 큰 소리로 제 시를 낭송하고 있었어요. 비명 소리를 듣고 밖으로 나갔어요. 진열장 옆에 한 소녀가 있었어요. 번개의 번쩍임과 어우러져 그것은 공포 영화 같았어요. 저는 겁이 나서 곧장 집으로 달려갔어요."

23 "창이 깨지는 소리를 들었나요?"

24 "아니요, 천둥소리가 너무 컸어요. 음, 제가 그런 게 아니에요. 저는 어쨌든 1등을 할 거였으니까요."

25 7학년인 Harry는 짧은 금발을 가지고 있었다.

26 그는 말했다. "이봐요, 사람을 잘못 짚었어요. 저는 제 춤 동작을 연습하고 있었어요. 저는 9시 조금 전에 집에 갔어요. 저는 그때까지 교실 밖으로 한 발자국도 나가지 않았어요."

27 "이상한 소리라도 들었나요?"

28 "제가 어떻게 듣겠어요? 제 음악 소리가 정말 컸어요."

29 "집에 가는 길에 누군가를 보았나요?"

30 "아니요, 누군가가 노래를 정말 끔찍하게 부르는 소리는 들었지만 누구도 보진 못했어요."

31 Shirley는 "더 이상 들을 필요는 없겠네요."라고 말했다. 그러고 나서 그녀는 도둑을 향했다.

32 "정말 곤경에 빠지기 전에 금메달을 돌려주는 게 어때요?"

※ 다음 우리말을 영어로 쓰시오.

1 Reese 교장은 젖은 운동장을 달려왔다.

➡ _____

2 "Shirley! Shirley! 네 도움이 필요하구나!"

➡ _____

3 Shirley는 Bakersville 중학교의 8학년 학생이었다.

➡ _____

4 그녀는 또한 그 마을 최고의 탐정이었다.

➡ _____

5 "무슨 일이 있나요?" Shirley가 물었다.

➡ _____

6 "누군가 장기 자랑 대회 금메달을 훔쳐갔어!"

➡ _____

7 Reese 교장은 Shirley를 범죄 현장으로 데려갔다.

➡ _____

8 유리창이 깨진 진열장이 있었다.

➡ _____

9 은메달과 동메달은 그곳에 그대로 있었다.

➡ _____

10 하지만 금메달은 사라졌다. 그 자리에는 시가 있었다.

➡ _____

11 내일은 장기 자랑 대회다. 금메달은 어디로 갔을까?

➡ _____

12 구석구석 찾아라. 당신은 나를 잡을 수 없어. 당신은 너무 느려.

➡ _____

13 Shirley는 "언제 이 사건이 일어났는지 말씀해 주시겠어요?"라고 물었다.

➡ _____

14 "어젯밤 9시가 조금 넘은 후에. 내가 순찰을 돌고 있었을 때 비명 소리가 들렸어. 나는 달려가서 Jocelyn과 이 상태인 진열장을 발견했지."

➡ _____

15 "어젯밤에 또 다른 누가 여기 있었는지 궁금해요."

➡ _____

16 "Sylvia와 Harry가 있었어. 그 두 사람 또한 장기 자랑을 위해 연습 중이었어. 내가 그들을 내 사무실로 부르마."

➡ _____

17 Jocelyn은 빨간색 짧은 곱슬머리를 가진 9학년 학생이었다.

➡ _____

18 "저는 제 노래를 연습하고 있었는데 목이 말랐어요. 저는 물을 가지러 교실 밖으로 나갔어요. 완전히 어두웠어요. 갑자기, 커다란 천둥소리가 났어요. 저는 도둑이 그 순간에 유리창을 깼다고 생각해요. 번개가 바로 뒤따랐고 1~2초 정도 밝아졌어요. 그때 저는 누군가가 진열장에서 도망치는 걸 봤어요."

➡ _____

_____

_____

19 "도둑의 얼굴을 봤나요?"

➡ _____

20 "아니요, 도둑의 뒷모습만 봤어요. 하지만 그 도둑은 짧은 머리였어요."

➡ _____

21 다음은 8학년 학생인 Sylvia였다. 그녀는 긴 검은색 머리에 키가 컸다.

➡ _____

22 그녀는 말했다. "저는 교실에서 큰 소리로 제 시를 낭송하고 있었어요. 비명 소리를 듣고 밖으로 나갔어요. 진열장 옆에 한 소녀가 있었어요. 번개의 번쩍임과 어우러져 그것은 공포 영화 같았어요. 저는 겁이 나서 곧장 집으로 달려갔어요."

➡ _____

_____

_____

23 "창이 깨지는 소리를 들었나요?"

➡ _____

24 "아니요, 천둥소리가 너무 컸어요. 음, 제가 그런 게 아니에요. 저는 어쨌든 1등을 할 거였으니까요."

➡ _____

25 7학년인 Harry는 짧은 금발을 가지고 있었다.

➡ _____

26 그는 말했다. "이봐요, 사람을 잘못 짚었어요. 저는 제 춤 동작을 연습하고 있었어요. 저는 9시 조금 전에 집에 갔어요. 저는 그때까지 교실 밖으로 한 발자국도 나가지 않았어요."

➡ _____

_____

27 "이상한 소리라도 들었나요?"

➡ _____

28 "제가 어떻게 듣겠어요? 제 음악 소리가 정말 컸어요."

➡ _____

29 "집에 가는 길에 누군가를 보았나요?"

➡ _____

30 "아니요, 누군가가 노래를 정말 끔찍하게 부르는 소리는 들었지만 누구도 보진 못했어요."

➡ _____

31 Shirley는 "더 이상 들을 필요는 없겠네요."라고 말했다. 그러고 나서 그녀는 도둑을 향했다.

➡ _____

32 "정말 곤경에 빠지기 전에 금메달을 돌려주는 게 어때요?"

➡ _____

※ 다음 우리말과 일치하도록 빈칸에 알맞은 말을 쓰시오.

Project

1. To the _____ _____,

2. Hello. We _____ _____ our treasure in the classroom. It is _____ _____.

3. Do you want to know _____ it is? Then _____ _____ _____.

4. First, _____ _____ a plant _____ the window. Look _____ the plant. You'll find a key.

5. Second, _____ _____ the key and _____ _____ _____ _____ of the classroom. You'll see the lockers.

6. The treasure is in the _____ _____ _____ _____ _____ _____.

7. It _____ _____, so use the key _____ _____ it. Got it? Help _____.

1. 보물 사냥꾼들에게,
2. 안녕. 우리는 교실에 우리 보물을 숨겼어. 그것은 맛있는 것이야.
3. 그것이 어디에 있는지 알고 싶니? 그러면 다음 단계를 따라 봐.
4. 우선, 창문 옆에 있는 식물을 찾아. 그 식물 아래를 봐. 너는 열쇠 하나를 찾을 거야.
5. 두 번째, 그 열쇠를 들고 교실 뒤쪽으로 걸어가. 너는 사물함을 볼 거야.
6. 보물은 왼쪽에서 세 번째 사물함 안에 있어.
7. 그것은 잠겼으니 그것을 열기 위해 열쇠를 사용해. 알겠지? 많이 먹으렴.

Think and Write

1. When Rapunzel was a baby, a witch _____ _____ _____ a tall tower.

2. Rapunzel _____ _____ in the tower. She had _____ _____.

3. The witch used it _____ _____ _____ the tower.

4. The witch always said, "The _____ _____ is very dangerous."

5. One day, a prince _____ _____ _____ _____ _____.

6. He said, "_____ _____. The world outside is wonderful."

7. Rapunzel said, "I don't know _____ _____ _____ _____ _____." Rapunzel _____ _____.

8. Finally, she _____ _____ her mind. She _____ her hair and _____ _____ from the tower.

9. When she _____ the world _____ _____ _____ _____ _____, she couldn't believe her eyes. "_____ _____ _____ _____!"

1. Rapunzel이 아기였을 때, 한 마녀가 그녀를 높은 탑에 가뒀다.
2. Rapunzel은 그 탑에서 자랐다. 그녀는 긴 머리카락을 가지고 있었다.
3. 마녀는 탑을 올라가기 위해 그 머리카락을 사용했다.
4. 마녀는 항상 "바깥세상은 매우 위험해."라고 말했다.
5. 어느 날, 한 왕자가 Rapunzel이 노래를 아름답게 부르고 있는 것을 들었다.
6. 그는 "내려와요. 바깥세상은 멋져요."라고 말했다.
7. Rapunzel은 "누가 사실을 말하고 있는지 모르겠어."라고 말했다. Rapunzel은 혼란스러웠다.
8. 마침내, 그녀는 결심했다. 그녀는 머리카락을 자르고 탑에서 내려왔다.
9. 그녀가 처음으로 세상과 마주했을 때, 그녀는 자신의 눈을 믿을 수 없었다. "정말 아름다운 세상이야!"

Check Up

1. A: Can _____ do _____ _____ _____ _____?

2. B: _____. What is it?

3. A: Can you _____ _____ _____ _____ these balloons?

4. B: No _____.

1. A: 부탁 하나 해도 될까?
2. B: 물론이지. 뭔데?
3. A: 이 풍선들을 부는 것 좀 도와줄 수 있니?
4. B: 좋아.

※ 다음 우리말을 영어로 쓰시오.

Project

1. 보물 사냥꾼들에게,
➡

2. 안녕. 우리는 교실에 우리 보물을 숨겼어. 그것은 맛있는 것이야.
➡

3. 그것이 어디에 있는지 알고 싶니? 그러면 다음 단계를 따라 봐.
➡

4. 우선, 창문 옆에 있는 식물을 찾아. 그 식물 아래를 봐. 너는 열쇠 하나를 찾을 거야.
➡

5. 두 번째, 그 열쇠를 들고 교실 뒤쪽으로 걸어가. 너는 사물함을 볼 거야.
➡

6. 보물은 왼쪽에서 세 번째 사물함 안에 있어.
➡

7. 그것은 잠겼으니 그것을 열기 위해 열쇠를 사용해. 알겠지? 많이 먹으렴.
➡

Think and Write

1. Rapunzel이 아기였을 때, 한 마녀가 그녀를 높은 탑에 가뒀다.
➡

2. Rapunzel은 그 탑에서 자랐다. 그녀는 긴 머리카락을 가지고 있었다.
➡

3. 마녀는 탑을 올라가기 위해 그 머리카락을 사용했다.
➡

4. 마녀는 항상 "바깥세상은 매우 위험해."라고 말했다.
➡

5. 어느 날, 한 왕자가 Rapunzel이 노래를 아름답게 부르고 있는 것을 들었다.
➡

6. 그는 "내려와요. 바깥세상은 멋져요."라고 말했다.
➡

7. Rapunzel은 "누가 사실을 말하고 있는지 모르겠어."라고 말했다. Rapunzel은 혼란스러웠다.
➡

8. 마침내, 그녀는 결심했다. 그녀는 머리카락을 자르고 탑에서 내려왔다.
➡

9. 그녀가 처음으로 세상과 마주했을 때, 그녀는 자신의 눈을 믿을 수 없었다. "정말 아름다운 세상이야!"
➡

Check Up

1. A: 부탁 하나 해도 될까?
➡

2. B: 물론이지. 뭔데?
➡

3. A: 이 풍선들을 부는 것 좀 도와줄 수 있니?
➡

4. B: 좋아.
➡

※ 다음 영어를 우리말로 쓰시오.

01 bark _____

02 spread _____

03 package _____

04 cover _____

05 date _____

06 agree _____

07 signature _____

08 borrow _____

09 cool _____

10 meaning _____

11 entire _____

12 perfectly _____

13 envelope _____

14 situation _____

15 graduate _____

16 punish _____

17 inside _____

18 local _____

19 mean _____

20 receive _____

21 article _____

22 funny _____

23 grade _____

24 classmate _____

25 nearby _____

26 reporter _____

27 extra _____

28 decide _____

29 pleased _____

30 excited _____

31 satisfied _____

32 vocabulary _____

33 war _____

34 dictionary _____

35 have no choice _____

36 be over _____

37 by the time _____

38 take out _____

39 hold up _____

40 be worried about _____

41 on the way home _____

42 be famous for _____

43 be excited about _____

단어 Test

※ 다음 우리말을 영어로 쓰시오.

01 (개가) 짖다 _____

02 의미하다 _____

03 봉투 _____

04 빌리다 _____

05 서명 _____

06 학년 _____

07 받다 _____

08 멋진 _____

09 날짜를 적다; 날짜 _____

10 기쁜, 기뻐하는 _____

11 의미 _____

12 처벌하다, 벌주다 _____

13 (신문의) 기사 _____

14 여분의, 추가의 _____

15 만족하는 _____

16 신이 난 _____

17 재미있는 _____

18 상황 _____

19 퍼지다, 확산되다 _____

20 졸업하다 _____

21 소포 _____

22 안에 _____

23 지역의, 지방의 _____

24 결정하다 _____

25 완벽하게 _____

26 기자 _____

27 사전 _____

28 보도하다, 덮다 _____

29 인근의, 가까이의 _____

30 재빨리, 빠르게 _____

31 전체의, 온 _____

32 어휘 _____

33 전쟁 _____

34 동의하다 _____

35 더욱 더, 갈수록 더 _____

36 ~로 유명하다 _____

37 선택의 여지가 없다 _____

38 쥐다, 잡다 _____

39 (사전 등에서) 찾아보다 _____

40 손을 쓸 수 없는 _____

41 그때까지, ~할 때까지 _____

42 집으로 가는 길에 _____

43 ~에 대해 걱정하다 _____

※ 다음 영영풀이에 알맞은 단어를 <보기>에서 골라 쓴 후, 우리말 뜻을 쓰시오.

1 _____ : to complete a course in education: _____

2 _____ : a flat paper container used for sending letters in: _____

3 _____ : to have the same opinion as somebody: _____

4 _____ : including everything, everyone or every part: _____

5 _____ : the idea that is represented by a word, phrase, etc.: _____

6 _____ : all the words that a person knows or uses: _____

7 _____ : more than is usual, expected, or than exists already: _____

8 _____ :a piece of writing about a particular subject in a newspaper: _____

9 _____ : a person who is or was in the same class as you at school or college: _____

10 _____ : a box, bag, etc. in which things are wrapped or packed: _____

11 _____ : a person who collects and reports news for newspapers, radio or television: _____

12 _____ : your name as you usually write it, for example at the end of a letter: _____

13 _____ : to take and use something that belongs to somebody else, and return it to them at a later time: _____

14 _____ : all the circumstances and things that are happening at a particular time and in a particular place: _____

15 _____ : to make somebody suffer because they have broken the law or done something wrong: _____

16 _____ : a book that gives a list of the words of a language in alphabetical order and explains what they mean, or gives a word for them in a foreign language: _____

보기			
vocabulary	dictionary	article	envelope
punish	entire	package	signature
reporter	borrow	situation	agree
extra	graduate	meaning	classmate

Step1

※ 다음 우리말과 일치하도록 빈칸에 알맞은 것을 골라 쓰시오.

1 Nick Allen was _____ about starting _____ _____, but he was _____ about one thing — Mrs. Granger's English class.

A. worried   B. grade   C. fifth   D. excited

2 Mrs. Granger was _____ _____ her _____ vocabulary _____.

A. lessons   B. famous   C. difficult   D. for

3 In the first _____, Mrs. Granger said, "Everyone should have a good _____. You can look _____ the _____ of new words in it."

A. meanings   B. class   C. dictionary   D. up

4 "Mrs. Granger? Who decides the _____ of words? I mean, who _____ that 'dog' _____ an animal that _____?" Nick asked.

A. means   B. meanings   C. barks   D. decided

5 "You did, Nick. You, me, and the _____ town and country. We all _____. That gives the word _____ _____."

A. agreed   B. meaning   C. entire   D. its

6 Nick wasn't _____. "When did I _____?" he said to _____.

A. agree   B. satisfied   C. himself

7 _____ the way home, he _____ to _____ Mrs. Granger's idea.

A. decided   B. on   C. test

8 He _____ _____ a pen and said, "_____ today, this is a *frindle*."

A. from   B. out   C. took

9 The next day, he _____ five friends to _____ the _____ *frindle*.

A. use   B. asked   C. word

10 _____ _____, Nick said, "Mrs. Granger, I _____ my *frindle* today."

A. forgot   B. class   C. during

11 His friend, John, _____ _____ a pen and said, "I have an _____ *frindle*. Do you want to _____ my *frindle*?"

A. up   B. extra   C. help   D. borrow

12 Mrs. Granger was _____ _____.

A. pleased   B. not

13 She said, "Your new word is cute, _____ it _____ has a _____ good name — a pen."

A. perfectly   B. already   C. but

14 Nick's classmates _____ this _____ and began to _____ the word _____ and more.

A. more   B. funny   C. use   D. found

15 _____ just three days, it _____ the _____ _____ at school.

A. word   B. in   C. cool   D. became

---

1 Nick Allen은 5학년이 시작되는 것이 신났지만, 한 가지가 걱정되었다. 그것은 Granger 선생님의 영어 수업이었다.

2 Granger 선생님은 어려운 어휘 수업으로 유명했다.

3 첫 번째 시간에 Granger 선생님은 말했다. "모두 좋은 사전을 가지고 있어야 해요. 여러분은 사전에서 새 단어의 뜻을 찾을 수 있어요."

4 "Granger 선생님? 단어의 뜻은 누가 정하나요? 그러니까, '개'는 짖는 동물을 뜻한다고 누가 정했나요?" Nick이 물었다.

5 "네가 그랬지, Nick. 너와 나, 그리고 온 마을과 나라가 말이야. 우리 모두가 동의했단다. 그게 그 단어에게 의미를 부여하는 거야."

6 Nick은 마음에 들지 않았다. "내가 언제 동의했지?" 그는 혼잣말을 했다.

7 집에 가는 길에 Nick은 Granger 선생님의 생각을 시험하기로 결심했다.

8 그는 펜을 하나 꺼내서 말했다. "오늘부터 이것은: 'frindle'이야."

9 그 다음날 Nick은 다섯 명의 친구들에게 단어 'frindle'을 사용해 달라고 부탁했다.

10 수업 중에 Nick이 말했다. "Granger 선생님, 오늘 'frindle'을 빠뜨리고 왔어요."

11 Nick의 친구인 John이 펜을 하나 들고서는 말했다. "나한테 여분의 'frindle'이 있어. 내 'frindle'을 빌리고 싶니?"

12 Granger 선생님은 즐거워하지 않았다.

13 선생님이 말했다. "너희들의 새 단어는 귀엽지만, 그건 이미 'pen'이라는 완벽하게 좋은 이름이 있단다."

14 Nick의 학급 친구들은 이것을 재미있어 했고 더욱 더 그 단어를 사용하기 시작했다.

15 단지 3일 만에 학교에서 그것은 멋진 단어가 되었다.

16 Mrs. Granger said to Nick after class, "This is _____ out of _____. Can you tell your friends to _____ _____ *frindle?*"

    A. hand   B. getting   C. saying   D. stop

17 "I'm sorry, but I can't _____ it. It started _____ my word, but now it's the students' _____."

    A. as   B. stop   C. word

18 "Very well. Then I _____ _____ _____."

    A. choice   B. no   C. have

19 Mrs. Granger _____ _____ an envelope and asked Nick to _____ and _____ the back.

    A. date   B. out   C. sign   D. took

20 She said, "I'll _____ this letter to you _____ all this is _____."

    A. over   B. give   C. when

21 Nick _____, "She really _____ me."

    A. hates   B. thought

22 _____ week, Mrs. Granger _____ a war _____ *frindle.*

    A. began   B. next   C. with

23 She said that she would _____ any student _____ _____ it.

    A. using   B. punish   C. for

24 But this _____ made _____ _____.

    A. only   B. worse   C. things

25 The students wanted _____ _____ the word _____ and more.

    A. use   B. more   C. to

26 *Frindle* quickly _____ _____ _____ middle and high schools.

    A. nearby   B. spread   C. to

27 _____ _____, a local newspaper reporter _____ an article on the situation and everyone in town _____ about it.

    A. wrote   B. after   C. knew   D. shortly

28 A month _____, a national television station _____ the news and everyone _____ _____ about *frindle.*

    A. out   B. covered   C. found   D. later

29 _____ the time Nick _____ _____ elementary school, most students in the country _____ the word.

    A. used   B. from   C. graduated   D. by

30 Time _____ _____ and Nick turned 21. _____ day, he _____ a package.

    A. received   B. by   C. flew   D. one

31 _____ it, he _____ a pen, an _____ and a dictionary.

    A. found   B. inside   C. envelope

32 The envelope had his _____ _____ fifth _____.

    A. grade   B. from   C. signature

33 The dictionary had a yellow _____. It _____, "_____ page 541."

    A. said   B. note   C. check

16 Granger 선생님은 수업 후에 Nick에게 말했다. "점점 손을 쓸 수 없게 되어 가는구나. 네 친구들에게 'frindle'을 말하는 것을 멈춰달라고 말해 줄래?"

17 "죄송하지만, 멈추게 할 수가 없어요. 그건 제 단어로 시작됐지만, 이제 그건 학생들의 단어예요."

18 "좋아. 그러면 선택의 여지가 없구나."

19 Granger 선생님은 봉투를 하나 꺼내더니 Nick에게 뒷면에 서명을 하고 날짜를 적게 했다.

20 선생님은 말했다. "이 모든 것이 끝나면 내가 이 편지를 너에게 줄게."

21 Nick은 생각했다. "선생님은 내가 정말 싫은가봐."

22 다음 주에 Granger 선생님은 'frindle'과의 전쟁을 시작했다.

23 선생님은 그 단어를 사용한다면 어떤 학생이든 벌을 줄 것이라고 말했다.

24 하지만 이것은 상황을 더 나쁘게 만들 뿐이었다.

25 학생들은 그 단어를 더욱 더 사용하고 싶어했다.

26 'frindle'은 근처의 중학교와 고등학교로 빠르게 퍼져 나갔다.

27 곧 지역 신문 기자가 그 상황에 관한 기사를 썼고, 마을의 모든 사람들이 그것에 관해 알게 되었다.

28 한 달 후에 한 전국 텔레비전 방송사에 서 그 소식을 다루었고, 모든 사람들이 'frindle'에 관해 알게 되었다.

29 Nick이 초등학교를 졸업할 때쯤에는 이 나라의 대부분의 학생들이 그 단어를 사용했다.

30 시간은 흘러 Nick은 21살이 되었다. 어느 날 Nick은 소포를 하나 받았다.

31 소포 안에는 펜 한 자루, 봉투 한 장, 그리고 사전 한 권이 있었다.

32 봉투에는 5학년 때의 그의 서명이 있었다.

33 사전에는 노란색 쪽지가 있었다. "541쪽을 확인해 봐."라고 적혀 있었다.

※ 다음 우리말과 일치하도록 빈칸에 알맞은 말을 쓰시오.

1 Nick Allen _____ _____ _____ starting _____ _____, but he _____ _____ _____ one thing — Mrs. Granger's English class.

2 Mrs. Granger _____ _____ _____ her difficult _____ _____.

3 In the first class, Mrs. Granger said, "Everyone _____ _____ _____ _____. You _____ _____ _____ the _____ of _____ _____ in it."

4 "Mrs. Granger? Who decides _____ _____ of words? I mean, who decided that 'dog' _____ an animal that _____?" Nick asked.

5 "You did, Nick. You, me, and the _____ _____ and country. We all _____. That gives the word _____ _____."

6 Nick wasn't _____. "When _____ _____ _____?" he _____ _____ _____.

7 _____ the way home, he _____ to test Mrs. Granger's idea.

8 He _____ _____ a pen and said, "_____ today, this is a *frindle*."

9 The next day, he _____ five friends _____ _____ the word *frindle*.

10 _____ _____, Nick said, "Mrs. Granger, I _____ my *frindle* today."

11 His friend, John, _____ _____ a pen and said, "I have an _____ *frindle*. Do you want _____ _____ my *frindle*?"

12 Mrs. Granger _____ _____ _____.

13 She said, "Your new word is cute, _____ it _____ _____ a _____ good name — a pen."

14 Nick's classmates _____ this _____ and began _____ _____ the word _____ _____ _____.

15 _____ just three days, it _____ the _____ _____ at school.

1 Nick Allen은 5학년이 시작되는 것이 신났지만, 한 가지가 걱정되었다. 그것은 Granger 선생님의 영어 수업이었다.

2 Granger 선생님은 어려운 어휘 수업으로 유명했다.

3 첫 번째 시간에 Granger 선생님은 말했다. "모두 좋은 사전을 가지고 있어야 해요. 여러분은 사전에서 새 단어의 뜻을 찾을 수 있어요."

4 "Granger 선생님? 단어의 뜻은 누가 정하나요? 그러니까, '개'는 짖는 동물을 뜻한다고 누가 정했나요?" Nick이 물었다.

5 "네가 그랬지, Nick. 너와 나, 그리고 온 마을과 나라가 말이야. 우리 모두가 동의했단다. 그게 그 단어에게 의미를 부여하는 거야."

6 Nick은 마음에 들지 않았다. "내가 언제 동의했지?" 그는 혼잣말을 했다.

7 집에 가는 길에 Nick은 Granger 선생님의 생각을 시험하기로 결심했다.

8 그는 펜을 하나 꺼내서 말했다. "오늘부터 이것은 'frindle'이야."

9 그 다음날 Nick은 다섯 명의 친구들에게 단어 'frindle'을 사용해 달라고 부탁했다.

10 수업 중에 Nick이 말했다. "Granger 선생님, 오늘 'frindle'을 빠뜨리고 왔어요."

11 Nick의 친구인 John이 펜을 하나 들고서는 말했다. "나한테 여분의 'frindle'이 있어. 내 'frindle'을 빌리고 싶니?"

12 Granger 선생님은 즐거워하지 않았다.

13 선생님이 말했다. "너희들의 새 단어는 귀엽지만, 그건 이미 'pen'이라는 완벽하게 좋은 이름이 있단다."

14 Nick의 학급 친구들은 이것을 재미있어 했고 더욱 더 그 단어를 사용하기 시작했다.

15 단지 3일 만에 학교에서 그것은 멋진 단어가 되었다.

16 Mrs. Granger _____ _____ Nick _____ _____, "This is _____ _____ _____ _____. Can you tell your friends _____ _____ _____ *frindle*?"

17 "I'm sorry, but I can't _____ _____. It started _____ my word, but now it's the _____ _____."

18 "Very well. Then I have _____ _____."

19 Mrs. Granger _____ _____ an envelope and _____ Nick _____ _____ and _____ the back.

20 She said, "_____ _____ this letter _____ when all this _____ _____."

21 Nick _____, "She really _____ me."

22 Next week, Mrs. Granger _____ a war _____ *frindle*.

23 She said that she would _____ any student _____ _____ it.

24 But this only _____ _____ _____.

25 The students wanted _____ _____ the word _____ _____ _____.

26 *Frindle* quickly _____ _____ _____ middle and high schools.

27 _____ _____, a local newspaper reporter _____ an article _____ the situation and everyone in town _____ _____ _____.

28 _____ _____ _____, a national television station _____ the news and everyone _____ _____ _____ *frindle*.

29 _____ _____ _____ Nick _____ _____ elementary school, _____ in the country _____ the word.

30 Time _____ _____ and Nick turned 21. _____ _____, he _____ a package.

31 _____ _____, he _____ a pen, an _____ and a _____.

32 The envelope had his _____ _____ _____ _____ _____.

33 The dictionary had a _____ _____. _____ _____, "Check page 541."

---

16 Granger 선생님은 수업 후에 Nick에게 말했다. "점점 손을 쓸 수 없게 되어 가는구나. 네 친구들에게 'frindle'을 말하는 것을 멈춰달라고 말해 줄래?"

17 "죄송하지만, 멈추게 할 수가 없어요. 그건 제 단어로 시작됐지만, 이제 그건 학생들의 단어예요."

18 "좋아. 그러면 선택의 여지가 없구나."

19 Granger 선생님은 봉투를 하나 꺼내더니 Nick에게 뒷면에 서명을 하고 날짜를 적게 했다.

20 선생님은 말했다. "이 모든 것이 끝나면 내가 이 편지를 너에게 줄게."

21 Nick은 생각했다. "선생님은 내가 정말 싫은가봐."

22 다음 주에 Granger 선생님은 'frindle'과의 전쟁을 시작했다.

23 선생님은 그 단어를 사용한다면 어떤 학생이든 벌을 줄 것이라고 말했다.

24 하지만 이것은 상황을 더 나쁘게 만들 뿐이었다.

25 학생들은 그 단어를 더욱 더 사용하고 싶어했다.

26 'frindle'은 근처의 중학교와 고등학교로 빠르게 퍼져 나갔다.

27 곧 지역 신문 기자가 그 상황에 관한 기사를 썼고, 마을의 모든 사람들이 그것에 관해 알게 되었다.

28 한 달 후에 한 전국 텔레비전 방송사에 서 그 소식을 다루었고, 모든 사람들이 'frindle'에 관해 알게 되었다.

29 Nick이 초등학교를 졸업할 때쯤에는 이 나라의 대부분의 학생들이 그 단어를 사용했다.

30 시간은 흘러 Nick은 21살이 되었다. 어느 날 Nick은 소포를 하나 받았다.

31 소포 안에는 펜 한 자루, 봉투 한 장, 그리고 사전 한 권이 있었다.

32 봉투에는 5학년 때의 그의 서명이 있었다.

33 사전에는 노란색 쪽지가 있었다. "541쪽을 확인해 봐."라고 적혀 있었다.

※ 다음 문장을 우리말로 쓰시오.

1 Nick Allen was excited about starting fifth grade, but he was worried about one thing
— Mrs. Granger's English class.

➡ _____

2 Mrs. Granger was famous for her difficult vocabulary lessons.

➡ _____

3 In the first class, Mrs. Granger said, "Everyone should have a good dictionary.
You can look up the meanings of new words in it."

➡ _____

4 "Mrs. Granger? Who decides the meanings of words? I mean, who decided that 'dog' means
an animal that barks?" Nick asked.

➡ _____

5 "You did, Nick. You, me, and the entire town and country. We all agreed.
That gives the word its meaning."

➡ _____
_____

6 Nick wasn't satisfied. "When did I agree?" he said to himself.

➡ _____

7 On the way home, he decided to test Mrs. Granger's idea.

➡ _____

8 He took out a pen and said, "From today, this is a *frindle* ."

➡ _____

9 The next day, he asked five friends to use the word *frindle*.

➡ _____

10 During class, Nick said, "Mrs. Granger, I forgot my frindle today."

➡ _____

11 His friend, John, held up a pen and said, "I have an extra *frindle* . Do you want to borrow my *frindle*?"

➡ _____

12 Mrs. Granger was not pleased.

➡ _____

13 She said, "Your new word is cute, but it already has a perfectly good name — a pen."

➡ _____

14 Nick's classmates found this funny and began to use the word more and more.

➡ _____

15 In just three days, it became the cool word at school.

➡ _____

16 Mrs. Granger said to Nick after class, "This is getting out of hand. Can you tell your friends to stop saying *frindle*?"

⇒ _____

_____

17 "I'm sorry, but I can't stop it. It started as my word, but now it's the students' word."

⇒ _____

18 "Very well. Then I have no choice."

⇒ _____

19 Mrs. Granger took out an envelope and asked Nick to sign and date the back.

⇒ _____

20 She said, "I'll give this letter to you when all this is over."

⇒ _____

21 Nick thought, "She really hates me."

⇒ _____

22 Next week, Mrs. Granger began a war with *frindle*.

⇒ _____

23 She said that she would punish any student for using it.

⇒ _____

24 But this only made things worse.

⇒ _____

25 The students wanted to use the word more and more.

⇒ _____

26 *Frindle* quickly spread to nearby middle and high schools.

⇒ _____

27 Shortly after, a local newspaper reporter wrote an article on the situation and everyone in town knew about it.

⇒ _____

28 A month later, a national television station covered the news and everyone found out about *frindle*.

⇒ _____

29 By the time Nick graduated from elementary school, most students in the country used the word.

⇒ _____

30 Time flew by and Nick turned 21. One day, he received a package.

⇒ _____

31 Inside it, he found a pen, an envelope and a dictionary.

⇒ _____

32 The envelope had his signature from fifth grade.

⇒ _____

33 The dictionary had a yellow note. It said, "Check page 541."

⇒ _____

※ 다음 괄호 안의 단어들을 우리말에 맞도록 바르게 배열하시오.

1 (Allen / Nick / excited / was / starting / about / grade, / fifth / but / was / he / about / worried / thing / one / — / Granger's / Mrs. / class. / English)
➡ _____

2 (Granger / Mrs. / famous / was / her / for / vocabulary / lessons. / difficult)
➡ _____

3 (the / in / class, / first / Granger / Mrs. / said, / "everyone / have / should / a / dictionary. / good // can / you / look / the / up / meanings / new / of / it." / in / words)
➡ _____

4 (Granger? / "Mrs. // decides / who / meanings / words? / of / the // mean, / I / decided / who / 'dog' / that / an / means / barks?" / that / animal // asked. / Nick)
➡ _____

5 (did, / "you / Nick. // me, / you, / and / entire / the / country. / and / town // all / we / agreed. // gives / that / word / the / meaning." / its)
➡ _____

6 (wasn't / Nick / satisfied. // "when / I / did / agree?" / said / he / himself. / to)
➡ _____

7 (the / on / home, / way / decided / he / test / to / Granger's / Mrs. / idea.)
➡ _____

8 (took / he / a / out / and / pen / said, / "from / today, / is / this / *frindle*." / a)
➡ _____

9 (next / the / day, / asked / he / friends / five / use / to / *frindle*. / word / the)
➡ _____

10 (class, / during / said, / Nick / Granger, / "Mrs. / forgot / I / today." / *frindle* / my)
➡ _____

11 (friend, / his / John, / up / held / pen / a / and / said, / "I / an / extra / have / *frindle*. // you / do / want / borrow / to / *frindle*?" / my)
➡ _____

12 (Granger / Mrs. / was / pleased. / not)
➡ _____

13 (said, / she / "your / word / new / cute, / is / it / but / already / has / perfectly / a / name / good / — / pen." / a)
➡ _____

14 (classmates / Nick's / this / found / funny / began / and / use / to / word / the / more / and / more.)
➡ _____

15 (just / in / days, / three / became / it / cool / the / school. / at / word)
➡ _____

1 Nick Allen은 5학년이 시작되는 것이 신났지만, 한 가지가 걱정되었다. 그것은 Granger 선생님의 영어 수업이었다.

2 Granger 선생님은 어려운 어휘 수업으로 유명했다.

3 첫 번째 시간에 Granger 선생님은 말했다. "모두 좋은 사전을 가지고 있어야 해요. 여러분은 사전에서 새 단어의 뜻을 찾을 수 있어요."

4 "Granger 선생님? 단어의 뜻은 누가 정하나요? 그러니까, '개'는 짖는 동물을 뜻한다고 누가 정했나요?" Nick이 물었다.

5 "네가 그랬지, Nick. 너와 나, 그리고 온 마을과 나라가 말이야. 우리 모두가 동의했단다. 그게 그 단어에게 의미를 부여하는 거야."

6 Nick은 마음에 들지 않았다. "내가 언제 동의했지?" 그는 혼잣말을 했다.

7 집에 가는 길에 Nick은 Granger 선생님의 생각을 시험하기로 결심했다.

8 그는 펜을 하나 꺼내서 말했다. "오늘부터 이것은 'frindle'이야."

9 그 다음날 Nick은 다섯 명의 친구들에게 단어 'frindle'을 사용해 달라고 부탁했다.

10 수업 중에 Nick이 말했다. "Granger 선생님, 오늘 'frindle'을 빠뜨리고 왔어요."

11 Nick의 친구인 John이 펜을 하나 들고서는 말했다. "나한테 여분의 'frindle'이 있어. 내 'frindle'을 빌리고 싶어?"

12 Granger 선생님은 즐거워하지 않았다.

13 선생님이 말했다. "너희들의 새 단어는 귀엽지만, 그건 이미 'pen'이라는 완벽하게 좋은 이름이 있단다."

14 Nick의 학급 친구들은 이것을 재미있어 했고 더욱 더 그 단어를 사용하기 시작했다.

15 단지 3일 만에 학교에서 그것은 멋진 단어가 되었다.

16 (Granger / Mrs. / to / said / after / Nick / class, / "this / getting / is / of / out / hand. // you / can / your / tell / to / friends / saying / stop / *frindle*?")
➡

17 (sorry, / "I'm / but / can't / I / it. / stop // started / it / my / as / word, / now / but / it's / word." / students' / the)
➡

18 (well. / "very // I / then / choice." / no / have)
➡

19 (Granger / Mrs. / out / took / envelope / an / and / Nick / asked / to / date / and / sign / back. / the)
➡

20 (said, / she / "I'll / this / give / letter / you / to / when / this / all / over." / is)
➡

21 (thought, / Nick / "she / hates / really / me.")
➡

22 (week, / next / Granger / Mrs. / a / began / war / *frindle*. / with)
➡

23 (said / she / that / would / she / punish / student / any / it. / using / for)
➡

24 (this / but / made / only / worse. / things)
➡

25 (students / the / to / wanted / use / word / the / and / more / more.)
➡

26 (quickly / *frindle* / to / spread / middle / nearby / and / schools. / high)
➡

27 (after, / shortly / local / a / reporter / newspaper / an / wrote / article / the / on / situation / and / in / everyone / knew / town / it. / about)
➡

28 (month / a / later, / national / a / station / television / covered / news / the / and / found / everyone / about / out / *frindle*.)
➡

29 (the / by / time / graduated / Nick / from / school, / elementary / students / most / the / in / country / word. / the / used)
➡

30 (flew / time / and / by / Nick / 21. / turned // day, / one / received / package. / a / he)
➡

31 (it, / inside / found / he / pen, / a / envelope / an / and / dictionary. / a)
➡

32 (envelope / the / his / had / from / signature / grade. / fifth)
➡

33 (dictionary / the / a / had / yellow / note. // said, / it / page / "check / 541.")
➡

---

16 Granger 선생님은 수업 후에 Nick에게 말했다. "점점 손을 쓸 수 없게 되어 가는구나. 네 친구들에게 'frindle'을 말하는 것을 멈춰달라고 말해 줄래?"

17 "죄송하지만, 멈추게 할 수가 없어요. 그건 제 단어로 시작됐지만, 이제 그건 학생들의 단어예요."

18 "좋아. 그러면 선택의 여지가 없구나."

19 Granger 선생님은 봉투를 하나 꺼내더니 Nick에게 뒷면에 서명을 하고 날짜를 적게 했다.

20 선생님은 말했다. "이 모든 것이 끝나면 내가 이 편지를 너에게 줄게."

21 Nick은 생각했다. "선생님은 내가 정말 싫은가봐."

22 다음 주에 Granger 선생님은 'frindle'과의 전쟁을 시작했다.

23 선생님은 그 단어를 사용한다면 어떤 학생이든 벌을 줄 것이라고 말했다.

24 하지만 이것은 상황을 더 나쁘게 만들 뿐이었다.

25 학생들은 그 단어를 더욱 더 사용하고 싶어했다.

26 'frindle'은 근처의 중학교와 고등학교로 빠르게 퍼져 나갔다.

27 곧 지역 신문 기자가 그 상황에 관한 기사를 썼고, 마을의 모든 사람들이 그것에 관해 알게 되었다.

28 한 달 후에 한 전국 텔레비전 방송사에서 그 소식을 다루었고, 모든 사람들이 'frindle'에 관해 알게 되었다.

29 Nick이 초등학교를 졸업할 때쯤에는 이 나라의 대부분의 학생들이 그 단어를 사용했다.

30 시간은 흘러 Nick은 21살이 되었다. 어느 날 Nick은 소포를 하나 받았다.

31 소포 안에는 펜 한 자루, 봉투 한 장, 그리고 사전 한 권이 있었다.

32 봉투에는 5학년 때의 그의 서명이 있었다.

33 사전에는 노란색 쪽지가 있었다. "541쪽을 확인해 봐."라고 적혀 있었다.

※ 다음 우리말을 영어로 쓰시오.

1 Nick Allen은 5학년이 시작되는 것이 신났지만, 한 가지가 걱정되었다. 그것은 Granger 선생님의 영어 수업이었다.

➡ _____

_____

2 Granger 선생님은 어려운 어휘 수업으로 유명했다.

➡ _____

3 첫 번째 시간에 Granger 선생님은 말했다. "모두 좋은 사전을 가지고 있어야 해요. 여러분은 사전에서 새 단어의 뜻을 찾을 수 있어요."

➡ _____

4 "Granger 선생님? 단어의 뜻은 누가 정하나요? 그러니까, '개'는 짖는 동물을 뜻한다고 누가 정했나요?" Nick이 물었다.

➡ _____

5 "네가 그랬지, Nick. 너와 나, 그리고 온 마을과 나라가 말이야. 우리 모두가 동의했단다. 그게 그 단어에게 의미를 부여하는 거야."

➡ _____

_____

6 Nick은 마음에 들지 않았다. "내가 언제 동의했지?" 그는 혼잣말을 했다.

➡ _____

7 집에 가는 길에 Nick은 Granger 선생님의 생각을 시험하기로 결심했다.

➡ _____

8 그는 펜을 하나 꺼내서 말했다. "오늘부터 이것은 'frindle'이야."

➡ _____

9 그 다음날 Nick은 다섯 명의 친구들에게 단어 'frindle'을 사용해 달라고 부탁했다.

➡ _____

10 수업 중에 Nick이 말했다. "Granger 선생님, 오늘 'frindle'을 빠뜨리고 왔어요."

➡ _____

11 Nick의 친구인 John이 펜을 하나 들고서는 말했다. "나한테 여분의 'frindle'이 있어. 내 'frindle'을 빌리고 싶니?"

➡ _____

12 Granger 선생님은 즐거워하지 않았다.

➡ _____

13 선생님이 말했다. "너희들의 새 단어는 귀엽지만, 그건 이미 'pen'이라는 완벽하게 좋은 이름이 있단다."

➡ _____

14 Nick의 학급 친구들은 이것을 재미있어 했고 더욱 더 그 단어를 사용하기 시작했다.

➡ _____

15 단지 3일 만에 학교에서 그것은 멋진 단어가 되었다.

➡ _____

16 Granger 선생님은 수업 후에 Nick에게 말했다. "점점 손을 쓸 수 없게 되어 가는구나. 네 친구들에게 '*frindle*'을 말하는 것을 멈춰달라고 말해 줄래?"

➡ _____

17 "죄송하지만, 멈추게 할 수가 없어요. 그건 제 단어로 시작됐지만, 이제 그건 학생들의 단어예요."

➡ _____

18 "좋아. 그러면 선택의 여지가 없구나."

➡ _____

19 Granger 선생님은 봉투를 하나 꺼내더니 Nick에게 뒷면에 서명을 하고 날짜를 적게 했다.

➡ _____

20 선생님은 말했다. "이 모든 것이 끝나면 내가 이 편지를 너에게 줄게."

➡ _____

21 Nick은 생각했다. "선생님은 내가 정말 싫은가봐."

➡ _____

22 다음 주에 Granger 선생님은 '*frindle*'과의 전쟁을 시작했다.

➡ _____

23 선생님은 그 단어를 사용한다면 어떤 학생이든 벌을 줄 것이라고 말했다.

➡ _____

24 하지만 이것은 상황을 더 나쁘게 만들 뿐이었다.

➡ _____

25 학생들은 그 단어를 더욱 더 사용하고 싶어했다.

➡ _____

26 '*frindle*'은 근처의 중학교와 고등학교로 빠르게 퍼져 나갔다.

➡ _____

27 곧 지역 신문 기자가 그 상황에 관한 기사를 썼고, 마을의 모든 사람들이 그것에 관해 알게 되었다.

➡ _____

28 한 달 후에 한 전국 텔레비전 방송사에 서 그 소식을 다루었고, 모든 사람들이 '*frindle*'에 관해 알게 되었다.

➡ _____

29 Nick이 초등학교를 졸업할 때쯤에는 이 나라의 대부분의 학생들이 그 단어를 사용했다.

➡ _____

30 시간은 흘러 Nick은 21살이 되었다. 어느 날 Nick은 소포를 하나 받았다.

➡ _____

31 소포 안에는 펜 한 자루, 봉투 한 장, 그리고 사전 한 권이 있었다.

➡ _____

32 봉투에는 5학년 때의 그의 서명이 있었다.

➡ _____

33 사전에는 노란색 쪽지가 있었다. "541쪽을 확인해 봐."라고 적혀 있었다.

➡ _____

MEMO

Come One, Come All

시험대비 실력평가 p.08

01 far 02 hometown 03 ①
04 (1) neighborhood (2) parade (3) advertise
(4) pile (5) regularly 05 ① 06 ⑤
07 (1) sled (2) colorful (3) arrow

01 주어진 단어는 반의어 관계를 나타낸다. far: 먼, near: 가까운
02 '당신이 태어나거나 자란 도시나 마을'을 가리키는 것은
hometown(고향)이다.
03 ①번 문장에서 sail은 '돛'을 의미한다. rake: 갈퀴로 긁다, 긁어
모으다
04 neighborhood: 근처, 이웃, parade: 퍼레이드, 행진,
advertise: 광고하다, pile: 더미, regularly: 규칙적으로
05 주어진 문장에서 live는 형용사로 '실황인, 라이브의'를 의미하
며 이와 같은 의미로 쓰인 것은 ①번이다. 나머지는 모두 '살다'
나 '살아 있다'를 의미한다.
06 주어진 문장에서 cross는 '건너다'와 '십자, X표'를 의미한다.
07 sled: 썰매, colorful: 형형색색의, arrow: 화살

서술형 시험대비 p.09

01 disappear 02 (1) live (2) fireworks (3) almost
(4) artwork 03 (1) to end (2) more and more
(3) come out (4) out of hand
04 (1) When will the music festival be held?
(2) I enjoyed decorating the Christmas tree.
(3) People gathered together to see the singer.
05 (1) People celebrate the festival everywhere for
two days.
(2) It was amazing to see my favorite singer in
person.
(3) People watch the artists shaping their works
from beginning to end.

01 주어진 단어는 반의어 관계를 나타낸다. appear: 나타나다,
disappear: 사라지다
02 live: 라이브의, 실황인, almost: 거의, fireworks: 불꽃놀이,
artwork: 예술 작품
03 from beginning to end: 처음부터 끝까지, more and
more: 더욱 더, come out: 나오다, out of hand: 손을 쓸 수
없는

04 hold: 개최하다, decorate: 장식하다, gather: 모이다, 모으다
05 (2) in person: 직접 (3) from beginning to end: 처음부터
끝까지

교과서 Conversation

핵심 Check p.10~11

1 (1) How can I get to
(2) Cross the street, go straight
(3) Is there a hospital / just around
2 (1) take about half an hour
(2) How long will it take to / by bus
(3) How long will it take to decorate the classroom /
take about two hours

교과서 대화문 익히기

Check(√) True or False p.12

1 T 2 F 3 T 4 F

교과서 확인학습 p.14~15

Listen and Speak 1-A
How can I get to the library / Cross, go straight, make

Listen and Speak 1-B
What's up / free / Why, ask / having / Let's, near / How
can I get there from the school / Come out, go straight,
Make a left, on your left / Let's meet / See, then

Listen and Speak 1-C
How can, get to / Go straight, make, be on your right /
far from / not

Listen and Speak 2-A
be late for / How long will it take to get to the theater /
take about, by bus / almost

Listen and Speak 2-B
excited / Me, too, advertise / about making / post
them, neighborhood / How long will it take to / take
about / come to

Real Life Talk
get to / over there / Take, get off / How long will it
take to get there / take about / the festival / it's a lot
of fun / have a great time

01 It will take about 5 minutes by car.

02 (B) → (E) → (C) → (D) → (A)

03 ⓒ → and 04 ⑤

02 (B) 길 묻기 → (E) 길 안내하기 → (C) 거리가 먼지 질문 →
(D) 대답 → (A) 감사 표현

03 between A and B: A와 B 사이에

시험대비 실력평가 p.17~18

01 How long will it take to get to the theater?

02 ① 03 why don't we have lunch together?

04 ⑤ 05 advertise 06 ⓐ the school festival

ⓑ the posters 07 ⑤

08 He will go there by bus.

09 Because he heard (that) it's a lot of fun.

10 He should take the number 11 bus.

11 (A) get (B) Go straight (C) a right (D) one
block (E) front

02 by bus: 버스로

03 how about ~?=why don't we ~?= ~하는 게 어때?

04 위 대화를 읽고 Emma가 Ming's까지 가는 데 걸리는 시간은
알 수 없다.

05 '사람들이 물건을 사게 만들도록 물건에 대해 대중에게 이야기
하다'를 가리키는 말은 advertise(광고하다)이다.

07 Andy와 Mike가 그들의 이웃들과 포스터를 게시할 것이라는
설명은 대화의 내용과 일치하지 않는다.

11 Green Street까지 직진하세요. 우회전하세요. 한 구역 곧장 간
후 길을 건너면 마켓이 당신 앞에 있을 것입니다.

서술형 시험대비 p.19

01 How can I get to the library?

02 make a left 또는 turn left 03 ⓐ → excited

04 They are going to advertise the school festival.

05 They are going to make posters.

06 (A) Go straight to 1st Street and make a right
(B) left

01 이어지는 대답으로 보아 길을 묻는 질문이 적절하다.

02 make a left: 왼쪽으로 돌다

03 exciting: 흥분시키는, excited: 신나는, 흥분한

04 Andy와 Mike는 학교 축제를 홍보할 것이다.

05 Andy와 Mike는 포스터를 만들 것이다.

06 극장에 가기 위해 1st Street까지 곧장 간 후 오른쪽으로 돌면
왼쪽에 있다.

교과서

Grammar

핵심 Check p.20~21

1 (1) It, to exercise (2) It, to drive (3) to lie

2 (1) felt, follow(ing) (2) saw, enter(ing)

(3) made[had], clean

시험대비 기본평가 p.22

01 (1) get → to get (2) to changing → to change

(3) said → say(또는 saying)

(4) to dance → dance(또는 dancing)

02 (1) fall 또는 falling (2) to go

(3) break 또는 breaking (4) to play

03 (1) I heard the baby cry(ing).

(2) It is a good idea for you to wake up early.

(3) Emma saw them swim(ming) around the island.

(4) People watch the artists create their works
from beginning to end.

01 (1) 가주어 it에 의미상의 주어 'for+목적격'이 쓰였으므로 진주
어로 to부정사를 쓰는 것이 옳다. (2) to부정사의 형태는 'to+동
사원형'이다. (3), (4) 지각동사의 목적어가 목적격보어의 행위
의 주체가 될 경우 목적격보어로 원형부정사나 현재분사를 쓰는
것이 옳다.

02 (1), (3) 지각동사의 목적격보어는 목적어와의 관계가 능동일
경우 원형부정사나 현재분사가 쓰인다. (2), (4) 진주어로 to부
정사를 쓸 수 있다.

03 (1), (3) '아기가 우는 소리', '그들이 수영하는 것'은 모두 목적
어가 목적격보어의 주체가 되므로 목적격보어로 원형부정사나
현재분사를 쓰는 것이 옳다. (2) 일찍 일어나는 것의 주체가 '너'
이므로 의미상의 주어로 '너'를 명시하여 for you를 써야 한다.
(4) 미술가들이 작품을 만드는 것을 지켜보는 것이므로 목적어
로 the artists, 목적격 보어로 create their works를 쓴다.

시험대비 실력평가 p.23~25

01 ③ 02 ② 03 ④

04 It is wrong to tell a lie. 05 ⑤ 06 ③

07 ④ 08 It is dangerous to ride a motorcycle
without a helmet. 09 ④ 10 ①

11 ② 12 anybody go(ing) out 13 ②

14 ⑤ 15 ⑤ 16 It is a lot of fun to
ride a horse. 17 ④ 18 ⑤ 19 ③

20 I saw her call(ing) someone. 21 ①, ④

01 ③ 모두 가주어 It이지만 ③번은 인칭대명사 It이다. 전자는 해석되지 않지만 후자는 '그것'이라고 해석된다.

02 see는 지각동사로 목적격보어로 원형부정사 혹은 현재분사, 과거분사를 받을 수 있다. 친구들이 축구를 하는 주체가 되므로 play(ing)가 빈칸에 들어가는 것이 적절하다.

03 '이 책을 읽는 것'이 주어이므로 to read this book이라고 쓰고 어려웠다는 것은 과거이므로 was difficult를 쓴다.

04 '거짓말을 하는 것'을 진주어로 하여 문장을 만든다.

05 make가 사역동사로 쓰였으므로 목적격보어로 원형부정사 형태를 쓰는 것이 옳다.

06 '부부가 싸우는 소리', '집이 흔들리는 것'이므로 ③번이 옳다.

07 listen to는 지각동사이다. 따라서 목적격보어로 원형부정사나 현재분사를 쓰는 것이 옳다.

08 to가 필요하다.

09 '최선을 다하는 것'이 주어이므로 to do your best를 써서 진주어를 만들고 가주어 It을 쓴 것이 답이다.

10 남자가 차에 타는 것이므로 get 혹은 getting을 쓰는 것이 옳다. dormitory: 기숙사

11 모두 주어로 쓰인 to부정사이지만 ②번은 부사로 쓰인 to부정사로 감정의 원인을 나타낸다.

12 누가 나가는 것을 보지 못했다는 의미이다. anybody는 go out의 주체가 되므로 go out 혹은 going out을 쓸 수 있다.

13 hear는 지각동사이며 you가 들어오는 것이므로 원형부정사 혹은 현재분사를 목적격보어로 써야 한다.

14 (A), (C) 목적어와의 관계로 보아 지각동사의 목적격보어로 원형부정사나 현재분사를 쓰는 것이 옳으며, (B) 진주어이므로 to부정사를 쓰는 것이 옳다.

15 주어진 문장의 It은 가주어이다. ①, ② 시간, 명암을 나타내는 비인칭 주어, ③, ④ 인칭대명사, ⑤ 가주어

16 '말을 타는 것'이 주어이므로 가주어 it을 활용하여 문장을 만든다.

17 '나는 Brad가 길을 걷고 있는 것을 보았다'가 옳다.

18 make는 목적격보어로 원형부정사를 취하여 사역동사의 의미를 갖는다.

19 네가 창문을 닫는 것을 내가 보았다는 의미가 된다. 따라서 ③번이 가장 적절하다.

20 '그녀가 누군가에게 전화하는 것'이므로 목적어로 her, 목적격보어로 call 또는 calling을 쓸 수 있다.

21 It is fun 다음에는 진주어로 동명사를 쓸 수도 있으며, see는 지각동사에 해당하므로 목적격보어로 원형부정사나 현재분사를 쓴다.

22 to부정사의 형태는 'to+동사원형'이다.

23 '나는 그 소년이 어제 나무에서 떨어지는 것을 보았다'라고 쓸 수 있다.

24 using을 대신하여 use를 써도 무방하다.

25 가주어 it과 진주어로 to부정사를 이용하여 문장을 만든다.

서술형 시험대비
p.26~27

01 you ride(또는 riding) a bike yesterday
02 It is bad to run on the stairs.
03 Did you see the accident happen?
04 It was true
05 It is not a good idea to allow students to use cell phones in school.
06 saw her cross(ing) the street
07 It is rude of you not to bow politely.
08 (1) To save water is important.
　 (2) It is important to save water.
09 open(ing) the window
10 It is difficult to shoot an arrow.
11 to reduce food waste in school cafeteria
12 musicians play(ing) beautiful live music, play(ing) catch, sing(ing) a song
13 It is easy to look up a word in a dictionary.
14 I heard someone play(ing) the piano.
15 It is important to be honest and fair.
16 잘못된 곳: to do → do(ing)　고친 이유: 지각동사의 목적격 보어로 원형부정사나 현재분사를 쓰는 것이 옳다.
17 It is not easy to be a doctor.
18 to watch them move the table
19 I felt someone follow(ing) me yesterday.

01 어제 네가 자전거를 타는 것을 보았기 때문이라고 답할 수 있다.

02 stairs: 계단

03 '사고가 발생하는 것을 보았니?'라는 문장으로 쓸 수 있다. happen: 발생하다

04 to부정사를 맨 뒤로 보낸 것으로 보아 가주어 it을 써야 함을 알 수 있다.

05 allow+목적어+to부정사: 목적어가 V하도록 허락하다

06 Susan이 길을 건너는 것을 보았다고 답하는 것이 적절하다. 'Susan이 길을 건너는 것'이므로 지각동사의 목적격보어로 원형부정사나 현재분사를 사용하여 답한다.

07 '예의 바르게 인사하지 않는 것'이 주어이다. to부정사의 부정은 to V 앞에 부정어를 써서 나타내므로 진주어를 not to bow politely라고 쓰는 것이 옳다.

08 '물을 절약하는 것'이 주어이므로 to save water라고 쓴다.

09 어떤 남자가 창문을 여는 것을 보았지만 그가 누구인지는 모른다고 답할 수 있다. 지각동사 see의 목적어로 창문을 여는 주체

인 a man이 쓰이고 있으므로 원형부정사나 현재분사를 목적격
보어로 쓰는 것이 옳다.

10 'To shoot an arrow is difficult.'라고 써도 무방하다.

11 학교에서 음식물 쓰레기를 줄이려는 것이 힘들었다는 대답이 들
어가는 것이 자연스럽다.

12 공원에서 너는 음악가들이 아름다운 즉석 연주를 하는 것을 들
을 수 있다. 또한 너는 아이들이 캐치볼 놀이를 하고, 커플들이
노래를 부르는 것을 볼 수 있다.

13 difficult의 반의어는 easy이므로 사전에서 단어를 찾는 것은
쉽다고 답할 수 있다. 'To look up a word in a dictionary
is easy.'라고 써도 좋다.

14 '누군가가 피아노를 연주하는' 소리이므로 목적어와 목적격보어
로 someone play(ing) the piano를 쓰는 것이 옳다

15 fair: 공정한

16 해석: Brady는 Clara가 무언가를 하는 것을 보았고 그녀가 무
엇을 하는지 궁금했다.

17 to become a doctor로 써도 무방하다.

18 move를 대신하여 moving을 써도 무방하다.

19 feel은 지각동사로 목적어와 목적격보어를 취하는 동사이
다. '누군가가 나를 따라오는 것'이라고 하였으므로 목적어로
someone을 쓰고 목적격보어로
follow 혹은 following을 쓰는 것이 옳다.

교과서 Reading

확인문제   p.28

1 T   2 F   3 F   4 T

확인문제   p.29

1 T   2 F   3 T   4 F   5 T

교과서 확인학습 A   p.30~31

01 Festival   02 from
03 the most popular   04 is usually
05 say goodbye, hello   06 celebrate, for
07 On, gather around, at night
08 begins the next day   09 chase each other
10 What, powder   11 to run around, throw, at
12 join street parades   13 White Nights
14 from   15 Have, heard of
16 amazing, happens

교과서 확인학습 B   p.32~33

1 Holi, the Festival of Colors
2 Amala from Delhi, India
3 Holi is the most popular festival in my country.
4 It is usually in March.
5 During the festival, we say goodbye to cold winter
   and hello to warm spring.
6 We celebrate the festival everywhere for two days.
7 On the first day, people gather around a big fire at
   night and sing and dance.
8 The main event begins the next day.
9 Children and adults chase each other with *gulal*.
10 What is *gulal*? It is blue, yellow, green and pink
   powder.
11 It's a lot of fun to run around and throw colorful
   powder at everyone.
12 We also join street parades!
13 White Nights Festival
14 Victor from St. Petersburg, Russia
15 Have you heard of the *White Nights*?
16 Every summer, this amazing thing happens in my
   hometown.
17 The night sky does not get completely dark.
18 During that time, we hold the White Nights
   Festival.
19 It usually starts in May and lasts for about a
   month.
20 During the festival, there is a ballet or an opera
   almost every night.
21 The most popular event is the Scarlet Sails
   celebration.
22 A boat with red sails slowly appears on the river.
23 Soon, fireworks begin and a water show follows.
24 You can also hear musicians playing beautiful live
   music.

17 does not get completely   18 During, hold
19 starts in, lasts, about
20 there is, almost every night
21 popular, celebration   22 appears on the river
23 begin, follows   24 hear, playing
25 Snow Festival   26 from
27 my favorite season because of
28 starts in the last week, goes on
29 The largest event   30 shape, into, other
31 watch, shaping, from, to 32 favorite activity
33 to fly through, on

25 Kiruna Snow Festival

26 Ebba from Kiruna, Sweden

27 Winter is my favorite season because of the Kiruna Snow Festival.

28 The festival starts in the last week of January and goes on for five or six days.

29 The largest event is the snow design competition.

30 The artists shape huge piles of snow into animals, buildings, and other beautiful artworks.

31 People watch the artists shaping their works from beginning to end.

32 My favorite activity is the dog sled ride.

33 It is amazing to fly through a world of snow on a dog sled.

01 ④   02 to run   03 ③

04 Holi is the most popular festival in India.

05 gather   06 ⑤   07 ②

08 the White Nights   09 ⑤

10 We can see a ballet or an opera almost every night.   11 shape (또는 shaping)   12 ②

13 ⑤   14 It lasts five or six days.   15 ②

16 ④   17 ⑤

18 chase[chasing] each other with gulal

19 We should go to the festival on the second day.

20 play(ing)   21 every summer   22 ⑤

23 ④   24 ②   25 ⑤

26 shaping their works   27 ④   28 ③, ⑤

01 at night: 밤에, throw something at someone: ~에게 ~을 던지다

02 가주어 it이 쓰이고 있으므로 진주어를 써야 한다. 병렬로 연결된 동사 throw의 형태로 미루어 보아 to run을 쓰는 것이 옳다.

03 주요 행사는 다음 날에 시작된다고 하였다. 따라서 ③번은 일치하지 않는다.

04 인도에서 가장 인기 있는 축제는 '홀리'라고 하였다.

05 사람들이 한 무리로 모이는 것은 gather이다.

06 colorful powder를 던진다고 하였다.

07 (A)에서 쓰인 현재완료는 '경험'이다. 따라서 '~에 가본 적이 있다'는 경험을 나타내는 has been to가 옳다.

08 '이 놀라운 것'이라는 것은 '백야'를 의미한다.

09 (C)는 '개최하다'는 의미로 쓰였다. ①, ③ ~을 쥐다, 잡다, ② 지탱하다, ④ (수화기를 들고) 기다리다, ⑤ 개최하다

10 축제 동안 거의 매일 밤 발레나 오페라가 있다고 하였다.

11 지각동사 watch의 목적격보어 자리이다. 목적어와 능동 관계에

있으므로 원형부정사 혹은 현재분사를 쓴다.

12 (A) 명사구가 이어지고 있으므로 because of (B) 복수명사가 이어지고 있으므로 other (C) 놀라움을 유발하는 것이므로 현재분사 amazing을 쓰는 것이 옳다.

13 ⑤ 몇 명의 미술가가 눈 디자인 대회에 참가하는지는 알 수 없다.

14 축제는 5~6일 동안 지속된다고 하였다.

15 (A) 출신을 나타내는 전치사 from, (B) 월, 연도 앞에는 전치사 in, (C) 특정 기간을 나타내어 '~ 동안'이라는 의미는 during

16 ④ 축제 첫 날 밤에 사람들이 큰 모닥불 주변에 모여 노래하고 춤을 춘다고 하였다.

17 join은 타동사이므로 전치사 없이 목적어를 취한다. 따라서 join이라고 쓰는 것이 어법상 옳다.

18 축제 마지막 날인 둘째 날에는 어린이들과 어른들이 gulal을 지니고 서로를 쫓아다니는 모습을 볼 수 있다.

19 둘째 날에 주요 행사가 있다고 하였다. 따라서 주요 행사만 보고 싶다면 둘째 날 축제에 가야 한다.

20 목적어와 능동 관계에 있으므로 지각동사 hear의 목적보어로 원형부정사나 현재분사를 쓸 수 있다.

21 백야 축제는 매년 여름마다 거행된다고 하였다.

22 배가 어디에서 오는지는 알 수 없다.

23 배가 서서히 나타난다고 하였으므로 ④번은 옳지 않다.

24 go on: 계속되다

25 ⑤ 눈 덩어리를 동물 모양으로 만드는 사람들은 미술가들이라고 하였다.

26 지각동사 see의 목적격보어 자리이므로 shape their works라고 써도 좋다.

27 ④ 미술가들은 눈덩이로 동물, 건물, 다른 아름다운 작품의 모양을 만든다고 하였다.

28 밑줄 친 (A)는 가주어 it이다. ①, ④ 인칭대명사 ② 비인칭 주어

01 They celebrate the festival for two days.

02 gather around, sing and dance

03 is a lot of fun to run around and throw, colorful powder at everyone.

04 India in March

05 It is blue, yellow, green and pink powder.

06 St. Petersburg, Russia

07 It usually starts in May and lasts for about a month.

08 The night sky does not get completely dark.

09 There are a ballet or an opera almost every night and the Scarlet Sails celebration.

10 slowly appear(ing) on the river

11 to fly

12 Winter is Ebba's favorite season because of the Kiruna Snow Festival.

13 Kiruna, the snow design competition

14 It lasts for five or six days.

15 I am watching the artist shaping a huge pile of snow into an elephant.

30 We can see the artists shape huge piles of snow into animals, buildings, and other beautiful artworks.　　　　31 ④

32 It is interesting to watch the artists shaping their works from beginning to end.　　　33 sled

01 축제는 이틀 동안 지속된다고 하였다.

02 gathering around, singing and dancing이라고 써도 좋다.

03 가주어를 이용하여 문장을 다시 쓸 수 있다.

04 홀리 축제를 보려면 3월에 인도로 가야 한다.

05 gulal은 파랑, 노랑, 초록, 분홍의 가루라고 하였다.

06 러시아 상트페테르부르크가 글쓴이의 고향이다.

07 빈도부사의 위치는 보통 일반동사 앞, be동사나 조동사 뒤이다.

08 밤하늘이 완전히 어두워지지 않는 것이 백야이다.

09 축제 행사로는 발레, 오페라, 붉은 돛 축하 행사가 있다고 하였다.

10 배가 강 위에 서서히 나타나는 것을 보았다고 쓸 수 있다. '배가 나타나는 것'이므로 지각동사의 목적어로 원형부정사나 현재분사를 쓰는 것이 옳다.

11 진주어이므로 to fly를 쓴다.

12 키루나 눈 축제 때문에 Ebba는 겨울을 가장 좋아한다고 하였다.

13 키루나 눈 축제를 보기 위해서 키루나를 방문할 것이라면 축제에서 가장 큰 행사인 눈 디자인 대회를 보아야 한다고 말하는 것이 옳다.

14 축제는 5일이나 6일 동안 계속된다고 하였다.

15 '미술가가 ~을 바꾸는 것'이므로 목적어로 the artist, 목적격보어로 shaping ~을 쓰는 것이 옳다.

01 주어진 단어는 반의어 관계를 나타낸다. dark: 어두운, bright: 밝은

02 '따라가서 잡으려고 노력하다'를 가리키는 말은 chase (뒤쫓다)이다.

03 ④번 문장에서 chase는 '뒤쫓다'를 의미한다.

04 make a left: 왼쪽으로 돌다, each other: 서로, get off: 내리다

05 주어진 문장에서 sail은 '돛'을 의미하며 이와 같은 의미로 쓰인 문장은 ②번이다. 나머지는 모두 '항해하다'를 의미한다. retirement: 은퇴, navigator: 항해사, extend: 펼치다

06 hometown: 고향, across from: ~ 건너편에, celebrate: 축하하다

08 민수는 학교에서 나와서 Green Street까지 곧장 간 후 왼쪽으로 돌아야 음식점을 찾을 수 있다.

10 Andy와 Mike가 포스터를 어디에서 만들지는 알 수 없다.

11 ⑤번을 제외한 나머지는 모두 감사에 대한 대답 표현이다.

12 (A)는 수원 화성에 어떻게 가는지 질문하는 문장이므로 get(도착하다)이 적절하다. (B) get on the bus: 버스를 타다, get off the bus: 버스에서 내리다 (C) 그곳까지 가는 데 소요 시간을 질문하고 있으므로 'How long will it take to ~?'가 적절하다.

13 Mina가 수원 화성 축제에 방문해 본 적이 있는지는 알 수 없다.

14 빈칸에는 목적격보어로 원형부정사를 쓰는 동사가 들어가야 한다. encourage는 목적격보어로 to부정사를 사용하는 동사이다.

15 모두 날씨, 날짜, 거리, 명암, 시간 등을 표현할 때 쓰이는 비인칭 주어 it이지만 ②번은 가주어 it이다.

16 누군가가 문을 열고 나가는 것이므로 open the door와 go out의 주체는 someone이 된다. 따라서 ④번이 옳다.

17 그가 누군가에게 소리 지르는 것을 보는 것은 놀라움을 주었다고 답하는 것이 자연스럽다.

18 ③ 소녀들이 공을 차는 주체가 되므로 kick 혹은 kicking을 쓰는 것이 옳다.

19 밑줄 친 부분은 진주어로 쓰인 to부정사이다. 각각의 to부정사는 ① 목적격보어로 쓰인 명사적 용법 ② 부사적 용법 중 목적 ③ 명사를 꾸미는 형용사 ④ 동사의 목적어로 쓰인 명사적 용법 ⑤ 진주어로 쓰인 to부정사이다.

20 진주어는 to부정사이다. 따라서 to hear로 쓰는 것이 옳다.

21 '영어를 배우는 것'이 주어이므로 to learn English를 진주어로 하여 문장을 만든다.

22 ⓒ listen to는 지각동사이므로 tell 혹은 telling을 쓰는 것이 옳다. ⓓ 지각동사 see가 쓰였으므로 목적격보어로 원형부정사나 현재분사를 쓰는 것이 옳다.

영역별 핵심문제　　　p.41~45

01 dark　　　02 ①　　　03 ④

04 (1) Go straight, make　(2) each other　(3) get off

05 ②　　　06 (1) Where is your hometown?

(2) It is across from the museum.

(3) My friends gathered to celebrate my birthday.

07 How can I get there from the school?

08 ④　　　09 I hope many people come to the festival.　　10 ⑤　　11 ⑤　　12 ④

13 ⑤　　14 ⑤　　15 ②　　16 ④

17 to see him shouting at someone　　18 ③

19 ⑤　　　20 to hearing → to hear

21 It is exciting to learn English.　　22 ②

23 ③　　　24 I felt someone touch(ing) my shoulder.　　25 celebrate　　26 ④

27 ③　　　28 ⑤　　　29 ③

23 첫 번째 빈칸은 진주어 자리이므로 to부정사를 쓰는 것이 옳으며, 두 번째 빈칸에는 지각동사의 목적격보어가 들어가야 하므로 ③번이 옳다.

24 '누군가가 내 어깨를 만지는 것'이므로 목적어로 someone, 목적격보어로 touch(ing)을 쓰는 것이 옳다.

25 중요한 행사나 명절을 위해 특별한 무언가를 하는 것은 '축하하다, 기념하다(celebrate)'이다.

26 아이들과 어른들이 gulal을 지니고 서로를 쫓아다닌다는 말이 먼저 나온 후 gulal이 무엇인지 설명해 주는 것이 자연스럽다.

27 ⓑ는 진주어로 쓰인 to부정사로 명사적 용법이다. 따라서 ③번이 옳다. ① 부사적 용법 중 목적 ② 감정의 원인 ④ 형용사적 용법 ⑤ 부사적 용법 중 형용사 수식

28 축제에 있는 사람들이 얼마나 많은 양의 gulal을 가지고 있는지는 알 수 없다.

29 go on은 '계속되다'는 의미이다. 따라서 continue가 옳다.

30 눈 디자인 대회에서는 미술가들이 거대한 눈 덩어리를 동물, 건물, 다른 아름다운 작품의 모양으로 만드는 모습을 볼 수 있다. shaping을 써도 무방하다.

31 가장 큰 행사는 개썰매 타기가 아니라 눈 디자인 대회라고 하였다.

32 지각동사 watch의 목적어와 목적격보어가 능동 관계에 있으므로 shape를 써도 무방하다.

33 '눈 위로 미끄러지는 데 사용되는 작은 탈 것'은 '썰매'이다.

단원별 예상문제　　　　　　　　p.46~49

01 bank(오른쪽 맨 위 건물)　**02** Go straight two blocks and make a left. The bakery is between the hospital and the bus stop.　**03** ⑤　**04** How long will it take to get there?　**05** ①
06 (A) make posters　(B) their neighborhood (C) about three hours　(D) the (school) festival
07 ④　　　**08** ⑤　　　**09** 1st Street까지 곧장 간 후 우회전하면 오른쪽에 우체국이 있다.
10 Is it far from here?　　**11** ③　　　**12** ③
13 I heard Kevin speak(ing) French.
14 ②　　　**15** ⑤
16 It is a good chance to hear her play(ing) the violin.
17 Do you see a boy swim(ming) in the lake?
18 ①　　　**19** ④　　　**20** ⑤　　　**21** ②
22 gulal

03 길을 묻는 질문에 소요 시간을 답하고 있으므로 ⑤번은 어색하다.

06 Andy와 Mike는 이번 주 금요일의 학교 축제로 매우 신이 났다. 이를 홍보하기 위해 그들은 포스터를 만들고 근방에 포스터를 붙이기로 결정한다. 포스터를 만드는 데 약 세 시간이 걸릴 것이다. 그들은 많은 사람들이 축제에 와서 즐기기를 원한다.

07 주어진 문장은 길을 안내해 주는 표현이므로 길을 묻는 표현 다음에 이어지는 (D)가 적절하다.

---

08 ⓐ의 get은 '도착하다'라는 의미로 이와 같이 쓰인 것은 ⑤번이다. ①번은 '가져오다', ②번은 '타다', ③, ④번은 '받다'는 의미로 쓰였다.

11 진주어로 to부정사를 쓸 수 있으며 지각동사의 목적격보어로 원형부정사나 현재분사를 쓰는 것이 옳다.

12 모두 가주어 it이지만 ③번은 It was ~ that 강조 용법이다.

13 'Kevin이 프랑스어를 말하는 것'이므로 목적어로 Kevin, 목적격보어로 speak(ing) French를 써야 한다.

14 '목표를 설정하고 최선을 다하는 것'은 to set a goal and (to) do your best이다. 따라서 ②번이 옳다.

15 watch는 지각동사이며 목적어와 목적격보어의 관계가 능동이므로 원형부정사나 현재분사를 쓰는 것이 옳다.

16 '그녀가 바이올린을 연주하는 것'이므로 목적어로 her, 목적격보어로 play(ing) the violin을 써서 문장을 만든다.

17 '한 소년이 수영하고 있는 것'이므로 목적어로 a boy, 목적격보어로 swim(ming)을 쓰는 것이 옳다.

18 빈칸 ⓐ에는 전치사 of가 들어간다. ① get tired of: ~에 싫증이 나다 ② come up with: ~을 떠올리다 ③ look after: ~을 돌보다 ④ look up to: ~을 존경하다 ⑤ put off: ~을 미루다

19 백야에 대해 들어봤느냐는 질문에 - [C] 백야 설명 (this amazing thing이 'the White Nights' 지칭) - [A] 백야 기간 동안 축제를 엶 - [D] 축제 기간에 행사를 하고, 가장 인기 있는 축제는 '붉은 돛 축하 행사'임 - [B] 붉은 돛 축하 행사 설명

20 축제에 몇 명의 음악가들이 있는지는 알 수 없다.

21 홀리 축제를 이틀 동안 기념한다고 말한 후 첫째 날과 둘째 날에 어떤 행사가 있는지에 대한 설명이 이어지는 것이 자연스럽다.

22 형형색색의 가루는 gulal이다.

서술형 실전문제　　　　　　　　p.50~51

01 They are going to have lunch together at the new Chinese restaurant, Ming's.
02 They are going to meet at 12 o'clock.
03 학교에서 나와서 Green Street까지 곧장 간 후 왼쪽으로 돌면 왼쪽에 있다.
04 call(ing) / called
05 It is essential to improve my English skill.
06 to have a balanced diet
07 Did you see the cat jump(ing) up onto the chair?
08 I saw the boy swimming in the pool.
09 It's a lot of fun to run around and throw colorful powder at everyone.
10 join street parades
11 People in India celebrate Holi in March.
12 It is in Gangneung.
13 We can see people swim(ming) at the beach.
14 It is soft and sweet.

---

04 someone은 나의 이름을 부르는 주체가 될 수 있으므로 현재분사나 원형부정사를 쓰고, 나의 이름은 '불리는 것'이므로 called를 쓰는 것이 옳다.

05 improve: 향상시키다

06 균형 잡힌 식사를 하는 것은 정말로 중요하다고 답할 수 있다. 다섯 단어이므로 to부정사로 만들어 답한다.

07 고양이가 의자로 뛰어오른 것을 보았는지 묻는 말로 쓸 수 있다.

09 'To run around and throw colorful powder at everyone is a lot of fun.' 혹은 'Running around and throwing colorful powder at everyone is a lot of fun.'으로 써도 무방하다.

10 이어지는 대답이 행진을 설명하는 말이므로 '거리 행진에 참가했니?'라고 묻는 것이 옳다.

11 홀리 축제는 3월에 있다고 하였다.

12 오죽헌은 강릉에 있다.

13 사람들이 해변에서 수영하는 것을 볼 수 있다.

14 감자떡이 어떤지를 묻는 말이다. 글쓴이는 감자떡이 부드럽고 달콤하다고 하였다.

창의사고력 서술형 문제   p.52

|모범답안|

01 Come out from the school and go straight to Green Street. Make a left, and the restaurant will be on your left.

02 (1) You can see many children chasing each other.
(2) I can see many merchants selling their things.
(3) I can hear people laughing happily at a festival.

03 (1) It is important to do your homework.
(2) It is necessary to obey the school rules.
(3) It is essential to pay attention to what a teacher says.
(4) It is dangerous to run in the hall.

단원별 모의고사   p.53~56

01 ②   **02** ②   **03** ⑤

04 (1) threw (2) competition (3) huge

05 (1) go on (2) More and more (3) because of
(4) in front of   **06** It will take about 15 minutes by bus.   **07** 이곳에서 수원 화성에 가는 것

08 off   **09** ⑤

10 (1) How long does it take to get to school from your house?
(2) How can I get to the bank?
(3) Cross the street and go straight one block.
(4) It will take about 10 minutes by subway.

11 (C) → (B) → (D) → (A)   **12** ①   **13** ④

14 ②   **15** She heard the rain fall(ing) on the roof.   **16** ③   **17** ①, ②, ④

18 James felt something biting his arm.

19 ④   **20** ②   **21** ②   **22** ③

23 It is amazing to fly through a world of snow on a dog sled.

01 '눈 위에서 미끄러지기 위해 사용되는 작은 탈 것'을 가리키는 말은 sled(썰매)이다.

02 주어진 문장에서 hold는 '개최하다, 열다'를 의미하며 이와 같은 의미로 쓰인 것은 ②번이다. ①, ③, ④번은 '잡다, 쥐다'를 의미하며 ⑤는 '맡다, 보유하다'를 의미한다. ⑤ 내 자리 좀 맡아 주실래요?

03 이어지는 대화로 보아 길을 묻는 표현이 적절하다. ⑤번은 소요 시간을 묻는 표현이다.

04 throw: 던지다, competition: 경쟁, 대회, huge: 거대한

05 go on: 지속되다, 계속되다, more and more: 더욱 더, because of: ~ 때문에, in front of: ~ 앞에

08 get off: 내리다

09 교실 장식의 소요 시간은 언급되지 않았다.

11 (C) 계획 질문 → (B) 계획 설명 → (D) 소요 시간 질문 → (A) 소요 시간 대답

12 학교에 어떻게 가는지 묻고 있으므로 ①번이 적절하다.

13 (a)는 부사로 쓰여 '거의, 대략'을 의미하며 이와 같은 의미로 쓰인 것은 ④번이다. 나머지는 모두 전치사로 '~에 관하여, ~에 대해'를 의미한다.

14 ② 지각동사의 목적격보어는 목적어와 능동의 관계에 있을 경우 원형부정사나 현재분사를 쓴다. 따라서 sing 혹은 singing을 쓰는 것이 옳다. pound on: ~을 마구 두드리다

15 '비가 지붕 위로 떨어지는 소리'이므로 목적어로 the rain, 목적격보어로 fall(ing)을 쓰는 것이 옳다.

16 두 문장 모두 지각동사의 목적격보어로 원형부정사나 현재분사를 쓸 수 있다. irritate: 짜증나게 하다

17 빈칸에는 목적격보어로 원형부정사를 취할 수 있는 동사가 와야 한다. 따라서 사역동사와 지각동사가 옳다.

18 '무언가가 그의 팔을 무는 것'이므로 목적어로 something, 목적격보어로 biting 혹은 bite을 써서 문장을 만든다.

19 (A) 명사가 따라오고 있으므로 전치사 During, (B) appear는 자동사이므로 수동태로 쓸 수 없다. (C) 연주자들이 연주를 하는 주체가 되므로 지각동사의 목적격보어로 원형부정사나 현재분사를 쓴다.

20 ② 밤하늘이 완전히 어두워지지 않는다고 하였으므로 무언가를 보는 것이 어렵다는 것은 글의 내용과 일치하지 않는다.

21 due to: ~ 때문에

22 눈 디자인 대회에서는 예술가들이 눈으로 특정한 모양을 만들며 겨룬다고 하였다.

23 fly through: ~을 날다

Lesson 6

In Outer Space

Conversation

p.62~63

핵심 Check

1 (1) who he is (2) Do you know what it is
(3) Guess 2 (1) What is it for (2) look at / for
(3) What are they used for

시험대비 실력평가

p.60

01 include 02 ⑤ 03 ①
04 (1) mission (2) Although (3) peel (4) look for
(5) several 05 ⑤ 06 (1) deaf (2) average
(3) applied 07 ⑤

01 주어진 관계는 반의어 관계를 나타낸다. include: 포함하다, exclude: 제외하다
02 나머지는 모두 행성을 가리키지만 ⑤번은 은하를 뜻한다.
03 특정한 목적을 위해 형성된 모임이나 사업과 같은 단체를 가리키는 말은 organization(조직, 단체)이다.
04 mission: 임무, although: ~이긴 하지만, peel: 껍질을 벗기다, look for: ~을 찾다, several: 몇몇의
05 organization: 조직, 단체
07 나머지는 모두 '우주'를 뜻하지만 ⑤번은 '공간'을 뜻한다.

교과서 대화문 익히기

Check(√) True or False

p.64

1 T 2 F 3 T 4 T

서술형 시험대비

p.61

01 (1) is good at (2) are curious about
(3) On average 02 (1) blind (2) curious
(3) difference (4) similar (5) exhibition
03 (1) We have very similar interests.
   (2) Water is necessary for life.
   (3) The length of the trip is five days.
04 blind
05 (1) I'll apply for the volunteer program.
   (2) I read three books a month on average.
   (3) This ball is half the size of that one.
06 electricity

01 be good at: ~을 잘하다, be curious about: ~을 궁금해 하다, on average: 평균적으로
02 curious: 호기심 많은, blind: 눈이 먼, exhibition: 전시회, similar: 비슷한, difference: 차이
04 '볼 수 없는'을 가리키는 말은 blind(시각 장애가 있는)이다.
06 나는 수미의 Soccket이 최고의 발명품이라고 생각한다. 우리가 이것을 갖고 놀 때, 이것은 전기를 만들어 낸다. 우리가 전기가 없을 때 이것은 매우 유용하다.

교과서 확인학습

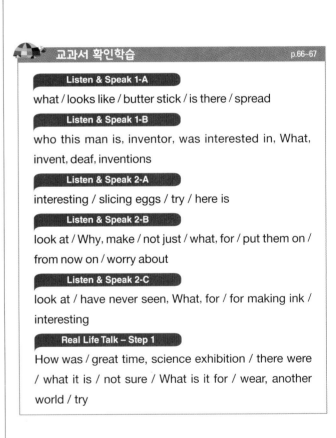

p.66~67

Listen & Speak 1-A
what / looks like / butter stick / is there / spread

Listen & Speak 1-B
who this man is, inventor, was interested in, What, invent, deaf, inventions

Listen & Speak 2-A
interesting / slicing eggs / try / here is

Listen & Speak 2-B
look at / Why, make / not just / what, for / put them on / from now on / worry about

Listen & Speak 2-C
look at / have never seen, What, for / for making ink / interesting

Real Life Talk – Step 1
How was / great time, science exhibition / there were / what it is / not sure / What is it for / wear, another world / try

시험대비 기본평가

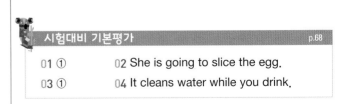

p.68

01 ① 02 She is going to slice the egg.
03 ① 04 It cleans water while you drink.

02 Jane은 달걀을 얇게 썰 것이다.

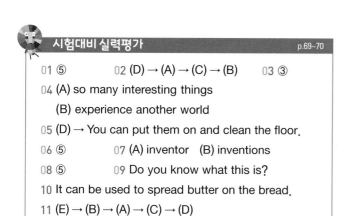
01 ⑤   02 (D) → (A) → (C) → (B)   03 ③

04 (A) so many interesting things

    (B) experience another world

05 (D) → You can put them on and clean the floor.

06 ⑤   07 (A) inventor   (B) inventions

08 ⑤   09 Do you know what this is?

10 It can be used to spread butter on the bread.

11 (E) → (B) → (A) → (C) → (D)

01   용도를 묻고 있는 질문에 '그것들은 비녀이다.'라고 대답하는 것은 어색하다.

02   (D) 용도 묻기 → (A) 용도 설명 → (C) 허락 요청 → (B) 대답

03   (A) 이어지는 주어가 복수이므로 were가 알맞다. (B) other 뒤에는 셀 수 있는 복수 명사가 이어진다. (C) 주어 That이 생략되어 있으므로 Sounds가 적절하다.

04   호진은 그의 남동생과 과학 전시회를 방문했다. 그는 경험할 흥미로운 것들이 매우 많았기 때문에 매우 신났었다. 그는 VR 헤드셋을 샀는데, 이것은 그를 다른 세계를 경험할 수 있게 만들어 주었다.

05   구동사(put on)의 목적어가 인칭대명사일 때 그 대명사는 동사와 부사(on) 사이에 위치한다.

06   Tom은 신고 청소할 수 있는 슬리퍼를 만들었으므로 엄마가 신을 수 있는 편리한 슬리퍼를 만들었다는 설명은 대화의 내용과 일치하지 않는다.

07   (A) inventor: 발명가, (B) make an invention: 발명품을 만들다

08   ⑤ 위 대화를 통해 Alexander Graham Bell의 전화기에 무슨 문제가 있었는지는 알 수 없다.

10   버터 스틱은 빵에 버터를 바를 때 사용될 수 있다.

11   (E) 모른다고 대답 및 설명 요청 → (B) 설명 → (A) 용도 질문 → (C) 용도 설명 → (D) 반응

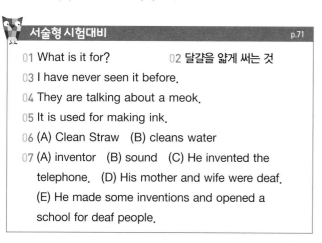
01 What is it for?   02 달걀을 얇게 써는 것

03 I have never seen it before.

04 They are talking about a meok.

05 It is used for making ink.

06 (A) Clean Straw   (B) cleans water

07 (A) inventor   (B) sound   (C) He invented the telephone.   (D) His mother and wife were deaf. (E) He made some inventions and opened a school for deaf people.

04   Irene과 Jane은 먹에 대해 이야기하고 있다.

05   먹은 잉크를 만드는 데 사용된다.

07   occupation: 직업, interest: 흥미, achievement: 업적, contribution: 기여

Grammar

1 (1) as fast as   (2) twice as good as

   (3) not as[so] brave as

2 (1) Although[Though]   (2) although[though], sleepy

   (3) Even though[if]

01 (1) Because → Although[Though]

   (2) hardly → hard   (3) bored → boring

02 (1) as interesting as   (2) as cool as

   (3) not as[so] pretty as   (4) Even though

03 (1) Although she was rich, she kept saving money.

   (2) Learning how to swim is not as difficult as it looks.

   (3) We are as sad as they are.

   (4) She is not as attractive as she used to be.

01   (1) 문맥상 양보의 접속사를 써야 한다. (2), (3) as ~ as 사이에는 형용사나 부사의 원급이 온다. hard는 '세게'라는 의미의 부사이며 hardly는 '거의 ~하지 않는'이라는 의미의 부사로 쓰인다. 연설은 지루함을 유발하는 것이므로 boring을 쓴다.

02   (1) 흥미를 유발하는 주체이므로 interesting을 쓰는 것에 유의한다. (4) Even if, Although, Though를 써도 무방하다.

03   (1) although를 주절 뒤에 배치할 경우 콤마 없이 쓴다. (2), (4) 동등비교의 부정을 써서 표현한다.

01 ④   02 ⑤   03 ①   04 ③

05 (1) David is not as[so] tall as Richard.

   (2) Richard is not as[so] short as David.

06 ④   07 ⑤

08 Barry is not as[so] rich as James.

09 Brad is not as[so] old as he looks.   10 ⑤

11 ②, ④   12 ③   13 ②

14 Though he has just cleaned his room, it is still dirty.

01 be동사의 보어가 빠져 있으므로 빈칸에는 보어 역할을 할 수 있는 형용사가 들어가는 것이 옳다. 따라서 부사는 답이 될 수 없다. ① 명사+ly: 형용사

02 '그것'이 기차만큼 빠르게 달릴 수 없다고 하였으므로 주어는 It으로 하고 can't run을 쓰는 것이 옳다.

03 ① what I said라는 명사절을 이끌고 있으므로 In spite of 혹은 Despite를 쓰는 것이 옳다.

04 모두 원인과 결과의 절을 이어주는 because나 as가 들어가지만, ③번에는 앞뒤로 상반되는 내용을 이어주는 although가 적절하다.

05 'David는 Richard만큼 크지 않다, Richard는 David만큼 작지 않다'라고 쓸 수 있다.

06 위 문장은 앞뒤 내용이 상반되는 내용을 이어주는 말이, 아래 문장은 원인과 결과를 이어주는 말이 들어가는 것이 적절하다.

07 ⑤ Although가 아닌 Because[As]가 들어가는 것이 적절하다.

08 James가 Barry보다 부자라고 하였으므로 Barry는 James만큼 부자가 아니라는 문장을 쓸 수 있다.

09 Brad는 보이는 것보다 젊다는 의미이므로 보이는 것만큼 늙지 않았다는 말로 쓸 수 있다.

10 비용이 70달러만큼 들지 않았다는 말은 70달러보다 적게 들었다는 의미이다.

11 주어진 문장에는 양보의 접속사가 들어가는 것이 옳다. 따라서 앞뒤가 상반된 내용인 ②, ④번이 답이다.

12 ③ 그의 외투와 나의 외투를 비교하는 것이므로 me가 아닌 mine으로 쓰는 것이 옳다.

13 전치사의 목적어 역할을 하는 what절이 이어지고 있으므로 In spite of, '조용히'라는 부사가 들어가는 것이 내용상 옳으며 I came in이 완전한 절이므로 부사 quietly, than이 있으므로 비교급

14 방 청소를 방금 완료했음에도 방이 여전히 더럽다고 하였으므로 양보의 접속사를 이용하여 문장을 만든다.

15 two times bigger than이라고 써도 무방하다.

16 James는 여전히 꽤 피곤하지만 어제 더 피곤함을 느꼈다고 하였으므로, James는 어제만큼 피곤하지 않다는 말로 쓸 수 있다.

17 ⓑ, ⓓ, ⓔ가 옳은 문장이다. ⓐ as creative as, ⓒ as much money as

18 노력에도 불구하고 목소리가 계속 떨렸다는 의미가 옳다. 명사구를 이끌고 있으므로 전치사(구)를 써야 한다.

19 내용상 양보의 접속사가 들어가는 것이 적절하다.

20 even though, although는 양보의 접속사로 완전한 절을 이끈다.

21 as와 as 사이에는 형용사나 부사의 원급이 온다.

22 생각했던 것보다 짧았다는 것을 동등 비교의 부정을 이용하여 '생각했던 것만큼 길지 않았다'라고도 쓸 수 있다.

🦉 서술형 시험대비　　　p.78~79

01 I didn't spend as[so] much money as you.

02 (1) as fast as　(2) not as[so] comfortable as
(3) as long as　(4) two times as heavy as

03 Although he is sick, Joe continues working.

04 BTS is as famous as Justin Bieber.

05 You are not as[so] wise as Bradley although you are as smart as he.

06 Although it rained a lot, we enjoyed our holiday. Although the traffic was bad, we arrived on time. Although we have an important job, we are not well paid.

07 (1) Turtles are not as[so] fast as rabbits.
(2) Turtles are slower than rabbits.

08 The new school was not as[so] far as Tom expected.

09 (1) In spite of　(2) though　(3) despite　(4) Although

10 David has not lived here as[so] long as I have.

11 Although[Though] she was poor, Helen never lost her sense of humor.

12 Although the story was silly, I enjoyed the film. But it was not as[so] silly as I expected.

13 Though he published a book, no one knew the fact.

14 is more expensive than the yellow car / is less expensive than the red car

15 I didn't eat anything although[though] I was hungry yesterday.

01 네가 나보다 돈을 더 많이 썼다고 하였으므로 '나는 너만큼 돈을 쓰지 않았다'는 문장으로 쓸 수 있다.

02 (1) 늦어서 죄송해요, 하지만 할 수 있는 한 빨리 이곳에 왔어요. (2) 침대만큼 편하진 않지만 나는 바닥에서 잘 거야. (3) 너는 네가 원하는 만큼 오래 이곳에 머물러도 좋다. (4) 나의 상자는 너의 상자보다 두 배나 무겁다. two times heavier than으로 써도 좋다.

03 Although 대신 Though, Even though, Even if 등을 써도 좋다.

04 동등 비교 표현을 이용하여 문장을 만들 수 있다. famous: 유명한

05 콤마를 사용하지 않으려면 양보의 부사절을 주절 뒤에 배치해야 하며, 양보의 부사절에서 Bradley 만큼 똑똑하지 않다는 내용을 이끌어야 한다. although를 대신하여 though나 even

though를 써도 무방하다.

06 Although를 대신하여 다른 양보의 접속사를 사용해도 좋다. 단, 부사절을 주절 뒤로 배치할 경우 콤마를 쓰지 않는 것에 유의한다.

07 동등 비교의 부정을 이용하여 문장을 만들 수 있으며, slow를 이용할 경우 비교급을 써서 나타낼 수 있다.

08 동등 비교의 부정문을 이용하여 같은 의미의 문장을 쓸 수 있다. 학교가 생각보다 가깝다고 하였으므로 생각만큼 멀지 않다고 말할 수 있다.

09 (1), (3)번 답과 (2), (4)번 답을 바꾸어 써도 무방하다. in spite of, despite는 전치사(구)로 명사구나 명사절을 이끌고, although와 though는 접속사로 부사절을 이끄는 것에 유의하여 답을 쓴다.

10 David는 이곳에서 꽤 오랫동안 살았지만 내가 그보다 더 오래 살았다고 하였으므로 'David는 나만큼 이곳에서 오래 살지 않았다'는 문장을 쓸 수 있다.

11 Despite와 같은 의미의 접속사는 although[though]이다.

12 양보의 부사절을 주절 뒤에 쓸 경우 콤마 없이 주절에 이어주는 것에 유의한다. 예상했던 것만큼 유치하지 않다는 것은 동등 비교의 부정문으로 표현할 수 있다.

13 publish: 출판하다

14 노란색 차는 빨간색 차만큼 비싸지 않다는 것은, 빨간색 차가 노란색 차보다 더 비싸다는 의미이다. 주어에 따라 more, less를 써서 같은 의미의 문장을 만들 수 있다.

15 I didn't eat anything 대신에 I ate nothing을 써도 무방하다. 부사절을 주절 앞에 배치할 경우 콤마를 쓰는 것에 유의한다.

교과서 Reading

확인문제 p.80

1 T 2 F 3 F 4 T

확인문제 p.81

1 T 2 F 3 F 4 T 5 T

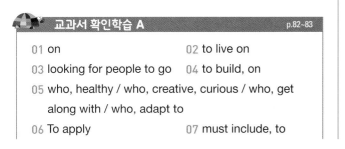

교과서 확인학습 A p.82~83

01 on
02 to live on
03 looking for people to go
04 to build, on
05 who, healthy / who, creative, curious / who, get along with / who, adapt to
06 To apply
07 must include, to

08 want to go / a good sense of / for this mission
09 a chance of, miss
10 the Second Earth
11 Although, many books, movies, yet
12 looking at, as
13 In fact, are trying to send
14 Can people live on
15 believe so
16 that, water
17 because, necessary for
18 hard land to build, on
19 is similar to
20 In addition, has four seasons
21 lead similar lives
22 very far
23 the second closest
24 however, some differences from
25 about half
26 the second smallest, solar
27 about twice as long as
28 much colder
29 On average
30 because, farther away
31 Although, answer, exciting to imagine
32 the first Korean on

교과서 확인학습 B p.84~85

1 Live on MARS!

2 Do you want to live on another planet?

3 The Korea Space Organization (KSO) is looking for people to go to MARS!.

4 Our mission is to build a city on Mars.

5 We are looking for someone… who is healthy. who is creative and curious. who can get along with others. who can adapt to a new environment quickly.

6 To apply, send us a short video.

7 The video must include the answers to the following questions:

8 Why do you want to go to Mars? / Do you have a good sense of humor? / Why are you the perfect person for this mission?

9 This is a chance of a lifetime, so don't miss out!

10 Mars, the Second Earth?

11 Although there are many books and movies about Mars, no one has been there yet.

12 These days, scientists are looking at Mars as a new home.

13 In fact, NASA and some companies are trying to send people there right now.

14 The big question is, "Can people live on Mars?"

15 Many scientists believe so for several reasons.

16 First, they think that there is water on Mars.

17 This is great because water is necessary for all life.

18 Second, Mars has hard land to build houses and buildings on.

19 Third, the length of day and night on Mars is similar to that on Earth.

20 In addition, Mars also has four seasons.

21 So, people can lead similar lives.

22 Lastly, Mars is not very far.

23 It is the second closest planet to Earth.

24 Mars, however, has some differences from Earth.

25 First, Mars is about half the size of Earth.

26 It is the second smallest planet in the solar system.

27 Second, a year on Mars is about twice as long as a year on Earth.

28 Third, Mars is much colder than Earth.

29 On average, it is about −60℃ on Mars.

30 This is because Mars is farther away from the Sun than Earth.

31 Although no one can answer the big question right now, it is exciting to imagine this new world.

32 Who knows? You could be the first Korean on Mars!

시험대비 실력평가
p.86~89

01 ⑤   02 ②   03 ④   04 ④

05 this is a chance of a lifetime   06 ⑤

07 ③   08 ⑤   09 Water is essential for all life.   10 ②   11 the length of day and night   12 ④   13 ⑤

14 It's because Mars has four seasons and the length of day and night on Mars is similar to that on Earth.

15 Mars is the second closest planet to Earth.

16 ⑤   17 화성의 기온이 약 섭씨 영하 60도인 것

18 ④   19 Mars   20 ④

21 to build (또는 building)   22 planet   23 ④

24 ③   25 ②

26 NASA and some companies are trying to send people to Mars right now.

27 ②   28 people can live on Mars

29 ⑤   30 ③

01 '~에 살다'는 의미로 live on이 가장 적절하다.

02 (B) look for: ~을 찾다 bring about: ~을 초래하다 care

for: ~을 돌보다, turn off: ~을 끄다, pick somebody up: ~을 태우러 가다, put on: ~을 입다

03 ④ 새로운 환경에 빨리 적응할 수 있는 사람을 찾는다고 하였으므로 Sheldon이 가장 거리가 멀다. have hard time Ving: ~하느라 힘든 시간을 보내다

04 ④ 동영상을 어디로 보내야 하는지는 위 글을 읽고 알 수 없다.

05 일생에 단 한번뿐인 기회이기 때문에 놓치지 말라고 하였다.

06 a great deal of는 셀 수 없는 명사를 수식한다.

07 believe so에서 so가 의미하는 것은 '화성에서 사람들이 살 수 있다.'이다.

08 ⑤ NASA에서 사람들을 화성으로 보내려고 노력하고 있다 하였다.

09 essential을 대신하여 necessary를 써도 좋다.

10 땅 '위에' 건물을 짓는 것이므로 전치사 on을 쓰는 것이 옳다.

11 낮과 밤의 길이를 가리킨다.

12 마지막 문장에서 화성과 지구는 다른 점이 몇 가지 있다고 하였으므로 이어질 내용으로는 ④번이 적절하다.

13 지구에서 두 번째로 가까운 행성이라고 하였다.

14 사람들이 화성에서 비슷한 생활을 할 수 있는 이유는 화성에 사계절이 있기 때문이다.

15 화성은 지구에서 두 번째로 가까운 행성이다.

16 (A) differences from: ~와의 차이점 (B) 태양계 '내에서'를 의미하므로 전치사 in (C) 주절과 부사절의 내용이 상반되므로 양보의 접속사 although

17 앞 문장의 내용을 가리키는 말이다.

18 가주어 it으로 쓰인 것은 ④번이다. 나머지는 모두 비인칭 주어이다.

19 화성을 의미하는 말이다.

20 지구의 평균 온도는 글을 읽고 알 수 없다.

21 be동사의 보어 자리이므로 to부정사나 동명사를 쓰는 것이 옳다.

22 우주에서 별 주변을 도는 크고 둥근 물체는 '행성(planet)'이다.

23 인터뷰가 아닌 영상에서 몇 가지 질문에 답해야 한다.

24 밑줄 친 (A)는 명사절을 이끄는 접속사로 완전한 절을 이끈다. ③번은 관계대명사로 쓰였으며 불완전한 절을 이끈다.

25 also라는 말로 화성과 지구의 유사점을 이어 말하고 있으므로 '게다가'가 들어가는 것이 옳다.

26 NASA와 몇몇 회사들은 화성에 사람들을 보내기 위해 바로 지금도 노력하고 있다고 하였다.

27 화성이 두 번째 지구가 될 수 있는지에 관한 글이다. 따라서 ②번이 적절하다.

28 몇 가지 이유로 과학자들은 화성에서 사람이 살 수 있다고 믿는다고 하였다.

29 단수명사 the length of day and night을 가리키는 지시대명사이므로 that이 옳다.

30 vital은 necessary와 동의어로 볼 수 있다.

01 화성으로 가서 도시를 세우는 것

02 a chance of a lifetime

03 healthy, have a good sense of humor

04 a short video to them

05 It must contain the answers to some questions.

06 There is water on Mars.   07 be similar to

08 although there are many books and movies about it

09 build houses and buildings on Mars

10 It has four seasons.   11 some differences

12 a year on Earth (또는 that on Earth)

13 Because it is farther away from the Sun than Earth.

14 not as[so] close   15 making friends

16 Give me the chance to live on Mars!

17 Because she can adapt to a new environment quickly.

01 화성으로 가서 도시를 세울 사람을 찾고 있다고 하였다.

02 chance: 기회, lifetime: 일생

03 동등 비교의 대상이 운동선수이므로 healthy가 적합하고, 사람들을 웃게 한다고 했으므로 유머 감각이 있다는 말이 들어가는 것이 적절하다.

04 지원하려면 짧은 동영상을 보내야 한다.

05 영상은 몇 가지 질문에 관한 답을 포함해야 한다고 하였다. contain: 포함하다

06 화성에 물이 있는 것이 좋다는 의미이다.

07 화성에서의 삶은 지구에서의 삶과 비슷할 것이다.

08 많은 책과 영화가 있긴 하지만 아직 화성에 가 본 사람은 없다고 하였다. although를 주절 뒤에 쓸 경우 콤마를 사용하지 않는 것에 유의한다.

09 화성은 단단한 땅을 가지고 있기 때문에 집과 건물을 지을 수 있다고 하였다.

10 화성은 사계절을 가지고 있다고 하였다.

11 some 대신에 several을 써도 무방하다.

12 비교 대상이 화성에서의 일 년과 지구에서의 일 년이다. 따라서 a year on Earth를 쓰는 것이 옳다.

13 화성이 지구보다 훨씬 더 추운 이유는 화성이 지구보다 태양에서 더 멀리 떨어져 있기 때문이다.

14 화성은 지구만큼 태양에 가깝지 않다는 의미이다.

15 enjoy는 동명사를 목적어로 취하는 동사이다.

16 '살 기회'이므로 to부정사가 the chance를 수식하도록 문장을 만든다.

17 새로운 환경에 빨리 적응할 수 있기 때문에 자신이 임무에 적합하다고 하였다.

01 ⑤   02 ①   03 ⑤   04 ③

05 (1) brave   (2) communicate   (3) spread

06 ③   07 ②   08 deaf

09 (B) → Do you know who this man is?

10 ③   11 ②

12 it looks like a glue stick. 13 ①   14 ⑤

15 Though[Even though, Although] it was cloudy, I put on my sunglasses.

16 ②   17 ①, ⑤   18 ④   19 ⑤

20 ③   21 ④   22 ②

23 watch TV as much as

24 Although tennis is not as popular as football, I like tennis more than football.

25 ①, ③   26 ②   27 ①   28 ④

29 Many scientists   30 twice as big[large] as

31 ①   32 ③   33 not as[so] small as

01 ⑤번을 제외한 나머지는 모두 사람의 성격을 묘사하는 형용사이다.

02 '과일, 야채 등으로부터 껍질을 제거하다'를 나타내는 말은 peel(껍질을 벗기다)이다.

03 Although: ~이긴 하지만

04 Mars: 화성

06 주어진 문장에서 lead는 '생활을 하다, 지내다'를 뜻하며 이와 같은 의미로 쓰인 것은 ③번이다. 나머지는 '이끌다'를 의미한다.

07 produce: 생산하다, 제작하다

08 어떤 것도 들을 수 없음을 나타내는 말은 deaf(귀가 먼)이다.

09 간접의문의 어순은 '의문사+주어+동사'이다.

12 look+형용사, look like+명사

13 주어진 문장은 주말이 어땠는지에 대한 질문에 대한 대답으로 적절하므로 (A)가 알맞다.

15 양보의 부사절을 주절 뒤에 쓸 경우 콤마를 사용하지 않는 것에 유의한다. put on: ~을 쓰다

16 절을 이끌며 원인과 결과를 나타내는 문장이므로 because, the noise는 명사로 전치사를 써야 하므로 despite가 옳다.

17 생각했던 것만큼 어렵지 않았다는 것은 생각했던 것보다 더 쉬웠다는 의미가 된다.

18 ④ 내용상 앞뒤가 상반되는 내용이므로 양보의 접속사로 이어주는 것이 좋다.

19 '머리가 전에는 더 길었다.'는 것은 지금은 전만큼 길지 않다는 의미이다. used to V: (과거에) ~이었다

20 ③ because → although{though}

21 '나는 너보다 고기를 덜 먹는다'는 말은 '나는 너 만큼 고기를 먹지 않는다.'는 의미이다.

22 앞뒤 절의 내용이 상반되는 ②번이 옳다. ①, ③ because[as] ④ since ⑤ if[when]

15

23 나는 너만큼 TV를 많이 보지 않는다는 말로 쓸 수 있다.

24 'Although football is more popular than tennis, I don't like football as much as tennis.'라고 써도 좋다.

25 앞뒤의 절이 상반된 내용이므로 양보의 부사절 접속사 although, even though가 들어가는 것이 옳다.

26 사람들이 비슷한 생활을 할 수 있다는 '결과를 이끄는 연결사'가 들어가는 것이 옳다.

27 (a)는 경험을 나타내는 현재완료이다. ① 경험 ② 완료 ③ 결과 ④ 계속 ⑤ 완료

28 화성으로 가는 데 얼마만큼의 시간이 걸리는지는 위 글을 읽고 알 수 없다.

29 앞 문장에 언급된 많은 과학자들을 가리키는 말이다.

30 '배수사+as+원급+as'를 이용하여 같은 의미의 문장을 쓸 수 있다.

31 (A) 비교급 강조부사 much (2) 원인을 이끌고 있으므로 This is because (3) 새로운 세상을 상상하는 것은 신나는 감정을 유발하는 것이므로 exciting을 쓰는 것이 옳다.

32 ⓑ는 진주어로 쓰인 to부정사이다. ③은 anything을 수식하는 형용사로 쓰인 to부정사이다.

33 화성은 태양계에서 두 번째로 작은 행성이라고 하였고, 수성이 가장 작은 행성이므로 화성은 수성만큼 작은 행성이 아니다.

단원별 예상문제   p.98~101

01 ②　　　　02 (C) → (B) → (E) → (D) → (A)

03 ⓒ → on

04 They are not just for wearing but also for cleaning the floor.　　　　05 ⑤

06 inventor　　07 He had an interest in sound.

08 He made some inventions for deaf people and opened a school for them.

09 ①　　　　10 이것을 갖고 놀 때 전기를 만들어 낸다.

11 ⑤　　　12 ③　　　13 ⑤

14 didn't play as[so] well as us[we did]

15 ③, ⑤　　　16 ④

17 Though the bread is not as[so] moist as it was yesterday, it is still delicious.

18 two times, high　　　19 ③　　　20 ①

21 ⑤　　　　22 Mars has four seasons.

23 [B]-[A]-[C]　　　　24 ④

25 Mars is not as far as I thought.　　　26 ②

---

01 (A) 명령문이므로 look, (B) 경험을 나타내는 현재완료 (have+p.p) 형태가 적절하다. (C) interesting: 흥미로운, interested: 흥미를 갖고 있는

02 (C) 알고 있는지 묻기 → (B) 추측 → (E) 정확한 설명 → (D) 버튼이 있는지 구체적인 질문 → (A) 대답

---

03 put off는 '미루다'는 뜻으로 문맥의 흐름상 '(신발을) 신다'를 나타내기 위해 'put on'이 적절하다.

04 Tom이 만든 슬리퍼는 신는 것뿐만 아니라 바닥을 청소하기 위한 것이다.

05 Tom이 과학 시간에 슬리퍼를 만들기 위해 무엇을 사용했는지 알 수 없다.

06 '무언가를 발명한 사람 또는 그의 직업이 무언가를 발명하는 사람'을 가리키는 말은 inventor(발명가)이다.

07 Alexander Graham Bell은 소리에 관심을 갖고 있었다.

08 Alexander Graham Bell은 청각 장애인들을 위한 몇몇 발명품도 만들고 그들을 위한 학교도 열었다.

11 ⓔ를 제외한 나머지는 모두 a Socckel을 가리킨다.

12 계단에서 넘어졌지만 다치지 않았다고 말하는 것이 가장 자연스럽다. 따라서 양보의 부사절 접속사를 쓰는 것이 옳다.

13 비교 대상이 배낭이므로 my backpack 혹은 mine이라고 쓰는 것이 옳다.

14 우리가 그들보다 더 잘했다는 것은 그들이 우리만큼 하지 못했다는 의미이다.

15 사과가 배만큼 크지 않다고 하였으므로 사과가 배보다 크지 않다고도 말할 수 있다.

17 moist: 촉촉한, 수분이 있는

18 후지산은 한라산보다 두 배만큼 높다는 의미이다.

19 (A)에는 양보의 부사절 접속사 although가 쓰인다. ① If ② while ③ Although ④ unless ⑤ since

20 과거를 나타내는 어구인 ago는 현재완료 시제와 함께 사용될 수 없다. ago → yet

22 사람이 화성에서 살 수 있다고 과학자들이 믿는 네 번째 이유로 화성에 사계절이 있기 때문이라고 하였다.

23 [B] 사람들이 비슷한 생활을 할 수 있는 마지막 이유로 지구에서 두 번째로 가까운 행성이라고 언급한 후 '그러나'로 차이점을 언급하며 첫 번째는 크기임 → [A] 화성은 태양계에서 두 번째로 작은 행성임을 언급하고 두 번째와 세 번째 차이(화성이 지구보다 훨씬 더 추움) 언급 → [C] 평균 온도가 섭씨 영하 60도임을 언급

24 ④번은 slice를 설명하는 말이다.

25 as+형용사/부사의 원급+as: ~만큼 …한

26 태양계에서 가장 작은 행성이 무엇인지는 글에 나와 있지 않다.

서술형 실전문제   p.102~103

01 He went there with his brother.

02 He bought a VR headset.

03 It is for experiencing another world.

04 He made them in science class.

05 He made a promise to clean his room from now on.

06 Although[Though] I turned on the air conditioner, the room is still hot.

07 Although[Though] Hannah invited Tom to her party, he didn't come without saying a word.

08 didn't get up as[so] early as Sally /
didn't get up as[so] late as James

09 (1) doesn't work as[so] hard as
(2) works harder than

10 is not as[so] important as health and happiness

11 ④번 → Mars has hard land to build houses and buildings on.

12 Many scientists think that there is water on Mars.

13 Mars is about half the size of Earth.

14 two times as long as

01 호진은 과학 전시회에 남동생과 같이 갔다.

02 호진은 과학 전시회에서 VR 헤드셋을 샀다.

03 VR 헤드셋은 다른 세상을 경험하기 위한 것이다.

04 Tom은 과학시간에 슬리퍼를 만들었다.

05 Tom은 엄마에게 이제부터 그의 방을 청소할 것을 약속하였다.

06 '에어컨을 틀었지만 방은 여전히 덥다'는 문장을 쓸 수 있다. although를 주절 뒤에 배치할 경우 콤마를 쓰지 않는 것에 유의한다.

07 해석: Hannah가 Tom을 파티에 초대했지만, 그는 말 한마디도 없이 오지 않았다.

08 Sally는 James보다 일찍 일어났다는 것은 Sally가 James만큼 늦게 일어나지 않았고, James는 Sally만큼 일찍 일어나지 않았다는 의미이다.

09 Amelia는 Jason만큼 일하지 않지만 Tom보다는 더 열심히 일한다. 일하는 시간을 비교해 보면 Jason은 Tom보다 두 배 만큼 많이 일한다.

10 건강과 행복은 돈보다 더 중요하다는 것은 '돈은 건강과 행복만큼 중요하지 않다'는 것이다.

11 build houses and building on hard land이므로 전치사 on을 쓰는 것이 옳다.

12 많은 과학자들이 화성에 물이 있다고 생각한다.

13 about: 대략 half: 절반

14 화성에서의 일 년은 지구에서의 일 년보다 약 두 배 길다고 하였으므로 two times as long as를 써서 나타낼 수 있다.

창의사고력 서술형 문제　　　　　　　　p.104

|모범답안|

01 (A) slippers　(B) cleaning the floor
(C) clean my room

02 (1) is not as[so] old as
(2) don't get up as[so] early as
(3) three times as much time as

03 (1) Although the length of day and night on Mars is similar to that on Earth, a year on Mars is about twice as long as a year on Earth.
(2) Although Mars has four seasons like Earth, Mars is much colder than Earth.
(3) Although Mars has hard land to build houses and buildings on, it is really expensive to build them on Mars.

01 오늘 나는 과학시간에 특별한 슬리퍼를 만들었다. 나는 어떤 천도 없이 바닥을 청소할 수 있는 아이디어를 생각해 냈다. 그래서 내 슬리퍼는 단지 신기 위한 것뿐만 아니라 바닥을 청소하기 위해 디자인되었다. 나는 엄마에게 스스로 내 방을 청소할 것을 약속했다.

02 (1) Jennifer는 Michael과 Christine만큼 나이 들지 않았다.
(2) Jennifer와 Christine은 Michael만큼 일찍 일어나지 않는다. (3) Christine은 직장에 가기 위해서 Michael보다 세 배나 더 많은 시간을 소비한다.

단원별 모의고사　　　　　　　　p.105~108

01 ②　　　02 (1) slice　(2) inventor
(3) organization　(4) deaf　(5) planets
03 (1) get along with　(2) sense of humor
(3) In addition
04 (E) → (A) → (C) → (B) → (D)　　05 ⑤
06 ②, ④
07 If you wear it, you can experience another world.
08 ③　　　09 ③　　　10 ④　　　11 ④
12 (1) Jimin doesn't seem to get along with his classmates.
(2) What is the biggest planet in the solar system?
13 ②　　　14 didn't run as[so] much(또는 far) as
15 ⑤
16 Although[Though] this cookie is not as[so] delicious as the cake, I will have this cookie.
17 because, although　　18 ②　　19 ③
20 Their[Its] mission is to build a city on Mars.
21 Do you have a good sense of humor?
22 ②　　　23 ③
24 ⑤번 → farther away from
25 Although Mars has some differences from Earth, scientists believe that people can live on Mars.

01 reason: 이유; 추론하다

02 inventor: 발명가, deaf: 청각 장애가 있는, planet: 행성, organization: 조직, 단체, slice: 얇게 썰다

04 (E) 과학 시간에 슬리퍼를 만든 것을 설명 → (A) 과학 시간에 만든 이유 질문 → (C) 용도 설명 → (B) 구체적인 용도 질문 → (D) 구체적인 용도 설명

05 태양 주위에서 움직이는 행성이나 태양을 일컫는 말은 solar system(태양계)이다.

06 용도를 묻는 표현이 들어가야 한다.

08 용도를 묻고 있으므로 이에 대한 대답인 ③번이 적절하다.

09 (A)는 의문사로 누구를 가리키는 'who' (B) be interested in: ~에 관심이 있다 (C) 동사 opened가 적절하다.

10 그가 무엇을 발명했는지 묻는 질문에 전화기를 발명했다는 대답이 이어지므로 ⓓ가 적절하다.

11 ④ Alexander Graham Bell이 가족을 위해 학교를 열었다는 설명은 대화의 내용과 일치하지 않는다.

13 ⓐ, ⓑ가 옳은 문장이다. ⓒ despite → although ⓓ you are → you do ⓔ as tidy than → as tidy as

14 나는 아빠만큼 많이 달리지 않았다는 말을 쓰는 것이 옳다.

15 as heavy as라고 쓰는 것이 옳다.

16 쿠키가 케이크만큼 맛있지 않다고 하였으므로 동등 비교의 부정문을 이용하여 문장을 만들 수 있다.

17 앞 문장은 원인과 결과를 이어주는 말이 들어가는 것이 옳으며, 뒷문장의 내용은 서로 상반되므로 양보의 부사절 접속사를 쓰는 것이 옳다. because 대신에 as, although 대신에 though나 even though를 써도 무방하다.

18 ⓐ 화성으로 갈 사람을 찾는 것이므로 look for ⓑ 새로운 환경에 빠르게 적응한다는 의미이므로 adapt ⓒ 질문에 대한 대답을 포함해야 한다는 의미이므로 include가 적절하다.

19 (A)는 부사적 용법 중 '목적'으로 쓰인 to부정사이다. 따라서 '~하기 위해서'라고 해석되는 ③번이 옳다.

20 그들의 임무는 화성에 도시를 세우는 것이라고 하였다.

21 a sense of humor: 유머 감각

22 앞 문단과 상반되는 내용이 이어지고 있으므로 역접의 접속부사 '그러나'가 옳다.

23 ③ 화성은 지구와 가깝고 사계절이 있다고 하였다.

24 화성이 지구보다 태양에서 더 멀기 때문에 더 추운 것이다.

25 Although절을 주절 뒤에 쓸 경우 콤마를 쓰지 않는 것에 유의한다.

Lesson 7

Can I Trust It?

Conversation

1 (1) recommend / How about (2) Can you suggest / Why (3) What do you think would be
2 (1) How do you like (2) I'm not satisfied with it
(3) What do you like

시험대비 실력평가 — p.112

01 simple   02 ②   03 ④
04 (1) express (2) advertisement (3) belief
05 ③   06 ①
07 (1) purple (2) beliefs (3) genre (4) friendship

01 주어진 단어의 관계는 반의어 관계를 나타낸다. simple: 간단한, complex: 복잡한
02 누군가가 한 무언가에 대한 돈 등과 같은 상을 가리키는 말은 award(상)이다. penalty: 벌금 fare: 운임 fee: 요금
03 prove: 증명하다
05 주어진 문장에서 touching은 '감동적인'을 뜻하며 이와 같은 의미로 쓰인 것은 ③번이다. 나머지는 모두 '만지다'를 의미한다.
06 navy: 해군, 남색
07 belief: 신념, purple: 보라색, genre: 장르, friendship: 우정

교과서 대화문 익히기

Check(√) True or False — p.116

1 T 2 T 3 T 4 F

서술형 시험대비 — p.113

01 difference 02 (1) lie (2) pocket (3) based
03 (1) traditional (2) desert (3) author
   (4) connection (5) award (6) fantasy
04 (1) From now on, let's start playing the soccer game.
   (2) Before you go out, check out the light again.
   (3) Who is the main character in this movie?
05 (1) Can you explain the rules of the game?
   (2) If you mix red with blue, you can get purple.
   (3) I can prove that he didn't break the window.
   (4) Did you see the advertisement on the newspaper?

01 주어진 빈칸에 different의 명사형 difference가 와야 한다.
02 lie: 거짓말하다, pocket: 주머니, be based on: ~을 바탕으로 하다
03 fantasy: 공상, traditional: 전통적인, connection: 연관성, author: 작가, desert: 사막, award: 상 primarily: 주로

교과서 확인학습 — p.118~119

Listen & Speak 1-A
recommend / yet / number one

Listen & Speak 1-B
help / backpack, recommend one / How about, these days / different / navy, pockets / take

Listen & Speak 2-A
got / like most about it / takes

Listen & Talk 2-B
like, trip / happy / Where else / wonderful place / perfect trip / walking up / worth it

Real Life Talk – Step 1
can you recommend / Why don't / about / delicious, recommend / the prices / think, too / Sounds like, How, the service / slow / check it out / problem, Enjoy

Real Life Talk – Step 2
recommend a book for me / about / What, like / main character, special / Sounds

---

시험대비 기본평가 — p.120

01 Can you recommend a good movie?
02 ⑤   03 What do you like most about it?
04 (B) the new smartphone (C) the camera

01 ④ → was   02 ②   03 ④

04 can you recommend a book for me?

05 She likes the main character.

06 ①   07 ⓐ Antonio's   ⓑ the service

08 ⑤   09 ②   10 ⑤   11 ③

12 ⑤

01 동명사가 주어로 쓰였으므로 동사는 단수 형태인 was가 적절하다.

02 문맥상 상반의 접속사 but이 알맞다.

03 ④ Jack은 석굴암까지 걸어 올라가는 것이 가치가 있었을 것이라고 믿었다.

06 주어진 문장은 식당을 추천하고 있는 표현이므로 (A)가 적절하다.

09 이어지는 대화에서 빨간색을 추천한 이유를 설명하고 있으므로 (B)가 적절하다.

10 소년의 오래된 배낭이 얼마나 많은 주머니를 갖고 있었는지는 알 수 없다.

11 (A)의 빈칸에 들어갈 말로 만족을 나타내는 표현이 알맞다. ③은 실망을 나타내고 있다.

12 ⑤ 위 대화를 통해 Tom이 언제 멋진 사진을 찍었는지 알 수 없다.

01 I haven't seen it yet.

02 She recommended *Star Wars*.

03 It's *Star Wars*.   04 It is red.

05 It has side pockets.

06 Because his old backpack was red.

07 (A) How   (B) Where   (C) Where

08 (A) Gyeongju   (B) Bulguksa   (C) Seokguram

02 Emily는 Brian에게 *Star Wars*를 추천하였다.

03 지금 1위 영화는 *Star Wars*이다.

04 요즘 가장 인기 있는 색은 빨간색이다.

05 남색 가방은 양옆에 주머니가 있다.

06 소년이 빨간색 배낭을 원하지 않는 이유는 그의 옛 배낭이 빨간색이기 때문이다.

08 나는 경주 여행을 갔다. 이곳은 정말로 멋지고 아름다운 도시였다. 나는 첨성대뿐만 아니라 불국사도 방문했다. 그들은 모두 훌륭한 곳이었다. 나는 석굴암까지 올라갔을 때 피곤했다. 그러나 그것은 가치있는 일이었다. 나는 경주로 간 완벽한 여행이 정말 마음에 들었다.

1 (1) so bright that   (2) so small that   (3) so lazy that

2 (1) that(또는 which) Elizabeth made

(2) that(또는 which) he lost   (3) that(또는 which) Molly really liked

(4) who(m)(또는 that) she saw

01 (1) who → which(또는 that)

(2) which → who(m)(또는 that)   (3) very → so

(4) so → too

02 (1) who(m) Tom likes   (2) so easy that

(3) so rich that, that   (4) that I sit on[in]

03 (1) She didn't touch the food that she didn't like.

(2) Those babies whom the woman is looking after look very cute.

(3) The shoes are so tight that my feet hurt.

(4) Her commute was so far that she bought a car.

01 (1), (2) 목적격 관계대명사가 쓰이고 있으므로 생략해도 무방하다. (3) 'so ~ that'은 원인과 결과를 나타내는 어구이며 that은 완전한 절을 이끈다. 'too ~ to V'는 '너무 ~해서 …할 수 없는'의 의미이다.

02 (1), (4) 'Tom이 많이 좋아하는 그 소녀', '내가 앉아 있는 이 의자'이므로 관계사절로 명사를 수식할 수 있다. (2), (3) 'so ~ that'은 원인과 결과를 나타내는 어구이다.

03 (1), (2) '좋아하지 않는 음식', '그 여자가 돌보고 있는 저 아기들'이므로 the food that she didn't like, the babies whom she is looking after로 쓰는 것이 옳다.

01 ④   02 ④   03 ②, ④

04 The book which[that] you borrowed from the library was written by my mother.

05 ③   06 ②   07 ⑤

08 The computer is so small that I can carry it around.

09 ③   10 ③

11 Julia studied so hard that she could pass the important exam.

12 The traffic was so heavy that I couldn't be here on time.

13 ③ 14 ⑤ 15 which[that] we
watched last week 16 ② 17 ②
18 that they sang together was beautiful 19 ⑤
20 ④ 21 I am so shy that I can't talk in front
of many people.
22 (1) which[that] I am interested
　　(2) which I am interested

01 피곤한 것이 원인이고 일찍 잔 것은 결과이므로 ④번이 옳다.

02 어제 만난 여자가 너무 상냥해서 친구가 되고 싶었다는 의미이
다. 원인과 결과를 나타내는 어구인 'so ~ that' 구문을 쓰는 것
이 옳다.

03 목적격 관계대명사가 적절하다. 사물이 선행사이므로 which나
that이 옳다.

04 목적격 관계대명사를 이용하면 '네가 도서관에서 빌린 그 책은
우리 엄마에 의해 쓰였다.'는 의미의 문장을 만들 수 있다.

05 'too ~ to V'는 '너무 ~해서 V할 수 없다'라는 의미이다. 'so
~ that ... can't'와 같다.

06 ② 핵심 주어인 자전거는 단수이므로 is라고 쓰는 것이 옳다.

07 hard는 부사로 '세게'라는 의미를 갖는다. hardly 역시 부사이
지만 '거의 ~하지 않는'이라는 의미이다. 두 번째 빈칸에는 목적
격 관계대명사가 쓰이므로 that 혹은 which가 온다.

08 컴퓨터가 너무 작은 것이 원인이 되어 내가 가지고 다닐 수 있게
되었다. 따라서 'so ~ that' 구문을 이용하여 문장을 만들 수 있
다. carry around: 휴대하다, 가지고 다니다

09 ③번은 주격 관계대명사이다. 목적격 관계대명사 혹은 '주격 관
계대명사+be동사'는 생략 가능하다. run across: 우연히 마주
치다

10 모두 완전한 명사절을 이끄는 접속사 that이지만, ③번은 불완
전한 절을 이끄는 관계대명사 that이다.

11 Julia가 공부를 열심히 해서 그 결과 시험에 합격할 수 있었다는
하나의 문장을 쓸 수 있다.

12 원인과 결과를 나타내는 어구를 이용하여 늦은 이유를 설명하면
된다. 주어진 단어를 이용한다면 '교통 체증이 너무 심해서 제때
에 올 수 없었다.'라고 쓸 수 있다.

13 결과를 나타내는 절을 이끌거나 목적격 관계대명사 역할을 할
수 있는 것은 that이다.

14 ⑤ 'Where is the dog which follows you all the time?'
이라고 쓰는 것이 옳다.

15 목적격 관계대명사이므로 that을 써도 무방하다.

16 'so ~ that'은 원인과 결과를 나타내는 어구이다. 같은 의미가
되기 위해서는 빈칸에 because를 쓰는 것이 옳다.

17 나를 슬프게 하는 것이 원인이고 라디오를 끈 것이 결과이므로
②번이 가장 적절하다.

18 목적격 관계대명사 that을 대신하여 which를 쓰거나 생략해도
무방하다.

19 'too ~ to V'는 '너무 ~해서 V할 수 없는'이란 의미이다. 따라
서 ⑤번이 옳다.

20 ① looks ② couldn't ③ whom(또는 that) ⑤ diligent

21 너무 수줍어서 많은 사람들 앞에서 말할 수 없다는 문장을 쓸 수
있다.

22 관계대명사 that은 전치사의 목적어로 쓰일 수 없는 것에 유의하
여 답을 쓴다.

🦉 서술형 시험대비　　　　　　　　　p.130~131

01 The girl whom you introduced to me is very
popular.

02 was so heavy that Sandra couldn't carry it 또는
was too heavy for Sandra to carry

03 which Ross wrote was so amazing that I was
moved to tears

04 (1) which(또는 that) (2) who(또는 that)
　(3) whom(또는 that)

05 (1) Penny couldn't eat anything because she was
　　very sick.
　(2) Penny was so sick that she couldn't eat
　　anything.

06 (1) which Tom is driving is not his
　(2) picked some roses which Catherine planted
　(3) know the person who(m) you took a trip with

07 so warm that he doesn't need to buy another coat

08 (1) Sally speaks English so well that you would
　　think it is her native language.
　(2) The music was so loud that you could hear it
　　from miles away.
　(3) Gabriel is so beautiful that any man would love
　　to be with her.

09 The soup was so hot that it burned my tongue.

10 Jody is the student who(m) Ms. Galler is looking
for.

11 (1) The boy who(m) you saw yesterday is my
　　brother.
　(2) The dress which she is wearing was designed
　　by a famous person.

12 The people whom I call most often are my mother
and my sisters.

13 so happy that

14 The party was so enjoyable that no one wanted to
leave.

15 She woke up so early that she was tired.

01 '네가 나에게 소개해 준 그 소녀'이므로 관계사절이 the girl을
수식하도록 문장을 만든다.

02 상자가 너무 무거워서 Sandra는 그것을 나르지 않았다고 쓸 수 있다.

03 which 대신 that을 쓰거나 또는 생략할 수 있다.

04 (1), (3)번에 쓰인 관계대명사는 목적격이므로 생략해도 무방하다.

05 Penny는 너무 아파서 아무것도 먹을 수 없었다는 의미이다.

06 목적격 관계대명사를 이용하여 하나의 문장으로 이어주었으므로 모두 that으로 쓰거나 생략해도 무방하다.

07 Avian의 외투가 너무 따뜻해서 다른 것을 살 필요가 없다는 문장을 쓸 수 있다.

08 원인과 결과를 나타내는 'so ~ that' 구문을 이용하여 문장을 하나로 만든다.

09 수프가 너무 뜨거워서 혀를 데였다는 문장으로 쓸 수 있다.

10 목적격 관계대명사이므로 that을 쓰거나 생략해도 무방하다.

11 모두 목적격 관계대명사이므로 that으로 쓰거나 생략해도 무방하다.

12 '내가 가장 자주 전화하는'이 '사람들'을 수식하고 있으므로 관계사절 The people whom I call most often이라고 쓰는 것이 옳다.

13 Jason에 따르면 Lisa는 너무 행복해서 방에서 춤을 추고 있다고 말할 수 있다.

14 파티가 너무 즐거워서 누구도 파티를 떠나고 싶어 하지 않았다는 문장을 쓸 수 있다.

15 원인과 결과를 나타내는 'so ~ that' 구문을 이용하여 문장을 만든다.

Reading

교과서

확인문제   p.132

1 T   2 F   3 T

확인문제   p.133

1 F   2 F   3 T   4 T

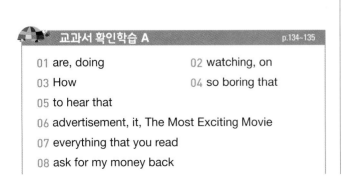

교과서 확인학습 A   p.134~135

01 are, doing   02 watching, on

03 How   04 so boring that

05 to hear that

06 advertisement, it, The Most Exciting Movie

07 everything that you read

08 ask for my money back

09 Hold on, lie because   10 not following you

11 express people's feelings   12 that, can be proven

13 For example, check that on the map

14 the connection with

15 Let me explain   16 It's

17 look for its advertisement

18 It says   19 uses facts unlike

20 the difference   21 exactly, says, says

22 Aren't, both opinions

23 words like, usually expressing opinions

24 which the movie won   25 that on the Internet

26 From now on, trust, with

27 that simple, mix, with

28 make a smart choice, both   29 to watch

30 the rest of

교과서 확인학습 B   p.136~137

1 Emma: What are you doing, Kyle?

2 Kyle: Oh, Emma. I'm watching the movie, *Y–Men 7* on my computer.

3 Emma: How is it?

4 Kyle: Don't ask. It's so boring that I want to cry.

5 Emma: I'm sorry to hear that.

6 Kyle: I'm so mad. The movie advertisement said it was "The Most Exciting Movie of the Year."

7 Emma: Well, you can't believe everything that you read.

8 Kyle: They lied on the advertisement. I'm going to ask for my money back.

9 Emma: Hold on, Kyle! They didn't really lie because they used opinions, not facts.

10 Kyle: Huh? I'm not following you.

11 Emma: Opinions express people's feelings like, "The desert is beautiful."

12 You can't say that it's true or not. But, facts can be proven.

13 For example, "The Atacama Desert is in Chile," is a fact. You can check that on the map.

14 Kyle: Okay.... But what's the connection with movies?

15 Emma: Let me explain. What's your favorite movie?

16 Kyle: It's *Forrest Gump*.

17 Emma: Okay. Let's look for its advertisement. What does it say?

18 Kyle: It says. "Winner of 6 Academy Awards including Best Picture."

19 Emma: See? It uses facts unlike the *Y-Men 7* advertisement.

20 Do you see the difference?

21 Kyle: Not exactly. The *Y-Men 7* ad says "Most Exciting Movie" and the *Forrest Gump* ad says "Best Picture."

22 Aren't they both opinions?

23 Emma: That's a great question, Kyle. When people use words like "best" or "most," they are usually expressing opinions.

24 But in the *Forrest Gump* ad, "Best Picture" is the award which the movie won.

25 We can check that on the Internet. That's a fact.

26 Kyle: Aha! From now on I'm only going to trust ads with facts.

27 Emma: It's not that simple. Most ads mix facts with opinions.

28 So you have to make a smart choice based on both of them.

29 Kyle: Got it! Emma, do you want to watch the rest of *Y-Men 7* with me?

30 Emma: Thanks, but no thanks. Enjoy the rest of the movie!

시험대비 실력평가
p.138~141

01 ①, ②　　02 ③　　03 opinions

04 It's because the movie is so boring.

05 ②　　06 ④　　07 아타카마 사막이 칠레에 있는 것　　08 ③　　09 ⑤　　10 a fact

11 ③　　12 facts and opinions　　13 ①

14 People usually express their opinions with words like "best" or "most."

15 ④　　16 ⑤　　17 ④

18 He is watching the movie, Y-Men 7 on his computer.　　19 ④

20 The movie advertisement said it was "The Most Exciting Movie of the Year."

21 ④　　22 ②　　23 an opinion, a fact

24 ④　　25 ⑤

26 (D) → (A) → (C) → (B)　　27 ③

28 영화 "Forest Gump"가 "Best Picture" 상을 받은 것

29 facts and opinions

01 사물을 선행사로 취하는 목적격 관계대명사가 들어가는 것이 옳다.

02 ③ Kyle은 영화에 만족하지 않는다. be fooled by: ~에 의해 속다

03 어떤 것에 대한 감정이나 생각은 '의견'이다.

04 Kyle이 울고 싶은 이유는 영화가 너무 지루하기 때문이다.

05 기다리라는 의미이다. 따라서 wait이 옳다. way to go: 잘 했어

06 앞 문장의 내용을 예를 들어 설명하고 있다.

07 "Atacama Desert is in Chile."를 가리키는 말이다.

08 Emma가 가장 좋아하는 영화는 글을 읽고 알 수 없다.

09 증명될 수 있는 것이 사실이다. 따라서 ⑤번이 사실이다.

10 의견과 사실의 차이점을 설명하는 글이다. 의견이 어떤 것인지를 설명한 후 사실에 관하여 설명하고 있다.

11 ① 오랫동안 ② 당분간 ③ 지금부터 ④, ⑤ 가끔

12 사실과 의견 둘 다 가리키는 말이다.

13 both 뒤에는 복수명사가 쓰인다.

14 사람들은 "best" 또는 "most"와 같은 말을 사용하여 그들의 의견을 표현한다.

15 ④ 대부분의 광고는 사실과 의견이 섞여 있다고 하였다.

16 ⓐ는 감정의 원인을 나타내는 to부정사이다. 따라서 ⑤번이 옳다.

17 그들이 거짓말을 한 것이 아니라는 이유를 설명하고 있으므로 because가 옳다.

18 Kyle은 컴퓨터로 영화 "Y-Men 7"을 보고 있다.

19 (A) 답변으로 미루어 보아 영화가 어떤지를 물었다고 볼 수 있으므로 how, (B) 지루함을 유발할 때에는 boring, (C) be going to V: V할 예정이다.

20 영화 광고에는 그 영화가 "올해의 가장 흥미진진한 영화"라고 쓰여 있었다.

21 that은 아타카마 사막이 칠레에 있다는 것을 받는다.

22 (A) 사실은 증명이 되는 것이므로 수동태, (B) 사역동사+목적어+원형부사: 목적어가 V하게 하다 (C) '~을 포함하여'라는 의미의 전치사가 쓰여야 하므로 including

23 글의 내용에 따르면, 그 아기가 가장 예쁘다는 것은 의견이고, 에베레스트 산이 세계에서 가장 높은 산이라는 것은 사실이라고 할 수 있다.

24 모두 확인 가능한 사실이지만 '혼자 해변 가에 가는 것은 안전하지 않다'는 것은 의견이다.

25 "Forest Gump"는 "Best Picture'를 포함하여 여섯 개의 아카데미상을 받았다고 하였다.

26 (D) 둘 다 의견이 아니냐는 질문 → (A) 의견과 사실의 차이를 설명 → (C) 이해한 후 사실만 있는 광고를 믿겠다고 말함 → (B) 보통 광고에는 사실과 의견이 섞여 있다고 말해 줌.

27 mix A with B: A와 B를 섞다. with: ~을 가진, ~을 포함한

28 영화가 상을 받은 사실을 인터넷을 통해 확인할 수 있다는 것이다.

29 대부분의 광고에는 사실과 의견 모두 있다고 하였다.

01 I am going to ask for my money back.

02 It's so boring that I want to cry.

03 They used not facts but opinions, so they didn't really lie.

04 It is *Y–Men 7*.   05 excited

06 be proven   07 We can check that on the map.

08 doesn't use facts

09 Did you see the movie that won 6 Academy Awards?

10 Kyle's favorite movie is *Forrest Gump*.

11 Aren't they both opinions?

12 "Best Picture" is the award. The movie won the award.

13 People who use words like 'best' or 'most' are usually expressing opinions.

14 base, facts and opinions

---

01 ask for ~ back: ~을 돌려달라고 청하다

02 원인과 결과를 나타내는 'so ~ that' 구문을 이용하여 문장을 만들 수 있다.

03 그들은 사실이 아니라 의견을 사용했으므로 꼭 거짓말을 한 것은 아니다. so는 결과를 이끄는 접속사이다. not A but B: A가 아니라 B(= B, not A)

04 Kyle이 보고 있는 영화의 제목은 "Y-Men 7"이다.

05 가장 흥미진진한 영화라는 광고와는 달리 Kyle은 흥미진진함을 느끼지 못했다고 말하는 것이 옳다.

06 사실은 '증명이 되는 것'이므로 수동태를 쓰는 것이 옳다. 조동사 뒤에 동사원형을 쓰는 것에 유의한다.

07 밑줄 친 문장이 사실이라는 것은 지도를 확인하여 알 수 있다.

08 "Y-Men 7" 광고와는 달리 사실을 사용하고 있다고 하였으므로 "Y-Men 7" 광고는 사실을 사용하지 않는다는 것을 알 수 있다.

09 관계대명사 that을 대신하여 which를 써도 무방하다.

10 Kyle이 가장 좋아하는 영화는 "Forest Gump"라고 하였다.

11 답변으로 미루어 보아 '둘 다 의견이 아니니?'라고 질문했음을 알 수 있다.

12 관계대명사를 이용하여 두 문장을 하나의 문장으로 쓴 것이다. 선행사를 이용하여 두 개의 문장으로 쓸 수 있다.

13 'best'나 'most'와 같은 말을 사용하는 사람이라고 하였으므로 관계사절이 people을 수식하도록 문장을 만든다.

14 대부분의 광고에는 사실과 의견이 섞여 있기 때문에 결정을 내릴 때 사실과 의견을 바탕으로 선택해야 한다.

01 full   02 ④   03 ④

---

04 (1) How do you like the present?

    (2) There is no evidence to prove his claim.

05 (1) make a choice   (2) check out   (3) full of

06 ③   07 ①   08 ②   09 ③

10 ②   11 ②   12 ⑤

13 How did you like your trip to Gyeongju?

14 worth   15 ⑤   16 ⑤   17 ⑤

18 ②   19 ①, ②, ⑤

20 It was so hot that we went swimming yesterday.

21 ②   22 ⑤

23 The drug that[which] the man stole was for his son.   24 ③

25 We eat the carrots which my grandfather grew on the farm.

26 There are so many leaves on a single tree that it is impossible to count them.

27 Tell me about the museum that you visited last week.

28 The movie that[which] Kyle chose used opinions in the advertisement.

29 ③, ⑤   30 ⑤   31 ①   32 ⑤

33 It's because most ads mix facts with opinions.

---

01 주어진 단어의 관계는 반의어 관계를 나타낸다. empty: 텅 빈, full: 가득 찬

02 사실이 아닌 무언가를 말하거나 쓰는 것을 가리키는 말은 lie(거짓말하다)이다.

03 worth: 가치가 있는

04 How do you like ~?: ~가 마음에 드니?, claim: 주장

05 make a choice: 선택하다, check out: 확인하다, be full of: ~로 가득 차다

06 주어진 문장에서 lie는 '거짓말하다'를 뜻하며 이와 같은 의미로 쓰인 것은 ③번이다. 나머지는 모두 '눕다'를 뜻한다.

07 worth: 가치가 있는, be worth ~ing: ~할 가치가 있다

10 여자와 소년은 점원과 손님의 관계임을 알 수 있다.

11 these days: 요즘에 = nowadays

14 무언가에 대해 충분히 중요하거나 좋거나 즐길 만한 것을 나타내는 말은 worth(가치가 있는)이다.

16 ⑤ 배낭의 무엇이 마음에 드는지에 대한 구체적인 답변이 이어져야 한다.

17 관계대명사 that과 접속사 that을 구별하는 문제이다. 관계대명사는 불완전한 절을 이끌고 접속사는 완전한 절을 이끈다는 사실에 유의하자.

18 날씨가 나빴기 때문에 우리 여행을 미루었다는 의미이다. 따라서 '날씨가 너무 나빠서 여행을 미루었다'는 ②번이 가장 적절하다.

19 목적격 관계대명사가 들어가야 한다. 사람이 선행사이므로 who, whom, that이 쓰일 수 있으며 생략도 가능하다.

20 너무 더워서 수영하러 갔다는 문장으로 쓸 수 있다. go Ving: V하러 가다

21 원인과 결과를 나타내는 문장이므로 because가 옳다.

22 모두 Maya가 비행을 너무 무서워해서 비행기로 여행할 수 없다는 의미이지만, ⑤번은 비행이 무섭다 할지라도 비행기로 여행한다는 의미이다.

23 that[which]은 생략할 수 있다.

24 목적격 관계대명사나 '주격 관계대명사+be동사'는 생략 가능하다.

25 which 대신 that을 쓰거나 생략해도 좋다.

26 한 그루의 나무에 잎이 너무 많아서 그것을 세는 것이 불가능하다는 문장으로 쓸 수 있다.

27 that을 대신하여 which를 쓰거나 목적격 관계대명사이므로 생략해도 무방하다.

28 'Kyle이 선택한 영화'라고 하였으므로 관계사절이 the movie를 수식하도록 문장을 만든다.

29 (A)는 인칭대명사로 the movie를 가리키는 말이다. it은 가주어, 비인칭 주어, 인칭대명사로 쓰일 수 있다.

30 Emma가 Kyle에 관해 어떻게 생각하는지는 알 수 없다.

31 모두 관계대명사 that이 들어갈 수 있으니 ①번에는 의문대명사 who나 what이 들어간다.

32 사실과 의견을 바탕으로 현명한 선택을 해야 한다고 하였으므로 ⑤번이 가장 적절하다.

33 대부분의 광고들은 사실과 의견을 섞기 때문에 사실로 이루어진 광고만 믿는다는 것은 간단한 일이 될 수 없다

단원별 예상문제
p.150~153

01 ⑤　　　02 (1) wisely　(2) recommend

(3) strongly　03 (1) number one　(2) look for

(3) right now　(4) Hold on　(5) worth it

04 (E) → (A) → (C) → (D) → (B)　　　05 ⑤

06 I was very happy with it.　　　07 ④

08 Cheomseongdae, Bulguksa

09 ⑤　　　10 ⑤　　　11 ③　　　12 ④

13 Can you give me back the pen that you
　　borrowed from me?

14 ②　　　15 ⑤

16 The barbell was so light that I could lift it up.

17 ②　　　18 ④　　　19 facts, opinions

20 They are mainly talking about the difference
　　between facts and opinions.　　　21 ③

22 The book was so touching that I read it many
　　times.　　　23 ⑤

24 Charlotte's Web is a children's novel which
　　E. B. White wrote.

01 무언가를 다른 무언가에 더하는 것을 가리키는 말은 mix(섞다)

이다.

03 (4) hold on: 기다리다 (5) worth it: 그만한 가치가 있다

04 (E) 도움 요청 → (A) 가방 추천 → (C) 거절 및 이유 설명 → (D) 다른 가방 추천 → (B) 반응 및 구매

05 이어지는 대화에서 자전거가 마음에 들지 않는 이유를 설명하고 있으므로 ⑤번처럼 무엇이 마음에 드는지 묻는 표현은 어색하다.

07 (A) How do you like ~?:~가 마음에 드니? (B)에는 주어 That이 생략되어 있으므로 Sounds, (C)에는 동명사 주어 walking이 적절하다.

09 주어진 빈칸에 들어갈 말로 추천하는 이유를 설명하는 표현이 적절하다.

10 Brian이 Antonio's에 가격이 좋은지 아닌지 확인하려고 갈 것이라는 설명은 대화의 내용과 일치하지 않는다.

11 관계대명사와 의문대명사를 구별하는 문제이다. 관계대명사는 해석되지 않으나 의문대명사는 '누구'라고 해석된다.

12 일을 열심히 한 것이 원인이고 그 결과로 그가 아프게 된 것이므로 ④번이 옳다.

13 '네가 나에게 빌려간 펜'이므로 the pen that you borrowed from me라고 쓰는 것이 옳다.

14 '의자에 앉다'는 표현은 sit on이다. 따라서 on which라고 쓰는 것이 적절하며 관계대명사 that은 전치사의 목적어로 쓰이지 않는 것에 유의하자.

15 전치사의 목적어로 관계대명사 that은 쓰일 수 없다. 따라서 to whom으로 쓰는 것이 적절하다.

16 가벼운 것이 원인이고 내가 들어 올릴 수 있었다는 것이 결과이므로 'so light that ~'을 쓴다.

17 Emma가 하는 말을 이해할 수 없다는 의미이다.

18 (B)는 명사절을 이끄는 접속사로 완전한 절을 이끈다. ④번은 불완전한 절을 이끄는 관계대명사 that이다.

19 사실은 증명될 수 있는 것이라고 하였다. 따라서 '사실과는 다르게 의견은 증명될 수 없다'라고 쓰는 것이 옳다.

20 사실과 의견의 차이에 관하여 주로 이야기하고 있다.

21 모두 확인할 수 있는 사실이지만 ③번은 의견이다.

22 '이 책은 너무 감동적이어서 나는 이 책을 여러 번 읽었다'의 의미이다.

23 Wilbur가 몇 명의 친구를 가지고 있는지는 알 수 없다.

24 which를 대신하여 that을 써도 무방하다.

서술형 실전문제
p.154~155

01 Her favorite restaurant is Antonio's.

02 She recommends the bulgogi pizza.

03 She thinks it is a little slow on the weekends.

04 (C) → (B) → (A) → (D)

05 I can't find the cup which my husband likes to use.

06 (1) The wind blew my hat off my head because it was strong.

   (2) The wind was so strong that it blew my hat off my head.

07 who[whom] Peter fell in love with left him / with whom Peter fell in love left him

08 that you baked / so delicious that

09 The jewel is so precious that it is priceless.

10 It says, "Winner of 6 Academy Awards including Best Picture."

11 She is using the advertisement of Forrest Gump.

12 의견은 진짜인지 아닌지 말할 수 없지만 사실은 확인할 수 있다.

13 opinions, facts

14 The book was so interesting that I couldn't put it down.

15 The genre of the book is fantasy.

01 미나가 가장 좋아하는 식당은 Antonio's이다.

02 미나는 불고기 피자를 추천하였다.

03 미나는 주말에는 서비스가 좀 느리다고 생각했다.

04 (C) 새 스마트폰을 갖게 된 것을 언급 → (B) 대답 및 만족 표현 → (A) 가장 마음에 드는 점 질문 → (D) 가장 마음에 드는 특징 설명

05 목적격 관계대명사이므로 생략해도 무방하며 that으로 써도 좋다.

06 원인은 바람이 강한 것이고, 그 결과로 내 머리에서 모자가 벗겨진 것이다.

07 'Peter가 사랑에 빠졌던 그 여자는 몇 주 전 그를 떠났다'는 문장을 쓸 수 있다. who[whom] 대신 that을 쓰거나 생략해도 좋다.

08 관계대명사 that은 생략하거나 which로 바꾸어 써도 좋다.

09 priceless: 값을 매길 수 없는, 대단히 귀중한

10 "Forest Gump" 영화 광고에는 "Winner of 6 Academy Awards including Best Picture."라고 쓰여 있다.

11 Emma는 Kyle이 가장 좋아하는 영화의 광고를 사용하여 사실과 의견의 차이점을 설명하고 있다.

12 의견은 사람의 감정을 나타내어 어떠한 것이 사실인지 아닌지 말할 수 없지만, 사실은 확인할 수 있는 차이가 있다고 하였다.

13 해석: 광고에는 우리가 믿을 수 없는 많은 의견들이 있다. 우리는 많은 사실을 가진 광고가 필요해.

14 원인과 결과를 이끄는 'so ~ that' 구문을 이용하여 문장을 만들 수 있다. 재미있는 것이 원인이고, 책을 놓을 수 없었던 것이 결과임에 유의한다.

15 책의 장르는 공상 소설(a fantasy novel)이라고 하였다.

|모범답안|

01 (A) the bulgogi pizza   (B) prices   (C) a little slow

02 (1) Tom was so busy that he couldn't answer the phone.

   (2) The waves were so high that we couldn't swim in the sea.

03 **Facts**

It is located in Yongin.

/ There are Korean traditional houses.

/ Visitors can watch nongak and jultagi.

Opinions

It's a fun place in Yongin.

/ Korean traditional houses are beautiful.

/ Nongak and jultagi are very exciting to see.

01 제가 가장 좋아하는 식당, Antonio's를 소개하고자 합니다. 이곳은 괜찮은 피자 식당이에요. 저는 불고기 피자를 추천합니다. 이것은 진짜 맛있어요. 만약 여러분이 주말에 이곳에 방문한다면, 서비스는 조금 느릴 수 있어요. Antonio's를 방문해 보는 게 어떨까요?

01 ⑤   02 ②

03 It was difficult for her.   04 ③   05 ⑤

06 (A) red   (B) a different color

   (C) a navy backpack   (D) side pockets

07 They are talking about Tom's new smartphone.

08 He is really happy with it.

09 He likes the camera most about his smartphone.

10 ⓓ → check it out   11 ⑤

12 (1) Mix the butter with the sugar.

   (2) Jack lifted the chair.

   (3) Are you telling the truth?

13 ④   14 ②

15 His speech was so famous that everyone knew about it.   16 ⑤

17 It is so cold that my mouth is frozen. 18 ③

19 ④   20 ⑤   21 ④

22 ① → unlike   23 fact, an opinion

24 ④   25 that I read is so touching that / recommend it to you

02 경주 여행에 매우 만족함을 알 수 있다.

03 Suji에게 석굴암까지 올라가는 것은 어려웠다.

04 이어지는 대화에서 추천하는 표현이 이어지므로 빈칸에 추천하는 표현이 적절하다. recommend: 추천하다

05 ⑤번을 제외한 나머지는 모두 추천을 하는 표현이다.

06 나는 오늘 새로운 배낭을 사서 기분이 좋았다. 나는 빨간색 배낭을 메곤 했었다. 그래서 나는 다른 색을 사고 싶었다. 점원은 내게 남색 배낭을 추천하였는데 이것은 양쪽에 주머니를 갖고 있었다. 나는 이것이 매우 마음에 들어서 샀다. 나는 내일 새 배낭을 메는 것을 기대하고 있다.

07 Tom과 Sue는 Tom의 새 스마트폰에 대해 이야기하고 있다.

08 Tom은 그의 스마트폰을 정말 만족스러워하고 있다.

09 Tom은 그의 스마트폰에서 카메라를 가장 좋아한다.

10 check out과 같이 '동사+부사'로 이루어진 구동사의 목적어가 인칭대명사일 때는 동사와 부사 사이에 목적어가 위치한다.

11 위 대화에서 Antonio's에서 불고기 피자가 얼마인지는 알 수 없다.

12 mix: 섞다, lift: 들어 올리다. tell the truth: 진실을 말하다

13 모두 날씨가 너무 좋아서 우리가 밖으로 나갔다는 의미이지만 ④번은 날씨가 너무 좋아서 밖으로 나갈 수 없었다는 의미이다.

14 모두 불완전한 절을 이끄는 관계대명사 that이지만 ②번은 접속사 that으로 완전한 절을 이끈다.

15 유명한 것이 원인이고 모두가 아는 것은 결과이다. 따라서 so famous that everyone knew about it이라고 쓰는 것이 옳다.

16 주어가 복수 명사인 The women이므로 are friendly라고 쓰는 것이 옳다.

17 너무 추워서 내 입이 얼었다는 문장으로 쓸 수 있다.

18 무엇을 하고 있는지 묻는 말에 ⓒ 대답 → ⓐ 영화가 어떠냐는 질문에 → ⓓ 너무 지루하다는 대답 → ⓑ 이 대답에 유감이라고 답하는 순서가 자연스럽다.

19 hold on: 기다리다

20 광고에는 사실과 의견이 모두 있다고 하였으므로 ⑤번이 글의 내용과 일치한다.

21 ④ "Forest Gump"의 광고를 가리키는 대명사이다.

22 "Y-Men 7" 광고에는 의견이 사용되었고 "Forest Gump" 광고에는 사실이 사용되었다고 하였으므로 unlike를 쓰는 것이 옳다.

23 어떠한 것이 증명될 수 있으면 사실이지만, 진실인지 아닌지 확인할 수 없는 것은 의견이라고 말할 수 있다.

24 ignore: 무시하다, 못 본 체하다

25 '내가 읽은 책'이라고 하였으므로 관계사절이 the book을 수식하도록 문장을 만든다.

Lesson 8

Be like Sherlock!

01 inside   02 ②   03 ②   04 ②

05 ②   06 (1) water   (2) thief   (3) talent

(4) take care of [look after]   (5) on the way home

(6) his rounds

01 주어진 단어의 관계는 반의어 관계를 나타낸다. inside: ~ 안에, outside: ~ 밖에

02 무언가를 잘하는 타고난, 특별한 능력을 가리키는 말은 talent(재능)이다.

03 lightning: 번개

04 주어진 문장에서 post는 '게시하다'를 뜻하며 이와 같은 의미로 쓰인 것은 ②번이다. 나머지는 모두 '우편, 우편물'을 의미한다.

05 문장에 공통으로 들어갈 말은 text이며 명사로 '본문, 문자메시지', 동사로 '문자를 보내다'를 의미한다.

06 water: 물을 주다, thief: 도둑, talent:재능, take care of=look after: ~을 돌보다, on the way home: 집에 오는 길에, make one's round: 순찰을 돌다

서술형 시험대비
p.165

01 lose   02 (1) refrigerator   (2) thunder   (3) clue

(4) afraid   (5) poem   (6) carry

03 (1) strange   (2) suddenly   (3) post

04 (1) His life was not happy anymore.

    (2) When we get into a trouble, we should try to overcome.

    (3) He won first place in the talent show.

05 (1) The crime rate is rising.

    (2) He showed a talent for dancing.

    (3) Her dog is afraid of thunder.

    (4) Could you mop the floor?

    (5) She hired a detective to solve the problem.

    (6) Her bag is as light as a feather.

01 주어진 단어의 관계는 반의어 관계를 나타낸다. find: 찾다, lose: 잃어버리다

02 afraid: 두려워하는, refrigerator: 냉장고, carry: 나르다, 옮기다, poem: 시, clue: 단서, thunder: 천둥

03 strange: 이상한, suddenly: 갑자기, post: 게시하다

04 not ~ anymore: 더 이상 ~ 않는, overcome: 극복하다, win first place: 일등을 하다

05 crime rate: 범죄율, be afraid of: ~을 두려워하다, mop: 닦다, detective: 탐정, feather: 깃털

핵심 Check
p.166~167

1 (1) favor / Can you help me   (2) favor / What is it / post / afraid

2 (1) Guess / I guess   (2) wrong   (3) Maybe

교과서 대화문 익히기

Check(√) True or False
p.168

1 T   2 F   3 T   4 F

교과서 확인학습
p.170~171

Listen and Speak 1-A

favor / wash the dishes

Listen and Speak 1-B

take care of / I'm sorry but I can't / what should I do / Why don't you / right now

Listen and Speak 1-C

do me a favor / help me mop / problem, can't

Listen and Speak 2-A

under the table / anymore / guess / he is

Listen and Speak 2-B

have passed, at the end of, wonderful year, a few, stranger, each other

Listen and Speak 2-C

what I'm doing / I guess / wrong / working on / right

Real Life Talk - Step 1

Can you help me / inside / texted / Where were / was making / somewhere / checked / let's check it again, it is, refrigerator / welcome

Real Life Talk - Step 2

help me find / did, see, last / guess, took, see its footprints

01 can I ask you a favor?   02 ⑤

03 Brian's baseball glove   04 ③

01 ①   02 ③, ⑤   03 ⑤

04 (E) → (C) → (A) → (D) → (B)

05 I guess a dog took your baseball glove.

06 ④   07 ⓐ → find (또는 to find)   08 ④

09 ③   10 classmates   11 ②

12 ⑤

01 (A)는 도움 요청에 대해 거절하는 표현으로 ①번과 바꾸어 쓸 수 있다.

02 (B)는 제안하는 표현이다.

04 (E) 야구 글러브를 보았는지 질문 → (C) 대답 및 설명 → (A) 그곳에 없음을 설명 → (D) 추측 표현하기 → (B) 야구 글러브 발견

06 ④ Jack이 야구 글러브를 갖고 도망가는 개를 보았다는 설명은 대화의 내용과 일치하지 않는다.

07 help는 준사역동사로서 목적보어로 동사원형 또는 to부정사를 취한다.

08 위 대화를 통해 Brian이 친구에게 왜 문자메시지를 보냈는지는 알 수 없다.

09 irritated: 짜증난, confused: 혼란스러워 하는, pleased: 기쁜, dissatisfied: 불만족한, nervous: 긴장된, upset: 화난

10 학교나 대학에서 당신과 같은 학급에 있는 사람들을 가리키는 말은 classmates(급우들)이다.

11 (A) 현재완료로 have passed, (B) 셀 수 있는 명사를 수식하는 a few, (C) each other: 서로

12 수진과 학급 친구들은 극소수만 같은 반이 될 것이다.

01 stranger   02 I guess only a few of us will be in the same class next year.

03 Can you help me find it?

04 He used it in the kitchen last.

05 It was in the refrigerator.   06 footprint

07 Because he can see its footprints on the bench.

01 당신이 모르는 사람을 가리키는 말은 stranger(모르는 사람)이다.

04 Brian은 그의 스마트폰을 부엌에서 마지막으로 사용하였다.

05 Brian의 스마트폰은 냉장고에 있었다.

06 발 또는 신발에 의해 남겨진 자국을 의미하는 것은 footprint(발자국)이다.

07 Jack이 Amy의 야구 글러브를 개가 가져갔다고 생각하는 이유는 그가 벤치 위에서 개의 발자국들을 볼 수 있기 때문이다.

Grammar

1 (1) something noisy   (2) something wrong
    (3) something strange

2 (1) when the movie starts   (2) what he ate
    (3) how much the watch is

01 (1) nice anyone → anyone nice
    (2) can I → I can   (3) to see pretty → pretty to see
    (4) that → if[whether]

02 (1) who she is   (2) what made her angry
    (3) something comfortable to sit on
    (4) how old she is   (5) there something cold

03 (1) I want to eat something sweet.
    (2) Do you have anything bigger than this?
    (3) Jason doesn't know how his mom found him.
    (4) We don't know when they will come.

01 (1), (3) -thing, -body, -one으로 끝나는 부정대명사는 형용사가 뒤에서 수식한다. 단, 이러한 대명사를 형용사와 to부정사가 동시에 수식하는 경우 '대명사+형용사+to부정사'의 어순임에 유의한다. (2), (4) 간접의문문의 어순은 '의문사+주어+동사'이며, 의문사가 없는 의문문의 간접의문문은 'if/whether+주어+동사'로 쓴다.

02 (1), (4) 간접의문문의 어순은 '의문사+주어+동사'이다. (2) what이 의문대명사로 주어로 쓰이고 있다. (3) 형용사와 to부정사가 동시에 something을 수식하는 경우 '대명사+형용사+to부정사'의 어순이다. (5) -thing으로 끝나는 부정대명사는 형용사의 수식을 뒤에서 받는다.

03 (1), (2) -thing으로 끝나는 부정대명사는 형용사의 수식을 뒤에서 받는다. (3), (4) 간접의문문의 어순은 '의문사+주어+동사'의 어순이다.

01 ⑤　　　　02 ②　　　　03 ④

04 She doesn't have anyone kind to talk with.

05 ⑤　　　　06 ④　　　　07 ①, ④

08 when we are going to meet

09 ⑤　　　　10 ④　　　　11 ③

12 There is something important to deal with.

13 ②　　　　14 ④　　　　15 ⑤

16 I wonder who he is talking with now.

17 ③　　　　18 ⑤

19 Could you tell me when this happened?

20 Do you know who brought this T-shirt?

21 ③　　　　22 ③　　　　23 ③

24 someone strong and healthy

01 주어진 우리말을 영어로 옮기면 'I want to see something colorful and beautiful.'이다.

02 간접의문문의 어순은 '의문사+주어+동사'이며 의문사가 주어 역할을 하는 경우는 '의문사+동사'의 어순이 가능하다.

03 -thing으로 끝나는 대명사는 형용사의 수식을 뒤에서 받으며, '신나는 것을 유발'할 때에는 현재분사를 쓰는 것이 적절하다. 간접의문문의 어순은 '의문사+주어+동사'이다.

04 -thing으로 끝나는 대명사가 형용사와 to부정사의 수식을 동시에 받을 때 '-thing+형용사+to부정사' 어순임에 유의하여 답을 쓴다.

05 빈칸에는 someone을 수식하는 형용사가 들어가는 것이 적절하다. ⑤는 부사이다.

06 ④번을 영어로 바르게 옮기면 Do you know who saw her?이다.

07 의문사가 없는 문장의 간접의문문은 if나 whether를 써서 만들 수 있다.

08 remember의 목적어로 '의문사+주어+동사' 어순의 간접의문문을 쓸 수 있다.

09 형용사와 to부정사가 동시에 something을 수식할 때에는 '형용사+to부정사'의 어순으로 수식하는 것이 일반적이다. 따라서 something fun to talk about이 적절하다.

10 대답으로 미루어 보아 길을 묻는 말이 들어가는 것이 가장 적절하다.

11 공을 찬 주체가 누구인지 궁금하다는 의미이므로 의문대명사 who를 이용하여 간접의문문을 완성할 수 있다.

12 important와 to deal with가 something을 동시에 수식하므로 something important to deal with 어순으로 쓴다.

13 -thing으로 끝나는 대명사를 수식할 때 '형용사+to부정사' 어순이며, remember라는 동사의 목적어로 간접의문문이 쓰이고 있으므로 '의문사+주어+동사' 어순으로 빈칸을 채운다.

14 ④번의 두 문장을 간접의문문으로 옮기면 I don't know who helped you.이다.

15 -one으로 끝나는 대명사 뒤에는 형용사가 수식한다. care는 명사이므로 빈칸에 쓰일 수 없다.

16 '그가 지금 누구와 이야기하고 있는지'가 wonder의 목적어이다. 따라서 간접의문문을 활용하여 who he is talking with now를 wonder의 목적어로 쓰는 것이 적절하다.

17 주어진 문장의 밑줄 친 who는 간접의문문을 만드는 의문대명사로 '누가'라고 해석된다. guess의 목적어로 간접의문문을 이끌고 있는 ③번이 답이다. 나머지는 모두 앞선 명사를 수식하는 관계대명사 who이다.

18 know의 목적어 역할을 하는 간접의문문이므로 who he is라고 쓰는 것이 적절하다.

19 간접의문문을 활용하여 '언제 이게 발생했는지'가 tell의 직접목적어가 되도록 문장을 만들 수 있다. '의문사+주어+동사'의 어순에 유의하여 답을 쓴다.

20 간접의문문의 어순은 '의문사+주어+동사'이지만, 의문사가 주어 역할을 하는 경우 '의문사+동사' 어순이다.

21 의문사가 없는 문장의 간접의문문은 if 혹은 whether를 써서 만든다.

22 ③ anything heavy라고 쓰는 것이 적절하다.

23 주어진 문장을 영어로 옮기면 He tries to do something good for others.이다.

24 답변으로 미루어 보아 의학 실험을 위해서 튼튼하고 건강한 누군가가 필요하다는 말을 했음을 유추할 수 있다. 긍정문이므로 someone을 쓰고 -one으로 끝나는 대명사이므로 형용사가 뒤에서 수식하도록 빈칸을 채운다.

01 I need someone reliable.

02 (1) Do you know how she bakes these cookies?

  (2) I'll ask Jason where he lives.

  (3) Do you remember what Brad's last name is?

  (4) I wonder if[whether] they will go abroad to study English.

  (5) Can you tell me if[whether] she is going to run or walk?

  (6) I don't understand what they wanted to do.

  (7) I want to know who made the decision last night.

03 Let me know how old he is.

04 when[what time] I came

05 A: I met someone interesting at a party yesterday.

  B: Tell me who he was.

06 Mike wanted to meet someone brave to be admired.

07 what the story is about

08 something strange / it is   09 if

10 I need something colorful to decorate this tree.

11 A: I don't know what he wants

   B: He wants something different.

12 Do you know what this word means?

13 something to drink

14 I don't remember where I put my purse yesterday.

15 A: what they are   B: something surprising

01 someone은 형용사의 수식을 뒤에서 받는 대명사이다.

02 간접의문문은 의문사가 이끄는 문장이 '의문사+주어+동사'의 어순으로 주절에서 명사 역할을 하는 것이다. 단, 의문사가 없는 경우 'if/ whether+주어+동사'의 어순임에 유의한다.

03 know의 목적어로 간접의문문 how old he is를 써서 문장을 완성한다.

04 답변으로 미루어 보아 '언제[몇 시에] 집에 왔는지를 기억할 수 없다'는 말이 들어가는 것이 적절하다.

05 someone을 수식하는 interesting은 뒤에서 someone을 수식한다. '그가 누구였는지'는 Tell의 직접목적어로 쓰여 '의문사+주어+동사' 어순으로 나타낼 수 있다.

06 '존경 받을 만한 용감한 누군가'라고 하였으므로 someone을 brave와 to be admired가 수식하도록 문장을 만든다. 이때 '형용사+to부정사'의 어순으로 대명사 someone을 뒤에서 수식하는 것에 유의한다.

07 그 이야기가 어떤 것에 관한 것인지 알고 싶다는 말에 대한 답변이 이어지고 있으므로 what the story is about이라고 쓰는 것이 적절하다.

08 이상하게 생긴 어떤 것을 발견했다고 하자, 정말로 이상하게 보인다며 무엇인지 아냐고 물어보고, 이에 모르겠다고 답하는 것이 자연스럽다.

09 조건의 부사절과 간접의문문을 이끌 수 있는 것은 접속사 if이다.

10 '이 트리를 장식할 다채로운 무언가'라고 하였으므로 colorful과 to decorate this tree가 something을 수식하도록 문장을 만든다. 이때, 'something+형용사+to부정사'의 어순임에 유의한다.

11 '그가 무엇을 원하는지'가 동사 know의 목적어이므로 I don't know what he wants.라고 쓴다. '다른 무언가'라고 하였으므로 부정대명사 something을 형용사 different가 뒤에서 수식하도록 문장을 만든다.

12 동사 know의 목적어로 간접의문문 what this word means를 써서 문장을 완성할 수 있다.

13 대답으로 미루어 보아 마실 것을 원한다는 말이 들어가는 것이 적절하다.

14 간접의문문의 어순은 '의문사+주어+동사'이다.

15 해석: A: 나는 그들이 무엇을 보고 있는지 궁금해. B: 그들은 극장에서 어떤 놀라운 것을 보고 있어.

Reading

확인문제   p.184

1 T   2 F   3 F   4 T

확인문제   p.185

1 F   2 T   3 T

교과서 확인학습 A   p.186~187

01 ran across   02 need, help

03 eighth grade   04 the best detective

05 something wrong   06 has stolen, for

07 took, to, scene   08 was, broken

09 were still there

10 missing, a poem, its place

11 Where did, go   12 high and low, too

13 when this happened

14 after, making my rounds, rushed over

15 who else was here

16 practicing, call them   17 ninth grade, curly

18 practicing, thirsty, stepped outside, to get, It, completely, Suddenly, thunder, broke, Lightning followed, running away

19 face   20 back, short

21 eighth grade, with long black

22 reading, aloud, next to, flash, like a horror movie, scared   23 hear, break

24 too loud, was going to win 25 short blonde

26 wrong, moves, a little before, take, outside, until

27 anything strange   28 How could

29 on the way home   30 singing

31 to hear anymore, turned to

32 bring the medal back

교과서 확인학습 B   p.188~189

1 Mr. Reese, the principal, ran across the wet playground.

2 "Shirley! Shirley! I need your help!"

3 Shirley was an eighth grade student at Bakersville Middle School.

4 She was also the best detective in the whole town.

5 "Is there something wrong?" asked Shirley.

6 "Someone has stolen the gold medal for the talent show!"

7 Mr. Reese took Shirley to the scene of the crime.

8 There was a case with a broken window.

9 The silver and bronze medals were still there.

10 But the gold medal was missing. There was a poem in its place.

11 Tomorrow is the talent show. Where did the gold medal go?

12 Look high and low. You can't catch me. You're too slow.

13 Shirley asked, "Could you tell me when this happened?"

14 "A little after nine last night. I was making my rounds when I heard a scream. I rushed over and found Jocelyn and the case like this."

15 "I wonder who else was here last night."

16 "Sylvia and Harry. They were also practicing for the talent show. I'll call them to my office."

17 Jocelyn was a ninth grade student with short curly red hair.

18 "I was practicing my song and I became thirsty. I stepped outside the classroom to get some water. It was completely dark. Suddenly, there was a loud sound of thunder. I think the thief broke the window at that moment. Lightning followed right after and it became bright for a second or two. Then I saw someone running away from the case."

19 "Did you see the thief's face?"

20 "No, I only saw the thief's back. But the thief had short hair."

21 Next was an eighth grade student, Sylvia. She was tall with long black hair.

22 She said, "I was reading my poem aloud in the classroom. I heard a scream and went outside. There was a girl next to the case. With the flash from the lightning, it was like a horror movie. I got scared so I ran straight home."

23 "Did you hear the window break?"

24 "No, the thunder was too loud. Well, I didn't do it. I was going to win first place anyway."

25 Harry, a seventh grader, had short blonde hair.

26 He said, "Hey, you got the wrong guy. I was practicing my dance moves. I went home a little before nine. I didn't take one step outside the classroom until then."

27 "Did you hear anything strange?"

28 "How could I? My music was really loud."

29 "Did you see anyone on the way home?"

30 "No, I heard someone singing really badly, but I didn't see anyone."

31 Shirley said, "I don't need to hear anymore." Then she turned to the thief.

32 "Why don't you bring the medal back before you get into some real trouble?"

시험대비 실력평가　　　　　　　　p.190~193

01 ②　　　　　02 in the case　　　　03 ④

04 Someone stole it.

05 Jocelyn, Sylvia and Harry　　　06 ③

07 ②　　　　　08 The thief had short hair.

09 thief　　　　10 ⑤

11 if[whether] you saw anyone on the way home

12 the thunder was too loud　　　　13 ③

14 when this happened　　15 ④, ⑤　　16 ②, ④

17 the gold medal　　　　18 ⑤　　　　19 ④

20 ③　　　　　21 Because she wanted to get some water.　　22 She was tall with long black hair.

23 ②　　　　　24 ③

25 He was practicing his dance moves.

01 위 글에서 금메달은 이미 사라지고 난 이후이므로 ②번은 위 글에서 찾아볼 수 없다.

02 진열장을 가리키는 말이다.

03 위 글에서 쓰인 case는 '진열장'을 의미한다.

04 누군가가 장기자랑 대회 금메달을 훔쳐갔다고 하였다.

05 어젯밤에 학교에 있었던 세 사람을 가리키는 말이다.

06 물을 가지러 교실 밖으로 나갔다고 하였으므로 교실 안에서 물을 마셨다는 것은 글의 내용과 일치하지 않는다.

07 ⓑ는 날짜, 날씨, 거리, 명암 등을 나타내는 비인칭 주어 It이다.
①, ④ 가주어 It ② 비인칭 주어 ③, ⑤ 인칭대명사

08 도둑이 짧은 머리인 것을 Jocelyn이 보았다.

09 다른 사람에게서 무언가를 훔치는 사람은 '도둑'이다.

10 음악 소리가 정말 커서 이상한 소리를 들을 수 없었다는 것이 자연스럽다.

11 집에 가는 길에 누군가를 보았느냐는 물음에 대한 답이 이어지고 있다. 의문사가 없는 의문문의 간접의문문은 if나 whether를 써서 만든다.

12 천둥소리가 너무 커서 창이 깨지는 소리를 듣지 못했다고 하였다.

13 Sylvia는 공포영화를 본 것이 아니라, 번개의 번쩍임에 본 진열장 옆의 소녀의 모습이 공포 영화 같았다고 하였다.

14 이어지는 대답이 '지난 밤 9시가 조금 넘은 후'라는 것으로 보아

언제 이 사건이 일어났는지 묻는 말이 들어가는 것이 가장 적절하다.

15 도둑이 쓴 시에 장기 자랑 대회가 내일이라고 적혀 있었다.

16 시의 내용으로 보아, 시를 쓴 사람은 도둑이며 학교 장기 자랑 대회는 사건 다음 날 개최될 예정이었다.

17 은메달과 동메달은 그대로 남아 있었다고 하였으므로 범인은 진열장에서 오직 금메달만을 가지고 갔다.

18 번개로 인하여 1~2초 정도 밝아졌을 때 범인이 진열장에서 도망치는 것을 보았다는 것이 자연스럽다.

19 공포영화를 본 것 같았다고 하였으므로 '무서움'을 느꼈다는 것이 적절하다.

20 천둥이 쳤을 때 Syliva는 교실 밖으로 나와 진열장 옆에 있던 소녀를 보고 있었다.

21 Jocelyn은 물을 가지러 교실 밖으로 나갔다고 하였다.

22 Sylvia는 길고 검은 머리를 가진 키가 큰 소녀이다.

23 (A) -thing으로 끝나는 대명사이므로 뒤에서 형용사의 수식을 받는다. (B) 지각동사의 목적격 보어로 원형부정사 혹은 현재분사이다. (C) Why don't you+동사원형 ~?

24 뒤에 이어지는 문장으로 보아 이상한 소리를 들을 수 없었다는 의미이다.

25 Harry는 교실 안에서 춤 동작을 연습하고 있었다고 하였다.

서술형 시험대비   p.194~195

01 Is there something wrong?
02 principal / eighth, best detective
03 They were in the broken case.
04 calling, Mr. Reese, stole the gold medal, broken, poem, the gold medal.   05 천둥소리가 나던 순간
06 what you were doing
07 Mr. Reese, Jocelyn, Sylvia, and Harry were in the school.
08 It was because his music was really loud.
09 She saw a girl next to the case.
10 Because she got scared.
11 The flash from the lightning did.
12 went home → went outside, heard → didn't hear
13 I found out who stole the gold medal.

01 무슨 일이 있는지를 묻는 표현이 들어가는 것이 적절하다. -thing으로 끝나는 부정대명사이므로 형용사의 수식을 뒤에서 받는 것에 유의한다.

02 Mr. Reese는 Bakersville 중학교의 교장 선생님이다. Shirley는 8학년이고 마을 최고의 탐정이다.

03 은메달과 동메달은 깨진 진열장 안에 있었다.

04 해석: 내가 걷고 있을 때, 누군가가 내 이름을 부르는 소리를 들었다. 그것은 Mr. Reese였다. 그는 누군가가 장기 자랑 대회

금메달을 훔쳤다고 말했다. 나는 그와 함께 범죄의 현장으로 갔다. 나는 진열장의 유리창이 깨져 있는 것을 보았다. 금메달 대신에 시가 있었다.

05 커다란 천둥소리가 났을 때 도둑이 유리창을 깼다고 생각한다는 의미이다.

06 비명소리를 들었을 때 Mr. Reese는 순찰을 돌고 있었다고 하였다.

07 교장 선생님, Jocelyn, Sylvia, Harry가 사건 당시에 학교에 있었다.

08 음악 소리가 너무 커서 이상한 소리를 듣지 못했다는 의미이다.

09 밖으로 나온 Sylvia는 진열장 옆에 있는 한 소녀를 보았다.

10 Sylvia는 무서웠기 때문에 곧장 집으로 달려갔다고 하였다.

11 번개의 번쩍임이 범죄 현장을 공포 영화처럼 보이게 만들었다고 하였다.

12 Sylvia는 비명소리를 듣고 밖으로 나갔다고 하였고, 커다란 천둥소리 때문에 창문이 깨지는 소리를 듣지 못했다고 하였다.

13 '누가 금메달을 훔쳤는지'가 find out의 목적어가 되어야 하므로 간접의문문을 이용하여 쓸 수 있다.

영역별 핵심문제   p.197~201

01 footprint   02 ⑤   03 ②
04 (1) thirsty (2) detective (3) footprint (4) broken
05 ②
06 (1) She gave me a silver necklace.
   (2) I'll carry your luggage to your room.
   (3) This story is about a witch who flies in the sky.
07 ⑤   08 Can you help me wash the dishes?
09 ⑤   10 ②
11 can you give me a hand?   12 ⑤
13 She is making her speech at the end of the school year.
14 She is asking them to say hello when they see each other.   15 ④   16 ④
17 ③   18 ②   19 ④
20 Do you know what color her bag is?   21 ⑤
22 ④   23 ⑤
24 She bought something special for her mother.
25 ③   26 I need someone trustful to depend on.   27 ③   28 ④   29 ②
30 She cut her hair.   31 ⑤

01 주어진 단어의 관계는 반의어 관계를 나타낸다. handprint: 손자국, footprint: 발자국

02 favor: 호의, 부탁

03 주어진 문장에서 principal은 '교장'을 뜻한다. ②번은 '주요한, 주된'을 의미한다.

33

04 broken: 깨진, 부서진, footprint: 발자국, thirsty: 목마른, detective: 탐정

05 pass는 각각 '통과하다, 합격하다, 건네주다, 지나다'를 의미한다.

06 silver: 은, necklace: 목걸이, luggage: 짐, witch: 마녀

07 위 대화의 밑줄 친 (A)와 나머지는 도움을 요청하는 표현이다. ⑤번은 도움을 제안하는 표현이다.

09 추측해 대한 반응으로 '그것 참 안됐구나.'라는 대답은 어색하다.

10 주어진 문장은 (B)의 앞에 나오는 Tony의 질문에 대한 답으로 적절하다.

12 위 대화를 통해 나래가 그녀의 개를 어떻게 돌보는지는 알 수 없다.

13 이 연설은 학년의 막바지에 하고 있다.

14 수진은 서로 만나면 인사말을 건넬 것을 부탁하고 있다.

15 ⓓ는 부엌을 가리키며 나머지는 모두 스마트폰을 가리킨다.

17 who found your purse라고 쓰는 것이 적절하다.

18 주어진 우리말을 영어로 옮기면 I want to do something exciting for my birthday party.이다.

19 '누가 너를 그 파티에 초대했는지'라고 하였으므로 의문대명사 who를 이용하여 간접의문문을 만든다.

20 의문사가 이끄는 문장을 동사 know의 목적어로 만든다. 이때 어순은 '의문사+주어+동사'의 어순임에 유의한다.

21 -thing으로 끝나는 부정대명사를 형용사와 to부정사가 동시에 수식할 때는 '형용사+to부정사' 어순으로 수식한다.

22 간접의문문의 어순은 '의문사+주어+동사'이고, -thing으로 끝나는 부정대명사는 '형용사+to부정사'의 어순으로 수식받는다. 의문사가 없는 의문문의 간접의문문은 if 혹은 whether를 써서 나타낸다.

23 부정대명사를 수식하는 어순은 '형용사+to부정사'이다. 따라서 nothing precious to keep이라고 써야 한다.

24 부정대명사는 뒤에서 형용사의 수식을 받는다. 따라서 something special이라고 쓰는 것이 적절하다.

25 그녀가 왜 늦었는지를 모르겠다는 말이 적절하다. 이때 간접의문문의 어순인 '의문사+주어+동사'에 맞게 빈칸을 채운다.

26 someone은 부정대명사이므로 '형용사+to부정사' 어순으로 뒤에서 수식받는다.

27 Mr. Reese가 범죄 현장으로 달려갔을 때 Jocelyn을 보았다고 하였으므로 그가 가장 먼저 도착했다고 볼 수 없다.

28 Mr. Reese는 학교에서 순찰을 돌고 있었다고 하였으므로 ④번은 글의 내용과 일치하지 않는다.

29 라푼젤은 긴 머리카락을 가지고 있었는데 (B) 마녀는 그것을 이용해서 탑으로 올라갔고 세상이 위험하다고 말함. 어느 날 지나가던 왕자가 그녀가 노래하는 것을 듣고 (A) 세상이 아름답다고 말하며 라푼젤에게 내려오라고 함 (C) 마침내 결심한 라푼젤은 탑에서 내려옴.

30 탑에서 내려오기 전에 라푼젤은 머리카락을 잘랐다.

31 탑에서 내려오기 위해서 라푼젤이 무엇을 사용했는지는 알 수 없다.

단원별 예상문제

p.202~205

01 ③   02 (C) → (B) → (D) → (A)
03 ④   04 ⑤
05 Can you take care of my dog this weekend?
06 ①, ③   07 ④   08 ⑤
09 She asks him to help her wash the dishes.
10 Can you give me a hand to wash the dishes?
11 ④   12 ③   13 ④   14 ⑤
15 warm to wear
16 Please ask him what time he can pick me up.
17 who built it   18 who is telling the truth   19 ④   20 ②
21 (C)–(B)–(A)–(D)   22 ⑤   23 ④
24 who stole, practicing her song, reading her poem
25 ⑤

01 구리와 주석을 포함한 황갈색의 금속을 가리키는 말은 bronze(청동)이다.

02 (C) 도움 요청하기 → (B) 대답 및 질문 → (D) 필요한 도움 설명 → (A) 승낙

03 주어진 문장은 어디에 있었는지에 대한 대답이므로 (D)가 적절하다.

04 Briain의 스마트폰이 냉장고에서 발견되었다는 설명이 대화의 내용과 일치한다.

07 ④번은 모르는 사람을 친구로 만드는 법을 배워야 한다는 것으로 Sujin이 학급 친구들에게 모르는 사람처럼 지내지 말고 내년에 서로 인사하며 지내자고 부탁하는 내용에 어색하다.

08 수진이 모르는 사람들을 만날 때마다 무엇을 해야 하는지는 알 수 없다.

09 Emily는 Jinsu에게 설거지를 도와줄 것을 요청한다.

10 give a hand: 도와주다

11 빈칸에는 간접의문문을 목적어로 받을 수 있는 동사가 쓰이는 것이 적절하다. know, tell, remember는 모두 목적어를 취할 수 있는 타동사이지만 happen은 자동사이다.

12 대답으로 보아 누가 깃발을 찾았는지 궁금하다는 말이 들어가는 것이 적절하다.

13 '형용사+to부정사'의 어순으로 부정대명사 something을 뒤에서 수식하는 ④번이 옳다. discuss: ~에 관하여 논의하다

14 ① who kicked the ball ② someone old ③ if she likes ④ what he would want라고 쓰는 것이 적절하다.

15 입을 따뜻한 무언가를 원한다는 말이 들어가는 것아 가장 적절하다.

16 ask의 직접목적어로 간접의문문을 활용하여 문장을 쓴다. 이때 '의문사+주어+동사'의 어순임에 유의한다.

17 대답으로 미루어 보아 누가 그것을 지었는지 아는지를 묻는 말이 적절하다.

18 간접의문문을 이용하여 문장을 완성할 수 있다. 이때 who는 의

문대명사로 의문사이자 주어 역할을 동시에 한다.

19 혼란스러웠지만 마침내 결정을 내렸다는 것이 가장 자연스럽다. 따라서 Finally가 가장 적절하다.

20 긴 머리를 가진 사람은 Rapunzel이다.

21 목이 말라서 (C) 물을 가지러 교실 밖으로 나옴 - (B) 갑자기 커다란 천둥이 치고 - (A) 바로 그 순간에 도둑이 창문을 깼다고 생각함. 이후에 번개가 쳤고 1~2초 정도 밝아짐 - (D) 그때 도둑이 진열장에서 달아나는 것을 봄

22 지각동사의 목적격 보어는 동사원형이나 현재분사이다.

23 Sylvia는 어쨌든 자신이 1등을 할 거였다고 말했으므로 Teo가 글의 내용을 제대로 이해하였다.

24 Shirley는 누가 금메달을 훔쳤는지 찾기를 원했고. Jocelyn은 사건 당시 노래를 연습하고 있었고, Sylvia는 시를 낭송하고 있었다고 하였다.

25 Sylvia가 비명소리를 몇 시에 들었는지는 알 수 없다.

서술형 실전문제　　　　　　　p.206~207

01 She asks him to take care of her dog this weekend.

02 Tony's mother doesn't like dogs.

03 Because Sumin's family loves dogs.

04 if[whether] Donna was satisfied with my[our] service

05 I wonder if[whether] she has something round.

06 I can't remember what it is called in English.

07 something sweet to eat[have]

08 I really don't understand why she is crying.

09 She used Rapunzel's long hair to climb up the tower.

10 Because the world outside was beautiful unlike what the witch said.

11 It happened at Bakersville Middle School last night.

12 He found Jocelyn and the case with a broken window.

13 He took her to the scene of the crime.

14 He is the principal of Bakersville Middle School.

15 the gold medal

01 나래는 Tony에게 이번 주말에 그녀의 개를 돌봐줄 것을 요청하였다.

02 Tony의 엄마는 개를 좋아하지 않는다.

03 Sumin의 가족은 개를 좋아하기 때문에 나래에게 추천하였다.

04 Donna가 서비스에 만족을 했는지 묻고 싶다는 말이 들어가는 것이 적절하다.

05 부정대명사 something은 형용사의 수식을 뒤에서 받는다.

06 동사 remember의 목적어로 간접의문문을 쓴다. 어순은 '의문사+주어+동사'이므로 'what it is called ~'라고 쓰는 것이 적절하다.

07 대답으로 미루어 보아 먹을 단것을 원한다고 말했음을 알 수 있다. -thing으로 끝나는 부정대명사의 수식은 '형용사+to부정사'의 어순임에 유의한다.

08 understand의 목적어로 간접의문문을 써야 하며, 이때 어순은 '의문사+주어+동사'이다.

09 마녀는 탑으로 올라가기 위해서 라푼젤의 긴 머리카락을 사용했다.

10 마녀가 말한 것과는 달리 바깥세상이 아름다웠기 때문에 그녀의 눈을 믿을 수 없었다는 이야기이다.

11 사건은 어젯밤 Bakersville 중학교에서 발생하였다.

12 교장 선생님이 달려와 발견한 것은 Jocelyn과 유리창이 깨진 진열장이었다.

13 교장 선생님은 Shirley를 범죄 현장으로 데리고 갔다.

14 그는 Bakersville 중학교의 교장 선생님이다.

15 금메달이 있던 자리에 시 한 편이 놓여 있었다는 의미이다.

창의사고력 서술형 문제　　　　　　p.208

|모범답안|

01 (A) take care of
　(B) his mother doesn't like dogs
　(C) her family loves dogs

02 who my favorite actor was / when he was born / if Tom Cruz was married

01 오늘 나는 내 개, Pony를 걱정했었다. 내가 이번 주말에 할머니를 방문해야 하기 때문에 나는 내 개를 돌보아 줄 수 있는 누군가를 찾아야 했다. 먼저 나는 Tony에게 내 개를 돌보아 줄 수 있는지 물어보았다. 불행히도, 그는 나를 도울 수 없었다. 왜냐하면 그의 엄마는 개를 싫어하기 때문이다. 나는 무엇을 해야 할지 몰랐다. 그 때, Tony가 수민을 추천해 주었다. 왜냐하면 그녀의 가족이 개를 매우 좋아하기 때문이었다. 나는 수민에게 전화를 했고 그녀에게 도움을 청했다. 그녀는 이번 주말 동안에 나를 도와줄 수 있다고 말했다. 나는 매우 기분이 좋았고 정말로 그녀에게 고마웠다.

단원별 모의고사　　　　　　p.209~212

01 ②

02 (1) win first place　(2) at the moment
　(3) rush over　(4) running across　(5) bring, back

03 ①

04 (1) A thief stole the gold medal yesterday.

　　(2) Can you help me blow up these balloons?

　　(3) Will you send me some pictures of our talent show?

05 ②, ④

06 He was looking for his baseball glove.

07 Spot took it.　　　　08 (C) → (A) → (B) → (D)

09 ⑤　　　　　　10 ③

11 (A) his smartphone　(B) the house

　　(C) a sandwich　(D) the refrigerator

12 ③　　　　13 ③　　　　14 ④

15 Can you tell me where he is?

16 something important　　17 ②　　　　18 ③

19 ②

20 She saw someone running away from the case.

21 He went home a little before nine.

22 "Did you hear the window break?"　　23 ⑤

01 다른 사람으로부터 무언가를 훔치는 사람을 일컫는 말은 thief(도둑)이다.

02 bring back: ~을 돌려주다, at the moment: 그때, rush over: 달려가다, 달려오다, run across: ~을 가로질러 뛰다, win first place: 일등을 하다

03 문장에 공통으로 들어갈 말은 flash이며 '섬광, 번쩍임' 또는 동사로 '번쩍이다, 빛나다'를 의미한다.

04 steal: 훔치다, blow up: ~을 불다, talent show: 장기 자랑

05 (A)는 추측을 나타내는 표현으로 ②, ④번과 바꾸어 표현할 수 있다.

06 Brain은 그의 야구 글러브를 찾고 있었다.

07 Spot이 Brian의 야구 글러브를 가져갔다.

08 (C) 도움 요청 → (A) 수락 및 질문 → (B) 대답 → (D) 추측 표현

09 ⑤번의 A는 도움을 요청하고 있으므로 이에 대한 대답이 이어져야 한다.

10 (A)는 동사 lost, (B)는 '문자를 보냈다'라는 과거동사 texted, (C)는 긍정문에서 '어딘가에'를 뜻하는 somewhere가 적절하다.

11 Brian은 그가 그의 스마트폰을 찾을 수 없어 혼란스러웠다. 그는 엄마에게 이것을 찾는 것을 도와주실 것을 요청하였다. Brain은 스마트폰이 집안에 있을 것이라고 확신하였다, 왜냐하면 그는 몇 분 전에 친구에게 문자 메시지를 보냈기 때문이다. 그는 부엌에서 샌드위치를 만들고 있었다. 그래서 그의 엄마는 부엌을 다시 한 번 확인했다. 마침내 그의 엄마는 이것을 냉장고 안에서 찾아내셨다.

12 Do you know how far the school is from here?라고 쓰는 것이 적절하다.

13 의문사가 없는 의문문은 if나 whether를 이용하여 간접의문문을

14 when she has to move out이라고 쓰는 것이 적절하다.

15 tell의 직접목적어로 '의문사+주어+동사' 어순의 간접의문문을 써서 문장을 완성할 수 있다.

16 -thing으로 끝나는 부정대명사는 형용사의 수식을 뒤에서 받는다.

17 두 문장 모두 시간과 관련된 것이므로 when이 적절하다. ⓐ에는 간접의문문을 이끄는 when이, ⓑ에는 시간의 부사절을 이끄는 when이 쓰인다.

18 범인이 누구인지 모르는 상황에서 학교에 있었던 학생들을 인터뷰하는 것으로 보아 ③번이 가장 적절하다.

19 (A)의 쓰임은 to부정사의 부사적 용법 중 목적에 해당한다. ① 명사적 용법 중 목적어 ② 부사적 용법 중 목적 ③ 진주어 ④ 형용사적 용법 ⑤ 명사적 용법 중 주어

20 번개가 쳤을 때 Jocelyn은 누군가가 진열장에서 달아나는 것을 보았다.

21 Harry는 아홉시 조금 전에 집으로 갔다.

22 창문이 깨지는 것이므로 지각동사 hear의 목적격보어로 완료를 나타내는 broken이 아니라 break가 적절하다.

23 장기 자랑 대회에서 누가 1등을 했는지는 위 글을 읽고 알 수 없다.

Lesson
Special

Frindle

教科書
Reading

확인문제   p.216

| 1 T   2 T |

확인문제   p.217

| 1 T   2 T   3 F   4 T   5 F |

교과서 확인학습 A   p.218~219

01 was excited about, was worried about

02 was famous for

03 should have a good dictionary, can look up

04 the meanings, means

05 entire town, agreed, its meaning

06 satisfied, did I agree, himself

07 On, decided   08 took out, From

09 asked, to use   10 During

11 held up, extra, to borrow   12 pleased

13 but, already has   14 found, funny, to use

15 In, became, cool word

16 said to, getting out of hand, to stop saying

17 stop it, as   18 no choice

19 took out, asked, to sign, date

20 I'll give, to you, is over   21 hates

22 began, with   23 punish, for using

24 things worse

25 to use, more and more   26 spread to nearby

27 Shortly after, wrote, on, knew about it

28 covered, found out about

29 By the time, graduated from, used

30 flew by, received   31 Inside it, found

32 signature from   33 yellow note . It said

교과서 확인학습 B   p.220~221

1 Nick Allen was excited about starting fifth grade, but he was worried about one thing—Mrs. Granger's English class.

2 Mrs. Granger was famous for her difficult vocabulary lessons.

3 In the first class, Mrs. Granger said, "Everyone should have a good dictionary. You can look up the meanings of new words in it."

4 "Mrs. Granger? Who decides the meanings of words? I mean, who decided that 'dog' means an animal that barks?" Nick asked.

5 "You did, Nick. You, me, and the entire town and country. We all agreed. That gives the word its meaning."

6 Nick wasn't satisfied. "When did I agree?" he said to himself.

7 On the way home, he decided to test Mrs. Granger's idea.

8 He took out a pen and said, "From today, this is a *frindle*."

9 The next day, he asked five friends to use the word *frindle*.

10 During class, Nick said, "Mrs. Granger, I forgot my *frindle* today."

11 His friend, John, held up a pen and said, "I have an extra *frindle*. Do you want to borrow my *frindle*?"

12 Mrs. Granger was not pleased.

13 She said, "Your new word is cute, but it already has a perfectly good name — a pen."

14 Nick's classmates found this funny and began to use the word more and more.

15 In just three days, it became the cool word at school.

16 Mrs. Granger said to Nick after class, "This is getting out of hand. Can you tell your friends to stop saying *frindle*?"

17 "I'm sorry, but I can't stop it. It started as my word, but now it's the students' word."

18 "Very well. Then I have no choice."

19 Mrs. Granger took out an envelope and asked Nick to sign and date the back.

20 She said, "I'll give this letter to you when all this is over."

21 Nick thought, "She really hates me."

22 Next week, Mrs. Granger began a war with *frindle*.

23 She said that she would punish any student for using it.

37

24 But this only made things worse.

25 The students wanted to use the word more and more.

26 *Frindle* quickly spread to nearby middle and high schools.

27 Shortly after, a local newspaper reporter wrote an article on the situation and everyone in town knew about it.

28 A month later, a national television station covered the news and everyone found out about *frindle*.

29 By the time Nick graduated from elementary school, most students in the country used the word.

30 Time flew by and Nick turned 21. One day, he received a package.

31 Inside it, he found a pen, an envelope and a dictionary.

32 The envelope had his signature from fifth grade.

33 The dictionary had a yellow note. It said, "Check page 541."

서술형 실전문제 p.222~223

01 agree

02 (1) bark (2) signature (3) envelope (4) package

03 (1) I was excited about the school trip to Jejudo.
   (2) I felt relaxed after the math test was over.

04 (1) David was so tired that he couldn't meet us last night.
   (2) They are so tall that they can touch the ceiling.

05 (1) I want you to eat vegetables.
   (2) The doctor advised my father to exercise regularly.

06 (1) to do (2) to borrow (3) interesting

07 He was excited about starting fifth grade.

08 She wanted her students to have a good dictionary.

09 Students can look up the meanings of new words in it.

10 *frindle*   11 He created a new word, *frindle*.

12 Mrs. Granger was Nick's English teacher.

13 친구들이 *frindle*을 말하는 것

14 (D)–(A)–(C)–(B)

15 She asked him to sign and date the back of the envelope.

01 주어진 단어는 반의어 관계를 나타낸다. agree: 동의하다, disagree: 반대하다

04 'so ~ that 주어 can't 동사원형'은 'too ~ to V'와 같으며 '너무 ~해서 …할 수 없는'이라는 의미로 쓰인다. '~ enough to V'은 'so ~ that 주어 can 동사원형'으로 풀어쓸 수 있고 '…하기에 충분히 ~한'이라는 의미이다.

05 want와 advise는 목적격보어로 to부정사를 취하는 동사이다.

06 (1), (2) encourage와 want는 to부정사를 목적격보어로 취하는 동사이다. (3) find는 5형식 동사이며 상황은 흥미를 유발하는 주체이므로 interesting이라고 쓰는 것이 옳다.

07 Nick은 5학년이 시작되는 것이 신났다고 하였다.

08 선생님께서는 학생들이 좋은 사전을 갖기를 원하셨다.

09 Granger 선생님에 따르면, 학생들은 새로운 단어의 뜻을 사전에서 찾을 수 있다.

10 Nick이 지어낸 *frindle*이라는 단어를 의미한다.

11 선생님의 생각을 시험하기로 결심한 Nick은 새로운 단어인 *frindle*을 만들었다.

12 Nick의 영어 선생님은 Mrs. Granger였다.

13 친구들이 *frindle*을 말하는 것을 멈춰달라고 말하는 선생님의 요청에 그렇게 할 수 없다고 답하고 있다.

14 (D) 선생님께서 *frindle*과의 전쟁을 시작 → (A) 그 단어를 사용하는 학생을 벌 줄 것이라 말함 → (C) 이것은 상황을 더 악화시킴 → (B) 학생들은 그 단어를 점점 더 사용하고 싶어 함

15 선생님은 봉투를 하나 꺼내어 Nick에게 뒷면에 서명을 하고 날짜를 적게 했다.

단원별 예상문제 p.224~228

01 ②   02 (1) took out (2) look up
(3) have no choice (4) out of hand (5) hold up

03 ①   04 ②   05 ③

06 (1) James spends more and more time playing the computer games.
   (2) My English teacher is famous for funny class.

07 ⑤   08 ③   09 ③   10 ⑤

11 ②   12 who gave you this letter 13 ③

14 The teacher makes me nervous.

15 decided the meanings of words   16 ③

17 She was famous for her difficult vocabulary lessons.   18 ④

19 He was worried about Mrs. Granger's English class.

20 ④   21 [C]–[B]–[A]

22 펜을 *frindle*이라고 부르는 것   23 ③

24 She was not pleased. 25 ③   26 ④

27 ②   28 ③   29 ②

30 She will give it to Nick when all this is over.

31 She said that she would punish any student for using the word, *frindle*.

32 The students wanted to use the word more and more.　　　　33 ⑤

34 Most students in the country used the word, *frindle*.

35 He found a pen, an envelope, and a dictionary.

36 ⑤

01 '누군가가 법을 어기거나 무언가를 잘못했기 때문에 고통을 주다'는 punish(처벌하다)를 말한다.

02 take out: 꺼내다, get out of hand: 손을 쓸 수 없게 되다, hold up: 잡다, look up: (사전 등에서) ~을 찾다, have no choice: 선택의 여지가 없다

03 date: (동) 날짜를 적다, (명) 날짜

04 주어진 문장에서 cover는 '보도하다'를 의미하며 이와 같은 의미로 쓰인 것은 ②번이다. 나머지는 모두 '덮다, 가리다'를 뜻한다.

05 pleased: 기쁜

06 more and more: 점점 더 많은

07 cause는 to부정사를 목적격보어로 취하는 동사이다. 따라서 to be more careful이라고 쓰는 것이 적절하다.

08 would like는 to부정사를 목적격보어로 취하는 동사이다. 따라서 '네가 나를 초대하면 좋겠다'고 하였으므로 would like you to invite me라고 쓰는 것이 적절하다.

09 'so ~ that 주어 can't 동사원형'은 'too ~ to 동사원형'과 같다.

10 make는 목적격보어로 동사원형을 취하는 사역동사이다.

11 의문사가 없는 의문문의 간접의문문은 의문사 대신 if나 whether를 사용하여 만들 수 있다.

12 의문사이자 주어 역할을 동시에 하는 의문대명사를 이용하여 간접의문문을 만들 수 있다.

13 let은 사역동사로 목적격보어를 동사원형을 취한다.

14 make는 5형식으로 쓰일 수 있다. 이때 목적어를 설명하는 목적격보어가 형용사임에 유의하자.

15 단어의 의미를 결정하는 것을 말한다.

16 온 마을과 나라가 동의한 것을 의미하므로 ③번이 가장 적절하다.

17 Mrs. Granger는 어려운 어휘 수업으로 유명했다.

18 누가 단어의 의미를 결정하는지 궁금해 한 것은 Nick이다.

19 Nick이 걱정한 것은 Mrs. Granger의 영어 수업이다.

20 ① agree ② difficult ③ new ⑤ famous의 반의어이며 ④는 entire와 같은 의미이다.

21 펜을 *frindle*이라고 부르기로 함 - [C] 친구들에게 단어 *frindle*을 사용해 달라고 부탁하고 수업시간에 *frindle*을 가져오지 않았다고 말함 - [B] 이에 친구가 *frindle*이라는 단어를 사용하며 빌리겠느냐고 물어봄 - [A] 이 말을 들은 선생님은

22 Nick이 요청한 대로 펜을 *frindle*이라고 부르는 것을 의미한다.

23 a perfectly good name은 pen을 의미하며 나머지는 모두 *frindle*을 의미한다.

24 선생님은 새로운 단어에 대해 즐거워하지 않았다.

25 '빌리다'라는 의미의 borrow라고 쓰는 것이 적절하다. lend는 '빌려주다'라는 의미이다.

26 Nick의 교실에 반 친구들이 몇 명이나 있는지는 알 수 없다.

27 get out of hand는 '감당할 수 없게 되다'라는 의미이다. 따라서 '제지할 수 없게 되다'라는 의미의 ②번이 가장 적절하다.

28 stop은 동명사를 목적어로 취하는 동사로 '~하는 것을 멈추다'라는 의미로 사용해야 하므로 saying, (B) ask는 to부정사를 목적격보어로 취하는 동사, (C) want는 to부정사를 목적어로 취하는 동사이다.

29 Nick은 자신의 단어로 시작된 것이 이제는 그 학생들의 단어가 되었다고 하였다. 따라서 ②번이 글의 내용과 일치한다.

30 이 모든 것이 끝나면 선생님이 이 편지를 Nick에게 주실 것이라고 하였다.

31 선생님께서는 *frindle*이라는 단어를 사용하면 어떤 학생이든 벌을 줄 것이라고 말했다.

32 선생님이 *frindle*과의 전쟁을 시작하자 학생들은 그 단어를 더욱 더 사용하고 싶어 하였다.

33 *frindle*이라는 단어가 인기를 얻었을 때 Nick의 감정은 위 글을 읽고 알 수 없다.

34 Nick이 초등학교를 졸업할 때쯤에는 그 나라의 대부분의 학생들이 그 단어를 사용했다.

35 Nick이 소포 안에서 발견한 것은 펜 한 자루, 봉투 한 장, 그리고 사전 한 권이었다.

36 ⓐ는 '보도하다, 방송하다'라는 의미로 쓰였다. ①, ③ ~을 덮다 ② ~을 씌우다 ④ (책의) 표지 ⑤ 방송하다, 보도하다

교과서 파헤치기

12 pile, 더미   13 advertise, 광고하다
14 shape, ~ 모양으로 만들다   15 celebrate, 축하하다
16 decorate, 장식하다

단어 TEST Step 1   p.02

01 화살	02 근처, 이웃, 인근	03 나타나다
04 어두운	05 해결하다	06 장식하다
07 먼, 멀리	08 폭죽, 불꽃놀이	09 따르다
10 모이다, 모으다	11 형태, ~ 모양으로 만들다	
12 놀라운	13 거대한	14 지속하다
15 광고하다	16 대회, 시합, 경쟁	17 축제
18 썰매	19 거의	20 완전히
21 게시하다	22 음악가	23 축하하다, 기념하다
24 야외의	25 뒤쫓다	26 더미
27 예술 작품	28 가루	29 성인, 어른
30 형형색색의	31 개최하다	32 던지다
33 고향	34 빵집, 제과점	35 서로
36 손을 쓸 수 없는	37 처음부터 끝까지	38 A와 B 사이에
39 지속되다, 계속되다	40 ~ 때문에	
41 더욱 더	42 ~의 오른편에	43 ~ 앞에

단어 TEST Step 2   p.03

01 bakery	02 celebrate	03 colorful
04 parade	05 take	06 during
07 sail	08 artwork	09 chase
10 hold	11 hometown	12 boat
13 cross	14 live	15 near
16 powder	17 outdoor	18 block
19 pile	20 adult	21 throw
22 decorate	23 gather	24 advertise
25 solve	26 last	27 appear
28 neighborhood	29 competition	30 firework
31 huge	32 arrow	33 completely
34 follow	35 more and more	
36 get off	37 each other	38 in front of
39 because of	40 next to	41 go on
42 between A and B		
43 from beginning to end		

단어 TEST Step 3   p.04

1 lift, 들어올리다   2 adult, 어른   3 chase, 뒤쫓다
4 artwork, 예술 작품   5 competition, 대회, 경쟁
6 festival, 축제   7 sled, 썰매   8 last, 지속하다
9 hometown, 고향   10 gather, 모이다   11 hold, 개최하다

대화문 TEST Step 1   p.05~06

Listen and Speak 1-A

How can I get to the library / Cross, go straight, make a left / Thank you

Listen and Speak 1-B

What's up / Are, free this Saturday / Why do, ask / about having lunch / Let's try, Chinese restaurant, near / How can I get there from the school / Come out, go straight, Make a left, be on your left / All right. Let's meet at / See you then

Listen and Speak 1-C

Excuse me, can, get to / Go straight, make a right, will be on your right / Is, far from / No, not / Thank you

Listen and Speak 2-A

hurry up, going to be late for / How long will it take to get to the theater / take about, by bus / almost ready

Listen and Speak 2-B

excited about, this Friday / Me, too, can, do to advertise / about making / can post them, neighborhood / How long will it take to / take about three hours / I hope, come to the festival

Real Life Talk

Excuse, How can, get to / easy, over there / I do / Take, get off / How long will it take to get there / take about 20 minutes / very much / problem, Are, going, the festival / its's a lot of fun / I hope, have a great time

대화문 TEST Step 2   p.07~08

Listen and Speak 1-A

Sora: Excuse me. How can I get to the library?
Tom: Oh, the library? Cross the street and go straight two blocks. Then make a left.
Sora: Thank you very much.

Listen and Speak 1-B

Minsu: Hi, Emma. What's up?
Emma: Hey, Minsu. Are you free this Saturday?
Minsu: Yes. Why do you ask?
Emma: Well, how about having lunch together?
Minsu: Sure.
Emma: Let's try the new Chinese restaurant, Ming's.

It's near the school.

Minsu: Okay. How can I get there from the school?

Emma: Come out from the school and go straight to Green Street. Make a left, and the restaurant will be on your left.

Minsu: All right. Let's meet at 12 o'clock.

Emma: Wonderful. See you then.

Listen and Speak 1-C

A: Excuse me. How can I get to the post office?

B: Go straight to 1st Street and make a right. It will be on your right.

A: Is it far from here?

B: No, it's not.

A: Thank you very much.

Listen and Speak 2-A

Amy: Jinho, hurry up. We're going to be late for the movie.

Jinho: Okay. How long will it take to get to the theater?

Amy: It will take about 15 minutes by bus.

Jinho: All right. I'm almost ready.

Listen and Speak 2-B

Andy: I'm so excited about the school festival this Friday.

Mike: Me, too. What can we do to advertise it, Andy?

Andy: How about making posters?

Mike: Great idea. We can post them in our neighborhood.

Andy: Right. How long will it take to make them?

Mike: Well, it will take about three hours.

Andy: Okay, I hope many people come to the festival.

Real Life Talk

Man: Excuse me. How can I get to Suwon Hwaseong from here?

Mina: It's easy. Do you see the bus stop over there?

Man: Yes, I do.

Mina: Take the No. 11 bus and get off at the sixth stop.

Man: How long will it take to get there?

Mina: It will take about 20 minutes.

Man: Thank you very much.

Mina: No problem. Are you going there for the festival?

Man: Yes. I heard it's a lot of fun.

Mina: I hope you have a great time.

본문 TEST Step 1   p.09~10

01 Festival, Colors
02 from Delhi
03 most popular, my
04 is usually in
05 During, say, hello
06 celebrate, everywhere for
07 On, gather around, at
08 main, begins, next
09 chase each other
10 What, green, powder
11 run around, throw, at
12 also join, parades
13 White Nights
14 from, Petersburg, Russia
15 Have, heard of
16 Every, amazing, happens
17 get completely dark
18 During, hold
19 in, lasts, about
20 there, almost every
21 most popular, celebration
22 with, appears on
23 begin, follows
24 also hear, playing
25 Kiruna, Festival
26 from Kiruna
27 favorite, because of
28 starts, last, goes on
29 largest event, competition
30 shape, into, other
31 watch, shaping, from, to
32 activity, sled ride
33 to, through, on

본문 TEST Step 2   p.11~12

01 Festival of Colors
02 from Delhi, India
03 the most popular festival
04 is usually in March
05 During, say goodbye, hello, warm spring
06 celebrate, for two days
07 On, gather around, at night, sing and dance
08 main, begins the next day
09 chase each other with
10 What, powder 11 to run around, throw, at everyone
12 also join street parades
13 White Nights
14 from, Russia
15 Have you heard of
16 amazing, happens
17 does not get completely dark
18 During, hold
19 usually starts in, lasts for about
20 During, there is, almost every night
21 most popular, celebration

41

22 appears on the river

23 fireworks begin, follows

24 also hear, playing   25 Snow Festival

26 from Kiruna, Sweden

27 my favorite season because of

28 starts in the last week, goes on for

29 The largest event, competition

30 shape huge piles, into, other

31 watch, shaping, from beginning to end

32 favorite activity, dog sled ride

33 It, amazing to fly through, on

---

1 홀리, 색의 축제

2 인도, 델리의 Amala

3 '홀리'는 우리나라에서 가장 인기 있는 축제예요.

4 그것은 보통 3월에 있어요.

5 축제 기간 동안에, 우리는 추운 겨울에게 작별 인사를 하고 따뜻한 봄을 맞는 인사를 해요.

6 우리는 이틀 동안 어디서든 축제를 기념해요.

7 첫째 날, 사람들은 밤에 큰 모닥불 주변에 모여 노래하고 춤을 춰요.

8 주요 행사는 다음 날에 시작돼요.

9 어린이들과 어른들이 'gulal'을 지니고 서로를 쫓아다녀요.

10 'gulal'이 무엇이냐고요? 그것은 파랑, 노랑, 초록, 분홍의 가루예요.

11 주변을 뛰어다니며 형형색색의 가루를 모든 사람들에게 던지는 것은 정말 재미있어요.

12 우리는 거리 행진에도 참가해요!

13 백야 축제

14 러시아, 상트페테르부르크의 Victor

15 '백야'에 대해 들어 봤나요?

16 매년 여름, 이 놀라운 일이 나의 고향에서 벌어져요.

17 밤하늘이 완전히 어두워지지 않아요.

18 그 시기 동안, 우리는 백야 축제를 열어요.

19 축제는 보통 5월에 시작되고 약 한 달 동안 지속돼요.

20 축제 기간 동안 거의 매일 밤 발레나 오페라 공연이 있어요.

21 가장 인기 있는 행사는 '붉은 돛 축하 행사'예요.

22 빨간 돛을 단 배가 강 위에 서서히 나타나요.

23 곧 불꽃놀이가 시작되고 물 쇼가 이어져요.

24 또한 여러분은 음악가들이 아름다운 라이브 음악을 연주하는 것을 들을 수 있어요.

25 키루나 눈 축제

26 스웨덴, 키루나의 Ebba

27 겨울은 키루나 눈 축제 때문에 내가 가장 좋아하는 계절이에요.

28 축제는 1월 마지막 주에 시작해서 5일이나 6일 동안 계속돼요.

---

29 가장 큰 행사는 '눈 디자인 대회'예요.

30 미술가들이 거대한 눈 덩어리를 동물, 건물, 다른 아름다운 작품의 모양으로 만들어요.

31 사람들은 미술가들이 그들의 작품을 만드는 것을 처음부터 끝까지 지켜봐요.

32 내가 가장 좋아하는 활동은 개썰매 타기예요.

33 개썰매를 타고 눈 세상을 날아가는 것은 정말 놀라워요.

---

1 Holi, the Festival of Colors

2 Amala from Delhi, India

3 Holi is the most popular festival in my country.

4 It is usually in March.

5 During the festival, we say goodbye to cold winter and hello to warm spring.

6 We celebrate the festival everywhere for two days.

7 On the first day, people gather around a big fire at night and sing and dance.

8 The main event begins the next day.

9 Children and adults chase each other with *gulal*.

10 What is *gulal*? It is blue, yellow, green and pink powder.

11 It's a lot of fun to run around and throw colorful powder at everyone.

12 We also join street parades!

13 White Nights Festival

14 Victor from St. Petersburg, Russia

15 Have you heard of the White Nights?

16 Every summer, this amazing thing happens in my hometown.

17 The night sky does not get completely dark.

18 During that time, we hold the White Nights Festival.

19 It usually starts in May and lasts for about a month.

20 During the festival, there is a ballet or an opera almost every night.

21 The most popular event is the Scarlet Sails celebration.

22 A boat with red sails slowly appears on the river.

23 Soon, fireworks begin and a water show follows.

24 You can also hear musicians playing beautiful live music.

25 Kiruna Snow Festival

26 Ebba from Kiruna, Sweden

27 Winter is my favorite season because of the Kiruna Snow Festival.

28 The festival starts in the last week of January and goes on for five or six days.

29 The largest event is the snow design competition.

30 The artists shape huge piles of snow into animals, buildings, and other beautiful artworks.

31 People watch the artists shaping their works from beginning to end.

32 My favorite activity is the dog sled ride.

33 It is amazing to fly through a world of snow on a dog sled.

구석구석지문 TEST Step 1   p.19

Listen and Speak 2 - C

1. will, do, class party
2. make sandwiches
3. How long, take to
4. Maybe, take about an hour

Think and Write

1. Love
2. live in
3. There are, neighborhood
4. a lot of, to swim
5. famous *hanok* in
6. is called, was born
7. The most famous food
8. Come and enjoy

Project Culture

1. to introduce
2. is held in, in July
3. many interesting events
4. see people do
5. it, to do, painting
6. Lastly, outdoor concert
7. hear musicians play

구석구석지문 TEST Step 2   p.20

Listen and Speak 2 - C

1. A: Chris, what will you do for the class party?
2. B: I'll make sandwiches.
3. A: Great idea. How long will it take to make them?
4. B: Maybe it'll take about an hour.

Think and Write

1. I Love Gangneung
2. I live in Gangneung.
3. There are beautiful beaches in my neighborhood.

4. It's a lot of fun to swim at the beach.
5. There is a famous hanok in Gangneung.
6. It is called Ojukheon. Yulgok was born there.
7. The most famous food in Gangneung is potato tteok.
8. It is soft and sweet. Come and enjoy Gangneung!

Project Culture

1. I want to introduce Boryeong Mud Festival.
2. It is held in Daecheon Beach in July.
3. There are many interesting events in the festival.
4. First, you can see people do Ssireum in mud.
5. Also it is fun to do colorful mud body painting on your body.
6. Lastly, there is an outdoor concert.
7. You can hear musicians play beautiful musics.

11 half, 절반   12 inventor, 발명가   13 adapt, 적응하다
14 stick, 나뭇가지, 막대   15 apply, 지원하다
16 organization, 조직, 단체

단어 TEST Step 1   p.21

01 발명가   02 마지막으로   03 지원하다
04 환경, 주위의 상황 05 시각 장애가 있는, 눈이 먼
06 약속하다   07 의사소통하다   08 비슷한
09 청각 장애가 있는, 귀가 먹은   10 평균
11 장식하다   12 우주, 공간   13 활발한
14 용감한   15 전시회   16 (비록)~이긴 하지만
17 더 먼, 더 멀리   18 친절한, 상냥한   19 포함하다
20 바르다, 펼치다   21 발명   22 다음에 나오는
23 몇몇의   24 기간, 길이   25 적응하다
26 필요한, 없어서는 안 될   27 조직, 단체
28 호기심이 많은, 궁금한   29 껍질을 벗기다
30 임무   31 차이   32 (얇게) 썰다, 자르다
33 전기   34 게다가   35 놓치다
36 평균적으로   37 지금부터   38 ~로 만들어지다,
~로 구성되다   39 ~와 잘 지내다
40 기운을 내다, ~을 격려하다   41 발명하다
42 ~에 대해 궁금해 하다   43 ~을 잘하다

단어 TEST Step 2   p.22

01 invention   02 blind   03 similar
04 electricity   05 deaf   06 average
07 decorate   08 promise   09 inventor
10 lastly   11 necessary   12 organization
13 slice   14 environment   15 curious
16 communicate   17 friendly   18 reason
19 solar system   20 peel   21 outgoing
22 stick   23 exhibition   24 brave
25 produce   26 mission   27 although
28 include   29 apply   30 following
31 several   32 length   33 adapt
34 difference   35 miss out   36 from now on
37 get along with 38 on average   39 in addition
40 be made of   41 be curious about
42 cheer up   43 have a great time

단어 TEST Step 3   p.23

1 blind, 시각 장애가 있는, 눈이 먼   2 length, 기간
3 mission, 임무   4 slice, (얇게) 썰다, 자르다
5 deaf, 청각 장애가 있는, 귀가 먹은   6 spread, 바르다
7 similar, 비슷한   8 peel, 껍질을 벗기다   9 difference, 차이

대화문 TEST Step 1   p.24~25

Listen & Speak 1-A
what this is / looks like / butter stick / is there butter in it / can spread butter, with

Listen & Speak 1-B
show and tell / who this man is / inventor, was interested in, What, invent, deaf, made some inventions, deaf people, opened

Listen & Speak 2-A
looks interesting, What, for / for slicing eggs / try / here is an egg

Listen & Speak 2-B
look at, in science class / Why, make / not just for wearing / what, for / put them on, clean the floor / will clean, from now on / Don't worry about

Listen & Speak 2-C
look at / have never seen, before, What, for / for making ink / interesting

Real Life Talk – Step 1
How was / had a great time, science exhibition with / heard there were / Look at, what it is / not sure / What is it for / wear, can experience another world / Sounds, try / Her, go

대화문 TEST Step 2   p.26~27

Listen & Speak 1-A
Brian: Do you know what this is?
Amy: Um, it looks like a glue stick.
Brian: No, it's a butter stick.
Amy: Oh, is there butter in it?
Brian: Yes, you can spread butter on the bread with it.

Listen & Speak 1-B
Ms. Lee: Hello, class! Jisu is today's speaker for show and tell. Jisu?
Jisu: Hi, class! Do you know who this man is? His name is Alexander Graham Bell. Bell was an inventor. He was interested in sound. What did he invent? Yes, the telephone! His mother and wife were deaf. So he also made some inventions for deaf people and opened a school for them.

Jane: This looks interesting. What is it for?

Mike: It's for slicing eggs.

Jane: Really? May I try it?

Mike: Sure, here is an egg.

Tom: Mom, look at these slippers. I made them in science class.

Mom: Why did you make slippers in science class?

Tom: They are not just for wearing.

Mom: Then, what are they for?

Tom: You can put them on and clean the floor.

Mom: Oh, so you will clean your room from now on?

Tom: Sure. Don't worry about my room, Mom.

A: Jane, look at this. It's a meok.

B: I have never seen it before. What is it for?

A: It's for making ink.

B: Oh, really? That's interesting.

Judy: How was your weekend, Hojin?

Hojin: I had a great time. I went to a science exhibition with my brother.

Judy: Did you? I heard there were so many interesting things.

Hojin: Yes. Look at this. I bought it there. Do you know what it is?

Judy: Well, I'm not sure. What is it?

Hojin: It's a VR headset.

Judy: A VR headset? What is it for?

Hojin: If you wear it, you can experience another world.

Judy: Sounds cool. May I try it?

Hojin: Sure. Here you go.

본문 TEST Step 1 — p.28~29

01 Live on

02 live on another

03 looking for, to

04 to build, on

05 healthy / curious / along / adapt

06 To apply, send

07 must include, to following

08 Why, want, go / good sense, humor / perfect, for, mission

09 chance, so, miss out

10 the Second Earth

11 Although, one, been, yet

12 These, looking at, as

13 In fact, trying, right

14 big, live on

15 believe so, several reasons

---

16 think, that, water

17 because, necessary for

18 hard land, build, on

19 lengt, similar to that

20 In addition, has, seasons

21 So, lead , lives

22 Lastly, very far

23 the second closest

24 however, differences from

25 about half, size

26 second smallest, solar system

27 year, about twice, as

28 much colder than

29 On average, about

30 because, farther away, than

31 Although, answer, exciting, imagine

32 be the, Korean on

본문 TEST Step 2 — p.30~31

01 Live on

02 to live on another

03 Korea Space Organization, looking for people to go

04 Our misson, to build, on

05 are looking for / who, healthy / who, creative, curious / who, get along with / who, adapt to new environment

06 To apply, send us

07 must include, to, following questions

08 want to go / a good sense of humor / perfect person for this mission

09 a chance of, don't miss

10 the Second Earth

11 Although, many books, movies, has been, yet

12 These days, looking at, as

13 In fact, are trying to send, right now

14 Can people live on

15 believe so, several seasons

16 that, water on

17 because, necessary for

18 hard land to build, on

19 length, is similar to that

20 In addition, has four seasons

21 can lead similar lives

22 not very far

23 the second closest planet

24 however, some differences from

25 about half

26 the second smallest, solar

27 about twice as long as

28 much colder than

29 On average, about

30 because, farther away from

31 Although, answer, right now, exciting to imagine

32 the first Korean on

45

1 화성에서 살아요!

2 다른 행성에서 살고 싶은가요?

3 한국 우주 기구(KSO)는 화성에 갈 사람들을 찾고 있습니다!

4 우리의 임무는 화성에 도시를 세우는 것입니다.

5 우리는 다음과 같은 사람을 찾고 있습니다. 건강한 사람. 창의적이고 호기심이 많은 사람. 다른 사람들과 잘 지낼 수 있는 사람. 새로운 환경에 빨리 적응할 수 있는 사람.

6 지원하려면 우리에게 짧은 동영상을 보내세요.

7 동영상은 다음의 질문에 관한 답을 포함해야 합니다.

8 1. 당신은 왜 화성에 가고 싶은가요?
　2. 당신은 유머 감각이 있나요?
　3. 왜 당신이 이 임무에 적합한 사람인가요?

9 이것은 일생에 단 한 번뿐인 기회이므로 놓치지 마세요!

10 화성, 제 2의 지구?

11 화성에 관한 많은 책과 영화가 있긴 하지만, 아직 화성에 가 본 사람은 아무도 없다.

12 요즘, 과학자들은 화성을 새로운 거주지로 보고 있다.

13 사실, NASA와 몇몇 회사들은 그곳에 사람들을 보내기 위해 바로 지금도 노력하고 있다.

14 중요한 질문은 "화성에서 사람들이 살 수 있는가?"이다.

15 많은 과학자들은 몇몇 이유로 그렇게 믿고 있다.

16 첫째, 그들은 화성에 물이 있다고 생각한다.

17 물은 모든 생명체에 필수적이기 때문에 이것은 중요하다.

18 둘째, 화성은 집과 건물을 지을 수 있는 단단한 땅을 가지고 있다.

19 셋째, 화성의 낮과 밤의 길이는 지구의 낮과 밤의 길이와 비슷하다.

20 게다가, 화성은 사계절도 있다.

21 그래서 사람들이 비슷한 생활을 할 수 있다.

22 마지막으로, 화성은 그렇게 멀지 않다.

23 화성은 지구에서 두 번째로 가까운 행성이다.

24 그러나 화성은 지구와 다른 점이 몇 개 있다.

25 첫째, 화성은 지구의 약 절반 크기이다.

26 화성은 태양계에서 두 번째로 작은 행성이다.

27 둘째, 화성에서의 일 년은 지구에서의 일 년보다 약 두 배 길다.

28 셋째, 화성은 지구보다 훨씬 더 춥다.

29 평균적으로, 화성의 기온은 약 섭씨 영하 60도이다.

30 이것은 화성이 지구보다 태양에서 더 멀리 떨어져 있기 때문이다.

31 비록 누구도 그 중요한 질문에 지금 당장 답할 수는 없지만, 이 새로운 세상을 상상하는 것은 신이 난다.

32 누가 알겠는가? 당신이 화성에 발을 디디는 첫 번째 한국인이 될 수도 있다!

1 Live on MARS!

2 Do you want to live on another planet?

3 The Korea Space Organization (KSO) is looking for people to go to MARS!.

4 Our mission is to build a city on Mars.

5 We are looking for someone… who is healthy, who is creative and curious, who can get along with others, who can adapt to a new environment quickly.

6 To apply, send us a short video.

7 The video must include the answers to the following questions:

8 Why do you want to go to Mars? / Do you have a good sense of humor? / Why are you the perfect person for this mission?

9 This is a chance of a lifetime, so don't miss out!

10 Mars, the Second Earth?

11 Although there are many books and movies about Mars, no one has been there yet.

12 These days, scientists are looking at Mars as a new home.

13 In fact, NASA and some companies are trying to send people there right now.

14 The big question is, "Can people live on Mars?"

15 Many scientists believe so for several reasons.

16 First, they think that there is water on Mars.

17 This is great because water is necessary for all life.

18 Second, Mars has hard land to build houses and buildings on.

19 Third, the length of day and night on Mars is similar to that on Earth.

20 In addition, Mars also has four seasons.

21 So, people can lead similar lives.

22 Lastly, Mars is not very far.

23 It is the second closest planet to Earth.

24 Mars, however, has some differences from Earth.

25 First, Mars is about half the size of Earth.

26 It is the second smallest planet in the solar system.

27 Second, a year on Mars is about twice as long as a year on Earth.

28 Third, Mars is much colder than Earth.

29 On average, it is about −60℃ on Mars.

30 This is because Mars is farther away from the Sun than Earth.

31 Although no one can answer the big question right now, it is exciting to imagine this new world.

32 Who knows? You could be the first Korean on Mars!

구석구석지문 TEST Step 1　　　　p.38

Real Life Talk - Step 2

1. what this is
2. No, don't, What, it
3. Clean Straw
4. What is it for
5. while you drink
6. that's great

Think and Write

1. from Korea, years old
2. want to, because, been curious about
3. friendly, enjoy making friends
4. good at taking
5. perfect person, adapt, new environment
6. Although, communicate well with others
7. the chance to live

Project

1. Neptune
2. moons, cold planet
3. named after, god of the sea
4. the farthest planet, the solar system

구석구석지문 TEST Step 2　　　　p.39

Real Life Talk - Step 2

1. A: Do you know what this is?
2. B: No , I don't . What is it?
3. A: It's a Clean Straw.
4. B: A Clean Straw? What is it for?
5. A: It cleans water while you drink.
6. B: Wow, that's great!

Think and Write

1. My name is Suji Lee from Korea. I'm 15 years old.
2. I want to go to Mars because I've been curious about space.
3. I'm friendly and I enjoy making friends.
4. I'm good at taking photos.
5. I'm the perfect person for this mission because I can adapt to a new environment quickly.
6. Although I'm young, I can communicate well with others.
7. Give me the chance to live on Mars!

Project

1. Neptune
2. It has 14 moons. It's a very cold planet.
3. It's named after the god of the sea.
4. It's the farthest planet from the Sun in the solar system.

단어 TEST Step 1　　　　p.40

01 작가	02 배낭	03 완벽한
04 관련성, 연관성	05 여행	06 상
07 차이점	08 섞다	09 믿다, 신뢰하다
10 모험	11 전통적인	12 설명하다
13 간단한, 단순한	14 우정	15 특히
16 ~와 달리	17 진실, 사실	18 거짓말하다
19 광고	20 가치가 있는	21 공상
22 신념, 생각	23 강력하게	24 들어 올리다
25 현명하게	26 식사	27 증명하다
28 나타내다, 표현하다		29 해결하다, 풀다
30 남색	31 추천하다	32 지루한
33 감동적인	34 의견	35 예를 들면
36 ~로 가득한	37 ~을 바탕으로	38 지금부터
39 기다려, 멈춰	40 선택하다	41 지금
42 ~을 확인하다	43 그만한 가치가 있는	

단어 TEST Step 2　　　　p.41

01 trust	02 author	03 perfect
04 touching	05 express	06 boring
07 trip	08 navy	09 adventure
10 purple	11 novel	12 opinion
13 advertisement	14 pocket	15 simple
16 award	17 worth	18 especially
19 meal	20 friendship	21 strongly
22 lift	23 solve	24 prove
25 explain	26 traditional	27 difference
28 mix	29 fantasy	30 recommend
31 belief	32 unlike	33 wisely
34 truth	35 check out	36 look for
37 from now on	38 make a choice	
39 for example	40 full of	41 based on
42 right now	43 hold on	

단어 TEST Step 3　　　　p.42

1 trust, 신뢰하다, 믿다　2 opinion, 의견　3 mix, 섞다
4 lift, 들어 올리다　5 truth, 진실, 사실　6 meal, 식사
7 express, 나타내다, 표현하다　8 lie, 거짓말하다
9 pocket, 주머니　10 recommend, 추천하다
11 advertisement, 광고　12 connection, 관련성
13 explain, 설명하다　14 prove, 증명하다

15 award, 상   16 desert, 사막

Listen & Speak 1-A

recommend a good movie / really liked / haven't seen, yet / number one, right now

Listen & Speak 1-B

help / looking for, backpack, recommend one / How about, the most popular color these days / My old backpack, different color / How about, navy, has side pockets, looks good, take

Listen & Speak 2-A

got, new smartphone / really happy with / What, like most about it / takes great pictures

Listen & Speak 2-B

How did, like, trip / happy with / Where, visit / visited / Where else did, go / wonderful place / Sounds like, perfect trip / walking up, was difficult / I'm sure, worth it

Real Life Talk – Step 1

can you recommend / Why don't, my favorite / What, like about / delicious, recommend / How, the prices / think, too / Sounds like, How, like the service / little slow / check it out / problem, Enjoy

Real Life Talk – Step 2

recommend a book for me / How about / What do you like / main character, special / Sounds, read

Listen & Speak 1-A

Brian: Can you recommend a good movie?
Emily: Try Star Wars. I really liked it.
Brian: Oh, I haven't seen it yet.
Emily: It's the number one movie right now.

Listen & Speak 1-B

W: May I help you?
B: Yes. I'm looking for a backpack. Can you recommend one?
W: How about this red one? Red is the most popular color these days.
B: My old backpack was red, so I want a different color.
W: How about this navy one? It has side pockets.
B: Oh, that looks good. I'll take it.

Listen & Speak 2-A

Sue: Tom, you got a new smartphone.
Tom: Yes, I did. I'm really happy with it.
Sue: What do you like most about it?
Tom: I love the camera. It takes great pictures.

Listen & Speak 2-B

Jack: Hi, Suji. How did you like your trip to Gyeongju?
Suji: I was very happy with it.
Jack: Where did you visit?
Suji: I visited Cheomseongdae. It was great.
Jack: Where else did you go?
Suji: Bulguksa. It was a wonderful place.
Jack: Sounds like the perfect trip.
Suji: Yeah, but walking up to Seokguram was difficult.
Jack: But I'm sure it was worth it.

Real Life Talk – Step 1

Brian: Mina, can you recommend a good pizza restaurant?
Mina: Why don't you try Antonio's? It's my favorite.
Brian: What do you like about it?
Mina: The food is delicious. I recommend the bulgogi pizza.
Brian: How are the prices?
Mina: I think the prices are good, too.
Brian: Sounds like a good restaurant. How do you like the service?
Mina: It's a little slow on the weekends.
Brian: Okay. I'll check it out. Thanks.
Mina: No problem. Enjoy your meal!

Real Life Talk – Step 2

Amy: Yujin, can you recommend a book for me?
Yujin: How about The Little Prince?
Amy: What do you like about the book?
Yujin: I like the main character. He is very special.
Amy: Sounds good. I'll read it.

01 are, doing
02 watching, on, computer
03 How, it
04 Don't, so boring that
05 sorry to hear
06 mad, advertisement said
07 believe everything that, read
08 lied on, for, back
09 Hold, lie because, opinions
10 not following you

11 express, feelings like

12 that, not, facts, proven

13 For example, check, on

14 the connection with

15 Let, explain, favorite　　16 It's, *Gump*

17 Let's, its advertisement, say

18 says, Awards including　　19 uses facts unlike

20 Do, see, difference　　21 exactly, says, ad

22 Aren't, both opinions

23 question, like, expressing opinions

24 ad, award, movie won　　25 check, on, fact

26 From, on, trust, with

27 that simple, mix, with

28 have, make, choice, both

29 Got, watch, rest, with

30 no thanks, rest

01 What are, doing

02 watching the movie, on

03 How, it

04 Don't, so boring that, to cry

05 sorry to hear that

06 mad, advertisement, it, The Most Exciting Movie

07 can't believe everything that you read

08 lied on, ask for my money back

09 Hold on, lie because, used opinions, facts

10 not following you

11 express people's feelings

12 that, true or not, can be proven

13 For example, check that on the map

14 the connection with

15 Let me explain　　16 It's

17 Let's look for its advertisement

18 It says, including　　19 uses facts unlike

20 the difference　　21 exactly, says, says

22 Aren't, both opinions

23 words like, usually expressing opinions

24 award which the movie won

25 check that on the Internet

26 From now on, trust, with

27 that simple, mix facts with opinions

28 make a smart choice based on both

29 to watch the rest

30 no thanks, the rest of

1 Emma: Kyle, 뭐 하고 있니?

2 Kyle: Emma. 나는 컴퓨터로 영화 "Y-Men 7"을 보고 있어.

3 Emma: 어때?

4 Kyle: 묻지 마. 너무 지루해서 울고 싶어.

5 Emma: 유감이야.

6 Klye: 난 정말 화가 나. 영화 광고에는 이것이 "올해의 가장 흥미진진한 영화"라고 쓰여 있었어.

7 Emma: 음, 넌 네가 읽는 것을 모두 믿을 수는 없어.

8 Kyle: 그들은 광고에 거짓말을 한 거야. 돈을 환불해 달라고 해야겠어.

9 Emma: 기다려, Kyle! 그들은 사실이 아닌 의견을 사용했기 때문에 꼭 거짓말을 한 것은 아니야.

10 Kyle: 뭐라고? 네 말을 이해하지 못하겠어.

11 Emma: 의견은 "사막은 아름다워."와 같이 사람들의 감정을 표현하는 것이야.

12 그것이 사실인지 아닌지 말할 수는 없어. 하지만 사실은 증명할 수 있어.

13 예를 들면, "아타카마 사막은 칠레에 있다."는 사실이야. 넌 그것을 지도에서 확인할 수 있어.

14 Kyle: 알겠어…. 하지만 그게 영화와 무슨 관련이 있니?

15 Emma: 설명해 줄게. 네가 가장 좋아하는 영화가 뭐니?

16 Kyle: "Forest Gump"야.

17 Emma: 좋아. 그 영화의 광고를 찾아보자. 뭐라고 쓰여 있니?

18 Kyle: "Best Picture를 포함하여 아카데미 6개 부문 수상작"이라고 쓰여 있어.

19 Emma: 알겠니? "Y-Men 7" 광고와는 달리 사실을 사용하고 있어.

20 차이를 알겠니?

21 Kyle: 잘 모르겠어. "Y-Men 7" 광고는 "Most Exciting Movie"라고 쓰여 있고 "Forest Gump" 광고는 "Best Picture"라고 쓰여 있잖아.

22 둘 다 의견 아니니?

23 Emma: 좋은 질문이야, Kyle. 사람들이 'best'나 'most'와 같은 말을 사용할 때, 그들은 대개 의견을 표현하는 거야.

24 하지만 "Forest Gump" 광고에서 "Best Picture"는 영화가 받은 상이야.

25 우리는 인터넷에서 그것을 확인할 수 있어. 그건 사실이야.

26 Kyle: 아하! 지금부터 사실로 이루어진 광고만 믿겠어.

27 Emma: 그렇게 간단하지는 않아. 대부분의 광고는 사실과 의견이 섞여 있어

28 그러니 그 둘을 바탕으로 현명한 선택을 해야 해.

29 Kyle: 알겠어! Emma, "Y-Men 7"의 남은 부분을 나와 함께 볼래?

30 Emma: 고맙지만 사양할게. 영화의 남은 부분 잘 봐!

1 Emma: What are you doing, Kyle?

2 Kyle: Oh, Emma. I'm watching the movie, *Y–Men 7* on my computer.

3 Emma: How is it?

4 Kyle: Don't ask. It's so boring that I want to cry.

5 Emma: I'm sorry to hear that.

6 Kyle: I'm so mad. The movie advertisement said it was "The Most Exciting Movie of the Year."

7 Emma: Well, you can't believe everything that you read.

8 Kyle: They lied on the advertisement. I'm going to ask for my money back.

9 Emma: Hold on, Kyle! They didn't really lie because they used opinions, not facts.

10 Kyle: Huh? I'm not following you.

11 Emma: Opinions express people's feelings like, "The desert is beautiful."

12 You can't say that it's true or not. But, facts can be proven.

13 For example, "The Atacama Desert is in Chile," is a fact. You can check that on the map.

14 Kyle: Okay.... But what's the connection with movies?

15 Emma: Let me explain. What's your favorite movie?

16 Kyle: It's *Forrest Gump*.

17 Emma: Okay. Let's look for its advertisement. What does it say?

18 Kyle: It says, "Winner of 6 Academy Awards including Best Picture."

19 Emma: See? It uses facts unlike the *Y–Men 7* advertisement.

20 Do you see the difference?

21 Kyle: Not exactly. The *Y–Men 7* ad says "Most Exciting Movie" and the *Forrest Gump* ad says "Best Picture."

22 Aren't they both opinions?

23 Emma: That's a great question, Kyle. When people use words like "best" or "most," they are usually expressing opinions.

24 But in the *Forrest Gump* ad, "Best Picture" is the award which the movie won.

25 We can check that on the Internet. That's a fact.

26 Kyle: Aha! From now on I'm only going to trust ads with facts.

27 Emma: It's not that simple. Most ads mix facts with opinions.

28 So you have to make a smart choice based on both of them.

29 Kyle: Got it! Emma, do you want to watch the rest of *Y–Men 7* with me?

30 Emma: Thanks, but no thanks. Enjoy the rest of the movie!

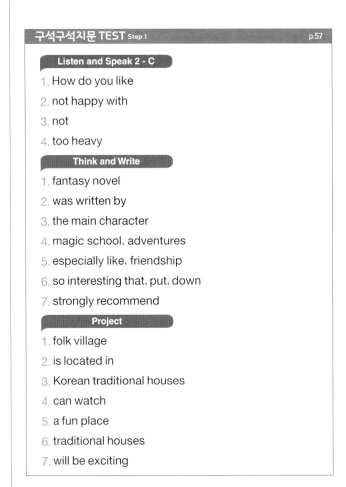

Listen and Speak 2 - C

1. How do you like

2. not happy with

3. not

4. too heavy

Think and Write

1. fantasy novel

2. was written by

3. the main character

4. magic school, adventures

5. especially like, friendship

6. so interesting that, put, down

7. strongly recommend

Project

1. folk village

2. is located in

3. Korean traditional houses

4. can watch

5. a fun place

6. traditional houses

7. will be exciting

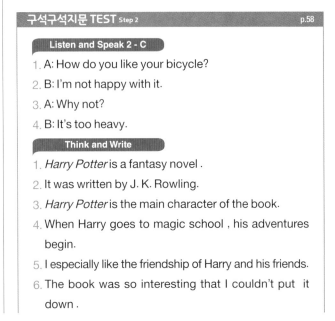

Listen and Speak 2 - C

1. A: How do you like your bicycle?

2. B: I'm not happy with it.

3. A: Why not?

4. B: It's too heavy.

Think and Write

1. *Harry Potter* is a fantasy novel .

2. It was written by J. K. Rowling.

3. *Harry Potter* is the main character of the book.

4. When Harry goes to magic school , his adventures begin.

5. I especially like the friendship of Harry and his friends.

6. The book was so interesting that I couldn't put it down .

7. I strongly recommend it to everyone.

Project

1. Korean folk village
2. Facts: It is located in Yongin.
3. There are Korean traditional houses.
4. Visitors can watch nongak and jultagi.
5. Opinions: It's a fun place in Yongin.
6. Korean traditional houses are beautiful.
7. Nongak and jultagi will be exciting.

Lesson 8

단어 TEST Step 1 p.59

01 공포	02 게시하다, 공고하다	
03 깨진, 부서진	04 목마른	05 청동
06 깃털	07 (급히) 움직이다, 서두르다	
08 섬광, 번쩍임	09 시	10 이상한
11 천둥	12 단서, 실마리	
13 걱정하는, 두려워하는		14 냉장고
15 문자 메시지를 보내다; 문자		16 손자국
17 ~ 안에	18 보물	19 범죄
20 위험한	21 훔치다	
22 낯선 사람, 모르는 사람		23 탐정
24 궁금해 하다	25 호의, 친절, 부탁	26 전화를 걸다, 부르다
27 갑자기	28 발자국	29 도둑
30 번개	31 나르다, 옮기다	32 대걸레로 닦다
33 교장	34 재능	35 ~을 돌보다
36 몇몇의, 조금의	37 지금, 곧, 당장	38 일등을 하다
39 더 이상 ~ 않다	40 집에 가는(오는) 길에	
41 달려가다	42 곤경에 빠지다	43 그 순간에, 그때에

단어 TEST Step 2 p.60

01 footprint	02 silver	03 bronze
04 lightning	05 stranger	06 carry
07 refrigerator	08 dangerous	09 suddenly
10 wonder	11 feather	12 broken
13 talent	14 crime	15 rush
16 poem	17 flash	18 clue
19 thief	20 lose	21 handprint
22 principal	23 favor	24 thirsty
25 horror	26 steal	27 strange
28 detective	29 inside	30 water
31 mop	32 treasure	33 post
34 thunder	35 a few	36 on the way home
37 not ~ anymore		38 right now
39 take care of	40 at the moment	
41 bring ~ back	42 get into trouble	
43 rush over		

단어 TEST Step 3 p.61

1 anyway, 어쨌든　2 footprint, 발자국　3 horror, 공포

4 principal, 교장　5 crime, 범죄　6 thief, 도둑

7 else, 또 다른　8 flash, 섬광, 번쩍임

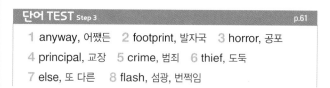

9 mop, 대걸레로 닦다 10 rush, (급히) 행동하다

11 talent, 재능 12 clue, 단서, 실마리

13 bronze, 청동 14 detective, 탐정 15 steal, 훔치다

16 lightning, 번개

대화문 TEST Step 1
p.62~63

Listen and Speak 1-A

ask, favor / Sure / wash the dishes / problem

Listen and Speak 1-B

do me, favor / take care of, going to visit / I'm sorry but I can't / what shoud I do / Why dont you, loves / call, right now

Listen and Speak 1-C

do me a favor / help me mop / problem, Sorry, can't

Listen and Speak 2-A

baseball glove / under the table / not, anymore / guess, took / he is

Listen and Speak 2-B

have passed, at th end of, wonderful year, a few, be in the same class, stranger, each other

Listen and Speak 2-C

what I'm doing / I guess, playing / wrong, Guess / guess, working on / right

Real Life Talk - Step 1

can't find, Can you help me / Are you sure, inside / texted, a few minutes / Where were, at the time / was making / somewhere / already checked / let's check it again, it is, refrigerator / greastest / welcome

Real Life Talk - Step 2

help me find / did, see, last / On / guess, took, see its footprints

대화문 TEST Step 2
p.64~65

Listen and Speak 1-A

Emily: Jinsu, can I ask you a favor?

Jinsu: Sure. What is it?

Emily: Can you help me wash the dishes?

Jinsu: No problem.

Listen and Speak 1-B

Narae: Tony, can you do me a favor?

Tony: Sure. What is it, Narae?

Narae: Can you take care of my dog this weekend? My family is going to visit my grandmother in Busan.

Tony: Oh, I'm sorry but I can't. My mom doesn't like dogs.

Narae: Oh, what should I do?

Tony: Why don't you ask Sumin? Her family loves dogs.

Narae: Okay. I'll call her right now.

Listen and Speak 1-C

A: Can you do me a favor?

B: Sure. What is it?

A: Can you help me mop the floor?

B: No problem. / Sorry, I can't.

Listen and Speak 2-A

Brian: Did you see my baseball glove?

Jane: Yes, I saw it under the table.

Brian: Really? It's not there anymore.

Jane: Then I guess Spot took it.

Brian: Oh, there he is. You bad dog, Spot!

Listen and Speak 2-B

G: Good morning, classmates! Nine months have passed so fast, and we are almost at the end of this school year. We all had a wonderful year. I guess only a few of us will be in the same class next year. Don't be a stranger. Say hello when we see each other, okay? Thank you.

Listen and Speak 2-C

A: Guess what I'm doing.

B: I guess you're playing the piano.

A: You're wrong. Guess again.

B: I guess you're working on the computer.

A: That's right.

Real Life Talk - Step 1

Brian: Mom, I can't find my smartphone. Can you help me find it?

Mom: Are you sure you lost it inside the house?

Brian: Yes, I just texted my friend a few minutes ago.

Mom: Where were you at the time?

Brian: In the kitchen. I was making a sandwich.

Mom: Then I guess you left it somewhere in the kitchen.

Brian: I already checked the kitchen, Mom.

Mom: Well, let's check it again. Oh, here it is. Inside the refrigerator.

Brian: Thanks, Mom. You are the greatest!

Mom: You're welcome, honey.

Real Life Talk - Step 2

A: Can you help me find my baseball glove?

B: Okay. Where did you see it last?

A: On the bench.

B: I guess a dog took your baseball glove. I can see its footprints on the bench.

01 ran across, wet　　　　02 need, help

03 eighth grade student

04 best detective, whole

05 something wrong　　　　06 has stolen, for

07 took, to, scene

08 case with, broken

09 bronze, still there

10 missing, poem, its place　　11 Where did, go

12 low, catch, too

13 when this happened

14 after, rounds, rushed over

15 wonder who else was

16 practicing for, call them

17 ninth grade, curly

18 thirsty, completely, thunder, away

19 see, thief's face

20 only, thief's back, short

21 eighth grade, with long

22 aloud, flash, like, scared

23 hear, break　　24 too loud, going, win

25 seventh, short blonde

26 wrong, moves, little, outside

27 anything strange

28 How could, loud

29 on, way home

30 heard, singing, badly, anyone

31 need, anymore, turned to

32 bring, back, into, trouble

01 ran across, wet

02 need your help

03 an eighth grade student

04 the best detective, whole

05 something wrong, asked

06 has stolen, for, talent show

07 took, to, scene

08 was a case, broken

09 bronze, were still there

10 missing, a poem, its place　　11 Where did, go

12 high and low, too slow

13 when this happened

14 after, making my rounds, rushed over, like

15 who else was here

16 practicing for, call them

17 ninth grade, with short curly

18 practicing, become thirsty, stepped outside, to get, It, completely, Suddenly, thunder, broke, Lightning followed, a second, two, saw, running away

19 thief's face

20 only saw, back, short

21 eighth grade, with long black

22 reading, aloud, went outside, next to, flash, like a horror movie, scared, ran straight

23 hear, break　　24 too loud, was going to win

25 seventh, short blonde

26 wrong, moves, a little before, take, outside, until

27 hear anything strange

28 How could　　29 on the way home

30 heard someone singing

31 need to hear anymore, turned to

32 bring the medal back, get into, trouble

1 Reese 교장은 젖은 운동장을 달려왔다.

2 "Shirley! Shirley! 네 도움이 필요하구나!"

3 Shirley는 Bakersville 중학교의 8학년 학생이었다.

4 그녀는 또한 그 마을 최고의 탐정이었다.

5 "무슨 일이 있나요?" Shirley가 물었다.

6 "누군가 장기 자랑 대회 금메달을 훔쳐갔어!"

7 Reese 교장은 Shirley를 범죄 현장으로 데려갔다.

8 유리창이 깨진 진열장이 있었다.

9 은메달과 동메달은 그곳에 그대로 있었다.

10 하지만 금메달은 사라졌다. 그 자리에는 시가 있었다.

11 내일은 장기 자랑 대회다. 금메달은 어디로 갔을까?

12 구석구석 찾아라. 당신은 나를 잡을 수 없어. 당신은 너무 느려.

13 Shirley는 "언제 이 사건이 일어났는지 말씀해 주시겠어요?" 라고 물었다.

14 "어젯밤 9시가 조금 넘은 후에. 내가 순찰을 돌고 있었을 때 비명 소리가 들렸어. 나는 달려가서 Jocelyn과 이 상태 인 진열장을 발견했지."

15 "어젯밤에 또 다른 누가 여기 있었는지 궁금해요."

16 "Sylvia와 Harry가 있었어. 그 두 사람 또한 장기 자랑을 위해 연습 중이었어. 내가 그들을 내 사무실로 부르마."

17 Jocelyn은 빨간색 짧은 곱슬머리를 가진 9학년 학생이었다.

18 "저는 제 노래를 연습하고 있었는데 목이 말랐어요. 저는 물을 가지러 교실 밖으로 나갔어요. 완전히 어두웠어요 갑자기, 커다란 천둥소리가 났어요. 저는 도둑이 그 순간에 유리창을 깼다고 생각해요. 번개가 바로 뒤따랐고 1~2초 정도 밝아졌어요. 그때 저는 누군가가 진열장에서 도망치는 걸 봤어요."

19 "도둑의 얼굴을 봤나요?"

20 "아니요, 도둑의 뒷모습만 봤어요. 하지만 그 도둑은 짧은 머리였어요."

21 다음은 8학년 학생인 Sylvia였다. 그녀는 긴 검은색 머리에 키가 컸다.

22 그녀는 말했다. "저는 교실에서 큰 소리로 제 시를 낭송하고 있었어요. 비명 소리를 듣고 밖으로 나갔어요. 진열장 옆에 한 소녀가 있었어요. 번개의 번쩍임과 어우러져 그것은 공포 영화 같았어요. 저는 겁이 나서 곧장 집으로 달려갔어요." "

23 "창이 깨지는 소리를 들었나요?"

24 "아니요, 천둥소리가 너무 컸어요. 음, 제가 그런 게 아니에요. 지는 어쨌든 1등을 할 거으니까요."

25 7학년인 Harry는 짧은 금발을 가지고 있었다.

26 그는 말했다. "이봐요, 사람을 잘못 짚었어요. 저는 제 춤 동작을 연습하고 있었어요. 저는 9시 조금 전에 집에 갔어요. 저는 그때까지 교실 밖으로 한 발자국도 나가지 않았어요."

27 "이상한 소리라도 들었나요?"

28 "제가 어떻게 듣겠어요? 제 음악 소리가 정말 컸어요."

29 "집에 가는 길에 누군가를 보았나요?"

30 "아니요, 누군가가 노래를 정말 끔찍하게 부르는 소리는 들었지만 누구도 보진 못했어요."

31 Shirley는 "더 이상 들을 필요는 없겠네요."라고 말했다. 그러고 나서 그녀는 도둑을 향했다.

32 "정말 곤경에 빠지기 전에 금메달을 돌려주는 게 어때요?"

---

1 Mr. Reese, the principal, ran across the wet playground.

2 "Shirley! Shirley! I need your help!"

3 Shirley was an eighth grade student at Bakersville Middle School.

4 She was also the best detective in the whole town.

5 "Is there something wrong?" asked Shirley.

6 "Someone has stolen the gold medal for the talent show!"

7 Mr. Reese took Shirley to the scene of the crime.

8 There was a case with a broken window.

9 The silver and bronze medals were still there.

10 But the gold medal was missing. There was a poem in its place.

11 Tomorrow is the talent show. Where did the gold medal go?

12 Look high and low. You can't catch me. You're too slow.

13 Shirley asked, "Could you tell me when this happened?"

14 "A little after nine last night. I was making my rounds when I heard a scream. I rushed over and found Jocelyn and the case like this."

15 "I wonder who else was here last night."

16 "Sylvia and Harry. They were also practicing for the talent show. I'll call them to my office."

17 Jocelyn was a ninth grade student with short curly red hair.

18 "I was practicing my song and I became thirsty. I stepped outside the classroom to get some water. It was completely dark. Suddenly, there was a loud sound of thunder. I think the thief broke the window at that moment. Lightning followed right after and it became bright for a second or two. Then I saw someone running away from the case."

19 "Did you see the thief's face?"

20 "No, I only saw the thief's back. But the thief had short hair."

21 Next was an eighth grade student, Sylvia. She was tall with long black hair.

22 She said, "I was reading my poem aloud in the classroom. I heard a scream and went outside. There was a girl next to the case. With the flash from the lightning, it was like a horror movie. I got scared so I ran straight home."

23 "Did you hear the window break?"

24 "No, the thunder was too loud. Well, I didn't do it. I was going to win first place anyway."

25 Harry, a seventh grader, had short blonde hair.

26 He said, "Hey, you got the wrong guy. I was practicing my dance moves. I went home a little before nine. I didn't take one step outside the classroom until then."

27 "Did you hear anything strange?"

28 "How could I? My music was really loud."

29 "Did you see anyone on the way home?"

30 "No, I heard someone singing really badly, but I didn't see anyone."

31 Shirley said, "I don't need to hear anymore." Then she turned to the thief.

32 "Why don't you bring the medal back before you get into some real trouble?"

Project

1. treasure hunters
2. have hidden, something delicious
3. where, follow the steps
4. look for, near, under
5. pick up, walk to the back
6. third locker from the left
7. is locked, to open, yourself

Think and Write

1. put her in
2. grew up, long hair
3. to climb up
4. world outside
5. heard Rapunzel singing beautifully
6. Come down
7. who is telling the truth, was confused
8. made up, cut, came down
9. faced, for the first time, What a beautiful world

Check Up

1. you, me a favor
2. Sure
3. help me blow up
4. problem

Project

1. To the treasure hunters,
2. Hello. We have hidden our treasure in the classroom. It is something delicious.
3. Do you want to know where it is? Then follow the steps.
4. First, look for a plant near the window. Look under the plant. You'll find a key.
5. Second, pick up the key and walk to the back of the classroom. You'll see the lockers.
6. The treasure is in the third locker from the left.
7. It is locked, so use the key to open it. Got it? Help yourself.

Think and Write

1. When Rapunzel was a baby, a witch put her in a tall tower.
2. Rapunzel grew up in the tower. She had long hair .
3. The witch used it to climb up the tower.
4. The witch always said, "The world outside is very dangerous."

5. One day, a prince heard Rapunzel singing beautifully.
6. He said, "Come down. The world outside is wonderful."
7. Rapunzel said, "I don't know who is telling the truth." Rapunzel was confused.
8. Finally, she made up her mind. She cut her hair and came down from the tower.
9. When she faced the world for the first time, she couldn't believe her eyes. " What a beautiful world !"

Check Up

1. A: Can you do me a favor?
2. B: Sure. What is it?
3. A: Can you help me blow up these balloons?
4. B: No problem.

55

Lesson S

10 package, 소포 11 reporter, 기자

12 signature, 서명 13 borrow, 빌리다

14 situation, 상황 15 punish, 처벌하다

16 dictionary, 사전

단어 TEST Step 1   p.78

01 (개가) 짖다	02 퍼지다, 확산되다	03 소포
04 보도하다, 덮다	05 날짜를 적다; 날짜	06 동의하다
07 서명	08 빌리다	09 멋진
10 의미	11 전체의, 온	12 완벽하게
13 봉투	14 상황	15 졸업하다
16 처벌하다, 벌주다	17 안에, 내부에	18 지역의, 지방의
19 의미하다	20 받다	21 기사
22 재미있는	23 학년	24 급우, 반 친구
25 인근의, 가까이의	26 기자	27 여분의, 추가의
28 결정하다	29 기쁜, 기뻐하는	30 신이 난
31 만족하는	32 어휘	33 전쟁
34 사전	35 선택의 여지가 없다, 대안이 없다	
36 ~이 끝나다	37 그때까지, ~할 때까지	
38 ~을 꺼내다	39 쥐다, 잡다	40 ~에 대해 걱정하다
41 집으로 가는 길에	42 ~로 유명하다	43 ~에 신이 나다

단어 TEST Step 2   p.79

01 bark	02 mean	03 envelope
04 borrow	05 signature	06 grade
07 receive	08 cool	09 date
10 pleased	11 meaning	12 punish
13 article	14 extra	15 satisfied
16 excited	17 funny	18 situation
19 spread	20 graduate	21 package
22 inside	23 local	24 decide
25 perfectly	26 reporter	27 dictionary
28 cover	29 nearby	30 quickly
31 entire	32 vocabulary	33 war
34 agree	35 more and more	
36 be famous for	37 have no choice	
38 hold up	39 look up	40 out of hand
41 by the time	42 on the way home	
43 be worried about		

단어 TEST Step 3   p.80

1 graduate, 졸업하다   2 envelope, 봉투

3 agree, 동의하다   4 entire, 전체의   5 meaning, 의미

6 vocabulary, 어휘   7 extra, 여분의

8 article, (신문의) 기사   9 classmate, 급우

본문 TEST Step 1   p.81~82

01 excited, fifth grade, worried

02 famous for, difficult, lessons

03 class, dictionary, up, meanings

04 meanings, decided, means, barks

05 entire, agreed, its meaning

06 satisfied, agree, himself

07 On, decided , test   08 took out, From

09 asked, use, word   10 During class, forgot

11 held up, extra, borrow   12 not pleased

13 but, already, perfectly

14 found, funny, use, more

15 In, became, cool word

16 getting, hand, stop saying

17 stop, as, word   18 have no choice

19 took out, sign, date   20 give, when, over

21 thought, hates   22 Next, began, with

23 punish, for using   24 only, things worse

25 to use, more   26 spread to nearby

27 Shortly after, wrote, knew

28 later, covered, found out

29 By, graduated from, used

30 flew by, one, received

31 Inside, found, envelope

32 signature from, grade   33 note, said, Check

본문 TEST Step 2   p.83~84

01 was excited about, fifth grade, was worried about

02 was famous for, vocabulary lessons

03 should have a good dictionary, can look up, meaning, new words

04 the meanings, means, barks

05 entire town, agreed, its meaning

06 satisfied, did I agree, said to himself

07 On, decided   08 took out, From

09 asked, to use   10 During class, forgot

11 held up, extra, to borrow   12 was not pleased

13 but, already has, perfectly

14 found, funny, to use, more and more

15 In, became, cool word

16 said to, after class, getting out of hand, to stop saying

17 stop it, as, students' word   18 no choice

19 took out, asked, to sign, date

20 I'll give, to you, is over   21 thought, hates

22 began, with   23 punish, for using

24 made things worse

25 to use, more and more   26 spread to nearby

27 Shortly after, wrote, on, knew about it

28 A month later, covered, found out about

29 By the time, graduated from, most students, used

30 flew by,One day, received

31 Inside it, found, envelope, dictionary

32 signature from fifth grade   33 yellow note, It said

1 Nick Allen은 5학년이 시작되는 것이 신났지만, 한 가지가 걱정되었다. 그것은 Granger 선생님의 영어 수업이었다.

2 Granger 선생님은 어려운 어휘 수업으로 유명했다.

3 첫 번째 시간에 Granger 선생님은 말했다. "모두 좋은 사전을 가지고 있어야 해요. 여러분은 사전에서 새 단어의 뜻을 찾을 수 있어요."

4 "Granger 선생님? 단어의 뜻은 누가 정하나요? 그러니까, '개'는 짖는 동물을 뜻한다고 누가 정했나요?" Nick이 물었다.

5 "네가 그랬지, Nick. 너와 나, 그리고 온 마을과 나라가 말이야. 우리 모두가 동의했단다. 그게 그 단어에게 의미를 부여하는 거야."

6 Nick은 마음에 들지 않았다. "내가 언제 동의했지?" 그는 혼잣말을 했다.

7 집에 가는 길에 Nick은 Granger 선생님의 생각을 시험하기로 결심했다.

8 그는 펜을 하나 꺼내서 말했다. "오늘부터 이것은 'frindle'이야."

9 그 다음날 Nick은 다섯 명의 친구들에게 단어 'frindle'을 사용해 달라고 부탁했다.

10 수업 중에 Nick이 말했다. "Granger 선생님, 오늘 'frindle'을 빠뜨리고 왔어요."

11 Nick의 친구인 John이 펜을 하나 들고서는 말했다. "나한테 여분의 'frindle'이 있어. 내 'frindle'을 빌리 고 싶니?"

12 Granger 선생님은 즐거워하지 않았다.

13 선생님이 말했다. "너희들의 새 단어는 귀엽지만, 그건 이미 'pen'이라는 완벽하게 좋은 이름이 있단다."

14 Nick의 학급 친구들은 이것을 재미있어 했고 더욱 더 그 단어를 사용하기 시작했다.

15 단지 3일 만에 학교에서 그것은 멋진 단어가 되었다.

16 Granger 선생님은 수업 후에 Nick에게 말했다. "점점 손을 쓸 수 없게 되어 가는구나. 네 친구들에게 'frindle'을 말하는 것을 멈춰달라고 말해 줄래?"

17 죄송하지만, 멈추게 할 수가 없어요. 그건 제 단어로 시작됐지만, 이제 그건 학생들의 단어예요."

18 "좋아. 그러면 선택의 여지가 없구나."

19 Granger 선생님은 봉투를 하나 꺼내더니 Nick에게 뒷면에 서명을 하고 날짜를 적게 했다.

20 선생님은 말했다. "이 모든 것이 끝나면 내가 이 편지를 너에게 줄게."

21 Nick은 생각했다. "선생님은 내가 정말 싫은가봐."

22 다음 주에 Granger 선생님은 'frindle'과의 전쟁을 시작했다.

23 선생님은 그 단어를 사용한다면 어떤 학생이든 벌을 줄 것이라고 말했다.

24 하지만 이것은 상황을 더 나쁘게 만들 뿐이었다.

25 학생들은 그 단어를 더욱 더 사용하고 싶어했다.

26 'frindle'은 근처의 중학교와 고등학교로 빠르게 퍼져 나갔다.

27 곧 지역 신문 기자가 그 상황에 관한 기사를 썼고, 마을의 모든 사람들이 그것에 관해 알게 되었다.

28 한 달 후에 한 전국 텔레비전 방송사에 서 그 소식을 다루었고, 모든 사람들이 'frindle'에 관해 알게 되었다.

29 Nick이 초등학교를 졸업할 때쯤에는 이 나라의 대부분의 학생들이 그 단어를 사용했다.

30 시간은 흘러 Nick은 21살이 되었다. 어느 날 Nick은 소포를 하나 받았다.

31 소포 안에는 펜 한 자루, 봉투 한 장, 그리고 사전 한 권이 있었다.

32 봉투에는 5학년 때의 그의 서명이 있었다.

33 사전에는 노란색 쪽지가 있었다. "541쪽을 확인해 봐."라고 적혀 있었다.

1 Nick Allen was excited about starting fifth grade, but he was worried about one thing—Mrs. Granger's English class.

2 Mrs. Granger was famous for her difficult vocabulary lessons.

3 In the first class, Mrs. Granger said, "Everyone should have a good dictionary. You can look up the meanings of new words in it."

4 "Mrs. Granger? Who decides the meanings of words? I mean, who decided that 'dog' means an animal that barks?" Nick asked.

5 "You did, Nick. You, me, and the entire town and country. We all agreed. That gives the word its meaning."

6 Nick wasn't satisfied. "When did I agree?" he said to himself.

7 On the way home, he decided to test Mrs. Granger's idea.

8 He took out a pen and said, "From today, this is a *frindle*."

9 The next day, he asked five friends to use the word *frindle*.

10 During class, Nick said, "Mrs. Granger, I forgot my *frindle* today."

11 His friend, John, held up a pen and said, "I have an extra *frindle*. Do you want to borrow my *frindle*?"

12 Mrs. Granger was not pleased.

13 She said, "Your new word is cute, but it already has a perfectly good name — a pen."

14 Nick's classmates found this funny and began to use the word more and more.

15 In just three days, it became the cool word at school.

16 Mrs. Granger said to Nick after class, "This is getting out of hand. Can you tell your friends to stop saying *frindle*?"

17 "I'm sorry, but I can't stop it. It started as my word, but now it's the students' word."

18 "Very well. Then I have no choice."

19 Mrs. Granger took out an envelope and asked Nick to sign and date the back.

20 She said, "I'll give this letter to you when all this is over."

21 Nick thought, "She really hates me."

22 Next week, Mrs. Granger began a war with *frindle*.

23 She said that she would punish any student for using it.

24 But this only made things worse.

25 The students wanted to use the word more and more.

26 *Frindle* quickly spread to nearby middle and high schools.

27 Shortly after, a local newspaper reporter wrote an article on the situation and everyone in town knew about it.

28 A month later, a national television station covered the news and everyone found out about *frindle*.

29 By the time Nick graduated from elementary school, most students in the country used the word.

30 Time flew by and Nick turned 21. One day, he received a package.

31 Inside it, he found a pen, an envelope and a dictionary.

32 The envelope had his signature from fifth grade.

33 The dictionary had a yellow note. It said, "Check page 541."

MEMO

적중 1⊙⊙ + 특별부록

Plan B

우리학교 최신기출

동아 · 이병민 교과서를 배우는

학교 시험문제 분석 · 모음 · 해설집

전국단위 학교 시험문제 수집 및 분석

출제 빈도가 높은 문제 위주로 선별

문제 풀이에 필요한 상세한 해설

중2-2
영어

동아 · 이병민

Lesson 5   Come One, Come All

Lesson 6   In Outer Space

Lesson 7   Can I Trust It?

Lesson 8   Be like Sherlock!

적중 **100** + 특별부록

Plan B

우리학교 최신기출

중2-2
영어

동아 · 이병민

Lesson 5   **Come One, Come All**

Lesson 6   **In Outer Space**

Lesson 7   **Can I Trust It?**

Lesson 8   **Be like Sherlock!**

◎ 선택형 문항의 답안은 컴퓨터용 수정 싸인펜을 사용하여 OMR 답안지에 바르게 표기하시오.
◎ 서술형 문제는 답을 답안지에 반드시 검정 볼펜으로 쓰시오.
◎ 총 30문항 100점 만점입니다. 문항별 배점은 각 문항에 표시되어 있습니다.

[서울 광진구 ○○중]

01 다음 중 밑줄 친 부분의 의미가 바르지 <u>않은</u> 것은?　(3점)

① The man <u>chased</u> her. (뒤쫓았다)

② The movie <u>lasted</u> for three hours. (지속되었다)

③ Don't <u>miss</u> a great chance! (그리워하다)

④ People <u>gathered</u> together to see her. (모였다)

⑤ Let's <u>celebrate</u> her birthday together. (축하하다)

[서울 노원구 ○○중]

02 다음 〈보기〉의 단어 풀이가 설명하는 것은?　(3점)

> **보기**
>
> to have a particular type of life

① peel　　　② lead

③ slice　　　④ chase

⑤ gather

[서울 노원구 ○○중]

03 다음 중 어법과 표현이 올바른 것은? (정답 2개)　(4점)

① She heard Tom sing a song in his room.

② I saw him to enter the house.

③ Jane watched her sister drawing a picture.

④ The teacher saw his students danced.

⑤ The hunter felt someone follows him in the woods.

[서울 노원구 ○○중]

04 다음 빈칸에 들어갈 말로 가장 알맞은 것은?　(3점)

> A: Excuse me. How can I get to the post office?
> B: Go straight to 1st Street and make a right. It will be on your right.
> A: _____ from here?
> B: No, it's not.
> A: Thank you very much.

① Is it far

② Is it long

③ Can you ride

④ Does it far

⑤ Does it long

[서울 마포구 ○○중]

05 다음 대화 중 자연스럽지 않은 것은?　(3점)

① A: How can I get to the library?
　B: ·Cross the street and go straight two blocks.

② A: How long is the science fair going to last?
　B: It is going to last for a week.

③ A: What will you do for the class party?
　B: I'll make some cookies.

④ A: How long will it take to get to the theater?
　B: No, it's not far from my house.

⑤ A: What about having lunch together?
　B: All right. Let's meet at 12 o'clock.

Man: Excuse me. (A)_____ Suwon Hwaseong from here?

Mina: It's easy. Do you see the bus stop over there?

Man: Yes, I do.

Mina: Take the No. 6 bus and get off at the eleventh stop.

Man: How long will it take to get there?

Mina: It will take about 20 minutes.

Man: Thank you very much.

Mina: No problem. Are you going there for the festival?

Man: Yes. I heard it's a lot of fun.

Mina: I hope you have a great time.

[인천 ○○중]

06 위 대화의 빈칸 (A)에 들어갈 말로 알맞지 <u>않은</u> 것은? (2개) (3점)

① How can I go to

② How can I get to

③ Why don't I go to

④ Where can I get to

⑤ Could you tell me the way to

[인천 ○○중]

07 위 대화의 내용과 일치하는 것은? (3점)

① The man should get off at the 6th stop.

② The man wants to go to the festival with Mina.

③ The man tells Mina where Suwon Hwaseong is.

④ Mina tells the man how long it will take to get to the bus stop.

⑤ It will take about twenty minutes to get to Suwon Hwaseong by bus.

[서울 광진구 ○○중]

08 위 대화를 읽고 다음 질문에 대한 답을 완성하시오. (3점)

Q: How will the man go there?

A: He will go _____ _____ _____.

A: _____ _____ _____

[9~11] 다음 대화를 읽고 물음에 답하시오.

(*A phone rings.*)

B: Hi, Emma. What's up?

G: Hey, Minsu. Are you free this Friday?

B: Yes. Why do you ask?

G: Well, (A)<u>how about having dinner together?</u> I am coming with Junho and Mina. Will you join us?

B: Sure.

G: Let's try the new Chinese restaurant, Ming's. It's near the school.

B: Okay. (B)_____

G: Come out from the school and go straight to Green Street. Make a left, and the restaurant will be on your left.

B: All right. Let's meet at 6 o'clock.

G: Wonderful. See you then.

*B: Minsu, G: Emma

09 위 대화에서 찾을 수 없는 정보는? (3점)

① 가려는 음식점 이름

② 식당에 함께 갈 친구들

③ 만나기로 한 시각

④ 민수의 토요일 일정

⑤ 대화하는 사람들의 이름

10 위 대화의 밑줄 친 (A)와 바꿔 쓸 수 있는 문장을 주어진 단어를 이용하여 쓰시오. (4점)

why / don't

→ _____

11 위 대화의 빈칸 (B)에 알맞은 것은? (3점)

① How can I get there from the school?

② Oh, is it the one in the red building?

③ How far is the restaurant?

④ Is 6 o'clock okay for you?

⑤ How long will it take from the school?

[12~14] 다음 대화를 읽고 물음에 답하시오.

Andy: ⓐI'm so exciting about school festival this Friday.

Mina: Me, too. ⓑWhat can we do advertise it, Andy?

Andy: How about making posters?

Mina: Great idea. ⓒWe can post them in our neighborhood.

Andy: Right. How long will it take to make them?

Mina: Well, ⓓit will take about three hours.

Andy: Hmm... that's too long. Why don't we just upload promoting videos on our social media? I have several videos from the last year on my laptop. It will take only 30 minutes to edit them.

Mina: That's much better I guess! If you send me the videos, I can create a post on my Facenote, too.

Andy: Okay, ⓔI hope many people came to the festival.

12 위 대화의 밑줄 친 ⓐ~ⓔ의 표현 중 어법상 올바른 것은? (답 2개) (4점)

① ⓐ　　　　② ⓑ　　　　③ ⓒ

④ ⓓ　　　　⑤ ⓔ

13 위 대화의 내용과 일치하지 <u>않는</u> 것은? (3점)

① Both Andy and Mina are interested in the school festival.

② The school is going to hold a festival this Friday.

③ Andy and Mina considered making posters to promote their school festival first.

④ The promoting videos will be sent to Mina later.

⑤ Andy will take videos of the school festival this year.

15 대화가 자연스럽게 이어지도록 바르게 배열한 것은? (3점)

(A) Great idea. How long will it take to make them?

(B) Chris, what will you do for the class party?

(C) I'll make sandwiches.

(D) Maybe it'll take about an hour.

① (A)-(C)-(B)-(D)

② (A)-(D)-(B)-(C)

③ (B)-(D)-(A)-(C)

④ (B)-(C)-(A)-(D)

⑤ (C)-(B)-(A)-(D)

[16~17] 다음 글을 읽고 물음에 답하시오.

14 위 대화를 읽고 〈조건〉에 맞게 빈칸을 완성하시오. (6점)

Mina and Andy will promote the school festival by (1)_____. This is because (2)_____ than making a poster.

조건
(1) 7단어, 본문의 단어를 활용할 것
(2) 6단어

(1) _____

(2) _____

What's your favorite holiday? My favorite holiday is Thanksgiving. In the United States, Thanksgiving ⓐis always celebrated on the fourth Thursday of November. There is a long weekend after Thanksgiving, so we just relax and spend time together with our family and friends.

ⓑOn Thanksgiving we have a big meal, the Thanksgiving dinner. We usually have turkey, potatoes and apple pie. ⓒAll of them are my favorites. It takes lots of time ⓓcook a turkey. I always help my mom ⓔprepare the dinner. At the dinner table we give thanks for our family and friends. After the dinner, we go out to see the big Thanksgiving parade, play sports in the yard, and take photos. There is also a big football game on TV, and of course, the men in my family love to watch it.

16 위 글의 밑줄 친 ⓐ~ⓔ 중 어법상 옳지 <u>않은</u> 것은? (3점)

① ⓐ   ② ⓑ   ③ ⓒ

④ ⓓ   ⑤ ⓔ

17 What do people do on the Thanksgiving weekend? (3점)

① They have a big meal.

② They watch a big football game on TV.

③ They go out to see the big Thanksgiving parade.

④ They usually have turkey, potatoes and apple pie.

⑤ They just relax and spend time together with their family and friends.

18 위 글의 내용과 거리가 먼 것은? (3점)

① Holi is a summer festival.

② Holi lasts for two days.

③ Holi is usually held in March.

④ Holi is a popular Indian festival.

⑤ Children and adults participate in the festival.

19 위 글의 밑줄 친 ⓐ~ⓔ 중 어법에 맞지 <u>않는</u> 것을 <u>모두</u> 고른 것은? (3점)

① ⓐ   ② ⓑ   ③ ⓒ

④ ⓓ   ⑤ ⓔ

20 위 글을 읽고 답할 수 <u>없는</u> 질문은? (3점)

① What is *gulal*?

② Where does Holi take place?

③ What kinds of food are there?

④ How long do people celebrate Holi?

⑤ What do people do on the first day?

[18~21] 다음 글을 읽고 물음에 답하시오.

Holi, the Festival of Colors

Amala from Delhi, India

Holi is a popular festival in my country. ⓐ<u>It is usually in March.</u> ⓑ<u>During the festival is held</u>, we say goodbye to cold winter and hello to warm spring. We celebrate the festival everywhere for two days. ⓒ<u>On the first day, people gather around a big fire at night and singing and dancing.</u> ⓓ<u>The main event begins on the second day.</u> Children and adults throw *gulal* at each other. What is *gulal*? (A)_____ ⓔ<u>It's a lot of fun to chase each other on the street.</u>

21 위 글의 빈칸 (A)에 들어갈 적절한 문장을 〈보기〉의 주어진 단어를 반드시 모두 포함하여 영작하시오. (4점)

> **보기**
>
> powder / blue / yellow / green / pink

→ _____

[22~26] 다음 글을 읽고 물음에 답하시오.

Ebba from Kiruna, Sweden
Winter is my favorite season ⓐbecause of the Kiruna Snow Festival. The festival starts in the last week of January and ⓑgoes on for five or six days. The largest event is the snow design competition. The artists shape huge piles of snow ⓒfor animals, buildings, and other beautiful artworks. People watch the artists (A)_____ their works ⓓwith beginning to end. My favorite activity is the dog sled ride. (가)It is amazing (B)_____ through a world of snow ⓔon a dog sled.

22 위 글의 밑줄 친 ⓐ~ⓔ 중, 쓰임이 <u>어색한</u> 것끼리 짝지어진 것은? (4점)

① ⓐ, ⓑ　　　　② ⓑ, ⓒ
③ ⓑ, ⓓ　　　　④ ⓒ, ⓓ
⑤ ⓒ, ⓓ, ⓔ

23 위 글의 빈칸 (A), (B)에 들어갈 말이 바르게 짝지어진 것은? (3점)

① shaping – to fly
② shaping – fly
③ shape – fly
④ shape – flied
⑤ shaped – to fly

24 위 글을 읽고 답할 수 <u>없는</u> 질문은? (3점)

① For what reason does Ebba like winter the best?
② How long does the festival last?
③ When does the Kiruna Snow Festival start?
④ What is Ebba's favorite activity in the festival?
⑤ How many artworks can you see during the festival?

25 위 글을 참고하여 다음 질문에 영어로 된 완전한 문장으로 답하시오. (4점)

Q: What do the artists shape into artworks at the Kiruna Snow Festival?
A: _____

26 위 글의 밑줄 친 (가)It과 쓰임이 같은 것은? (3점)

① <u>It</u> was dark in the classroom.
② How far is <u>it</u> from here to the church?
③ <u>It</u> is not easy to do my English homework.
④ <u>It</u> is the backpack that I told you before.
⑤ My smartphone is too old. I don't like <u>it</u>.

Victor from St. Petersburg, Russia

Have you @heard of the *White Nights*? Every summer, this amazing thing happens in my hometown. The night sky does not get completely dark. During that time, we hold the White Nights Festival. It usually ⓑstarts in May and lasts ©for about a month. During the festival, there is a ballet or an opera almost every night.

The most popular event is the Scarlet Sails celebration. A boat with red sails slowly ⓓappears on the river. Soon, fireworks begin and a water show follows. You can also hear musicians ⓔplayed beautiful (A)live music.

27 위 글의 밑줄 친 @~ⓔ 중, 어법상 어색한 부분을 바르게 고쳐 쓴 것은? (3점)

① @ heard of → hear of

② ⓑ starts → start

③ © for → during

④ ⓓ appears → appear

⑤ ⓔ played → playing

28 위 글의 밑줄 친 (A)와 같은 뜻으로 쓰인 것은? (4점)

① Long live, the King!

② I live my life to the full cheerfully.

③ I will live in Songdo for five years.

④ I watched live streaming sports all night long.

⑤ Don't live in the past. Learn from it and move on.

29 위 글의 White Nights Festival에서 찾아볼 수 없는 것은? (3점)

① ballet

② fireworks

③ water show

④ the Scarlet Sails celebration

⑤ deep dark nights

30 위 글의 내용과 일치하는 문장끼리 짝지어진 것은? (3점)

ⓐ During the White Nights, you can see a completely dark night sky.

ⓑ The White Nights Festival lasts for about a month.

© During the festival, there isn't a ballet or an opera almost every night.

ⓓ The Scarlet Sails celebration includes fireworks and a water show.

① ⓐ, ⓑ   ② ⓐ, ©

③ ⓑ, ©   ④ ⓑ, ⓓ

⑤ ©, ⓓ

◎ 선택형 문항의 답안은 컴퓨터용 수정 싸인펜을 사용하여 OMR 답안지에 바르게 표기하시오.
◎ 서술형 문제는 답을 답안지에 반드시 검정 볼펜으로 쓰시오.
◎ 총 30문항 100점 만점입니다. 문항별 배점은 각 문항에 표시되어 있습니다.

[울산 ○○중]

01 다음 영영풀이에 해당하는 영어 단어가 <u>아닌</u> 것은? (순서 상관 없음) (4점)

- a fully grown person
- an event or contest in which people compete
- a small vehicle used for sliding over snow
- to tell the public about goods to make people buy them
- a mass of something that has been placed somewhere

① competition   ② pile
③ advertise   ④ adult
⑤ parade

[서울 노원구 ○○중]

02 빈칸 ⓐ~ⓔ에 들어갈 단어로 옳지 <u>않은</u> 것은? (3점)

- She is ____ⓐ____ her new book.
- The painting is my son's ____ⓑ____ artwork.
- I enjoy ____ⓒ____ the Christmas tree with my mom.
- The 1988 Olympic Games were ____ⓓ____ in Seoul, Korea.
- The kid went down a hill on a ____ⓔ____.

① ⓐ advertising
② ⓑ latest
③ ⓒ decorating
④ ⓓ hold
⑤ ⓔ sled

[인천 ○○중]

03 다음 중 단어의 영어 의미가 올바른 것은? (3점)

① blind: unable to hear
② scarlet: a bright blue color
③ several: only one
④ chase: to buy something to give to somebody them
⑤ necessary: that is needed for a purpose or a reason

[충북 ○○중]

04 다음 빈칸에 들어갈 말로 가장 적절하지 <u>않은</u> 것은? (3점)

A: I'm so excited about the school festival this Friday.
B: Me, too. What can we do to advertise it, Andy?
A: _____
B: Great idea.

① Why don't we ask our classmates?
② Why do you ask me instead of yourself?
③ Let's make a video clip for the school festival.
④ What about making posters about the school festival?
⑤ How about putting the festival poster on the school bulletin board?

05 다음 중 대화가 가장 <u>어색한</u> 것은? (3점)

① A: Let's meet at 12 o'clock.

B: I'm sorry. This clock is not mine.

② A: How about having lunch together?

B: Are you asking me out on a date?

③ A: How long will it take to get to the theater?

B: It will take about 15 minutes on foot.

④ A: Jinho, hurry up. We're going to be late for the movie.

B: I'm almost ready. Just wait a second.

⑤ A: Are you free this Saturday?

B: No, I have to study all day for the mid term test.

06 위 대화를 읽고, 대답할 수 <u>없는</u> 질문은? (3점)

① When is the school festival?

② What are they talking about?

③ How will they advertise the festival?

④ How long will it take to make the posters?

⑤ How many people will come to the festival?

07 위 대화의 (A)~(D)의 순서로 가장 적절한 것은? (3점)

① (A) - (C) - (D) - (B)

② (A) - (D) - (C) - (B)

③ (B) - (C) - (D) - (A)

④ (C) - (A) - (B) - (D)

⑤ (C) - (B) - (A) - (D)

[6~7] 다음 대화를 읽고 물음에 답하시오.

A: I'm so excited about the school festival this Friday.

B: Me, too. What can we do to advertise it, Andy?

(A) How about making posters?

(B) Well, it will take about three hours.

(C) Great idea. We can post them in our neighborhood.

(D) Right. How long will it take to make them?

A: Okay, I hope many people come to the festival.

[8~10] 다음 대화를 읽고 물음에 답하시오.

Man: Excuse me. How can I get to Suwon Hwaseong from here?

Mina: It's easy. Do you see the bus stop over there?

Man: Yes, I do.

Mina: Take the No. 11 bus and get off at the sixth stop.

Man: (A)[get / how / will / take / it / to / there / long]?

Mina: It will (B)take about 20 minutes.

Man: Thank you very much.

Mina: No problem. Are you going there for the festival?

Man: Yes. I heard it's a lot of fun.

Mina: I hope you have a great time.

08 위 대화의 (A)의 단어를 배열하여 문장을 완성하시오. (4점)

→ _____

09 위 대화의 밑줄 친 (B)의 의미와 같은 것은? (3점)

① <u>Take</u> your books out on your desk.

② My mom will <u>take</u> me to the nearest park.

③ It will <u>take</u> seven days to finish the project.

④ You should <u>take</u> the subway to go there.

⑤ Next month I will <u>take</u> an English exam.

10 위 대화의 내용과 일치하지 <u>않은</u> 것은? (3점)

① There is a festival in Suwon Hwaseong.

② The man is going to Suwon Hwaseong.

③ Mina knows the way to go to Suwon Hwaseong.

④ Mina and the man are going to Suwon Hwaseong.

⑤ It will take about 20 minutes to get to Suwon Hwaseong.

11 다음 대화문의 빈칸에 가장 알맞은 표현을 고르시오. (3점)

> A: Excuse me. How can I get to the post office?
> B: Go straight to 1st Street and make a right. It will be on your right.
> A: _____
> B: No, it's not. It is close.
> A: Thank you very much.

① Is it far from here?

② Can you tell me where it is?

③ Would you like to go there with me?

④ Is it going to be raining?

⑤ Are they close?

[12~13] 다음 대화를 읽고 물음에 답하시오.

> (*A phone rings.*)
> B: Hi, Emma. What's up?
> G: Hey, Minsu. Are you free this Saturday?
> B: Yes. Why do you ask?
> G: Well, how about having lunch together?
> B: Sure.
> G: Let's try the new Chinese restaurant, Ming's. It's near the school.
> B: Okay. (A)<u>내가 학교에서 거기까지 어떻게 갈 수 있니?</u>
> G: Come out from the school and go straight to Green Street. Make a left, and the restaurant will be on your left.
> B: All right. Let's meet at 12 o'clock.
> G: Wonderful. See you then.

12 위 대화를 읽고 답할 수 <u>없는</u> 것은? (3점)

① Where is the new restaurant?

② Why did Emma phone Minsu?

③ What time are they going to meet?

④ What are they going to do after lunch?

⑤ What's the name of the new restaurant?

13 위 대화의 밑줄 친 (A)의 우리말을 영작하시오. (4점)

> 조건
> • 주어진 단어를 모두 사용하되 필요시 새로운 단어를 추가할 것
> • 8단어로 쓸 것

(can, how, get, the)

→ _____

14 다음 글의 밑줄 친 문장 ⓐ~ⓔ 중, 어법상 옳은 것만 있는 대로 고른 것은? (4점)

What's your favorite holiday? ⓐ<u>My favorite holiday is Thanksgiving, which is celebrated on the fourth Thursday of November in the United States.</u> ⓑ<u>People usually can relax and spend time together with their family and friends after that.</u> ⓒ <u>It is possible because Thanksgiving is followed by a long weekend.</u> ⓓ<u>On Thanksgiving we have a big meal, the Thanksgiving dinner.</u> We have turkey, potatoes and apple pie. All of them are my favorites. It takes lots of time to cook a turkey. ⓔ<u>I help my mom preparing the dinner all the time.</u> At the dinner table, we give thanks for our family and friends.

① ⓐ, ⓑ   ② ⓐ, ⓒ, ⓔ

③ ⓑ, ⓒ, ⓓ   ④ ⓐ, ⓒ, ⓓ

⑤ ⓒ, ⓓ, ⓔ

[15~16] 다음을 읽고 물음에 답하시오.

Hi, my name is Leila. I live in Delhi, India. I'm going to introduce Diwali, the Festival of Light. Diwali is usually in November. We celebrate Diwali for five days. We don't go to school (**A**)[until / by] the festival finishes, but we do many other things at home. On the first day of the festival, we get up early, clean the house, and decorate it with lots of lights. We also prepare food and drinks for a big party. It is not easy (**B**)[make / to make] the food, but it is fun. While we celebrate Diwali, we don't eat meat or fish. We eat only vegetarian food. It is delicious! We also wear new clothes and visit our friends and family. People dance together and watch fireworks, and children eat lots of sweets and candies. The festival is full of fun and everyone (**C**)[enjoy / enjoys] it.

15 위 글의 괄호 (A), (B), (C) 안에서 어법상 옳은 것은? (3점)

	(A)	(B)	(C)
①	until	to make	enjoys
②	until	to make	enjoy
③	until	make	enjoys
④	by	make	enjoys
⑤	by	to make	enjoy

16 위 글을 읽고 답할 수 <u>없는</u> 것은? (3점)

① What is Diwali?

② For how many days do people celebrate Diwali?

③ What do people eat while they celebrate Diwali?

④ What do people do on each day of the festival?

⑤ What do people decorate their houses with during Diwali?

[17~19] 다음 글을 읽고 물음에 답하시오.

Kiruna Snow Festival
Ebba from Kiruna, Sweden

Winter is my favorite season (A)[because / because of] the Kiruna Snow Festival. The festival starts in the last week of January and goes on (B)[for / during] five or six days. The largest event is the snow design competition. The artists shape huge piles of snow (C)[into / out] animals, buildings, and other beautiful artworks. ⓐ<u>사람들 은 처음부터 끝까지 예술가들이 그들의 작품을 만드는 과정을 본다</u>. My favorite activity is the dog sled ride. It is amazing to fly through a world of snow on a dog sled.

17 위 글의 괄호 (A), (B), (C) 안에서 문맥에 맞는 낱말로 가장 적절한 것은? (4점)

	(A)	(B)	(C)
①	because of	during	into
②	because of	for	into
③	because of	for	out
④	because	during	out
⑤	because	during	into

18 위 글의 밑줄 친 ⓐ와 서로 의미가 통하도록 다음 〈보기〉의 단어들을 사용하여 〈조건〉에 맞게 영작할 때 7번째로 올 단어로 알맞은 것은? (4점)

┌─ 보기 ─────────────────────┐
the beginning / people / end / from / the artists / watch / shaping / their / works / to
└──────────────────────────┘

┌─ 조건 ─────────────────────┐
• 문장은 반드시 people로 시작할 것
• 문장은 반드시 end로 끝낼 것
└──────────────────────────┘

① from

② shaping

③ works

④ beginning

⑤ the

19 위 글을 읽고 답할 수 <u>없는</u> 질문은? (3점)

① When does the festival begin?

② How long does the festival last?

③ What is the largest event of the festival?

④ What is Ebba's favorite season and activity?

⑤ What are the meanings of the beautiful snow artworks?

White Nights Festival

Visitor from St. Petersburg, Russia

ⓐHave you hear of the *White Nights*? ⓑEvery summer, this amazingly thing happens in my hometown. (A)_____ During (가)that time, we hold the White Nights Festival. ⓒThe festival usually starts in May and it lasts for about a month. During the festival, there is a ballet or an opera almost every night.

The most popular event is the Scarlet Sails celebration. ⓓA boat with red sails slowly appear on the river. Soon, fireworks begin and a water show follows. ⓔYou can also hear musicians play beautiful live music.

20 위 글의 내용과 일치하는 것은? (3점)

① 백야 축제는 2년마다 한 번씩 열린다.

② 백야 현상은 5월에만 일어나는 현상이다.

③ 축제 기간 동안 거의 밤마다 예술 공연이 있다.

④ 백야 축제가 끝나면 뒤이어 붉은 돛 축제가 있다.

⑤ 붉은 돛 축하 행사의 오프닝은 물 쇼이다.

21 위 글의 밑줄 친 (가)가 가리키는 것을 우리말로 구체적으로 설명하시오. (4점)

→ _____

22 위 글의 밑줄 친 ⓐ~ⓔ 중 어법에 맞는 것을 모두 고른 것은? (3점)

① ⓐ   ② ⓑ   ③ ⓒ

④ ⓓ   ⑤ ⓔ

23 위 글의 빈칸 (A)에 들어갈 적절한 문장을 주어진 두 단어를 반드시 포함하여 영작하시오. (3점)

get / completely

→ The night sky does not _____.

24 위 글의 내용을 바탕으로 다음 질문에 완전한 영어 문장으로 답하시오. (4점)

Where does the White Nights Festival take place?

→ _____

[25~30] 다음 글을 읽고 물음에 답하시오.

Holi, the Festival of Colors

Amala from Delhi, India

ⓐHoli is the most popular festival in my country. ⓑIt is usually ㉠_____ March. During ⓒthe festival, we say goodbye ㉡_____ cold winter and hello to warm spring. We celebrate the festival everywhere ㉢_____ two days. On the first day, people gather around a big fire ㉣_____ night and sing and dance. (가)The main event begins the next day. Children and adults chase each other ㉤_____ *gulal*. What is *gulal*? ⓓIt is blue, yellow, green and pink powder. ⓔIt's a lot of fun (A)_____ around and throw colorful powder at everyone. We also join street parades!

25 위 글을 읽고 대답할 수 <u>없는</u> 문장은? (3점)

① Where can I buy *gulal*?

② How long does Holi last?

③ In what month is Holi held?

④ Which country do you go to join Holi?

⑤ Why do people call Holi the festival of colors?

28 위 글의 빈칸 (A)에 들어갈 말로 가장 적절한 것은? (3점)

① to run   ② run

③ ran   ④ runs

⑤ running

29 위 글의 빈칸 ㉠~㉤에 들어갈 말로 <u>어색한</u> 것은? (3점)

① ㉠ in

② ㉡ to

③ ㉢ in

④ ㉣ at

⑤ ㉤ with

26 위 글의 밑줄 친 (가)가 가리키는 것으로 가장 알맞은 것은? (4점)

① Making *gulal* with family

② Saying hello to warm spring

③ Decorating houses with colorful things

④ Running around and throwing *gulal* to people

⑤ To gather around a big fire singing and dancing

30 위 글의 내용과 일치하면 T, 일치하지 않으면 F로 표현할 때, 순서대로 짝지어진 것은? (4점)

- *Gulal* is a colorful cake for Holi.
- During the festival, people in India can feel the season changing.
- The main event takes place for two whole days.
- People can take part in street parades on the first day of the festival.

① F-T-T-T

② F-T-F-F

③ F-F-T-T

④ F-F-T-F

⑤ F-T-T-F

27 위 글의 밑줄 친 ⓐ~ⓔ 중 가리키는 것이 같은 것끼리 짝지어진 것은? (3점)

① ⓐ, ⓓ

② ⓐ, ⓑ, ⓒ

③ ⓐ, ⓒ, ⓔ

④ ⓑ, ⓓ

⑤ ⓑ, ⓒ, ⓔ

2학년 영어 2학기 중간고사(6과) 1회

반		점수	
이름			

문항수 : 선택형(27문항) 서술형(3문항)　　20 ．　．　．

◎ 선택형 문항의 답안은 컴퓨터용 수정 싸인펜을 사용하여 OMR 답안지에 바르게 표기하시오.
◎ 서술형 문제는 답을 답안지에 반드시 검정 볼펜으로 쓰시오.
◎ 총 30문항 100점 만점입니다. 문항별 배점은 각 문항에 표시되어 있습니다.

[울산 ○○중]

01 다음 중 단어의 영영풀이가 올바른 것은?　　(3점)

① deaf: not able to hear anything
② lead: to cut something into thin pieces
③ mission: to have a particular type of life
④ half: more than two but not very many
⑤ average: not able to see

[서울 성북구 ○○중]

02 다음 〈보기〉의 영문 뜻풀이에 해당하는 단어로 가장 적절한 것은?　　(3점)

┌─ 보기 ─────────────────────┐
│ move something from one place to another │
└──────────────────────────┘

① peel
② carry
③ chase
④ slice
⑤ decorate

[서울 노원구 ○○중]

03 〈보기〉 문장들의 빈칸에 들어갈 단어가 <u>아닌</u> 것은? (순서 관계 없음)　　(4점)

┌─ 보기 ───────────────────────────┐
│ • Babies are _____ about everything.
│ • I have to _____ quickly to the new school.
│ • Many companies _____ electrical goods in Korea.
│ • The book tells me the way to _____ a happy life.
└──────────────────────────────────┘

① lead　　　　　② adapt
③ spread　　　　④ curious
⑤ produce

[서울 노원구 ○○중]

04 어법상 옳지 <u>않은</u> 것은? (정답 2개)　　(4점)

① She sings as well as he is.
② My boss is as busy as a bee.
③ Sumi can't run as fast as Jiho.
④ The pear is as sweeter than the apple.
⑤ I have two times as many shoes as she.

[서울 노원구 ○○중]

05 다음 빈칸에 알맞은 것은?　　(3점)

┌──────────────────────────────┐
│ A: Look at this. It's a _____.
│ B: What is it for?
│ A: It's for carrying things.
│ B: Oh, really? That's interesting.
└──────────────────────────────┘

① Hanji　　　　② Meok
③ Binyeo　　　④ Jige
⑤ Gama

[6~7] 다음 대화를 읽고 물음에 답하시오.

Judy: How was your weekend, Hojin?

Hojin: I had a great time. I went to a science exhibition with my brother.

Judy: Did you? I heard there were so many interesting things.

Hojin: Yes. Look at this. I bought it there. (A)너는 그것이 무엇인지 알고 있니?

Judy: Well, I'm not sure. What is it?

Hojin: It's a VR headset.

Judy: A VR headset? What is it for?

Hojin: If you wear it, you can experience another world.

Judy: Sounds cool. May I try it?

Hojin: Sure. Here you go.

[8~10] 다음 대화를 읽고 물음에 답하시오.

Yerin: Mom, look at these slippers. I made them in science class.

Mom: ⓐWhy did you make slippers in science class?

Yerin: ⓑThey are not just for wearing.

Mom: Then, (A)_____?

Yerin: Look! ⓒYou can put them on and clean the floor.

Mom: Oh, ⓓso you will clean your room from now on?

Yerin: ⓔSure, I won't. Don't worry about my room, Mom.

[인천 ○○중]

06 위 대화의 (A)를 바르게 영작한 것은? (3점)

① What do you know it is?

② What do you know is it?

③ Do you know what it is?

④ Do you know what is it?

⑤ Do you know it was what is?

[서울 노원구 ○○중]

08 위 대화의 ⓐ~ⓔ 중 흐름상 어색한 것은? (4점)

① ⓐ   ② ⓑ   ③ ⓒ

④ ⓓ   ⑤ ⓔ

[경기 ○○중]

09 위 대화의 흐름상 빈칸 (A)에 가장 알맞은 것은? (3점)

① what is it like

② what are they for

③ who are you talking to

④ do you know what they are

⑤ why didn't you make real slippers

[인천 ○○중]

07 위 대화의 내용과 일치하는 것은? (3점)

① Hojin은 남동생과 함께 과학 박람회에 다녀왔다.

② Hojin은 과학 박람회가 즐겁지 않다고 이야기했다.

③ Hojin은 과학 박람회에서 VR헤드셋을 경품으로 받았다.

④ Judy는 VR헤드셋이 무엇인지 정확히 알고 있었다.

⑤ Hojin은 Judy에게 VR헤드셋을 빌려주지 않을 것이다.

[서울 성북구 ○○중]

10 위 대화의 주제로 가장 적절한 것은? (3점)

① How to Make Slippers

② Slippers for Science Class

③ Wearing Slippers Every Day

④ Giving Slippers as a Present

⑤ Slippers for Cleaning the Floor

11 아래 광고문에서 찾고 있는 사람으로 가장 거리가 먼 것은?
(3점)

> We're looking for someone...
>   who is healthy.
>   who is creative and curious.
>   who can get along with others.
>   who can adapt to a new environment quickly.
>   who has a good sense of humor.

① 사람들을 잘 배려하고 어울리는 재석
② 신체 건강한 국가 대표 출신의 장훈
③ 어느 곳에서나 빠르게 적응하는 희철
④ 무슨 음식이든 잘 먹는 긍정적인 호동
⑤ 유쾌하고 유머 감각이 뛰어난 수근

[12~13] 다음 글을 읽고 물음에 답하시오.

> Today I will tell you about Alexander Graham Bell. He was an inventor. He was interested in sound. He invented the telephone. In addition, his mother and wife were _____ . So he also made some inventions for _____ people and opened a school for them. I hope to become a great inventor like him.

12 위 글을 읽고 아래의 설명을 근거로 빈칸에 공통으로 들어갈 알맞은 단어는?
(3점)

> • unable to hear anything or unable to hear very well
> • someone who is unable to hear because their ears are damaged

① deaf
② blind
③ artist
④ inventor
⑤ scientist

13 위 글을 통해 알 수 없는 내용은?
(3점)

① Alexandar Graham Bell은 발명가였다.
② Alexandar Graham Bell은 딸이 있었다.
③ Alexandar Graham Bell은 학교를 열었다.
④ Alexandar Graham Bell은 소리에 관심이 있었다.
⑤ 나는 Alexandar Graham Bell과 같은 훌륭한 발명가가 되기를 희망한다.

14 다음 글의 ⓐ~ⓔ 중 내용상 어색한 문장은?
(4점)

> My name is Suji Lee from Korea. I'm 15 years old. ⓐI want to go to Mars because I've been curious about space. ⓑI'm friendly and I enjoy making friends. I'm good at taking photos. ⓒTo apply, send us a short video which includes the answers to the following questions.
> ⓓI'm the perfect person for this mission because I can adapt to a new environment quickly. ⓔAlthough I'm young, I can communicate well with others. Give me the chance to live on Mars!

① ⓐ
② ⓑ
③ ⓒ
④ ⓓ
⑤ ⓔ

Dear Teacher Mike,

(A)When I came back home after school, I was thirsty. So I put some ice in a glass and poured some water in ⓐit. When I drank ⓑit, (B)I saw that there were little water drops outside the glass. Where did the water drops come from? There were no water drops when I poured the water in ⓒit. Thank you.

From Minjun

Dear Minjun,

(C)You can't see it with your eyes, but there is a little bit of water in the air. Because you put ice in the glass, the glass became cooler than the air around ⓓit, and ⓔit cools the air. (D)When the air is cooled, it changes from water to gas. So you can see the small water drops. (E)Science can explain the everyday happenings around us. (가)네가 질문을 할 때, 과학으로 가는 문은 언제나 열린단다. So don't be afraid to wonder "Why?"

From Teacher Mike

15 위 글의 밑줄 친 ⓐ~ⓔ 중 가리키는 것이 <u>다른</u> 것은? (3점)

① ⓐ   ② ⓑ   ③ ⓒ

④ ⓓ   ⑤ ⓔ

16 위 글의 밑줄 친 (A)~(E) 중 흐름에 맞지 <u>않는</u> 문장은? (3점)

① (A)   ② (B)   ③ (C)

④ (D)   ⑤ (E)

17 위 글의 밑줄 친 (가)의 우리말을 주어진 단어를 바르게 배열하여 영작하시오. (4점)

the / you / to / question / when / opens / ask / science / door / a / always

→ _____

18 주어진 글의 다음에 이어질 글의 순서로 가장 적절한 것은? (4점)

I'm going to talk about Mars. Scientists at NASA are trying to change Mars into another Earth.

(A) The next thing is to grow plants for food and air. On Earth, NASA is already growing plants on rocks from Mars. Scientists think plants and air will be able to change the red planet into a blue planet.

(B) And they think Mars is the answer. Changing Mars will not be an easy thing to do. The most important thing is to make Mars warm. Then the ice under the ground will turn into water.

(C) They don't think people can live on Earth forever. So people will have to move to another planet someday.

So, do you think scientists can change Mars?

We only know a little about Mars. It's only the beginning. But someday people will go to Mars. It won't be easy. It will be a long trip. But we already went to the moon. Mars is next.

① (A)-(B)-(C)   ② (A)-(C)-(B)

③ (B)-(C)-(A)   ④ (C)-(A)-(B)

⑤ (C)-(B)-(A)

ⓐMars, however, has some differences from Earth. First, ⓑMars is about half the size of Earth. It is the second smallest planet in the solar system. Second, a year on Mars is (가)약 두 배 길다 a year on Earth. Third, ⓒMars is much colder than Earth. On average, it is about -60℃ on Mars. This is because ⓓMars is farther away from the Sun than Earth.

(A)비록 우리가 지금 당장 화성에서 살 수 있다고 말할 수는 없지만, it is exciting to imagine this new world. ⓔWho knows? You could be the first Korean on Mars!

19 위 글의 밑줄 친 ⓐ~ⓔ와 의미가 전혀 <u>다른</u> 문장은?　(3점)

① ⓐ: Mars and Earth are different in some ways.

② ⓑ: Mars is twice as big as Earth.

③ ⓒ: Earth is much warmer than Mars.

④ ⓓ: Earth is closer to the Sun than Mars.

⑤ ⓔ: No one knows.

20 위 글의 밑줄 친 (A)의 우리말과 의미가 같도록 〈보기〉의 주어진 단어를 모두 포함하여 바르게 영작하시오.　(4점)

> say / although / can / right

→ _____

21 위 글의 밑줄 친 (가)를 as ~ as 구문을 활용하여 우리말 뜻에 맞게 영작하시오. (4 words)　(4점)

→ _____

Mars, ⓐthe Second Earth?

Although ⓑthere are many books and movies about Mars, no one has been ⓒthere yet. These days, scientists are looking at Mars as ⓓa new home. In fact, NASA and some companies are trying to send people ⓔthere right now.

The big question is, "Can people live on Mars?" Many scientists believe so for several reasons. First, they think that there is water on Mars. This is great because water is necessary for all life. Second, Mars has hard land to build houses and buildings on. Third, the length of (1)_____ (2)_____ (3)_____ (4)_____ (5)_____ on Earth. In addition, Mars also has four seasons. So, people can (가)lead similar lives. Lastly, Mars is not very far. It is the second closest planet to Earth.

22 위 글의 밑줄 친 ⓐ~ⓔ 중, 지칭하는 대상이 <u>다른</u> 하나는?　(3점)

① ⓐ　　　② ⓑ　　　③ ⓒ

④ ⓓ　　　⑤ ⓔ

23 위 글의 내용과 일치하는 것은?　　　　　　(3점)

① 화성에는 3개의 계절이 있다.

② 화성에 가 본 지구인들이 있다.

③ 화성은 지구에 첫 번째로 가까운 행성이다.

④ 과학자들은 화성에 물과 단단한 땅이 있다고 믿는다.

⑤ 과학자들은 화성에 사람이 살기 어렵다고 생각한다.

25 위 글의 밑줄 친 (가)lead의 의미는?　　　　(3점)

① 적용하다　　　　② 생활하다

③ 안내하다　　　　④ 생산하다

⑤ 지원하다

---

24 위 글의 빈칸 (1)~(5)를 다음 주어진 〈보기〉를 이용하여 완성할 때, (5)에 들어갈 표현으로 알맞은 것은?　(4점)

보기
that / is / day and night / on Mars / similar to

해석
화성의 밤낮 길이는 지구의 밤낮 길이와 비슷

① that　　　　　② is

③ day and night　④ on Mars

⑤ similar to

[26~30] 다음 글을 읽고 물음에 답하시오.

Live on MARS!

(A)_____

　The Korea Space Organization (KSO) is looking for people to go to MARS! Our mission is to build a city on Mars.

We're looking for someone...
- (B)_____ is healthy.
- (B)_____ is creative and curious.
- (B)_____ can get along with others.
- (B)_____ can adapt to a new environment quickly.

　To apply, send us a short video. The video must include the answers to the following questions:

1. Why do you want to go to Mars?
2. Do you have a good sense of humor?
3. Why are you the perfect person for this mission?
4. What are you good at?

This is a chance of a lifetime, so don't miss out!

26 위 글의 흐름상 (A)에 들어갈 말로 가장 적절한 것은? (3점)

① Why is Mars the second Earth?

② Do you want to live on another planet?

③ Are you interested in studying the solar system?

④ Why don't you apply to NASA to be an astronaut?

⑤ What do you know about the most mysterious planet?

29 다음 글을 읽고 대답할 수 <u>없는</u> 질문은? (3점)

① What is KSO's mission?

② What is KSO doing these days?

③ How can KSO send people to Mars?

④ What kind of people is KSO looking for?

⑤ What content does the video need to include?

27 위 글의 Mars에 관한 광고문의 내용과 일치하지 <u>않는</u> 것은? (3점)

① 지원자는 젊고 건강에 문제가 없어야 한다.

② 지원하기 위해 비디오를 찍어 제출해야 한다.

③ 창의적이고 호기심이 많은 지원자를 찾고 있다.

④ 화성에서 도시를 건설할 지원자를 모집하고 있다.

⑤ 지원자는 새로운 환경에 빨리 적응할 수 있어야 한다.

30 위 글을 보고 작성한 지원서입니다. 빠진 내용은 무엇일까요? (4점)

My name is Suji Lee from Korea. I'm 15 years old. I want to go to Mars because I've been curious about space. I'm good at taking photos. So I can take a beautiful picture of Mars.

I'm the perfect person for this mission because I can adapt to a new environment quickly. Although I'm young, I can use my power and energy to build a city on Mars. Give me the chance to live on Mars!

① Why do you want to go to Mars?

② Do you have a good sense of humor?

③ Why are you the perfect person for this mission?

④ What are you good at?

⑤ 빠진 내용이 없음.

28 위 글의 빈칸 (B)에 들어갈 적절한 말은? (3점)

① what   ② who

③ which   ④ where

⑤ how

2학년 영어 2학기 중간고사(6과) 2회

문항수 : 선택형(25문항) 서술형(5문항)   20 . . .

◎ 선택형 문항의 답안은 컴퓨터용 수정 싸인펜을 사용하여 OMR 답안지에 바르게 표기하시오.
◎ 서술형 문제는 답을 답안지에 반드시 검정 볼펜으로 쓰시오.
◎ 총 30문항 100점 만점입니다. 문항별 배점은 각 문항에 표시되어 있습니다.

[인천 ○○중]

01 다음 중 빈칸에 공통으로 들어갈 단어로 가장 적절한 것은?
(3점)

> • I usually _____ up early in the morning.
> • We are looking for someone who can _____ along with other people.

① help   ② get   ③ do
④ bring   ⑤ buy

[경기 ○○중]

02 다음 밑줄 친 부분의 의미가 같은 것은?
(4점)

① It will take about 30 minutes.
   What do you think about that?
② People can lead similar lives.
   She leads a peaceful life in her village.
③ The sky doesn't get completely dark.
   How can I get to the subway station?
④ She studied very hard to pass the test.
   Mars has hard land to build a house on.
⑤ This action movie lasts for two hours.
   What did you do on weekends last year?

[서울 광진구 ○○중]

03 다음 중 밑줄 친 단어의 쓰임이 어색한 것은?
(3점)

① He peels butter on bread.
② The average of 10, 8, and 6 is 8.
③ Alice grew up in a good environment.
④ We collected dry sticks for the campfire.
⑤ There is a reason why they don't want to come.

[서울 노원구 ○○중]

04 어법상 옳은 것은? (정답 2개)
(3점)

① During she was reading, I cooked the dinner.
② They arrived while we were having dinner.
③ She joined the meeting even if her sickness.
④ Despite of being tired, he stayed up all night.
⑤ Although the weather was bad, we went on a picnic.

05 대화의 흐름이 자연스러운 것은? (3점)

① A: Can you recommend a good movie?
   B: Try *Star Wars*. I didn't really like it.

② A: Have you ever seen a movie *Titanic*?
   B: Yes, I haven't seen it yet.

③ A: Is the post office far from here?
   B: No, it's not.

④ A: How long will it take to get to the bank?
   B: All right. I am almost ready.

⑤ A: Excuse me. How can I get to the library?
   B: Oh, the library? Cross the street and you can find it next to the hospital.
   A: You're welcome.

06 위 대화를 통해 알 수 있는 것은? (3점)

① 호진에게는 여동생이 한 명 있다.
② Judy는 과학 전시회에 갔다.
③ 호진은 오래전부터 VR 헤드셋에 대해 알고 있었다.
④ 호진은 VR 헤드셋의 작동 원리를 정확히 알고 있다.
⑤ VR 헤드셋을 통해서 신세계를 경험할 수 있다.

07 위 대화의 밑줄 친 (A), (B)를 다음의 〈조건〉에 맞게 영작하시오. (4점)

> **조건**
> 1. what / be / do / know / for / it / you
> 2. 필요한 경우 단어의 형태를 변화시킬 것.

(A) _____

(B) _____

[6~7] 다음 대화를 읽고 물음에 답하시오.

Judy: How was your weekend, Hojin?
Hojin: I had a great time. I went to a science exhibition with my brother.
Judy: Did you? My best friend told me that there were so many interesting things.
Hojin: Yes. Look at this. I bought it there. (A)너 이게 뭔지 알아?
Judy: Well, I'm not sure. What is it?
Hojin: It's a VR headset.
Judy: A VR headset? (B)이건 어디에 쓰는 건데?
Hojin: If you wear it, there will be a new world.
Judy: Sounds cool. May I try it?
Hojin: Sure. Here you go.

08 (A)에 들어갈 말로 가장 자연스러운 것은? (3점)

> M: Jane, look at this. It's a Jige.
> W: I have never seen it before. What is it for?
> M: (A)_____
> W: Oh, really? That's interesting.

① It's for making ink.
② It's for carrying people.
③ It's for decorating your hair.
④ It's for carrying many different things.
⑤ It's for slicing vegetables and fruit regularly.

[9~10] 다음 글을 읽고 물음에 답하시오.

Teacher: Hello, class! Sihyun is today's speaker for show and tell. Sihyun?

Sihyun: Hi, class! (A)_____? He is ⓐAlexander Graham Bell. Bell was a scientist and inventor who was interested in sound. What did he invent? Yes, the telephone! His mother and wife were deaf, so he also made some inventions for deaf people and opened a school for them.

Teacher: Excellent, Sihyun! Do you guys have any questions?

[서울 성북구 ○○중]

09 위 글의 ⓐ에 대한 설명으로 **틀린** 것은? (3점)

① 과학자이자 발명가였다.

② 소리에 관심이 있었다.

③ 전화기를 발명하였다.

④ 어머니와 부인이 시각장애인이었다.

⑤ 특정 장애를 가진 사람들을 위한 학교를 세웠다.

[서울 성북구 ○○중]

10 위 글의 (A)에 들어갈 문장을 다음 〈보기〉의 단어를 모두 사용하여 완성하시오. (단어 추가나 변형 없이 배열만 하시오.) (4점)

> 보기
>
> do / is / man / you / who / know / this

→ _____

[부산 ○○중]

11 자연스러운 대화가 되도록 (A)~(E)를 바르게 배열하시오. (4점)

(A) Do you know what this is?

(B) Oh, is there butter in it?

(C) Um, it looks like a glue stick.

(D) Yes, you can spread butter on the bread with it.

(E) No, it's a butter stick.

① (A)-(B)-(C)-(D)-(E)

② (A)-(C)-(E)-(B)-(D)

③ (A)-(C)-(B)-(E)-(D)

④ (A)-(E)-(D)-(B)-(C)

⑤ (A)-(E)-(B)-(D)-(C)

[12~13] 다음 글을 읽고 물음에 답하시오.

Do you want to live on another planet? The Korea Space Organization (KSO) is ⓐlooking for people to go to MARS! Our mission is to build a city on Mars. So, we need someone who is healthy, creative and curious, can ⓑget along with others and adapt to a new environment quickly.

To apply, send us a short video. The video must include the answers to ⓒthe following questions:

1. Why do you want to go to Mars?

2. Do you have ⓓa good sense of humor?

3. Why are you the perfect person for this mission?

This is ⓔa chance of a lifetime, so don't miss out!

12 위 글의 밑줄 친 ⓐ~ⓔ 중 우리말 뜻이 잘못된 것은? (3점)

① ⓐ: 사람들을 찾고 있다

② ⓑ: 다른 사람들과 잘 지내다

③ ⓒ: 불필요한 질문들

④ ⓓ: 뛰어난 유머 감각

⑤ ⓔ: 일생일대의 기회

[14~16] 다음 글을 읽고 물음에 답하시오.

When Minjun came back home after school, he was thirsty. So he put some ice in a glass and poured some water in ⓐit. When he drank it, he saw that there were little water drops outside the glass. He wondered where the water drops outside the glass came from because there were no water drops when he poured the water in the glass. What happened to the glass?

(A) Although we can't see it with our eyes, there is a little bit of water in the air. (B) Because Minjun put ice in the glass, the glass became cooler than the air around ⓑit. (C) And the glass cools the air outside the glass. (D) When the air is cooled, ⓒit changes from gas to water. (E) Science can explain the everyday happenings around us. The door to science opens when we ask a question. So don't be afraid to wonder "Why?"

---

13 위 글에 따라 수지가 KSO에 보낼 동영상의 대본을 다음과 같이 준비하였다. 내용에 비추어 볼 때, ⓐ~ⓔ 중 가장 적절하지 않은 것은? (4점)

My name is Suji Lee from South Korea. I'm 15 years old. I'm the perfect person for this mission. Let me tell you the reasons.

ⓐFor my health, I exercise regularly. I am very serious in everything, so ⓑI don't usually make jokes and laugh at funny things. I really want to go to Mars because ⓒI've been curious about space. I'm friendly and ⓓI can communicate well with others. ⓔI also like making new friends in a new place.

Give me the chance to live on Mars!

① ⓐ　　　② ⓑ　　　③ ⓒ

④ ⓓ　　　⑤ ⓔ

---

14 위 글의 흐름으로 보아, (A)~(E) 중 주어진 문장이 들어가기에 가장 적절한 곳은? (3점)

So there were the small water drops outside the glass.

① (A)　　　② (B)　　　③ (C)

④ (D)　　　⑤ (E)

15 위 글의 밑줄 친 ⓐ~ⓒ가 가리키는 것을 본문에서 찾아 쓰시오. (3점)

ⓐ: _____

ⓑ: _____

ⓒ: _____

[17~21] 다음 글을 읽고 물음에 답하시오.

> Mars, however, has some ⓐ_____ from Earth. First, Mars is about half the size of Earth. (A) It is the second smallest planet in the solar system. Second, a year on Mars is about twice as long as a year on Earth. (B) Third, Mars is much colder than Earth. (C) This is because Mars is farther away from the Sun than Earth. (D) ⓑ_____ no one can answer the big question right now, it is exciting to imagine this new world. (E) Who knows? (가)_____
> _____

17 위 글의 빈칸 ⓐ, ⓑ에 들어갈 표현으로 올바른 것은? (3점)

	ⓐ	ⓑ
①	differences	Although
②	differences	In spite of
③	similarity	Although
④	similarity	In spite of
⑤	similarity	Despite

16 위 글의 내용과 일치하는 것은? (3점)

① No one could give the answer to Minjun's question.

② The everyday happenings around us can't be explained by science.

③ Minjun wanted to know where the water drops outside the glass came from.

④ Before ice was put in the glass, the glass became cooler than the air around it.

⑤ When Minjun was thirsty, he saw that there were little water drops outside the glass.

18 위 글의 흐름으로 보아 주어진 문장이 들어가기에 가장 적절한 곳은? (3점)

On average, it is about –60°C on Mars.

① (A) ② (B) ③ (C)

④ (D) ⑤ (E)

19 위 글을 읽고 대답할 수 없는 질문은? (3점)

① What is the second smallest planet in the solar system?

② How much bigger is Earth than Mars?

③ How much longer is a year on Mars than a year on Earth?

④ What is the average temperature on Mars?

⑤ How far is it from Mars to the Sun?

20 위 글의 빈칸 (가)에 들어갈 가장 적절한 말은? (3점)

① Mars won't be our next home in the future!

② New world isn't always pleasant for us!

③ Our imagination does not take us far!

④ You can't answer all the questions!

⑤ You could go to Mars for the first time!

21 위 글을 읽고 화성이 지구와 다른 점 세 가지를 찾아 우리말로 쓰시오. (6점)

(1) _____

(2) _____

(3) _____

[22~26] 다음 글을 읽고 물음에 답하시오.

(A)Live on MARS!

Do you want ⓐto live on another planet?

The Korea space Space Organization (KSO) is (B)looking for people ⓑto go to MARS! Our mission is ⓒto build a city on Mars.

We're looking for someone...
who is healthy.
who is (C)creative and curious.
who can (D)get along with others.
who can adapt to new environment quickly.

ⓓTo apply, send us a short video. The video must include the answers ⓔto the following questions:

1. Why do you want to go Mars?
2. Do you have a good sense of humor?
3. Why are you the perfect person for this mission?

This is a chance of a lifetime, so don't (E)miss out!

22 위 글의 밑줄 친 ⓐ~ⓔ 중 쓰임이 다른 하나는? (3점)

① ⓐ   ② ⓑ   ③ ⓒ

④ ⓓ   ⑤ ⓔ

23 What is the genre of this text? (3점)

① diary

② interview

③ advertisement

④ poem

⑤ novel

26 위 글의 내용과 일치하지 <u>않는</u> 것은? (4점)

① KSO has a mission to build a city on Mars.

② KSO is looking for people who can get along with others.

③ The video must include why you want to go to Mars.

④ People who want to apply must send a short video to KSO.

⑤ The video must include the way you can adapt to a new environment quickly.

24 위 글의 (A)~(E) 중 의미가 옳은 것은? (3점)

① (A) Live: 생방송인

② (B) look for: ~을 돌보다

③ (C) creative: 의사소통을 잘하는

④ (D) get along with: ~와 잘 지내다

⑤ (E) miss out: 후회하다

[27~30] 다음 글을 읽고 물음에 답하시오.

25 위 글을 통해 답할 수 <u>없는</u> 질문을 <u>모두</u> 고른 것은? (3점)

① What does KSO mean?

② What is KSO's mission?

③ How can the city on Mars be built?

④ How can people apply for KSO's mission?

⑤ What should people do when they miss the chance?

Mars, the Second Earth?

Although there are many books and movies about Mars, no one has been there yet. These days, scientists are looking at Mars as a new home. In fact, NASA and some companies are trying to send people there right now.

The big question is, "(A)_____"
Many scientists believe so for several reasons. First, they think that there is water on Mars. This is great because water is necessary for all life. Second, (B)Mars has hard land to build houses and buildings on. Third, the length of day and night on Mars is similar to that on Earth. (C)_____, Mars also has four seasons. So, people can lead similar lives. Lastly, Mars is not very far. It is the second closest planet to Earth.

27 위 글의 빈칸 (A)에 들어갈 알맞은 말은? (3점)

① Can people live on Mars?

② Should people travel into space?

③ Can scientists complete the mission?

④ Do humans need a new place to live?

⑤ What do people need for living in Mars?

29 위 글의 화성에 대한 내용과 일치하는 것은? (3점)

① It is not like Earth.

② It has only one season.

③ Scientists have been there.

④ NASA wants to send people there.

⑤ The length of day is longer than that of night.

28 위 글의 밑줄 친 (B)와 같은 의미의 문장이 되도록 주어진 단어를 사용하여 바르게 영작하시오. (4점)

> Mars / to / possible / land / because / has / it / it / houses / is / hard / build / buildings / and / on

→ _____

_____

30 위 글의 빈칸 (C)에 들어갈 알맞은 말은? (3점)

① However

② In short

③ For example

④ Therefore

⑤ In addition

반		점수	
이름			

문항수 : 선택형(28문항) 서술형(2문항)　　　20 ． ． ．

◎ 선택형 문항의 답안은 컴퓨터용 수정 싸인펜을 사용하여 OMR 답안지에 바르게 표기하시오.
◎ 서술형 문제는 답을 답안지에 반드시 검정 볼펜으로 쓰시오.
◎ 총 30문항 100점 만점입니다. 문항별 배점은 각 문항에 표시되어 있습니다.

[경기 ○○중]

01 다음 단어의 우리말 뜻풀이가 옳은 것은?　　(3점)

① mix: 섞다
② explain: 쉬다
③ prove: 감추다
④ lie: 진실을 말하다
⑤ express: 안내하다

[서울 양천구 ○○중]

02 다음 주어진 두 문장을 〈조건〉에 맞게 같은 의미가 되도록 완성하시오.　　(4점)

조건
• 한 칸에 한 단어만 쓸 것.
• 어법상 자연스러운 문장이 되도록 쓸 것.

She was too tired to do her homework.
→ She was ＿＿＿＿＿ ＿＿＿＿＿
＿＿＿＿＿ ＿＿＿＿＿ her homework.

[서울 마포구 ○○중]

03 다음 중 어법상 올바른 문장은?　　(4점)

① I visited a museum where is located in New York.
② Look at the baby that is crying in the stroller.
③ You can order anything what you want.
④ He was the third student which passed the exam.
⑤ I'm making a calendar which are full of our pictures.

[서울 송파구 ○○중]

04 다음 두 사람의 대화 중 빈칸에 들어가기에 가장 적절한 것은?　　(2점)

A: ＿＿＿＿＿＿＿＿＿＿＿＿＿＿＿＿
B: It was really nice.

① How was your trip?
② How about going on a trip?
③ What did you like about the trip?
④ Where will you go for your trip?
⑤ Why did you like the trip?

[경북 ○○중]

05 다음 짝지어진 대화 중 어색한 것은?　　(3점)

① A: You got a new smartphone.
　B: Yes, I did. I'm really happy with it.
② A: Guess what I'm doing.
　B: I guess you're playing the piano.
③ A: May I help you?
　B: Yes. I'm looking for a backpack.
④ A: Can you help me clean the board?
　B: No problem. I have to go.
⑤ A: How about this navy backpack?
　B: Oh, that looks good. I'll take it.

M: Mina, can you recommend a good pizza restaurant?
W: Why don't you try Antonio's? It's my ⓐ _____ .
M: What do you like about it?
W: The food is delicious. I ⓑ_____ the bulgogi pizza.

(A): Okay, I'll check it out. Thanks.
(B): How are the prices?
(C): It's a little slow on the weekends.
(D): How do you like the service?
(E): I think the prices are good, too.

*M: Brian, W: Mina

06 위 대화의 빈칸 ⓐ, ⓑ에 들어갈 단어로 알맞게 나열된 것은?

(3점)

	ⓐ	ⓑ
①	best	steal
②	favorite	recommend
③	business	command
④	bad	suggest
⑤	love	advise

07 위 대화에서 미나의 말 다음에 이어지는 (A)~(E)의 대화를 순서대로 가장 자연스럽게 나열한 것은? (4점)

① (E)-(D)-(A)-(C)-(B)
② (C)-(D)-(B)-(A)-(E)
③ (A)-(B)-(C)-(D)-(E)
④ (B)-(E)-(D)-(C)-(A)
⑤ (D)-(C)-(A)-(E)-(B)

08 다음 대화의 내용과 일치하는 것은? (3점)

① Brian이 Antonio's 식당을 추천하고 있다.
② Brian은 Antonio's 식당의 불고기 피자를 좋아한다.
③ Mina는 Antonio's 식당의 가격대에 대해서 부정적으로 평가하고 있다.
④ Mina는 Antonio's 식당의 서비스에 대해서도 평가를 내리고 있다.
⑤ Antonio's 식당은 주말에는 문을 닫는다.

[9~10] 다음 대화를 읽고 물음에 답하시오.

B: Hi, Suji. How did you like your trip to Gyeongju?
G: I was very happy with it.
B: Where did you visit?

(A) Bulguksa. It was a wonderful place, too.
(B) Where else did you go?
(C) I visited Cheomseongdae. It was great.

B: Sounds like the perfect trip.
G: Yeah, but walking up to Seokguram was difficult.
B: _____

09 위 대화가 자연스럽도록 (A)~(C)를 바르게 배열한 것은? (3점)

① (A)-(C)-(B)
② (A)-(B)-(C)
③ (B)-(A)-(C)
④ (B)-(C)-(A)
⑤ (C)-(B)-(A)

10 위 대화의 마지막 말에 이어질 남자의 대답으로 가장 적절한 것은? (3점)

① I don't really like going to Gyeongju.

② I will never to go Seokguram again.

③ Maybe, it was a good experience for you.

④ It's probably waste of time to walk there.

⑤ Maybe you should have visited Seokguram.

[11~13] 다음 대화를 읽고 물음에 답하시오.

A: May I help you?

(A) How about this navy one then? It has side pockets.
(B) Yes. (가)I'm looking for a backpack. Can you recommend one?
(C) My old backpack was red, so I want a different color.
(D) How about this red one? Red is the most popular color these days.

A: Oh, that looks good. (나)I'll take it.

11 위 대화의 (A)~(D)를 흐름에 맞게 가장 잘 배열한 것은? (4점)

① (B) - (A) - (D) - (C)

② (B) - (D) - (C) - (A)

③ (C) - (B) - (A) - (D)

④ (D) - (A) - (B) - (C)

⑤ (D) - (C) - (B) - (A)

12 위 대화의 밑줄 친 (가)와 바꾸어 쓸 수 <u>없는</u> 표현은? (3점)

① I can see a backpack.

② Do you have a backpack?

③ I'd like to buy a backpack.

④ Where can I find a backpack?

⑤ I'm trying to find a backpack.

13 위 대화의 밑줄 친 (나)가 뜻하는 것은? (3점)

① I will buy it.

② I will lend it.

③ I will send it.

④ I will refund it.

⑤ I will borrow it.

14 다음 대화의 (A), (B), (C)에 들어갈 단어를 알맞게 짝지은 것은? (3점)

A: Hey, can you (A)[order / recommend] a good musical for me?
B: How about *The Lion King*? The dancing is (B)[boring / amazing].
A: Okay. Sounds good.
B: I'm sure you'll (C)[like / fail] it.

	(A)	(B)	(C)
①	order	boring	like
②	order	amazing	fail
③	recommend	boring	like
④	recommend	amazing	like
⑤	recommend	amazing	fail

15 다음 글의 종류로 가장 적절한 것은? (3점)

Title: Harry Potter
Genre: fantasy
Author: J. K. Rowling
Rating: ★★★★☆

Harry Potter is a fantasy novel. It was written by J. K. Rowling. Harry Potter is the main character of the book. When Harry goes to magic school, his adventures begin. I especially like the friendship of Harry and his friends. The book was very interesting, so I couldn't put it down. I strongly recommend it to everyone.

① play ② review ③ letter
④ article ⑤ advertisement

16 다음 글을 참고하여 주어진 문장(ⓐ~①)을 Opinion과 Fact로 분류하여 기호를 쓰시오. (5점)

Opinions express people's feelings like, "The desert is beautiful." You can't say that it's true or not. But, facts can be proven. For example, "The Atacama Desert is in Chile," is a fact. You can check that on the map.

ⓐ Steven Spielberg is a living legend.
ⓑ Steven Spielberg directed the movie *A.I.: Artificial Intelligence*.
ⓒ Steven Spielberg made a film about the shark.
ⓓ Steven Spielberg was born on December 18, 1947 in Ohio, U.S.
ⓔ My favorite director is Steven Spielberg.
① Steven Spielberg is most likely the best moviemaker the Hollywood has ever known.

→ (1) Opinion - _____
(2) Fact - _____

[17~19] 다음 글을 읽고 물음에 답하시오.

Ads don't always tell the truth. Here are the ads from two pizza restaurants. The first one says, "Once you eat, you can't stop." The second one says, "8 ⓐout of 10 customers come back to our restaurant." ⓑWhich one would you order from? The second restaurant ⓒmight seem a little boring. Maybe you would order from the first one.

What's the difference between the two ads? One uses an opinion and the other uses a fact. Facts are true information. You can ask the question, "Is it true or not?" (A)_____, opinions express people's feelings. We can't say they're true or false. They're just someone's thoughts. (B)_____, the first ad expresses an opinion and ⓓthe second ad give a fact.

Most ads have both facts and opinions in them. So be more careful when you read advertisements. You have to make a smart choice ⓔbased on both facts and opinions.

17 위 글의 빈칸 (A), (B)에 들어갈 말로 가장 적절한 것은? (4점)

(A)	(B)
① In case	Instead
② As a result	For instance
③ For example	In this way
④ Nevertheless	However
⑤ On the other hand	Therefore

18 위 글의 ⓐ~ⓔ 중 어법상 옳지 않은 것은? (3점)

① ⓐ ② ⓑ ③ ⓒ
④ ⓓ ⑤ ⓔ

19 위 글의 제목으로 가장 적절한 것은? (3점)

① Make Pizza Properly

② Requirements of Good Advertisements

③ Be a Wise Consumer by Analyzing Ads

④ Various Ways of Making Advertisements

⑤ Just Trust the Information from Advertisements

20 다음 대화를 읽고 Emma에 대해 알맞게 표현한 것은? (4점)

Emma: What are you doing, Kyle?

Kyle: Oh, Emma. I'm watching the movie, *Y-Men 7* on my computer.

Emma: How is it?

Kyle: Don't ask. It's so boring that I want to cry.

Emma: I'm sorry to hear that.

Kyle: I'm so mad. The movie advertisement said it was "The Most Exciting Movie of the Year."

Emma: Well, you can't believe everything that you read.

① She thinks Kyle should believe *Y-Men 7* advertisement.

② She thinks *Y-Men 7* is a great movie and everything about the movie is true.

③ She believes there may be lies or exaggerations in everything she reads.

④ She thinks everything in the world is so simple that she can believe what she reads.

⑤ She believes people can lie easily but when you read something, you should trust what you read.

[21~25] 다음 글을 읽고 물음에 답하시오.

Making Good Choices

Emma: What are you doing, Kyle?

Kyle: Oh, Emma. I'm watching the movie, *Y-Men 7* on my computer.

Emma: How is it?

Kyle: Don't ask. (A)그것이 너무 지루해서 울고 싶어.

Emma: I'm sorry to hear that.

Kyle: I'm so mad. The movie advertisement said it was "The Most Exciting Movie of the Year."

Emma: Well, you can't believe everything that you read.

Kyle: They lied on the advertisement. I'm going to ask for my money back.

Emma: Hold on, Kyle! They didn't really lie because they used opinions, not facts.

Kyle: Huh? (B)I'm not following you.

Emma: Opinions express people's feelings like, "The desert is beautiful." You can't say that it's true or not. (가)_____ For example, "The Atacama Desert is in Chile," is a fact. You can check that on the map.

21 위 글을 읽고 답할 수 없는 질문은? (3점)

① Why is Kyle mad?

② What does Emma want to ask for?

③ How does Kyle like the movie, *Y-Men 7*?

④ What did the advertisement say about *Y-Men 7*?

⑤ Why is the sentence, "The Atacama Desert is in Chile", a fact?

22 위 글의 밑줄 친 우리말 (A)를 영어로 가장 바르게 옮긴 것은?

(3점)

① It's bored to want to cry.

② It's so bored that I want to cry.

③ It's so boring that I want to cry.

④ It is boring that I wanted to cry.

⑤ It was boring, so that I wanted to cry.

23 위 글의 (B)가 의미하는 바로 가장 적절하지 <u>않은</u> 것은? (4점)

① I don't get it.

② I don't understand you.

③ I will not follow your tips.

④ I can't understand it clearly.

⑤ It is difficult to understand.

24 위 글의 빈칸 (가)에 들어갈 말로 가장 적절한 것은? (3점)

① But, facts can be proven.

② Some ads don't tell the truth.

③ We don't need to check the fact.

④ So we shouldn't believe opinions.

⑤ It depends on what people believe.

25 위 글의 Emma의 설명으로 미루어 볼 때, Fact를 말하고 있는 사람은? (3점)

① 재국: Frozen is a wonderful movie.

② 지선: Paris is one of the cities in France.

③ 현정: Korean food is the best in the world.

④ 경재: It's fun to solve puzzles with friends.

⑤ 유리: History is the most important subject.

[26~30] 다음 글을 읽고 물음에 답하시오.

Kyle: Okay.... But what's the ⓐconnection with movies?

Emma: Let me explain. What's your favorite movie?

Kyle: It's *Forrest Gump*.

Emma: Okay. Let's look for its ⓑadvertisement. What does it say?

Kyle: It says, "Winner of 6 Academy Awards including Best Picture."

Emma: See? It uses **(A)**_____ unlike the *Y-Men 7* advertisement. Do you see the difference?

Kyle: Not exactly. The *Y-Men 7* ad says "Most Exciting Movie" and the *Forrest Gump* ad says "Best Picture." Aren't they both opinions?

Emma: That's a great question, Kyle. When people use words like "best" or "most," they are usually ⓒexpressing **(B)**_____. But in the *Forrest Gump* ad, "Best Picture" is the ⓓaward which the movie won. We can check that on the Internet. That's a fact.

Kyle: Aha! From now on I'm only going to trust ads with facts.

Emma: It's not that simple. Most ads ⓔmix facts with **(C)**_____. So you have to make a smart choice based on both of them.

Kyle: Got it! Emma, do you want to watch the rest of *Y-Men 7* with me?

Emma: Thanks, but no thanks. Enjoy the rest of the movie!

26 위 글의 밑줄 친 단어 ⓐ~ⓔ의 영영풀이로 옳지 <u>않은</u> 것은?

(3점)

① ⓐconnection: ideas or feelings about something

② ⓑadvertisement: a notice, picture or short film telling people about something

③ ⓒexpress: to show what you think or feel

④ ⓓaward: a prize such as money, etc. for something that somebody has done

⑤ ⓔmix: to add something to something else

27 위 글을 읽고 답할 수 <u>없는</u> 것은? (3점)

① What is Kyle's favorite movie?

② What does the advertisement say about *Forrest Gump*?

③ What can we check if the "Best Picture" is an award?

④ When did *Forrest Gump* receive the Academy Award?

⑤ Will Kyle and Emma watch the movie *Y-Men 7* together?

28 위 글의 빈칸 (A)~(C)에 들어갈 말이 바르게 짝지어진 것은?

(4점)

	(A)	(B)	(C)
①	facts	facts	facts
②	facts	opinions	facts
③	facts	opinions	opinions
④	opinions	facts	facts
⑤	opinions	facts	opinions

29 위 글을 읽고 아래의 질문에 대한 답으로 가장 적절한 것은?

(4점)

> Q: I need to watch a good movie. What kind of ads can I trust?

① Don't trust ads because they are full of lies.

② Watch only movies that use facts in their ads.

③ Watch only movies that use opinions in their ads.

④ Check both facts and opinions and choose wisely.

⑤ Check the facts of movies because facts can be proven.

30 위 글의 내용과 일치하는 질문과 대답은? (3점)

① Q: What is Kyle's favorite movie?

A: It's *Y-Man 7*.

② Q: What does *Y-Men 7*'s advertisement say?

A: It says, "Winner of 6 Academy Award."

③ Q: When do people use words like "best" and "most"?

A: They usually use them for expressing facts.

④ Q: What is "Best Picture" in the *Forrest Gump* ad?

A: It is the award which the movie won.

⑤ Q: Will Kyle and Emma watch the rest of *Y-Men 7*?

A: Yes. They will enjoy it together.

◎ 선택형 문항의 답안은 컴퓨터용 수정 싸인펜을 사용하여 OMR 답안지에 바르게 표기하시오.
◎ 서술형 문제는 답을 답안지에 반드시 검정 볼펜으로 쓰시오.
◎ 총 30문항 100점 만점입니다. 문항별 배점은 각 문항에 표시되어 있습니다.

[서울 양천구 ○○중]

01 다음 〈보기 1〉의 (A)~(E)에 들어갈 각 단어의 영영풀이를 〈보기 2〉에서 골라 바르게 연결한 것은? (4점)

보기 1
- Water (A)_____ at 0℃.
- His (B)_____ health is good.
- Mercury is the smallest (C)_____.
- My uncle was a professional (D)_____.
- I'm just (E)_____. I don't know exactly.

보기 2
ⓐ viewed as a whole
ⓑ to turn into ice by cold
ⓒ a person who competes in sports
ⓓ a large, round object in space that travels around a star
ⓔ to give an answer about something without knowing the exact answer

① (A) - ⓔ   ② (B) - ⓑ
③ (C) - ⓐ   ④ (D) - ⓒ
⑤ (E) - ⓓ

[서울 광진구 ○○중]

02 다음 중 단어와 영영풀이가 어색한 것은? (4점)

① mix - to add something to something else
② express - to show what you think or feel
③ opinion - ideas or feelings about something
④ explain - to talk about something in an easy way
⑤ prove - something that helps a person find something

[서울 마포구 ○○중]

03 다음 중 어법상 맞는 것은? (3점)

① You can choose any color that you want.
② Things bad do not happen to good people.
③ Much Hollywood films are sold to all the world.
④ My room is two as large as my brother's room.
⑤ I didn't know that you will eat Italian food.

[서울 마포구 ○○중]

04 다음 대화 중 자연스럽지 않은 것은? (3점)

① A: What do you like most about the novel?
   B: I like the main character. She is creative.
② A: How do you like your sneakers?
   B: I'm happy with them. They're so comfortable.
③ A: Guess what I'm doing.
   B: I guess you're dancing.
④ A: Can you help me cook dinner?
   B: I'm afraid I can't. I'm busy.
⑤ A: Can you recommend a book for me?
   B: Why don't you go to the library?

[5~6] 다음 대화를 읽고 물음에 답하시오.

> W: May I help you?
> M: Yes. I'm looking for a backpack. Can you recommend one?
>
> (A) Oh, that looks good. I'll take it.
> (B) My old backpack was red, so I want a different color.
> (C) How about this red one? Red is the most popular color these days.
> (D) How about this navy one? It has side pockets.

05 다음 남자의 말에 이어질 대화를 가장 알맞게 배열한 것은? (3점)

① (A)-(B)-(D)-(C)
② (A)-(C)-(B)-(D)
③ (C)-(B)-(D)-(A)
④ (C)-(D)-(B)-(A)
⑤ (D)-(B)-(A)-(C)

06 Why does the woman recommend a red colored backpack? (4점)

① She loves the color red the most.
② She thinks the man hates the color red.
③ She believes the color red brings a good luck.
④ She has only red colored backpacks in her shop.
⑤ She thinks red is the most popular color recently.

[7~9] 다음 대화를 읽고 물음에 답하시오.

> Brian: Mina, can you recommend a good pizza restaurant?
> Mina: Why don't you try *Antonio's*? It's my favorite.
> Brian: (A)그곳의 무엇이 마음에 드니?
> Mina: The food is delicious. I recommend the bulgogi pizza.
> Brian: How are the prices?
> Mina: I think the prices are good, too.
> Brian: Sounds like a good restaurant. How do you like the service?
> Mina: It's a little slow on the weekends.
> Brian: Okay. I'll check it out. Thanks.
> Mina: No problem. Enjoy your meal!

07 위 대화의 내용과 가장 일치하는 것은? (3점)

① Brian recommends *Antonio's* for Mina.
② Mina thinks the prices of *Antonio's* are not good.
③ *Antonio's* is Mina's favorite because the food is tasty.
④ The service of *Antonio's* is a little slow except on the weekends.
⑤ Brian will check out another restaurant because of some problems.

08 위 대화에서 말하는 음식점에 대해 알 수 <u>없는</u> 정보는? (3점)

① 상호　　　　　② 위치
③ 가격　　　　　④ 서비스 수준
⑤ 판매하는 음식

09 위 대화의 밑줄 친 (A)를 우리말에 맞도록 〈보기〉의 단어를 배열하여 문장을 완성하시오. (4점)

┌─ 보기 ──────────────────────────┐
│ it / like / what / do / about / you │
└────────────────────────────────┘

→ _____

10 다음 중 어법상 올바른 것을 2개 고르면? (3점)

① He is the boy which I met in New York.

② I have a friend that I share everything with.

③ This is the movie whom I watched last Sunday.

④ That is the new car which I bought yesterday.

⑤ Australia is a country whom a lot of people want to visit.

11 다음 대화의 B의 응답에 적절한 A의 질문으로 옳은 것은? (3점)

A: He was a doctor. He helped sick people in Africa. _____
B: Yes, I do. He is Albert Scheweitzer.
A: That's right.

① Do you know who you are?

② Do you know where he lives?

③ Do you know who he is?

④ What is his name?

⑤ Where does he live?

12 다음 대화가 자연스럽게 이어지도록 (A)~(D)에 〈보기〉의 ⓐ~ⓓ를 넣으려고 할 때, 가장 적절한 배열은? (4점)

┌────────────────────────────────┐
│ Jay: How did you like your trip to │
│   *Gyeongju*? │
│ Lena: (A)_____ │
│ Jay: Where did you visit? │
│ Lena: I visited *Cheomseongdae*. It was │
│   great. │
│ Jay: (B)_____ │
│ Lena: *Bulguksa*. It was a wonderful place. │
│ Jay: (C)_____ │
│ Lena: Yeah, but walking up to *Seokguram* │
│   was difficult. │
│ Jay: (D)_____ │
└────────────────────────────────┘

┌─ 보기 ──────────────────────────┐
│ ⓐ Sounds like a perfect trip. │
│ ⓑ I was really happy with it. │
│ ⓒ Cool. Where else did you go? │
│ ⓓ But I'm sure it was worth it. │
└────────────────────────────────┘

　　(A)　(B)　(C)　(D)

① ⓐ　ⓑ　ⓒ　ⓓ

② ⓑ　ⓒ　ⓐ　ⓓ

③ ⓑ　ⓓ　ⓐ　ⓒ

④ ⓒ　ⓐ　ⓓ　ⓑ

⑤ ⓒ　ⓓ　ⓑ　ⓐ

Ms. Han: All right, everyone. ⓐWe will go on a school field trip next month. Where would everyone like to go? Any opinions?

Hana: How about Gyeonju? I want to see Bulguksa and Seokguram because I have only seen them in a textbook.

Jinsu: Well, ⓑI agree that Gyeongju is a great place to go to. But most schools go there for school field trips. Our school should go somewhere special. For example, how about Jeju-do? ⓒThere are many things we can do them on the island. We can hike up Mt. Halla, ride horses, and swim at the beach. We can enjoy all these things in one place.

Minho: Well, I'd love to go to Jeju-do, too. But we can only get there by plane or ship. ⓓIt's too expensive to afford it. I suggest Sokcho instead. We can visit beautiful mountains and beaches there.

Sumi: Sokcho sounds great, but it takes too much time to get there. Why don't we go camping near our town? I want to go fishing and cook some food for my friends. I also want to sit by a campfire and talk. ⓔWe'll get to know and understand each other much better.

Ms. Han: I'm glad to hear your opinions. Now, let's vote!

[서울 송파구 ○○중]

13 위 대화의 밑줄 친 ⓐ~ⓔ 중 어법에 맞지 않는 것을 고르면? (2개) (4점)

① ⓐ ② ⓑ ③ ⓒ
④ ⓓ ⑤ ⓔ

[서울 송파구 ○○중]

14 다음 빈칸에 들어가기에 가장 적절한 것은? (3점)

Q: What are they mainly talking about?
A: They are talking about _____
_____.

① wonderful historical places in Korea
② what they can do in Jejudo together
③ the best place for their school field trip
④ how to agree with each other
⑤ the most beautiful city in Korea

[서울 송파구 ○○중]

15 위 대화를 통해 알 수 없는 것은? (3점)

① The students are sharing opinions on the school field trip.
② Hana saw Bulguksa and Seokguram in her textbook.
③ Jinsu wants to do many things in Jeju-do.
④ Minho thinks visiting Jeju-do by plane or ship is expensive.
⑤ Sumi thinks there is no camping place in Sokcho.

16 다음 중 대화의 흐름상 <u>어색한</u> 부분은? (3점)

> B: Hi, Suji. How did you like your trip to Gyeongju?
>
> G: ⓐI'm satisfied with it.
>
> B: Where did you visit?
>
> G: I visited Cheomseongdae. ⓑIt was perfect.
>
> B: Where else did you go?
>
> G: Bulguksa. It was a wonderful place.
>
> B: ⓒIt looks like a horrible trip.
>
> G: Yeah, but ⓓwalking up to Seokguram was not easy.
>
> B: But ⓔI think it was worth visiting there.

① ⓐ   ② ⓑ   ③ ⓒ

④ ⓓ   ⑤ ⓔ

17 다음 글의 문맥상 빈칸 (A)에 들어갈 수 있는 것은? (3점)

> Opinions express people's feelings like, "(A)_____."
> You can't say that it's true or not. But, facts can be proven. For example, "The Atacama Desert is in Chile," is a fact. You can check that on the map.

① Dogs cannot see red.

② The story is really touching.

③ Cats have four legs and two ears.

④ Dogs can smell better than humans.

⑤ *Harry Potter* was written by J.K Rowling.

[18~19] 다음 글을 읽고 물음에 답하시오.

> ⓐAds don't always tell the truth. Here are the ads from two pizza restaurants. The first one says, "Once you eat, you can't stop." The second one says, "ⓑ8 out of 10 customers come back to our restaurant." Which one would you order from? The second restaurant might seem a little boring. Maybe you would order from the first ⓒone.
>
> What's the difference between the two ads? One uses an (A)_____ and the other uses a fact. Facts are true information. You can ask the question, "Is it true or not?" Opinions express people's feelings. We can't say they're true or not. They're just someone's ⓓthoughts. ⓔ_____, the first ad expresses an opinion and the second ad gives a fact.
>
> Most ads have both facts and opinions in them. So be more careful when you read advertisements. You have to make a smart choice based on both facts and opinions.

18 위 글의 (A)에 들어갈 단어에 대한 설명으로 옳은 것은? (3점)

① It helps us make a smart choice by telling us the truth.

② It expresses people's feelings like "Once you eat, you can't stop."

③ It's someone's thought that gives a fact which makes us bored.

④ It is a true information that we can ask whether it is true or not.

⑤ Most ads use this in them, so you can get true information about the products.

19 위 글에 대한 설명으로 옳지 <u>않은</u> 것만을 〈보기〉에서 있는 대로 고른 것은? (4점)

> **보기**
>
> ㄱ. ⓐ means that ads always tell lies.
> ㄴ. ⓑ means 80% of customers want their money back.
> ㄷ. ⓒ means a customer.
> ㄹ. ⓓ는 think의 과거형으로 사용되었어.
> ㅁ. We can put Though instead of Therefore in the place of ⓔ.

① ㄱ, ㄴ   ② ㄱ, ㄴ, ㄷ

③ ㄱ, ㄷ, ㄹ   ④ ㄱ, ㄴ, ㄷ, ㄹ

⑤ ㄱ, ㄴ, ㄷ, ㄹ, ㅁ

Emma: It's not that simple. Most ads mix facts with opinions. So (나)＿＿＿＿＿＿.

Kyle: Got it! Emma, do you want to watch the rest of *Y-Men 7* with me?

Emma: Thanks, but no thanks. Enjoy the rest of the movie!

*consider 생각하다, 고려하다

20 위 글의 빈칸 (A)~(D)에 들어갈 말로 가장 적절한 것은? (4점)

	(A)	(B)	(C)	(D)
①	opinion	fact	fact	opinions
②	opinions	opinion	facts	fact
③	opinions	opinions	fact	facts
④	opinions	fact	facts	opinions
⑤	opinion	opinions	facts	fact

[20~24] 다음 글을 읽고 물음에 답하시오.

Emma: Okay. Let's look for ad of *Forrest Gump*.

Kyle: It says, "Winner of 6 Academy Awards including Best Picture."

Emma: See? It uses facts unlike the *Y-Men 7* advertisement. Do you see the difference?

Kyle: Not exactly. The *Y-Men 7* ad says "Most Exciting Movie" and the *Forrest Gump* ad says "Best Picture." Aren't they both (A)＿＿＿＿＿?

Emma: That's a great question, Kyle. When people use words like "best" or "most," they are usually expressing (B)＿＿＿＿＿. But in the *Forrest Gump* ad, (가)<u>"최우수 작품상"은 그 영화가 수상했던 상이야.</u> We can check that on the Internet. That's a (C)＿＿＿＿＿.

Kyle: Aha! From now on I'm only going to trust ads with (D)＿＿＿＿＿.

21 위 글의 내용으로 가장 올바른 것은? (3점)

① *Forrest Gump*는 가장 재미있는 영화이다.

② *Y-Men 7*은 "Best Picture" 상을 수상하였다.

③ 모든 광고에는 반드시 fact와 opinion이 섞여 있다.

④ Emma는 Kyle이 자신에게 영화를 보자고 말한 것에 진심으로 고마워하고 있다.

⑤ 똑똑한 선택을 하기 위해서는 fact와 opinion 둘 다 고려해야 한다.

22 위 글의 밑줄 친 (가)를 올바르게 영작한 것은? (3점)

① The movie which won "Best Picture" is Forrest Gump.

② "Best Picture" is which the movie won.

③ The award who the movie won is "Best Picture."

④ "Best Picture" is the award which the movie won.

⑤ Which the movie won is the award, "Best picture."

23 위 글의 내용으로 옳은 것만을 〈보기〉에서 있는 대로 고른 것은? (4점)

> 보기
>
> ㄱ. *Y-Men 7* used facts in its advertisement.
>
> ㄴ. Kyle wants to watch *Y-Men 7* with Emma and so does she.
>
> ㄷ. In the ad of *Forrest Gump*, "Best Picture" is the fact not opinion.
>
> ㄹ. Be careful because most ads always use only opinions about their products.
>
> ㅁ. After all, Kyle understands the difference between facts and opinions.

① ㄱ, ㄴ

② ㄷ, ㅁ

③ ㄴ, ㄷ, ㄹ

④ ㄷ, ㄹ, ㅁ

⑤ ㄱ, ㄴ, ㄷ, ㄹ, ㅁ

24 위 글의 빈칸 (나)에 들어갈 주제 문장으로 가장 알맞은 것은? (3점)

① you have to believe facts only

② you may choose the movie with opinions

③ you can't find the difference between facts and opinions

④ you don't trust the movies because they are full of lies

⑤ you should make a smart choice based on both facts and opinions

[25~30] 다음 글을 읽고 물음에 답하시오.

Emma: What are you doing, Kyle?

Kyle: Oh, Emma. I'm watching the movie, *Y-Men 7* on my computer.

Emma: How is it?

Kyle: Don't ask. (A)It's so boring that I want to cry.

Emma: ⓐI'm sorry to hear that.

Kyle: ⓑI'm so mad. ⓒThe movie advertisement said it was "The Most Exciting Movie of the Year."

Emma: Well, you can't believe everything (B)that you read.

Kyle: ⓓThey lied on the advertisement. ⓔI want to get my money back.

Emma: Hold on, Kyle! They didn't really lie because they used opinions, not facts.

Kyle: Huh? (C)I'm not following you.

Emma: (가)_____ express people's feelings like, "The desert is beautiful." You can't say that it's true or not. But, (나)_____ can be proven. For example, "The Atacama Desert is in Chile," is (다)_____. You can check that on the map.

25 위 글의 밑줄 친 (A)의 해석으로 올바른 것은? (3점)

① 영화가 너무 지루해서 나는 울고 싶어.

② 내가 울고 싶다는 사실은 너무 지루해.

③ 내가 울고 싶다고 해서 영화가 지루해졌어.

④ 그것은 지루했지만 나는 그것을 보고 울었어.

⑤ 영화가 지루한 이유는 나를 울고 싶게 하기 때문이야.

26 위 글의 밑줄 친 (B)와 바꿔 쓸 수 있는 것은? (3점)

① which   ② who

③ what   ④ why

⑤ when

27 위 글의 (가)~(다)에 들어갈 단어를 문맥에 맞도록 올바르게 짝지은 것은? (4점)

	(가)	(나)	(다)
①	Facts	facts	an opinion
②	Facts	opinions	a fact
③	Opinions	facts	an opinion
④	Opinions	facts	a fact
⑤	Opinions	opinions	a fact

28 위 글의 밑줄 친 ⓐ~ⓔ 중, "fact"에 해당하는 것은? (3점)

① ⓐ   ② ⓑ   ③ ⓒ

④ ⓓ   ⑤ ⓔ

29 위 글의 (C)의 의미로 가장 적절한 것은? (3점)

① I can get your point.

② I'm not running after you.

③ I'm not going to follow you.

④ I don't want to talk to you now.

⑤ I don't understand what you are saying.

30 위 글의 내용과 일치하는 것은? (3점)

① Kyle went to a theater with Emma.

② Kyle liked the movie, *Y-Men 7*.

③ Emma paid for the movie, *Y-Men 7*.

④ Emma thinks that Kyle should get a refund.

⑤ Emma said facts can be proven.

2학년 영어 2학기 기말고사(8과) 1회

문항수 : 선택형(29문항) 서술형(1문항)   20 . . .

◎ 선택형 문항의 답안은 컴퓨터용 수정 싸인펜을 사용하여 OMR 답안지에 바르게 표기하시오.
◎ 서술형 문제는 답을 답안지에 반드시 검정 볼펜으로 쓰시오.
◎ 총 30문항 100점 만점입니다. 문항별 배점은 각 문항에 표시되어 있습니다.

[울산 ○○중]

01 다음 각 문장에 들어갈 단어가 올바르게 짝지어진 것은? (4점)

- I'll [carry / post] your luggage to your room.
- This information is a valuable [flash / clue].
- I have no musical [taking / talent].
- I didn't [win / water] the plants today.
- Many children are [afraid / awake] of the dark.

① carry, clue, talent, water, wrong
② post, clue, taking, win, wrong
③ carry, flash, talent, win, wrong
④ carry, clue, talent, water, afraid
⑤ post, flash, taking, water, afraid

[서울 성북구 ○○중]

02 다음 빈칸에 공통으로 들어갈 단어로 가장 적절한 것은? (3점)

- I like the movie *Frozen*. The story is really _____.
- The skirt is too long. It is almost _____ the floor.

① washing   ② exciting
③ touching   ④ watching
⑤ surprising

[경기 ○○중]

03 다음 중 올바른 문장은? (3점)

① I wonder who is your favorite singer.
② Do you know how much is the car?
③ Don't you remember what color her hat is?
④ Can you tell me what this called in English?
⑤ Please ask him what time can he pick me up.

[서울 송파구 ○○중]

04 다음 대화의 빈칸에 들어가기에 <u>어색한</u> 것은? (3점)

A: _____
B: Sure, what is it?
A: I can't find my phone.

① Can you help me out?
② Can you do me a favor?
③ Can you give me a hand?
④ Do you have a favor to ask?
⑤ Please help me with this.

[인천 ○○중]

05 다음 중 대화가 자연스럽지 <u>않은</u> 것은? (3점)

① A: Guess what I'm doing.
   B: Maybe you're fishing.
② A: Can you give me a hand?
   B: Sorry, I can't.
③ A: Jiho, can you do me a favor?
   B: Sure. What is it?
④ A: I guess you are playing the piano.
   B: You're right.
⑤ A: Would you mind helping me make sandwiches?
   B: Yes, I would. I really like cooking.

Brian: Mom, I can't find my smartphone. Can you help me find it?

Mom: Okay. (가)집 안에서 잃어버린 것이 확실하니? (A)

Brian: Yes. I just texted my friend a few minutes ago.

Mom: Where were you at the time? (B)

Brian: In the kitchen. (C) I was making a sandwich.

Mom: (D) Then I guess you left it somewhere in the kitchen.

Brian: I already checked the kitchen, Mom.

Mom: Well, let me check it again. (E) Inside the refrigerator.

Brian: Thanks, Mom. You are the greatest!

Mom: You're welcome, honey.

06 위 대화를 다음과 같이 요약할 때, 빈칸에 들어갈 말로 가장 적절한 것은? (4점)

His mother thought Brian's smartphone was (A)_____ in the kitchen. But Brian couldn't remember when and where he (B)_____ his smartphone. So they looked for it here and there. Finally, his mother was (C)_____. It was inside the refrigerator.

	(A)	(B)	(C)
①	somewhere	had left	right
②	sometimes	leaves	alright
③	anywhere	have left	alright
④	someplace	had left	wrong
⑤	somewhere	have left	wrong

07 위 대화의 흐름으로 보아, 다음 문장이 들어갈 가장 적절한 곳은? (3점)

Oh, here it is.

① (A)   ② (B)   ③ (C)
④ (D)   ⑤ (E)

08 위 대화를 읽고, 다음 질문에 대한 답을 쓰시오. (반드시 괄호 안의 조건과 해석을 참고하여 쓸 것) (8점)

(A) What was Brian's problem?

(1) He _____. But he couldn't find it.
(lose를 이용)

(2) So he _____ it.
(ask가 포함된 5단어)

(3) He looked c_____ at first, but later he was p_____ to find his smartphone.
(주어진 첫 자로 시작)

(B) Where did Brian use his smartphone last?

(4) He used it _____.
(3단어)

(C) (가)를 아래와 같이 표현할 때, 빈칸에 들어갈 말을 쓰시오.

(5) _____ inside the house?
(sure를 이용하여 6단어)

09 다음 대화의 빈칸에 들어갈 말로 알맞지 <u>않은</u> 것은? (4점)

> A: _____
> B: Yes. What is it, Sumin?
> A: Can you help me post this notice on the board?
> B: No problem. When I finish my homework, I'll do it.

① Can you help me?

② Can I ask you a favor?

③ Can you do me a favor?

④ Can you give me a hand?

⑤ Would you mind helping me?

11 어법상 올바른 문장은 <u>모두</u> 몇 개인가? (3점)

> • I wonder why she came late.
> • I don't know where did the book go.
> • Do you know when Sam's birthday is?
> • Could you tell me when the school trip is?
> • I'll ask Mary how does she come to school.

① 1개   ② 2개   ③ 3개

④ 4개   ⑤ 5개

10 다음 연설문에 대한 설명으로 옳은 것은? (3점)

> Good morning, classmates! Nine months have passed so fast, and we are almost at the end of this school year. We all had a wonderful year. I guess only a few of us will be in the same class next year. Don't be a stranger. Say hello when we see each other, okay? Thank you.

① 연설문의 청중은 낯선 사람들이다.

② 연설문은 학년 초에 적합한 내용이다.

③ 연설자는 내년에 중학교 3학년이 된다.

④ 연설자는 다음 해에도 인사하고 지내기를 원한다.

⑤ 연설문의 목적은 같은 반이 된 학급 친구들에게 자기소개를 하는 것이다.

[12~14] 다음 대화를 읽고 물음에 답하시오.

> Tony: Hey, Narae. What's wrong?
> Narae: My family is going to visit my grandmother in Busan this weekend, but we are worried about the dog, Spot. So, can you take care of my dog this weekend?
> Tony: (A)_____ My mom doesn't like dogs.
> Narae: Oh, what should I do?
> Tony: Why don't you ask Sumin? Her family loves dogs.
> Narae: Okay. I'll call her right now.

12 위 대화의 빈칸 (A)에 들어갈 문장으로 적절한 것은? (3점)

① Of course.

② No problem.

③ That's great.

④ Sure, I'd love to.

⑤ I'm afraid but I can't.

13 위 대화에서 Tony가 Narae의 부탁을 거절한 이유로 적절한 것은? (3점)

① 부산 여행을 가야 해서
② 수민이와 약속이 있어서
③ 할머니 댁을 방문해야 해서
④ 엄마가 개를 싫어하셔서
⑤ 과학 프로젝트를 완성해야 해서

14 위 대화의 내용과 일치하는 것은? (3점)

① Tony doesn't like dogs.
② Sumin's family loves dogs.
③ Tony will take care of Narae's dog.
④ Narae asked Sumin to take care of her dog.
⑤ Narae won't visit her grandmother in Busan this weekend.

[15~18] 다음 글을 읽고 물음에 답하시오.

The Jewel Robber

There was a robbery at Mr. Goldstein's jewelry shop. Shirley rushed over to the shop. It was big and warm. When Shirley opened the front door, a silver bell on it rang to welcome her. Inside, free coffee and doughnuts were on a table. Shirley asked Mr. Goldstein what happened.

"I was robbed! When I was cleaning the jewelry case, a man came behind me with a gun," said Mr. Goldstein. (A)He looked nervous and anxious.

"Was anybody with you in the store? Shirley asked.

"No, I was alone."

"Did you see the robber's face?"

"No, I couldn't see his face because he was ⓐ facing toward me. I felt a gun in my back. He put a bag over my head and ⓑunfasten my hands and feet with a rope."

"How long were you tied up?"

"I'm not sure. It sounded like he was opening the jewelry cases. Then it became very quiet. I thought he was still there. So, I stayed quiet. After a few hours, I managed to ⓒtie the rope and ⓓtake off the bag."

"Was anything missing?"

"The robber took the ⓔcheapest diamond, the Hope Diamond. It was on loan from the city museum because I can't afford it alone. Oh, he also stole a couple of doughnuts. Shirley, do you think you can catch the robber?"

Shirley replied, "Of course. That bell on the door is pointing right at you! If the robber went out through the front door, the bell must have shaken and rung. Jingle! Jingle! But, you said it was quiet. You lied."

15 위 글을 읽고 Goldstein의 사건에 대한 설명으로 거리가 먼 것은? (3점)

① 강도가 들어왔을 때 그는 보석 진열장을 청소하고 있었다.

② 그는 총을 든 강도의 얼굴을 확인하지 못했다.

③ 그는 강도가 보석 진열장을 여는 듯한 소리를 들었다.

④ 그는 스스로 밧줄을 풀 수 없어 Shirley에게 도움을 요청해서 겨우 빠져나왔다.

⑤ 사라진 물건은 비싼 다이아몬드와 도넛 두 개다.

16 위 글의 밑줄 친 ⓐ~ⓔ 중 문맥상 어휘의 쓰임이 옳은 것은? (3점)

① ⓐ   ② ⓑ   ③ ⓒ

④ ⓓ   ⑤ ⓔ

17 위 글에서 Shirley가 범인이 누구인지 추리할 때, 가장 결정적인 역할을 한 단서로 옳은 것은? (3점)

① the bell

② the gun

③ doughnuts

④ the diamond

⑤ the rope and the bag

18 위 글에서 범인이 누구인지 고려했을 때, 밑줄 친 (A)의 이유로 가장 적절한 것은? (3점)

① Because he was sick.

② Because he felt guilty.

③ Because he ate too many doughnuts.

④ Because his diamond has been stolen.

⑤ Because his business was getting worse.

19 다음 중 문장을 올바르게 바꾸어 쓴 것은? (3점)

① She said to me, "Is Tom at home?"

→ She asked me Tom was at home.

② I said to him, "What is Jessica looking at?"

→ I asked him what Jessica is looking at.

③ He said to me, "Who are those people?"

→ He asked me who are those people.

④ He said to me, "When will she be back?"

→ He asked me when she would be back.

⑤ I said to her, "Who is going there with John?"

→ I asked her who there is going with John.

[20~25] 다음 글을 읽고 물음에 답하시오.

Mr. Reese, the principal, ran across the wet playground. "Shirley! Shirley! I need your help!"

Shirley was an eighth grade student at Bakersville Middle School. She was also the best detective in Bakersville, the town. "(가)잘못된 일이 있나요?" asked Shirley. "ⓐSomeone have stolen the gold medal for the talent show!" Mr. Reese took Shirley to the scene of the crime. ⓑThere was a case with a breaking window. ⓒOnly the gold medal was missing. ⓓThe other two medals were still in the case. There was a poem in its place.

Tomorrow is the talent show.
Where did the gold medal go?
Look high and low.
You can't catch me. You're too slow.
(A)_____

Shirley asked, "Could you tell me when this happened?" (B)_____ Mr. Reese explained. Then Shirley said, (C)_____ "I rushed over and found Jocelyn and the case ⓔlike these." She said (D)_____ He answered right (나)_____, (E)_____ Then he continued, saying "I'll call them to my office."

21 위 글의 밑줄 친 ⓐ~ⓓ 중 어법에 맞는 것을 <u>모두</u> 고른 것은? (4점)

① ⓐ, ⓒ   ② ⓑ, ⓓ

③ ⓒ, ⓓ   ④ ⓐ, ⓑ

⑤ ⓑ, ⓒ, ⓓ

22 위 글의 내용과 일치하지 <u>않는</u> 것은? (3점)

① Mr. Reese는 Shirley에게 사건을 의뢰했다.

② Shirley는 Bakersville 중학교 8학년 학생이다.

③ Shirley는 Bakersville 마을의 최고의 탐정이다.

④ Shirley는 운동장에서 시가 적힌 쪽지를 발견했다.

⑤ Shirley는 금메달 도난 사건의 수사를 맡게 되었다.

23 위 글에서 시의 단어들의 각운을 고려해 볼 때, 빈칸 (A)에 들어가기에 적절한 것을 <u>모두</u> 고르면? (3개) (3점)

① I am the fastest as you know.

② In this town who is the best?

③ I would hide it under the rainbow.

④ My move is just like an arrow.

⑤ Shirley, Shirley, you never find me.

20 위 글의 (가)를 올바르게 영작한 것은? (3점)

① Is it anything wrong?

② Is there wrong nothing?

③ Is there nothing wrong?

④ Is there wrong something?

⑤ Is there something wrong?

24 위 글의 빈칸 (나)에 알맞은 것은? (3점)

① on   ② from

③ away   ④ with

⑤ along

25 위 글의 빈칸 (B)~(E)에 들어갈 문장을 〈보기〉에서 차례로 나열한 것은? (3점)

> **보기**
>
> (가) "Who else was here last night?"
> (나) "Sylvia and Harry. They were also practicing for the talent show."
> (다) "Oh, really? So, what did you do then?"
> (라) "A little after nine last night. I was making my rounds when I heard a scream."

① (라)-(다)-(가)-(나)
② (가)-(나)-(다)-(라)
③ (라)-(나)-(가)-(다)
④ (가)-(다)-(나)-(라)
⑤ (다)-(가)-(라)-(나)

[26~30] 다음 글을 읽고 물음에 답하시오.

Jocelyn was a ninth grade student with short curly red hair.

"I was practicing my song and I became thirsty. I stepped outside the classroom to get some water. It was completely dark. Suddenly, there was a loud sound of thunder. I think the thief broke the window at that moment. Lightning followed right after and it became bright for a second or two. ⓐThen I saw someone strange to run away from the case."

"Did you see the thief's face?"

"No, I only saw the thief's back. But the thief had short hair. Then, the principal arrived at the crime scene."

Next was an eighth grade student, Sylvia. She was tall with long black hair. She said, "I was reading my poem aloud in the classroom. I heard a scream and went outside. ⓑThe girl whom I saw was standing next to the case. With the flash from the lightning, it was like a horror movie. ⓒIt was so terrified that I ran straight home."

"Did you hear the window break?"

"No, the thunder was too loud. Well, I didn't do it. I was going to win first place anyway."

Harry, a seventh grader, had short blonde hair. He said, "Hey, you got the wrong guy. I was practicing my dance moves."

"ⓓI wonder what time did you go home."

"When did I go home? I went home a little before nine. I didn't take one step outside the classroom until then."

(가)"이상한 소리 들었어요?"

"How could I? My music was really loud."

"No, I heard someone singing really badly, but I didn't see anyone."

Shirley said, "I don't need to hear anymore." Then she turned to the thief.

"ⓔWhy don't you bringing the medal back before you get into some real trouble?"

26 위 글의 종류로 가장 적절한 것은? (3점)

① a poem
② an advertisement
③ a detective novel
④ an invitation card
⑤ a recommendation letter

27 위 글의 밑줄 친 ⓐ~ⓔ 중 어법상 옳은 것은? (3점)

① ⓐ   ② ⓑ   ③ ⓒ
④ ⓓ   ⑤ ⓔ

28 다음 글은 Shirley가 작성한 사건 일지이다. 사건이 발생한 순서대로 바르게 배열한 것은? (4점)

<Detective Shirley's Note>

(A) Harry finished practicing his dance moves.

(B) The thief appeared to steal the gold medal.

(C) The principal found Jocelyn hanging around the case.

(D) Harry heard someone singing terribly on his way home.

(E) Sylvia witnessed the thief with the flash of lightning and ran away.

---

① (A)-(B)-(D)-(C)-(E)
② (A)-(D)-(B)-(E)-(C)
③ (B)-(E)-(D)-(C)-(A)
④ (C)-(D)-(A)-(B)-(E)
⑤ (D)-(A)-(E)-(B)-(C)

29 위 글의 밑줄 친 (가)를 다음 단어들을 참고하여 영작할 때, 4번째에 올 단어는? (2점)

---
hear / did / strange / you / anything
---

① anything   ② you   ③ did
④ hear   ⑤ strange

30 다음 글은 Shirley가 범인을 밝혀내기 위해 추리한 내용이다. 괄호 (A), (B), (C) 안에 들어갈 말로 알맞게 짝지어진 것은? (4점)

First of all, Jocelyn states that the thief had short hair. Then, among the three suspects, those who have short hair are Jocelyn and (A)[Sylvia / Harry].

Second, we have to prove who was really at school when the robbery happened. Although it can't be proven that Sylvia and Harry truly went home around 9 o'clock, Jocelyn, you were spotted by the principal at the crime scene.

Finally, Jocelyn and Sylvia, you told me that both of you heard a loud sound of thunder and also saw a flash of lightning last night. However, Jocelyn stated there was a thunder first and right then lightning followed. Unfortunately, that's scientifically wrong. Although lightning and thunder occur at the exact same time at the sky, lightning always strikes (B)[after / before] thunder. It is because the light travels much (C)[faster / slower] than the sound. The speed of light is 300 million meters per second while the speed of sound is only 340 meters per second.

Therefore, Jocelyn, you're the thief. If you dream of a perfect crime, read more science books first!

	(A)	(B)	(C)
①	Sylvia	before	slower
②	Sylvia	after	slower
③	Harry	before	slower
④	Harry	after	faster
⑤	Harry	before	faster

◎ 선택형 문항의 답안은 컴퓨터용 수정 싸인펜을 사용하여 OMR 답안지에 바르게 표기하시오.
◎ 서술형 문제는 답을 답안지에 반드시 검정 볼펜으로 쓰시오.
◎ 총 30문항 100점 만점입니다. 문항별 배점은 각 문항에 표시되어 있습니다.

[서울 성북구 ○○중]

01 다음 설명에 해당하는 단어를 고르면? (4점)

something that helps you to solve a problem or answer a question

① clue
② guess
③ feather
④ footprint
⑤ lightning

[서울 마포구 ○○중]

02 다음 중 어법상 맞는 것은? (3점)

① Where do you suppose he come from?
② Why do you think she quitted school?
③ Please tell me why didn't you agree with him.
④ I wonder if is that man my new biology teacher.
⑤ Could you tell me when the nearest subway station is?

[울산 ○○중]

03 다음 중 자연스러운 대화가 되도록 주어진 단어를 바르게 배열할 때 필요 없는 단어는? (3점)

A: _____?
(ask, you, a favor, can, I, me)
B: Sure. What is it?

① ask
② you
③ a favor
④ I
⑤ me

[경기 ○○중]

04 다음 두 사람의 대화가 자연스럽지 않은 것은? (3점)

① A: What do you like most about your sneakers?
   B: I'm really happy with them.
② A: Can you help me mop the floor right now?
   B: I'm afraid I can't.
③ A: Do you want to watch the movie with us?
   B: Thanks, I really want to watch the movie.
④ A: How do you like the service of the restaurant?
   B: It's a little slow on the weekends.
⑤ A: Can you recommend a good pizza restaurant?
   B: Why don't you try Antonio's?

[5~8] 다음 대화를 읽고 물음에 답하시오.

G: Tony, ⓐ_____
B: (A) Sure. What is it, Narae?
G: Can you take care of my cat this Friday? (B) My family is going to visit my grandmother in Wonju.
B: (C) My mom doesn't like cats.
G: Oh, what should I do? (D)
B: Why don't you ask Sumin? (E) Her family loves cats.
G: Okay. I'll call her right now.

[경북 ○○중]

05 다음 대화의 흐름으로 보아 다음 문장이 들어갈 곳은? (2점)

Oh, I'm sorry but I can't.

① (A)
② (B)
③ (C)
④ (D)
⑤ (E)

06 위 대화의 빈칸 ⓐ에 들어갈 말로 알맞지 <u>않은</u> 것은? (3점)

① Can you give me a hand?

② Can you help me out?

③ Please can I help you?

④ Can I ask you a favor?

⑤ I have a favor to ask.

[9~11] 다음 대화를 읽고 물음에 답하시오.

Brian: Mom, I can't find my smartphone. Can you help me find it?

Mom: ⓐ<u>Are you sure you lost it inside the house?</u>

Brian: Yes. I just ⓑ<u>have texted my friend a few minutes ago.</u>

Mom: Where were you at the time?

Brian: In the kitchen. I was making a sandwich.

Mom: Then I guess ⓒ<u>you left it somewhere in the kitchen.</u>

Brian: I ⓓ<u>already checked the kitchen,</u> Mom.

Mom: Well, let's check it again. Oh, here it is. Inside the refrigerator.

Brian: Thanks, Mom. You are ⓔ<u>the greatest</u>!

Mom: You're welcome, honey.

07 나래가 Tony에게 말하는 목적으로 알맞은 것은? (3점)

① 부산 여행을 제안하려고

② 친지 방문을 요청하려고

③ 친구 전화번호를 물어보려고

④ 고양이 돌보는 것을 부탁하려고

⑤ 할머니의 건강 상태를 알려 주려고

09 위 대화의 밑줄 친 ⓐ~ⓔ 중 어법상 알맞지 <u>않은</u> 것은? (3점)

① ⓐ   ② ⓑ   ③ ⓒ

④ ⓓ   ⑤ ⓔ

08 위 대화의 내용으로 올바른 것은? (3점)

① Tony는 이번 주 금요일에 원주에 갈 예정이다.

② Narae네 가족은 이번 주 금요일에 할아버지 댁에 간다.

③ Narae의 어머니는 개를 좋아하신다.

④ Sumin의 가족은 고양이를 좋아한다.

⑤ Sumin의 부모님은 개를 좋아하신다.

10 위 대화를 읽고, 주어진 질문에 알맞은 답을 쓰시오. (3점)

> Q: Where did Mom find Brian's smartphone?
>
> A: She _____ it _____.

11 위 대화의 내용과 일치하는 것은? (3점)

① Brian was looking for his smartphone.

② Brian helped his mom to clean the kitchen.

③ Brian found his smartphone in the refrigerator.

④ Brian was making a sandwich in the kitchen with his mom.

⑤ Brian's mom thought Brian had lost his smartphone in his room.

[12~13] 다음 글을 읽고 물음에 답하시오.

Good morning, classmate! Nine months have passed so fast. ⓐNow, we are almost at the end of this school year. ⓑWe all had a wonderful year. ⓒ Only a few of us will be in the same class next year. ⓓDon't be a stranger. ⓔWe should be careful when we meet strangers. Say hello when we see each other, okay? Thank you.

12 위 글에서 전체 흐름과 관계<u>없는</u> 문장은? (3점)

① ⓐ   ② ⓑ   ③ ⓒ

④ ⓓ   ⑤ ⓔ

13 위 글을 읽고 글쓴이가 학생들에게 부탁하는 내용 중 하나를 찾아 우리말로 쓰시오. (4점)

→ _____

[14~15] 다음 대화를 읽고 물음에 답하시오.

Frank: Marie, ⓐcan you do me a favor?

Marie: Sure, what is it?

Frank: (A)내가 바닥을 대걸레질하는 것을 도와줄 수 있어?

Marie: Of course, Frank, I also need your help. (B)내가 이 공지를 저 게시판에 붙이는 것을 도와줄 수 있어?

Frank: No problem. Let's help each other!

14 위 대화의 밑줄 친 ⓐ와 바꾸어 쓸 수 있는 것은? (3점)

① can I help you?

② can I ask you a favor?

③ can I give you a hand?

④ can I help you with that?

⑤ do you need any help?

15 위 대화의 밑줄 친 우리말에 맞도록 (A)와 (B)에 들어갈 문장을 쓰시오. (단어는 추가 없이 배열만 하시오.) (6점)

me / can / mop / the / you / help / floor

(A): _____ ?

me / on / can / the / you / help / help / post / this / board / notice / bulletin

(B): _____
_____ ?

16 다음 대화의 빈칸에 들어갈 알맞은 말은? (3점)

> A: _____
> B: I guess you're working on the computer.

① I'm going to play the piano.

② Can you guess what it is?

③ What are you doing?

④ I don't know how to use it.

⑤ Guess what I'm doing.

17 위 글의 (A), (B), (C)에 들어갈 말을 짝지은 것 중 적절한 것은? (4점)

	(A)	(B)	(C)
①	broken	playing	anywhere
②	broken	played	anywhere
③	broken	playing	somewhere
④	breaking	played	somewhere
⑤	breaking	playing	somewhere

[17~18] 다음 글을 읽고 물음에 답하시오.

It was Sunday and Shirley went to Mr. Shoppe's store. He sounded upset.

"Shirley, someone broke my window!"

"Calm down and tell me everything," said Shirley.

"This morning, I made a 'Sale' sign. After I put it up around 9 o'clock, I went to the basement. Suddenly, I heard something. So I ran back quickly, and I found the window (**A**)[broken / breaking]."

"Did you see anyone?"

"Yes. I saw a young boy. He ran away really fast. So I didn't see his face."

"Hmm... I saw two boys (**B**)[playing / played] basketball in the park just now. They looked rather suspicious."

Shirley went to the boys. She explained the situation and asked them where they were that morning.

Rooney answered, "I woke up and came straight here."

"Me too, I didn't go (**C**)[somewhere / anywhere] near the store today," said Messi.

18 위 글을 읽고 답할 수 있는 질문은? (3점)

① What time does the store open?

② What does Mr. Shoppe's store sell?

③ Where were the two boys yesterday morning?

④ What made the boys look suspicious to Mr. Shoppe?

⑤ Where was Mr. Shoppe when he heard the window break?

The suspicious students were questioned about what they did last night when the gold medal was stolen.

The first suspect was Jocelyn, a ninth grade student with short curly red hair. "I was practicing my song and I became @thirst. I stepped outside the classroom to get some water. It was completely dark. Suddenly, there was a loud sound of thunder. I think the thief broke the window at that moment. Lightning followed (가)right after and it became ⓑ brightly for a second or two. Then I saw someone ⓒto run away from the case."

"Did you see the thief's face?" asked Shirley.

"No, I only saw the thief's back. But the thief had short hair."

Next was an eighth grade student, Sylvia. She was tall with long black hair. She said, "I was reading my poem aloud in the classroom for the talent show. I heard a scream and went outside. There was a girl ⓓnext the case. With the flash from the lightning, it was like a horror movie. I got ⓔscared so I ran straight home."

"Did you hear the window break?"

"No, the thunder was too loud. Well, I didn't do it. I was going to win first place anyway."

19 위 글의 @~ⓔ 중 어법상 옳은 것은? (4점)

① @ ② ⓑ ③ ⓒ
④ ⓓ ⑤ ⓔ

20 다음 글을 읽고 대답할 수 없는 질문은? (4점)

① What grade is Sylvia in?
② What was Sylvia doing in the classroom?
③ What did Sylvia do when she heard a scream?
④ What horror movie does Sylvia like?
⑤ Who does Sylvia think will win the first place?

21 위 글의 내용과 일치하는 것은? (3점)

① Jocelyn was an eighth grader with short curly red hair.
② Sylvia went outside the classroom to drink some water last night.
③ Sylvia was reading her poem silently in the classroom for the talent show.
④ The first suspect said she was practicing her song when the crime happened.
⑤ The second suspect couldn't hear the window break because of someone's loud scream.

22 위 글의 밑줄 친 (가)right와 같은 의미로 쓰인 것은? (3점)

① He was <u>right</u> in front of the goal.
② What's the <u>right</u> time?
③ He has a <u>right</u> to know the truth.
④ I hope we're doing the <u>right</u> thing.
⑤ Take a <u>right</u> turn at the intersection.

[23~25] 다음 글을 읽고 물음에 답하시오.

Mr. Reese took Shirley to the scene of the crime. There ⓐwas a case with a broken window. The silver and bronze medals were still there. But the gold medal was (A)[missed / missing]. There was a ㉠_____ in its place.

Tomorrow is the talent show.
ⓑWhere the gold medal go?
Look high and low.
You can't catch me.
You're too (B)[slow / fast].

Shirley asked, "Could you tell me when this happened?" "A little after nine last night. I was making my ⓒrounds when I heard a scream. I rushed over and found Jocelyn and the case ⓓlike this." "I wonder (C)[else who / who else] was here last night." "Sylvia and Harry. They were also practicing for the talent show. I'll call ⓔthem to my office."

24 위 글의 밑줄 친 ⓐ~ⓔ 중, 어법상 <u>어색한</u> 것은? (3점)

① ⓐ   ② ⓑ   ③ ⓒ

④ ⓓ   ⑤ ⓔ

25 위 글의 괄호 (A), (B), (C) 안에서 문맥에 맞는 낱말로 가장 적절한 것은? (4점)

	(A)	(B)	(C)
①	missed	slow	else who
②	missing	fast	else who
③	missed	fast	who else
④	missing	slow	who else
⑤	missed	slow	who else

23 위 글의 빈칸 ㉠에 들어갈 다음 영어 설명에 해당하는 단어로 알맞은 것은? (3점)

> a piece of writing that expresses emotions, experiences, and ideas, especially in short lines using words that rhyme (=end with the same sound)

① poem   ② talent

③ difference   ④ connection

⑤ trouble

[26~27] 다음 글을 읽고 물음에 답하시오.

Harry, a seventh grader, had short blonde hair. He said, "(A) Hey, you got the wrong guy. (B) I was practicing my dance ⓐ_____. (C) I went home a little before nine. (D)"

"Did you hear anything strange?"

"How could I? (E) My music was really loud."

"Did you see anyone on the way home?"

"No, I heard someone ⓑ_____ really badly, but I didn't see anyone."

Shirley said, "I don't need ⓒ_____ anymore." Then she turned to the thief.

26 다음 (A)~(E) 중 주어진 문장이 들어갈 수 있는 곳으로 가장 알맞은 것은? (3점)

> I didn't take one step outside the classroom until then.

① (A) 　　② (B) 　　③ (C)

④ (D) 　　⑤ (E)

28 위 글의 빈칸 (A), (B)에 들어갈 단어가 바르게 짝지어진 것은? (3점)

	(A)	(B)
①	to	for
②	to	with
③	from	with
④	from	in
⑤	for	in

27 위 글의 흐름에 맞게 빈칸 ⓐ~ⓒ에 들어갈 말이 바르게 짝지어진 것은? (4점)

	ⓐ	ⓑ	ⓒ
①	moving	singing	hearing
②	moves	singing	to hear
③	to move	to sing	hear
④	moves	to sing	hearing
⑤	moving	sing	to hear

29 위 글의 내용을 보고 대답할 수 있는 질문은? (4점)

① When did someone steal the gold medal?

② Who was the best principal in the whole town?

③ Where did Shirley go across the wet playground?

④ What happened to the gold medal for the talent show?

⑤ How did Shirley become the best detective in the town?

[28~30] 다음 글을 읽고 물음에 답하시오.

Mr. Reese, the principal, ran ⓐunderline{across} the wet playground. "Shirley! Shirley! I need your ⓑhelp!" Shirley was an eighth grade student at Bakersville Middle School. She was also the ⓒbest detective in the whole town. "Is there ⓓsomething wrong?" asked Shirley. "Someone ⓔhas stolen the gold medal for the talent show!"

Mr. Reese took Shirley (A)_____ the scene of the crime. There was a case (B)_____ a broken window. The silver and bronze medals were still there. But the gold medal was missing.

30 위 글의 밑줄 친 ⓐ~ⓔ에 대한 설명 중에서 올바른 설명이라고 할 수 <u>없는</u> 것은? (3점)

① ⓐ '~을 가로질러서'의 뜻

② ⓑ '도움'의 뜻을 가진 명사

③ ⓒ '가장 착한'의 뜻을 가진 최상급

④ ⓓ something을 wrong이 뒤에서 수식

⑤ ⓔ have+p.p.의 현재완료 구문

정답 및 해설

Lesson 5 (중간)

1회

01 ③ **02** ② **03** ①, ③ **04** ① **05** ④ **06** ③, ④

07 ⑤ **08** there by bus **09** ④

10 why don't we have dinner together?

11 ① **12** ③, ④ **13** ⑤

14 (1) uploading promoting videos on their social media
(2) editing them will take shorter time

15 ④ **16** ④ **17** ⑤ **18** ① **19** ②, ③ **20** ③

21 It is blue, yellow, green, and pink powder.

22 ④ **23** ① **24** ⑤

25 They shape huge piles of snow into artworks.

26 ③ **27** ⑤ **28** ④ **29** ⑤ **30** ④

---

01 ③ miss는 '그리워하다'라는 뜻이 아니라 '놓치다'라는 뜻으로 사용되었다.

02 특정한 종류의 삶을 살다'라는 영영영풀이가 가리키는 단어는 ② lead: (특정한 유형의) 생활을 하다이다.

03 ② to enter → enter / ④ danced → dance / ⑤ follows → follow로 고쳐야 어법상 적절한 문장이 된다.

04 위 대화에 따르면, A의 질문에 대한 B의 대답이 그렇지 않다 ("No, it's not.")고 했다. 따라서 빈칸에 들어갈 말로 가장 적절한 것은 ① Is it far?(그곳은 먼가요?)이다.

05 극장에 가려면 얼마나 걸리냐는 A의 질문에 대해 "아니, 그곳은 우리 집에서 멀지 않아."라는 B의 대답은 흐름상 자연스럽지 않다.

06 위 대화에서 화자들은 수원 화성에 가는 길을 묻고 그곳에 가는 방법을 알려주고 있다. 따라서 위 글의 빈칸 (A)에 들어갈 말로 적절하지 않은 것은 ③, ④이다.

07 위 대화에 따르면, 미나는 현재 위치에서 수원 화성에 가는 것이 약 20분 걸린다고("It will take about 20 minutes.") 대답했다.

08 위 대화에 따르면, 남성은 수원 화성에 가는 방법을 물어봤고 미나는 6번 버스를 타고 가는 방법을 설명해 주었다. 따라서 남성은 버스를 타고 갈 것이다.

09 위 대화에 따르면, 민수는 Emma에게 이번주 금요일에 저녁을 먹으러 가자고 제안했다. 민수의 토요일 일정에 대해서는 대화에서 언급된 바 없다.

10 Why don't we ~? : ~하는 것이 어때?

11 G가 B에게 밍 식당에 가는 방법을 알려 주었다.

12 ⓐ exciting → excited / ⓑ advertise → to advertise / ⓔ

---

came → come으로 고쳐야 어법상 적절한 문장이 된다.

13 위 글에서 Andy가 올해 학교 축제에서 비디오를 찍는다는 이야기는 언급 되어 있지 않다.

14 위 글에 따르면, 미나와 Andy는 학교 축제를 홍보하기 위해 소셜 미디어에 동영상을 게시할 것이라고 한다. 왜냐하면 이것은 포스터를 만드는 것보다 시간이 덜 걸리기 때문이라고 한다.

15 A가 B(Chris)에게 학급 파티에서 무엇을 할 것이냐고 묻자(B), B는 샌드위치를 만들 것이라고 대답한다(C). 이에 A는 그것이 좋은 생각이라고 말하면서 샌드위치를 만드는 데 얼마나 걸리냐고 물어보자(A), B는 약 1시간 정도가 걸린다(D)고 대답하는 순서로 이어지는 것이 문맥상 가장 자연스럽다.

16 가주어 It이 쓰인 문장이므로 ⓓcook는 to cook으로 고쳐야 어법상 적절하다.

17 위 글에 따르면, 사람들은 추수감사절 주말에는 휴식을 취하고 가족, 친구들과 시간을 함께 보낸다고 ('There is a long weekend after Thanksgiving, so we just relax and spend time together with our family and friends.') 언급되어 있다.

18 위 글에 따르면, 홀리 축제는 주로 봄인 3월에 열린다고('It is usually in March.') 한다.

19 ⓑDuring → While / ⓒ singing and dancing → sing and dance로 고쳐야 어법상 적절한 문장이 된다.

20 ③ What kinds of food are there?(무슨 종류의 음식이 있는가?)에 대한 내용은 위 글에서 언급되어 있지 않다.

21 위 글에서는 gulal이 무엇인가라고 질문했으므로 이에 대한 대답은 'It is blue, yellow, green, and pink powder.'가 되어야 자연스럽다.

22 ⓒfor → into / ⓓwith → from으로 고쳐야 어법상 적절한 문장이 된다.

23 (A) 지각동사 watch는 목적보어로 동사원형이나 현재분사를 취한다. / (B) 가주어 It이 쓰인 문장이므로 to fly가 들어가는 것이 적절하다.

24 ⑤ How many artworks can you see during the festival? (얼마나 많은 예술 작품들을 축제 동안 볼 수 있는가?)에 대한 내용은 위 글에서 언급되어 있지 않다.

25 위 글에 따르면, 예술가들은 크게 쌓인 눈을 예술 작품으로 만든다고('The artists shape huge piles of snow into animals, buildings, and other beautiful artworks.') 언급되어 있다.

26 (가)It은 to부정사 구문을 대신하는 역할을 하는 가주어이다. 따라서 이와 쓰임이 같은 것은 ③ It is not easy to do my English homework.(영어 숙제를 하는 것은 쉽지 않다.)이다.

27 지각동사 hear는 목적보어로 동사원형이나 현재분사를 취한다. 따라서 ⓔ played는 play나 playing으로 고치는 것이 어법상 적절하다.

28 (A)live는 '라이브의', '실시간의'라는 뜻으로 사용되었다. 이와 쓰임이 같은 것은 ④ I watched live streaming sports all night long.(나는 밤새 라이브로 하는 스포츠 중계를 보았다.)이다.

29 위 글에 따르면, 백야 축제에서는 밤하늘이 완전히 어두워지지 않는다고('The night sky does not get completely dark.') 했으므로, ⑤ deep dark nights가 정답이다.

30 위 글에 따르면, 백야 축제는 한 달간 지속되며, 가장 인기 있는 행사인 스칼렛 항해 기념 행사에서는 불꽃놀이와 물 쇼가 진행된다고 한다.

Lesson 5 (중간)

01 ⑤	**02** ④	**03** ⑤	**04** ②	**05** ①	**06** ⑤	**07** ①

08 How long will it take to get there? **09** ③ **10** ④ **11** ①
12 ④ **13** How can I get there from the school? **14** ④
15 ① **16** ④ **17** ② **18** ③ **19** ⑤ **20** ③
21 밤하늘이 완전히 어두워지지 않는 때 **22** ③, ⑤
23 gct complctcly dark **24** It takcs placc in Russia. **25** ①
26 ④ **27** ② **28** ① **29** ③ **30** ②

01 영영풀이가 가리키는 것은 위에서부터 adult, competition, sled, advertise, pile이다.

02 수동형 동사가 쓰인 문장이므로 ⓓ hold는 held로 고쳐야 어법상 적절한 문장이 된다.

03 blind 맹인의 / scarlet 자주색의 / several 여러 개의 / chase 쫓다

04 B가 A에게 "학교 축제를 홍보하기 위해 무엇을 할 수 있을까?"라고 물어보았다. 이에 대한 A의 대답으로 가장 적절하지 않은 것은 ② Why do you ask me instead of yourself?(왜 너 자신 말고 나에게 물어보는 거니?)이다.

05 12시에 만나자는 A의 말에 대해 "미안, 이 시계는 내 것이 아니야."라는 B의 대답은 흐름상 자연스럽지 않다.

06 ⑤ How many people will come to the festival?(얼마나 많은 사람들이 축제에 올 것인가?)에 대해서는 위 대화에서 언급된 바 없다.

07 B가 A에게 "학교 축제를 홍보하기 위해 무엇을 할 수 있을까?"라고 물어보았다. 이에 대해 A는 포스터를 만드는 것은 어떠냐고 제안하고(A), B는 그것이 좋은 생각이라고 말한다(C). A가 포스터를 만드는 데 얼마나 걸릴 것이냐고 묻자(D), B가 약 3시간 정도 걸릴 것이라고 대답하는 순서로 이어지는 것이 흐름상 가장 자연스럽다.

08 "How long will it take to ~?"는 "~하는 데 얼마나 걸리니?"라는 의미로 어떤 일의 시간이 얼마나 경과하는지에 대해서 묻는 표현이다.

09 (B)take는 '(시간이) 걸리다'라는 뜻으로 사용되었다. 이와 동일한 의미로 쓰인 문장은 ③ It will take seven days to finish the project.(그 프로젝트를 끝내는 데 7일이 걸릴 것이다.)이다.

10 미나가 수원 화성에서 열리는 축제에 갈 것이라는 내용은 언급된 바 없다.

11 위 대화에서는 우체국에 가는 길을 묻고 그곳에 가는 방법을 대답하고 있다. B의 대답인 "아뇨, 멀지 않아요."("No, it's not. It is close.")로 미루어 볼 때, 빈칸에 들어갈 말로 가장 적절한 것은 ① Is it far from here?(그곳은 여기서 먼가요?)이다.

12 ④ What are they going to do after lunch?(Emma와 민수는 점심 식사 후에 무엇을 할 예정인가?)라는 질문에 대한 내용은 위 대화에서 언급되어 있지 않다.

13 How can I get there from ~? : ~에서 그곳까지 어떻게 갈 수 있니?

14 ⓑ usually can → can usually / ⓔ preparing → (to) prepare로 고쳐야 어법상 적절한 문장이 된다.

15 (A) until: ~할 때까지 / (B) 가주어 It이 쓰인 문장이므로 to부정사구인 to make가 들어가야 어법상 적절하다. / (C) 주어가 단수인 everyone이므로 enjoys가 적절하다.

16 ④ What do people do on each day of the festival?(축제의 각각의 날에 사람들은 무엇을 하는가?)에 대한 내용은 위 글에서 언급되어 있지 않다.

17 (A) because of+명사(구): ~ 때문에 / (B) for+기간의 길이: ~ 동안에 / (C) shape A into B A를 B로 조각하다

18 주어진 우리말을 영작하면, People watch the artists shaping their works from the beginning to end.가 된다.

19 ⑤ What are the meanings of the beautiful snow artworks?(눈으로 만든 아름다운 예술 작품의 의미는 무엇인가?)에 대해서는 위 글에서 언급되어 있지 않다.

20 첫 문단에서 '축제 기간 동안에는, 거의 매일 밤마다 발레나 오페라 공연이 있다'('During the festival, there is a ballet or an opera almost every night.')고 언급되어 있다.

21 '그 시기'가 가리키는 것은 문맥상 밤하늘이 완전히 어두워지지 않는 백야 시기이다.

22 ⓐ hear → heard / ⓑ amazingly → amazing / ⓓ appear → appears로 고쳐야 어법상 적절한 문장이 된다.

23 get ~하게 되다 / completely 완전히

24 백야 축제가 열리는 곳은 러시아라고 언급되어 있다.

25 ① Where can I buy gulal?(gulal을 어디서 살 수 있는가?)에 대한 내용은 위 글에서 언급되어 있지 않다.

26 (가)The main event는 사람들이 gulal이라는 형형색색의 가루

를 서로에게 뿌리는 놀이라고 한다.

27 ⓐ, ⓑ, ⓒ는 모두 Holi festival을 가리킨다. ⓓ는 gulal, ⓔ는 사람들에게 gulal 가루를 던지고 노는 것을 가리킨다.

28 빈칸 (A)가 포함된 문장은 가주어 It이 쓰인 문장이기 때문에 to부정사구인 to run이 들어가야 어법상 적절하다.

29 ⓔ in이 아니라 for(~ 동안)이 들어가야 적절하다.

30 Gulal은 형형색색의 가루이며, 주요 행사는 두번째 날에 한다고 언급되어 있다. 또한 사람들이 축제 첫날 거리 행진에 참여할 수 있는지에 대해서는 언급 되어 있지 않다.

Lesson 6 (중간)

1회

01 ① **02** ② **03** ③ **04** ①, ④ **05** ④ **06** ③ **07** ①
08 ⑤ **09** ② **10** ⑤ **11** ④ **12** ① **13** ② **14** ③ **15** ②
16 ④
17 When you ask a question, the door to science always opens.
18 ⑤ **19** ②
20 Although we can't say we can live in Mars right now
21 twice as long as **22** ② **23** ④ **24** ① **25** ① **26** ②
27 ① **28** ② **29** ③ **30** ①

01 '어떤 것도 들을 수 없는'이라는 영영풀이가 가리키는 단어는 ① deaf(청각 장애의)이다.

02 '어떤 것을 한 곳에서 다른 곳으로 옮기다'는 영영풀이가 가리키는 것은 ② carry(옮기다)이다.

03 빈칸 맨 위에서부터 순서대로, curious(궁금해하는), adapt(적응하다), produce(생산하다), lead(살다)가 들어가는 것이 문맥상 자연스럽다.

04 ① is → does / ④ as sweeter than → as sweet as로 고쳐야 어법상 적절한 문장이 된다.

05 용도가 무엇이냐는 B의 질문에 대해 A가 물건들을 실어나르는 것이라고 대답했다. 따라서 빈칸에 들어갈 말로 가장 적절한 것은 ④ Jige(지게)이다.

06 간접의문문이 포함된 문장을 이용해 의문문을 만들 때, 어순은 '의문사+주어+동사' 형태가 된다.

07 위 글에 따르면, 호진이는 남자 형제와 함께 과학 박람회에 갔다왔다("I went to a science exhibition with my brother.")고 언급했다.

08 엄마가 예린이에게 앞으로 네 방 청소를 할 것이냐고 물었고, 이에 대해 예린이가 ⓔSure, I won't.(네, 안 그럴 거예요.)라고 대답하는 것은 적절하지 않다.

09 엄마의 말에 대한 예린이의 대답이 슬리퍼의 용도를 가르쳐 주는

것이었다. 따라서 빈칸에 들어갈 엄마의 말로 가장 적절한 것은 ② what are they for(그건 용도가 무엇이니?)이다.

10 위 글에서는 예린이가 과학 시간에 만든 청소하는 슬리퍼에 대해서 이야기하고 있다.

11 위 광고문에 따르면, 무슨 음식이든 잘 먹는 긍정적인 성격에 대해서는 언급되어 있지 않다.

12 '들을 수 없거나 잘 들을 수 없는', '귀가 손상되어서 들을 수 없는 사람'이라는 영영풀이가 가리키는 단어는 ① deaf(청각 장애의)이다.

13 위 글에 따르면, Alexandar Graham Bell의 말에 대해서는 언급된 바 없다.

14 위 글에서 수지는 화성에 가고 싶은 이유에 대해서 설명하고 있다. 따라서 ⓒTo apply, send us a short video which includes the answers to the following questions.(지원하려면, 다음의 질문에 대한 대답을 포함한 짧은 영상을 보내 주세요.)라는 문장은 글의 흐름과는 어색하다.

15 ⓑit는 물을 가리킨다. 나머지는 모두 the glass(유리컵)를 가리킨다.

16 위 글에서는 (D)When the air is cooled, it changes from water to gas.(공기가 차가워지면, 액체에서 기체로 바뀐다.)는 문장은 차가워진 공기가 컵 표면에 물을 만들어 내는 과정에 대해서 설명하고 있는 글의 흐름과는 관계 없는 문장이다.

17 ask a question 질문을 하다

18 첫 문단에서 NASA의 과학자들이 화성을 또 다른 지구처럼 변화시키기 위해 노력하고 있다고 이야기하자, (C)에서 지구에서 영원히 살 수는 없기 때문에 다른 행성으로 옮겨가려 한다고 그 이유를 설명한다. (B)에서는 화성이 그 대안이라고 설명하면서 화성을 변화시키는 첫 번째 방법으로 화성을 따뜻하게 만드는 방법을, 이어서 (A)에서는 두 번째 방법으로 식물을 기르고 있다고 설명하는 순서로 이어지는 것이 흐름상 가장 자연스럽다.

19 ⓑMars is about half the size of Earth.(화성은 지구 크기의 약 반이다.)라는 의미의 문장이다. ② Mars is twice as big as Earth.(화성은 지구보다 두 배 만큼 크다.)라는 문장과는 반대되는 내용이다.

20 접속사 Although는 '~이긴 하지만'이라는 뜻으로, 주절과 종속절이 반대되는 내용일 때 사용할 수 있다. 이와 같은 표현으로는 접속사 Even though, Though 등이 있다.

21 '~만큼 …한'이라는 동등 비교 표현은 'as (형용사/부사) as ~'의 형태로 쓸 수 있다. 이때 '두 배 만큼 기다란'이라는 표현은 'twice as long as'이라고 쓸 수 있다.

22 ⓑ는 부사로 '~이 있다'라는 문장에서 사용된다. 나머지는 모두 화성을 가리킨다.

23 두 번째 문단에 나와 있듯이, 과학자들은 화성에 물이 있다고 생각

하며, 집과 건물을 지을 수 있는 단단한 땅이 존재한다고 믿는다.

24 주어진 우리말을 영작하면, The length of <u>day and night on Mars is</u> <u>similar to that on Earth</u>.가 된다.

25 (가)lead는 '살다', '생활하다'라는 의미로 사용되었다.

26 위 글에서는 화성 탐사 임무를 할 사람을 모집하고 있는 글이다. 따라서 위 글의 빈칸에 들어갈 말로 가장 적절한 것은 ② Do you want to live on another planet?(다른 행성에 살아보고 싶은가요?)이다.

27 지원자가 젊어야 한다는 내용은 위 글에서 언급된 바 없다.

28 선행사 someone이 쓰인 문장이므로 관계대명사는 사람이 선행사일 때 쓰는 ② who가 들어가는 것이 어법상 가장 적절하다.

29 ③ How can KSO send people to Mars?(KSO는 어떻게 사람들을 화성에 보낼 수 있는가?)에 대한 내용은 위 글에서 언급된 바 없다.

30 본문에서 질문한 ② Do you have a good sense of humor? (좋은 유머 감각이 있는가?)에 대해서는 대답하지 않았다.

Lesson 6 (중간)

01 ② **02** ② **03** ① **04** ②, ⑤ **05** ③ **06** ⑤
07 (A) Do you know what it is? (B) What is it for? **08** ④
09 ④ **10** Do you know who this man is **11** ② **12** ③
13 ② **14** ⑤ **15** ⓐ: the glass / ⓑ: the glass / ⓒ: the air
16 ③ **17** ① **18** ③ **19** ⑤ **20** ⑤
21 화성은 지구의 약 절반 크기이다. / 화성에서 1년은 지구에서의 1년보다 약 2배 더 길다. / 화성은 지구보다 훨씬 더 춥다.
22 ⑤ **23** ③ **24** ④ **25** ③, ⑤ **26** ② **27** ①
28 It is possible to build houses and buildings on Mars because it has hard land.
29 ④ **30** ⑤

01 get up: 일어나다 / get along with: ~와 잘 지내다

02 ②lead는 모두 '살다', '생활하다'라는 뜻으로 사용되었다. / ① 약, 대략; ~에 대해서 / ③ ~이 되다; 도착하다 / ④ 열심히; 단단히 / ⑤ 지속되다; 지난

03 ①peel(껍질을 벗기다) 대신 spread(바르다, 펼치다)가 들어가는 것이 문맥상 더 자연스럽다.

04 ① During → While / ③ even if → despite / ④ Despite of → In spite of로 고쳐야 어법상 적절한 문장이 된다.

05 "우체국은 여기서 먼가요?"라는 A의 질문에 대해 "아니, 그렇지 않아요."라는 B의 대답은 흐름상 가장 자연스럽다.

06 VR 헤드셋의 용도를 묻는 Judy의 질문에 대해 호진이는 "If you wear it, there will be a new world."(그걸 쓰면, 신세계를 경

험할 수 있어.)라고 대답했다.

07 (A) 간접의문문이 쓰일 때 문장의 순서는 '의문사+주어+동사'의 형태가 되어야 어법상 적절하다. / (B) "What are they for?" 혹은 "What is it for?"는 "그것은 무엇을 위한 거니?"라는 의미로 어떤 사물이나 일의 목적이나 쓰임을 묻는 표현이다.

08 W가 지게의 용도를 물어봤으므로 이에 대한 M의 대답으로 가장 적절한 것은 ④ It's for carrying many different things.(많은 것들을 싣고 가는 용도야.)이다.

09 ⓐAlexander Graham Bell의 어머니와 부인은 청각 장애인 ("His mother and wife were deaf")이었다고 언급되어 있다.

10 간접의문문이 쓰일 때 문장의 순서는 '의문사+주어+동사'의 형태가 되어야 어법상 적절하다.

11 A가 이것이 무엇인지 아냐고 묻자, B는 딱풀 같이 보인다고 대답한다. 그러자 A는 이것이 버터 스틱이라고 말해 주고 B는 그 안에 버터가 있냐고 묻는다. 이에 A는 이것을 이용해 빵에 버터를 바를 수 있다고 대답하는 순서로 이어지는 것이 대화의 흐름상 가장 자연스럽다.

12 ⓒthe following questions는 '다음에 오는 질문들'이라는 뜻이다.

13 본문에서, "Do you have a good sense of humor?"라고 물어보았다. 따라서 수지의 대답인 ⓑI don't usually make jokes and laugh at funny things.(별로 농담을 하지 않고 웃기는 것에 웃지 않는다.)는 적절하지 않다.

14 '그래서 유리 컵의 표면에 작은 물방울들이 있었다.'라는 문장이 들어가기에 가장 적절한 곳은 차가워진 공기가 기체를 물로 변화시킨다고 설명하는 곳인 (E)이다.

15 ⓐit은 앞서 언급된 the glass(유리컵)를 가리킨다. / ⓑ it은 앞서 언급된 the glass(유리컵)를 가리킨다. / ⓒ it은 앞서 언급된 the air(공기)를 가리킨다.

16 위 글에 따르면, 민준이는 유리컵 표면의 물방울이 어떻게 생긴 건지 알고 싶어 한다('What happened to the glass?').

17 ⓐ differences: 차이점 / ⓑ although+주어+동사: ~이긴 하지만

18 '평균적으로, 화성의 기온은 약 영하 60도이다.'라는 문장이 들어가기에 가장 적절한 곳은 화성이 지구보다 태양에서 멀기 때문이라고 설명하고 있는 곳인 (C)이다.

19 ⑤ How far is it from Mars to the Sun?(화성에서 태양까지의 거리는 얼마인가?)에 대해서는 위 글에서 언급된 바 없다.

20 마지막 문단에서 화성이라는 새로운 세계를 상상하는 것은 즐겁다고 이야기하면서 "누가 아나?"라고 말하고 있다. 따라서 빈칸에 들어갈 말로 가장 적절한 것은 ⑤ You could go to Mars for the first time!(당신이 처음으로 화성에 갈 수 있다!)이다.

21 첫 문단에 나와 있듯이, 화성은 지구 크기의 절반이며, 화성의 1년

은 지구의 약 두 배라고 한다. 또한 화성은 태양에서 더 멀기 때문에 춥다고 한다.

22 ⓔ는 '~에'라는 의미의 전치사로 사용되었다. 나머지는 모두 to부정사이다.

23 위 글에서는 화성 탐사 임무를 갈 사람을 모집하고 있다. 따라서 위 글의 종류로 가장 적절한 것은 ③ advertisement(광고)이다.

24 (A) live 살다 / (B) look for ~을 찾다 / (C) creative 창의적인 / (E) miss out 놓치다

25 ③ How can the city on Mars be built?(어떻게 화성에 도시를 지을 수 있는가?)와 ⑤ What should people do when they miss the chance?(사람들이 기회를 놓쳤을 때 무엇을 해야 하는가?)라는 질문에 대한 내용들은 위 글에서 언급되어 있지 않다.

26 ⑤ The video must include the way you can adapt to a new environment quickly. (영상에는 당신이 새로운 환경에 빠르게 적응하는 방법에 대해 담겨 있어야 한다.)는 위 글에서 언급되지 않았다.

27 위 글에서는, 화성을 새로운 거주지로 생각한다고 이야기하면서 화성에 사람들을 보내려고 한다고 언급한다. 따라서 위 글의 빈칸 (A)에 들어갈 말로 가장 적절한 것은 ① Can people live on Mars?(인간이 화성에서 살 수 있는가?)이다.

28 가주어 It-진주어 to 구문을 이용해 'It is possible to build houses and buildings on Mars because it has hard land.' 라고 영작할 수 있다.

29 위 글에 따르면, NASA는 현재 화성에 사람을 보내기 위해 노력하고 있다('NASA and some companies are trying to send people there right now.')고 언급되어 있다.

30 두 번째 문단에서는 화성을 두 번째 지구, 혹은 새로운 거주지로 생각하면서 화성과 지구의 유사점에 대해서 설명하고 있다. 따라서 빈칸 (C)에 들어갈 수 있는 말로 가장 적절한 것은 ⑤ in addition(게다가)이다.

Lesson 7 (기말) 〔1회〕

01 ①	**02** so tired that she couldn't do		**03** ②	**04** ①
05 ④	**06** ②	**07** ④	**08** ④	**09** ⑤ **10** ③ **11** ② **12** ①
13 ①	**14** ④	**15** ②	**16** (1) ⓐ, ⓔ, ⓕ / (2) ⓑ, ⓒ, ⓓ	
17 ⑤	**18** ④	**19** ②	**20** ③	**21** ② **22** ③ **23** ③ **24** ①
25 ②	**26** ①	**27** ②	**28** ③	**29** ④ **30** ④

01 ② 설명하다, ③ 증명하다, ④ 거짓말하다, ⑤ 나타내다, 표현하다

02 '너무 ~해서 …했다'라는 문장은 'so+형용사[부사]+that +주어+동사'의 형태로 쓸 수 있다. 이는 원인과 그에 따른 결과를

서술할 때 쓰인다.

03 ① where → which / ③ what → that / ④ which → who / ⑤ are → is로 고쳐야 어법상 적절한 문장이 된다.

04 A의 질문에 대한 B의 대답이 "그건 정말 좋아서."였다. 따라서 A의 질문으로 가장 적절한 것은 ① How was your trip?(네 여행은 어땠니?)이다.

05 칠판을 치우는 것을 도와줄 수 있냐는 A의 질문에 대해 "문제 없어. 난 가야 해."라는 B의 대답은 흐름상 자연스럽지 않다.

06 ⓐ favorite 가장 좋아하는 / ⓑ recommend 추천하다

07 미나가 Antonio's 식당을 추천하면서 그곳의 불고기 피자가 맛있다고 말한다. Brian은 음식에 이어 가격을 물어보고, 미나는 그곳의 가격도 좋다고 대답한다. Brian이 서비스는 어떠냐고 묻자, 미나는 주말에는 서비스가 조금 느리다고 대답하고 Brian은 확인해 보겠다고 말하면서 고맙다고 대답하는 순서로 이어지는 것이 흐름상 가장 자연스럽다.

08 위 대화에 따르면, 미나는 Antonio's 식당의 서비스에 대해 "주말에는 조금 느려."("It's a little slow on the weekends.")라고 평가를 했다.

09 B가 G에게 어디를 방문했냐고 물어보고 G는 첨성대를 방문했다(C)고 대답한다. B가 또 어디를 방문했냐고 묻자(B), G는 불국사를 방문했는데 그곳도 너무 좋았다고 대답하는 순서로 이어지는 것이 대화 흐름상 가장 자연스럽다.

10 G가 석굴암에 올라가는 것은 너무 힘들었다고 말한다. 이에 대한 B의 대답으로 가장 적절한 것은 ③ Maybe, it was a good experience for you.(아마도 그건 너에게 좋은 경험이었을 거야.)이다.

11 A가 "무엇을 도와줄까?"라고 물어 보았고, B는 가방을 찾고 있다고 말하면서 추천을 해달라고 요청한다. A는 빨간색이 요즘 가장 인기 있다고 말하면서 추천을 해주자, B는 자신이 이미 빨간색을 갖고 있기 때문에 다른 색을 원한다고 대답한다. 이에 A는 네이비 색을 추천해 주고 옆에 주머니가 달려 있다고 말하자 B는 그것이 마음에 든다고 하면서 구매하겠다고 말하는 순서로 이어지는 것이 흐름상 가장 자연스럽다.

12 (가)I'm looking for a backpack.은 "가방을 찾고 있어요."라는 의미의 문장이다. 이와 바꿔 쓸 수 없는 표현은 ① I can see a backpack.(난 가방을 볼 수 있다.)이다.

13 "I'll take it."은 "그걸로 살게요."라는 뜻으로 ① I will buy it. 과 바꿔 쓸 수 있다.

14 (A) recommend 추천하다 / (B) amazing 놀라운, 멋진 / (C) like 좋아하다

15 위 글에서는 해리 포터라는 소설책에 대해서 소개하면서 그 책을 읽고 느낀 점에 대해서 이야기하고 있다. 따라서 위 글의 종류로 적절한 것은 ② review(서평)이다.

16 위 글에 따르면, 의견은 사람들의 감정을 표현하는 반면에, 사실은 증명될 수 있는 것이라고 한다.

17 (A) On the other hand 반면에 / (B) Therefore 그러므로

18 ⓓthe second ad give a fact.에서 주어인 the second ad는 단수 명사이기 때문에 동사는 give가 아니라 gives가 되어야 어법상 적절하다.

19 위 글의 마지막 문단에서 언급되어 있듯이, 대부분의 광고는 사실과 의견을 섞기 때문에 광고를 볼 때 좀 더 주의해야 한다고 주장한다. 따라서 위 글의 제목으로 가장 적절한 것은 ③ Be a Wise Consumer by Analyzing Ads(광고를 분석함으로써 현명한 소비자가 되어라)이다.

20 Emma는 Kyle에게 읽는 모든 것을 믿지 말라고 조언했다. 따라서 Emma에 대해서 알맞게 표현한 것은 ③ She believes there may be lies or exaggerations in everything she reads.(그녀는 그녀가 읽는 모든 것에 거짓이나 과장이 있다고 믿는다.)이다.

21 위 글에 따르면, ② What does Emma want to ask for?(Emma는 무엇을 요청하고 싶어 하는가?)에 대해서는 언급되어 있지 않다.

22 '너무 ~해서 …하다'라는 문장은 'so+형용사[부사]+that+주어+동사'의 형태로 쓸 수 있다. 이는 원인과 그에 따른 결과를 서술할 때 쓰인다.

23 "I'm not following you."는 상대방의 말을 이해하지 못할 때 쓸 수 있는 표현이다. "I don't get it.", "I don't understand.", "It is difficult to understand." 등으로 바꿔 쓸 수 있다.

24 (가) 뒤에서 '아타카마 사막은 칠레에 있다'라는 문장은 사실이라고 예시를 들었다. 따라서 (가)에 들어갈 문장으로 가장 적절한 것은 ① But, facts can be proven.(그러나, 사실은 증명될 수 있다.)이다.

25 위 글에 따르면, 사실은 의견과는 달리 증명될 수 있다고 한다. 따라서 사실을 말하고 있는 사람은 ② 'Paris is one of the cities in France.(파리는 프랑스에 있는 도시 중 하나이다.)'이라고 말한 지선이다.

26 ⓐconnection은 '연관성'이라는 뜻을 가진 단어이다.

27 ④ When did *Forrest Gump* receive the Academy Award?(영화 포레스트 검프는 언제 아카데미 상을 받았는가?)라는 질문에 대한 내용은 위 글에서 언급된 바 없다.

28 (A) 영화 포레스트 검프의 광고는 '최고 영화상'을 포함한 아카데미 상 6개를 받았다고 했으므로 이것은 사실에 해당한다. / (B) 위 글에 따르면 "제일의", "최고의"라는 단어는 의견을 표현하는 단어들이다. / (C) 위 글에 따르면, 대부분의 광고들은 의견과 사실을 섞는다고 언급되어 있다.

29 "좋은 영화를 보고 싶은데 어떤 영화 광고를 믿어야 하는가?"라고

물어보았다. 위 글의 내용으로 미루어 볼 때, 현명한 선택을 하기 위해서는 사실과 의견 모두를 똑똑하게 확인해야 한다. 따라서 ④ Check both facts and opinions and choose wisely.가 가장 적절한 답이다.

30 위 글에 따르면, 영화 포레스트 검프는 아카데미 시상식에서 "최고의 영화상"을 받았다고 한다.

Lesson 7 (기말) 2회

01 ④	**02** ⑤	**03** ①	**04** ⑤	**05** ③	**06** ⑤	**07** ③	**08** ②
09 What do you like about it?		**10** ②, ④			**11** ③	**12** ②	
13 ③, ④		**14** ⑤	**15** ⑤	**16** ③	**17** ②	**18** ②	**19** ⑤
20 ③	**21** ⑤	**22** ④	**23** ②	**24** ⑤	**25** ①	**26** ①	**27** ④
28 ③	**29** ⑤	**30** ⑤					

01 (A) - boils, (B) - mental, (C) - planet, (D) - athlete, (E) - curious가 들어가는 것이 문맥상 가장 자연스럽다.

02 ⑤ prove는 '증명하다'라는 뜻을 갖는 단어이다.

03 ② Things bad → Bad things / ③ Much → Many / ④ two → twice / ⑤ you will eat the Italian food → you would eat the Italian food로 고쳐야 어법상 적절한 문장이 된다.

04 좋은 책을 추천해 달라는 A의 질문에 대해 "도서관에 가는 건 어때?"라는 B의 대답은 흐름상 자연스럽지 않다.

05 M이 가방을 찾고 있다고 하면서 하나 추천해달라고 요청했다. 이에 W는 빨간색 가방을 추천해 주면서 빨간색이 요즘 가장 인기 있는 색이라고 말한다. 이에 M은 자신이 갖고 있는 가방이 빨간색이라고 말하면서 다른 색을 원한다고 대답한다. W는 네이비 색을 추천하면서 옆에 주머니가 있다고 말한다. 이에 M은 그게 좋아보인다면서 그 가방을 사겠다고 대답하는 순서로 이어지는 것이 흐름상 가장 자연스럽다.

06 위 대화에 따르면, 점원은 빨간색이 요즘 가장 인기 있는 색이라고 말하면서 빨간색 가방을 추천해 주었다.

07 위 대화에 따르면, 미나는 Antonio's 식당을 추천하면서 그곳이 자신이 가장 좋아하는 식당("Why don't you try Antonio's? It's my favorite.")이라고 말했다.

08 위 대화에 따르면, Antonio's 식당이 어디에 위치하는지에 대해서는 언급된 바 없다.

09 "What do you like about it?"은 "그것의 무엇이 마음에 드니?"라는 의미로 어떤 사물이나 일에 대한 상대방의 선호를 묻는 표현이다.

10 ① which → who(m) / ③ whom → which / ⑤ whom → which로 고쳐야 어법상 적절한 문장이 된다.

11 B의 대답으로 미루어 볼 때, A가 한 말로 가장 적절한 것은 ③ Do

you know who he is?(그가 누군지 아니?)이다.

12 Jay가 Lena에게 경주 여행은 어땠냐고 묻자, Lena는 매우 행복했다(ⓑ)고 대답한다. Jay가 첨성대 말고 다른 어디를 방문했는지 묻고(ⓒ), Lena는 불국사를 방문했고 좋았다고 대답하자, Jay가 완벽한 여행이었겠다(ⓐ)고 말한다. Lena는 석굴암에 올라가는 것이 힘들었다고 말하자, Jay가 그래도 보람이 있었겠다(ⓓ)고 말하는 순서로 이어지는 것이 흐름상 가장 자연스럽다.

13 ⓒThere are many things we can do them on the island.는 There are many things we can do on the island.로, ⓓIt's too expensive to afford it.는 It's so expensive that we can't afford it.으로 바꾸는 것이 어법상 적절하다.

14 대화 초반 한 선생님의 말에 따르면, 다음 달에 있을 수학 여행에 어디를 갈지 정하기 위해 이야기를 나누고 있다.

15 수미가 속초에는 캠프를 할 장소가 없다고 생각하는지에 대해서는 위 대화에서 언급된 바 없다.

16 위 대화에서 G는 경주 여행을 갔다왔고 매우 만족해했다고 한다. 따라서 B가 한 말인 ⓒIt looks like a horrible trip.은 It looks like a wonderful trip.으로 고치는 것이 문맥상 자연스럽다.

17 빈칸 (A)에는 의견을 나타내는 문장이 들어가야 한다. 따라서 빈칸에 들어갈 문장으로 적절한 것은 ② The story is really touching.(그 이야기는 정말 감동적이다.)이다.

18 빈칸 (A)에는 opinion(의견)이 들어가는 것이 문맥상 가장 자연스럽다.

19 ⓐ는 광고가 항상 진실을 말하는 것이 아니라는 의미이다. / ⓑ 80%의 고객들이 다시 식당에 방문한다는 의미이다. / ⓒ는 restaurant을 가리킨다. / ⓓthoughts는 think의 명사형으로 '생각'이라는 뜻으로 사용되었다. ⓔ는 Therefore가 들어가야 한다.

20 (A) opinions 의견들 / (B) 위 글에 따르면 "제일의", "최고의"라는 단어는 의견을 표현하는 단어들이다 / (C) 내용을 증명할 수 있는 것은 사실이다. / (D) facts 사실들

21 위 글에서는 대부분의 광고는 사실과 의견이 섞여 있기 때문에 그 둘 모두에 바탕을 두고 현명한 선택을 해야 한다고 주장한다.

22 선행사를 the award로, 관계대명사 which를 사용해 ④ "Best Picture" is the award which the movie won.이라는 문장으로 영작할 수 있다.

23 위 글에 따르면, 영화 Y-Men 7의 광고는 의견을 사용했으며, Kyle이 Emma와 함께 Y-Men 7을 보고싶어 하는지에 대해서는 언급된 바 없다. 또한 대부분의 광고에서는 사실과 의견을 함께 사용한다고 언급되어 있다.

24 위 글에서는 대부분의 광고는 사실과 의견이 섞여 있기 때문에 그 둘 모두에 바탕을 두고 현명한 선택을 해야 한다고 주장한다.

25 'so ~ that 주어+can't[could't]' 구문은 '너무 ~해서 …할 수

없다'라는 의미이다. 주어진 문장을 해석하면 ① '영화가 너무 지루해서 나는 울고 싶어.'가 된다.

26 관계대명사 that은 선행사가 사람, 사물일 경우 모두 쓸 수 있다. 이 경우에서 선행사가 everything이므로 which로 바꿔 쓸 수 있다.

27 (가) opinions 의견들 / (나) facts 사실들 / (다) a fact 사실

28 위 글에 따르면, 사실은 그 내용이 증명될 수 있다고 한다. 따라서 위 글에서 사실인 문장은 ⓒThe movie advertisement said it was "The Most Exciting Movie of the Year."(그 영화의 광고는 그 영화가 "올해의 가장 재밌는 영화"라고 말했다.)라는 문장이다.

29 "I'm not following you."는 상대방의 말을 이해하지 못할 때 쓸 수 있는 표현이다.

30 위 글에 따르면, Emma는 사실은 증명될 수 있다고 말했다.

Lesson 8 (기말) 1회

| 01 ④ | 02 ③ | 03 ③ | 04 ④ | 05 ⑤ | 06 ① | 07 ⑤ |

08 (1) lost his smartphone / (2) asked his mom to find / (3) confused, pleased / (4) in the kitchen / (5) Are you sure you lost it

09 ⑤	10 ④	11 ③	12 ⑤	13 ④	14 ②	15 ④	16 ④
17 ①	18 ②	19 ④	20 ⑤	21 ③	22 ④	23 ①, ③, ④
24 ③	25 ①	26 ③	27 ②	28 ②	29 ①	30 ⑤

01 carry ~을 들고 가다 / clue 단서 / talent 재능 / water 물을 주다 / afraid 두려워하는

02 touching 감동적인, touch 닿다

03 ① who is your favorite singer → who your favorite singer is / ② how much is the car → how much the car is / ④ what this called → what this is called / ⑤ can he pick me up → he can pick me up으로 고쳐야 어법상 적절한 문장이 된다.

04 ④ Do you have a favor to ask?는 "너는 부탁할 게 있니?"라는 뜻으로 상대방에게 도움을 요청하는 표현이 들어가야 하는 빈칸에는 적절하지 않다.

05 샌드위치 만드는 것을 도와줄 수 있냐는 A의 질문에 대해 "싫어. 난 요리하는 걸 정말 좋아해."라는 B의 대답은 흐름상 자연스럽지 않다.

06 (A) somewhere 어딘가에 / (B) had left (과거완료) / (C) right 옳은

07 "오, 그거 여기 있다."라는 문장이 들어가기에 가장 적절한 곳은 Brian이 찾지 못하던 핸드폰을 엄마가 냉장고 속에서 찾아서 건네

주고 있는 (E)이다.

08 (1) lose의 현재완료형은 has lost이다 / (2) ask A to B A에게 B를 요청하다 / (3) confused 혼란스러운, pleased 즐거운 / (4) 위 대화에 따르면 부엌에서 마지막으로 사용했다고 한다 / (5) "Are you sure that~?"은 "~라는 것은 확실하니?"라는 표현으로 상대방에게 어떤 사실에 대해 확신하냐고 묻는 표현이다.

09 B가 Yes.로 대답하고 있으므로 ⑤ Would you mind helping me?(나를 도와 주지 않을래?)는 적절하지 않다.

10 위 글의 후반부에 언급되어 있듯이, 화자는 내년에도 학생들이 모른 척하지 말고 인사를 하며 지내자고 조언하고 있다.

11 where did the book go → where the book went / how does she come → how she comes로 고쳐야 어법상 적절한 문장이 된다.

12 주말 동안 자신의 개를 돌봐 줄 수 있겠냐는 나래의 부탁에 Tony는 자신의 어머니가 개를 싫어하신다고 대답했다. 따라서 빈칸 (A)에 들어갈 말로 가장 적절한 것은 ⑤ I'm afraid but I can't.(미안하지만 안 되겠어.)이다.

13 위 대화에 따르면, Tony의 어머니가 개를 싫어하신다("My mom doesn't like dogs.")고 말하며 나래의 요청에 거절했다.

14 위 대화에 따르면, Tony는 수민이의 가족은 개를 좋아한다고 ("Why don't you ask Sumin? Her family loves dogs.") 언급했다.

15 Goldstein 씨는 스스로 손과 발에 묶인 줄을 풀었다고 한다.

16 ⓐ facing toward → turning away from / ⓑunfasten → tied up / ⓒtie → untie / ⓔcheapest → the most expensive로 고쳐야 문맥상 적절한 문장이 된다.

17 글의 후반부에 나와 있듯이, 정문의 벨이 울리지 않았다는 말을 듣고 Shirley는 다이아몬드 도난 사건은 Goldstein 씨가 지어낸 것이라고 추리했다.

18 Goldstein이 초조하고 불안해 보였던 이유는 다이아몬드 도난 사건을 자신이 지어내어 죄책감을 느꼈기 때문이었다.

19 ① Tom was → if Tom was / ② is looking → was looking / ③ who are those people → who those people are / ⑤ who there is going with John → who is going there with John으로 고쳐야 어법상 적절한 문장이 된다.

20 something, anything, nothing, everything은 형용사가 뒤에서 꾸며 준다.

21 ⓐ have stolen → has stolen / ⓑ breaking → broken / ⓔ like these → like this로 고쳐야 어법상 적절한 문장이 된다.

22 위 글에 따르면, Shirley가 시가 적힌 쪽지를 발견한 것은 메달이 있던 곳이다.

23 범인이 남긴 시에 들어갈 문장으로 적절한 것은 show / go / low / slow 등과 운이 맞는 know / rainbow / arrow로 끝나는 ①,

③, ④이다.

24 right away 곧바로, 즉시

25 Shirley가 교장 선생님에게 언제 도난 사건이 일어났느냐고 물어 보았으므로 (B)에는 (라)가 들어가는 것이 자연스럽다. / 교장 선생님의 대답으로 미루어 볼 때, (C)에는 (다)가, (D)에는 (가), (E)에는 (나) 순서로 들어가는 것이 흐름상 가장 자연스럽다.

26 위 글은 장기 자랑 대회의 금메달이 도난 당한 사건을 해결하려는 Shirley라는 학생 탐정에 대해서 이야기하고 있다. 따라서 위 글의 종류는 ③ a detective novel(탐정/추리 소설)이다.

27 ⓐ to run → run[running] / ⓒ terrified → terrifying / ⓓ what time did you go home → what time you went home / ⓔ bringing → bring으로 고쳐야 어법상 적절한 문장이 된다.

28 위 글에 따르면, Harry가 춤 연습을 끝내서 9시 조금 전에 집에 갔고, 가는 길에 누군가 엉망으로 노래하는 것을 들었다고 진술했다. 또한 도둑이 나타났고 Sylvia가 번개와 함께 그것을 목격하고는 현장에서 달아났으며, 나중에 온 교장 선생님은 금메달 보관함에서 Jocelyn을 보았다.

29 주어진 우리말을 영작하면 "Did you hear anything strange?"가 된다.

30 (A) Sylvia는 긴 어두운 색깔의 머리라고 한다. / (B) 번개는 항상 천둥이 치기 전에 발생한다. / (C) 빛이 소리보다 빠르기 때문이다.

Lesson 8 (기말) 【2회】

01 ①	02 ②	03 ⑤	04 ①	05 ③	06 ③	07 ④	08 ④

09 ②　10 found, inside the refrigerator　11 ①　12 ⑤

13 모르는 사람처럼 지내지 말자.14 ②

15 (A) Can you help me mop the floor / (B) Can you help me post this notice on the bulletin board

16 ⑤	17 ①	18 ⑤	19 ⑤	20 ④	21 ④	22 ①	23 ①
24 ②	25 ④	26 ④	27 ②	28 ④	29 ④	30 ③	

01 '문제를 해결하게 도와주거나 질문에 대답하게 도와주는 어떤 것'이라는 영영풀이가 가리키는 것은 ① clue(단서)이다.

02 ① come → comes / ③ didn't you → you didn't / ④ if is that man → if that man is / ⑤ when → where로 고쳐야 어법상 적절한 문장이 된다.

03 주어진 단어를 흐름에 맞게 배열하면 "Can I ask you a favor?"가 된다.

04 운동화의 어떤 점이 제일 좋으냐는 A의 질문에 대해 "운동화 때문에 정말 행복해."라는 B의 대답은 흐름상 자연스럽지 않다.

05 "오, 미안하지만 안되겠어."라는 문장이 들어가기에 가장 적절한

곳은 금요일에 고양이를 봐달라는 나래의 요청을 Tony가 거절하고 있는 (C)이다.

06 위 대화의 문맥상 나래가 Tony에게 할 말로 적절하지 않은 것은 ③ Please can I help you?(내가 도와줄까?)이다.

07 나래는 Tony에게 자신이 집을 비울 동안 고양이를 돌봐달라고 부탁하고 있다.

08 Tony에 따르면, 수민이네 가족은 고양이를 좋아한다고("Why don't you ask Sumin? Her family loves cats.") 한다.

09 'a few minutes ago.'라고 과거를 지칭하는 어구가 같이 쓰였다. 따라서 현재완료 ⓑhave texted가 아니라 과거형 texted로 고쳐야 어법상 적절한 문장이 된다.

10 위 대화에 따르면, Brian의 엄마는 Brian의 핸드폰을 주방의 냉장고 안에서 찾았다.

11 위 대화에 따르면, Brian은 잃어버린 핸드폰을 찾기 위해 엄마에게 도움을 부탁했다.

12 위 글에서는 화자는 같은 반 학생들에게 내년에 다른 반이 되더라도 모른 척하지 말고 인사를 하며 지내라고 조언하고 있다. 따라서 ⓔWe should be careful when we meet strangers.(낯선 사람을 만날 때에는 조심해야 한다.)라는 문장은 글의 내용과는 관계없다.

13 화자는 같은 반 학생들에게 내년에 다른 반이 되더라도 모른 척하지 말고 인사를 하며 지내라고("Don't be a stranger. Say hello when we see each other, okay?") 말하고 있다.

14 "can you do me a favor?"는 '부탁 하나 들어줄래?'란 뜻으로, 상대방에게 부탁하는 표현이다. 이와 쓰임이 같은 것은 ② can I ask you a favor?이다.

15 사역동사 help는 'help+목적어+목적보어(동사원형 또는 to부정사)' 순으로 쓰여서 '목적어가 목적보어하는 것을 돕다'라는 뜻으로 쓰인다.

16 "내가 추측하기엔, 너는 지금 컴퓨터를 하고 있어."라는 B의 대답으로 미루어 볼 때, A가 한 말로 가장 적절한 것은 ⑤ Guess what I'm doing.(내가 지금 뭐 하고 있는지 추측해 보렴.)이다.

17 (A) broken: 동사 find의 목적보어로 the window를 수식하므로 과거분사형인 broken이 들어가는 것이 적절하다. / (B) playing: 지각동사 see의 목적보어이므로 동사원형 또는 현재분사형이 들어가는 것이 적절하다. / (C) anywhere 어디에도

18 ⑤ Where was Mr. Shoppe when he heard the window break?(Shoppe 씨는 창문이 깨지는 소리를 들었을 때 어디 있었는가?)에 대한 대답은 글 초반에 나와 있듯이, 지하에 있었다고 한다.

19 ⓐthirst → thirsty / ⓑbrightly → bright / ⓒto run → running / ⓓnext → next to로 고쳐야 어법상 적절한 문장이 된다.

20 ④ What horror movie does Sylvia like?(Sylvia는 무슨 공포 영화를 좋아하는가?)에 대해서는 위 글에서 언급된 바 없다.

21 위 글에 따르면, 첫 번째 용의자인 Jocelyn은 금메달 도난 범죄가 일어났을 때 노래를 연습하고 있었다고("I was practicing my song") 말했다.

22 (가)right는 '바로', '곧'이라는 뜻으로 사용되었다. 이와 쓰임이 같은 것은 ①이다.

23 '감정이나 경험, 생각 등을 표현하는, 특히 운을 맞춘 단어를 사용한 짧은 글이 가리키는 단어는 ① poem(시)이다.

24 ⓑWhere the gold medal go? → Where did the gold medal go?로 고쳐야 어법상 적절한 문장이 된다.

25 (A) missing 실종된 / (B) slow 느린 / (C) who else 다른 누군가가

26 "나는 그때까지 교실 밖으로 한 발짝도 나가지 않았어요."라는 문장이 들어가기에 가장 적절한 곳은 9시 조금 전에 집에 돌아가기 전까지는 안무를 연습했다고 말하고 있는 곳인 (D)이다.

27 ⓐ moves: 동작, 춤 / ⓑ singing: 지각동사 hear는 목적보어로 동사원형 또는 현재분사를 취한다. / ⓒ to hear, doesn't need to: ~할 필요가 없다

28 (A) take A to B A를 B로 데려가다 / (B) with ~가 있는

29 위 글에 따르면, 장기 자랑 대회를 위한 금메달을 누군가가 훔쳐 갔다고("Someone has stolen the gold medal for the talent show!") 한다.

30 ⓒ '가장 착한'의 뜻을 가진 최상급이 아니라 '최고의'라는 뜻으로 사용된 최상급이다.